Helen Faucit
Fire and Ice on the Victorian Stage

Head of Helen Faucit by Sir Frederick Burton
(by courtesy of the Folger Shakespeare Library)

Helen Faucit
Fire and Ice on the Victorian Stage

by Carol Jones Carlisle

THE SOCIETY FOR THEATRE RESEARCH
LONDON

First published 2000
by The Society for Theatre Research,
c/o The Theatre Museum,
1E Tavistock Street,
Covent Garden,
London WC2E 7PA

ISBN 0854 30 0678

General Editor: Dr. Richard Foulkes

Volume Editors: Dr. Richard Foulkes, Dr. Russell Jackson

Printed by Woolnough Bookbinding
Church Street, Irthlingborough, Northants

"Mary Coleridge told us much of Helen Faucit. She is full of strength and grace, and though cold in surface there is burning Etna beneath."

Journals of Caroline Fox, 2 July 1849

"With remarkable deliberation she joins intense emotion; and … we see the passions coursing up and down the blue veins of the living marble."

Morning Post, 17 July 1851

TO DOUGLAS

Jamais arrière

Contents

Acknowledgements

The "Afterpiece" in this book incorporates a considerable amount of material previously published in three of my essays: "Passion Framed by Art: Helen Faucit's Juliet," *Theatre Survey*; "Helen Faucit's Rosalind" and "Helen Faucit's Lady Macbeth," *Shakespeare Studies*. I appreciate being allowed to repeat the material in a new form.

I am grateful for the gracious permission of Her Majesty Queen Elizabeth II to publish quotations from manuscripts in the Royal Archives at Windsor Castle. I also acknowledge, with thanks, permission to quote from manuscripts in the following libraries and special collections: the Shakespeare Centre Library: Royal Shakespeare Company collections; the Theatre Museum (a branch of the Victoria and Albert Museum), Covent Garden, London; the Raymond Mander and Joe Mitchenson Theatre Collection; the National Library of Scotland; the Harvard Theatre Collection, Houghton Library; the Armstrong Browning Library, Baylor Unlversity, Waco, Texas; the H.H. Furness Memorial Library Manuscript Collections, University of Pennsylvania Library; and the Osborn Collection, Beinecke Library, Yale University Library. I thank the Master and Fellows of Trinity College Cambridge for permission to quote extracts from diary entries in the Munby Collection, as published in Derek Hudson's *Munby: Man of Two Worlds*. Although the Folger Shakespeare Library and the Huntington Library did not require formal permission to quote from their manuscripts, I thank them both. Like countless other scholars, I have revelled in the hospitable atmosphere of these fine libraries and the efficient help so cheerfully given by their staffs. I have also received some much-appreciated assistance at numerous other libraries and repositories in Great Britain, Ireland, and the United States. Some of these are named in the bibliography under "Clipping Files and Scrapbooks" and "Playbills"; among those unnamed but very important is the British Library's Newspaper Library at Colindale.

I am grateful to the various institutions and individual owners that have allowed me to reproduce pictures in their collections.

I should like to thank the Department of English, University of South Carolina, and the University administration for two sabbatical leaves and for a semester as Research Professor; also the Research Committee of the University for several travel grants. I thank Mlle. Claire Bourel of the University's International Programme for Students for criticising my French translations. I have grateful memories of the help I received in earlier years from two diligent research assistants: Ellen Lane Haggar and Dr. Carolyn Ellison Stringfellow.

This book, because of my passion for thoroughness, has been many years in the making and has had to undergo several slimming operations. In the process it and here has benefited from the help and encouragement of numerous friends, colleagues, and other scholars. I regret that I have space to mention only a few. (Some are listed in the bibliography under "Letters" and "Interviews.") I particularly appreciate the generosity of Jack Reading, theatrical scholar and collector, who sent me copies of some manuscripts in his possession, with his permission to quote from them. Several friends to whom I owe most are no longer with us. Professor Arthur Colby Sprague's inspiration, information, and wise counsel were especially important to me, as to so many others. Dr. Kathleen Barker, good friend as well as dedicated scholar, not only sent me information but voluntarily read the unwieldy first draft of this biography and made some practical suggestions. Professor Charles Shattuck gave me copies of numerous theatrical reviews, and those eminent critics John and Wendy Trewin sent me helpful materials.

I thank the Society for Theatre Research for undertaking the publication of this biography. I am grateful, in particular, to Dr. Russell Jackson for his interest in it and his help in bringing it to the light of day. He read the work in its penultimate form, gave me the benefit of his acute judgment, and began the editing of the book despite many other obligations. I am very grateful, too, to Dr. Richard Foulkes, General Editor of Publications, for being willing to take over the editing of this volume in addition to his other duties; his calm efficiency and tolerance in dealing with the exigencies of publication, including the vagaries of the author, have been remarkable.

Finally, I am thankful for the love and understanding of my family, especially my husband. True to the Douglas motto, he is never behind – not only in his own accomplishments but also in his encouragement and support of all my undertakings.

Carol Jones Carlisle

University of South Carolina

Illustrations

Note: There are very few illustrations of Helen Faucit in Shakespearean characters since she refused to sit for portraits of "Helen Faucit as Juliet," etc., thinking they would detract from the illusion that she *was* that person while onstage.

Forms of Reference

1. Shakespeare's works are cited from *The Riverside Shakespeare*, ed. G. Blakemore Evans et al., 2nd ed. (Boston: Houghton Mifflin, 1997).
2. The two following books, frequently referred to throughout, are cited only by the authors' names:
   Sir Theodore Martin: Sir Theodore Martin, *Helena Faucit* (*Lady Martin*) (Edinburgh: Blackwood, 1900).
   Helena F. Martin : Helena Faucit, Lady Martin, *On Some of Shakespeare's Female Characters*, 4th ed., new and enlarged. (Edinburgh, 1891).
   Other writings by Martin and by Helen Faucit/Helena Martin are cited in the usual way.
3. 'Theatre Royal' is abbreviated as 'T.R.'
4. The following designations are used for major or frequently cited libraries and collections:
   BL: British Library
   HTC: Harvard Theatre Collection
   NLS: National Library of Scotland
   PRO: Public Record Office, London
   RA: Royal Archives, Windsor Castle
   Folger: Folger Shakespeare Library
   Baylor Univ.: Armstrong Browning Library, Baylor University
   Theatre Museum: Theatre Museum, Covent Garden, London
   Mander and Mitchenson: The Raymond Mander and Joe Mitchenson Theatre Collection, London

Prologue

HELENA FAUCIT Saville, later Lady Martin (1814-1898), was best known to her contemporaries as Helen Faucit, the stage name that she retained professionally even after marriage. She was always Helen to family and friends, especially in her early years, though she later used her baptismal name, Helena, for social and literary purposes. Since it would be awkward, in writing of her, to switch back and forth, she will generally be called Helen Faucit in this biography – or, to sound a more personal note, just Helen – except when the context absolutely demands something else.

Helen Faucit, whose life almost spanned the nineteenth century, typified her period in many ways. In her best-known stage portrayals she seemed to countless devotees the incarnation of ideal womanhood. At the height of her career, young men were enraptured by her, middleaged scholars acknowledged her influence, and women, seeing in her their own best selves, offered her affection as well as praise. She was particularly admired in Shakespeare's characters and in the romantic heroines of the contemporary poetic drama. Socially, she was an intimate friend, both before and after marriage, of talented and influential people in the major cities of Great Britain. As Mrs. Theodore Martin, later Lady Martin, she broadened her acquaintance in elite circles, including, ultimately, that of courtly society. Her essays on Shakespeare's heroines won her a certain literary reputation.

Seventeen years after her professional retirement, and nine years after her final stage appearance, Robert W. Lowe, the theatrical editor and bibliographer, still called her "the most notable actress of modern times." And several years after her death at age 84, the popular theatrical critic Joseph Knight wrote that she was "the greatest interpreter of the poetical drama in living memory."[1]

Why, then, is she not better known today? The only previous biography of her was written by her husband, Sir Theodore Martin, shortly after her death.

Ironically, his book, which enshrines her as a paragon among women and a flawless model for actresses, has done much to discourage any interest in Helen Faucit's life. This was inevitable, for Sir Theodore, in addition to adoring his wife, believed that a responsible biographer should present his subject in an ideal way – that is, he should ignore incidental details in order to concentrate upon the essential "truth." When writing the life of William Aytoun, for example, he would not include "one sentence that did not bear … on [his] friend's literary career, or did not tend to heighten the impression of his admirable qualities as a man among men…" Too many biographers had violated "the sanctities of friendly intercourse," he thought, and had detracted from the dignity of their subject by quoting "chance sayings" from informal conversations.[2] As with words, so with incidents that did not reflect the essential truth. Sir Theodore probably did not know about some of his wife's early experiences; others that he did know about he glossed over as irrelevant to the "true" woman.

Actually, Helen Faucit did have her share of personal problems – not strongly dramatic, perhaps, but psychologically interesting and, in addition, highly relevant to her development as an actress. Before achieving her status as ideal woman, offstage as well as on, she had suffered an early loss of family stability, an unhappy relationship with her mother, a sense of shame over a long-standing scandal in her family, an intensely frustrating experience of unrequited love, and a near-scandal in her own life. Professionally, too, she had faced difficulties. Overcoming the handicaps of physical delicacy and limited resources required extraordinary determination and hard work. The subtle, poetic style so effective in "womanly" parts did not come naturally; it was a hard-won accomplishment. It was not even the style at which she originally aimed, but, rather, the one for which her physical endowments suited her. There were many fluctuations in the critics' responses before she achieved sustained success.

Whatever the details of her life, an actress who fascinated the audiences and critics of her period, over as long a period of time and in as many different places as Helen Faucit did, would be worth studying. In fact, one of the values of such a study is the panoramic view that it offers of theatrical and social life in Victorian Britain. Although "life and times" may have an old-fashioned ring, there can be no real sense of a person's life without some context of place, society, contemporary attitudes, and so on. In a theatrical biography, the conditions under which the acting was done are important – size of theatre, for example, kind of audience, proficiency of colleagues. Since acting is a joint enterprise, the triumphs and failures of a particular actor in a particular part cannot be meaningfully reported without some mention of other performances in the same production. Similarly, the dramas in which the acting was done must be more than names. It is meaningless, for example, to say that Helen Faucit's most popular character was Pauline in *The Lady of Lyons* unless the reader knows what the play was like. The world has frequently been compared to a theatre; since theatre embraces so many aspects of the world to which it belongs, the comparison works both ways.

In Helen Faucit's case, even after she married – indeed, even after she left the stage entirely – her personal and theatrical worlds overlapped to a great extent. Although she tried to keep her professional life distinct from her private one, her dramatic interests were too absorbing to relegate to a single area of experience – she took them with her into an increasingly enlarged social sphere, where she was an effective emissary of the theatre. So, although her acting career must be the main focus of this biography, her life outside the theatre demands some attention.

The most basic point about Helen Faucit is that she was not simply a representative of the "ideal woman": she was a real woman living with the practical advantages (few) and disadvantages (many) of that ideal. She was unusually fortunate in that, while enjoying its benefits, she managed to evade most of its traps. Although this biography does not focus narrowly on feminist concerns, it necessarily touches on many aspects of Victorian life that presented problems for women – in education, employment, health, marriage and divorce, property rights, and so on – and it gives special attention, of course, to problems faced by actresses.

I suppose every biographer discovers that the subject was a paradox. From the "character sketches" we write in school to the police "profiles" of criminals we read about later, the assumption seems to be that a personality consists of a coherent set of characteristics. In everyday life we confidently describe the people we know – honest or dishonest, warm-hearted or distant, generous or parsimonious. Even if we speak glibly of "complexity" and "ambiguity," we are shocked when a close acquaintance does something "out of character." In studying the life of someone we never knew, however, we discover, not simply aberrations in times of crisis, but consistent contradictions.

These are found abundantly in the records of Helen Faucit's life. A particularly intriguing paradox, already implicit in much I have said, deserves stressing: that an actress, who could be branded by her profession as "no better than she should be," achieved acceptability – even admiration – in the best society. Mary Jean Corbett, in her book *Representing Femininity*, argues that, despite a popular Victorian notion that a theatrical woman was the epitome of unconventionality, certain actresses, by publicly portraying "the middleclass ideal of womanhood," made the actress "a respectable public woman." Julie Hankey, in her essay "Helen Faucit and Shakespeare: Womanly Theater," suggests that the revered name of Shakespeare gave the actress a refuge from criticism and endowed her with legitimacy.[3] Although I think both scholars are correct, as far as they go, I must pursue the matter farther. Granted that a reputation for portraying ideal womanliness could counteract, to some extent, the stigma of a stage career, how did Helen Faucit acquire such a reputation in the first place? And, having done so, how did she maintain it offstage, in view of such business-world necessities as financial arrangements and publicity?

An interest in these and related questions has determined my varied approaches to different parts of Helen Faucit's life. In the first nine chapters, which deal with her formative years – a lengthy period that reached completion well after her fame was secure – I follow her progress step-by-step; this allows me to show her twists and turns in response to early influences but, all the while, her gradual development of a distinctive personality and style. In Chapter 10 I abandon the strictly chronological account for a comprehensive description of her life as a woman star and her ways of coping with its problems. The rest of the biography covers her life after marriage, when she played a variety of roles – wife, actress, social figure, and literary critic. I concentrate on each of these in a separate chapter, but I also note their interrelatedness and the permeation of them all by her theatrical interest. My last chapter gives a loosely chronological account of major events in her final years. In the Afterpiece, the reconstructions of several character portrayals demonstrate, among other things, how Helen Faucit depicted such "dangerous" passions as erotic love, ambition, and pride without losing her reputation for womanliness.

Returning to the subject of paradoxes, we find some interesting ones in Helen Faucit's personality and in her acting. A "reconciliation of opposites" is usually easy where her acting is concerned. Take the opposing traits of passion and formality, for instance: although some writers stress one and some the other, many witnesses show that in the best of her mature performances she held the two in balance and created an artistic synthesis. As for her personality, reports of it are so divergent as to suggest an explanation rooted in her background and early life. I think I have found the right one, but how can anyone be certain?

As all historians know, the evidence for recreating the past is necessarily flawed. The subjectivity that makes diaries and reminiscences particularly interesting also raises questions about their accuracy in reporting events. Biographies, even serious, well-documented ones, can be slanted to fit some overriding thesis. The two published works most essential for any biographer of Helen Faucit illustrate these problems. They are: (1) Helena Faucit, Lady Martin's own book of essays interspersed with personal reminiscences, *On Some of Shakespeare's Female Characters*, 4th edition (Edinburgh, 1891); and (2) Sir Theodore Martin's *Helena Faucit (Lady Martin)* (Edinburgh, 1900). Lady Martin began writing her essays in 1880, only a year after her last stage performance and nine years after her professional retirement, but between forty and fifty years after most of the events she describes in the autobiographical passages. In some cases she had her diaries to help her, but in others she apparently relied on unaided memory. The descriptions of her stage performances present little difficulty, but several reminiscences of early life contain details at odds with information from other sources. When I first noticed these discrepancies, I suspected Lady Martin of indulging in imaginative reconstructions for herself as she did for Shakespeare's heroines. After checking the questionable stories as well as possible, however, I concluded that, although three showed signs of romantic embroidery, none had been cut from whole cloth. In the biography I give slightly edited versions of two such accounts and explain my changes in the notes; but, for the third, most important one, I tell Helen Faucit's story, then analyze the evidence and give my interpretation. Sir Theodore's biography of his wife is invaluable in providing otherwise unobtainable material, such as extracts from her diaries (the originals were evidently destroyed). It is frustrating, however, not only because of the over-idealization mentioned earlier, but also because of the occasional misrepresentations. For example, in discussing Helen Faucit's first London performance of Belvidera, Martin says that "severe notices" were published in "some of the minor journals" (21), thus ignoring the adverse reviews in such notable periodicals as the *Morning Post* and the *Examiner*; he also attributes a laudatory quotation to a "leading journal" without naming it or mentioning its place of publication – New York, not London. His quotations, though often inexact, do not usually alter the basic meaning of the original, but in at least one instance the quotation is wholly fabricated. When discussing the Festival Performance of *Macbeth* in 1858, Martin says that the "most interesting" critique of Helen Faucit's portrayal was published in the *Art Journal*, and he quotes a long, enthusiastic passage (251-53). That journal has no such article, however; instead, a large portion of Martin's "quotation" is lifted, almost verbatim, from a review published in the *Scotsman* on 26 April 1845. In my biography I habitually quote reviewers' comments only from the original articles. When I do borrow from Martin an interesting passage unavailable to me elsewhere, I document it "as quoted by Martin" – *caveat lector.*

Two essential but partly unreliable sources for theatre history and biography are promptbooks and theatrical reviews. Promptbooks, especially those used over a period of time, are often ambiguous and inadequate as evidence, yet, in conjunction with information from other documents, they can be very helpful. (See Afterpiece.) Theatrical reviews present various problems. As we know from our own experience, two critics can describe a performance so differently that it is hard to believe they saw the same one. Although conflicting testimonies may simply reflect the writers' ingrained ideas about a character or play, they may also reflect variations in acting if the critics saw the production on different nights. Changes in a performance, even if not deliberately introduced during a run, may occur spontaneously, sparked by something in the actor's mood, in the interplay between actors, or in the audience's response.[4] Thus Lady Martin remarks that the "inspiration of the scene" often clarifies what has not been previously "dreamed of"; in acting, she recalls, she tried to keep her mind open to such "revealings" rather than mechanically repeat previous performances

(108). Sometimes an actor, without consciously altering an interpretation, creates a wholly new impression simply by having matured the portrayal.[5] In her early years Helen Faucit, a highly-strung actress, was particularly volatile. When playing a role famous for its grand effects, she was excessively nervous on opening night, and, in trying to meet conventional expectations, she strained her voice to the point of ranting. During the run of the production, however, she suited the role to her own abilities and produced impressive effects of a new kind. First-night reviews obviously give an inadequate idea of such portrayals.

Journalistic and personal biases are other impediments to the accurate reporting of performances. A newspaper's political policy, for example, might affect a reviewer's attitude.[6] The *Examiner*, a weekly periodical with Whig sympathies, was likely to favour plays, playwrights, and actors that upheld democratic principles, whereas *John Bull*, a weekly with Tory orientation, was likely to attack these. There was no consistent connection, however, between theatre criticism and political views. (Indeed the political views themselves were sometimes inconsistent.)[7] Macready, who was stoutly democratic in principles, was a frequent victim of *John Bull*'s vituperation. Yet he also suffered from assaults by some Whiggish weeklies, which branded him a "Tory" because he kept company with baronets, dined with wealthy families, and discriminated against the "popular" press.[8] Certain newspapers, though strongly political, had equally strong interests of other kinds. For example, The *Sunday Times*, besides being "savage with the Tories" and "equally savage" with the Socialists, was sternly moralistic and so fervidly patriotic as to condemn foreign drama at English theatres.[9] Writers were sometimes influenced by personal friendships and antipathies. John Forster, who was theatrical reviewer for the *Examiner* during Helen Faucit's early London period, was a personal friend of Macready's, whereas Charles Westmacott, editor of *The Age*, was his enemy, being friendly instead with Macready's *bête noir*, Alfred Bunn. As a theatre manager, Macready denied free passes to particularly hostile reviewers, like those for the *Weekly Dispatch* and the *Satirist*, who thus became all the more hostile.[10] Actors in his company, including Helen Faucit, could suffer or gain in the reviews by association with their manager. A critic who was partial to a particular actor might judge a rival with undue harshness, especially in roles associated with the favourite. On the other hand, reviewers could be unusually benevolent on occasion. John Hollingshead, dramatic critic for the *Daily News* during Helen Faucit's latest London performances, admits that he occasionally gave a "friendly 'lift'" – "as we all do" – to someone who asked for it. He adds, however, that as a rule his reviews were "as honest as [he] could make them."[11] The *Athenaeum* prided itself on its completely candid reviews, and *The Times* had a similar policy.[12] Fortunately for Helen Faucit, the provincial reviews in her starring days showed little effect from political bias, though they occasionally revealed a partisanship for another actress.

I have tried, despite this confusing state of affairs, to get reasonably close to Helen Faucit's performances as most people saw them. In order to achieve a balanced perspective I have collected many reviews of each production, supplemented first-night reviews (whenever possible) with later ones, and coordinated the testimony of newspaper critics with evidence from other sources. Though alert to signs of prejudice, I have not ignored the tainted reviews. With due allowance for exaggeration, even malicious criticism can sometimes be enlightening. Reviews, whatever their flaws, are the materials on which we chiefly rely when attempting to reconstruct past performances. When used judiciously, with due respect for the language and ideas of their time, they can do much to help us visualize a performance and imagine the audience's response.

In one of Simon Brett's theatrical mysteries, Charles Paris contemplatively soaks up the atmosphere of an old theatre, whose Grave Trap, Star Trap, and Corsican Trap speak intriguingly of performances long gone by. He is indulging in "that pleasingly painful feeling of hopeless nostalgia which always comes from the knowledge that, however much one exercises the imagination, however much one researches, it is never possible to know what the earlier times were really like."[13] True. Even if the evidence were not flawed, we would still see it reflected in the mirror of our own experiences and prejudices. To go through the looking-glass is an impossible fantasy. Yet at fleeting moments a crack opens up in it, revealing in perfect clarity a living person – a lonely child – a young woman torn with conflicting emotions – a brilliant star – a Court lady splendidly gowned and bejewelled. Then the glassy surface closes once more over that other world. I have experienced many such moments while working on this biography. I hope the same will be true for its readers.

PART I: "Apt To Learn and Thankful for Good Turns"

The Taming of the Shrew, 2.1.165

Chapter 1

Beginnings

In 1880, when Helena Faucit Martin became Lady Martin by virtue of her husband's knighthood, friends reminded her that her title was nothing new.[1] From her earliest days as Helen Faucit, the actress, she had attracted nicknames like Ladybird, Lady Helen, even Princess. They seemed hers by right because of her distinctive combination of fastidiousness, grace, and imperiousness.

But they implied no aristocratic heritage. She was simply the fifth of six children in an ordinary family of actors – not even "aristocrats of the theatre." Although she belonged, on her mother's side, to the third generation of players, the Diddears never had the distinction of a dynasty. As for her father, John Faucit Savill[e], although he begat a whole tribe of thespians, he never succeeded in playing a patriarchal role, much less a kingly one. The nearest Helen Faucit came to theatrical royalty was through her stepfamily, the Farrens.

Nevertheless her family background was important. As with many other stars, her brilliance seemed to concentrate within itself all the lesser brightnesses inherited from her forebears or reflected from her environment. Relatives associated with the stage included grandfather, parents, stepfather, sister and brothers, half-brothers, aunt and uncle, cousins, nieces, nephews, and various other connections by law or courtesy. They represented, among them, almost every kind of dramatic activity, from classical acting to performing in burlesques and pantomimes, and almost every kind of theatrical affiliation, from the great patent theatres to the London minors, from Royals in major provincial towns to fairground booths and struggling companies on the poorer circuits. Perhaps awareness of the lower levels of the profession added impetus to Helen Faucit's naturally strong ambition to reach the highest. She attained her goal, thanks to her own talents and determination, but thanks also to the encouragement of the professional-minded Farrens, who provided her early theatrical training, bargained energetically on her behalf, and imposed upon her the discipline of unsparing criticism. Although she specialized in tragedy, high comedy, and romantic drama, her performances may have reflected, on occasion, influences from the fine melodramatic acting of several close relatives.

Personally, as well as professionally, she can be understood, in part, as the product of family influences and incidents of family life. Friends saw in their offstage princess something like the harmonizing of opposite traits that critics noticed in her best acting: power and grace, passion and reticence, grandeur and delicacy. For unsympathetic associates, however, the grandeur seemed outright arrogance; the delicacy, mere affectation; the reticence, frigidity. The family story helps to explain such disparities.

Family Background

The most stable presences in Helen's early childhood were her maternal grandparents, John Diddear (c. 1761-1841) and his wife Elizabeth (1763?-1838). Since mother and father rarely had time for the children, Helen depended for her sense of security on these "dear grandparents," who, as she later wrote, were "real parents to me in all my earliest years."[2]

At the time she referred to, Diddear was in semi-retirement after years of varied experiences. He was evidently of French extraction, if not literally of "French origin," but nothing is known of his family except that his uncle was the "celebrated Major La Valeire" – now, alas, a forgotten hero. According to early accounts, Diddear began his career (evidently in his teens) as a merchant in the West Indies; after heavy losses in the island of Antigua, he became a silk mercer in London, and, when that venture failed, turned to the theatre.[3] He had considerable experience as a "utility" actor in the provinces, his longest stint being nine years on the Exeter circuit. The rest of his career was spent largely in management (sometimes alone, sometimes with Robert Copeland) in towns like Brighton, Margate, Richmond (Surrey), Dover, Sandwich, and Deal.[4] Diddear's abilities shone particularly at the fashionable Theatre Royal, Brighton, which he managed alone for three seasons (1796-98) with much *éclat* – no mean feat, considering the sophisticated and demanding audience. Ultimately, though, his industry brought no commensurate success: a lack of financial shrewdness and a naive trust in his associates made him vulnerable to manipulation.[5] Like other provincial managers, he exploited his children – to their professional benefit. Helen would find in him the moral support she needed at a critical moment in her early career.[6]

Elizabeth Diddear was a Quaker who had lost membership in her church by "marrying out," yet retained its beliefs, including opposition to the theatre. As the wife of a manager, however, she had to compromise: she never entered a theatre herself, but she sometimes sold tickets from the adjoining house; she lent her name to an occasional benefit; and when her children performed on the stage, she probably prayed for their success, as she would later do for her granddaughter's. Perhaps Helen's simple but genuine religious faith was a legacy from her.[7]

The Diddears had at least four children: Harriet Elizabeth, Elizabeth Isabella, Martha Louise, and Charles Bannister (named for the well-known comedian); all except Martha had longtime careers in the theatre. Harriet, who became the mother of Helen Faucit, was the most prominent; Elizabeth (later Mrs. Sheppard) had a successful provincial career, especially in York; and Charles, after some years in the provinces, became a well-known though secondary actor in London. Despite Helen's lack of closeness to her mother – indeed partly because of her longing for a closeness she did not have – there was no stronger force in her youth than the one exerted, both positively and negatively, by this woman. Although Helen was removed in childhood from her father's direct influence, his personal traits and early experiences must be taken into account, if only because of her mother's responses to them. The disruption of the parental relationship, with its consequences in the lives of the children, would have left a lasting impression on a sensitive child.

The explanation of these influences must begin with Helen's mother, whose experiences as a child actress probably did much to mould her formidable personality. Harriet Diddear (1789-1857) was born at Penzance, in Cornwall, while her father was acting on the Exeter circuit.[8] She was not quite seven when she made her debut on 5 July 1796, her father's opening night as manager at Brighton; as the boy Edward in Mrs. Inchbald's *Everyone Has His Fault* she astonished the audience by her "extraordinary abilities." "Little Miss Diddear" continued to enchant the playgoers both in dramatic parts and in pertly appealing prologues and epilogues. She was a particular favourite of the aristocrats who patronized her father's theatre: on one occasion, the Duke and Duchess of Marlborough led the whole house in repeated applause; on another, the Duchess of Galway patronized her benefit night, and the theatre was "crouded with all the fashion of Brighton."[9] If the clever little girl had her head permanently turned, it was no wonder. And if success in the theatre became a criterion of personal worth for her, that was hardly surprising either. During her years of transition from precocious child to adolescent woman she was eclipsed by more experienced actresses, but by 1804, when she had reached fifteen, she was taking some fairly substantial roles in comedy and farce. In this year, while acting at Richmond, she met the young actor, "Mr. Faucit," who was to become Helen Faucit's father.

Mr. Faucit's real name may have been John Faucit Saville (or Savill, as he usually spelled it). All but one of the official records I have seen for him and his children support this possibility, but, lacking his baptismal record, I cannot be sure. Since the documents giving "Savill[e]" as the children's last name also include "Faucit" as the middle name, presumably a double, though

The Richmond Theatre in 1804, John Diddear's period
(by courtesy of the London Borough of Richmond-upon-Thames)

unhyphenated, surname is intended.[10] Helen Faucit's paternal grandparents have eluded all attempts to trace them. Perhaps the family originated in the West Riding of Yorkshire, which was particularly rich in both Faucits and Savilles (each spelled in a variety of ways); John, however, may have grown up in East London, where he first appeared on the theatrical scene. As far as I know, he was not related to the theatrical Fawcetts.

John Faucit Saville, or possibly John Saville Faucit (c.1783-1853), came to the Richmond theatre from the travelling company of the eccentric "Muster Richardson," which toured from one fair to another, acting in a large, ingeniously-constructed booth that could be taken apart and reassembled at need. He had joined the company at Stepney Fair while still in his teens and had stayed with it for two seasons or more. His fairground experience in constantly-repeated mini-dramas, written to formula, fostered stereotyped impersonations, and the manager's exaggerated notions of "bould" speech encouraged a tendency to rant. But John also learned, under the Great Showman, to carry himself with assurance, to act with precision as part of an ensemble, and to become a genuine artist in pantomime. Occasionally he had an opportunity for more ambitious acting, for Richardson sometimes followed a successful fairground visit with a day or two of regular productions in the same town. In fact, "Saville Faucit," as Richardson called him, reportedly owed his engagement at the Richmond theatre to his performance of Young Norval in a post-fair production of *Douglas*.[11]

The new member of the Richmond company, though too short for the ideal gallant (he was about the size of Edmund Kean), may well have seemed a romantic figure to fifteen-year-old Harriet Diddear. A young man of twenty-one, with some unusual experiences behind him, he was easy to confuse with the sophisticated roles in which he was sometimes cast. Harriet, young as she was, must have shown signs of developing the "fine figure" for which she was later admired, and her face, with its bold, lustrous eyes, framed in dark, curly hair, was strikingly handsome. Her appearance and poise would have created the effect of a maturity beyond her years. A mutual attraction developed, but apparently the Diddears did not approve an early marriage. In the following summer, when John was again at Richmond and Harriet was in her father's company at Margate, the lovers eloped to London and, on 2 September 1805, they were married in St. George's Church, Southwark. Although Harriet had only recently celebrated her sixteenth birthday, she was able to pass for "full age" and thus to marry without her parents' consent. The Diddears soon became reconciled to the fait accompli, and bride and groom began acting, as "Mr. and Mrs. Faucit," at Margate.[12]

In the following year the Faucits joined a relatively prosperous company on the large Norwich circuit, which embraced seven towns. Except for one brief hiatus they remained with it for the next seven years.[13] During this period their first four children were born: John (1807), Harriet (1808), Edmund Henry (1811), and Alfred (1812).[14] All would have careers in the theatre. Life cannot have been easy for Mrs. Faucit, often pregnant, as she met the constant demands of study, performance, and travel while, at the same time, caring for her growing family and keeping their wardrobe, personal and theatrical, in order. (Provincial actors often "found their own clothes," and actresses always did.) She did needlework for her children behind the scenes, laying it aside when her presence was required onstage and resuming it the moment she came off.[15] Such domesticity was no sign of contentment, however, for Harriet's theatrical ambitions were unassuaged. Although she eventually became the leading actress of the Norwich company, her sights were on London. John Faucit, who acted principal parts in pantomime but only the "second juvenile line" in regular drama, acknowledged his wife's superior talents and humbly tried to promote her interests. Half a dozen of his letters, written to Drury Lane and the Haymarket, give touching evidence of such efforts: they apply for positions for both himself and his wife but emphasize the latter's talents; two have postscripts saying that if a position can be offered to Mrs. Faucit only, that will be "no bar to an agreement."[16]

Eventually the Faucits did get a London engagement, not at Drury Lane but at the other great patent theatre, Covent Garden. Mrs. Faucit made her debut on 6 October 1813 as Desdemona to the Othello of "Handsome Conway," a recent arrival from Dublin. Major journals took little notice, but some of the lesser ones published interesting reviews. In general they praised the new actress's figure, face, voice, and knowledge of the stage but censured her mispronunciations, her smug self-assurance, and her tendency to play to the audience. Mrs. Faucit went on to act other important roles. Although she shone with no special brilliance (she was eclipsed, in fact, by Eliza O'Neill's sensational success in the following season), she did firmly establish herself on the metropolitan stage. Throughout her career she would be associated with one of the major theatres. Her greatest successes were in melodrama, comedy, and regal but matronly roles like Gertrude in *Hamlet* and Queen Elizabeth in *Richard III.* In the greater characters she was too much of a tragedy queen, and even in her best parts she sometimes antagonized the critics by her seeming arrogance.[17]

Mr. Faucit, whose roles at Covent Garden were infrequent and usually minor, began devoting much time to provincial management. Later he also achieved a certain success as a dramatist – for example, in *The Miller's Maid.*

Mrs. Faucit as Queen Gertrude in *Hamlet*
(anonymous print 1828: Harvard Theatre Collection, Houghton Library)

Among his early theatres was the little playhouse on the London Road, Greenwich. This property included a dwelling-house for the manager, which made a convenient residence for the family when Mrs. Faucit's presence was not required at Covent Garden. The Faucits were well liked in Greenwich, except by some anti-theatrical Dissenters. Mr. Faucit was considered "unimpeachable" as "a man, father, and neighbour," and his wife's presence was reportedly "coveted" in good society.[18]

According to a manuscript statement (author unknown) in the Local History Library of Greenwich, Helen Faucit was born in Greenwich in 1814. The year has proved correct (not 1817, as her husband states): she was born on 11 October 1814. If the family had established residence in Greenwich by that time, it may well have been her birthplace. It is possible, however, that the future actress was born in the heart of theatrical London, in lodgings at No. 9, Great Newport Street, Leicester Square. That was the residence recorded when six-month-old Helena Faucit Saville (known familiarly as Helen) was baptized on 5 May 1815 at the Church of St. Martin-in-the-Fields.[19]

The Faucits' sixth and last child, Charles, was born in Greenwich in 1816. According to Theodore Martin, he was "educated as a doctor" and "died in Australia." If he did study medicine, he probably never practised it. (His brother Edmund served an apprenticeship to a surgeon, but then embraced the family profession.) Charles did go to Australia, but his career there is uncertain. He appeared on the Sydney stage at least once, however (in 1838), and, despite bad reviews, he may well have remained in the theatre.[20]

The Rupture in Family Life

By the time Helen was two and a half years old the Faucits were spending the late summer months (July-September) at the seaside. For by 1817, if not earlier, Mr. Faucit had assumed the management of the Theatre Royal, Margate, rich in honeymoon memories, and Mrs. Faucit, billed as a Covent Garden star, was acting off-season in her husband's productions. John Diddear was back in his old haunts, taking charge of the box-office for his son-in-law, and Mrs. Diddear was probably caring for her grandchildren. Family enterprise and family living at the seashore – this all sounds very pleasant. By 1819, however, there were signs of erosion: Mrs. Faucit, who had accepted starring engagements at Birmingham and elsewhere that summer, made only a few appearances on the Margate stage.[21] Family life would continue in some fashion through the Margate season of 1820, but the agents of destruction had been at work for some time.

Mrs. Faucit was a proud, ambitious, strong-willed woman. Though not without affection, she was even less capable than most people of loving without imposing demands and qualifications. Not only she but those who belonged to her must succeed. Mr. Faucit seems to have had a softer, more sentimental nature. He obviously loved the theatre, but his ego was satisfied with small successes. His wife's ambition demanded a London stage; his own financial opportunities lay in the provinces. Husband and wife often maintained separate establishments; sometimes they did not see each other for as much as two months.[22] Even if the once-romantic Faucit had not fallen short of his wife's expectations, the lack of a shared domestic routine posed some danger to their marriage. The immediate cause of its rupture, however, was another man.

Mrs. Faucit's new interest was the famous comedian William Farren (1786-1861), with whom she had become acquainted when he joined the Covent Garden company in 1818. Farren had grown up in a relatively privileged London household: his father, the first William Farren, though an actor of only moderate accomplishments, had been able with the aid of a wealthy benefactor to support his family in a gentlemanly style. The younger William's career, prior to his Covent Garden engagement, had been entirely provincial; in recent years he had acted at the Theatre Royal, Dublin, where he had built up a reputation in his chosen line of "old men." On 10 September 1818 he made a successful London debut as Sir Peter Teazle in *The School for Scandal*, and he went on to win acclaim in other parts, notably Lord Ogleby in *The Clandestine Marriage.* He remained in London, where he enjoyed a long and eminent career.[23]

William Farren in costume, caricature by "Sem" (by courtesy of the Folger Shakespeare Library)

Though a remarkable actor, Farren had some personal traits that interfered with his popularity among colleagues. He was accused of being opinionated, egotistical (calling himself the "only cock-salmon in the market"), overly fond of money, and selfishly inclined to monopolize the audience's attention. He had the reputation of driving a hard bargain and of rarely doing a favour without expecting one in return. Jokes about his miserliness were only half-true, however: he pinched no pennies on the creature comforts; in fact, he was sometimes envied for his handsome style of living. Farren did have some attractive traits, though, to balance his foibles. He good-naturedly endured the practical jokes that were frequently played on him, and he had an easy, courteous, and friendly manner when not "on his high horse."[24]

Farren may have been less attractive than Faucit, but he was reasonably good-looking, and he clearly outshone his rival in wealth and professional reputation. Just how soon the two did become rivals is unknown; Faucit had no warning, apparently, until it was too late. Farren himself had a wife, a "very handsome young lady of good family," not an actress, whom he had met in Dublin, but her charms could not compete with the voluptuous attractions of Mrs. Faucit. Although he had the reputation of a child-hater, Farren reportedly jested, in the then-popular jargon of phrenology, that he had left his childless wife because of a belated rising of his "bump of philoprogenesis."[25]

Gossip, which may well have been true, said that he made arrangements for Mrs. Faucit and himself to star at several of the same theatres and that their affair began during one of the journeys together. Evidently it was well advanced when Faucit had Farren at his Margate theatre for the first time, on 4 September 1820, to act for Mrs. Faucit's benefit. Later, after his wife had left Margate, Faucit received the news of her "delinquency and his own disgrace." According to "all the talk," he was stunned: on the night he found out, he left the theatre in great agitation, shaking off many people who spoke to him, and went to the home of a close friend. Here he consumed "upwards of two bottles of wine, without being visibly affected" – a surprising aberration in this normally temperate man.

> He paced the room, and seemed unconscious of the presence of anyone. To his friend's inquiries he made no reply. He once said, "My heart is almost broke, but you will soon know why." He quitted the house at two o'clock, and wandered round the rocks for some hours … He has never reproached her; but his silence speaks for him.[26]

This sounds like imaginative reconstruction, but, even if details of the picture are suspect, the central figure gives the impression of reality.

The next act in the Faucits' domestic drama seems as improbable as anything they might have played on the stage. On 11 May 1821, the Consistorial and Episcopal Court of London initiated the trial of a case known as "Diddear falsely called Faucit, otherwise Savill against Faucit." After being a wife for fifteen years and bearing six children, Harriet was trying to have her marriage annulled. Only the sketchiest records of the trial are extant, but evidently the chief ground alleged for annulment was her having married under the legal age without her parents' consent. On 13 July the judge's decision was handed down: predictably, Harriet had lost her bid for freedom.[27]

Her annulment attempt must have been intended as a first step toward a legal union with Farren, but, unless Farren could have had his own marriage annulled, any hope of that would have been vain. Divorce was out of the question: aside from other difficulties, Farren had no grounds for a suit, and, although Mrs. Farren could certainly charge adultery, in practice it was virtually unheard-of for a woman to be granted a divorce. (Unlike a man, she had to prove aggravating circumstances in addition to adultery – and even wife-beating was not aggravating enough.) Perhaps if Harriet's suit had succeeded, Farren would have tried to have his marriage annulled on some pretext relating to its childlessness. But, since his own parents had created a happy home without being legally married, he might have thought Harriet was making an unnecessary fuss.[28]

The mature lovers probably lived circumspectly until Harriet's case had been decided and Mrs. Farren had been established in a new home,[29] but at some point they set up housekeeping together and Farren became the acknowledged "stepfather" of the Faucit girls, Harriet and Helen. The house where they lived for many years, No. 30 Brompton Square, was pleasant and commodious, for No. 26, which must have resembled it, had six bedrooms, two drawing-rooms, two parlours, and "every needful convenience." The neighbourhood was congenial, too, for a number of theatrical people lived there. The Farrens had several live-in servants, and they kept their own carriage – a smart green equipage, which offended one righteously-indignant writer as a sign that the wicked were not only flourishing but flaunting their prosperity.[30]

It is doubtful that Mrs. Faucit "bitterly regret[ted]" leaving her husband for William Farren, as *Oxberry* sentimentally alleges, but she probably did regret being unable to put the new alliance right in the eyes of the world, the family, and the church – especially the last. Galling as the "world's" disapproval might have been to this woman who thrived on admiration, she could face down any jests, moralizings, or slights with regal self-assurance. Other problems would have been more difficult. By deciding to live with Farren she had given up some part of her rights in the Faucit children; apparently her husband was amenable to a compromise, but no complete solution was possible. A few years later there were two Farren children to think of: William, born in 1825, and Henry, 1827. Their illegitimacy and her own irregular union with Farren must have caused her enduring anxiety, for she had a high regard for the sacraments of the church. Happily for her peace of mind, she and Farren would outlive their respective spouses and would be able, in their declining years, to make their union legal.[31]

An obituary of John Faucit Saville states that he was "legally divorced" from his first wife and that he married again twice. The "divorce" was certainly a polite fiction, and any other marriages were necessarily bigamous. To be free to remarry John would have had to be granted a separation in the ecclesiastical court, then to win damages against Farren in a civil court for "criminal conversation," and finally to petition Parliament successfully for an absolute divorce by Private Act. Leaving aside the unpleasantness and complication, he could not have afforded this extremely expensive process.[32] He probably acted in as much good faith as he could, but, like many of his contemporaries, he was frustrated by an outmoded system. John's second "wife" was "the widow of an actor named Amthos, the daughter of a country manager named Collier." She was obviously the "Mrs. Faucit Savill" whose name appeared in the Margate playbills in 1822 and the years following, for the former "Mr. Faucit" was now listed in those same bills as "Mr. Faucit Savill." (Though this was possibly the correct form all along, he undoubtedly made the change so as to dissociate himself from Harriet, who continued to use "Mrs. Faucit" professionally.) After the death of his second mate, John was "united," it is said, to "the daughter of a Yorkshire clergyman." This must have been the Emily Moody whose marriage with John Faucit Saville is recorded as having taken place on 11 April 1829 at St. Clement Danes. He had at least two children, Ann and Phoebe, after the breakup of his first family, but Helen, who never saw her father again, would not have known these half-sisters of hers.[33]

Sir Theodore Martin (3) states that after the Faucits' separation the girls were reared by their mother, the boys by their father. There was more contact between mother and sons, however, than he implies. In the early days, according to *Oxberry* (III: 133), Mrs. Faucit contributed "largely to the support of her children, most of whom [were] with her, or under her controul," but the eldest son (John, Jr.) was with his father. Perhaps the younger boys stayed with their Diddear grandparents at first but joined their father after he had established a second family. Whatever the arrangements, brothers and sisters were not completely separated emotionally. Helen, though brought up with the Farrens, would always be particularly close to her brother John.

The professional careers of Helen's brothers reflected their mother's influence as much as their father's. Although they used the name "Saville" after becoming established actors, they all began their careers as "Faucits," thus exploiting their relationship with a London actress. Moreover, at least two of them, and probably all (barring Charles, the unknown quantity), maintained a friendly relationship with Farren. John, a provincial actor-manager, engaged him as a star for his theatres; and Alfred, a mostly provincial actor, specialized in Farren's line of "old men," imitated his manner, and even (reportedly) wore his cast-off costumes.[34] Edmund, who lived in London for many years, was, geographically, the brother closest to his mother's household, but, being the most successful one – he was an outstanding melodramatic actor at the Victoria, the Surrey, and the City of London – he was least dependent on Farren's help.[35]

Growing Up: Schooldays and Holidays

In the long run, then, family feeling as well as practical considerations prevailed over possible hurt and resentment. But what of the immediate damage done by the family rupture to the child Helen? Just six when the annulment suit was in progress, she would not have understood the implications of her mother's actions, even if twelve-year-old Harriet did. It was at this time, most likely, that she was enrolled in the Greenwich boarding school that she attended with Harriet, evidently Miss Kimbell's School in King Street.[36] But the new life, though it helped her escape some awkward family scenes, might well have brought tensions of its own. It is hard to say how much theatrical gossip would have reached the families of Helen's schoolmates or how the attitudes of censorious parents would have influenced their daughters' treatment of "those Faucit girls." (Even the children of respectable theatrical families were sometimes unwelcome as associates for the other students.)[37] Mrs. Faucit, instead of helping young Helen bridge the gap between the old life and the new, made only rare appearances, always as "a great lady, beautifully dressed"; even then, she actually "repelled rather than wooed the daughter's demonstrations of affection." The Faucit sisters often spent holiday periods with their grandparents rather than with their mother.[38]

In later life Helen would recall the smothering sense of claustrophobia that haunted her in her youth and the nights of insomnia when, in lonely wakefulness, she "look[ed] round on the little beds to see the others asleep." Perhaps these problems were due to something more than circulation difficulties or "weak action of [the] heart." Although she never outgrew them completely, she would always associate them with boarding-school memories.[39]

Helen's one firm centre in this time of change was her merry-spirited, resilient sister, "Harry," who assumed a motherly responsibility toward her. Though "too fond of fun" to understand the strange daydreams of little "Birdie," as she called her, she cheered her as no one else could do.[40]

The boarding school at Greenwich became Helen's chief home, probably until well past her fourteenth birthday; it also provided all the formal education she was to receive. Miss Elizabeth Kimbell, the head mistress (or "governess," as Helen called her), conducted the school in a house that had been her own home. The pupils here must have varied widely in age, as they often did in such establishments – "some very little ones, and some fifteen, sixteen, and seventeen years of age" – for Harriet and Helen received all their education under one roof.[41] The cost of boarding and instruction was about 30 guineas a year with 3 guineas more for laundry and possibly other fees if drawing, music, and so on were considered "extras." Although moderate compared with the charges at the more expensive schools, where one might pay 100 guineas or more,[42] this was a substantial sum for Mrs. Faucit, particularly during the five or six years when both daughters were students.

Miss Kimbell's school would have offered no training in classical languages, as the best boys' schools did, for women never went on to a university at that time and never entered a profession like law or medicine. Higher mathematics, too, was probably, though not necessarily, omitted from her curriculum. Helen evidently read some history, however, and she may have been lightly exposed to a science or two, neglected though such subjects often were.[43] The subjects most likely stressed at Miss Kimbell's were those conventionally associated with boarding schools for girls: poetry and other literature (at least a smattering, sometimes much more), French, and such "accomplishments" as music, drawing, dancing, calligraphy, and what might loosely be called "social conduct" (grace of posture and movement, propriety of manners, and so on). There was probably some emphasis on moral and religious instruction as well.

The strongest appeal to young Helen's imagination came from literature. Although her recollections of favourite books refer most specifically to those read on her own, at least some were met through her studies: for example, a blank-verse translation of Dante's *Inferno*.[44] Her training in French was at least adequate, for, when supplemented by some free lessons from Madame Sala (a singer who was also a personal friend), it would enable her to hold her own in the fashionable salons of Paris.[45] An "accomplishment" that she shone in and loved all her life was dancing. As a young woman she considered no party complete without it: "I wish all people were as fond of it as I am," she wrote after an evening's disappointment, "they would be capering eternally." And in later years, when visiting Scotland with her husband, she would join enthusiastically in the Northern Meeting Balls, holding out "gallantly" in the long Highland reels.[46] She studied piano and voice, of course, and she even tried her hand at composing. Although her musical talents were not equal to Harriet's, she could perform pleasingly enough in a party of friends.[47] Drawing was probably not a strong point – there is an amateurish sketch of Harriet as Mary, Queen of Scots, which may have been drawn by the youthful Helen[48] – but somehow, at school or later, she developed an understanding and appreciation of art. Her love of great painting and sculpture would have a strong influence on her mature acting. Judging by her performance after leaving school, "social conduct" was one of her best subjects, calligraphy her very worst. Finally, with or without Miss Kimbell's encouragement, young Helen developed a strong idealistic tendency.

Although this boarding school, like most contemporary schools for women, would today be considered inadequate or worse, the education it provided was at least superior to what most actresses received. It was generally true that "the real aim of a girl's education . . . was to make her more superficially attractive because the only course open to her was marriage,"[49] but some of the much-derided "accomplishments" could have practical value in a theatrical career. It was in the intellectual realm that Helen, a girl with a good mind and a soaring but undisciplined imagination, needed something more than her limited formal education could provide. For this she would have to depend on private study, sometimes self-directed but often undertaken on the advice of a chosen mentor.

Some years later, overwhelmed by the superior education of her idol, Macready, Helen would feel despondent about her own limited knowledge. Macready would comfort her by the assurance that education of real value is "for the most part self-acquired. We merely gain a certain start by early tuition, but we teach ourselves most rapidly, and learn most, after our minds have `grown up.'"[50] Helen never lost her interest in self-improvement, and as a result she finally acquired with some critics an excessive reputation for scholarly learning and artistic taste. A good indication of her real accomplishments at the time of her early maturity (1845) is found in an admiring but reasonably objective description of her by Sir Archibald Alison, the historian. She lacked some cultural advantages, like proficiency in foreign languages, enjoyed by carefully-tutored or widely-travelled women of his family: at that time she knew only French, and her reading of Dante, Schiller, and Calderon, whose works she discussed with him, had been limited to English translations. Yet, as Alison later recalled, this young woman, "without any advantages of fortune or situation, was not only fully equal, but in many respects superior, in conversation to a man of fifty whose life had been spent with the aid of far greater facilities in the constant study of literature and the arts."[51]

The school-time experiences that Helen remembered best were the extra-curricular activities. Especially prophetic of her future was a performance of the cave scenes from Shakespeare's *Cymbeline* that a group of girls got up in honour of their "governess's" birthday. Helen managed to be cast as Princess Imogen (disguised here as the page Fidele), leaving her schoolmates to play the male parts: old Belarius, the courtier-turned-recluse, and the two young princes whom he had stolen in their infancy and reared as hunters in the Welsh mountains. The girls must have ransacked their trunks for costumes, for they dressed the cave-dwelling princes in "all the fur trappings, boas, cuffs, muffs, &c.,[they] could muster." Then there was the problem of "simulating Belarius's 'ingenious instrument'" that plays, unbidden, for Imogen's supposed death. As Helen recalls: "Our only available means . . . was a guitar; but the girl who played it had to be apart from the scene, and, as she would never take the right cue, she was always breaking in at the wrong place." She says nothing about her own performance, but she does report that her "governess" later saw her act Imogen professionally.[52] It would always be a favourite role.

There were no playing fields at schools like Miss Kimbell's, for team sports were considered unsuitable for girls. Instead, for health and recreation, the students were taken on walks, often to Greenwich Park, with its herds of tame deer, its grand avenue of Spanish chestnuts, and its famous Observatory. Then there was Blackheath Common, notorious for its legends of Wat Tyler and Macheath-like highwaymen, but in the Faucits' time the scene of cricket games, donkey rides, and coconut shies. Helen especially enjoyed the donkey rides, but she complained that they were "much too rare."[53] A silhouette picture of her as a child, wearing a riding habit and holding a little whip, is preserved in her sister's album, now in the Folger Library.

Helen Faucit as a child, in riding habit, silhouette cut from life (by courtesy of the Folger Shakespeare Library)

Among Helen's favourite walks was one to "Lee churchyard" – that is, the burial ground of St. Margaret's Church in the village of Lee, about two miles southeast of Greenwich. The church itself was modern (it had replaced an ancient one on the same site), but its cemetery had some venerable monuments. One of these took a special hold on Helen's imagination: which one is hard to tell from her later description, but it may have been the imposing Dacre tomb, which is enclosed by iron fencing.[54] With her was her favourite school-friend, a German girl who shared her "dread of the terrible" and also her "attraction … towards it." The two girls would stand and peer through the railings, describing to each other, with delighted shivers, what they imagined to lie underneath the ornate bulk of the monument. As they talked and stared, they could almost see the slimy green steps leading down to the vault, where a "massive door" with "open iron-work at the top" was all that stood between them and – Juliet! For they had named this "Juliet's Tomb," and while their gothic fancies flourished, unchecked, they half believed it was.[55]

Harriet Faucit, who reached her eighteenth birthday in December 1826, must have left school by that time. According to Sir Theodore Martin (2), Helen remained there for several years after the older sister's departure, deeply lonely for the companionship that had taken the place of maternal care. "She was thus early thrown upon the resources of her always grave and thoughtful nature." An even gloomier report, published during Helen's early years as an actress, says she had "a melancholy temperament in girlhood" and "estrange[d] herself from her companions at school," devoting their hours of play to "self-communion." The author, Mrs. C. Baron Wilson, might have received her information from Anna Maria Hall, a mutual friend of hers and Helen Faucit's. She attributes Helen's schoolgirl "morbidness of feeling" to "domestic events of a painful nature" – an obvious reference to the Faucit-Farren scandal. Ellen Braysher, a friend in whom the young actress certainly confided, was so moved by passages in Helen's early diaries that their revelations of a "sad, uncherished youth" haunted her memory for many years.[56] There was plenty of reason for periods of melancholy. Mrs. Wilson's explanation is certainly plausible: Helen, a budding adolescent at the time she lost Harriet's companionship, might well have become more sensitive than ever to her family's unconventional situation; perhaps she "estranged herself" from schoolmates because of some half-formed fear of rejection. Yet, as Mrs. Braysher's word "uncherished" suggests, her deepest sense of alienation came from a rejection nearer home.

At its worst, however, the picture could not have been completely dark. References to "our dear governess" suggest that Miss Kimbell was sympathetic and affectionate; the German friend's zestful participation in Helen's gloomy fancies would have effectively reduced their morbidity; and a sense of companionship and fun shines through the *Cymbeline* story.

According to Helen Faucit's own statement, she was taken "early away from school, because of delicate health" and "often sent to spend months at the seaside."[57] Her precarious health was a lifelong problem. She took colds easily, had severe bouts of coughing, was particularly subject to "affection of the chest," and suffered from painful nervous disorders. The usual prescription was rest, especially at the seaside. At such times in her girlhood Helen stayed at Brighton, in the home of "kind but busy people" (otherwise unidentified), under the care of someone named Kate.[58] Among the friends whom she undoubtedly saw in Brighton was her brother John, for her teenage visits coincided with the period when he was acting, as "Mr. Faucit," at the Theatre Royal there (1828-31). She would also have come to know Marianne Hobden, who, though only two years older than she, was already an actress ("Miss Fox") and who became

John's wife in 1830, at age eighteen.[59] The warm relationship that would always exist between Helen and her eldest brother's family was undoubtedly fostered by such early experiences.

A resident of Brighton whom Helen knew in her youth and continued to cherish as a friend was the Reverend Henry Michell Wagner, vicar of the ancient Church of St. Nicholas. Being "a High Churchman and a Tory in a largely Whig community," this colourful, strong-minded man was often involved in controversies with leading citizens, including his own vestry. But, for all his militancy and dogmatism as a public figure, Wagner was sympathetic and kind to his young parishioner Helen Faucit. His encouragement followed her into the theatre: in her early London years "he never missed an opportunity of seeing her on the stage." They agreed that if ever she married he would perform the ceremony.[60]

During her Brighton periods, Helen later recalled, she spent many hours on the beach with her books, alone except for "the great dog of the house" that accompanied her. All her life she loved the sea: she "could sit by [it] watching the wonderful life and motion of it for hours." There was plenty of time here for day-dreaming, time for reading and rereading her favourite passages, acting out the scenes in her imagination. Milton's Satan was, she writes, "my great hero. I think I knew him by heart. His address to the council I have often declaimed to the waves, when sure of being unobserved."[61] Another favourite passage was one of Dante's that she still remembered (though not with strict accuracy) more than fifty years later: "Up! be bold!/ Vanquish fatigue by energy of mind!" Like some of Satan's speeches, it inspired her with its ideal of unconquerable soul. "How often since," she exclaims in true Victorian fashion, "in life's hard struggles and trials, have these lines helped me!" But it was true: such lines were talismans for her; she even jotted some down in her promptbooks as oblique directions to herself. *The Arabian Nights*, with its visions of the strange and marvellous, found its proper setting in Brighton, where one could look, even with the outward eye, on a pinnacled Pavilion, exotic in its Eastern splendour yet so airy and graceful it might have floated in on the foam. Very different was her volume of *The Pilgrim's Progress*, with its tedious passages full of allegorical names – yet romantic in its own way, with its exciting combat between Christian and bat-winged Apollyon and its dreadful dungeon guarded by Giant Despair. Helen's books, though "a strange medley," satisfied her youthful cravings, filling her imagination with images of "the gorgeous, the wonderful, the grand, the heroic, the self-denying, the self-devoting."

Such was the context of her first intensive reading of Shakespeare. Since the edition she had "begged" from home was an acting version by John Philip Kemble, she received an incomplete and, occasionally, a distorted view of some plays. *Romeo and Juliet*, for example, had the Garrick version of the tomb scene, in which Juliet awakens in time for an ecstatic reunion with Romeo (poisoned but not yet dead), followed by an anguished farewell.[62] At Brighton, where Shakespeare need no longer compete with irregular verbs and musical scales, Helen could relive in luxuriant detail the ordeals of her old favourites, Juliet and Imogen, dwelling anew on the courage and faithfulness of these devoted women. And she could create in her imagination whole lives for such freshly-discovered heroines as Ophelia, whom she found fascinating "partly, perhaps, from the mystery of her madness," and Desdemona, into whose life she "entered with a passionate sympathy" that she could never recall without emotion. Here was a character who embodied all the qualities she most admired: "A being so bright, so pure, so unselfish, generous, courageous – so devoted to her love, so unconquerable in her allegiance to her 'kind lord,' even while dying by his hand ..."[63]

Memories of her youthful sympathy for Desdemona had a lifelong power over her because they evoked emotions associated with her own experiences. Most of Shakespeare's young heroines are motherless, a fact pathetically stressed by the mature Helen Faucit in some of her essays. But in the essay on Desdemona (also motherless) the greatest emphasis is on the deprivation of emotion in her relationship with her father:

> Absorbed in state affairs, he seems to have been at no pains to read his daughter's nature, to engage her affections or her confidence. Thus a creature, loving, generous, imaginative, was thrown back upon herself. ... Making so small a part of her father's life, and missing the love, or the display of it, which would have been so precious to her, she finds her happiness in dreams of worth more exalted than any she has known, but which she has heard and read of in the poets and romancers ...

This imaginative reconstruction of Desdemona's early life served two purposes in Helen Faucit's interpretation: it explained Brabantio's misreading of his daughter's character without making Desdemona herself seem deceitful, and it explained Desdemona's readiness to fall in love with the heroic Othello, who is the fulfilment of her romantic dreams. But it also served a private, less conscious purpose as the surrogate story of Helen's own youth. The parents' roles are reversed: Helen's father, long missing from her life, is the "dead" parent; her mother, present but inclined to repel demonstrations of affection, is the one who drove the daughter "back upon herself," her reading, and her dreams. Helen Faucit's explanation of Brabantio makes this truth inescapable:

> There is a kind of proud frowardness in some natures which, as I have known, even while loving dearly, will yet hold aloof from, keep at a distance, the objects of their love. They claim as a right that which will not grow without care and fostering, without some responsive looks, some tender words.

"*As I have known* ..." She has drawn here a picture of her own mother.

Another aspect of Desdemona's story also seized on Helen's imagination: because of her own horror of being smothered, which gripped her at "the very thought of being in a crowd" or of having "any pressure near [her]," the manner of Desdemona's death had a "fearful significance" for her.[64] In that long-ago time at Brighton the younger Helen would not have formulated her ideas so clearly, but she was drawn with a "passionate sympathy" to Shakespeare's heroine because, if only subconsciously, she identified herself with the noble but misvalued Desdemona.

Helen's family, which now included two little half-brothers, regularly spent their summer vacations in Richmond (Surrey). Here, in a "small house on the Green," the children were often left with an elderly servant in charge while the Farrens were in London or on tour. Helen was always happier in Richmond than anywhere else in her youth, and in later years she liked to take drives there with her husband, catching fresh glimpses of the house which, even then, "looked to her like a home."[65] That Richmond "home" seems to have been a boarding-house on the south side of the Green, owned by Mr. George Ellard. In his old age Mr. Ellard often recalled how Helen Faucit used to stay in his house and how "some great actor (one of the Kembles)" would come there and give her lessons.[66] (The tutor was Percy Farren, but perhaps the old man's memory was better in other respects.) Judging by the property assigned to Ellard in the Rate Books, Helen and her family stayed in what is now called Gothic House (No. 3, The Green). It is larger than her description suggests, but it would have been less imposing in her day: the front rooms and "battlemented" façade were added later.[67]

Gothic House, though a near neighbour of the present theatre, sits obliquely across the Green from the place where the theatre stood in Helen's youth. In that earlier building her grandfather had once served as manager, and his family had lived in the bow-windowed cottage attached to it. It was there, too, that her parents had met and fallen in love. In a few years it would become a landmark in her own life.

"Nothing could be so beautiful!" the teenaged Helen exclaimed about Richmond. Looking back later, she wrote: "Every step of the Green, the river-banks, the fields round Sion House, the Hill, the Park, the Twickenham Meadows, were all loved more and more as each summer enlarged my sense of beauty."[68] In her early memories, her love of natural scenery, a lifelong trait, was as closely linked with Richmond as her love of books was with Greenwich and Brighton.

Chapter 2

Trial Flights

IT IS commonly said that Helen's family kept her away from the theatre in early youth because they did not wish her to become an actress.[1] This is, almost certainly, pure romance. Her grandmother undoubtedly disapproved of a theatrical career, but it is hard to imagine her mother's opposition. Besides, women had few other dependable means of support, and, except for a literary or artistic career open to a few fortunate ones, none that better rewarded their talents and efforts. Walter Donaldson, a provincial actor of Macready's age who had spent some time in France, observed in his autobiography that French women could get positions, like that of shop assistant, which in England would usually have been held by men; English women were mostly limited to employment as governesses, house-maids, or grossly-underpaid seamstresses.[2] (He ignored some kinds of jobs, such as those in factories, but none that the Farrens would have considered.)[3] Although actors had some advantages over actresses, Donaldson was substantially correct in saying that the stage provided the only situation "where woman [was] perfectly independent of man, and where, by her talent and conduct, she obtain[ed] the favour of the public."[4] True, theatrical people had an equivocal status, both professionally and socially, but so, to a lesser extent, did many artists, musicians, and writers. Actresses, of course, were especially vulnerable to their profession's stigma of dubious morality – as a class, indeed, they were often considered little better than prostitutes. Yet some outstanding ones, like Fanny Kemble, had attained not only respectability but social prominence, especially in artistically-inclined groups which included established professionals like lawyers and academicians.[5]

Even so, an actress who valued a reputation for "womanliness," as defined by middle-class standards, had good reason to encourage the story that she had not been intended for the stage – or indeed for any work outside her home. The ideal woman avoided the public arena, where exposure to the darker side of human nature would coarsen the personality and weaken the moral and spiritual ideals; safe in her domestic realm, she preserved those ideals for her family in their pristine purity and, by her own refinement, charm, and inspiration, provided her menfolk with a redemptive haven from their struggles in a ruder world.[6] Even her social life must be of a properly protected kind; organizations and functions traditionally associated with masculine activities were inappropriate for her. Women were generally excluded from public dinners, for example, though they might be allowed to look on from a spectators' gallery. Ironically, this applied even to actresses, who had already flouted the feminine ideal: at the annual dinners benefiting the Royal General Theatrical Fund (held at the height of Helen Faucit's career and long afterwards), only men were seated at the table; the women spectators usually got nothing to eat, though occasionally they were served a "preliminary repast" before being seated "advantageously" near the vocalists or decoratively amid "palms, ferns, and flowers."[7] A gentlewoman whose circumstances deprived her of the ideal life could survive respectably by living with relatives or by working as a governess, the least demeaning of positions open to women; in either case, however, she had a dependent and ambiguous relationship with her hosts. In that society, a woman who had been propelled onto the stage by a sudden discovery of her extraordinary talent – as Helen Faucit supposedly had been – might well have seemed less aggressively unfeminine than one who had deliberately sought a public career. In fact, however, she did not stumble upon the stage by accident; she was trained for it.

The Farrens' strategy for promoting their daughters' careers differed sharply from that of the average theatrical family. Harriet and Helen would not enter some provincial company in their teens, hoping to rise by stages to leading lady and eventually to win a trial in London. Instead, after an education that would fit them to be ornaments of both stage and society, they would be trained for the theatre by an experienced actor. A convenient tutor was Farren's elder brother Percy, stage manager of the Haymarket Theatre; since chronic asthma had curtailed his acting, he had leisure for other work. When his pupil was sufficiently advanced, her talents would be displayed on the stage in as favourable circumstances as possible; though named only as "A Young Lady," she would be heralded by grapevine as a debutante worth watching. She might be tested then in some provincial engagements, too few to mark her as a "country actress." Finally, William Farren would press the manager of a major London theatre to allow his *protégée* a place in the company. If she succeeded, she would enhance the family's reputation and contribute to its bank account.

The plan was only a qualified success in young Harriet's case.[8] She did make a creditable debut at the Haymarket in 1828 on her stepfather's benefit night, and, after some provincial experience, she did get an engagement at Drury Lane beginning with the season 1829-30. Although she remained there four seasons, however, she achieved no outstanding success. When she tried the provincial theatres, she did very well. Miss Faucit, as she was known on the stage (later Mrs. Bland), had great versatility – she succeeded in all kinds of drama, from tragedy to burlesque, and she performed adequately in opera – but she was best in comedy and in domestic melodrama, where she aroused pathos by natural rather than exaggerated means. Although she had inherited her mother's Junoesque figure (as Helen had not), her acting style was very different from Mrs. Faucit's: no one accused her of arrogantly "parading" the stage or of giving "the vulgar outline of tragic effect" without any "delicate filling-up."[9] She had charm, sensitivity, and a certain amount of power. Although she was not, as sometimes maintained, equal in talent to her more famous sister, she was a very good actress.

At the time Harriet began her engagement at Drury Lane, Helen had left school and was living at home, under Percy Farren's tutelage. The sisters, much separated in recent years, could now resume their closeness, and Helen's own studies could receive constant reinforcement from the practical experiences of her beloved Harry. It is even possible that Harriet's relatively strong interpretation of Ophelia (her best Shakespearean role) influenced Helen's conception of the character.[10]

In training for the theatre Helen would have studied elocution and the arts of expressing the passions by look, gesture, and carriage; later she would have prepared herself in certain roles considered essential to a leading lady's repertoire. Farren must have described to her great moments in her predecessors' portrayals, for, although she later denied any knowledge of other actresses' "points," several of her striking pieces of business can be traced to former impersonations. Apparently, however, he encouraged the imaginative young woman to develop her own ideas as well.

Though an exacting taskmaster, Percy Farren was a kind, understanding teacher, more patient with his young charge than her mother was and more interested in her as a person than her stepfather. Her dreaminess and romantic emotionalism did not make him laugh as they did even Harriet. The teenaged girl became deeply attached to him; he called her his "child," and she obviously found in him the father she had missed. But the master-apprentice relationship was important to her, too: she needed someone whose approval she valued to direct her and demand her best efforts. She would always be grateful to the man who first filled that need:

> He … taught me much of what I learned, after my delicate health took me from school … and to him and him only could I confide, with the assurance of perfect sympathy, all my devotion for the heroines of Shakespeare. He taught me the value of the different metres in blank verse and rhyme, as I recited to him many of Milton's poems, the

> "Lycidas," large portions of "Paradise Lost," and Byron's "Darkness". . . . He made me understand the value of words, nay, of every *letter* of every word, for the purpose of declamation. Nothing was to be slighted. This true friend – a man of varied and large acquirements, a humourist, too, and a wit – never refused, although most delicate in health, to give me largely of his time. (Helena F. Martin 92)

The statement, occasionally made by critics, that Helen Faucit was trained in the "Kemble school" was evidently true as far as elocution went: the rhythmic speech and unusual precision of enunciation mentioned in her own account were certainly associated with the Kembles.[11] So, too, was the over-elaborate use of gesture to enforce meaning, noticed by critics of her early acting. On the other hand, there was not much Kemble stateliness in Helen's youthful demeanour (some of that would come later); she was likely to be accused of extravagance rather than of coldness. One must remember, of course, that the Kemble women were more dynamic than the Kemble men[12] and that Helen had not only heard wonders about Mrs. Siddons but had almost certainly seen Fanny, whose brief but memorable reign at Covent Garden coincided with Harriet's first three seasons at Drury Lane. Even so, the stormier tendencies in Helen Faucit's acting may have owed their strongest inspiration to Edmund Kean.

Kean's connection with her family went a long way back. According to "Muster" Richardson, "Saville Faucit" and Edmund Kean (using the name "Master Carey") had been in his company at the same time. There seems little reason to question this; in fact, Helen's brother Edmund may well have been named in honour of the early friendship.[13] The Faucit sisters became acquainted with Kean, however, in the last few years of his life, when Harriet acted with him during his starring engagements at Drury Lane. In 1831, when the Farrens moved into their summer quarters at Richmond, Kean had become their neighbour across the Green: he had leased the King's Theatre, as it was then called, and was occupying the manager's cottage. Harriet was a member of his Richmond company, which had a summer season, and when Kean himself chose to appear she sometimes acted with him.[14] Though his acting had sadly deteriorated, he still had moments when he could make the lightning flash. Sixteen-year-old Helen, knowing he was the "pet hero" of her adored sister, would have been awestruck at his very name. Here in the tiny Richmond theatre, where his expressive face imposed itself clearly upon every spectator, she must have been mesmerized.

Helen Faucit gives no account of such experiences – they would have destroyed the fiction that she was forbidden the theatre in her youth –but she vividly recalls a personal meeting with the famous actor. He was hobbling across the Green with the help of his tall, grey-haired "aunt," Miss Tidswell, when the Faucit girls contrived to encounter him "by chance" so that Helen could meet him. (Kean drove himself hard, despite his weakened condition, but when he relaxed between bouts of feverish activity, his debility became obvious.)[15] As they approached, Helen, a shy girl, nearly retreated before the strange, unnerving sight. She saw a "small pale man," wearing, in spite of summer weather, "a fur cap, and wrapped in a fur cloak. He looked … as if come from the grave. A stray lock of very dark hair crossed his forehead, under which shone eyes which looked dark, and yet bright as lamps. So large were they, so piercing, so absorbing, [she] could see no other feature." Kean greeted the sisters kindly, but his voice "seemed to come from so far away – a long, long way behind him." He tried to draw Helen out by quoting whimsical verses and asking questions, but she was too spellbound to respond. Only when he asked how she liked Richmond did enthusiasm loosen her tongue.[16]

A few months after Kean's death, in 1833, the happy accident occurred which, according to Helen Faucit, determined her career as an actress. When her family arrived in Richmond for the summer, a new manager, Willis Jones, had taken over the little theatre. One hot afternoon Harriet and Helen, en route to the river, stopped to rest in the cool, dark theatre, which was deserted on off-days like this one. (Performances were held there only a few times a week.) The sisters noticed on the stage "a flight of steps, and a balcony, left standing no doubt after rehearsal." Impulsively Harriet exclaimed, "Why this might do for Romeo and Juliet's balcony! Go up, birdie, and I will be your Romeo." And so, with "much laughter, and with no little stumbling over the words," they acted their impromptu balcony scene. Afterwards they learned, to their chagrin, that the manager, "having occasion to go from the dwelling-house to his private box," had overheard the "merry rehearsal." Impressed with the Juliet's voice and figure, he persuaded the Farrens to let her have a trial on his stage. "Thus," the actress concludes her story, "did a little frolic prove to be the turning-point of my life."[17]

The implication that Helen had not previously been intended for the stage must, of course, be rejected. If the Farrens needed persuasion to let her try her wings as an actress, they must have had misgivings about her readiness. Perhaps her age and her emotional temperament gave them pause: although she would soon be nineteen, she was nearly a year younger than Harriet had been at her debut, and her response to the challenge of a public appearance was unpredictable. Of course, Helen's story may be romance from beginning to end. There are two reasons, however, for accepting some version of it: first, the physical arrangements of the theatre and the attached cottage made it possible for the manager, while in his house, to hear sounds on the stage – which he would naturally investigate; and, second, Helen's debut at Richmond had none of the *éclat* of a launching planned by the Farrens. I suggest that Helen, ambitious then as later, was eager to begin her career and that the sisters cleverly arranged an "audition" in the guise of a lark.

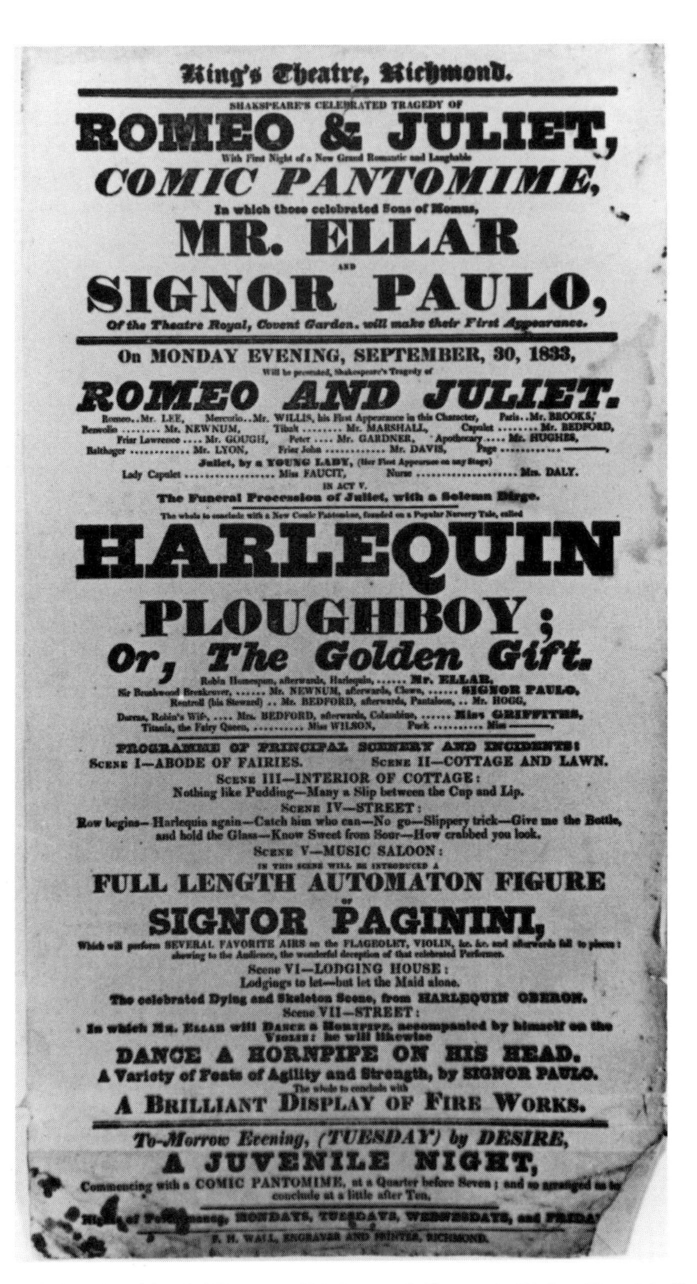

Playbill for the King's Theatre, Richmond (Surrey): Helen Faucit's first appearance on any stage, as "A Young Lady", in *Romeo and Juliet* (by courtesy of the London Borough of Richmond-upon-Thames)

Whatever the prologue, on Monday evening, 30 September 1833 – exactly five years, to the day, after Harriet's debut – "a Young Lady" made "Her First Appearance on any Stage" at the King's Theatre, Richmond, in the character of Juliet. Romeo was played by Mr. Lee, Mercutio by Mr. Willis (i.e. Willis Jones,the manager), the Nurse by Mrs. Daly, and Juliet's mother, Lady Capulet, by the Young Lady's sister, Miss Faucit. (Harry had taken this matronly role so as to provide moral support, but her genuinely maternal anxiety made her almost as nervous as the debutante.) The playbill listed, enticingly, as part of the fourth act, "*The Funeral Procession of Juliet with a Solemn Dirge,*" and, more enticingly still, the delights promised by the afterpiece, *Harlequin Ploughboy; or The Golden Gift* – including a "Full Length Automaton Figure" of Paganini, the famous violinist, which was "to perform several favourite airs," then "fall to pieces."

In honour of her debut Helen was allowed to dress in the parlor of the manager's dwelling-house – a room where Edmund Kean had sometimes prepared for the stage. His toilet articles were displayed in a glass case nearby, reminders of the greatness that was gone. Or not completely gone, perhaps? Responsive to atmosphere, the slender, dark-haired girl could almost sense Kean's sympathetic presence as she stood, waiting, in her white satin dress. As curtain time approached and she heard the instruments being tuned in the theatre nextdoor, she discovered a new kind of claustrophobia. She would never forget her first experience of stagefright:

> I felt a most unaccountable sensation stealing over me. This feeling grew and grew until it nearly overcame me. I saw my mother looking very anxiously at me. ... I begged her to leave me to myself for a few minutes. At first she did not gather what was in my mind, and tried to rally my courage; but again I begged to be left, for I knew well that when alone I could more freely seek the help [I needed] ...

Mrs. Faucit and her companions finally did as Helen asked. When they returned to call her for the stage, they found her composed but pensive. As she was leaving the room, someone asked whether she had left anything behind. She turned for a farewell look at her talismans in their glass case. It felt like a farewell to life itself.

On stage Helen was shocked by a sense of unfamiliarity. After only daytime rehearsals, the auditorium lights perplexed her (at that time they could not be dimmed during performance), and the faces in the audience seemed unexpectedly close. As the panic-stricken girl looked about, her gaze fixed on a single face – Percy Farren's – whose agitation mirrored her own. Miraculously, his fears calmed hers. She would not disappoint her "dear master." Self-control eventually merged into self-forgetfulness, as the new actress became increasingly absorbed in Juliet's story. So absorbed that in the potion scene her sympathetic horror caused her unconsciously to clench her hand and crush the glass phial she was holding. When she saw the blood, she fainted away, creating a dramatic conclusion to the scene. Fortunately the family doctor, who was present for the debut, lost no time in binding up the wound.[18] The new Juliet completed the play successfully and was rewarded with "most cordial" applause – no less hearty, of course, for the accident.

Mrs. Cornwall Baron Wilson, who was present, later recalled: "Though evidently struggling with that nervous timidity so natural to her novel situation, her personation . . was far above the common run of *débutantes*; and there were points in it that gave bright promise of future excellence."[19]

Another member of the audience was Anna Maria Hall (née Fielding), known at that time for her popular *Sketches of Irish Character* and later for a prolific output of stories, novels, and travel books. She and her husband, Samuel Carter Hall, also a writer and later an editor of several important journals, became lifelong friends of Helen's. These indefatigable do-gooders, who delighted in encouraging young artists, writers, and other creative people, were influential acquaintances. The wife had all the effusive charm associated with her native Ireland, and the husband, though he had spent only part of his youth there, outdid her in blarney; but beneath her frothiness and his humbug were a genuine devotion to art and friendship. Anna Maria, at that time a pretty little woman of thirty-three, lost no time in telling Helen of her enthusiastic approval. In her impulsive way she was soon calling her "Ladybird," a pet name borrowed from Juliet's Nurse but reminiscent, too, of Harriet's "Birdie." (Later it was picked up by Helen's other close friends.) No doubt she did much to publicize her *protégée*'s talents.[20]

Pleased with the interest aroused by his new actress, Willis Jones had her repeat Juliet on the next acting night, 2 October. This time a wooden phial was provided, and there were no mishaps.[21] The Farrens had removed their household to London by now, but the Faucit sisters, ensconced in smaller lodgings, remained for an abnormally protracted Richmond season.[22] Although Harriet, as a member of the company, acted regularly, Helen's further appearances were delayed in favour of a rival novelty, seven-year-old Master Mangeon, "the American Roscius." At last, however, on 28 October, for the benefit of Mr. Lee, "the YOUNG LADY who made so successful a debut in … JULIET" undertook a new role, Fanny Kemble's popular character of Julia in Sheridan Knowles's *The Hunchback*. How she fared is unknown, but Julia would later assume an important place in her career. Her fourth appearance, on 6 November, was in the difficult part of Mrs. Haller in *The Stranger*, Benjamin Thompson's adaptation of a German drama by August von Kotzebue. The play, seen perennially since 1798, had often been attacked because of its subject matter, but it remained on the boards for the sake of its strong roles. Mrs. Haller, a fallen wife who redeems herself through penitence and good works and, at the end, is reconciled to her husband, was a ludicrously inappropriate character for the virginal novice. Since it was a standard test of tragic merit, however, Helen was put through her paces in Mrs. Siddons's old part. The little theatre must have been packed that night, for Harriet was having her benefit and William Farren had come from the Haymarket to play two of his popular roles. Word of the new actress had been circulating in London, too, and this time a critic for the *Athenaeum* was in the audience. Thus the first review of Helen Faucit's acting was published in this important weekly periodical (9 November 1833: 315). Although it did not proclaim the advent of a star, it was very encouraging. The critic approved the novice's naturalness, grace, and "freshness," but, most of all, her "rare merit" of responding to other actors' words as if hearing them for the first time – her face took their "impress" and her answer seemed "the spontaneous effusion of her own mind." He (or she) concluded that, although she had "much to learn," she evidently had "both the inclination and the capability to learn it."

The Young Lady's fifth appearance was for Willis Jones's benefit on 18 November, announced as the season's closing night. She acted Mariana in Knowles's *The Wife,* a play introduced at Covent Garden barely seven months before. The heroine, originally intended for Fanny Kemble but actually "created" for the British stage by Ellen Tree, is a virtuous wife whose husband, the Duke of Mantua, refuses to believe his treacherous cousin's report of her adultery. According to Miss Kemble, she herself could not make anything of the part and she never heard of anyone else who could do so.[23] Whatever Helen made of it, Willis Jones was pleased enough to keep his theatre open for a repetition of *The Wife,* on 25 November. There may have been some additional performances.[24] Thus Helen's trial run, which comprised six or more performances in four very diverse characters, was a limited but genuine test of her abilities.

Audiences and theatre manager had been enthusiastic, but Percy Farren was not. After her last performance, Helen recalls, "I was sure something was wrong. He was very silent, and when I begged to have his opinion, whatever it might be, he told me I had not improved, – that I had disappointed him. I was not in the character throughout, and he feared I had not the true artistic power to lose myself in the being of another." Shocked into numbness, she only looked at him in silence; but, back in her room, she wept all night. Harriet tried to comfort her, assuring her of her great talent and berating Farren for his cruelty, but none of this helped. Helen had worked hard and done her best. And, much as she longed to be a great actress, her primary thought had been to please her master. When they met again the next morning, he was "deeply pained" by her response to his censure, which he belatedly tried to soften. After all, he said, he had expected too much too soon; what she needed was more time to mature. They talked things over with Mrs. Faucit, who decided that Helen must not be launched on her career until better prepared. The delay would reflect no discredit on her, for she had been represented as "very young."

In a moment of candour Helen Faucit later confessed, "I certainly was never a precocious child."[25] This was true. Her adolescent attitudes were prolonged to an unusual extent; indeed they contributed to her charm. Her frequent periods of illness and her early dependence on Harriet were partly responsible, no doubt, but so, too, was her unusually privileged preparation for the stage. Protracted study brought a certain depth of interpretation, but it denied her the mundane experience and the consequent self-reliance that regular provincial engagements could have given her.

A year later, after quietly working at home, Helen was allowed another trial at Richmond, this time abandoning her anonymity. Beginning on 29 September 1834, "Miss HELEN FAUCIT" appeared for three successive nights, each time in a different character: Juliet, Mariana, then Mrs. Beverley in Edward Moore's *The Gamester*. (There may have been other roles later.)[26] Mrs. Beverley, long-suffering wife of a compulsive gambler in an eighteenth-century domestic tragedy, offers the actress only two good "situations": when she repels the advances of the villain, Stukely, and when her husband dies in her arms after taking poison in debtor's prison. Yet Mrs. Siddons, besides electrifying her audiences in these scenes, had also aroused their admiration by her dignity and devotion in less dramatic ones.[27] Remembering this, successive actresses hopefully attempted the role, and a few, like Ellen Tree (later Mrs. Charles Kean), made it convincingly their own. Helen Faucit, while keeping it in her repertoire for twenty-five years, would never find it very rewarding. She could denouce Stukely with ringing sincerity, but she had trouble sympathizing with a weak-willed husband.

Percy Farren must have been pleased with his pupils's latest efforts, for he allowed a further test of her powers, shortly afterwards, at the larger Theatre Royal, Brighton. She faced a genuine challenge here. This theatre, though no longer so generously supported by the aristocracy as in her grandfather's day, had many sophisticated and fastidious patrons, including a number of visiting or retired actors. Besides, any tragic actor encountered resistance in the pleasure-loving atmosphere of Brighton. Audiences here wanted to be amusingly diverted or spectacularly entertained, not deeply stirred.[28] To protect Helen's reputation in case of failure, the Farrens, in announcing her first performance (29 December 1834), reverted to the anonymous "A YOUNG LADY" and even added, mendaciously, "being her first appearance on any stage."[29] They need not have worried. She was gratifyingly successful, and the billing was immediately changed to "Miss Helen Faucit."

Helen remained in Brighton through early February 1835, acting in at least eight parts: Juliet, Mrs. Beverley, and six that were new to her. Only three of the latter had a lasting place in her career. Jane Shore, that pathetic penitent in Nicholas Rowe's old blank-verse tragedy, would be a standard part of her repertoire but only as a filler. The others, Lady Teazle in Sheridan's *The School for Scandal* and Lady Townly in Vanbrugh and Cibber's *The Provoked Husband*, represented a new departure. Comedy of manners proved much more difficult for Helen Faucit, however, than tragedy and romantic tragicomedy. And, ladylike as she was in everyday life, she would soon find that even Shakespeare's shrewish Kate was more congenial in performance than the genteel parts so delightfully portrayed by her sister Harriet. She lacked the lightness of touch, the charmingly artificial manner required for such roles. Eventually she would act Lady Teazle with much success, but this time William Farren as Sir Peter must have wished for the other Miss Faucit.

The "Theatre" columnist who reported Helen Faucit's first appearance (*Brighton Herald* 3 January 1835), after compliments on her physical endowments and her "excellent readings," declared that she bore "the promise of much future greatness." Other notices were brief but very favourable.

Helen Faucit had now been tested on three occasions, at two different theatres, in at least a dozen roles, and her reception had always been good. The Farrens were finally ready to seek an opportunity for her at one of London's great patent houses, Drury Lane and Covent Garden. (Except for the smaller Haymarket, open mostly in the summers, these had a legal monopoly on Shakespeare and other "legitimate" drama in London, though the minor theatres sometimes broke the law with impunity.) Drury Lane, where William Farren would be acting in 1835-36, was out of the question for Helen's debut, for Ellen Tree would be there – and, now that Fanny Kemble had left the British stage for an American husband, Miss Tree was considered the most promising actress of the day. Covent Garden was in a precarious situation. It had recently been dropped by Alfred Bunn, who had struggled to manage both patent theatres at once, and D.W. Osbaldiston, former manager of the Surrey (known for nautical melodrama and opera), had taken it. His first move was to cut the prices of tickets by nearly one-half, thereby (as some thought) cheapening the reputation of a great national theatre.[30] Perhaps the Farrens waited for the situation to clarify before making a proposal. The time was propitious in one way, however. Charles Kemble was back at this theatre for the first time since leaving for America in 1832 – back without Fanny, whose loss would thus be felt afresh. The major actresses here were Mrs. W. West, the "heavy" lead, and Harriet Taylor, a talented if rather artificial performer but no star. An exciting new actress might do much to raise the theatre's fortunes.

Late in 1835 Osbaldiston agreed to give Helen a chance: she could perform Juliet, her chosen character, provided her acting in rehearsals was approved by Charles Kemble and other judges. She passed the test, but, two days after an advance announcement about Juliet, her role was changed to Julia in *The Hunchback*.[31] George Bennett, the prospective Romeo, had seemed too old for her at rehearsals, she was told. A more pressing reason may have been the imminent engagement of Sheridan Knowles, author of *The Hunchback* and first actor of the title part; with Charles Kemble and Miss Taylor to act Sir Thomas Clifford and Helen, respectively, the original cast of this play could be duplicated in its prominent parts – except for the heroine herself. In Julia, as much as in Juliet, a successful new actress would seem like another Fanny Kemble. Such strategy was far from the debutante's mind, however. Juliet, her favourite character since girlhood, had been the first role in every trial engagement; denying it to her now seemed ominously unfair.[32]

Disappointment was soon swallowed up in excitement. Time was short, and necessary preparations were demanding – dress-fittings, study, rehearsals. On the real preparation, however, years had already been spent. Soon everyone would know whether those years had been wasted.

Chapter 3

Uncertain Glory

AT A time when new plays were prevailingly melodramatic or farcical, *The Hunchback*, a romantic comedy in vigorous if awkward verse, stood out as an unusually successful legitimate drama. The plot, though easy to laugh at now, provided some strong situations for actors. Julia, sweetly naive ward of a hunchback, Master Walter, becomes affectedly worldly overnight when her cousin Helen introduces her to the giddy pleasures of London society. Rejected by her fiancé, Sir Thomas Clifford, who has overheard a flippant reference to himself, she agrees to marry the profligate Earl of Rochdale. She immediately repents, but Walter insists she must keep her promise. When Clifford loses his title and estate, Julia reveals her genuine love for him, but she checks his ardent response until she can be honourably his. After a stormy scene with Walter, in which she threatens suicide unless he rescues her from a hateful marriage, she asks Rochdale to release her. The marriage contract is invalid, anyway, for Walter proves to be the true Earl of Rochdale and also Julia's father, a relationship kept secret for fear she could not love a hunchback. A mature Julia can now be united with a Clifford who values her more than ever.

The Hunchback had several good roles, but, despite the title, the great one was Julia – a spirited heroine whose wilful behaviour entertained audiences without threatening their values since they knew her false pride would ultimately be subdued and her true womanliness revealed. This was a bravura part for the actress, requiring her to be, by turns, artless, flippant, indignant, desperate, and loving. Fanny Kemble considered it "by far the finest conception of female character . . . since the old golden dramatic age."[1] Helen Faucit, though less enthusiastic at first, was soon identifying herself with Julia and doubting that she could ever enter into another character "with all her heart and soul as she did into this."[2]

Helen Faucit by Clara Lane, from
Sir Theodore Martin's *Helena Faucit* (*Lady Martin*)

On the eve of her debut, Helen fretted nervously over her own deficiencies. After only three rehearsals, she was uncertain about some of her stage business, and she was worried about her appearance. She and Kate, her Brighton friend, had experimented with coiffures and settled on a neat, simple fashion with the hair centre-parted, drawn back behind the ears, and allowed to fall in loose curls to the shoulders. But nothing could be done about her main concern, her face. Though picturesque in its contrasts – fair skin and dark hair, blue-grey eyes framed with black lashes, – it was, except for the undeniably lovely eyes, more piquant than "handsome"; the cleft chin, imperfect nose, and generous mouth did not fit the current ideal of beauty. Such a face "never could have been intended for the stage," she wrote in her diary, "the features are so – well, I won't worry myself any more about it." But she continued to scribble compulsively until Kate scolded her off to bed.[3]

A novice might well have been overwhelmed by the thought of acting at the imposing Theatre Royal, Covent Garden, with its great portico and massive columns, its grand marble foyer and elegant promenades, and, most impressive of all, despite the grime that partially obscured the ornamentation, its vast, five-tiered auditorium that could hold nearly three thousand spectators.[4] Having acted only in Richmond's tiny theatre and Brighton's medium-sized one, could Helen even make herself heard here? And how would all those people respond?

Covent Garden audiences, though much more democratic than those of earlier periods, still followed to some extent the old classifications. The roughest spectators sat in the cheap gallery seats of the two top tiers. Many of these waited until the half-price hour to arrive, since they were less interested in the main production than in the afterpiece (usually a farce, pantomime, or other light entertainment, with perhaps music and dance). The boxes, which filled the first three tiers, had the most expensive seats in the house, especially the "dress boxes" of the lowest tier. Traditionally they had been occupied by aristocrats and members of the upper middleclass. Now the aristocrats had largely abandoned the drama for Italian opera. Many middleclass people had also stopped attending, repelled by the increasing number of uneducated, ill-behaved spectators – including prostitutes, whose presence had become more obvious than before. This trend, often noticed by stage historians, can be overemphasized, however. Respectable people, women as well as men, did attend the theatre in the 1830s and 40s to see admired actors in important revivals or appealing novelties. The ones with families preferred the private boxes with separate entrances, though some of those boxes could also be used for illicit purposes. On the ground floor, separated from the stage by the orchestra, were the benches of the pit, with their medium-priced places. Here sat the newspaper critics and other experienced theatregoers. Although some pittites could rival the gallery "gods" in shouts and hisses, the quiet ones were most dangerous. Their judicious censure could lastingly damage an actor's reputation.[5]

Covent Garden's stage, much larger than any other except Drury Lane's, could also be intimidating to a young actress. Its apron, the locus for most of the acting, projected about 12 feet beyond the curtain line; behind it, the proscenium arch, about 38 feet wide, framed and partly closed in the huge stage (more than 67 feet deep and 81 feet wide) that accommodated the scenery.[6] Like other theatres, Covent Garden still used the old scenic system of flats, wings, and borders, which permitted quick changes in view of the audience. Pairs of removable grooves, spaced at regular intervals, ran across the stage floor, with matching grooves above. The spaces between them, called "entrances," were the places through which actors normally entered or left the stage. (Traps in the stage floor allowed, at need, for entrances from below.) Two flats, with half a picture painted on each, would slide in grooves from opposite sides of the stage and meet to form a whole. When this scene was placed in the upstage area, it was supplemented with wings, set in the forward grooves, and borders (representing the sky or the ceiling of a room), hung from above in the forward "entrances." Sometimes "cut flats" were used for perspective and other special effects: for example, cut-out spaces between "trees" offered glimpses of a distant scene on a painted backcloth; or an arch cut in the "wall of a room" revealed another room behind it. It was possible to add "set pieces," either three-dimensional or profiled, to represent, for example, a building or a hill. Special productions might have an occasional "set scene" – an elaborate arrangement of individual pieces set in different planes, put in place behind a flat and revealed when the latter was drawn off. Although the scenery partly encompassed the actors at times, it served mostly as a pictorial background – not always an appropriate one. Generic scenes from the stock room – a prison, a palace, a forest – were considered good enough for regular dramas, as contrasted with new and elaborate sets for pantomimes and operas. Costumes, too, were often unsuitable. The gaslight, however, was up-to-date; it gave a consistent view of the stage and could be varied to suggest time of day.[7] With experience Helen would learn to use this theatre's facilities to advantage, but experience was, at the moment, exactly what she lacked.

On Tuesday evening, 5 January, playgoers were surprised to see the enormous theatre "filled to the slips [the seats at each end of the gallery] before the curtain drew up" – a remarkable sight in an age when the boxes were often deserted and the galleries were rarely crowded so early in the evening. Although there had been little newspaper puffery for the new actress (indeed some reviewers supposed Harriet Faucit was to play Julia), the grapevine must have been busy.[8] In the audience was Helen's grandfather, John Diddear, who was allowed, because of deafness, to occupy the orchestra leader's seat near the stage. Grandmother Diddear had given Helen her blessing, but, true to her Quaker principles, she remained at home "in an agony of suspense."[9]

Waiting in the wings for her entrance, the debutante had "most need of blessing." For, as the painted flats depicting the first scene slid away, to be replaced by "a garden before a country house," she stood frozen with stagefright. Harriet Taylor, who played the fictional Helen, put her arm around the real one and, when the "terrible moment" came, propelled her forward, whispering as the audience thundered its welcome, "Curtsey to the applause – again! again!" Helen, overcome by the cordial greeting, stood there trembling and faint. Rallying, she managed "indistinctly to articulate her first sentences, and by degrees she gained her self-possession." Only the mechanics were working, though, and they were not enough. Remembering the strength she had gained at Richmond by "acting to" her master, Helen searched for him desperately but could not distinguish him from the crowd.[10] With her powers all but paralyzed, she limped through the first act.

During the interval she was too distraught to respond to her colleagues' reassuring words, and when she was given sal volatile she spilled most of it on her dress. Her mother "looked sad and disappointed, the dear old dresser very pitiful." Percy Farren asked about her at the dressing-room door but, despite her pleas, could not trust himself to come in. She never forgot the "hopeless anguish" of that half hour.

Helen Faucit as Julia in Sheridan Knowles's *The Hunchback*
(*Illustrated London News* 6 March 1852, during a later performance)

The second act had begun. Helen had exchanged the ingénue's white satin for the city finery of Julia's new phase; a long, trailing feather in her hair gave her a dashing look, at odds with her mood. Once more the audience greeted her with encouraging applause. And this time her eye fell on her white-haired grandfather, whom, unaccountably, she had not seen before, close at hand though he was. She had, at last, the audience she needed. Instantly, it seemed, she grew calm and her voice "gained tone." As she threw herself into the spirited words and gestures of her part, the spectators saw not only a new phase of Julia's character but an entirely new actress. When she came to the words "I'll shine, be sure I will!" they broke into delighted applause. The rest of the evening was a fulfilment of that prophecy. So continuous and resounding was the audience's acclaim that Osbaldiston sought out the Farrens after the third act and offered a three-year engagement for Helen; they would sign a contract for her the next morning. Although she was actually twenty-one, the fiction that she was "much underage" allowed William Farren, a clever bargainer, to hold out for terms – thirty pounds a week – that the novice could hardly have won for herself.[11]

The deafening ovation at the end of the play left no doubt of Helen Faucit's conquest. At her curtain call she seemed "deeply affected," and a journalist who rushed backstage saw her lean against the scenery in tears. The "excitement of her success," as he expressed it, was as overpowering for this highly strung young woman as the fear of failure had been earlier.[12] At home, in the privacy of her room, she let her feelings gush forth in her diary, schoolgirl fashion:

> IT IS OVER, IT IS OVER, this as yet the most important day of my life, and, *I thank God well over* – at least I hope and trust so. It seems even now like a dream to me. I can remember nothing, think of nothing, but that it is over. Oh, happy, happy girl! and most of all happy in making those I love happy. Oh that some bird could whisper to my Harry! … I can remember *seeing nothing*, but my dear old grandfather … I will now bless the Almighty for having supported me through my (I must say it, because I felt it so) *fearful trial*, and try to go calmly to sleep. *Again and again. thank God it is over*! (quoted by Sir Theodore Martin 13)

The new actress's success was exuberantly celebrated in the newspapers. No other first performance within memory had been more triumphant, reviewers declared – not even Fanny Kemble's or (for those with longer memories) Eliza O'Neill's![13] Her physical and mental endowments were approved: her figure, voice, and face (expressive though admittedly not "handsome"); her taste, understanding, and conception of character.[14] As at Richmond, she was praised for her freshness and spontaneity – for her naturally-flowing words, her "free and unrestrained" action, and her "faith in herself, or rather … in the truth and force of the passion" she was portraying. Even her attempt to do too much, a problem that would draw fire later, seemed endearing.[15]

Inevitably the débutante's Julia was compared with the original one. Helen Faucit, like Fanny Kemble, effectively portrayed Julia's conflicting emotions, but, by unexpectedly introducing the softer feelings, she gave unusual complexity to some passages. In responding to Clifford's rejection (Act 2), instead of "bit[ing] his head off' as her predecessor had done, she mixed anger and hurt with lingering love and a consciousness of her own fault; and in their climactic interview (Act 4) she said, "Clifford! why don't you speak to me?," not in a "reproachful and violent manner," but in a tone of "tender entreaty." Critics were captivated, particularly in the latter scene. "Well as we know the play," wrote one, "and blunted as our dramatic feelings are by continual hacking, we found our heart thrilled by her natural and touching performance" here.[16] Only in the fifth act was Helen Faucit generally considered inferior to Fanny Kemble. In the desperate plea to Walter, "Do it! nor leave the task to me!" she knew she would be on trial. Winding herself up to her highest pitch, she tried to match the first Julia's ringing tones. She did receive excited applause, but, as critics pointed out, her voice lacked the power and modulation required for the thrilling effect she intended. She had better forget Fanny Kemble and suit the passage to her own abilities.[17]

Delighted with Helen Faucit's success as Julia, Osbaldiston had her act it thirteen times in her first three weeks and once more after that before appearing in a different role. No wonder; for, if the *Observer*'s reports are correct, on each of her first five nights the receipts fell "little short" of 350 pounds, the greatest sum a full house could bring at current prices, and each perfomance in her first three weeks brought an average of 150 pounds above expenses.[18]

Though she remained popular with the public, however, Helen encountered some unexpected hostility from reviewers at the end of her second week. On 16 January the *Spectator* critic, explaining that he had originally been overly excited by the "pleasure of surprise," published a second review that retracted much of his former praise. After coolly scrutinizing a later performance, he reported that imitation of Fanny Kemble seemed more widespread than before and that "plaintive tenderness" had lapsed, on repetition, into "whining, canting affectation." As if to make up for the earlier enthusiasm, the *Spectator* became one of Helen Faucit's harshest critics from then on. On 17 January, John Forster of the *Examiner*, who had previously been silent about the new actress, wrote that he was "sorry" he could not agree with all the "pleasant things" his colleagues had been saying about her. She was "clever and intelligent," but she was "not a fine actress" nor "likely, at present, to become one." Her "theatrical vein" was "forced, pampered, sophisticated" (witness her "sailing before the footlights" during Julia's agitated soliloquy after accepting Rochdale's proposal), and her attempt to present "everything, great or small, under the most taking aspect" made harmony and consistency impossible.

How can these delayed charges of artificiality be reconciled with the former praise of Helen Faucit's naturalness? Her impulsive temperament was often reflected in her early acting, giving the impression of spontaneity, but her arduous attempts at self-improvement sometimes counteracted it; perhaps, in responding to critical praise for her "plaintive tenderness," she over-cultivated this essentially delicate effect. Despite the occasional obtrusiveness of well-practised techniques, however, her intuitive identification with her character created, for sympathetic spectators, a sense of verisimilitude; thus the restless pacing, so reminiscent of Mrs. Faucit's tragedy-queen style,[19] probably communicated, however imperfectly, Julia's inner turmoil. The *Spectator* conceded that "her passionate emotions, if sometimes artificially expressed, appear to be spontaneously and vividly felt," and even Forster reported that the audience, evidently feeling these emotions with her, followed her portrayal with an "interest and delight" which familiarity with the play could not "destroy."

Forster was possibly influenced by the criticism of his friend William Charles Macready, who, after seeing Helen Faucit's Julia, wrote in his diary (11 January): "she had some force and some intelligence, but no elegance, little real abandonment [i.e. self-forgetfulness] and little true pathos – occasionally violent, flurried *larmoyante* and almost always *stagey* ..."[20] Macready, though recognized since Kean's death as England's foremost tragedian, was notoriously jealous of the success of other players, hence inclined to belittle them. Even so, the professional opinion of this severe but discriminating judge carries weight. Helen would have been crushed had she known of it, for her own diary (16 February) bears witness to her enthusiasm for Macready's acting: "somehow he always carries my heart and soul along with him, there is such earnestness and meaning about everything he does..."[21] An unconscious "dialogue" of the two diaries, begun in these antithetical passages, would later develop into a full-scale drama.

Meanwhile Helen Faucit had attempted a second role, Belvidera in Thomas Otway's blank-verse tragedy *Venice Preserved.* Virtually every tragic actress during the past century and a half had undertaken it, but for recent critics the ideal had been set by the beautiful and tender Eliza O'Neill. Her interpretation, as recollected through the rosy mists of fifteen years, was the one by which any new Belvidera would be tested. The plot of *Venice Preserved* centres on the involvement of the heroine's husband, Jaffier, in a conspiracy to assassinate the senators (including her father), burn the city, and institute a new government; Belvidera persuades him to reveal the plot, and, when Jaffier kills himself in remorse for having betrayed his friends, she goes mad. Although this role was full of strong situations for the actress, Helen considered it "overdrawn and unnatural"; she had to "force [her] feelings" in an effort at identification.[22]

On the first night of its performance (27 January) she had a gratuitous problem; her costume, ready only at the last moment, proved so tight she had to be worked into it by "squeezing and screwing" while the audience hissed at being kept waiting and Mrs. Faucit had hysterics. Sent onstage "like a stuffed turkey," expecting the seams to split at any moment, Helen was not at her best in the first scene, but she soon recovered her composure, and, as she thought, "got on *pretty fairly*." The audience, which had filled the theatre to see her new portrayal, applauded loudly and rose *en masse* when she took her curtain call. Charles Kemble assured her she had done well, and friends congratulated her on another triumph.[23]

This time, however, the press reported no triumph. Most reviews were either mixed or downright censorious. *The Times*, for example, remarked that every beauty had been immediately followed by a defect, and the *Morning Post* stated categorically that, on the evidence of her Belvidera, Helen Faucit could never be a great actress. A major problem was that her delicate constitution and limited vocal resources, only slightly noticed in Julia, were revealed as serious weaknesses in the heavier, more demanding part of Belvidera. (The tight costume could not have helped.) Several journals complained of inaudibility in the softer passages and shrill tones in the more vehement ones. The *Examiner* described her "screams" as "formidably repulsive, the more so as coming from so slight and delicate a person." Faults of delivery, too, were more obtrusive than before: monotony in the quieter passages (a "Kemble" fault) and too-abrupt transitions from one mood to another (an inept attempt at Kean's technique).[24] Helen's worries about her face, temporarily dispelled by reviews of her Julia, were now justified by an ungallant reference to her irregular profile and even a complaint that one could not tell from her countenance what passion she was representing. Her Belvidera suffered, predictably, from comparison with Miss O'Neill's: she had not moved the audience to tears or captured their affections with "thrilling touches of nature" as her lovely predecessor had done. But the most hurtful criticism, striking at her "dear master" as well as herself, blamed her "laboured and conventional" acting on over-training in an artificial style and declared that the sooner she left her present instructor, the better.[25]

With her lack of sympathy for Belvidera and her inexperience in transforming old-fashioned rhetoric into "natural" speech, Helen Faucit could hardly have been so convincing in this part as in Julia. But could her acting have deteriorated to the degree suggested by some reviews? Perhaps critics, disappointed of their unreasonable expectations, exaggerated her faults. Anyhow, the verdict, though general, was not unanimous. At issue was what constituted natural acting. What the *Examiner* deplored as extravagant, hence artificial, behaviour – "flinging herself into attitudes" and shocking the audience with "hysterics" – appealed to the *Morning Chronicle* as uninhibited, hence natural. One reminded the actress that "it is the intention of tragedy to exhibit mental passion and not bodily agony," but the other encouraged her to ignore such restrictions:

> What we mainly and most of all like in Miss Helen Faucit is the fearlessness with which she throws herself into the passion of the part … and she does not care a straw about making unbecoming … faces, if by an ugly face she can accomplish what she wishes better than by a pretty one.

The latter review, far from agreeing that Miss Faucit's face was inexpressive, paid lyrical tribute to its "varied and powerful characters" and its ocean-like changes from calm to storm.[26] It was such disagreements, perhaps, that led the *Athenaeum* critic to suggest that "practice, operating upon natural good sense," would do more to improve her "clever" but unequal performance than "either teaching or newspaper criticism."

Helen herself was too shocked by the unexpected attacks to respond to the more encouraging reviews. She wept over the "horrid newspapers" until she could scarcely see out of her swollen eyes. In her humiliation she feared to go onto the stage for a second performance, but, to her astonishment, the audience welcomed her as cordially as ever. Whatever the critics said, the London public would cheer her in all she did. That night she wrote in her diary: "I certainly acted much better to-night than last night. No doubt there was a great deal of truth in what was said against me, but still I think it is rather hard critics should see and judge you so severely on a *first* appearance ..."[27] Her Belvidera did improve on a second and third performance (even the *Post* grew more favourable in later reviews), but only after some years would it become an outstanding success.

Just a few nights after her first performance of Belvidera, Helen Faucit was brought out as Mrs. Haller in *The Stranger*, a part in which she had shown much promise at Richmond. Unlike Belvidera, Mrs. Haller was only too realistic for her. The family parallel probably disturbed her more than it did her mother. Whether to allay some inner qualm or to placate the critics, who had become increasingly censorious toward *The Stranger*, she changed the ending to avoid rewarding a fallen woman: instead of having husband and wife rush into each other's arms, she had Mrs. Haller, after tearfully embracing her children, fall in a dead faint at her husband's feet as the curtain came down. She continued to use this ending in later performances. Many years afterwards Sir Archibald Alison would recall his disappointment in missing the "well-remembered rush of the long-severed parents," and, though crediting its omission to Helen Faucit's "high standard of moral feeling," would express doubt that the touching sight could produce "any but the most virtuous emotions." As for Helen, even with her "moral" conclusion, she privately considered Mrs. Haller a "heart-breaking, hopeless, miserable part."[28]

After only two rehearsals *The Stranger* was produced on 8 February. The actress thought she "got through pretty well," but the next day there was a different story. The critics had cut her up "frightfully," she wrote in despair. "They say it is the worst thing I have done, even worse than Belvidera. Ah me, ah me! what am I to do? I am sure I strive hard enough to please ..."[29] Actually the reviews in general were no worse than before, though a few of them were exceptionally harsh. Despite the new conclusion, the prevailing attitude toward the play itself – "nauseous trash," as *The Times* called it – clouded the criticism of the performance. Helen's physical inadequacies, especially her incongruously immature appearance, were deplored; the *Sunday Times* oddly stated that she was "both morally and physically unfitted" for Mrs. Hailer, as if she must have become a fallen woman herself in order to play the part. Praise was mixed with blame, however. *The Morning Herald* pointed out that in Miss Faucit's "most excited" scenes her "spontaneous and fine conceptions of emotion" had counteracted "the effect of redundant action and much-schooled accentuation." More than one critic noticed her strong impression on the audience and the abundant tears she elicited.

"I'm sure I strive hard enough to please" – that childlike sentence is revealing as well as pathetic. The too-obvious striving after effect, which was the chief fault of her early acting, was something she did not know how to mend; all she could do was "strive" harder. Some faults for which she was censured in Mrs. Haller, like meaningless variations in tone, were obvious attempts to overcome others, like monotony, previously deplored in Belvidera. Her attitude of a pupil trying to please a teacher, a child trying to please a parent, is not surprising. When she went home after an evening's performance, the family dissected her acting and told her where she had fallen short; the next day, apparently, they went over the newspaper criticisms with her. When her Mrs. Haller was attacked, she got no comfort from her censorious mother. After the reviews came out, Helen did not get to bed until four in the morning.[30]

Helen Faucit's first original part was in a tragedy by Joanna Baillie, a poetic dramatist who had long held a high literary reputation but whose plays were largely unacted. Early in 1836, after years of silence, she published a new collection of dramas, ten of which had not been in print before. Critics were ecstatic.[31] Charles Kemble was reportedly eager to act the title role in *Henriquez*, the critics' favourite, but Helen Faucit preferred *The Separation*, which had a more prominent heroine. Journalists sneered about "Lady Helen's" whims, but Kemble, despite qualms about the play's theatrical chances, deferred to her wishes.[32] Drury Lane then decided to produce *Henriquez*. In the event, Kemble lost nothing by his graciousness: neither play answered to expectations, but the Covent Garden production proved much more attractive than its rival.[33] *The Separation* is not one of Joanna Baillie's "plays on the passions," but it resembles them in uniformity of tone and slightness of plot. When Lady Margaret discovers that her husband, Garcio, is the murderer of her brother (who had opposed their marriage), she insists, though she loves him still, that they live apart; at the end, Garcio saves his wife from a rejected suitor who is storming the castle, but he is mortally wounded in the fight. Helen Faucit was delighted with Margaret's "noble and beautiful" character. "It requires a lofty and yet gentle bearing," she reminded herself, "a decision of manner and carriage …" Despite Kemble's misgivings – and her own, which grew during five rehearsals, – she hoped, unrealistically, for a hit.

When the important night came, 25 February, the theatre was crowded with Miss Baillie's friends and admirers as well as Helen Faucit's loyal public. Unfortunately Helen was on the verge of illness, but she fought it off determinedly and got through the performance. Afterwards she wrote in her diary that the play had "gone off very well indeed"; she added ironically that she could not tell how she had acted but she would be "*sure to hear all about it tomorrow*."[34]

She must have been pleasantly surprised by the reviews, for her acting received more praise than it had done in recent weeks. Apparently she was less shrill in Margaret than she had been, for example, in Belvidera, and more convincing in her emotional outbursts. As in her Julia, she effectively portrayed conflicting passions – for example, "the gradual working of doubt upon love." According to the *Literary Gazette*, "where the situations allowed for tragic power, she was eminently impressive," and, at the end, her "falling senseless from the couch of her dead husband" was "original and fine." Lady Margaret enhanced Helen Faucit's reputation, but the play itself could be called, at best, a "*succès d'estime*." Critics agreed that it was full of beautiful poetry but, except for the powerful confession scene in Act 3, it did not lend itself well to dramatic representation. *The Separation* was performed six times within less than two weeks and was repeated on four other occasions – a good record for that play but not the run Helen had hoped for.

Her public recognition as the creator of a new role seemed complete when the young actress delightedly discovered in the Soho Bazaar a doll wearing a costume like hers and labelled "Miss Helen Faucit as the Lady Margaret in *Separation*." Suddenly life was much happier: the critics had been unexpectedly "indulgent"; she had received numerous fan-letters, including one that she would always cherish for its early confidence in her future ("Go on and prosper, noble, intellectual, and most interesting Helen!"); and, at long last, "darling Harry" had finished her season at Brighton and come home to her. Harriet's letter to a friend reflects her maternal pride in and concern for her sister:

> She looks so beautiful and acts so beautifully, so simply, so feelingly, and so powerfully … I wish she possessed as much strength of body as of mind … She has been very ill since this new part … It is dreadfully cold, too. My darling suffers from this, – the fatigue is so great, – and though we wrap her up when she leaves the stage, yet it is impossible to help a chill.[35]

Helen now enjoyed at home the appreciation and coddling she had been missing.

Having established herself with the London audience and made a second start with the critics, she was finally allowed, on 10 March, to act her favourite character, Shakespeare's Juliet. The only available Romeo was the "vehement" George Bennett, a "fine, ranting, roaring, vaulting Cavalier," who shook the tomb so violently with his crowbar that Harriet insisted on immuring herself with her sister so as to hold up the structure from collapsing.[36] Thus any romantic effect in the play must have depended on Juliet herself. Since Helen Faucit was no longer a novelty and since stock productions of old plays were often ignored, there were relatively few reviews. There was some praise, however, for the originality of the new Juliet (*Morning Post*) as well as some predictable comparison with favourite portrayals of the past. For both the *Sunday Times* (13 March) and the *Morning Chronicle* (11 March) Eliza O'Neill's Juliet remained the ideal, but the *Chronicle* drew an interesting contrast between the

Kemble and Faucit portrayals: Fanny Kemble had a "want of loveableness and lovingness" that made her scenes unlike a reader's conception of them, but "there was so much mind about her performance … that she simply made up for any deficiencies"; Helen Faucit, on the other hand, was "extremely loveable," and she did not keep her Romeo "at such arms' length."

The Faucit sisters spent Passion Week at Brighton (mostly watching the rain), after which they parted once more, Harriet to become leading lady at the Theatre Royal, Liverpool. Back at Covent Garden, Helen chafed at having to act the "stupid part" of a Jewess, Donna Florinda, in a melodramatic play from the French, *Don Juan of Austria*: a "poor injured innocent" who stabs herself to escape being burned at the stake when Philip II, rejected as a lover, turns her over to the Inquisition. Some speeches were "so affected and ridiculous" that she hardly had the patience to repeat them. Yet, according to critics, she spoke the "commonplace passages" with great effectiveness, and the play proved successful with the audience.[37]

On 29 April William Charles Macready, who had been acting at Drury Lane, made his famous assault upon the manager, Alfred Bunn, an enterprising philistine who had insulted the actor's artistic pride once too often. With his engagement terminated and a lawsuit pending, the "Eminent Tragedian" accepted an offer from Osbaldiston to join the Covent Garden company. Many people, though they did not condone the assault, understood the provocations and sympathized with Macready. Helen's faith in him was unconditional: "it would be impossible for him to commit any act that would be derogatory to the high character of a gentleman."[38] His gentlemanliness did not necessarily include amiability, however, as she soon discovered. On the morning of 18 May, when the two met for the first time to rehearse *The Stranger* for that night's performance, he congratulated her "very kindly" on her success, yet she felt in his manner something "cold," "distant, and almost repulsive." That night, after the play, the audience called for Macready, who was now the great star of the theatre. He gallantly led Helen Faucit onstage to share in the applause, but his haughty manner convinced her that "he thought it a great bore." "I feel very much afraid of him," she wrote in her diary, … I don't think I shall ever like him."[39] She was never more wrong.

Before his abrupt departure from Drury Lane, Macready had planned to introduce a new tragedy, *Ion*, by his friend Thomas Noon Talfourd, and Ellen Tree had agreed to act Clemanthe in it. These plans were now transferred to Covent Garden, but, since Miss Tree could not perform there except for Macready's benefit, another actress was needed after the first night. When Helen Faucit was asked to take over Clemanthe, the Farrens were incensed: any credit this negligible part could afford would go to its first representative, Miss Tree. Helen, however, eventually gave in to the pleas of Macready and Talfourd.[40]

Ion is a slight but skilfully-wrought drama, written in pleasing if overly-polished verse. Its romantic treatment of "classical" scenes and characters sets up echoes of Guarini, Fletcher, and Shelley. The atmosphere is remote and legendary, the passion etherealized. The theme of patriotic self-sacrifice is poetically uplifting, but the sacrifice at the end, though a literal one, affects the reader like a pretty piece of symbolism. No doubt the passion seemed more robust, however, and the incidents less visionary when Macready acted Ion. The noble young saviour of his people was exactly the hero to stir Helen's imagination, but the insipid Clemanthe – the sweet love that Ion gives up, along with power, to fulfil his destiny – merely bored her.

Ellen Tree did garner the rewards of participating in an auspicious occasion, but, though she was applauded and fêted along with Macready, she was probably glad to be rid of her thankless role. Her real interest was in the character of Ion: before long, becomingly clad in a chlamys, she would make the idealistic young prince one of her finest impersonations. Meanwhile Helen Faucit was left with the drudgery of acting Clemanthe.

Macready did not help her. At her first rehearsal she was so unnerved by his "freezing and proud coldness" that she found her voice trembling. "I wonder if I shall ever get over this silly feeling," she wrote in her diary. "I fear not; for I think … *he dislikes me* …" A sense of constraint, which persisted at the next rehearsal, left her "very, very low spirited." Her intuition was correct, for that night Macready grumbled to his diary about the "uncomfortable addition of a strange actress, Miss H. Faucit, whom I do not like; she wants heart."[41] Accustomed to receiving encouragement and help from Charles Kemble, Helen found it impossible to show much "heart" in the inhibiting presence of her new stage partner. No wonder the *Morning Post* (2 June) found her Clemanthe "cold, tame, spiritless, uninteresting." Helen had to drag herself through this wretched part seven times before Macready's departure for the provinces temporarily freed her from it – and from the "awful" but fascinating man who would shortly become the strongest influence in her life.

Of the other roles she acted before the season closed, on 22 June, Lady Townly, Mariana, and Mrs. Beverley were familiar from provincial experience; the only new one, Kate in *Catherine and Petruchio* (a shortened adaptation of *The Taming of the Shrew*) was the first of her comic heroines from Shakespeare.

During her first six months on the London stage Helen Faucit had performed seventy-four times in eleven characters, the most popular of which, by far, was Julia in *The Hunchback*. This crucial half-season, despite its brilliant beginning, could not be called a great critical success, but it was undoubtedly a great popular success. Even with the reviewers Helen had made many gains, particularly after *The Separation*: learning by experience, she was winning her way back toward the acclaim she had initially enjoyed. So far she was an uneven, rather erratic actress. Sensitive and highly strung, she was extraordinarily responsive to the moods and attitudes of others. She had to "act to" someone in particular, to feel a rapport with her fellow actors as well as her audience; she could not master her feelings in performance. Only later would she learn to make capital out of her emotions, to turn a liability into one of her greatest assets. Her early critics often said she tried too hard. She did, yet the ambition, determination, and diligence that drove her to do this were essential factors in her development.

In late July Helen accompanied her stepfather to Ireland, where they had starring engagements in Cork and Galway. She acted several of her Covent Garden characters, and, because of William Farren, she attempted some comic roles, such as the Widow Cheerly in *The Soldier's Daughter*, which she would never repeat. George Bennett, who was at Cork for the summer, played the male leads in most of her serious plays there. [42]

When the new season opened at Covent Garden on 12 September, the company had been strengthened by several prominent additions: William Farren and Mrs. Glover in comedy, John Vandenhoff in tragedy. Macready had wished for Ellen Tree as well (he plainly preferred her to Helen Faucit), but she was preparing for an American tour that would keep her away for several years. Both Macready and Charles Kemble were still at Covent Garden, but the latter would soon be leaving to become Examiner of Plays.

The most remarkable characteristic of the 1836-37 season was the unusual number of Shakespearean productions and the enthusiasm they aroused. Contributing factors were the tremendous public interest in Kemble's farewell performances, many of which were Shakespearean, and the theatre's rivalry with Drury Lane, where Edwin Forrest, the American tragedian, was winning success in some of Macready's great roles. These circumstances gave Helen Faucit an opportunity to act nine Shakespearean characters, most of them for the first time. Of these, Queen Catherine was the least important to her career; since it was thought to require a substantial figure, the slender Miss Faucit soon gave it up. Hermione, which she acted only twice this season, would be in later years among her most impressive parts. The ones that did most for her at this time, Constance and Beatrice, we will return to shortly. First, though, several other roles important to her professional development – Portia, Kate, Desdemona, Juliet –deserve some mention.

Only sketchy remarks about these were published by journalistic critics, whose attention was focused on the tragic heroes. Fortunately, however, these can be supplemented with passages from private "reviews" in the notebooks of a stagestruck young man named Charles Rice. It is good to have, for example, his account of Helen Faucit's first Portia, acted on 24 September 1836 to Charles Kemble's Shylock. Rice was struck, naturally enough, by her mercy speech, but he found the "lighter parts" of the portrayal "equally fine in their way." This comment, together with his later chuckle that Miss Faucit's Kate (8

April 1837) was in every way "worthy of her honoured lord," Petruchio, tells us something of her increasing success in comic acting.[43] The press, as well as Rice, noticed Helen Faucit's first performance of Desdemona, on 21 October, with Macready as Othello, Vandenhoff as Iago, and Charles Kemble as Cassio, but Rice "reviewed" a later one as well.[44] Desdemona, though a favourite heroine of hers since girlhood, was overshadowed theatrically by hero and villain, particularly at a time when the "willow scene" was omitted. The *Morning Post* (22 October) stated, typically, that the part contained little to challenge the powers of a great actress but did require "judgment, combined with feminine dignity and grace"; Helen Faucit had "succeeded entirely," winning "warm and general" approbation. This was too tame for Rice. In his second review, written 3 June 1837 (when Macready was still acting Othello, though other roles were less strongly cast), he declared that Helen Faucit's Desdemona was "the best performance of the evening."[45] His review of her "faultless" Juliet (17 December 1836, with Charles Kemble in the penultimate performance of his famous Mercutio) contained this prophetic appraisal: "unlike many who when they reach a certain degree of mediocrity imagine themselves stars, she still keeps improving, and will, I have no doubt, very shortly be confessed the first actress on the London boards."[46] Rice, an experienced and observant playgoer, offers interesting evidence of the popular response to Helen Faucit's portrayals.

The role of Constance in *King John* which Helen first acted on 6 October 1836, marked a turning-point for her. Since John was one of Macready's finest characters and the Bastard one of Charles Kemble's, the theatre was "crowded to the slips" for this production. There were doubts about the prospective Lady Constance, however: the "fragile and delicate" Helen Faucit could hardly rise to the "proud indignation of the queenly woman, the … stormy grief of the bereaved mother." Those who remembered Mrs. Siddons "laughed at the idea of a *raw* girl … attempting such a character."[47] For several critics these doubts were sustained, but for others the performance was astonishingly good. Although Helen Faucit did not look the part, said one, "her *conception* … did her infinite credit"; she threw her "whole soul" into Constance and "proved that there was more beneath her usual gentleness than we had hoped for." Another declared that in no other part had she "exhibited such decided originality of talent."[48] Six years later (25 October 1842), when reviewing another *King John*, the *Morning Chronicle* recalled that it was Helen Faucit's Constance "which first made the public feel that she really was a Shakespearian actress."

What Constance did for Helen in tragedy Beatrice did in comedy. The glamour of the occasion, Charles Kemble's Farewell (23 December 1836), which brought a surging crowd to the theatre several hours before opening time, gave a special prominence to her success in this new character. Helen Faucit had felt "unqualified" for Beatrice, but Charles Kemble had taught her the stage business and had brought out her latent talents with encouragement and direction. The result, as reviews indicate, was reassuring. The "force and fire" of her "Kill Claudio!" were to be expected, but the "pleasant archness" of her repartee showed a new facility in comedy of manners. The most notable characteristic of this first Beatrice, in fact, was her treatment of the sarcastic passages, which she delivered "with much point and meaning" yet "without any … shrewishness of manner."[49] Liveliness devoid of malice would always be the hallmark of her interpretation. This time even the *Examiner* (25 December) was "surprised" by the "merit" of Helen Faucit's Beatrice. 'There were some charming points in it. Too much effort … but still a pleasing version …"

The occasion was important to Helen, not only in demonstrating her unsuspected versatility as an actress, but also in bringing her into closer relationship with her second mentor, Charles Kemble. After the performnces were over, after the farewell speech had been made and the cheering, waving audience had departed,[50] the actors, emotional in their leave-taking, begged Kemble for mementos (a glove, a feather). Helen asked, amid her sobs, for the book from which he had studied Benedick. "You shall have it, my dear," he promised, "and many more." Later he gave her two volumes containing a number of promptbooks that had belonged to his daughter Fanny, with an inscription reading, in part: "To you alone do these Parts, which were once Fanny Kemble's, of right belong; for from you alone can we now expect the most efficient representation of them."[51] More important, he told Mrs. Faucit she might bring her daughter to see him whenver she thought he could be helpful. After that he read over several new parts with Helen and advised her about her acting. As she recalls:

> One thing he impressed upon me I never forgot. It was, on no account to give prominence to the merely physical aspect of any painful emotion. Let the expression be genuine, earnest, but not ugly. He pointed out to me how easy it was to simulate distortions – for example, to writhe from the supposed effect of poison, to gasp, to roll the eyes, &c. These were melodramatic effects. But if pain or death had to be represented, or any sudden or violent shock, let them be shown in their mental rather than in their physical signs. The picture presented might be as sombre as the darkest Rembrandt, but it must be noble in its outlines … never repulsive, mean, or commonplace. It must suggest the heroic, the divine in human nature, and not the mere everyday struggles or tortures of this life … Under every circumstance the ideal, the noble, the beautiful, should be given side by side with the real. [52]

To the impulsive young actress who had been "flinging" herself about, going into "hysterics" with her emotional acting, and making "ugly faces" when she thought the situation called for them, this doctrine of ideal acting was a revelation. *The Times* and the *Examiner* had already advised her against excessive physical action, but when her "generous and sympathetic" preceptor explained the theory behind the advice, it touched a chord in her own idealistic nature.

Beginning early in 1837 Helen Faucit acted in four new plays. Two, Sheridan Knowles's *Brian Boroihme* and Edward Fitzball's *Walter Tyrrel*, were unimportant: although termed "historical" plays, they were outright melodramas.[53] The others, however, represented serious, if disappointing, attempts by literary men, Sir Edward Lytton Bulwer and Robert Browning (both friends of Macready), to write for the theatre.

Bulwer's poetic drama, *The Duchess de la Vallière* was based on a novel by the Comtess de Genlis. Louise de Ia Vallière first idealizes King Louis XIV, then falls in love with him and becomes his mistress; her former fiancé, the soldierly Marquis de Bragelone, persuades her to repent and fly to a convent, but Louis pursues her and brings her back to court; eventually, though loving him still, she renounces him and takes the veil.

Since *La Vallière* was the first dramatic work of a well-known novelist, its production was an event in the literary as well as the theatrical world. On opening night (4 January 1837) a large and fashionable audience assembled, hoping to witness the rejuvenation of the British drama. Unfortunately, the play was too long (it began at "a quarter before Seven, & ended at a quarter after Eleven!");[54] it contained some "blasphemous" phrases and a scene in which Louis, virtually under a crucifix, wooed Louise back to a life of sin (there were hisses here); worst of all, despite some passionate and touching moments, it was boring. Although Bulwer's admirers applauded whenever they could, the play was at best an "equivocal success."[55] Despite immediate textual revisions, the production never took on much life. Its wobbling run, interrupted by Helen Faucit's illness,[56] ended after eight performances.

The critics generally attacked the play, not only for its "revolting" Gallic subject matter, but also for its underdeveloped characters and its weak, disconnected incidents. They unanimously praised Macready's Bragelone (the only character they liked), gave qualified approval to Helen Faucit's La Vallière, but usually condemned the other performances. As they realized, Miss Faucit was hardly responsible for the insipidity of her lachrymose character; even the *Spectator* admitted her "grace and propriety" in a "trying part" and her success in such passionate scenes as the dramatist allowed her.[57] No-one could have believed that in less than a year Bulwer would provide the most popular role of her career.

Robert Browning's *Strafford*, a tragedy written in irregular blank verse, deals with the fall of Thomas Wentworth, First Earl of Strafford, originally a leader of Parliamentary opposition to Charles I but later his loyal supporter; when condemned by Parliament, he expects Charles to save him, but the latter weakly consents to his friend's death and Strafford is executed. Helen Faucit's role was Lucy Percy, Countess of Carlisle, a fictional character introduced for the sake of feminine interest; evidently in love with Strafford (though he does not realize this), she gives him sympathetic support throughout and helps in an abortive rescue attempt.

Although young Robert Browning had not yet made his reputation as a major poet, the theatre was crowded on the first night of *Strafford* (1 May), perhaps because the name of a new dramatist promised an interesting novelty. At least some enthusiasts – literary, artistic, and professional – were there, however, because Browning's long philosophical poem, *Paracelsus*, had so impressed them that they expected wonders from his first drama.[58] The audience's disappointment has been amusingly described by the artist William Bell Scott:

> My admiration of Paracelsus was so great I determined to go and to applaud, without rhyme or reason; and so I did, in the front of the pit. From the first scene it became plain that applause was not the order. The speakers had every one of them orations to deliver, and no action of any kind to perform … Still I kept applauding … till the howling was too overpowering, and the disturbance so considerable that for a few minutes I lost my hat.[59]

An exaggeration, maybe, but there were certainly some hisses when the play was announced for repetition. Although applause predominated and the major actors were given curtain calls, the handwriting was on the wall. *Strafford* was acted only three times more.

The reviewers, too, were disappointed, though several saw a promise of better things; they deplored the play's faulty structure and the characters' "fragmentary" expression of their thoughts.[60] They were more impressed by some of the staging, especially the appearance of Macready, who looked exactly like Van Dyke's portrait of Strafford coming alive. (Helen Faucit's dress, too, was designed from a Van Dyke picture, even to the kind of fur used for the trim.)[61] As for performances, they generally agreed with Browning himself, who thought Macready "acted very finely – as did Miss Faucit," that Vandenhoff as John Pym was "tolerable" (some gave him a better rating), but that the rest were hopeless. Macready was, of course, the great star, but Helen Faucit received some warm commendations.[62] Later she recalled her problem in making the audience, but not Strafford himself, aware of the Countess's feeling for him.[63] The *Athenaeum*'s praise was reassuring: she had filled in the author's mere outline of character with feeling, delicacy, and skill and had made "intelligible that which he had left very indistinct." The young actress was learning the value of subtlety.

The 1836-37 season was of great value in Helen Faucit's development as an actress and her steady rise in reputation. Much of this was due to the presence of Macready, without which some of the most important productions would not have been staged. Personally as well as professionally, Macready's influence took root during this period. He must have unbent toward Helen at some point, for she obviously lost her fear of him while at the same time increasing her admiration. His diaries hint that her hero-worship was already turning into romantic attachment. (Her own journal for this period, if she kept one, was evidently destroyed.) One night while acting Clemanthe, she cast such an adoring look at Ion that Macready suspected her of having "designs" on him but decided it was "all the truth of acting." Later, as Desdemona, she disconcerted Othello in the same way. And at a rehearsal of *La Vallière*, her "frank . . . expression of admiration" made Macready wonder whether it was inspired by "simplicity, deceit, coquetry, or passion."[64] Helen often did assume a coquettish expression – the ability to do so in a demure, ladylike manner was among the arts of a charming woman – but there was no simple coquetry in her attitude toward Macready. From the first she had felt uplifted by the power and beauty of his acting; as Alan Downer has perceptively remarked, "Like many another young and impressionable spectator, she could not separate the emotions evoked by the actor in character from the personality of the man …"[65] Now that she was participating in his scenes, her response had become more immediate and, by degrees, more personal. Whatever their origin, the emotions inspired by Macready would become as real, as powerful, and as long-lasting in their effects as anything she ever experienced.

Macready at this time was nearly forty-four, about twice Helen's age. He had a tall, angular form and a square-jawed face with massive brow, expressive eyes, and somewhat rugged features. Despite many remarks about his homeliness, his portraits show an interesting, by no means ugly face. When illumined by dramatic passion, it could be powerfully attractive. (Helen was not the first to feel his magnetism. The handsome and forceful actress Mary Amelia Huddart, later Mrs. Warner, had already fallen under his spell.) His remarkably controlled voice was clear and musical except when he deliberately introduced growls, grunts, or staccato phrasing for emotional effects.[66] Although the son of an actor-manager, he had attended Rugby and had been intended for the law until his father's financial misfortunes compelled him to leave school for the stage. He felt degraded by his association with many ignorant and slovenly people (as he thought), and, despite the respect of his literary and professional friends, he was bitterly conscious of an actor's anomalous social position; even so, he had a high regard for the art of acting at its best. He was the devoted head of a large family, and, jealousy and temper aside, he was a model Victorian gentleman.[67]

If Macready had become increasingly conscious of Helen Faucit's admiration during the 1836-37 season, he had also become concerned over her possible rivalry. After a performance of *King John*, for instance, he grumbled that he had been "much less applauded than either Miss Faucit or Kemble," and, after playing Pierre to Helen Faucit's Belvidera, he refused a curtain call, thinking it "no compliment" because she had received one first. Once, during a performance of *La Vallière*, he even suspected her of trying to "play some tricks" in order to ruin his "effects."[68] Unlikely as that was, she probably did attempt an "effect" of her own. There are signs that her hero-worship was far from passive, that it inspired her to emulation.[69] Emotional excitement gave her a certain buoyancy and self-confidence that she had lacked before. Throughout her apprenticeship to Percy Farren and her discipleship to Charles Kemble she was reverential, hard-working, and eager to learn. With Macready her reverence intensified to adoration, but she also felt in him a challenge to which her ambitious spirit responded.

Covent Garden closed its season in June. On the 20th of that same month a more momentous event occurred: King William IV died, and eighteen-year-old Princess Victoria ascended the throne. As Queen Victoria she would restore dignity and respect to the crown, bring about a new age for Great Britain, and become known as one of her country's greatest monarchs. On a less exalted level, she would gradually bring theatrical attendance back into fashion. Eventually she would extend her personal interest and favour to Helena Martin (the quondam Helen Faucit). At the moment, however, she had little use for the young actress, so "plain and thin," who, as she said, "rants and screams too much."[70]

In July, Helen, who was in Liverpool caring for her ill sister, received a letter from Macready. Having decided to take over the management of Covent Garden, he was asking the actors to accept reduced salaries so as to minimize his risks; he offered her fifteen pounds a week, exactly half what her contract with Osbaldiston called for. She replied that she would be "*proud* and *happy*" to serve under one for whom she had "such warm feelings of respect and regard" but that since her engagement had been arranged by Farren and her services were "*entirely*" at her mother's disposal, she would have to consult with her "friends."[71] As she remarked, she was "not at liberty" to answer for herself. She was still living with the Farrens; her stepfather was managing her financial affairs, and she was receiving an allowance out of her salary for "pocket money."[72] The following month Farren called on Macready and argued with him for several hours about Helen's articles of agreement. Realizing the value of her engaging with the Eminent Tragedian, he swallowed his Lovegold qualms and agreed to the salary cut, but he refused to rescind the stipulation that "in every Tragedy or serious play performed … Miss Faucit shall have the choice of the principal character with the privilege of refusing any and every one which she may deem detrimental to her interest to perform …" Macready, though convinced that his managerial rights were infringed by this clause, was forced to accept it.[73]

On 11 September Macready began a starring engagement at Liverpool, and Helen Faucit, now relieved by Harriet's recovery, was "also engaged." Seizing his chance, Macready explained his problem with her contract, and she, "seriously affected," promised to strike out the "objectionable clause" after coming of age on 11 October.[74] Her only new part at Liverpool was one she never acted again, the sinful Evadne in *The Bridal*, an adaptation of Beaumont and Fletcher's *The Maid's Tragedy*. Though a much-softened version of the original, the play retained enough of a "terrible moral," as Macready thought, to deter any sensitive actress of Evadne from an adulterous love. Yet he was astonished, on the very evening of that play, by Helen's naive request that their discussion of the prospective Covent Garden season be held in his dressing room rather than hers since she shared hers with another person. She seemed to have "an *unconsciousness of wrong*," he told his diary, yet what did she intend? Did she "think" or only "*feel*"? He determined not to give in to "vanity or weakness." "I really like her much as a friend," he wrote, "and I will be a friend to her."[75] He was true to that promise.

Chapter 4

Working for Macready

INFATUATION WITH Macready, at first an invigorating force, brought, with its increasing domination, anxiety and mixed emotions. Virtue, in the sense of valorous dedication to the highest good, had a strong emotional attraction for Helen, reinforced as it had been by images from allegory and romance. Sexual purity, though by no means its equivalent, was an indispensable part of the ideal; but so, too, was love – love so great that it justified any sacrifice. Only now, when the ideal was tested by reality, it displayed an impossible dichotomy. Intensely affectionate but discouraged from expressing her feelings outwardly, she had been late in maturing. Now the emotions she had dreamily associated with Juliet and Desdemona had become disturbingly her own, bringing undreamed-of sensations.

The conflict between her cherished ideals and her obsession with Macready was exacerbated by ambiguous feelings toward her irregular household. Acutely aware of her family's unacceptable situation, she had learned to substitute "my friends" for the normal expression "my parents." Time and custom might have made her less sensitive if not for continued reminders that the Farrens had no right to hold their heads high. Jeering at them had become a habit, still good for a smile when nothing racier was at hand. Three months before the birth of her first Farren son, Mrs. Faucit, by continuing to act during her pregnancy (a common habit), had provoked the mirth of a critic who might normally have been more tactful: "Mrs. Faucit tried to look *big*," he wrote, punningly referring to her tragedy-queen style, "and she was successful." Now, as late as 1837, a writer for a popular magazine was still sneering about her size as well as her morals (her voluptuous figure must have gone out of control), reminding readers that an unnamed actor – obviously Farren – had "quitted his amiable but childless wife for the arms of the fat lady" and that this "precious couple," though "doubly violating the holy vow," were revelling in "every luxury."[1] Farren jokes still appeared in theatrical journals, and even Helen had become fair game – as when a list of actors, facetiously paired with dramatic titles, included "*The Adopted Child* Miss Helen Faucit."[2] Besides, much as she benefited professionally from the Farren connection, she sometimes suffered on its account. Witness this attack in the moralistic *Sunday Times* (28 January 1838):

> Miss H.FAUCIT ... is the daughter of Mr. Faucit Saville, of Margate; when that gentleman's wife eloped with Mr. W. Farren, the children were protected by their mother. Miss Faucit's theatrical education has been derived from her mother and Mr. W. Farren ... [she has] sustained her station by outrageous puffs and family influences. She is, like all persons who have been parroted into all they know, an unequal and inefficient artiste, totally devoid of mind ...

Living in a glass house, even a less idealistic young woman might have thought twice before offending the moral code.

Yet, legality aside, her family's life seemed respectable enough: her "friends" behaved like any husband and wife, and her half-brothers, William and Henry, were developing into "spruce young gentlemen" (twelve and ten respectively), whose handsome appearance in their "Eton round jackets ... and shiny top-hats" could stir a sister's pride.[3] In such an environment, Macready mused, it was "scarcely to be wondered at" that Helen "should be keenly alive to the influences of passion – but it is not right." Even he felt the need for a "sterner rule of conduct ... if I wish to be ... at peace with myself."[4]

Professionally, as well as personally, Helen was tugged in two directions. Both ambition and desire to please her mother aligned her with the Farrens, who insisted that she refuse parts unlikely to raise her reputation; yet attraction to Macready and respect for his artistic aims made her susceptible to opposing pressures. As 11 October approached (when her majority would be publicly acknowledged), Macready watched to see whether she would alter her contract, but the day passed with no sign from her.[5] The Farrens' influence or her own reluctance had intervened. Six days later Macready, about to act the hero in Knowles's "classical" tragedy *Virginius*, asked her to play Virginia, the Roman maiden whose father kills her to save her from a lustful official. Even in her first London season she had considered this slight part "*infra dig.*"[6] Should she condescend to act it now? Macready was persuasive, and, though "her mother was very much against it," she agreed. This willingness to oblige evidently convinced him of her pliability. When she came to him on the 26th, ready, after all, to strike the objectionable clause, he decided, quixotically, to rely on her word instead.[7] As a result he sometimes had to remonstrate and cajole, but he usually got his way.

All omens were good as Macready began his first season of management. The theatre had been cleaned, its boxes reupholstered, and back-rests installed in the pit; the gilded ornaments (rose, thistle, shamrock) gleamed, the great chandelier and the stars and rosettes in the ceiling sparkled as they had not done in years. A strong company had been assembled. Although Vandenhoff and Farren had left, there were fine new actors like Samuel Phelps and James Anderson (a much-needed jeune premier); Helen's uncle, Charles Diddear, was a substantial addition in characters of lesser importance.[8] Two of the new members would be influential, for good or ill, in Helen's personal life. The courtly Edward William Elton, an asset in roles of second and third rank, became her avuncular friend; they exchanged teasing nicknames – he was "Cruel Father" (he played Priuli to her Belvidera), and she was "Spring Morning" (suggesting both youthful freshness and April-weather moods).[9] Miss Huddart (soon to become Mrs. Warner), an impressive "heavy" actress, became her particular enemy.

Critics soon noticed some remarkable improvements in the Covent Garden productions. Particularly striking was the "homogeneousness and unity of effect," both in the acting, which showed "the pervading influence of one mind," and in the costumes and scenery, whose "sober elegance and appropriateness of every thing" gave a sense of "completeness to the *ensemble*."[10] There were none of Osbandiston's incongruities, such as a dress with a train for Nerissa and a "deficient" one for Portia.[11] No more were legitimate dramas denied the enhancement of appropriate scenic effects. Macready made imaginative use of traditional scenery (painted by fine artists) and supplemented it with "set pieces" and even "set scenes" more often than was usual in productions of the old classics. To Helen Faucit, his artistry was a revelation. Later she maintained that scenery and costume, as he used them, had intensified the effect of the performance by stimulating the imagination of actors as well as spectators. Her own imagination had been so stirred, in fact, that she remembered the "beautiful gardens" and "enchanted woods" of Macready's stage as if they had been realities. His emphasis on ensemble acting impressed her, too, as it did her colleagues, though the despotism with which it was implemented often antagonized them. "His will was law," she later wrote; any complaint was met by earnest reminders of "your duty to sacrifice yourself to the general good."[12] Only he was spared that sacrifice.

Macready's rehearsals were longer, more numerous, and far more meticulous than usual. They began at ten in the morning and often continued until three or four in the afternoon; important new plays and grand revivals were sometimes rehearsed for several weeks.[13] In "drilling" the players (his word), Macready corrected them about their interpretations, their speech, and their acting.[14] Helen Faucit recalls him as constantly saying, "My dear, you are entirely wrong in this conception." Very different from Charles Kemble, who softened his criticisms with "the balm of encouragement," Macready was "merciless to the feelings," a "surgeon, who 'cuts beyond the wound to make the cure more certain.'" But young Helen "believed in him, and could not act by his side without being moved and influenced by his intense earnestness and power."[15]

Whatever his foibles, Macready did make a determined effort to "regenerate the drama." As Alan Downer points out (176), during the 1837-38 season there was, "for the first time in many years," a favourable balance of legitimate performances as opposed to performances of opera and pantomime. Of the 209 legitimate ones Helen Faucit acted in 119 (about 52%), 23 of which were in Shakespeare, 17 in old non-Shakespearean dramas, and 79 in new plays.

Her first Shakespearean role was Hermione in a handsome production of *The Winter's Tale* that opened Macready's management on 30 September 1837. Macready's Leontes was most memorable in the statue scene, where his passionate joy seemed "so sudden, so overwhelming" that his leading lady "cried out hysterically" and had to be admonished to control herself.[16] Helen Faucit's Hermione was praised for her combination of queenliness and sweet femininity; as the "statue," she was "noble and imposing," and, even when she began to move, "she looked still like marble in action."[17]

Macready staged two grand Shakespearean revivals during the season: *King Lear* and *Coriolanus*. There was no role for Helen in the latter (Volumnia was considered a "heavy" part), and in her opinion there was none in *Lear* either. She refused to play Cordelia at first but agreed ungraciously after receiving a "kind note of remonstrance" from Macready.[18] No doubt she resented being given a part with so few lines and so little possibility of making an "effect."

This 1838 *Lear*, which opened on 25 January, is one of the best-known productions in Shakespearean stage history because of its return, in large part, to the original play after a century and a half of adaptations. The omission of Nahum Tate's "love story" for Cordelia and Edgar, the restoration of the Fool (surprisingly assigned to Priscilla Horton), and the tragic ending – all this has frequently been recounted;[19] so, too, have the marvels of the staging – the grandeur of the scenery, the effectiveness of the storm. In retrospect Helen Faucit was probably proud of having been part of this history-making production. Critics approved her Cordelia's sweetness and simplicity but deplored its near-inaudibility.[20] She had forgotten that the low-voiced Cordelia of Shakespeare's imagination did not have to make herself heard in Covent Garden. Later she found ways to deepen her characterization. When *Lear* was revived the following season, she drew praise for her delicate hints of emotional depths underlying Cordelia's terse speeches and for such suggestive bits of business as her "parting glance at the familiar objects in the old hall" as she was leaving her father's palace forever (*Morning Chronicle* 5 February 1839).

Of her four other Shakespearean plays this season, all of which she had acted in before, her favourite was also the most noteworthy. At last, with Anderson's arrival, Helen Faucit's Juliet was matched with a "gallant Romeo"; the fiery

Bennett was now cast as Tybalt. Macready, breaking his custom, took a minor role and turned Friar Lawrence's sententious speeches into "melodious word music," but he vowed that this was his "first and last time" of making such a "sacrifice."[21] The *Literary Gazette* (5 May 1838: 283) spoke warmly of Helen Faucit's acting, especially in the balcony scene, which now bore marks of "superior cultivation." Not everyone admired such cultivation, however. Miss Faucit had done very well in the "violent passages," said the *Morning Post* (1 May), especially the "heartbreaking" final scene (Garrick's version of the tomb scene), but in the love passages she should have been content with a "sweet, *distinct*, simple recitation" instead of resorting to "strange pauses," "puzzling intonations," and "staccato" delivery. If only unconsciously, she had begun to imitate Macready.

This season Helen Faucit acted two new comic roles in established classics, Violante in Mrs. Centlivre's *The Wonder* and Mrs. Oakly in the elder Colman's *The Jealous Wife*. Mrs. Oakly, who was merely jealous, did not interest her, but Violante, who must keep her friend's secret at the peril of her own reputation, allowed for greater complexity in the acting than "genteel comedy" usually did. Miss Faucit's Violante was too solemn for critics who preferred their comedy light (*Morning Herald* 29 Jan. 1838), but for the *Morning Post* (29 January) she was exactly what the author must have intended.

The new plays, however, were most important to her reputation. Or, rather, two of them were: Bulwer's *The Lady of Lyons*, which ran for thirty-three nights, and Knowles's *Woman's Wit*, which ran for thirty-one. Of her other new plays, William Dimond's *The Novice* and T. J. Serle's *The Parole of Honour* were nonentities, and Lord Byron's *The Two Foscari* was important chiefly in enhancing Macready's prestige.

The Lady of Lyons; or Love and Pride had its premiere on 15 February 1838 and remained popular throughout most of the century. Although usually described as a melodrama, it is easily superior to most plays in that category. It was intended seriously, for serious actors, and it elicited some of the finest acting of that period. Charles H. Shattuck describes the play as "a charming and durable fable ruined by superficial writing."[22] No doubt he is right, yet the dialogue, though banal in some passages and extravagant in others, might have been very effective on the stage. The prose, in which much of the play is written, has an easy, speakable quality, and the verse, noticeable mainly in the more emotional passages, seems by comparison romantic and passionate if the meaning is not examined too closely.

The "fable," set in France in the late 1790s, goes like this: Pauline Deschappelles, daughter of a wealthy merchant, is so beautiful that her foolish mother determines she must marry a nobleman – a foreigner, perforce, since the French aristocrats have lost their titles in the Revolution. Pauline is curious about the unknown admirer who has been sending her flowers, but when she

Helen Faucit as Pauline and Macready as Claude in Sir Edward Bulwer's *The Lady of Lyons*, Act 5, sketch by M. S. Rolls (by courtesy of the Folger Shakespeare Library)

finds it is Claude Melnotte, a gardener's son, she scornfully rejects his love. While smarting from her cruelty, he accedes to a plot devised and financed by another rejected suitor, the proud and bitter Beauseant (a former marquis).

Claude poses as the Prince of Como, wins Pauline's love, and marries her. In the climactic third act, he takes his bride to the cottage where he lives with his widowed mother, and Pauline's shocked disillusionment erupts in passages of intense emotional excitement. Claude, now deeply penitent, promises to arrange a divorce. In his absence Beauseant offers to rescue Pauline from poverty; she indignantly spurns him, and Claude returns just in time to save her from enforcement. Pauline discovers that she loves Claude in spite of everything, but he will not claim her until he has proved his worth. With her uncle, Colonel Damas, he joins Napoleon's army in Italy. Two and a half years elapse between Acts 4 and 5. The French army has been victorious, Damas is now a general, and Claude, under the assumed name of Morier, has won honour, rank, and wealth. Back in Lyons, they find Pauline about to sign a marriage contract with Beauseant in order to save her father from bankruptcy. "Morier," overjoyed to hear that Pauline still loves Claude, pays her father's debts, reveals his identity, and is ecstatically reunited with the wife he can now claim. Native worth has proved itself, and love has triumphed over pride.

Bulwer, who imagined Claude to be the centre of interest in his play, clearly underrated the theatrical potentialities of his heroine. (Macready discovered them, to his "surprise and regret," less than two weeks before opening night.)[23] He did not even realize the kind of heroine he had created. He originally suggested an actress "light in hand" to play the part, "something like Vestris only with more feeling," perhaps Mrs. Nisbett – a vivacious comedienne, in other words, not a strongly dramatic actress. "Miss Faucit freezes me," he declared strangely, and she had been "perfectly inaudible as Cordelia."[24] The arrogant beauty of Lyons, forced to discover her own emotional depths, was very different from Helen Faucit's soft-spoken Cordelia, and no one knew this better than the actress herself. Percy Farren told her that, whereas her Shakespearean characters had challenged her to rise to their level, this role required her to lift it "by tone and manner and dignity of expression" to her own level.[25] He did not suggest for one moment, however, that she refuse it. At last she had a new part that she could get her teeth into.

Since Bulwer's liberal politics made him vulnerable to Tory attacks, the author of *The Lady of Lyons* was not announced until its success was assured. Although the "rapturous applause" at its premiere signalled a triumph, attendance on subsequent nights was smaller than Macready had anticipated. After six performances, however, success was clear enough to warrant revealing the author's identity.[26] Among the congratulatory letters showered on Bulwer was one by Mary Shelley, who had felt the "charm of nature and high feelings" throughout the play; she thought Bulwer, following Shelley's advice to Byron, had "left the beaten road of old romance, so worn by modern dramatists, and idealised the *present*."[27] Once *The Lady of Lyons* had caught on, the public could not get enough of it.

Critics, however, would always be divided about the merits of the play. The first reviewers generally praised the artful construction, the unflagging interest, and the dramatic situations, but they did not agree about the characterization, the language, or the political sentiments ("clap-traps," as some called them).[28] The *Examiner* pronounced *The Lady of Lyons* the "most charming" play since *The Hunchback*, but the *Morning Post* called it a "foolish play" which had been saved from condemnation by some "striking situations ... some direct appeals to the most evident sources of strong feeling ... but, above all, the very excellent acting of Miss HELEN FAUCIT."

The production was visually beautiful, with its scenes of terrace, garden, and elegant interiors and its graceful, slightly adapted period costumes. Pauline's dresses, made of "fine muslin, with lace *fichus*, ruffles, broad sashes," were trimmed, in the "Prince of Como" scenes, with real roses, to illustrate Helen Faucit's idea that Pauline "loved flowers passionately."[29] These were supplied by friends and admirers, particularly Ellen Braysher, who faithfully sent a fresh bouquet every night.[30]

In *The Lady of Lyons* Helen had, for the first time, an ardent, fully developed love scene with Macready. She would never forget that second act on 3 March 1838, when Macready told her softly that this was his birthday. Thirty years later, on the eve of the anniversary, she recalled the occasion in clear but dreamlike detail – "even his very words. We were walking in the beautiful gardens of M. and Mme. Deschappelles."[31] A lifelong admiration for Macready shines through her description of his Claude Melnotte. Although he was too old for the part, she writes, his "elastic figure" and his "buoyancy of manner" overcame any impression of age. He made the character "one of nature's exceptional gentlemen and in this way prepossessed his audience, despite the unworthy device to which Claude lends himself in the first frenzy of wounded vanity."

In telling of her own performance Helen Faucit dwells on the cottage scene in the third act, when Pauline finds that she is married to a peasant rather than a prince:

> As I recalled to Claude, in bitter scorn, his glowing description of his palace by the Lake of Como, I broke into a paroxysm of hysterical laughter, which came upon me ... as the natural relief from the intensity of the mingled feelings of anger, scorn, wounded pride, and outraged love ... The effect upon the audience was electrical ... But well do I remember Mr. Macready's remonstrance with me ... No one ... should ever, he said, hazard an unrehearsed effect. I could only answer that I could not help it ... and if the impulse seized me again ... I must act the scene in the same way.

The "unrehearsed effect" of her first performance (if, indeed, it was so) immediately became a part of the stage business of the scene.[32]

Critics in general were enthusiastic about Helen Faucit's Pauline. Some, predictably, chided her for excessive vehemence, but the *Spectator*, though among the severest of these, actually praised her "hysterical burst" in the third act.[33] Other reviewers admired the "*abandon*" with which she had thrown herself into her character's emotions; as a result, they said, her "passionate and touching" portrayal had moved the audience to tears and its truthfulness had "seemed to rise far above all art."[34] No performance by Helen Faucit since her debut in Julia had caused so much excitement.

Years later James Anderson would write that Pauline was the part that "made" Helen Faucit. She was already "a charming young woman," he recalled, "with all the attributes of a fine artiste," yet she made "no real impression on the public till she played Pauline." Her portrayal was "a triumph, a splendid rendition of the proud and haughty beauty of Lyons, which has never been surpassed. She became that night the brightest ornament of the British stage."[35] That is obviously an exaggeration – Helen Faucit had never lacked the enthusiastic support of the general public, nor did she now achieve the steady acclaim of the critics – but it is true that her reputation as an actress of major importance was established by her brilliant success as Pauline. She would continue to act it throughout her career – more often, in fact, than any other role – and, though hundreds of other actresses would appear in this enduringly popular character, it would always be identified with her name.

The other great hit of the season, *Woman's Wit; or, Love's Disguises*, opened on 23 May 1838. Like many of Knowles's dramas, it was written in "Elizabethan" verse and set in some unspecified period of the past; its double structure was reminiscent of Shakespeare. In the serious plot, Helen Mowbray's reputation, lost through the machinations of the libertine Lord Athunree, is finally restored and her former suitor, Lord Walsingham, finds that the "boy Eustace," of whom he has become increasingly fond, is really Helen. Macready and Harriet Taylor redeemed the sentimentalism and improbability by their excellent acting, and Charles Diddear scored a minor hit by his believable portrait of Lewson, Athunree's wretched henchman. In the comic plot, Sir Valentine de Grey loves Hero Sutton but becomes disenchanted because of her lively participation in a sensuous "foreign dance" at a ball; she teaches him a lesson by impersonating a "Quaker cousin," Ruth, who carries simplicity and otherworldliness to the extreme. The scene in which Sir Valentine meets "Ruth" for the first time is amusing even to a modern reader. When the "Quaker maid" naively asks her courtly visitor what dancing is and insists that he demonstrate by dancing for her, Hero has a chance to show her mischievous delight in putting her prudish lover through his paces while at the same time maintaining her role of wondering observer of his "worldliness." As several reviewers attested, Helen Faucit and James Anderson took full advantage of their opportunities here. One considered this scene among "the most delightful" he had ever seen.[36]

The production was, as the *Times* reported, "exceedingly beautiful." The brilliant opening scene depicted "a grand saloon and ballroom beyond, lighted up and crowded with guests" (*Morning Post*). A watercolour sketch owned by James Anderson, done in gold, aquamarine, rose-red, and ivory, suggests the splendor of Macready's first stage picture. There is a large, handsome room with columns, ornate moldings, and mirrors that must have flashed with colour and light when the crowd of merry-makers was in motion; at the back, an arched door opens upon an outdoor scene with terrace, trees, and a crescent moon.[37]

Although *Woman's Wit* was acted nearly as many times as *The Lady of Lyons* in the season when both were produced, it was never revived by Macready, and it was rarely performed by other actors. Anderson, who enjoyed a success as Sir Valentine, could never understand why the play did not keep its place on the stage.[38] That question is easily answered, however. The comic plot, though charming, is too slight for a whole play, and the serious plot is incongruously melodramatic. The storms of applause that greeted the performances can be explained by the splendid staging, the superior acting, and the popularity of the author. Some critics deplored the flaws in the play but enjoyed it anyway. As the astute manager knew, their tolerance would have waned along with the production's novelty.

Meanwhile Helen Faucit enjoyed a personal triumph. Although all the major performances won the critics' praise, her Hero obviously gave the greatest pleasure.[39] The role was a professional windfall: it both challenged and displayed her versatility to an unprecedented extent. Best known as a tragic and romantic actress, she was now being appreciated for her unexpectedly rich "vein of comic humour." Even her old enemy the *Sunday Times* declared that in *Woman's Wit* Miss Faucit had become "a new woman." Never before had she had a chance to play two characters in one as she did now – an art she would later exploit more fully as Shakespeare's Rosalind. Her transformations from Hero to Ruth and back were "electric, and drew down the loudest plaudits."[40] Forster of the *Examiner* was reminded of her Beatrice, for in both "the cordial truth of the feeling of the part itself elicited, with delightful force and effect, the truth of her own nature."

Although Helen acted Hero with charm and ease, she had evidently been under some strain while studying the part and had possibly tried to give it up. For some reason she was temporarily at odds with Harriet Taylor, but luckily Macready did not have the two exchange roles, as he once contemplated.[41] On the first night of *Woman's Wit* she was still behaving badly. When she and Miss Taylor were called for, Anderson, though he had not yet been called, took the actresses' hands to "lead them on" – a gallant gesture, but interpreted by Helen as pretending to a call he had not received. She pulled away, snatched Miss Taylor's hand from his, and "forced" her fellow heroine onto the stage with her.

Macready was "much offended" with her.[42] Helen's tantrums can be partially explained, perhaps, by personal unhappiness, for her "Quaker" part coincided with the death of her beloved Quaker grandmother. Elizabeth Diddear died on 14 May, five days after the parts for *Woman's Wit* had been distributed, and was buried on the 20th, three days before the play opened.[43] But, whatever the excuse, Helen Faucit was obviously not free from petty jealousies.

In the previous months concern for her professional status had brought her into conflict with Thomas Noon Talfourd, but in that case her manager had been sympathetic. The author of *Ion* had written another "classical tragedy," *The Athenian Captive.* Macready, who disliked the play, agreed to produce it only to placate his friend. Creusa, the character intended for Helen Faucit, is a sweet nonentity, much like Clemanthe in *Ion*; the only role with any possibilities for an actress is Ismene, a proud, vengeful queen, designed for Mrs. Warner. Helen wished to refuse her part, but, on Macready's advice, she wrote to Talfourd accepting it under protest. Apparently her reluctance infuriated Mrs. Talfourd, but it did not disturb the dramatist himself; when preparing the play for publication he named Helen Faucit as Creusa in the cast list, mentioning in the preface her "sacrifice" in accepting a part beneath her talents. Nature intervened, however, and invalidated the published information. During the rehearsal period, the pregnant Mrs. Warner went into labour prematurely. In desperation Talfourd asked Helen to take over Ismene, but his wife wrote a hysterical letter to Macready forbidding this. *The Athenian Captive* was temporarily shelved.[44] When it was finally brought out at the Haymarket that summer, with Macready and Mrs. Warner but without Helen Faucit, this heavy, pretentious drama was surprisingly successful.[45]

Shortly before the Covent Garden season ended (on 6 July 1838), London became for awhile one vast festival, culminating on 28 June with a spectacle unrivalled on the stage, the coronation of Queen Victoria. As Lady Morgan noticed, the city resembled "the last scene in a pantomime, all transformed," and the scaffolded buildings along the processional route carried out the theatrical metaphor on a grand scale.

> Every house, from Hyde Park Corner to the Abbey, cased up with wooden platforms, canopied balconies. The... great houses in Piccadilly, which have courts before them, have superb boxes erected as in a theatre, all draped and gilt. The whole front of the Ordnance ... is fitted up as an amphitheatre, decorated with the Queen's arms and crown.[46]

Helen must have been caught up in the general excitement, but the threat of claustrophobia would have kept her away from the "thronging, bustling, gaping" mob that lined the streets to see the show.[47] There was no place for her, at that time, in the "superb boxes," and even she did not dream of the days when she would be a welcome guest at Windsor.

During the summer Helen went with her friend Mrs. Braysher for a holiday visit to Scarborough, the Yorkshire resort. Picturesquely situated on successive ledges of rock which rose like an amphitheatre about a bay open to the sea, it was very different from Margate and Brighton. Its water was colder but also clearer than theirs, and it boasted a spa at the end of the impressive Cliff Bridge. But Helen's favourite recreation, here as in the south, was horseback riding. Since Ellen Braysher, too, was an ardent equestrienne, they spent much of their holiday riding in the nearby countryside.[48]

When Macready began his second season in early autumn, Helen Faucit was again in his company. There had been considerable haggling between them; Macready had insisted that if he met Helen's demands (for a private dressing room, the right to refuse parts, etc.) he "would not be manager," after which she had signed a fresh contract – presumably on his terms.[49] Whatever these were, the relationship between manager and leading lady changed very little. True, she accepted without demur the part of Miranda in *The Tempest*, slight though it was for an ambitious actress. But she tried, most stubbornly, to avoid the relatively weak role of Lady Catherine in *Ruthven*, a new tragedy by James Haynes. Macready was to play Ruthven, a leader in the murder of David Rizzio, and Mrs. Warner was to be Mary, Queen of Scots. Here was *The Athenian Captive* over again. A tug-of-war ensued, with Helen declining the part, Macready insisting upon it, Helen returning the script, Macready sending it back. Finally, after a personal appeal by Prospero to Miranda during an act-break in *The Tempest*, she capitulated. Ironically, Macready then began worrying about the effectiveness of his own character and he eventually persuaded the author to withdraw *Ruthven* for rewriting.[50] It was more than a year before the altered version, renamed *Mary Stuart*, was brought out – at Drury Lane, without Helen Faucit.

If the leading lady was on her guard against the "heavy" actress, the latter was also jealous and resentful of her. Once, when Helen Faucit was to act Kate in the afterpiece *Catherine and Petruchio*, Mrs. Warner's name was accidentally inserted in the playbill. When notified of the mistake, she assumed that Macready had originally intended her to have the part but had given in to Helen's request for it. She paid him two stormy visits over this misunderstanding.[51]

Macready had another problem with his actresses, the conflict between effective costuming and womanly scruples, but in Helen's case he handled it adroitly. Her first performance of the season was to be in Shakespeare's Imogen. Having acted no other breeches part, and this one only three times before, she still felt uneasy about exposing her legs. To lessen her embarrassment, she designed a long, tunic-like garment reminiscent of some worn by earlier actresses. Macready insisted on its alteration, however, to make clear that it was a boy's costume.[52] Perhaps more than modesty accounted for Helen's embarrassment; she might have been painfully aware that her legs did not meet the standards of shapeliness set by such popular actresses of "breeches parts" as Madame Vestris. Realizing the problem, Macready tactfully suggested "on the supposition that her legs were rather thin, the use of a pair of fleeced stockings `such as Malibran used to wear.'" The glamorous name of Malibran was an inspiration. Helen was "reconciled" to the "experiment," and Macready himself bought the stockings for her. Apparently she liked them, for later in the season she wanted some for Rosalind in *As You Like It.*[53]

Helen Faucit's timidity was not unusual. Several other actresses – Mrs. Warner, Harriet Taylor, Priscilla Horton – also caused difficulties for Macready because of their feminine qualms.[54] This is hardly surprising. In 1838 a respectable woman of the middle or upper class never showed her legs in public, whatever the occasion, and never wore a garment without a skirt. When she took a dip in the sea, the umbrella-like hood of a bathing machine hid from curious eyes even the swelling folds of her voluminous bathing dress; when she went riding (side saddle, of course), her habit had a long, trailing skirt.[55] A young actress, especially a boarding-school alumna, might well have had trouble adjusting to a radical infringement of social convention. To some extent her apprehensions were justified: many masculine spectators were conditioned to go beyond the audience's general sense of daring excitement and, regardless of dramatic context, respond according to the "codes" of contemporary pornography.[56] Yet, depending on the actress, there must have been some sublimation of coarser thoughts in plays like *Cymbeline* and *As You Like It.* Helen Faucit's breeches costumes, as described in later years, were delicate in material and colour, and they made no attempt to disguise her female figure. Judging by the written responses (which cannot, of course, tell the whole story), genteel playgoers enjoyed the titillating spectacle of a shapely actress in revealing tights, but they often idealized their pleasure, emphasizing the effects of poetry, romance, and "daydream."[57]

During the Covent Garden season that began on 24 September 1838 and ended on 16 July 1839, Helen Faucit acted in 81 of the 118 Shakespearean performances (more than 60%) and in 75 of the 114 performances of other legitimate plays (52%).[58] Actually, two parts – Miranda in *The Tempest* and Julie in Bulwer's new drama, *Richelieu* – accounted for about 77% of all her performances, and repetitions of *The Lady of Lyons* accounted for another 12%. The only new role she had, besides Miranda and Julie, was Rosalind. The rest were characters in which she was now well known.

Macready's *Tempest,* which opened on 13 October 1838 and ran for 55 nights, was the most spectacular of all his revivals. Insofar as possible, his attempt to "realize" Shakespeare's poetic vision through sights and sounds was triumphantly successful. Critics were ecstatic over the storm and shipwreck, the enchanted island walled with "stupendous cliffs … against the roaring surge," the magic of the intermittent strains of music and the dimly-seen spirit shapes, the graceful singing and flitting about of Priscilla Horton's Ariel. They generally praised the acting as well: Macready "gave a human heart to the mystic personage" of Prospero; Bennett made Caliban a shaggy, "portentous"-looking brute; Anderson and Helen Faucit were charming as the lovers – at least, most people thought so. A few critics, however, considered Miss Faucit too artificial: as the *Morning Post* said, "when acting unaffectedness [she] was most affected of all."[59]

Bulwer's *Richelieu; or, The Conspiracy* was produced with great success on 7 March 1839 and ran for 37 nights. Richelieu, written for Macready, is the great role; all the others are relatively minor. Helen Faucit did not care for her part, Julie de Mortemar, which, as she said, "promises a great deal, and ends in doing nothing."[60] Julie, an orphaned ward of the Cardinal's, is in love with and later marries the Chevalier de Mauprat (played by Anderson). In her big scene she pours out to her guardian, with grief and indignation, the news that the King intends her to be his mistress – and the report (false) that her husband consents. The play's most famous theatrical effect occurs later when Richelieu draws a circle around her and invokes the "curse of Rome" on anyone who dares to violate that boundary. But Julie's story is of secondary interest. Much more important are a conspiracy against Richelieu and the King, the old man's increasing feebleness as he sees his power fading, and, finally, when the truth comes out and he is restored to power, his sudden regeneration.

Never did Macready prepare more thoroughly for a production. He studied accounts of Richelieu and his period, conducted numerous rehearsals, and held private tutoring sessions with several actors. The result was a uniformly excellent production.[61] One aspect of the rehearsals could not have been helpful, though. Bulwer was often present, and once he invited Lady Blessington and Count D'Orsay to come.[62] Macready was annoyed at this, but he himself frequently allowed other friends the same privilege – Browning, Dickens, Maclise, Fox, Forster. James Anderson tells of a rehearsal of *Henry V* when, to the "disgust and horror" of the actors, all these people and others were sitting close to the prompter's table and offering their criticisms. Under such circumstances Helen would become cold and mechanical. (Later, in rehearsing another Bulwer play, she "walked through" her part and was sharply reprimanded by the author.)[63]

Covent Garden Theatre was mobbed on *Richelieu*'s opening night. Westland Marston tells how, as a young man, he fought his way to the pit door and waited for two hours amid a "human sea" that "swayed and roared … against that grim, all-ignoring barrier" before he finally got inside and managed to secure a seat.[64] No one who reads Marston's description of Macready's performance can wonder at the immense success of *Richelieu*, which continued to be acted throughout the century. Slight though the character of Julie is, Helen Faucit received a curtain call for her performance. Reviewers praised her as passionate, natural, "exquisite"; they particularly admired the "strength and dignity of INSULTED VIRTUE" with which she poured out her troubles to Richelieu and her "filial air" in the last scene as she led in "the apparently fainting Cardinal."[65] Queen Victoria, appreciating the womanly virtues depicted here, considered Julie's character "beautiful" and, for once, approved of Helen Faucit.[66] Bulwer himself was pleased with her grace and delicacy, but he urged her to create a grander effect in one scene – to let her form "dilate" and her head "tower."[67] There was such a thing as being *too* natural.

The only strong role in which Helen Faucit appeared with any frequency this season was Pauline in *The Lady of Lyons*, which she acted almost as many times as in its first run. Since Drury Lane coincidentally featured Van Amburgh, a famous animal trainer, and his exhibition of wild animals, a favourite jest of the day concerned the rival "lions" at the two patent theatres. Laman Blanchard, editor of the *Courier*, elaborated it into an amusing set of pun-laden verses, which reappeared in several other journals. For all its heavy-handed wit, it contained a graceful compliment to Helen Faucit:

> Sweet Lady of Lyons! What lions of his,
> Van Amburgh's, could move us like thee to applaud?
> While he is avoiding a scratch on the phiz,
> We seeing you, wish – yes, we wish to be Claude.[68]

Young Queen Victoria was in ecstasies over Van Amburgh's lions. In January, 1839, she visited Drury Lane four times to see them, and once she remained after the entertainments to watch them being fed. The poor beasts, which had been starved for thirty-six hours, acted impressively wild and ravenous.[69] On 1 February the Queen attended Covent Garden in state to see *The Lady of Lyons*, but, as she wrote in her journal afterwards, she was "much more amused at Drury Lane …"[70] She liked the play, but she never cared for Helen Faucit's Pauline, who, as she wrote of an earlier performance, "screamed, and I may say ROARED."[71] Such lack of restraint was exciting in lions but deplorable in a lady.

Helen Faucit's one important new role this season was Rosalind in *As You Like It*, which she first attempted for her benefit on 18 April 1839. She had never before given this character a thought, for Rosalind neither sacrifices herself nobly for love nor suffers some terrible fate like live burial or madness. Looking back later on this first performance, she realized that she had barely scratched the surface of the character; only experience could reveal the "infinite development" of which it was capable.[72] Although she acted Rosalind only four times this season, she would later make it her best Shakespearean character and, next to Pauline, the most popular role of her career.

The production had an excellent cast, not only in Jaques (Macready), Orlando (Anderson), and Touchstone (Harley), but throughout.

A large crowd was present for Helen's benefit; according to the records of John Vandenhoff (back at Covent Garden this season), the receipts were 312 pounds as compared to 260 for Macready's benefit.[73] The audience applauded enthusiastically, and Helen went home feeling she had done very well. She found, on arriving, that her family thought otherwise. Their charge that she had been "merely playing, not acting" referred, perhaps, to the superficiality she later acknowledged herself, but their complaint that she had not "made out what were generally considered the great points in the character" meant that she had not lived up to the tradition established by Dorothy ("Dora") Jordan.[74] That actress's sprightly, somewhat hoydenish Rosalind had delighted the London audiences between 1787 and 1814 and had furnished the model for most of the Rosalinds ever since. Helen Faucit, however, had formed a rather more romantic and "feminine" view of the character. Later she would establish a tradition of her own, but for the moment her conception seemed merely incorrect.

John Forster's review in the *Examiner* (21 April 1839) is illuminating. "It was a pretty performance," he wrote, with "womanly grace and some effective passages of sharp and salient comedy," and it avoided "vulgar or offensive smartness."

> But it was not Rosalind. Of the buoyant wilfulness and passionate volubility, on the sparkling stream of which that tender and triumphant woman's soul is borne so magnificently along … we could discover little or nothing. Another word in all good humour let us add. When the true *Rosalind* put on doublet and hose she declared that … whatever fear lurked in her heart, she'd have a swashing and a martial outside. … Now Miss Faucit put on the hose and forgot the heartiness. … She walked about with so continued and uneasy a sense of the exposure of her legs, that we thought her anxious, at every step, to conceal the one behind the other.

Forster's conception of the "true" Rosalind seems to have been a transitional one, combining something of Mrs. Jordan's robustness with something of Miss Faucit's "womanly grace," but closer to the new Rosalind than to the old. He was probably thinking of Ellen Tree's portrayal, which must have been "transitional" at that time, though it evidently became more refined later. Helen Faucit's Rosalind would never have much of the heartiness he wished, but it would have plenty of buoyancy and passion.

While keeping up with her theatrical work, Helen was now enjoying an active social life. Her personality blossomed as her circle of friends expanded and her enthusiastic audiences continued to provide moral support. She would never completely overcome her vulnerability to possible rejection or attack, but the strong sense of her own worth that had always fuelled her ambition now rose triumphant over the self-distrust with which it so incongruously coexisted. She had built a protective wall around her emotions, excluding with a cold, formal manner those people she distrusted; for friends and admirers, however, she opened the gates wide, allowing a new young woman to emerge – warm-hearted, vivacious, and delightful.

She was a welcome guest at evening parties, with their inevitable musical performances – including, sometimes, her own. On one such occasion, dressed in white crepe and brand-new pearls, she attended a dinner party at Dr. Ure's house and remained to mingle with the large crowd of guests who came afterwards. Sarah Flower Adams, author of the hymn "Nearer, My God, to Thee," sang "two of her Scotch songs with all her usual feeling and sweetness."[75] Helen was regularly invited to the Carter Halls' "evenings" at their "doll-house" home, The Rosery, which was so packed with guests that getting from one room to another was a struggle.[76] Here one could meet "lions," great and small, including a large number of artists. It was at the Halls', probably, that Helen first encountered the Foley brothers, Edward Arlington and John Henry, both sculptors. The latter, at this time a long-faced, pensive-looking youth, would later achieve a high reputation for his work on the Albert Memorial. He would become a longtime friend of Helen's and would capture her likeness in several works of art – notably a marble bust, now in the National Portrait Gallery.[77] Other personal friends, often found at the Halls', were Ronald Robert M'Ian, an actor as well as a painter of Scottish historical subjects, and his wife, Fanny, also an artist. M'Ian, who jestingly called himself Helen's "oldest professional friend" (he was thirty-five in 1838), was the life of the party, with his lively narration of old legends and his humorous performance of Scottish ballads (rather different, one suspects, from those Sarah Adams knew). Once, during a party at the Halls', he imitated drunken behaviour so convincingly while singing "Willie Brew'd a Peck o' Maut" that the waiter asked in an anxious whisper whether he should call a cab to take the gentleman home.[78]

The gossip-mongers had begun to speculate about romance and marriage for Helen Faucit: a certain Member of Parliament was to be the lucky man.[79] They could not know that the man of her choice was unavailable.

The final months at Covent Garden were marred by a disagreeable situation. Macready discovered that a technicality in his contract deprived him of real authority and that his treasurer had been secretly turning over the theatre's income to the proprietors.[80] He decided to finish out the season, anyway, and the grateful actors agreed to sign a resolution condemning the proprietors; their document was so weakly worded, however, that Macready made a speech complaining of their injustice.[81] Helen, in distress, wrote him to express her gratitude for his "honourable and kind" treatment and the hope that he did not extend to her "a censure … so truly undeserved." Naively she disclaimed "any feeling … towards you but what you could wish me to entertain."[82]

Even before this unpleasantness Macready had decided to give up his management, believing his acting had suffered from the dissipation of his energies. He accepted a lucrative offer from Benjamin Webster of the Haymarket and recommended to him several other actors of the company. Helen Faucit, despite Farren's urgent advice, declined an engagement with Madame Vestris, the prospective new manager of Covent Garden, and eventually agreed to join the Haymarket.[83] After Covent Garden closed (on 16 July), she had just a month before beginning her new duties. She would need all the strength she could recruit during this holiday, for the severest trial of her life lay just ahead.

Chapter 5

Turmoil and Triumph

THE THEATRE Royal, Haymarket was the smallest "legitimate" theatre in London. Its stage was narrower than Covent Garden's by about 15 feet at the proscenium opening and 24 feet overall; it was shallower by approximately 25 feet. Its accommodations suffered by comparison, too, though Macready's complaints about this "dog-hole of a theatre" were hyperbolic. Benjamin Webster, a chubby, genial man whose frank manner matched his innocent look,[1] was no perfectionist, but he was a sensible, fair-minded manager. In his company Helen Faucit found such former colleagues as Phelps, Anderson, Mrs. Warner, and William Farren, but she was disturbed by the engagement of Ellen Tree – as Macready was by that of Charles Kean.

Ellen Tree, a well-liked actress whose London career had begun a decade before Helen Faucit's but had been interrupted by a three-year American tour, was now returning, richer in both money and reputation.[2] Londoners, not to be outdone by foreigners, were ready to receive the heroine with an unprecedented ovation. The *Era*, declaring that no actress since Mrs. Siddons could compete with her, welcomed her home "to adorn – nay to be the principal ornament – of the British stage" (8 September 1839: 591). The younger actress was naturally discouraged by this sudden threat to her hard-won position. Even Macready, once an admirer of Ellen Tree, was offended by the fulsome praise: she "left us a mediocre actress," he grumbled unfairly, "and having been puffed in her absence returns to be an attraction." Noticing Helen's depression and rightly divining the cause, he offered the consolation that "her griefs were unreasonable discontents."[3] Cold comfort, but typical.

Ellen Tree was at this time a tall, well-proportioned woman of thirty-three, with shapely legs ideal for breeches parts; she had abundant light brown hair, large hazel eyes, and an aquiline nose. Although even weaker than Helen Faucit in physique and vocal resources, she rarely attempted anything that would strain her powers. Despite her success in the male part of Ion, she was especially valued for her "womanliness" – a trait for which Helen Faucit would later be supremely praised. But, fine as she was in depicting "self-devotion and tenderness," she was equally natural, according to Westland Marston, in "mirth and humour."[4] She would long remain a competitor, though never the threat she seemed now.

On 19 August 1839, the Haymarket was "crammed in every part, and the pit and galleries almost to suffocation" for the production of *Othello* with which the Covent Garden contingent began their performances. Helen Faucit (Desdemona) received a curtain call, as did Macready (Othello) and Phelps (Iago). Some critics saw in this Desdemona the "delicate earnestness" and "simplicity of affection" that they expected, but others were offended by her unconventional vigour in the murder scene. One said she lacked pathos; another sneered that her "scream" belonged to "some untamed shrew."[5] The scream, though possibly exaggerated by the reviewer, was appropriate to Helen Faucit's conception.

Desdemona, she believed, was a stronger character than she was usually represented – a pure but warm-hearted idealist who defied petty conventions to choose a man that matched her vision of heroic worth and, having dedicated herself to him, never wavered in her love. In acting the death scene, Helen Faucit made Desdemona "very hard to kill" (as Macready approvingly said) because, as she explained, speaking in her dual voice of character and actress:

> I *would not* die dishonoured in Othello's esteem. This was bitterer than fifty thousand deaths! Then I thought of all his after-suffering, when he should come to know how he had mistaken me! The agony for him … as well as the mortal agony of death, which I felt in imagination, made my cries and struggles … very vehement and very real.[6]

Piteous appeals and gently reproachful looks might have produced more tears, yet a fragile young woman desperately struggling against overwhelming odds could create her own kind of pathos: Thomas Carlyle felt "quite hurt … to see the fair, delicate creature so brutally used." Helen's actor-friend Mr. Elton declared that her spirited Desdemona "restored the balance of the play" and thus enabled him to see the tragedy "for the first time in its true *chiaro-oscuro*."[7] But tradition-minded critics would always consider her performance too strong – like the one who tutted, "she could scarcely tame herself down to the due point of meekness and resignation" (*Brighton Herald*, 8 October 1842).

Most of Helen Faucit's performances this season were in just three characters: Pauline in *The Lady of Lyons*, which remained so popular that Webster was "unwilling to change the bill" when Juliet was requested;[8] Portia in *The Merchant of Venice*, important chiefly for Macready's innovative Shylock; and Violet in Bulwer's *The Sea-Captain*, a melodramatic new play about a mother who hated one son but loved the other. Violet, a sweet young thing beloved by the elder son (Macready's character), was aptly described as "a walking lady with one scream."[9] Helen had been caught at last in a weak role paired with a strong, if unsympathetic, one for Mrs. Warner (the mother). After twice trying to relinquish it but giving in to Macready's pleas, she finally succeeded, and Priscilla Horton took it over.[10]

Meanwhile Mrs. Warner was becoming increasingly jealous. She resented the special playbill announcements about Helen Faucit,[11] and she was upset by Macready's private interviews with her. There were discussions in his room at the theatre, and, on one occasion, at his London house, where Helen went by invitation for "some instructions in Portia." According to Macready's diary, he gave her "some very excellent advice," then "dismissed her very kindly and properly" – meaning, perhaps, that he restricted himself to a handshake.[12] But Mrs. Warner suspected him of worse improprieties than a parting kiss.

On 21 November Macready noticed that Helen "seemed low-spirited and unwell." When questioned, she reluctantly admitted hearing of a "malignant" discussion by Mrs. Warner, Ellen Tree, and Harriet Taylor (now Mrs. Walter Lacy) about her habit of going to his room. He tried to reassure her, reminding her that other people had been admitted during their interviews and that he had always told both Webster and Mrs. Macready about them. The next day, to "show her sense" of the true situation, Mrs. Macready invited Helen to a dinner party and musical evening at the family home, a large country mansion at Elstree. Among the distinguished guests were the writer Bryan Waller Procter ("Barry Cornwall") and the barrister and dramatist Zouch Troughton, who would be friends of Helen's for years to come. Despite Mrs. Macready's gesture, however, the gossip went on.[13]

Its effect was to intensify Macready's interest in his protégée. He continued to advise her about her performances, but "behind the scenes" rather than in his room. Once he invited her to his home for a morning of instruction, where Mrs. Macready welcomed her and looked in on her several times.[14] Macready was never so happy as when he was teaching others, and Helen was extraordinarily docile at this time.

Meanwhile he had become increasingly alarmed about her health. Finally, at his urging, she consulted her physician, Dr. Guy Babington, who ordered her, on 30 December, to discontinue her acting immediately.[15] She obeyed, thereby missing the two final weeks of that Haymarket season and, in the event, nearly six weeks of the next one.[16]

The symptoms of Helen's illness, which, according to Dr. Babington, was "of a hysterical character," were described by him as "a severe pain in the chest, especially on the left side, accompanied by a general debility, and a loud, dry, and almost incessant cough." In early January Dr. Babington held consultations about Helen with the Macreadys' physician, Dr. John Elliotson, who noted the morbid sensitivity of "the nerves of the outer part of the chest, and of the air tubes of the lungs." Apparently he concurred in his colleague's recommendation that the patient go to Hastings, a seaside resort in Sussex. While there, Helen was under the care of a Dr. William Duke, who compared the pain in her chest to that of *angina pectoris*. All three physicians believed that her "professional exertions" were at least partly responsible for her condition.[17]

The periodic bouts of illness that had plagued Helen since childhood were evidently similar in nature and treatment; only in the present instance, however, are the physicians' reports available. Now, if ever, there is a chance to understand her malady.

Although the reports list a number of symptoms, none gives a specific name to Helen's illness. The nearest approach is Dr. Babington's descriptive phrase "of a hysterical character." What did he mean?

The pathological condition called hysteria (from the Greek word for *womb*) had been associated in ancient times with the notion of a freely-moving uterus, which, when deprived of its proper function, could rise and press against other organs. Although this concept had been abandoned following a better knowledge of anatomy, the symptoms once explained by it were still associated with irregularities in a woman's reproductive system. (Men, admittedly, could be victims of a similar disorder, but hysteria was generally considered a woman's problem.) By Helen Faucit's time, there were conflicting ideas about the causes of "hysterical" symptoms:[18] for example, some theorists thought the locus was the brain and the nerves while others gave a gynecological explanation; there were also various sub-theories and combinations of theories. It was believed that the disorder, whatever its origin, could attack the weakest part of the body and produce symptoms characteristic of that part.[19] An idea held by some doctors, but more emphasized in later years, was that too much use of the brain could weaken a woman's reproductive system, producing unfortunate mental and physical results.[20] Although nymphomania had largely replaced sexual frustration as a supposed cause of hysteria, the latter was still considered important among repressed gentlewomen. Victorian theories aside, symptoms of "hysteria" among intelligent, ambitious women were surely due to a deadlier kind of repression: the restricted lives decreed for them by society.[21]

The manifestations of hysteria could vary, from a general malaise or mild depression to rapid swings in mood and uncontrollable fits of laughter, weeping, or coughing, to such severe conditions as epileptic-like seizures, temporary blindness, deafness, muteness, or paralysis. A particularly characteristic symptom was the *globus hystericus*, the sensation of a ball rising in the oesophagus to choke the sufferer.[22]

Although there was no generally-accepted medical view of hysteria at the time of Dr. Babington's diagnosis, one may guess why Helen was considered a victim of this disorder. Her sensitive, highly strung nature and her frustrating situation with Macready (if this was known) suggested vulnerability; her chronic fear of suffocation and her current paroxysms of coughing were symptomatic. The physicians' statements partly blaming her illness on her professional exertions undoubtedly alluded to problems like fatigue, exposure to temperature changes, and the effects of over-excitement; but possibly, too, they implied fears about the consequences of brain work. A doctor whom Helen consulted in Paris several years later told her that "the brain had been suffered to prey upon the body in a cruel manner."[23] Actually, though she drove herself hard and might well have overtaxed her constitution at times, she normally found acting very exhilarating. At any rate, she did not suffer because of stifled talents.

Since "hysteria" is no longer a generally-accepted medical term, it may be interesting to know the hypothetical diagnoses of two modern experts. Both have studied the reports of Helen's doctors as well as some notes about her life. According to a specialist in pulmonary medicine, her recurring bouts of coughing and her anxiety about suffocation are most consistent with asthma (a relatively mild form), as is her long life in spite of her illnesses; tuberculosis could have caused the coughing but not the chest pain, and *angina pectoris* would be unlikely in a woman of her age.[24] A specialist in neuropsychiatry notes evidence of Helen's "avoidant personality"; he suggests that her acting served as a defence against "shyness and insecurity," her relationship with Macready fulfilled some "unmet needs" from earlier years, and the stresses connected with this relationship "triggered" the illness of 1839-40. Her recuperative holidays had relieved her from childhood stresses, and she continued to use "somatization as a defensive mechanism to keep her anxieties and depressions out of her awareness."[25]

It is interesting that only one of Helen's physicians described her illness as "hysterical." Since he was the one who knew her best, however, his opinion carries weight. Whether or not it was medically valid, it is a reminder of personal traits which, when brought under control, became valuable assets in her acting. The extraordinary sensitivity that made her vulnerable to any hint of rejection, any atmosphere of hostility, also enabled her to enter imaginatively into each moment of her character's life and to exercise a suggestive power in conveying its essence. Critics would later speak of her "full-toned sensibility, vibrating at the slightest breath" and making the nerves of her spectators "vibrate" in response.[26]

Whatever the precise nature of Helen's illness, its effects were so painful that she immediately made preparations for the recommended stay at Hastings. Before leaving she attended a small dinner at the Macreadys' home (Robert Browning was one of the few guests), after which Macready gave her two books to read during her exile and promised to send her some rules of good acting to study. He "felt very low at parting with her," for he had not realized before "how deep and tender an interest" he felt for her.[27] Her own spirits were lower still, for she was obliged to leave her two great loves behind – her idolized profession and the human idol who represented it. She left behind her reputation as well: the school for scandal was still at work upon that.

On New Year's Day, as the first playbills were announcing her "severe indisposition," the "women in the dressing rooms" were saying that Miss Faucit had to leave the theatre because she was "in the family way." Macready was, of course, outraged.[28] The gossip soon spread. On 12 January the "Dramatic Intelligence" column of the *Observer*, after some news about Macready, added equivocally:

> Meanwhile … Miss Helen Faucit (for their names, probably from so frequently performing together, are usually coupled) is to proceed to the Continent for the recovery of her health, which has been seriously impaired in consequence of the severe duty she has undergone with Macready. We are very sorry to lose her … and on every account we hope that, at longest, it will only be until the re-opening of the Haymarket …

Macready believed, no doubt correctly, that this "trash" was "intended to convey gross insinuations."[29] Since the same column expressed in its next number (19 January) the hope that there would be "no disposition," as in the past, to "run down" Mrs. Warner's acting for the sake of any other performer, one may guess at the Lady Sneerwell behind the previous little paragraph. On 26 January the *Observer* followed a comment about Macready with another carefully-worded attack: "This reminds us of Miss Faucit. What is become of her? … She is said to be unwell, but why this silence and seclusion? Everybody has an interest in her, for … she is unquestionably our best young and unmarried actress." The writer – evidently John Payne Collier – was too clever to italicize "unmarried," but for those who knew the gossip he did not need to do so. The *Satirist* was less circumspect in its hints: on 1 March the column of "Theatrical Chit-Chat" included an item about Helen Faucit's "delicate state of health, arising from arduous professional exertions while engaged under the 'Eminent Tragedian'"; the writer added blandly, "Miss Faucit is not attended, as reported, by Mr. Macready's family physician."

By that time Helen had been established at Hastings for some weeks, attended by her friend Mrs. Braysher. One would like to know more about Ellen Drew Braysher, who provided endless bouquets for the Lady of Lyons, shared her bracing holidays with the work-weary actress, and now left home and husband to care for her sick friend. She obviously cherished a strong romantic devotion to Helen Faucit. She showered her with gifts: among them, a "beautiful little riding-whip" and several specially-bound copies of plays, elegantly covered in blue or rose watered silk and richly embellished with gold emblems, gold lettering, and gilt-edged pages.[30] She evidently idealized the actress as an incarnation of the beauties, charms, and virtues of the heroines she represented. Years later, in a letter dated 17 March 1880, Mrs. Braysher recalled Helen's acting in words that are puzzling, yet clearly charged with personal meaning: "your own charming exertions in your own beautiful art, on so many occasions, when the great help you gave *where help was needed*, was hardly exceeded even by the delight in the perfection of those impersonations …"[31] Why had help been so sorely needed, and how had Helen Faucit given it through her acting? Speculation is idle, but one thing is clear: after such generous giving of her own, Ellen Braysher remembered only what she had received from her friend.

"I do love to attract women, do I not?" Helen once wrote. In his biography of her Sir Theodore Martin explains: "To influence [women], to make them see and feel with her as to her heroines, was at all times her highest pride" (142). In later years an unknown woman admirer ("E. de C.") wrote that the emotion Helen Faucit inspired was "no mere passing admiration … but a deeper and truer feeling for one whom I cannot but look upon as the type of all that is most excellent in woman."[32] By that time Helen would have received countless similar tributes from men, but their tone was rather different; apparently her acting made women feel *themselves* to be more attractive, more worthwhile, more exalted in nature.

The period of rest prescribed by Helen's physicians was nothing like the notorious "rest cures" later used by some doctors, which required the patient to remain bedridden and mentally inactive for long periods.[33] Even so, the sudden change in her life was depressing. In youth she had contentedly read and dreamed on the beach at Brighton for hours at a time, but after four hectic years in the theatre such isolation and passivity seemed alien to her. Later, looking back on this time, she wrote:

> … despite the love and care of a dear friend … it was a weary time, this banishment – this separation from the art which was all in all to me; from which I had derived almost the only happiness … I could not but see, too, that my friends [i.e. the Farrens] did not expect I should grow better. I do not think I very much cared. … But oh, the inaction, the enforced care and thought for myself, the wearing cough by night, the sameness of the dreary days![34]

Her only comfort was the flow of solicitous letters from Macready – sending news of the theatre, suggesting books to read, and bidding her to get well because she was sorely missed.[35] Once, after receiving a despondent letter from her, he wrote:

> You grieve me very much in throwing a doubt upon the resumption of your art, for independently of the strong personal interest which I must always take in you, I have looked on you as one in whom I could hope to see left a surviving specimen of the purer style of the theatrical art … I … perceive no intelligence or sensibility among those engaged in our theatres to lend the least encouragement to hope beyond yourself.[36]

Most of Helen's letters pleased Macready, but one, though "nicely written," sent him into an emotional tailspin because of a single word she had used in signing her name. Even at the theatre, "all the day, and all the night, through the whole play, [he] was haunted by one word."[37]

Early in February Mrs. Braysher, acting on Macready's advice, evidently visited Collier of the *Observer* and informed him where Helen was and why. Collier, though slow to respond, finally reported in his "Dramatic Intelligence" column of the 23rd that Helen Faucit's health had been "much restored by residence on our southern coast." It was after this, however, that the *Satirist* published its barbed paragraph (1 March). Finally William Farren, after conferring with Macready and Mr. Braysher,[38] had Helen's lawyer, Thomas Hanson Peile, draw up a statement denying the reports "prejudicial to her moral character" and announcing her "directions" to adopt all legal measures for punishing those who had "so wantonly and cruelly attacked it." The statement, dated 9 March 1840 and signed by Peile, was posted in the greenroom of the Haymarket Theatre, together with detailed medical reports from the three doctors. Webster, the Haymarket manager, then sent copies of these documents to the *Observer*. They were published in the next number, 15 March. In his column that day Collier professed ignorance of the scandal, questioned the advisability of public denials, but said, by way of unacknowledged apology, that Helen Faucit was "a most valuable young lady to the stage" and he believed her to be "most reserved and irreproachable in her conduct." Other periodicals expressed indignation about the slander – for example the *Era* and the *Theatrical Journal* – and public sympathy for Helen seemed to be general. After this the Farrens let the matter drop.

By the latter part of March Helen was strong enough to resume her horseback riding, and, despite a temporary setback, she returned to London the following month.[39] On 25 April she was warmly welcomed back to the Haymarket as Pauline in *The Lady of Lyons*. According to reviewers, she played with "her usual judgment" but seemed weak, as if still suffering from the effects of illness.[40] She remained frail and spiritless for some time. Listlessness had never before been a problem in her performances – quite the reverse, in fact – but now Macready had to remonstrate with her about her "languid" acting.[41]

Such vitality as she had was consumed by personal emotions. No longer did she try to hide her feelings from Macready or to speak in euphemisms about her love. Distressed for her sake, he begged her not to "widow" her heart by allowing it to dwell on someone with "no power of recompensing her tenderness." Helen declared that, although her family wished her to marry, she could not "think of any person as a husband." Then all her stored-up griefs came pouring out, all her sufferings from her family – "so wearing, so sordid, so vulgar, so cruel." During her illness, she said, she had learned more than ever what he meant to her; her love for him was all she had to live for. On 9 July came a climactic renunciation scene. Playing her noblest, most self-sacrificing role, Helen vowed to overmaster the "absorbing passion which swell[ed] her heart almost to bursting." Macready replied that he "*dared not*" wish her to take any other course but that it wrung his "very soul to witness the agony it cost her." He gave her one little kiss, on the forehead, as a "remembrance." This was by no means the end of her sufferings, however. Unable to carry out her promise, she incessantly berated her weakness, "racking and prostrating herself mentally and physically."[42]

Macready's remedy was to focus her attention on the improvement of her acting. She responded obediently to his essays, lectures, and criticisms, making a valiant effort to change her style in accordance with his suggestions.[43] The principles he tried to instill were aimed primarily at overcoming her tendency toward exaggeration. "Passion does not require a loud tone of voice," he admonished her, "nor wide, nor violent gesticulation." And, as Charles Kemble had done, he advised her not to let passion "disturb the grace of the deportment"; in particular, "There should be no *moving* or *jerking of the head*, the noblest part of the body." She had already achieved some success in substituting earnestness for vehemence, but Macready encouraged even greater subtlety. And, although her transitions from one emotion to another had recently been praised, he thought she could make them still better by taking more time – a suggestion resulting in some "Macready pauses."[44]

Helen's attempts to follow these precepts were met with an outbreak of attacks in the press. On 24 May, when she had been back in the theatre barely a month, the *Observer* censured her for excessive imitation of Macready, saying that "all her stops, breaks, and pauses" were "caught from him." The next day the *Morning Herald* complained that her style had lost its "impulse and freshness" and she seemed "withering under some baleful tutelage." She would do well to forswear her newly-acquired tricks, "for at present Miss Faucit is lost to us, and in her place we have only – Miss Macready." From then on, as long as she was associated with Macready, Helen would be taxed at times with imitating his "mannerisms." In her usual way of doing nothing by halves, she probably exaggerated the very methods intended to tame her exaggeration. In time, removed from his magnetic personality, she would adapt some of his precepts to her own purposes and discard those she found ineffective.

During her second season at the Haymarket Helen Faucit gave 158 performances, 63 percent of which were in Bulwer's *Money*, one of her three new plays. Among her old characters, Pauline remained the most popular, with Rosalind next, though well below. More at ease in Rosalind than when she had played it at Covent Garden, she now won the approval of John Forster (*Examiner* 16 August 1840), but she was "not humorous and joyous enough" to satisfy Macready.[45]

The first of the new plays, Talfourd's blank-verse tragedy *Glencoe; or, The Fate of the Macdonalds*, was introduced on 23 May 1840 and acted 21 times. Despite its historical trappings – the setting in late-seventeenth-century Scotland, the depiction of the Macdonalds' massacre by the Argyll Campbells, – it is actually a fictitious story of two Macdonald brothers who love the same girl, Helen Campbell. Helen Faucit's friend R.R. M'Ian, an expert on Scottish tartans – and also a fanatically proud descendant of the Macdonalds – gave advice on the costumes.[46] As several critics noticed, the play has only "one part," that of the elder brother, Halbert (played by Macready). Although Helen Faucit disliked her role of Helen Campbell, her performance of this "amiable nobody" won critical approval for its sweetness, delicacy, and "feeling."[47]

The least popular of the new plays, Serle's *Master Clarke*, was first acted on 26 September 1840 and had nine performances. This unpretentious work in competent blank verse deals sympathetically with Richard Cromwell (son and successor of Oliver): at the beginning he is still in power, though having trouble with the army; at the end, after saving the King from a conspiracy, he happily contemplates a peaceful retirement under his alias "Master Clarke." His wife, Lady Dorothy Cromwell, is a strong, aggressive woman who later becomes more docile. Some critics were pleased by Helen Faucit's contrasting portrayal of "pride and ambition" at first and "humble and affecting tenderness" at last. Others, however, thought she should have toned down Lady Dorothy's stronger qualities, remembering, for example, that a woman's expression of confidence must be "trustful," not "robustly rejoiceful."[48] Helen Faucit had overcome her listlessness, only to find herself unwomanly.

Bulwer's *Money*, first performed on 8 December 1840 and acted 68 times, was Webster's most successful production, by far, this season. Actually Webster only provided the pounds, shillings, and pence for the production. Macready's directing hand was noticeable throughout: not only was the *mise en scène* more sumptuous and appropriate than usual for the Haymarket, but the performance had the kind of unity and smoothness associated with Macready's Covent Garden productions.[49]

Money, written in facile, sometimes lively prose, stands out as a successful comedy of manners in an age almost devoid of such plays. Its moralizing and sentimentality are balanced by satirical humour, realism, and commonsense. The heroine's nobility, for example, is made deliberately unromantic.[50] Though the basic plot is simple and predictable, the situations are well contrived; and, though the principal characters are hardly striking,[51] some colourful secondary ones provide variety – platitudinous politicians, a gentlemanly gambler, a merry widow, and a gloomy widower.

Clara Douglas (Helen Faucit) loves Alfred Evelyn (Macready) but refuses his proposal of marriage on account of his poverty. Shortly afterwards, Evelyn unexpectedly inherits a fortune. He becomes engaged to the frivolous Georgina Vesey, but, when he pretends to have lost his estate in gambling, she shifts her allegiance to the foppish Sir Frederick Blount. Clara, however, sends money anonymously to Evelyn and, defying convention, pays him a consolatory call.

When confronted with her former mercenary attitude, she explains that memory of the hardships suffered by her parents, who had married without money, had determined her not to let the man she loved repeat her father's experience. Evelyn is overjoyed to find she loves him, and the play ends happily.

Except in journals friendly to Bulwer and Macready, most early reviews were unenthusiastic about *Money*; critics complained that Bulwer had ruined a good subject by trite treatment. Charles Dickens declared, however, that no other comedy since Goldsmith's *The Good-Natured Man* was "so full of real, distinct, genuine character,"[52] and the *Literary Gazette* correctly remarked that the "power" of the play was in "holding the mirror up to society."[53] Even critics who disliked *Money* admitted that it was theatrically effective. Although attendance built slowly, in a few weeks *Money* had become one of the most successful plays of its day.[54] Now, said a common joke, Webster was the only manager in London with any money.[55] Many others would soon emulate him, however, and the comedy would be acted for years to come. Even after its original popularity had faded, there would be successful revivals. The Bancrofts would produce it in 1872 for a 200-night run and would bring it back at least twice after that. Charles H. Shattuck's belief that it would "have validity on the stage today" was justified when the Royal Shakespeare Company revived it in 1981.[56]

The role of Clara Douglas had none of the brilliance and power of Pauline, but it offered some challenges to an actress trying to improve her psychological suggestiveness. Clara must hide her distress when refusing Evelyn's proposal and her shock and dismay when hearing of his engagement to Georgina; only later, when Lady Franklin (her patroness) makes a bold guess at her secret, is her reserve temporarily destroyed. Helen Faucit was very successful in suggesting the conflict between Clara's surface manner and her inner emotions: the *Spectator* (more friendly than usual) praised her for the "simple, touching earnestness with which she depicted the suppressed grief and assumed calmness of the heart-broken girl, and her modest frankness when the kinswoman's regard breaks through the constraint of her maidenly reserve." Her greatest effect, however, came in the final act, especially in the speech about her parents' poverty. After so much repression, this forthright expression of emotion was doubly effective: even the *Morning Herald*, which had been plaguing her about Macreadyism, admitted her "natural pathos" and "true impulse of the heart."[57]

In January 1841, during a recurrence of Helen's illness, Fanny Stirling, a young forerunner of realistic acting, successfully played Clara. The new interpretation was evidently more ingenuous and straightforward than the original one, more likely to win immediate sympathy but less likely to suggest the character's inner life. For example, Mrs. Stirling's rejection of Evelyn's proposal seemed to arise from simple embarrassment and surprise, whereas Helen Faucit "threw something of hauteur and temper into the refusal" – intended, no doubt, as a blind to hide her true emotions. Although Macready normally encouraged attempts at psychological acting, he was impressed by Mrs. Stirling's effective simplicity. "She speaks with freshness and truth of tone," he wrote, "that no other actress in [sic] the stage now can do."[58]

Alan Downer suggests that this judgment was not wholly disinterested since Macready had become annoyed by Helen Faucit's demands as to salary and billing. He had been annoyed in other ways as well. On the first night of *Money* he noted in his diary: "In the last scene Miss Faucit, as I had anticipated, had quite the advantage over me; this was natural." But as the play ran on his tolerance waned, and he grumbled about the "unfair advantages" she had taken.[59] Her ambition was making a new stand against the docility produced by physical weakness and emotional frustration.

The Haymarket closed on 15 March 1841, but the new season was to begin less than a month later, on Easter Monday. (As in the preceding year, the Lord Chamberlain had allowed this "summer theatre" to extend its season through the winter months, thus becoming, in effect, a year-round theatre.) During the vacation Helen Faucit, at Macready's suggestion for broadening her theatrical experience, made her first visit to Paris. She had wished Ellen Braysher to accompany her, but, when thwarted by Mr.Braysher's adamant objection, she persuaded her brother John to go.[60] Armed with a letter from Macready, she met the courtly Marcellin de Fresne, who had been "under the Restoration ... Secrétaire-Général of the Prefecture of the Seine"; the two were charmed with each other and became lasting friends. Under de Fresne's auspices Helen was introduced to such writers and artists as Chateaubriand and Delaroche and also to "the best society of the Quartier St. Germain." She established an immediate rapport with Mme. Georgiane Colmache, whose husband had been Talleyrand's secretary. The two carried on a cordial correspondence afterwards and remained close friends.

In visits to the theatre Helen Faucit was strongly attracted to Rachel.[61] This remarkable young woman had burst upon the Parisian scene less than three years before, and her greatest accomplishments lay in the future; yet, despite a temporary setback, she was already the most important actress in France.[62] Helen must have found in her performances some of the excitement once aroused by Edmund Kean's. In the fashionable salons, where Rachel was the "lionne" of the day, the two actresses met and became acquainted. Rachel had delicate features, thick, curly hair, and a fragile form, whose meagreness was disguised by a high-necked gown of rich, heavy material. Her ladylike behaviour made everyone wonder how "this young girl, without education or knowledge of good society," had so easily "seized its manner and tone." Helen, who found her charming, responded with pleasure to Rachel's cordial interest in her.[63]

A memorable part of the Parisian visit was her tour of the great art galleries, particularly the gallery of ancient sculpture at the Louvre. Seeing the Venus de Milo was like a religious experience: she was filled with wonder as her ideals of beauty and nobility took tangible form before her. When revisiting Paris several years later, she was again profoundly moved by the "glorious Venus of Milo" but in a somewhat different way. As she explained in a letter:

> Never was anything so simply grand, and quietly yet eloquently graceful … The figure is much larger than life, and yet loses nothing in delicacy and chasteness. I am so delighted to find that my enthusiasm for all great things *increases*. When I was here last I should have thought this impossible … but I have now less of wonder and more of positive and appreciating enjoyment. If it did not seem presumptuous, I could say that I was conscious of a kindred spirit …[64]

That was because she saw here in perfection an achievement she was aiming toward in her acting: embodiment of the ideal in the actual.

The Haymarket, freshened with amber paint and yellow silk draperies, reopened on 12 April 1841,[65] but, because of Webster's plans for visiting stars, Helen Faucit was not scheduled to appear until 3 May. (One of the expected stars, Tyrone Power, went down with his ship en route from America.) Her season was unusually fragmented: she was idle during much of Charles Kean and Ellen Tree's engagement (from mid-May to the end of June), and absent because of illness from early September to mid-October. In this season she acted only 81 times. Novelties were her performances in two Sheridan roles opposite Henry Placide, visiting American comedian: Lady Teazle to his Sir Peter and Julia to his Bob Acres. Her most frequent appearances were in *Money*, *The Lady of Lyons*, and Zouch Troughton's new blank-verse tragedy, *Nina Sforza*.

During the early part of this season, in May 1841, Mlle. Rachel visited London for the first time and played an engagement at Her Majesty's Theatre. Helen met her socially at the Macreadys' home, and she undoubtedly went to see the French plays. Rachel was frequently seen at the Haymarket, too. During a performance of *The Lady of Lyons* she went behind the scenes and presented Helen with a gold thimble, containing a "secret bottle of smelling salts," which she had often worn on her own finger. (Years later, when Mary Anderson was playing Pauline, Helen passed the gift on to her.) Unfortunately, some critics, in their enthusiasm for the French tragedienne, denigrated the best British actresses: compared with Rachel, said the *Satirist*, Helen Faucit was "a vulgar hoyden."[66]

British competitors, however, were of more immediate importance to Helen Faucit. Although still uneasily aware of Ellen Tree's prominence, she had less to fear from this actress than had once seemed likely. Miss Tree had been engaged at Covent Garden during the previous season, but, as the *Observer* pointed out, Madame Vestris, the manager, had not made the best use of her talents. At the Haymarket, although she and Charles Kean attracted good audiences, they did not always please the critics. The *Athenaeum*, for example, called their *Macbeth* "less than ordinarily effective" and spoke disparagingly of Kean's "Romeo

Furioso" and Ellen Tree's "mature and discreet" Juliet. The *Examiner*, which had blown hot and cold about Miss Tree, praised her "affecting" performance of Mrs. Haller but remarked that Juliet was "out of her sphere."[67] (The reviewers' impressions of Kean may have influenced their criticisms of his leading lady: the two would soon be married, and they were already being treated as a pair.) The *Observer*'s shifting attitude toward Ellen Tree might not have been typical, but it was one of the straws in the wind. On 9 May the "Dramatic Intelligence" writer had expressed pleasure in the opportunity she would have at the Haymarket of "re-establishing her character as our first tragic actress," but by 31 October, evidently influenced by Helen Faucit's success in *Nina Sforza*, he was proclaiming:

> Miss H. Faucit is a young lady of great individual merit, of much personal beauty, and, we do not scruple to add, of higher tragic talents than any competitor now upon the stage. We consider Ellen Tree as gone from us – we know not where; and she forms another instance of … great abilities … rendered of little avail by mismanagement.

Ellen Tree, at thirty-five, had not "gone"; her "great abilities" would continue to show themselves as she and her husband cooperated for years to come in impressive productions of Shakespearean and other plays. But her beauty had reached its peak and her style its maturity before now. Helen Faucit, though only nine years younger, was still in the youthful stage of change, development, and noticeable upward progress.

Helen Faucit's one new play of the season, Troughton's *Nina Sforza*, did more for her reputation than any other since *The Lady of Lyons* and *Woman's Wit*. It was introduced on her benefit night, 1 November 1841, to a crowded and enthusiastic audience and was performed for eighteen nights. It would undoubtedly have run longer if Macready had not left the Haymarket early in December to prepare for his management of Drury Lane. Helen evidently expected him to revive it there after she joined him, and, when he failed to do so, she suspected him of trying to hold her down[68]. But since he was very successful in the play, he would hardly have let it die because of jealousy. More likely he doubted its survival power. Helen, however, never lost her enthusiasm for *Nina Sforza*: forty years later she was still describing it as "one of the finest plays of our time."[69]

The scene is Renaissance Genoa, where, in a feud between two great families, the Spinolas have been crushed by the Dorias. Hiding his deadly hatred, Ugone Spinola becomes the inseparable companion of the magnanimous young Raphael Doria and seeks his ruin by encouraging dissolute habits. Doria happily marries the lovely Nina Sforza, but eventually he succumbs to an old weakness and takes a mistress. When Spinola reports this to Nina, she indignantly spurns him, but he insists on offering proof. He takes her into the city, where, under cover of darkness, they watch Doria as he goes to his mistress's house. Nina, in an agony of grief, takes poison. When the repentant Doria discovers her, dying, she forgives him before expiring on his breast. He stabs himself, and Spinola exults over his dying enemy.

Most critics found some flaws in the play – poor construction, too little relation between Spinola's villainy and the catastrophe – but also pointed enthusiastically to its merits. The *Morning Post* called it "one of the purest and noblest tragedies that modern dramatic genius has put upon the stage." Several critics noticed similarities to Shakespeare: Nina was like Juliet, Spinola like Iago; the scene between these two was a "moonlight reflection" of the great temptation scene in *Othello*. All the reviewers reported the success of the theatrical production – the greatest in recent years, according to *The Times*. Certain scenes had been unforgettably vivid, especially the one in which Nina and Spinola watch for Doria in the darkened streets. According to the *Morning Chronicle*, the "group" formed here by Macready and Helen Faucit – "her crouching, earnest, agonised figure and he in his dusky cloak, with the light on his exulting countenance" – was "amongst the most beautiful of stage pictures." More than one critic imagined Macready as a serpent in this scene and Helen Faucit as its victim – Eve about to be crushed by the "arch enemy," a "fluttered dove" caught in the scaly toils.[70]

All the principal actors were much applauded, all received curtain calls, all were praised by most reviewers. J.W. Wallack succeeded as a gallant, spirited, and "feeling" Doria. Macready's diabolical Spinola, dressed to resemble Mephistopheles, almost mesmerized his audiences.[71] Helen Faucit's Nina, though it owed much of its impressiveness to Macready's acting and to their joint effects, was also, per se, an unusually accomplished portrayal. Critics particularly admired the intensity and effectiveness with which Nina's variegated emotions were depicted – "the vehement bursts of scorn and anger ... the anguish of her doubts, her agonising gaze of horror ... the blank of hopeless despondency ... the fondness of pitying forgiveness" (*Spectator*). An article in the *Theatrical Journal* (11 December 1841: 398-99), devoted exclusively to her portrayal, is full of details showing her revelations of thought through facial expression, vocal tone, attitude, and gesture. For example, when Nina tensely watched her husband approach his mistress's house, earnestly willed him to pass it, then released a sigh of painful recognition as he went in,

> the expression of her *figure* no less than of her face, was thrilling. She seemed turning to stone before our eyes, until the extremity of her suffering spoke in tones of the wildest despair ... her "*pass* – *pass* – ah!" those who have heard it once will never forget.

In 1841 Helen's personal life was less traumatic than in the preceding year, but continued emotional instability probably intensified her recurring illness. During her six-week absence from work in the autumn, she paid a recuperative visit to Brighton, where her brother John had recently entered the management of the Theatre Royal. On returning to London, she was happily reunited with Harriet, who, along with Humphrey Bland (a Liverpool actor whom she had married in 1839), was newly affiliated with Covent Garden.[72]

When Macready, in recruiting his Drury Lane company, offered Helen Faucit an engagement, she insisted on the thirty pounds a week that she was receiving at the Haymarket; he was "obliged to say *yes*."[73] Although he officially assumed the management on 4 October, he did not open his 1841-42 season until 27 December. Helen remained at the Haymarket through 15 January 1842, then prepared to join in his new venture.

Chapter 6

Macready's Management Again

HELEN FAUCIT had agreed to a short engagement at her brother John's theatre in Brighton before joining Macready at Drury Lane; at the last moment, however, she postponed it until March. Although the probable excuse was illness, there was a more disturbing reason.[1] On 15 January, a few days before her first scheduled appearance, Henry Michell Wagner, Vicar of Brighton, had assaulted a seven-year-old urchin, and the case brought against him by the boy's father was to be tried on the 20th. Acting in Brighton would have been an ordeal for Helen during this time of humiliating publicity for her long-time friend. Behind this incident lay a contemporary controversy over the fairness of "church rates" – that is, the traditional taxes to support the established Church of England. Wagner had become frustrated by his vestry's refusal to impose new rates for essential repairs. When he retaliated by allowing St. Peter's Clock to run down, children began jeering at him, chanting "Who stopped the clock?" This happened once too often, and the outraged Vicar gave the latest offender several lashes with his horsewhip. Although he was let off with a light fine, Wagner was undoubtedly punished by remorse; for, despite his crusading fury in defending the church's rights, he was a kindly man by nature.[2] It must have seemed strange to Helen that two men whom she particularly loved and admired, both with strong religious principles, had allowed their tempers to erupt in sordid acts of violence.

Drury Lane, being the older of the two great patent theatres, was thus the premier national theatre, with an obligation to uphold the best of British drama. More often than not, however, that responsibility went unfulfilled – certainly under the previous manager, Alfred Bunn. Macready was determined to redeem the reputation of Old Drury and even to give it new lustre. He began with the physical plant. The outside remained as it was – its neoclassical colonnade, still a familiar sight today, had been added in 1831 – but the interior underwent considerable renovation. Changes in the accommodations were made, for example, in the interests of comfort and decency: pittites now had individual, handomely upholstered seats; prostitutes made do with spartan facilities, completely separate from the rest of the theatre.[3] As at Covent Garden, Macready's scenery and costumes were artistic and appropriate. His aim, as always, was the worthy production of the best classics and new plays of high quality. His problem, as always, was to find such new plays.

Among the Drury Lane actors were some recent recruits, like Mrs. Stirling and the Keeleys, but also many former members of Macready's Covent Garden company. One of the latter was Mrs. Warner. Macready had become reconciled with her out of sympathy when Webster fired her in December 1840, but "Miss Faucit" was still a "sore subject."[4]

On 25 January 1842, while en route to the theatre for her first performance, Helen Faucit became ill and had to be replaced in the cast.[5] She finally appeared on 14 February, acting Belvidera in *Venice Preserved* to Anderson's Jaffier and Phelps's Pierre. This role, which had cost so many tears of her own in 1836, was now making spectators weep with its "overpowering" emotions.[6]

During the rest of the season, in addition to reviving several other old parts, she acted in three new productions, none with a strong role for her. The first and most interesting, Gerald Griffith's *Gisippus*, opened on 23 February 1842. The play, based on an old love-versus-friendship tale, popular in the Renaissance, lacks the interest of complexity, but it has some good poetry and several effective scenes. Gisippus, a Greek, gives up his prospective bride, Sophronia, when he discovers that she and his Roman friend Fulvius are in love; after a period of estrangement, in which Gisippus suffers hardship and danger, the friends are reunited. Macready's production was visually appealing, with its classical costumes and its striking scenes of ancient Athens and Rome. Macready and Anderson, respectively, were effective in Gisippus and Fulvius, and Helen Faucit, with her musical delivery and graceful performance, gave a surprising charm to the slender part of Sophronia.[7] Although the play had less drawing power than Macready had hoped, its run was stretched out to twenty nights. The next new play, George Darley's *Plighted Troth*, was the greatest failure of Macready's managerial career (what had seemed to him a powerful drama turned out to be ludicrous melodrama), and the heroine, Maddalen, had no redeeming moments whatever.[8] It was acted only once (20 April). Lord Byron's *Marino Faliero*, introduced on Macready's benefit night (20 May), was repeated only once and was revived the following season for just two performances. Its scenes of fourteenth-century Venice were impressive, and Macready's acting of the title role was admirable, but the production was more respected than enjoyed. Helen Faucit as Angiolina had little to do, but did it "extremely well" (*Morning Post* 21 May).

The very short season at Drury Lane ended early, on 23 May 1842. Two days later Helen left for Dublin, where, on the 28th, she began a joint engagement with Macready at the Theatre Royal. The journey, though it took the best part of a day and a night (to Liverpool by train, then to Ireland by packet), was considerably easier than it would have been several years earlier, before the railroad from London to Liverpool was opened.[9] This was Helen's first visit to Dublin, but her way was smoothed by Calcraft, manager of the Theatre Royal, who had secured some apartments for her "adjoining the Theatre," and by Anna Maria Hall, who had arranged for Helen to meet some of her Irish friends. One of these, Mrs. Hutton of Elm Park, was an accomplished, socially prominent woman, in whose home Helen became acquainted with "leading literary and scientific men," including some Trinity College professors.[10]

In a few years Dublin would prove a second home for Helen, giving her some of her greatest successes and warmest friendships. In 1842, though, she was seeing for the first time such landmarks as the Castle, ancient centre of political and social life; the Bank of Ireland, with its beautiful Ionic colonnade (the site of an Irish parliament in earlier years); and Trinity College, with its fortress-like buildings of grey granite set in a contrastingly lush expanse of well-kept lawns. For the first time she was acting at the large, handsome Theatre Royal on Hawkins Street, known for its excellent acoustics and its ornate but classically inspired decor – lyre-shaped auditorium, fluted gold columns, and box-front decorations "adapted from" Grecian temples. One of the designs, "the Grecian chain, twined with the shamrock," typified the attitude Helen would find among the artists, scholars, and literary people of Dublin.[11]

In the Dublin engagement of 1842 Helen Faucit, being "also engaged," with Macready as the great star, had major roles on only half of her fourteen nights. The most important, by far, was Lady Macbeth. She had feared to attempt it before, and with good reason. Sarah Siddons's towering Lady Macbeth, still a vivid memory for many people, including Macready, was the ideal toward which all her successors aspired: "a being of a superior order [who] had dropped from a higher sphere to awe the world with [her] majesty."[12] Helen, an ambitious tragedienne, would feel obliged to undertake the role someday, but not until she could do justice to it – and to herself. Alarmed as she was at the prospect, however, she agreed to support Macready in *Macbeth* as best she could.[13]

A week beforehand Macready gave her some "general notions about Lady Macbeth" and went over several scenes with her, but the only complete rehearsal was on the day of performance, 6 June. He was "very much struck" by her rehearsal, which "surprised and gratified" him. Despite her "absolute terror" before going onstage, Helen must have done very well that night, for Macready, who never bestowed praise lightly, pronounced her acting "*remarkably* good." He wanted her to share his curtain call but was annoyed to find that, in her relief to be through with the ordeal, she had hurried to her room and discarded her costume immediately.[14]

Macready told Helen that the banquet scene and sleepwalking scene were the best parts of her performance, that her first scene and her reception of Duncan were "promising," but that her "after scenes with him" were "very tame."[15] Her Lady Macbeth would always be best in the most sympathetic parts of the character. In scenes where Mrs. Siddons's Lady Macbeth had been most imperious, bringing her powerful will to bear upon her shrinking husband, Helen Faucit was least effective – especially when she tried to act them in the Siddons manner.

She would essay Lady Macbeth twice more before returning to Drury Lane: later in June, during a five-night engagement at Birmingham with Macready and James Anderson, and several months afterwards, during a joint engagement with J.W. Wallack at Brighton. On the latter occasion the *Sussex Advertiser* would remark (4 October 1842): "Lady Macbeth is not a part adapted to Miss Faucit's genius. A kind heart and a noble thinking mind, which constitute the character of this lady, looked through the masque of Lady Macbeth, and destroyed the illusion which we look for …" Later the actress would fit the character to her particular talents and would create one of her most interesting – if controversial – impersonations. For some people, however, the role could never be reconciled to her personality. When she first acted it, in Dublin, her new friend Mrs. Hutton was shocked by the incongruity: "My dear," she exclaimed, "I will never see you again in that terrible character."[16]

This first visit to Dublin was memorable not only for social and theatrical successes but also for some pleasant Sunday excursions (chaperoned by her maid) with Macready and Calcraft. On 5 June they went by carriage to Glendalough, a wooded glen amid the Wicklow Mountains, where they visited the site of St. Kevin's legendary hermitage, the ruins of several ancient churches, and an imposing waterfall. Awestruck as they were by the scenery, "most sad and stern and beautiful," they were in high spirits because of the fresh air, the genial company, and the sense of release from daily worries. A week later they took a similar drive through the scenic countryside of Enniskerry.[17] Unfortunately Helen's delight in these experiences was short-lived. The innocent comradeship, instead of satisfying her, only added fuel to the "ardour of her passion." Macready began to fear, anew, that "in *youth* … there is no love without an intermingling of sexual love. It is therefore *dangerous* and to be *avoided*."[18]

Between her Birmingham and Brighton engagements Helen had a holiday at Scarborough with the Brayshers and visited "elsewhere in the country." While she was in Brighton her infant niece and namesake, Eliza Helena Saville (youngest of John and Marianne's three children), was baptized, and Helen very likely served as godmother.[19] Like the middle sister, Kate, Eliza would become an actress, leaving the eldest, Maria, as the only member of the family who was not on the stage.

Macready's second, and last, season of management at Drury Lane began on 1 October 1842, but Helen Faucit did not appear until the 5th. She participated that season in 49 of the 96 Shakespearean performances (51%) and 56 of the 177 performances of other plays (31.6%).[20] Constance, in a grand revival of *King John*, was her most frequently acted Shakespearean character, and Desdemona was next; but Imogen, in an interesting new production of *Cymbeline*, was more important for her career as a whole despite its brief run. Her only new Shakespearean part was the inconsiderable one of Portia in *Julius Caesar*, which she never acted afterwards. Ironically, she appeared as Rosalind only three times and as Beatrice only once in a season when those characters (later among her most famous) were seen frequently at Drury Lane. Eight of her non-Shakespearean characters were old ones, acted only two or three times each except for the still-popular Pauline. Of the others, two were in special revivals of old plays, Congreve's *Love for Love* and Milton's *Comus*, and four were in new plays: Westland Marston's *The Patrician's Daughter*, Robert Browning's *A Blot in the 'Scutcheon*, Sheridan Knowles's *The Secretary*, and William Smith's *Athelwold.* Although none except *Comus* and *The Patrician's Daughter* had significant runs, several others were of interest to her career.

Macready introduced the season with an unusually attractive revival of *As You Like It*, his own favourite among all his productions.[21] Audiences found the woodland scenes enchanting: they saw huge old trees with interlacing branches, a rushing stream, a sheepfold; and they heard, intermittently, the sounds of birdsong, sheepbell, and hunting horn.[22] There was an outstanding cast: Macready as Jaques, Anderson as Orlando, Mrs. Nisbett as Rosalind, Mrs. Stirling as Celia, the Keeleys as Touchstone and Audrey. Amid general surprise that Helen Faucit was not cast as Rosalind, one journalist explained that her load had to be lightened because of delicate health.[23] Actually, her portrayal of Rosalind was not frolicsome enough for Macready's ideal of the character, based on youthful memories of Dora Jordan. Louisa Nisbett, a beautiful comedienne with a silvery laugh, was the best modern equivalent of Mrs. Jordan. When Macready succeeded in engaging her this season, he had the Rosalind (and the Beatrice) he wanted.[24]

He did not realize that attitudes were changing, that the saucy tomboy of the past could no longer satisfy the critics. Thus he was not prepared for the *Athenaeum*'s comment that Mrs. Nisbett's Rosalind did not "sound the depths of the character" (8 October: 876) or the complaint in *The Times* (3 October) that it lacked "that graceful sensibility without which it loses all its poetry." The *Examiner* was silent about Mrs. Nisbett's performance, though it had much to say about the production as a whole. Eventually Macready himself admitted that her Rosalind had been the only weak part of his production. Actually it must have been delightful in its way. Clearly it pleased her audiences, and even critics who considered it shallow found it engaging.[25] As Charles H. Shattuck points out, however, the *Zeitgeist* required a new interpretation. Helen Faucit's Rosalind suited its demands exactly[26] – but more of that later.

On 24 October Macready opened his second grand revival of the season, *King John*. This historical tragedy was impressively staged in every respect – artistic scenery, authoritative costumes, effective groupings of actors, and skilful management of lights and music to produce changes of mood.[27] Critics were virtually unanimous in applauding both the production as a whole and the acting of Macready's King John, Phelps's Hubert, and little Miss Newcombe's Prince Arthur; they differed, however, in assessing Anderson's Bastard (some thought him too coarse) and Helen Faucit's Constance.

Critiques of the latter covered a wide spectrum,[28] from praise for one of her best efforts (*Era*) to condemnation for a "huge mistake" (*Morning Post*). Some complaints were that Helen Faucit had sacrificed dignity and sublimity for violence and noise, that her grief was too full of pain to arouse sympathy, and that she made the audience applaud more than weep.[29] The most common judgment, however, was that her conception was very good, as were the more tender, womanly, and pathetic passages of her performance, but that a lack of physical power had made complete success impossible. *The Times* said, for example, that the portrayal had "rage, grief, irony, all well intended, but … a constant effort to attain the unattainable." Some reviewers considered her "intellectual intensity" and "consummate truth" in portraying Constance's feelings more important than her admitted physical limitations.[30] The painful sense of overstrained resources could be partially accounted for by an attack of influenza from which Helen was suffering when the play opened.[31] Her most serious problem, however, was the spectre of Mrs. Siddons, whose Constance, though it had not been seen for thirty years, was still recalled as the ideal portrayal. Helen Faucit sacrificed the effectiveness of her normal delivery in a desperate attempt to achieve the grandeur and power of that legendary Constance.

Although she received frequent applause during the first-night performance and a curtain call at the end, she was "much depressed."[32] She knew she had tried too hard and failed. As she had done in other instances, however, she "found herself" after the production was underway. She could hardly have attained the powerful effects at which she originally aimed, but she achieved a more harmonious performance by increased control over her resources and greater emphasis on those parts of the role best suited to her talents. Several months after the opening of *King John*, George Fletcher wrote an enthusiastic tribute to her Constance. Her physical power was "adequate" rather than great, he granted, but she compensated with "*elastic* force" and effective use of contrast

– as when she punctuated lofty or furious speeches with moments of tenderness. According to him, she made "*feeling*, not *pride*, the mainspring of the character"; she showed that Constance's "effusions of bitterness" were repugnant to her true nature and that she found relief in every look and word addressed to her beloved Arthur. Fletcher's detailed description of the performance reveals a complex interpretation that made the character both heroic and feminine.[33] His praise of Helen Faucit's Constance (discounting a certain extravagance due to his personal interest in the actress) is supported by the recollections, many years later, of other playgoers who had found it unforgettable. One recalled her voice as clear and mellow, "somewhat of a low pitch, but very distinct, with a passionate expression" – very different from the first-night descriptions. He vividly remembered several of her scenes, especially the one in which Constance sank with slow grandeur to the ground and said with "mournful cadence," "Here I and sorrow sit;/ Here is my throne, bid kings come bow to it."[34] Another, who was only a boy when he saw this Constance, wrote more than forty years later that he could "still hear in imagination the pathetic tones of Helen Faucit" in these lines.[35]

According to Theodore Martin, George Fletcher was a scholarly recluse whose friends persuaded him to go to the theatre and see Helen Faucit; he found her Shakespearean portrayals – and, later, her conversations – illuminating.[36] The two may have met through the Brayshers, who entertained them both, along with the Macreadys and others, at a dinner party on 16 March 1841. Macready took a violent dislike to the pedantic Fletcher (a "wretched 'dust'") and lost his temper during a discussion with him.[37] Helen, however, found in her sentimental, literary admirer a sympathetic friend. Fletcher's essays on Shakespearean characters, first published in the *Athenaeum* and the *Westminster Review*, were republished, with some changes, in a book, *Studies of Shakespeare* (1847), whose preface acknowledges his "obligations" to Helen Faucit.

One of Helen's most successful Shakespearean impersonations in her early years was Imogen in Macready's Drury Lane revival of *Cymbeline*, first seen on 21 January 1843. The staging, though less elaborate than in *As You Like It* and *King John*, was very effective, especially that of a banquet scene, full of jocund hilarity, during which the wager was made. The varied characters were well portrayed, from Macready's jovially voluptuous Iachimo and Anderson's manly if vehement Posthumus to Phelps's rugged but kind-hearted Belarius, Compton's pompously foppish Cloten, and Elton's quietly loyal Pisanio. Helen Faucit's Imogen received high praise from all but a few critics.[38] Typical reviews described it as one of her best creations, a succession of triumphs, unrivalled in its "pathos and natural beauty."[39] Her best acting was in response to Posthumus's letter ordering Pisanio to kill her. Here, said *The Times*, the "faltering of her eye and voice," the "sheer bewildered incredulity," the "trembling which overcame her, and her fall at last on the ground, were equal to some of the best effects of

Rachel." Other salient parts of her performance were the interview with Iachimo (though some critics thought her indignation too vehement for the "gentle Imogen"), the amusing trepidation in approaching the cave, the "quiet excellencies" of the scene with her unknown brothers, and the "sublime" reconciliation with Posthumus. Several reviewers gave very full descriptions of her acting, and George Fletcher wrote a detailed analysis. Obviously this "womanly" role brought out qualities in her acting that most appealed to her contemporaries.

Helen Faucit's most disappointing experience in Shakespeare was her first London attempt at Lady Macbeth. Macready had scheduled *Macbeth* for Easter Monday (17 April) 1843), to be followed by the real attraction of the evening, *Fortunio, and His Seven Gifted Servants*, a spectacular new burlesque. (Oddly enough, such festive entertainments were often preceded on their opening night by a tragedy – which the audience, restless with anticipation, suffered through impatiently and sometimes loudly.) Mrs. Warner, who had always acted Lady Macbeth, could not be available that night, and Helen, having gained a measure of confidence in the part, agreed to take her place. Macready held several discussions with her before the regular rehearsal, eager to "raise and dilate her mind to the conception of the full grandeur of the character." He did not realize that the majestic vision he was trying to impart might intimidate rather than inspire her. On the night of performance Helen was so overcome by the thought of acting Mrs. Siddons's greatest part before a London audience that, as Macready said, she "lost all management of herself." Her nerve-storm seems to have made her ill for several days afterwards.[40]

Even so, her portrayal must have had its merits. Immediately after the performance R.R. M'Ian wrote a warmly congratulatory letter, declaring she had made "quite a new thing" of Lady Macbeth, "different in feeling and effect from any one else's": "The banquet scene, strange to say, was *terribly pathetic* … But the sleeping scene … was better than it has ever been acted before. … You must have felt how much you had hold of our very souls …"[41] It is unlikely that M'Ian, however inclined to exaggerate his young friend's success, would have written in such an exuberant mood if the performance had been a failure. The mixed review in the *Morning Chronicle* (18 April) must have been near the mark: Miss Faucit had shown "admirable judgment" in most of her readings and a surprisingly "powerful … control over her physical disqualifications for the part," but she had been guilty of "flagrant … bad taste" in her "over-strained and even ranted" invocation to the spirits and her impulsive, undignified dismissal of the guests in the banquet scene; she was best in the murder scene, where both conception and execution were remarkable. On the whole, despite the "over-excited nervousness of the moment," Helen Faucit's performance was "full of mind, and a perfect understanding . . . of her author"; one hoped to see in her, before long, the best representative of this difficult character. (Her unqueenly agitation at the banquet, however indecorous, may have contributed to the pathetic effect noticed by M'Ian.) Most critics, however, simply ignored the new Lady Macbeth. The production they wanted to see was *Fortunio*. As the *Sunday Times* observed, there was "great relief" when the "sad and solemn tragedy" was "disposed of" and everyone could settle down to enjoy the new burlesque.

Chagrined by her lack of command over herself, Helen Faucit was eager for a second chance to act Lady Macbeth. But, despite her pleas, Macready refused to deprive Mrs. Warner of her usual part. Helen sulked, but he was adamant: he "would not do an injustice for *any* one."[42]

The least satisfactory of her non-Shakespearean roles this season was Angelica in Macready's discreet adaptation of Congreve's *Love for Love*, first seen on 19 November 1842. Her portrayal was complimented for its quiet archness and "graceful self-possession" but was generally considered deficient in "airiness" and brilliance. After four performances Helen Faucit relinquished Angelica to Miss Ellis so as to act in a new play.[43]

The season's other non-Shakespearean revival, Milton's *Comus*, gave her a more congenial part. This most beautiful of "afterpieces" was first performed for Macready's benefit on 24 February 1843, following a new production of *Much Ado about Nothing*. Though denied the role of Beatrice in the main play, Helen was thrilled to be cast as Milton's virtuous heroine. Macready's much-cut version of *Comus* ran just an hour, even with some interpolated songs using other Miltonic poetry. The magnificent scenery and the artistically directed movements of the actors – especially those in the huge crowd of bacchanals, seemingly wild yet carefully orchestrated – were among his most memorable achievements in staging.[44] No spectator was more impressed by these wonders than was the Lady on the stage:

> The enchanted wood … with its dense, bewildering maze of trees, … with the fitful moonlight casting deep shadows … the Hall of Comus . … a kind of Aladdin's garden, all aglow with light and colour … the rabble-rout, so gay, so variously clad, some like Hebes, some like hags; figures moving to and fro, some beautiful as Adonis, others like Fauns, and bearded Satyrs … the weird fascination of the music, … the rampant joyousness, the tipsy jollity! All served to quicken in me the feeling with which the poet has inspired the lonely "lady," when she sees herself, without means of escape, surrounded by a rabble-rout full of wine and riot, and abandoned to shameless revelry.[45]

Learning to represent the Lady involved some intensive practice in applying the principle of repose. In youth Macready, like Helen, had been taught to illustrate his words with many gestures, but later he rejected that system as unnatural. To achieve his desired effect, he practised repeating some of Shakespeare's most violent passages while in a rigidly immobile position or "under the supposed constraint of whispering them."[46] One result was his extraordinary ability to indicate suppressed emotion. Recently he had encouraged Helen to make similar efforts. Now, in acting the climactic scene of *Comus*, she found his method essential. When Comus eloquently urged her to drink from the cup, she had to reply with a lofty passage of virtuous indignation; it so inspired her that she could never speak it without "a thrill that seemed to dilate [her] whole frame, and to give an unwonted fulness and vibration to … [her] voice." The emotion made it difficult to sit immobile, yet the Lady is supposed to be in an enchanted chair, bound by a paralyzing spell. The experience helped Helen overcome a tendency toward "redundancy of action."[47]

Since the major event of the evening was the performance of *Much Ado*, with Macready's first attempt at Benedick, critical reaction to *Comus* was relatively sketchy. As Charles H. Shattuck has noted, the fullest and most interesting review was in the *Spectator* (4 March 1843: 204) – unfortunately so for Helen Faucit. The writer bemoaned the actors' tendency to treat *Comus* like any other play, degrading the verbal music to the level of "pert and flippant dialogue," and he named Helen Faucit as the worst offender. It is hard to imagine her speaking the lines flippantly, for she had loved Milton's poetry since her early youth. Perhaps she did sacrifice some lyricism for theatrical effects, but her real offence, one suspects, was to act as a verse-speaking character rather than a reciter of verse pure and simple. No dramatic production of *Comus* could have satisfied this reviewer, for he objected to the "bandy[ing]" of the lines "from mouth to mouth" – as if arias should have replaced dialogue. Other critics were more complimentary. Charles Dickens, writing for the *Examiner*, said that Helen Faucit had given "the best piece of level recitation" he had ever heard from her, and several critics praised her scene in the enchanted chair, with its "eloquent and impressive speech."[48]

Among the new plays of the season *The Patrician's Daughter*, by Westland Marston (first acted on 10 December 1842), stands out as a landmark in theatrical history. Although it fell far short of its ambitious purpose, to revitalize poetic tragedy by giving it contemporary significance, this blank-verse tragedy with a modern setting and a hero from common life was among the day's most interesting dramatic experiments.

The theme, to quote Marston, is "the conflict between the pride of Aristocracy and that of Democracy, with the evils resulting from their collision."[49] Excessive pride of birth, the aristocratic flaw, is exemplified in the Earl of Lynterne and his arrogant sister, Lady Lydia; excessive sensitivity to insult marks the democratic pride of Edgar Mordaunt, a high-minded poet and orator who has risen from a working-class background to become a Member of Parliament; the victim of the conflict is Lady Mabel, the Earl's daughter. Mordaunt visits the Lynterne estate at the invitation of the politically-minded

Helen Faucit as Lady Mabel in Act 5 of Westland Marston's *The Patrician's Daughter*, with Mrs. Warner (kneeling) as Lady Lydia (*Illustrated London News* 17 December 1842)

Earl. He and Mabel fall in love, but they are tricked by Lady Lydia into a misunderstanding that results in Mabel's denying that she loves him. Five years later, Mordaunt, now a great man with a title, is engaged to Mabel with her father's approval; but, as the marriage settlement is about to be signed, he publicly rejects her, reminding the Lynternes of the treatment he received in humbler days. Mabel, shocked and heart-broken, goes into a decline. When Lady Lydia confesses her perfidy, Mordaunt is appalled at what he has done. He exchanges declarations of love with Mabel, who dies in his arms.

Flaws in plot and character development are obvious, even in a summary; but, for the reader of the play, its most annoying characteristic is the frequent use of archaic and self-consciously "poetic" expressions – intended, no doubt, to dignify the style, but very incongruous in a drama of contemporary life. There is much of value in *The Patrician's Daughter*, however: some strong situations, passages of good poetry, and a seriousness of purpose that commands one's respect. Considering that it is a first play, written by a naive twenty-two-year-old, it is remarkable. It attracted widespread and controversial interest, both at its publication (1841) and at its production. Critics noticed all the obvious faults, and they were particularly disturbed by Mordaunt's ungentlemanly behaviour. They differed widely on whether a genuine tragedy could be written with a contemporary setting and on whether blank verse was incongruous in the mouths of modern characters. There were some enthusiastic responses to the play, however: *The Times*, for example, confidently pronounced it a "first step toward a better order of things."[50]

Whatever the critics thought of the play, they were impressed by Macready's production. The scenery was pleasing and appropriate, the cast very strong – Macready as Mordaunt, Phelps as the Earl, Mrs. Warner as Lady Lydia, Helen Faucit as Lady Mabel. Most critics agreed that the acting was admirable, though some complained that Macready should have softened down Mordaunt's rejection scene instead of playing it for all it was worth. Despite the excellence of the production, however, and the warmth of the first-night applause, *The Patrician's Daughter* had only a moderate run.

The greatest beneficiary of this production was Helen Faucit, whose reviews were particularly enthusiastic. Critics predictably approved of Mabel as a character, for she is an ideal Victorian woman who, once she has committed herself to love, remains steadfast in spite of all consequences – if the man rejects her or proves unworthy, she can only suffer and die. It is one thing to approve an ideal, however, and quite another to find its theatrical embodiment interesting. Helen Faucit succeeded in Mabel because she made her a convincing human being whose final disintegration really mattered to the audience. Her charm and vivacity in the early scenes were appreciated, as was her psychological truthfulness in the renunciation scene; it was her emotionally harrowing acting in the last act, however, that overcame any adverse effects of contrived plot and thin characterization. Here Mabel's "shattered frame and broken spirit" moved the audience to tears, and her intensity of feeling in the dying scene created a "painfully thrilling effect." However disappointing as a tragedy and flawed as a play, *The Patrician's Daughter* gave Helen Faucit one of her greatest successes with the London critics.[51]

Equally notable among the new plays, but even more disappointing, was Browning's poetic tragedy *A Blot in the 'Scutcheon*, first acted on 11 February 1843. It is much more dramatic than *Strafford*, his first drama, but its excellent potentialities are never realized. Improbabilities abound; characters are sketchily drawn and unnaturally motivated; the whole seems a preliminary draft that Browning never bothered to develop. Yet the play has both power and charm. Lord Tresham, who dotes on his young sister, Mildred, is shocked when he is told by an old retainer that a man has been entering her window at night.

In a dramatic interview, Mildred confesses her sin but refuses to name her lover. That night Tresham lies in wait and catches the young Earl of Mertoun, who has recently become engaged to Mildred but has been visiting her secretly for some time. Tresham, enraged at the loss of honour, insists on fighting, but Mertoun, who idolizes the older man, allows himself to be killed rather than attack his hero. Sickened by what he has done, Tresham takes Mertoun's dying message to Mildred; she forgives him, then dies, presumably of a broken heart. Tresham takes poison.

The part of Tresham was designed for Macready, but, since he could not undertake it until later and Browning wanted an immediate production, the role was given to Phelps. Anderson was cast as Mertoun, Helen Faucit as Mildred, and Mrs. Stirling as Mildred's cousin Gwendolen. There were various problems with the production, and the consequent hard feelings between Browning and Macready interrupted their friendship for many years.[52] The play was acted only three nights. Surprisingly enough, if Browning's friend Joseph Arnould is right, the rude gallery "gods" were the most appreciative part of the audience: they "*took* all the points" as quickly as the intellectuals in the pit, and they entered into the "feeling and interest of the action" far more than the gentlefolk in the boxes – some of whom were shocked at being "betrayed into so much interest in a young woman who had behaved as improperly as Mildred." According to Arnould, although the first night was a "triumph," only the gallery was full on the second night (the boxes were "desolate"), and the "miserable great empty house" on the third night was an obvious sign of the end.[53] Helen Faucit believed that if Macready had given more personal attention to the play the actors would have brought out its power more effectively, and Arnould had "no doubt whatever" that Macready's name in the cast would have attracted better audiences.[54] But, as most reviewers agreed, *A Blot in the 'Scutcheon*, however replete with poetic genius, simply is not a good play for the stage.[55]

Macready, after seeing the first night's performance, wrote that the play was "badly acted in Phelps's and Mrs. Stirling's parts – pretty well in Anderson's, and very well in Helen Faucit's."[56] Phelps was judged more favourably than this by reviewers, however, and his performance of Tresham later received am enthusiastic tribute from Westland Marston.[57] Evaluations of Helen Faucit's acting were coloured in a few instances by the critics' moral judgment of Mildred, as when the *Spectator* commented that the shame and wretchedness of the guilty girl were depicted with an intensity that would have been pathetic if there had been any room for sympathy. It was generally agreed that the confession scene was the strongest part of the play, and Miss Faucit's acting here, where she sank "senseless to the ground on her brother's reproaches," was considered particularly effective. Her final scene, however, though less exciting, was evidently more imaginative: when Tresham arrives to tell Mildred of Mertoun's death but cannot bring himself to speak, her "pause before her silent brother, in which she instinctively arrives at the knowledge of her misery – the dashing open of the window, and her frantic gaze into the night gloom, as well as the mute inquiry with which she examines Tresham's empty scabbard, were . . . conceived with a finely poetic spirit, and executed with a finely artistic power."[58]

On 24 April 1843 a new play by Sheridan Knowles was performed for the first time: *The Secretary*, based on G. P. R. James's novel *The King's Highway*. It has a few good scenes and a certain romantic dash, emphasized by the vigorous blank verse, but, on the whole, it is much inferior to Knowles's best plays. All the predictable ingredients are present: a hero who is ignorant of his birth (he is the rightful heir to an earldom), a wicked uncle who has usurped the hero's rights, a duke's daughter who falls in love with the hero despite his humble status as secretary to the wicked uncle. There are various melodramatic complications, but, largely through the efforts of a mysterious Colonel Green, all is satisfactorily resolved.

The Secretary was well acted, especially by Macready as Colonel Green (an unusual part for him) and Helen Faucit as Lady Laura Gaveston; Anderson in trying to give life to the admirable but dull hero, Wilton Brown, was rather too loud and energetic. The performance was frequently applauded on the first night, and there were curtain calls for Macready, Helen Faucit, and the author. The play was not enough of a hit, however, to justify extending it beyond the three days that Macready, because of his full calendar, had allotted it.[59]

Lady Laura is the most interesting character in the play, by far, but her flouting of social conventions made the role rather hazardous for the actress. When Wilton, because of his lowly position, refrains from declaring his love, Laura takes the initiative in the wooing, and she persists in her attachment despite her father's dismay. Later, when Wilton discovers that he is of noble blood but (as he thinks) illegitimate, he deplores the thought of blotting Laura's family escutcheon with his bastardy; Laura, however, cares nothing for such niceties – she will gladly marry the man of her choice, whatever his origin. Such a heroine was bound to shock fastidious critics, for, theoretically, a well-bred woman should be reticent about her emotions and should even suppress any romantic impulses until the man's intentions had been manifested.[60] Helen Faucit, who evidently enjoyed playing Laura, offended some critics by her spirited portrayal. The *Morning Post*, for example, expressed disgust for the "effrontery" and "impudence" of Knowles's creation and the "coarseness" of Miss Faucit's performance: instead of softening down her character's prominent features so as to make the portrayal "endurable," she had emphasized them.[61] Several reviewers recognized that the character posed a problem for the actress but complimented Helen Faucit on the delicacy and skill that had enabled her to avoid its pitfalls.[62] The *Sunday Times* critic, however, was delighted with the character as well as the performance. Miss Faucit, he proclaimed (30 May), availed herself "gloriously" of the "magnificent opportunity" Knowles had given her. "She was ... a creature of impulse and passion; a woman whirled onwards by a love that defied restraint ..." He had nothing but scorn for "'Niminy, Piminy'" critics who considered Laura "'unmaidenly'": "Bah! she depicts human nature, and acts like a woman."

The last new play in which Helen Faucit appeared during the 1842-43 season was William Smith's blank-verse "tragedy" *Athelwold*, introduced on her benefit night, 18 May 1843, and repeated once. Actually the play, though it ends with the death of its titular hero, is more unpleasant than tragic, and its heroine is the most unsympathetic one that Helen ever attempted. Athelwold, sent by the Saxon King Edgar to see whether Lady Elfrida is as beautiful as he has heard, falsely reports that she is not, then marries her himself. The two are happy at first, but, when Athelwold confesses his deception, Elfrida is indignant at having been cheated of a chance to become Queen. The King comes to visit, is charmed by Elfrida, and determines to rid himself of Athelwold and marry her. At first she encourages him, but later she visits her imprisoned husband, now under threat of death, and begs his forgiveness. When he scornfully repudiates her, she offers to kill the King. Athelwold replies, "My soul recoils in horror, shrinks from thee." Furious, she flings open the prison gates to admit the executioners. Smith originally ended his play with Elfrida sadly but arrogantly accepting her loss of innocence and embracing her new life of power. On the stage, however, his final passages were omitted, and Elfrida, in a new revulsion of feeling, shrieked and threw herself upon her husband's corpse. *Athelwold* is heavily written, with long speeches that required ruthless pruning. The violent changes in Elfrida's character and emotions seem entirely arbitrary.

No doubt Macready, who knew the author, originally proposed the production, and he altruistically undertook the thankless part of Athelwold. As Theodore Martin points out, Elfrida was hardly a character Helen would normally have chosen.[63] But perhaps, once it had been suggested, she became interested in what she could do with a role so unusual for her. After all, it did give her an opportunity to express "different states of unbridled passion." She met the challenge boldly, skilfully, and (for most people) convincingly. Significantly, several critics of her performance were reminded of the tempestuous Rachel.[64] Although her resources were severely taxed by Elfrida, Helen Faucit overcame the difficulties better than one would have expected. Most reviewers, even those who cordially disliked both play and character, found much to admire in her portrayal. A blatant exception was the one for the *Sunday Times*, who always loved or hated. This time he hated: *Athelwold* was "indecent," Elfrida was a "phrenetic strumpet," and Miss Faucit's performance was a "complete failure . . . a blending of the horrible and the ludicrous." A milder remonstrance came from the *Illustrated London News*, whose critic simply did not like to see her in wicked characters: "Everything bad sits badly upon Miss Faucit ... everything good derives additional virtue from her impersonation ..." More typical reviews, like those in the *Morning Post* and the *Athenaeum*, declared that the actress had done far more for her character than the author had, lifting it, at certain moments, "out of the unnatural conception into actual beauty." The *Examiner* credited her with creating a convincing whole out of ill-assorted materials and even declared Elfrida "the most even of all her late performances."

The role most important in Helen Faucit's later career, however, was neither new nor frequently acted by her this season. It was Rosalind, in which she replaced Mrs. Nisbett on three occasions, twice in December and once in June. Many spectators attended the popular production of *As You Like It* more than once; those who saw both actresses as Rosalind had two very different interpretations put before them. George Fletcher, who preferred Helen Faucit's because of its depth and complexity, praised the actress for "infus[ing] into the part ... all the tender though lively grace which the poet has made its principal attribute ... breathing the soul of elegance, wit, and feeling through that noble forest pastoral."[65] This is an apt description of Helen Faucit's Rosalind as it would be known throughout her career – except that "feeling" is too mild for the ardent emotion that would give her later performances their incandescent quality.

Macready closed his second and final season at Drury Lane on 14 June 1843, but Helen's last appearance was on the previous evening, when she acted Beatrice to his Benedick for the first and only time. This proved an important milestone in her life, not only her last night under Macready's management but also her last as a regular member of a London company. More impressive at the time, however, was her penultimate night, 12 June, when Queen Victoria made a state visit to Drury Lane. As always on such occasions, an enormous crowd assembled to look and to cheer. They were not disappointed. The royal box was "gorgeously fitted up in the form of a tent, with hangings of rich crimson falling from the top." The Queen, gowned in black velvet with the ribbon of the Garter, was resplendent with diamonds: they sparkled in tiara, necklace and bracelets, and even cascaded in clusters down the front of her dress. In contrast, her attendant ladies blossomed in pastels, like flowers in a summer garden. Prince Albert was in full military uniform, with ribbon, badge, and star of the Garter.[66] *As You Like It* had been commanded as the main piece of the evening; thus the admired production that had opened the season was now virtually closing it – except that Helen Faucit, not Louisa Nisbett, was playing Rosalind. She pleased everyone, even the fastidious young Queen, who admitted: "what surprised us most of all was the really beautiful acting of Miss H. Faucit as 'Rosalind.' She looked quite pretty in male attire & was so lively & 'naive.'"[67] This thoroughly satisfactory event makes a grand finale to Helen Faucet's seven successive years on the London stage, with *Much Ado* on the following night as a delightful afterpiece.

The season had been an excellent one for Helen. Except for rare occasions, like her first London appearance as Lady Macbeth, there had been no incapacitating bouts with nervous illness. Her performances had shown more maturity, self-confidence, and consistency than in previous years. The audiences had been as enthusiastic as ever, and the critics, after the ups and downs of the past, were according her the respect due to a leading actress of the English theatre. Some considered her *the* leading actress.

Her personal life had brought some good things, like close proximity to Harriet and Humphrey (who had been engaged, respectively, as leading lady at the Adelphi and a minor actor at Drury Lane), but it had also brought the "first great sorrow" of her life in the death of Percy Farren. He had been unwell for some time, but Helen, though worried, did not realize how near the end was. She was working hard to memorize a long versified address for a benefit (to raise funds for a Siddons memorial), and when Farren died on the very day of performance (29 May) she was not told. To keep her isolated from possible news-bearers, Macready had her join him as soon as she reached the theatre, share his "little dinner," and go over her speech with him. After the performances he gave her a letter, ostensibly on business, saying she should read it in the morning when she was less tired. She did not get a night's rest, however, for on the way home she stopped at Percy Farren's house and learned the sad news. Macready's letter expressed his sympathy and allowed her several days' absence from the theatre – an inconvenience to him so near the season's end. Helen never forgot his "gentle kindness"[68]: if anything could have comforted her in the loss of her first, most fatherly mentor, it was the affectionate sympathy of her last, most adored one.

Macready had originally planned to continue his management for another season, but, when faced with unacceptable terms from the proprietors' committee, he decided to tour America instead.[69] Although the closing of his management was a bad omen for Drury Lane, its timing could hardly have been better for Helen Faucit's development as an actress. Working under Macready's direction had been of incalculable benefit, but she would soon have reached the point of diminishing returns. Now twenty-eight years old, she had always been under the influence of some "dear master," some kindly advisor, some exacting director. It was time to strike out on her own.

PART II: "Happy Star Reign Now!"

The Winter's Tale, 1.2.363

Chapter 7

Capturing the Provinces

HEALTHY THOUGH the break with Macready would prove, Helen felt it as the shattering of her world.[1] Both career and personal life had lost their centre. What could she do? At a London theatre without Macready she could expect few careful revivals of classics, few experiments in new poetic dramas. The alternative, starring in the provinces, threatened her with frequent travel, uncertain accommodations, and inferior working conditions; on the other hand, it promised independence and opportunities for greater wealth and fame. Eventually she rejected several proposals of fixed engagements, including one at Drury Lane under the new management, and decided to try her luck as a star.[2]

When Drury Lane closed on 14 June 1843, she had not settled this matter, but she and James Anderson had arranged several summer engagements at provincial theatres, with herself in top billing. The first, at the Theatre Royal, Dublin (19 June – 11 July), proved an unpropitious beginning. Although Helen Faucit acted several of her best roles and, as a novelty, Lady Mabel in *The Patrician's Daughter* (never seen here before), the attendance was disappointingly small. As Anderson later explained, they could not compete with "that brilliant rival star, Daniel O'Connell, the Great Liberator, who was drawing hundreds of thousands from all parts of Ireland to Donnybrook Green to hear him lecture on the repeal of the Union."[3] The Dublin newspapers offer ample confirmation: "Repeal" and "O'Connell" are on every page. The greatest attention the theatre received was due, not to the stars, but to an unrehearsed performance that interrupted their *Macbeth* on 3 July. In the second scene, when John Calcraft entered as Macduff, a young man in the gallery shouted, "Damn you, Calcraft, you are a villain!" and hurled a glass filled with gunpowder, brass buttons, broken glass, and lucifer matches. None of the actors was hurt, but the would-be assassin, after sliding down a pillar into the middle gallery, leapt toward the stage, brandishing a knife, fell into the pit instead, and was mortally injured. After this bizarre incident, even *Macbeth* seemed anticlimactic.[4]

Though unsuccessful professionally, the Dublin visit was made pleasant by the hospitality of Helen's friends. As Anderson reports, "Dinners, suppers, and picnics, were of every day occurrence." Especially attentive hosts were "the charming family of the Huttons," the "cheery manager, John Calcraft," and "Dr. Wilde"[5] – that is, William Robert Wilde (later Sir William), a successful eye and ear surgeon, who would one day become the father of Oscar Wilde. In 1843 Wilde was in his late twenties, still a bachelor, and very much interested in Helen Faucit. He was notoriously ugly: his few good features – luxuriant black hair, a well-shaped nose – were offset by pale, rather prominent eyes, sensual-looking lips, a receding chin, and a short figure whose disproportionately long arms gave him a simian look. Despite all this he was very attractive to women. He was an odd but engaging escort for Helen – if she watched her step.[6]

Carte de Visite photograph of Helen Faucit, probably in her starring days (by courtesy of the Folger Shakespeare Library)

The Faucit and Anderson team next went to Birmingham for an engagement at the Theatre Royal. Beginning on 21 July, they offered a diverse bill of fare, including both classics (mostly Shakespearean) and recent plays (*The Patrician's Daughter* and *The Lady of Lyons*). On their last night (31 July), when *Hamlet* was performed for Anderson's benefit, Helen Faucit acted Ophelia for the first time in her career – a generous gesture for "this occasion" only. Though emotionally attracted to Ophelia, she was too intent on stardom to play regularly a role overshadowed by Shakespeare's most famous hero. In Birmingham the stars enjoyed the success they had missed in Dublin: the theatre was crowded every night with enthusiastic audiences. Unhappily, Anderson caught a severe cold, followed by an attack of typhoid fever that kept him from the next engagement.[7]

After several weeks' rest, Helen Faucit made her first appearance at the Theatre Royal, Bristol, which had long been under the management of Macready's stepmother, Mrs. Sarah M'Cready. Beginning with Belvidera on 28 August, the opening night of the new season, she gave six performances in five successive nights, concluding with a double bill of Lady Mabel and Violante (her only comic role). She was supported in the heroes' parts by Mr. H. Cooke of Dublin on the first night and, after that, by William Creswick, recently returned from America. The generally-favourable reviews are most interesting in discussing Belvidera's mad scene. According to the *Bristol Times and Bath Advocate* (2 September), it was "almost too grand; the terrific portraying of maniacism and despair was appalling, and her wild shrieks had less the appearance of mere acting than of horrible reality." But the *Bath Mercury* (2 September), emphasising the harmoniousness of the impersonation, declared that even the mad scene, which usually seemed to "stand out in distorted and revolting proportions," contained nothing that did not accord with the general tenor of the character." Though not completely contradictory, these critiques do point up a problem faced by the poetic (as opposed to the melodramatic) actress: how to make painful elements theatrically effective without offending critical sensibilities. Unfortunately, the would-be star was less successful with Bristol audiences than with Bristol critics. The crowds were never large, even on her benefit night.[8]

After this discouraging experience, a week of relaxation at Brighton was a welcome respite before her brief engagement at the Theatre Royal there. Relatives were present in force, for brother John (J. F. Saville) was still managing the theatre and Harriet and Humphrey (Mr. and Mrs. W. H. Bland) were members of his company. John had also arranged for Edmund (E. F. Saville) to have a limited engagement. During Helen's engagement, which began on 11 September, attendance was poor, and her choice of *The Patrician's Daughter* for her concluding benefit on the 16th disgusted the critic for the *Brighton Herald*. He was shocked by Mordaunt's "ungentlemanly conduct," and he was "sorry to see

Miss Faucit throw away her great abilities on such a poor creature as Lady Mabel." During the following week E. F. Saville put aside his usual melodramatic characters and stepped forth as a Shakespearean hero. When he took his benefit on 21 September, Helen played Juliet to his Romeo. But, although she might have been, as the *Herald* said, "certainly the best Juliet on the stage," the frivolous Brightonians were no more tempted by Shakespeare than they had been by Marston.[9] By this time Helen had planned to continue her starring efforts, but, having failed in three out of her four engagements, she must have been wondering whether this was a wise decision.

October brought other anxieties, William Farren, in the midst of a performance, had a severe stroke and was unable to speak. Although he eventually recovered, he was never so clearly articulate as before. Helen herself became ill about the same time, but by November she was ready to face the world again.[10] Early that month she had her spirits restored by a short engagement at Birmingham in which she repeated her earlier success there, winning recognition as Birmingham's "greatest favourite as a tragic actress" since Miss O'Neill.[11] Here was one city, at least, where her claim to stardom had been validated.

And now it was time for the real trial – at the Theatre Royal, Edinburgh. Helen must have anticipated this with mingled excitement and dread. She had heard of the cold audiences of Edinburgh, whom even Macready could not rouse to enthusiasm, yet she knew that the Theatre Royal there was among the best of the provincial theatres. To succeed as a star she must conquer the "modern Athens." There was one comfort, however. Harriet had recently joined the Edinburgh company as its leading lady. The prospect of her affectionate presence made that *terra incognita* loom less ominously.

It would not take long for the strangeness to vanish. Soon Edinburgh would be as familiar to Helen as London, and Number 7, North St. David Street, where she lodged during each of her early visits, would begin to seem like home. It was a convenient location. A short walk southward brought her to Princes Street, principal thoroughfare of the "new town," from which she looked across a garden-filled ravine to a tall grey line of "old-town" buildings, imposing at their higher level, and to the Castle, solid yet magical, on its craggy height. From Princes Street an easy walk, southeasterly, would bring her to the Theatre Royal in Shakespeare Square (site of the General Post Office today). Still farther east and dominating the skyline would be the Calton Hill, landmark for Edinburgh, "old" and "new", and favourite strolling place for inhabitants and visitors. Looking up at it Helen would see a varied pattern of buildings and monuments on its slopes – most of them classical, as befitted "modern Athens," but some reminiscent of a gothic past – and, crowning the whole, the tall "inverted telescope" of Nelson's monument and the twelve great pillars of the National Memorial, that massive fragment of a Parthenon.[12]

The Theatre Royal, Edinburgh, built in the eighteenth century, was a simple structure, ornamented only by a columned portico and, its most striking feature, three sculptured figures at the top – Comedy and Tragedy at the respective front corners and Shakespeare at the pinnacle of the pointed roof. The handsome interior, which was acoustically excellent, held about twelve hundred people, less than half of Drury Lane's capacity.[13] The stock company was unusually good for the provinces. William H. Murray, brother of Mrs. Henry Siddons (daughter-in-law of the great Mrs. Siddons), was a good manager and a fine character actor,; Edmund Glover, son of the famous comic actress Mrs. Julia Glover, was a very competent leading man; H. F. Lloyd, the principal low comedian, was a handsome little cockney whose drolleries were popular with the audience. Among the younger actors were two who would later achieve prominence, Mr. Leigh (i.e. Leigh Murray) and Mr. Sullivan (Barry Sullivan).[14] The leading lady was, of course, Mrs. W. H. Bland, but, according to custom, she was not asked to perform with a starring actress – even her sister.

The playbills for 14 November 1843 announced that the "Celebrated Actress, MISS HELEN FAUCIT" was engaged for twelve nights and would make her first appearance this evening as Pauline in *The Lady of Lyons*; Edmund Glover was to play Claude for the first time. When Helen saw the audience, however, she was dismayed to find how little "celebrated" she was here: the theatre was far from full, and there were numerous gaps in the dress circle, where ladies of good society sat when they came at all. Even worse was her first experience with the "cold Edinburgh audience." The spectators gave her a heartening welcome, but afterwards they sat like statues, providing none of that psychological sustenance to which a London actress was accustomed. They seemed to be merely absorbing the vitality she flung at them so generously instead of returning it with its force renewed. At one point they were shocked into response – the hysterical outburst in the third act "electrified" them – but apparently the subtler effects that were cheered elsewhere went unacknowledged here. At last, however, when Claude had thrown off his disguise and Pauline had responded with a burst of ecstatic joy, the curtain came down to a resounding thunder of applause.[15] Helen would soon realise that the spectators were not cold in feeling, that their silence often bespoke deep attentiveness, perhaps even deep emotion. But, understandable as their behaviour might be in theory, it was hard for a spirit-starved actor to accept it in practice.

When Murray saw how his new star had taken hold of the audience, he assured her that she need not worry about future attendance. His prediction proved true: within a week the ladies were taking their places in the dress circle and "every class of an audience, from orchestra to ceiling, now crowd[ed] to see her performances."[16] Their enthusiasm grew each night. When she answered the curtain call after her first appearance in *The Patrician's Daughter* (25

November), the audience rose en masse, cheering and waving their hats and handkerchiefs.[17] (The play itself was disliked in Edinburgh, as elsewhere, but Helen Faucit's acting caused a furore of admiration.) By this time there was such excitement over the new actress that Murray announced an extension of her engagement by six nights.

He was amply justified. The critics' reaction quickly mounted from approval to ecstasy: Helen Faucit was now "at the head of British actresses"; not since Miss O'Neill had Edinburgh witnessed "such soul-searching delineations of women"; young spectators need no longer regret having missed seeing Mrs. Siddons, "for we have seen Miss Faucit."[18] The last-quoted reviewer brazenly asserted that his tribute was "no hyperbole … but the deliberate opinion of cool reflection." Oh, those cold audiences and coolly reflective critics of Edinburgh! Helen Faucit's star never burned more brilliantly than in the frosty air of that northern climate.

According to Theodore Martin, who lived in Edinburgh at the time, Helen Faucit's acting had a remarkable appeal to the city's intellectual people, and the "usual theatrical criticisms of the journals were superseded by eloquent expositions of Miss Faucit's art from pens accustomed to higher work."[19] There were indeed some such reviews. A certain "Mephistopheles," who sprinkled his writing with Greek phrases, began on 23 November a sporadically published series of critiques for the *Caledonian Mercury* entitled "Our Standard Plays, and Their Representation at the Edinburgh Theatres." The first essay, devoted to *The Hunchback*, described Helen Faucit's Julia as an "intellectual treat," and several later ones eulogised her performances of other characters. The articles on Helen Faucit in the *Observer*, also very different from ordinary reviews, were obviously by a lover of the arts with a strong literary bent. Among his extravagant tributes were these: her "high art," though evidently attained by a study of great painting, sculpture, and poetry, had become so much a part of her that art and nature were now one; her performances were "poems" and she herself "our greatest living poet" (28 November); her portrayal of Lady Macbeth threw "more light upon the character than all the commentaries of the best critics – Coleridge, Schlegel, and Tieck not excepted" (5 December). For all his excesses, this critic made some unusually interesting observations about Helen Faucit's Lady Macbeth, notably the murder scene and the sleepwalking scene (see Afterpiece). He was so enthralled by her Lady Mabel that he reviewed it twice.[20] A letter of Helen Faucit's thanking an unnamed writer for his "kindly flattering notice" of her "poor Mabel" is dated 28 November 1843, the day on which the *Observer*'s first review of this performance was published; its tone suggests that the addressee is a personal acquaintance.[21] Perhaps it was Theodore Martin himself.

Helen's first visit to Edinburgh, though eminently satisfying, was also exhausting. She acted every night the theatre was open, six nights a week, in some of her most strenuous characters – Pauline, Mrs. Haller, Julia, Juliet, Lady Macbeth, Lady Mabel – some of them three, four, or five times. The lightest part was Lady Townly, which must have been chosen simply for variety. The abandon with which she threw herself into her acting took its toll. By 27 November she had collapsed completely and had to plead "indisposition," but she resumed her gruelling schedule the next day. After her last night, 5 December, she gave in to her illness and postponed an imminent engagement in Glasgow.[22]

Helen had hardly found her bearings in Edinburgh before she was warmly welcomed into an elite group of new acquaintances. This was partly the result of letters written by mutual friends in London. Charles Dickens, for example, wrote a letter about her to Sir William Allan, eminent painter and President of the Royal Scottish Academy.[23] Sir William, now sixty-eight, was best known for his scenes from Scottish history, but his early paintings of more exotic subjects reflected a ten-year experience in the interior of Russia; so, too, did the Turkish scimitars and Circassian armour that Helen would see on the walls of his studio when she posed for a portrait some time later. In the home of this genial and popular man she would meet not only his fellow artists but also many literary and academic people.[24] Another letter, which produced lastingly happy results, was written by R. R. M'Ian to an "intimate friend" of Theodore Martin, who in turn introduced Martin to Helen Faucit.[25] The person in question was very likely William Aytoun. When Helen met him he was practising law, but two years later he would be appointed to the chair of Rhetoric and Belles Lettres at the University of Edinburgh. Aytoun's homely looks, the butt of many jests, were offset by his witty personality. The little house where he and his family lived (he had not yet married) was frequently crowded with friends of his and his attractive sisters, Margaret and Isabella. It is easy to imagine Helen as a recruit for the hilarious charades that were the Aytouns' favourite diversion – like the notorious one in which William impersonated Queen Victoria.[26] Although her first Edinburgh engagement left little leisure for social life, the friends she made then would entertain her royally during later visits.

Theodore Martin, who would prove the most important person in Helen's later life, was at this time a neat, fashionably dressed young man of twenty-seven, often seen with a roguish twinkle in his eye. Though rather heavy-handed in his humour, he was an engaging conversationalist, knowledgeable about music, theatre, and literature. Martin had a privileged background: he was born on 16 September 1816 to James and Mary (Reid) Martin, who were, respectively, a well-to-do solicitor and a shipowner's daughter. After a classical education at the Royal High School of Edinburgh and the University of Edinburgh, he was "bred to the law."[27] For some time now he had been one of the Writers to the Signet, a group of lawyers next in importance to the Advocates (that is, the barristers, from whose ranks judges were appointed).[28] He

Theodore Martin as a boy, by Thomas Duncan (by courtesy of the Scottish National Portrait Gallery)

Sir Theodore Martin in later life (by courtesy Mrs. Cathrine Aird, Sir Theodore's great-grand niece)

was already known as a man of letters, proficient in both verse and prose: in addition to publishing pieces of his own, he was collaborating with Aytoun on translations of Goethe for *Blackwood's Edinburgh Magazine* and on humorous verses ascribed to a fictitious character named Bon Gaultier. Martin thought of himself as an intellectual liberal (Voltaire was his early hero), but his political inclinations were conservative. He was a member of the Episcopal Church, strongly opposed to the narrowness and fanaticism that he saw in some devotees of the Scottish Kirk. Although basically honest, he was not above deviousness in a good cause. He was completely sincere, however, in his romantic idealism and in the loyalty of his personal attachments.

Martin had first seen Helen Faucit at the Haymarket in September, 1840, when he was in London on business. Though he had admired her then, he was astonished now by her great advance in "the mastery of her art." Night after night he returned to the theatre, delighted with her voice, her face, her figure, her "genius" as an actress, and, above all, the "charm in her personality, that spoke of a pure and lofty spirit."[29] When he met her in person, the magic was stronger than ever. Helen must have been grateful for his admiration, especially at the beginning of her starring career, but there was nothing new about young men who thought they were in love with her. Only after years of Martin's unshaken devotion would she finally acknowledge his unique importance in her life.

In going from Edinburgh to Glasgow, Helen had to travel only forty miles, yet she must have felt, on arriving, that she was in another country. Glasgow's difference from the "modern Athens" was apparent at first sight; the Trongate, the thoroughfare by which one entered the city, offered an impressive vista of "huge black structures, rising on either side many stories into the air, but diversified, all along with very picturesque breaks and lights – pillars, turrets, spires." It was the behaviour of the people, however, that most distinguished Glasgow from Edinburgh. The "vast hum, and bustle, and jostling" in its streets spoke of an intense preoccupation with commence and industry.[30] As Helen would soon find out, the same concerns were reflected in the cliques and coteries of the social life. From the "Sugar Aristocracy" at the top of the social scale, down to the "iron and coal masters" at the bottom, the families of each trade tended to live exclusively within their own circle. According to Archibald Alison, the historian, when he and his wife moved to Glasgow in 1835, they, as strangers, were welcome in each group, but it was impossible to arrange a dance for as many as twenty-five couples who would condescend to be introduced to each other. (They found this strange after living in Edinburgh, where all "persons of respectability" became like "one great family" during the social season.) The country society, however, proved the best in Scotland, especially in autumn, when many families of the English nobility visited the local estates for the hunting.[31]

Sir Archibald Alison, by Robert Scott Lauder
(by courtesy of the Scottish National Portrait Gallery)

Archibald (later Sir Archibald) Alison, son of a prominent Episcopal clergyman of the same name, had been a member of the legal hierarchy, but, seeing that party politics made promotions uncertain, he had accepted the office of Sheriff of Lanarkshire. He was well known as a writer, his most important work being a ten-volume *History of Europe during the French Revolution.*[32] This scholarly and cultivated man, fifty-one years old when Helen met him, was an ideal patron for the new actress. His access to all groups in Glasgow's stratified society gave her an advantage – as did his willingness to write an occasional newspaper review. During her second visit to Glasgow, a few months after the first, the Alisons became personally acquainted with her and, after that, often entertained her at Possil House, their spacious home several miles from Glasgow. Here she could read from a wide choice of books, which overflowed every room, stroll with her hosts in the garden, watch "the lambs playing around the trees" in the large wooded park, and relax from professional cares.[33]

Such escapes were delightful, but in Glasgow, as everywhere else, the theatre remained the heart of Helen Faucit's existence. The Theatre Royal, on Dunlop Street, was a handsome building 90 feet long and 40 feet wide, with the usual portico supported by Doric columns and surmounted by two busts – the obligatory one of Shakespeare, paired with a vainglorious likeness of the current manager, the eccentric John Henry Alexander. The interior was attractive and well appointed. Alexander had made extensive alterations when he took over the forty-five-year-old theatre in 1829, and apparently he kept it in good repair. In other respects, however, he was known for his cheese-paring economy. It took boundless energy to save money in Alexander's style: he was his own secretary, stage manager, scene designer, and business manager, as well as the director of rehearsals and one of the principal actors. It is little wonder critics were sometimes dissatisfied with the way plays were staged. They were even more disgruntled about the acting, which they often described as execrable.[34] Alexander paid whatever was necessary to attract stars, but he must have economised severely on the salaries of regular performers.

The most versatile actor in the company was the manager himself. Though strongest in character parts, he would undertake anything that needed playing – even Romeo, despite abusive jokes from the gallery. The "gods" enjoyed exchanging insults with Alexander, but he could always restore their good will be performing "Alick's Lilt," his own version of the Highland Reel. Although the Lilt was not required during any of Helen Faucit's engagements, on one occasion some gallery boys did shower Alick with vegetables after Helen had received her lavish tribute of flowers.[35] The best of the other actors was Mun Noble Paumier, the leading man. He was an impressive figure, immensely tall but graceful and attractive. Now in his late thirties, he was a respectable actor, though not an inspiring one, and when he did attempt a storm of passion it was likely to degenerate into rant. He was very successful, however, in certain characters, notably Claude Melnotte. Helen Faucit evidently found him acceptable, for she later took him as a supporting actor on a number of tours.[36]

Miss Faucit's first engagement in Glasgow was announced for ten nights only, but a "re-engagement" extended it to seventeen (11-30 December, excluding Sundays and Christmas Day). She appeared in all her Edinburgh characters except Lady Townly but acted some of them less often, and she added two others, Mariana (in *The Wife*) and Rosalind. News of her recent success had preceded her here and playbills were embellished with extracts from the Edinburgh reviews. The critic for the *Glasgow Herald* (15 December) wrote that before seeing Helen Faucit he had distrusted such "eulogiums" but now he realised that they had fallen short of the reality. He was not alone: his colleagues at the *Citizen* and the *Chronicle* rivalled the Edinburgh critics in praise of the new actress.

As in Edinburgh, all the characteristics of her acting admired elsewhere were enthusiastically praised here. One, however, was more appreciated in Scotland than anywhere else: its ideality. Helen Faucit's intellectual qualities, though noticed since her early days, were now described in more lofty and spiritual terms – as when the *Glasgow Herald* spoke of the "soul to conceive … all those noble impulses and passions," as well as the "judgment to temper, and the skill and energy to embody" them. Some writers, in both Scottish cities, even claimed for her performances an inspirational power over the minds and lives of her audiences. For example, Edinburgh's "Mephistopheles," in countering a clergyman's attack on the theatre, cited a performance of hers as evidence of the drama's power to teach moral lessons, thereby making the spectators "better and wiser."[37] And a few months later, during her second Glasgow engagement, the *Scotch Reformer's Gazette* (20 April 1844) declared that there was "a contagious elevation of thought … proceeding from this young lady, which, next to devotion itself, [tended] powerfully to confirm man in the paths of virtue." In Scotland, where the theatre was so often consigned to the devil, it was pleasant for a theatre-lover to discover that it was actually on the side of the angels.

It was not through moral lessons, however, that Helen Faucit's ideal acting had its effect; it was through portraying human emotions so as to suggest, at moments, something transcendentally beautiful or sublime. William Black, who saw her performance of Juliet in Glasgow during his early youth, wrote to her years after becoming a successful novelist:

> I was brought up among one of the very rigidest sects of Scotch Puritans, who seemed to consider the expression of affection, even between parents and children, as a sort of weakness; and your Juliet was an extraordinary revelation to me of womanly tenderness and grace and beauty and passion. It . . . made the world quite different…[38]

Even terrible or painful emotions, such as those of Lady Macbeth's sleepwalking scene and Lady Mabel's dying scene, had ultimately an exalting effect for some spectators. It is not surprising that young men were particularly susceptible to her influence – like the dashing twenty-three-year-old who declared, "I did not know I had a soul, till I saw Helen Faucit."[39]

Soul and body were, of course, not far apart. As more than one Glasgow writer implied, there was a direct relationship between the actress's physical charms and the nobility of the ideal that she suggested in her acting.[40] At twenty-nine, but passing for twenty-five or less, Helen Faucit had become a figure of glamour and beauty for thousands of people, despite her irregular nose and her overly-generous mouth. Archibald Alison's description of her suggests the romantic vision that many of his countrymen saw when they looked at her:

> Her leading characteristic ... is the elegance which invariably distinguishes all her movements ... the proportions of her figure, which is uncommonly fine, charm the eye not less than the deep intonations and flexible richness of voice penetrate the heart. Without entire regularity of feature, her countenance possesses the whole beauty arising from powerful and changing expression. A profusion of jet-black locks, curling over a fine bust, add the contrast of dark shade and light. ... The different phases [of her facial expression] are so various, and yet so riveting, that it is often scarcely possible to believe that they belong to the same individual, or that so much fascination can have proceeded from one set of features.[41]

What had happened since those early days when the young Victoria had described Helen Faucit as "plain and thin," the *Morning Herald* had sneered about her profile, and the *Observer* had recommended a less "angular" use of her arms? Helen was still slender, but her figure had filled out satisfactorily, and the increasing grace of her movements had enhanced its attractiveness. Now that she had left the enormous patent houses of London for the smaller provincial theatres, the expressiveness of her mobile face was more effective than ever and her voice was less subject to strain. No doubt the excitement of her Scottish successes contributed to the radiance of her look and personality. There was no longer the nervous tension deriving from fruitless efforts to please both mother and manager, no longer the presence of Macready to inspire but also to inhibit and frustrate. (Helen still hoped to rejoin him later, but meanwhile her energies were flowing in newer, less obstructed channels.) Independence, maturity, and the joys of conquest had transformed her.

During Helen Faucit's first Glasgow engagement, the critics were most impressed with her Julia and her Juliet, especially the latter.[42] In the context of her whole history, however, her most important role was Rosalind, which she acted on 21 December for the first time in Scotland. Its popularity would increase quickly after this; rarely would she appear in either Glasgow or Edinburgh without including it. Personally, as well as professionally, this performance was a landmark. Theodore Martin, who had followed Helen to

Helen Faucit, by Kenneth Macleay
(by courtesy of the Scottish National Portrait Gallery)

Glasgow, saw her Rosalind and was so poignantly affected that he dashed off some verses describing his "dream" of being Orlando.[43] Not long afterwards Martin and Aytoun, in a fictional colloquy of "Bon Gaultier and His Friends" (*Tait's Magazine*, February 1844), had a participant read Martin's verses to cap the following tribute:

> Through all the joyousness of Rosalind's spirit, you see the extreme gentleness.... She is the reconciler of differences ... she lives in an atmosphere of loving-kindness. All this is admirably shadowed out by Miss Helen Faucit, while the delicious wit of Rosalind breaks from her with a graceful gaiety, as fascinating as it is rare. (123)

Theodore Martin was not the first critic to call attention to the romantic, feminine side of Helen Faucit's Rosalind, but he was among the early ones.

Meanwhile, back in London, the *Theatrical Journal* had been carrying glowing reports of Miss Faucit's success in Glasgow: the house was "crammed to the ceiling nightly"; her attraction was so great that "the orchestra was turned into stalls, and the band played behind the scenes. . . ." As Walter Baynham wrote later in his history of the Glasgow stage, Helen Faucit was from first to last "Glasgow's favourite actress."[44]

After a two-week holiday, spent, very likely, in Edinburgh, Helen travelled to Newcastle-on-Tyne for her first engagement at the Theatre Royal there. This theatre, only seven years old at the time, was an imposing structure with six large Corinthian columns supporting the inevitable portico, and, inside the main entrance, a "magnificent rotunda . . . consisting of two storeys separated by a circular stone gallery." The auditorium, with its elegant curve of crimson-lined boxes, its twelve slender gilt pillars, and its cut-glass chandelier, would hold nearly two thousand people.[45] The company, which included James Bennett as leading man, Miss Saker as leading lady, and Mr. Hudspeth as low comedian, must have been at least as good as Glasgow's.

Engraving of Kenneth Macleay's full-length portrait of Helen Faucit
(by courtesy of the Harvard Theatre Collection, Houghton Library)

Helen Faucit, announced for five nights only, opened as Pauline on 15 January and had a last appearance advertised on the 19th, when she acted Lady Mabel for her benefit. The following Monday, however (the 22nd), a "re-engagement" of five nights was begun, which concluded on Friday with another benefit (a performance of Julia). Although "re-engagements" were often fictitious, having been agreed on in advance, this one was probably genuine. According to the *Newcastle Journal* (20 January), "whatever may have been her attractions elsewhere," Helen Faucit did not draw "even a moderate house" here until the 19th, "when she appeared in a less favourable character and yet the house was crammed." That night's crowd convinced the manager, James Munro, that the new actress had caught on and would continue to draw. He was evidently right.

All the reviews were favourable, but those in the *Newcastle Advertiser* gave the most thoughtful analyses. Particularly interesting is a passage about the last act of *The Patrician's Daughter* (1 February): "Miss Faucit exhibits one quality of rare excellence. She cares nothing for personal appearance, when the requirements of the scene [decree otherwise]." "[A]shy pale, with open mouth and strained eyeballs," she created, for the shocked but approving critic, "the picture of death." This review, though strongly reminiscent of one in the *Morning Chronicle* nearly eight years before, has a significant difference – the comparison to a picture. The *Chronicle* had gloried in her "abandon" (making ugly faces when necessary), but other London critics had deplored her lack of control. The Newcastle review suggests her way of reconciling abandon and artistic discipline. By creating a "picture" she could idealise pain and ugliness, even while depicting them in repulsive detail.

During one of her visits to Newcastle, perhaps this first one, Helen became friendly with George William Armstrong (later Lord Armstrong), now remembered for his invention of the hydraulic lift and the Armstrong guns, and his wife, Margaret. A few years later the Armstrongs' home would become a haven for her during an emotional crisis.[46]

For Helen Faucit's second Edinburgh engagement, in mid-February, Murray ensured consistently large audiences with a double attraction: her plays were followed by melodramatic afterpieces featuring T. P. Cooke, famous actor of nautical parts. At this time, on 15 February, Helen first acted Rosalind here, charming both audience and critics. Mephistopheles, a good representative of the latter, pronounced this "the most intellectual, and at the same time, the most fascinating performance" that had been seen in Edinburgh for many years (*Caledonian Mercury* 19 February). So popular was Helen Faucit's Rosalind that she gave it four times to once or twice for any other role.

Only a week intervened between this engagement and a third one at the same theatre, already announced by Murray. As Helen wrote to her Parisian friend, Mme. Colmache, she was caught up in Edinburgh's social life. Her long, exuberant letter, dated 26 February 1844, covers the four sides of a folded sheet of stationery, then continues by "crossing" the first part of the message. As the following extract shows, it vibrates with energy and self-confidence.

> You see I am still in Scotland – the good people are feting & making a little Queen of me – The change of climate, notwithstanding the intense severity of the weather, has happily benefited my health. … This is their great season here, & balls & parties beset you at every turn. … my second engagement was even more successful than the first – it closed on Saturday night & I commence a *third* on the 4th of March – After this I repeat my Glasgow visit & then I hope home to England. When I left I looked to be away at most a month, & I think it will be nearer *six*…
>
> There is nothing stirring in the dramatic world in London therefore I dare say my stay will be short, for you know I *must work* while I am young & my sun is shining. Mr Macready I hear returns from America in the autumn – another winter it is most likely I shall be under his management again. I wish he, or *some one* would take a Theatre in Paris for the English drama & bring forward Shakespeare's plays – Louis Philippe should *command* it. … I do not think I am likely to marry a Scotch Laird, nor has your English Millionaire come forward yet, or at least one to my fancy – I suppose I have *no time* for such things. I am sure it is only idle people who are constantly falling in love – I hope I *shall some day*, but I suppose I must *bide my time*.[47]

Helen Faucit began her third Edinburgh engagement with *Nina Sforza*, which had not been acted since its initial run at the Haymarket in 1841. She needed some new attraction, for three starring engagements in the same city within a few months could test the faithfulness of her strongest admirers. Luckily the principal male roles could be reasonably well cast. Edmund Glover, who had seen Macready's chilling performance of the villain Spinola, did his best to reproduce its effects. Young Leigh Murray was at least handsome and graceful as the erring husband, Doria; Helen Faucit took pains to coach him in the part, and he responded well.[48] The production, if only a weak reflection of Macready's, was surprisingly well done for a provincial theatre. At the end there was the same kind of standing ovation and waving of everything wavable that *The Patrician's Daughter* had received on its first night in Edinburgh.[49] In both instances, however, a few scenes had caused all the excitement; neither play was effective enough to justify frequent repetitions.

During this engagement Helen introduced two Shakespearean roles that she had not previously acted here: Imogen in *Cymbeline* and Portia in *The Merchant of Venice*. Portia she acted only once, and she did not return to it for a year. Imogen she acted twice during the present engagement, but, as far as I know, she did not revive it again in Edinburgh for thirteen years. Considering the favourable reception of her portrayal here, this is puzzling. The manager may well have been responsible: since *Cymbeline* was not in the usual stock-company repertory, it was as troublesome to produce as a new play but did not have the same advertising value.

No performance was more pleasing than her Imogen, however, to Mephistopheles. In an essay on *Cymbeline* for the *Caledonian Mercury* (9 March 1844) he praised among other things, Miss Faucit's "exquisite sensibility," her effective use of byplay and facial expression, and the touching way in which she spoke some of the short, simple lines. He added that the "more susceptible" of his sex had better stay away from her performances of Imogen since seeing them was "likely to prove dangerous."

The jest was not without substance. It must have been about this time that someone, now unknown, got temporary possession of Helen's promptbook of *Cymbeline* and wrote two sonnets on a blank page at the end. (I fancy I can make out the date "10 March /44" in a faint scrawl at the bottom of the page.) The handwriting does not look like Theodore Martin's. The poems are not simply copied from some other source; the cancelled lines and written-over words proclaim them to be extemporaneous. The first one, which describes the poet's melancholy plight before the advent of his lady and ends with an epiphany, is sufficiently represented by these lines:

My soul had lost its wings – and crouched in shade
When thou my angel, to these eyes wast given
In snowy robes of purity arrayed
And glowing from thy brows the hues of heaven.

The other is a conventional love poem with a single ingenious twist: the final couplet completes the sentence begun in the first two quatrains as well as the one begun in the third. The lover celebrates such attractions of his lady as "tresses where the amorous winds do play" and "eyes serenely gay/Proud of the joyous witchery they flung."[50] Despite their dubious poetic quality, these compositions are an interesting fragment of Helen's story: they typify the Scottish idealisation of her; they are written in an unusual but appropriate place (Imogen was one of her most ideal characters); and they raise an intriguing question, "Who was this particular rival of Theodore Martin's?"[51]

Before returning to Glasgow, Helen Faucit went up to Dundee to act for five nights at the Yeaman Shore Theatre. Dundee, former Covenanter stronghold and still a centre of puritanical prejudice, had never been a good theatre town, and now attendance was worse than ever because of depressed economic conditions; Helen's visit was particularly ill-timed, during Lent, when even Episcopalians scanted their theatre-going. A disappointing first-night audience reflected these conditions, but soon Helen Faucit's performances were the talk of Dundee, and her benefit was a "bumper."[52] One young girl and her brother, whose parents were hostile to the theatre, heard so much about the actress that they braved the "den of wickedness" to see her. The girl had laughed scornfully when warned of an emotional experience, but, as she later recalled, "I wasna lang there before the tears were running down my cheeks in streams."[53] This response was not confined to young girls. According to the *Dundee Courier* (26 March and 12 April 1844), the "most obdurate" spectators were moved by Miss Faucit's Juliet and even the "callous" wept with her Mrs. Haller.

Helen Faucit's second Glasgow engagement began on 9 April when the Theatre Royal reopened after a brief recess; although announced for "twelve nights only," it stretched out to twenty-one nights or more. Belvidera, which Helen had never acted in Scotland before, was introduced on the first night of the "re-engagement" and repeated on the last. Her "touching and forcible" impersonation made this the most successful of her "new" parts, although, as often happened elsewhere, one critic found the concluding scene "almost too terrible" (*Glasgow Citizen* 24 April). Other roles that she acted here for the first time were Nina Sforza, Jane Shore, and, surprisingly, Desdemona (rarely included in her starring bills). *Nina Sforza* must have disappointed the enormous audience that assembled to see it. Since it could hardly have been produced satisfactorily at Alexander's theatre, the play's "want of development" and "weariness of speech," complained of by the *Argus* (18 April), were very obvious here. Helen Faucit's acting, however, was described as a "brilliant display of genius," among "her noblest efforts."

The engagement was a huge success. Both benefits were brilliantly patronised and were concluded by vociferous curtain calls and showers of wreaths and bouquets.[54] The critics were, if possible, more enthusiastic than before, particularly a writer for the *Scotch Reformer's Gazette* (Alison?). There was "no resisting the power of her representations," he wrote (13 April); she truthfully portrayed "the warm, buoyant, and fascinating qualities of dear woman" (20 April, 2nd. ed.); her acting revealed "intellect of the highest creative order – full-toned sensibility ... and a heart swelling ... with every noble emotion..." (4 May). And more, much more.

In mid-May, on her way toward home, Helen stopped for six nights at Newcastle. Her Lady Macbeth, which was new here, attracted attention for its originality: it was "less stately" than the usual portrayal, wrote a discerning critic, but "full of feeling," a "powerful display of nature in an ambitious yet loving wife" (*Newcastle Chronicle* 25 May). Her womanly interpretation was gradually winning its way.

Helen Faucit returned from Scotland a different woman than she had been six months earlier. In the two great cities of the once-alien North she had proved herself and found her own strength. Never again would she be anyone's obedient pupil or adoring disciple. Back in London, she established her own living quarters – no longer with the Farrens in Brompton Square but at 13 Michael's Place.[55] As a still-dutiful daughter, however, she acted the uncongenial part of Miss Dorrillon in *Wives as They Were and Maids as They Are* for William Farren's benefit (at the Haymarket, 10 June). Her reward was the "immense applause" that greeted her and "lasted for some minutes" before the play could proceed.[56] London had not forgotten her.

About this time, if not earlier, she learned that John Mitchell, manager of the St. James's Theatre (home of the French drama in London), was planning to take an English company to Paris in the autumn and that he wanted her as Macready's leading lady. Negotiations continued for some time, but, of course, she accepted the terms that proved necessary.[57]

Meanwhile, late in July, she travelled to Cork, in Ireland, a city she had not visited since 1836. Frank Seymour, manager of the Theatre Royal there, was reminiscent of his counterpart in Glasgow: nicknamed "Chouse" for his pronunciation of "Chaos" in Othello's "Chaos is come again," he rivalled Alexander in eccentricities. In fact, he and Alexander had once engaged in an epic struggle over a theatre in Glasgow that could furnish a plot for a comic opera. Now, in his sixties, he was back in his native Cork, a fine, Falstaffian figure of a man, always in good spirits but always short of cash. Gossip told of artful tricks by which he withheld money from salaries, but Helen seems to have had no trouble with him.[58] The theatre itself had acceptable accommodations for the audience, but its too-shallow stage was much in need of improvement. The same could be said of the company. At least there were enough members to cast the plays – something that was not always true.[59] Despite his tubby figure, Seymour himself was considered a very good Ghost in *Hamlet* (his voice was properly sepulchral), and Mrs. Seyton, who had long served as the "first old woman," was admired as Gertrude – though not, one would think, as a strong temptation for Claudius.[60] Helen had taken no chances on her leading man: Mun Noble Paumier, who accompanied her, was at least a known quantity.

Helen Faucit made her first appearance on 29 July as Pauline. Although originally advertised for six nights only, she actually remained (according to a now-familiar scenario) for twenty-one; on her final night, 23 August, she played Jane Shore for Seymour's benefit, the proceeds to be used for improvements to the theatre. Her roles were the same ones she had acted in Glasgow with the addition of Mrs. Beverley and Ophelia.

Her performance of the latter, on 10 August, was billed as "the first time on any stage" – though, strictly speaking, it was the second. Never part of her repertory, Ophelia was included as an "experiment" to determine whether she should play it, as she she had been asked to do, in Paris. Poor Paumier as Hamlet was badly "cut up" by the *Cork Examiner* (12 August), but Helen Faucit's Ophelia, described as "nature itself," was particularly praised for "grace of expression and action" in the mad scene. To Theodore Martin, with whom she was now corresponding regularly, Helen wrote:

> How I wish you had been present! I can form no idea of the impression it made. I have no one to tell me of my failures. How sadly I miss a discerning and analytic critic … I was terribly frightened, and my voice trembled excessively. Still I might perhaps get over this, and then I think I could do something with it.[61]

If she really trembled in this relatively simple role, it was from apprehensiveness about the judgment of Paris. There this delicate and pathetic character was forever associated with the beautiful Harriet Smithson, who had entranced everyone – especially Hector Berlioz – when performing with the English actors in 1827-28. To play Ophelia in Paris was to challenge a cherished memory.

The Cork engagement was overwhelmingly successful. The journalists constantly reported crowded, fashionable, and enraptured audiences. Enamoured young men poured out streams of verse about Helen Faucit, some of which was published in the *Cork Examiner* (5 and 12 August). One or two poems were rather pretty, and several were ingenious – like the twenty-six-line *tour de force* ending all the even lines with "Helen Faucit" and all the odd ones with rhymes like "cross it." Hardly less poetic, were the theatrical reviews, whose impressionistic, often hyperbolic language makes them distinctive, even in an age of effusive writing.

In Cork, as elsewhere, Helen Faucit's facial acting was much admired: a reviewer declared that in Lady Macbeth "her very features were altered; and … so wonderful was the change of expression from that of Juliet, Rosalind, etc. … that many asked with astonishment – 'Is that Miss FAUCIT? – *can it be* Miss FAUCIT?" '[62] The most notable passage of criticism, however, was a poetic tribute to her evocative power:

> In the little *traits* of character, that could not be noticed, only felt, HELEN FAUCIT shines. A tone, a gesture, a look are glorious with eloquence. The smell of a forgotten rose leaf, a half-uttered note of music – a tiny bit of tint in the sky of a landscape – put them before us unexpectedly, and how are we stirred? How are all the sleeping and mysterious emotions of our hearts awakened? HELEN FAUCIT does all this.[63]

Reluctant to let a good thing go, Seymour took his stars, along with his company, to Limerick, where he had once been an actor-manager, and opened the New Theatre for a series of performances. The small port on the Shannon estuary was abnormally filled with noise and activity during part of this visit, for Daniel O'Connell's release from prison inspired rejoicing here as in the rest of Ireland. On the night of 6 September the countryside around Limerick, as far as the eye could see, was illuminated in his honour, and in the town there were tar-barrels and piles of turf blazing at every corner. Shouting mobs paraded the streets, shots were fired almost continuously, and Temperance bands added to the cacophany with their martial music.[64] But this demonstration, unlike the earlier agitation over O'Connell in Dublin, had little effect on theatre attendance. Helen Faucit's benefit attracted the "fullest and most respectable house" that had ever been seen at the New Theatre.[65]

After a three-week holiday at the Killarney lakes and another short engagement at Cork, Helen returned home to prepare for her trip to Paris. In the sixteen months since Macready had closed his management her progress as a star had been extraordinary. It was about to receive a new and forceful impetus.

Chapter 8

Captivating Paris

ACCORDING TO Mitchell's original plan (made in the spring, 1844), the English actors would have a three-month season in Paris. Macready, still touring in America, agreed through his henchman T. J. Serle, but he cautioned that plays like *The Lady of Lyons* would not attract a Parisian audience. He recommended major Shakespearean dramas and other powerful plays "single in their effect," like *Virginius*, whose secondary parts would not require firstrate (hence expensive) actors.[1] But, though most of his suggested plays had no strong part for an actress, Macready wanted Helen Faucit as leading lady. She might be "large in her demand," he wrote, "yet if no dramatic Theatre in London is open, the eclat, as well as a *fair* remuneration, might have strong inducements for her."[2] Mitchell, knowing the proposed bill of fare would offend her, promised Helen Faucit that if she would act Virginia and Ophelia in "Macready's plays" he would include some of her special plays as well.[3]

Although Helen undoubtedly wished to act in Paris with Macready, she was wary of a long engagement, perhaps for fear of losing the momentum she had gained in Scotland. Macready, unaware of the magnitude of her recent successes, was shocked by her proposal of a partial engagement. "Of course she is beyond compare the best English actress," he wrote Serle, "– and her co-operation – in the *effect* of the plays – would be most valuable,"[4] but a partial engagement would mean a weakening of effect in her absence.

In the event there was no such problem, for Mitchell had to reduce his Parisian season to little more than four weeks. The English actors were to appear at the Salle Ventadour, home of the Italian opera, on the Italians' off-nights. Unfortunately Léon Pillet, director of another operatic theatre, the Opéra, appealed to the Minister of the Interior, adducing a "privilege" that had been granted to protect the Opéra from undue competition: by its terms the Italian company was restricted to three nights a week, the other nights being reserved, as far as opera was concerned, for Pillet's establishment; it was thus impossible, he argued, to admit a second troupe to the Italians' venue, Salle Ventadour. Specious as his reasoning was, the Minister compromised by limiting the English actors to twelve performances.[5] Mitchell, though disappointed, proceeded with his plans, hoping to get an extension later.

The date of the Paris opening, originally set for 18 November 1844, was delayed at Macready's request, pending the arrival of John Ryder, a former Drury Lane actor, and Charlotte Cushman, the American actress, who were *en route* from the United States. His attitude toward Miss Cushman had changed dramatically since 28 September, when he had questioned her wisdom in planning to visit England since methods effective with the American "Masses" would not serve her here;[6] now he was eager to include her in the Parisian company – as competition for his leading lady. Since returning to England he had learned of Helen Faucit's recent triumphs, and, as always, he found it difficult to tolerate a rival. The newly-arrived Miss Cushman, however, advised by a mentor to "beware," turned down Macready's urgent offer.[7]

When Helen Faucit arrived in Paris, on 26 November, after a stormy crossing followed by a twenty-four hour drive through freezing weather, she was ill with a chest cold that plagued her, off and on, throughout the visit. Macready, further delayed by an accident, left England more than a week later. Meanwhile Helen had leisure to visit her Parisian friends and to spend time with her nineteen-year-old half-brother, William, who was living here (perhaps as a student). Without her expected income, she had to call on Mitchell for an advance.[8]

Pillet's action against Mitchell's company reflected no general hostility, but, as the French scholars B. Juden and J. Richer point out, the political climate was not propitious for the visit.[9] The strong tensions that had existed between England and France during much of 1844 still left their mark, despite the peaceful settlement of the situations causing them. It was popularly believed that François Guizot, chief Minister of Louis-Philippe, had allowed himself to be duped and humiliated by the British. Luckily, Parisian journalists took the lead in welcoming the "dramatic missionaries" – an oblique reference to a Francophobic missionary in Tahiti who had been deported by French authorities but later promised an indemnity. A cultural *entente cordiale*, declared the journalists, was more honourable than a political one.[10]

Helen Faucit had been looking forward to her reunion with Macready, but it proved worse than disappointing. Although he called on her in Paris and congratulated her on her successes, he added that Mitchell should not have engaged the two of them together.[11] This was bad enough, but Mitchell's news was even more hurtful: Macready had insisted on his own list of plays, which excluded all her requests. Since the terms of her agreement had been broken, she threatened to leave. Mitchell talked her into staying, but her relations with her former idol progressively worsened.[12]

The English actors' appearances began at last on 16 December 1844 with a performance of *Othello.* The Salle Ventadour was brilliantly filled, the magnificent chandelier shedding its light on people who were luminaries in their own right. Fashionably dressed ladies and gentlemen lounged in the crimson-lined boxes, and the first gallery, basket-like with its stamped brass openwork, bloomed with appropriate colours.[13] Yet, for all its beauty, the auditorium was better suited to opera than to drama: not only was it too large but the seats were so far from the stage that, as Macready expressed it, the spectators were beyond the range of his "electric current." When he complained of the undemonstrative audience, Helen Faucit at first agreed with him.[14] With more experience, however, she changed her mind: despite the lack of "noisy applause," she felt "an indescribable atmosphere of sympathy" surrounding her. "Every tone was heard, every look was watched, felt, appreciated."[15] Except for the two stars the company was disappointing. John Ryder, accustomed to parts like the Banished Duke in *As You Like It,* was a weak Iago; Robert Wyndham, at this time young and inexperienced, was "painful" to watch as Cassio. The acting improved after the first night, however.[16]

The costumes and *mise en scène* caused much discussion, not always complimentary. Gautier, who thought Othello should be a true Moor, not a Negro, considered Macready's makeup too dark and his costume ridiculously inappropriate, giving no suggestion of the Orient (*La Presse,* 23 December).[17] According to Mme. Colmache, Helen Faucit's costumes for Desdemona were praised for their historical accuracy.[18] The one for the murder scene, however, and indeed the whole arrangement of that scene, caused some raised eyebrows. "That little white bed at the back of that vast room; Desdemona, not reclining on a sofa, and symmetrically draped in the folds of a tunic, but lying in her bed, in a nightdress" – "*mon Dieu oui! en vrai cami-sole!*" – was a "strange spectacle" to those not accustomed to the English stage. Perhaps such realism entailed a loss of tragic dignity, but it certainly added to the emotional effect – so concluded John Lemoinne, temporarily replacing Jules Janin as critic for the *Journal des débats.* "When the implacable Moor pounced upon the frail victim, an impression of terror reigned throughout the theatre," and the ladies could bear to look no more.[19]

The audiences were generally too polite to respond disrespectfully when confronted with such offences to French taste.[20] But, as the poet Gerard de Nerval pointed out in *L'Artiste* (22 December 1844), although educated people now paid lip-service to Shakespeare, most of them did not understand him well. Besides the language barrier, conflicting traditions of tragic art stood in their way[21] – this despite the "romantic revolution" in French drama during the previous two decades.

Many spectators at the English performances in 1844 had probably seen Macready during his visit to Paris in 1828. At that time he had astonished his audiences with a new experience of Shakespearean tragedy; some critics had found him even more thrilling than Edmund Kean.[22] Now he caused less excitement than before: Rolle of *Le Constitutionnel* (23 December) said that, like Lekain in his later days, he had moderated his old "superabundance of warmth and force" and had developed a more finished art. Most critics praised Macready very generously, however.[23] If he was disappointed by the response to his acting, it was less because it was undervalued than because, in his opinion, his leading lady's acting was overrated.

It was Helen Faucit's turn to bring the excitement of novelty and surprise. Her reputation in England was unknown to most Parisians, but, wrote Edouard Thierry in *Le Messager des chambres*, the first night's performance convinced the public that London had sent, not only a great tragedian but also a great tragedienne. By the end of the fourth act Miss Faucit was a stranger no longer: she was one of their own – "a truly French actress." When the play was over, she received a call with Macready.[24] Considering the slightness of Desdemona's role, especially in the stage version, Helen Faucit's Parisian debut was remarkably successful.

Thierry considered her a "French actress" partly because her delivery of dialogue was smoother and more fluent than Macready's, but in other ways she represented for him something universal. She was a tall and slender young woman, he wrote, without the "bloom of the flesh" that one expected (unlike the French actresses, she used little makeup) and, at first sight, she apparently lacked "the seduction necessary to an actress." But as soon as she began to walk, to make a gesture or assume an attitude, a charming grace revealed itself; she had the "irresistible attraction of the woman." When she spoke, her voice had the caressing sound that perfectly accompanied the caress (so to speak) of her look and manner. Indeed, wrote Thierry in his enthusiasm, "*Elle est femme*." Gautier, too, was struck by Helen Faucit's feminine grace and charm, but he considered them "English" in style. Miss Faucit, he wrote, was "a young woman, not exactly pretty, but expressive and gracious, with that slightly mannered English grace of the keepsakes and books of beauty. You know the kind of thing: the vague smile, the misty eye, the weeping hair, the undulant shoulder, the satiny shimmer on the flesh, something ruffled and glittering in the dress, an often-felicitous casualness of gauze and ribbons and feathers." Her manner, though somewhat affected, was by no means displeasing:

> for, today, under pretext of being simple, women too often fail in grace and suppleness … besides, it is natural to be mannered: women, cats and birds have, in their movements, certain innate affectations … Women are corrected of them by … the boarding school and the corset; but cats and birds retain them – that is what assures their superiority.[25]

Flippant and condescending as these remarks are, they have some pertinence to Helen Faucit's acting style. She would often be accused of "mannerism" by some critics, yet praised for "naturalness" by others.

Not all reviewers were impressed by the new actress's personality and art. Rolle of *Le Constitutionnel* (23 December) described her acting as "more sweet than passionate," though he admitted that her "gift of simple tears and naive sorrows" had a powerful effect on the heart. *La France théâtrale* commented briefly, "Miss Helen Faucit has qualities, but where is the grace of our French actresses?" And the "incurably Anglophobe" *Courrier des spectacles* declared that her qualities were more esteemed in her own country than in France, where there was a demand for "more naturalness and a more communicative sensitivity."[26] Even so, there was far more praise than blame.

Specific comments on Helen Faucit's Desdemona were almost entirely complimentary. In the early acts, according to Nerval, she was "gracious and interesting." In the scene where Desdemona pleads for Cassio's reinstatement, she circled about Othello, showing, as Gautier wrote, a "timorous caressing, a fondness a little like what one might have for a tamed tiger," but her intercessions had "all the audacity of virtue sure of itself." Both Nerval and Gautier deplored the omission of the willow scene, which, as the latter noted, is dramatic in itself and also contributes to the catastrophe by showing Desdemona's premonition of death. The murder scene was the great one for Helen Faucit: Lemoinne's reference to her "harrowing accents" as Desdemona struggled "in that narrow alcove against the pitiless vengeance of the Moor" helps to explain the wild applause she received.

Londoners were kept informed of the English productions in Paris by a correspondent for the *Sunday Times*. Macready had not been a favourite with this journal for several years past, nor had he become one now: his acting of Othello was only mechanically applauded, wrote the reviewer, except in a few passages. But Helen Faucit, though she had often been abused by the *Sunday Times* in earlier years, was now enthusiastically praised: her "natural powers" had been "wonderfully" developed since she had last appeared with Macready; she now "exaggerate[d] less" and in the parts requiring delicacy she "refine[d] with infinitely more care and truth." "Indeed, so much did her Desdemona interest the feelings of the audience that many of the boxes emptied immediately after her death ..." Despite the unfairness to Macready, the report probably contains some truth. At least one French critic thought the play should end with Desdemona's death and Othello's simultaneous realization, as if by a bolt of lightning, that she had been innocent.[27]

The second English production was *Hamlet* on 18 December. Macready, after watching Helen Faucit rehearse Ophelia, complimented her on her "original feeling and conception of the part." But "alas! alas!" she wrote to Martin before the performance, "goodness only knows what it will be like to-night."[28] She was freshly alarmed, that evening, to find several singers from the Italian opera company in the stage box; she would have to sing before *them*![29]

Helen's "sweet and plaintive voice" proved effective in Ophelia's songs – as one critic pointed out, they were not meant to be sung by a prima donna[30] – and, although she never exorcised Harriet Smithson's ghost, the new Ophelia enjoyed a success of her own. On the morning after the performance Helen added a note to her letter to Martin, telling how well her acting had gone in the mad scenes. "There are some new thoughts in it," she wrote, "that were particularly felt, but which I cannot now describe. If we ever meet and talk it over, I can make you feel with me."[31] Years later, in her essay on Ophelia, she tried to express the "new thoughts" that had informed her impersonation.

In her madness, she wrote, Ophelia imagines she is paying honour to her father's grave "in country fashion." Her brother, "of whom she had said before, most significantly, that he should 'know of it,'" is present, but he has "passed out of her memory . . . . She has no thought but to bury the dead – *her dead love* – her old father taking the outward form of it." In her acting, Helen Faucit had "ventured" to give, unobtrusively, a certain "character" to "Ophelia's treatment of her brother" here:

> When Laertes approaches Ophelia, something in his voice and look brings back a dim, flitting remembrance; she gives him of her flowers, and motions him to share in the obsequies she is paying. When her eyes next fall upon him, she associates him somehow with the "tricks i' the world." A faint remembrance comes over her of his warning words [against Hamlet's love], of the shock they gave her, and of the misery which came so soon afterwards. These she pieces together with her "half sense," and thinks he is the cause of all. She looks upon him with doubt, even aversion; and, when he would approach her, shrinks away with threatening gestures and angry looks. All this was shown only at intervals, and with pauses between – mostly by looks and slight action – a fitful vagueness being indicated throughout.[32]

If this sounds more modern than 1844, it is because of Helen Faucit's attempt to explain, through the workings of the subconscious mind, the relationships between Ophelia's experiences while sane and her words and actions while mad. Earlier in the essay she suggests that the "country" burial customs ("At his head a grass-green turf,/ At his feet a stone") have lingered, unthought-of, in Ophelia's memory since childhood; for, as the actress imagines, Ophelia's mother had died in childbirth and the baby Ophelia had been placed with a rural family for nurture during her early years. Courtly life would have temporarily banished the thought of her childhood experiences, but with madness the memory would return. The same explanation is given for the snatches of bawdy song, which in Miss Faucit's period should have been unknown to a young woman of Ophelia's class: the child Ophelia must have heard the peasants sing them. The death of her father and the death of her love find their pathetic expression in the early memories that have floated to the top of her disordered mind.[33] Helen Faucit's Ophelia was a subtle, seemingly intuitive piece of acting, but it had an intricate groundwork of careful thought.

The critics were all but unanimous in praising her performance. (The most important exception was the *Journal des débats*, which merely commented on the "formidable precedents" Miss Faucit had faced in the role and the ineffaceable memory of Harriet Smithson's Ophelia.)[34] Gerard Nerval even declared in *L'Artiste* (22 December), "We have actors who are able to equal Macready in Hamlet, but we doubt that any of our young actresses is able to play Ophelia as well as Miss Faucit."[35] Most reviewers concentrated on her mad scenes, and several spoke of the "silent acting," as she called it, by which she conveyed much of her interpretation. Nerval wrote that she spoke and sang Shakespeare's words admirably but was, at the same time, "a perfect mime." "How she reveals to you all the poetry in the madness of Ophelia!" exclaimed the *Revue Britannique*, " … the pantomime, the expressions of the face and the tones of voice speaking of it more than the verse and prose of Shakespeare."[36] Her poetic acting inspired critics with a lyricism of their own. "There is nothing more touching," said Rolle of *Le Constitutionnel* (23 December), "than Ophelia under the features of Miss Helen Faucit, reciting with a broken voice the plaintive love song with which she accompanies her madness." Gautier, in *La Presse* (23 December), vividly recalled: "How softly the flowers would slip from those hands [no longer controlled by the will]! what sickly and fatal grace in those incoherent couplets that would recur to her by fragments – and how pale she [was] already with her future death!"[37] Unfortunately, once the Parisian engagement was over, the practical requirements of stardom kept Helen Faucit from ever acting Ophelia again.

After a repetition of *Othello*, the English players performed Sheridan Knowles's *Virginius* on 23 December. Macready, who on previous occasions had grumbled about the unsympathetic audience, could now rejoice in an unalloyed triumph,[38] and the *Sunday Times* (29 December) could forget its hostility in enthusiasm for this "magnificent and powerful" Virginius. Virginia, on the other hand, was too slight a part to shine in. There was cold comfort for the ambitious Miss Faucit in Thierry's praise for her "self-abnegation,"[39] but consolation in Hippolyte Lucas's assertion, in *Le Siècle*, that only the charming presence of Mlle. Helene had given the production any interest.[40]

Christmas Day was spent by Helen with friends, visiting Notre Dame Cathedral and paying homage to the Venus de Milo at the Louvre – a happy time except for nervousness and fits of coughing, signs of worsening illness.[41]

Two days later, though ill, Helen Faucit dragged herself once more through Virginia, but, on doctor's orders, she missed a second performance of Ophelia (Mrs. Serle temporarily replaced her). A production of Byron's *Werner*, a play in which she never acted, brought a further respite. Despite Macready's fame in the title role, however, the audience was so "bad and unsympathetic" that *Werner* was not repeated.[42] Instead, Helen Faucit having recovered, the popular *Hamlet* was brought back.

On 5 January, Helen wrote Theodore Martin that *Macbeth*, to be performed the following night, would be the last play introduced into the series. "My *own* plays, therefore, which were to be of my own selection, we shall not arrive at. Well! Imperfectly as I shall be known here, I hope not to leave an unfavourable impression."[43] Meanwhile Martin, already indignant over the treatment she had received, had publicized it, citing instances from her letters. This, at least, is the likeliest explanation of an article in an Edinburgh paper which, according to Macready, "vilified and calumniated" him in order to "raise the name of Miss Helen Faucit." Some things in the article, Macready thought, must have come "directly or indirectly" from Helen herself.[44] He did not know that this rival star had a champion who would fight all challengers for her sake.

Meanwhile the most serious threat to Helen's Parisian reputation probably remained unknown to her. Charlotte Cushman, though she had originally refused to become involved, had come to Paris, after all, to look over the situation. Macready received her with open arms and once more urged her to join the English company. As Joseph Leach writes in his biography of Miss Cushman (139-40), she seemed just "the replacement – or competition – he needed for the tall dark lady who dared to reap an undue portion of the applause." But the shrewd American, reluctant to challenge the "brightest name on the British stage" before proving herself in England, again declined Macready's offer and, to escape temptation, returned to London. Had Charlotte Cushman been substituted for Helen Faucit in Lady Macbeth, the most substantial heroine in the Parisian series, Helen would have lost her best chance of demonstrating her histrionic powers in Paris.

Macbeth was performed on 6 January to "the greatest house of the season," according to the *Sunday Times* (12 January), the theatre being "crammed from the stalls to the roof"; the audience was warmly enthusiastic, and Helen Faucit's Lady Macbeth created a "profound sensation." According to the English writer, however, the portrayal, though "a beautiful piece of art," was "not 'the' Lady Macbeth": the actress's comparatively weak physique prevented her from exercising "that dominant metaphysical influence over the character of the tragedy" that Lady Macbeth "ought to assert." At least one major French critic agreed: John Lemoinne, in the *Journal des débats* (12 January), declared that Miss Faucit's very perfection in Ophelia and Desdemona convinced him that the "superhuman" role of Lady Macbeth was beyond her physical powers. In his view the character is "too much outside of nature to arouse sympathy," for she actually is what she prays the "murderous spirits" to make her (that is, unsexed and full of direst cruelty); she never regains her womanhood, and her sleepwalking scene, though gripping, inspires no moral emotion – merely physical terror. (This interpretation could hardly have been more opposed to Helen Faucit's.)[45] Mrs. Siddons's Lady Macbeth as described by Hazlitt was his ideal, and Rachel was, in his opinion, the only modern actress with the necessary characteristics. By comparison Helen Faucit seemed "too sweet and too girlish," lacking Rachel's "concentrated force … hidden energy, and …inner throbbing of passion."

Other critics, however – such as Gerard de Nerval (*La France musicale*), Edouard Thierry (*Le Messager des chambres*), Hippolyte Lucas (*Le Siècle*), and Jean-Toussaint Merle (*La Quotidienne*), – were much more impressed by Helen Faucit's performance.[46] Some of their comments read almost like replies to Lemoinne. Thierry pointed out, for example, that, difficult as it is to imagine how the same actress could satisfactorily impersonate both Virginia and Lady Macbeth, the "sense of truth takes the place of physical qualities in the genuine artist." And Merle, who held the same view of Lady Macbeth as Lemoinne, actually placed Helen Faucit in the Siddons tradition; giving only "flat compliments" to Macready, he awarded the evening's honours to this "great tragedienne … simple, noble, and terrible."[47]

Two of Helen Faucit's scenes attracted special attention. In the last moments of the banquet scene, according to Mme. Emile Girardin (wife of *La Presse*'s editor and a writer herself), this Lady Macbeth led her husband from the table "but never once look[ed] at him, turning her head as if in dread of meeting his glance." The loss of marital closeness indicated here was doubly pathetic in Miss Faucit's interpretation since it could be traced to Lady Macbeth's original love for her husband. It was the sleepwalking scene, however, that most profoundly moved the audience and drew the critics' strongest praise. "That gloomy fixity of the look," wrote Gautier, "those automatic movements, that sleeping, obedient body, without consciousness of what makes it act, with the soul kept on watch by an obsessing thought, produced an effect of high tragic terror …"[48]

Macready was deeply disturbed by the amount of applause given to Helen Faucit's performance. His annoyance on the first night of *Macbeth* led to his flouting of theatre etiquette: instead of "taking the lady on" to share in his curtain call, he left her to take a separate call alone. The snub was much talked about: "I hear he is in great disgrace with the Parisian public for his … discourtesy," Helen wrote to Theodore Martin; the *Sunday Times* reported the incident in London (12 January). Serle tried to warn Macready, on the second night of *Macbeth*, not to repeat the offence, "for it was noticed," but received the surly rejoinder, "When I want your advice I will ask for it!" After the performance that night Macready wrote in his diary:

> Acted Macbeth with effort, not so well as on Monday, but … I think with power and discrimination. It is, however, certain … that the audience applauded Miss Faucit's sleeping scene much more than anything else in the play. Again I had to observe the small portion of applause … that the audience gave to my performance; it would not have been so, I think – I am sure – before an English audience.

He was better pleased when his third performance of Macbeth (10 January) was rewarded by a wreath of bay followed by hearty applause.[49]

By this time the two stars were no longer friendly. Helen bitterly resented Macready's intransigence, as she saw it, in refusing to honour her choice of plays. She suspected, too, that he had tried to interfere with the effectiveness of her acting: a friend recalled his standing with cape spread wide in the senate scene of *Othello*, thus screening her "beautiful kneeling figure" from the audience, and Helen herself was depressed during a performance of *Macbeth* by his apparent "desire to keep everything and everybody down" except himself.[50] Macready's behaviour angered her admirers and probably produced retaliations. On 13 January, the last regular night of the engagement, Macready was hissed twice during the final scene of *Hamlet*. (He guessed the offender was Hippolyte Lucas of *Le Siècle*.) The audience counteracted the insult by calling for him and applauding cordially, but the incident rankled.

Mitchell told Macready that the "envious clique" that had tried to annoy him was composed of "friends of Miss H. Faucit," and Hely Bowes of *Galignani's Messenger* (an English-language newspaper in Paris) warned him that her friends were his enemies.[51] MM. Juden and Richer, after considering the possibility of a cabal to raise Helen Faucit's reputation and lower Macready's, conclude that, although it cannot be dismissed, Helen Faucit's tremendous success in Paris need not be explained by this theory (23-24). Some of her admirers were at least active on her behalf – witness an article in *Le National* (9 January) expressing regret that the English troupe would leave without allowing Parisians to see Miss Faucit in *The Lady of Lyons* and *Romeo and Juliet*.

Meanwhile Mitchell had petitioned the Minister of the Interior for an extension of his permit, but, after an appeal by Pillet alleging a violation of his vested interest, the request had been denied.[52] (Helen Faucit heard at the time that the Parisian actors had "appealed to the authorities to prevent the prolongation," but M. Regnier, the eminent comedian, later assured her that the French actors had been far too interested in the English performances to have made any such move.)[53] There was a slight stretching of the allotted twelve nights, however, for special occasions: on 16 January the company gave a command performance at the Tuileries; on the 17th Mitchell was allowed to take a benefit at the Salle Ventadour; and on the 20th some of the company (but not Helen Faucit) acted in a benefit for the Society of Dramatic Authors at the Opéra Comique.

The evening at the Palais des Tuileries was an elegant occasion: in addition to the King and Queen there was a brilliant audience of courtiers, military officers, and other eminent people. The performances – *Hamlet* with the afterpiece *A Day after the Wedding* – went off well, but, as decorum decreed, there was no applause in the royal presence. Louis-Philippe signified his pleasure, however, by sending members of his suite to thank the principal actors and to present gifts on his behalf. Helen's new bracelet was her first – but not her last – gift from royalty.[54]

For his benefit night Mitchell chose the fourth act of *II Henry IV*, a compressed version of *Romeo and Juliet*, and *A Day after the Wedding*. The entertainments did not end until 1:00 a.m., but they were highly successful. A handsome young actor named Graham, who had played at Drury Lane in parts like Oliver in *As You Like It* and Malcolm in *Macbeth*, now had his moment of glory as Prince Hal to Macready's Henry IV and Romeo to Helen Faucit's Juliet. Macready's acting was evidently very effective, but it was *Romeo and Juliet* that called forth "torrents of applause" and enough bouquets to fill a cart. During the curtain call the inexperienced Graham, instead of gathering up some of Miss Faucit's bouquets and presenting them to her, amused the audience by standing stolidly erect and letting her stoop to pick them up. Gautier, in reporting this "*sang froid tout britannique*," explained that Graham was unacquainted with French customs, but in truth the poor young man was unacquainted with curtain calls anywhere.[55] The *Sunday Times* (26 January) told Londoners that *Romeo and Juliet* "must fairly be regarded as the great success of the season," and Helen wrote jubilantly to her faithful Theodore that the play had gone off "immensely" and she herself had created "quite a *furore*."[56]

The critics, like the audience, were carried away with Helen Faucit's performance. Some spectators had seemed surprised by the eagerness and energy of her portrayal, but Gautier reminded them that, despite her tender years, Juliet is "not a little boarding-school pupil making sandwiches for tea; she is a loving, ardent Italian." In Juliet, as in Ophelia, Helen Faucit impressed him with the artistry and suggestiveness of her pantomime. Astonished by the variety of her attitudes, he declared that an artist would fill several sketchbooks if he tried to capture them all.[57]

Two of her scenes were most appreciatively described by Thierry. In the coaxing scene he, like the general public, was charmed with her byplay (so new to the French stage), and in the balcony scene he was enchanted with the expressiveness of her voice and face. Listening, "all the world understands Shakespeare, as all the world understands love"; watching, it is the same, for "her countenance explains everything, tells everything, understands everything; it is an open book, a magic book ... where each is able to read in his own language."[58] For everyone, however, she was most impressive in the potion scene, which won a "triple salvo of applause."[59] Both Thierry and Gautier admired her powerful evocation of Juliet's horror as she brought her fearful imaginings to life through pantomime and facial expressions.[60] Though using Garrick's tomb scene, she made it much quieter than usual: her Juliet, apparently still partly drugged, retained throughout the "dazed wonder of lethargy" (Thierry).

This Juliet, for all its energy and passion, had for some spectators a quality of ideality, of life transfigured by art or imagination. Gautier found in its misty grace ("*grace vaporeuse*") a reminder of engravings made from the aquatints of Angelica Kauffmann, and Georgianne Colmache, looking back on the performance in later years, called it "a vision of entrancing beauty such as must be produced by *haschisch*."[61]

One sees references occasionally to the "failure" of the English performances in Paris in 1844-45.[62] These performances were far from being a failure. They were very well attended; except for *Werner* they were enthusiastically applauded; and, as Victor Leathers says in *British Entertainers in France* (113), the critics, with very few exceptions, were "almost embarrassingly generous in their praise."[63] Both Macready and Helen Faucit were visited, entertained, and complimented by leaders of the theatrical and literary worlds.

Only the financial aspect of the Parisian venture was less than completely successful, and even here the word "failure" is incorrect. Apparently the box office receipts were excellent,[64] but, since Mitchell needed a longer season in order to make his anticipated profit, the denial of his request for an extension was a blow. According to Juden and Richer, however, Louis-Philippe compensated for it by sending a gift of 3,000 francs, thus ensuring financial success (9).

Why, then, should the notion of "failure" have arisen? Apparently its chief source was the brevity of Mitchell's season in Paris. Although Pillet's appeal for protection against the English competition is, if anything, a testimony to its success, the quick termination of the performances was so reported, sometimes, as to indicate the opposite. For example, the correspondent for the *Sunday Times* (19 January), patriotically indignant over the French government's rebuff of the English actors – and over Mitchell's simultaneous plan to reopen the St. James's Theatre in London with a French company, – called the Parisian "speculation" a "dire failure." As his subsequent explanation makes clear, he meant a financial failure for the "speculator," not a failure in the prestige or the drawing power of the English actors. When even this proved incorrect, the writer admitted (26 January) that Mitchell had actually made a profit, though not as great a one as he deserved. But the average newspaper reader might well remember the phrase "dire failure" without recalling its limitations or noticing its subsequent correction.

One of the chief propagators of the "news" that the performances had failed was Edwin Forrest, America's most eminent tragedian and Macready's chief rival during the latter's recent tour of the United States. Forrest had determined to join the English company at Paris, and some American newspapers had even announced that he would act there; apparently he had attempted no arrangements with Mitchell, however, thinking that an engagement could be worked out after his arrival. Had he been successful, Macready would have faced just such a situation as he had tried to contrive for Helen Faucit with Charlotte Cushman. But Forrest, unaware of the limitation placed on the English performances, did not arrive in Paris until after the twelfth performance. Mitchell could still have included him in the bill for his own benefit night, but he evaded Forrest's repeated attempts to see him.[65] Forrest, chagrined by his failure to carry out his previously announced intentions, evidently explained to friends at home that the English company had performed for twelve nights to "indifferent houses" and that Mitchell, having lost a large sum of money, was compelled to end his venture abruptly. A letter to this effect was published in the New York *Evening Post* (29 January 1845), and Forrest's admirers readily believed that he had lost his opportunity in Paris because his British rival had attracted too little interest to keep the venture going.[66]

For Helen Faucit the visit to Paris was an unqualified success. Not only did she receive continual assurance of her charm and power as an actress, but she was made much of by Parisian society. Mme. Colmache proudly watched her young friend's triumphs, particularly at a soirée of Mme. Ancelot's "where all literary and diplomatic Paris was invited to meet Miss Helen Faucit." Helen looked lovely "with a drooping branch of frosted leaves and flowers in her hair," and she impressed the distinguished guests with her youthful grace: François Guizot exclaimed as he kissed her hand, "*Mais c'est une enfant!*" – astonished that this "gentle girl" could have been the Lady Macbeth everyone was raving about.[67]

Only one regret clouded Helen's memories of her social triumphs in Paris: her failure to respond to the overtures of Rachel, the great tragedienne, who was ready to resume the friendly relations the two had enjoyed in 1841. According to Sir Theodore Martin (81), de Fresne and other friends told Helen that it was impossible for the acquaintance to be renewed, Rachel's conduct having now excluded her from the circles in which they had formerly met. Some of Rachel's genteel friends had indeed dropped her after her affair with Dr. Veron became public knowledge and others after she bore an illegitimate child to Count Walewski, natural son of Napoleon. Some influential people, however, including the elderly Mme. Recamier, never gave up Rachel's friendship, and after a while her affairs would cease to cause excitement. Perhaps if the birth of Rachel's son had not been so recent (only a few weeks before Helen's arrival in Paris), less attention would have been paid to her moral unworthiness.[68] Helen, with her own family background, must have felt herself in a false position; besides, she liked Rachel, and she never stopped admiring her as an actress. Unhappily, as a stranger taking her cue from hosts and sponsors, she dared not follow her own inclinations.

The only real failure of the Paris venture was the failure of her friendship with Macready. At the end of the engagement she wrote: "Either Mr. Macready has grown more selfish and exacting, or I am less capable of bearing with such ungenerous conduct. In either case I am far better away from him."[69] Macready's behaviour had been doubly shocking to the young woman who had long loved and admired him. Having triumphantly proved herself during the past year, she had assumed he would accept her as a worthy co-star; his rejection, though apparently professional, seemed like a personal blow. Perhaps it was personal, in part: the transformation of adoring pupil into presumptuous rival may have struck him as a betrayal.

The breach between the two was perpetuated by their respective friends. From time to time news of Helen's detraction of him would come to Macready – from Hely Bowes, from an anonymous writer, from a provincial actress, from Mrs. Warner.[70] Some of this tale-bearing was self-serving, some merely gossip-mongering; but some was due to the intense loyalty of Helen's friends, who, indignant at any slight she received, publicized and perhaps exaggerated things she had told them in confidence. Her busiest supporter was Theodore Martin, who contrived, indirectly or otherwise, to deepen the rift between her and Macready. As her self-appointed publicity agent, he attacked anyone who seemed to be holding her back, and, as her persistent suitor, he undoubtedly discouraged her "almost affectionate esteem" for any other man.[71]

Yet a certain wistfulness remained. Whatever their respective resentments, Helen Faucit would never break the bond of Macready's influence and her admiration; and, as his diaries show, he would never lose interest in her. There would be a healing of the breach at last, many years in the future, but the two never acted together again.

Chapter 9

The Hellenic Vision

"COVERED WITH laurels of her recent triumph in Paris" – so began a review of Helen Faucit's first performance at the Theatre Royal, Dublin in February 1845. In 1843 she had been virtually ignored here; now, after a succession of victories elsewhere, she would make Dublin capitulate too. This engagement would be among the most brilliant in her career.

Although she opened with Belvidera and included several other familiar characters, the real attraction was Antigone, which she introduced on 22 February and acted on ten of her sixteen nights. Upon returning from Paris, she had visited Covent Garden with John Calcraft to see the Vandenhoffs in an English version of *Antigone* by William Bartholomew, using Mendelssohn's music; they were sufficiently impressed to plan a similar production at Dublin. In the few weeks left before her engagement there, Helen, with the help of classically-educated Theodore Martin, had made an intensive study of Greek tragedy. Now Martin had come to Dublin, to see his Helen in Hellenic guise.[1]

It became her, as if her true nature had been newly discovered. After all, she had found a "kindred spirit" in the Venus de Milo. Images of the Louvre's sculptures, fresh in her mind, would have helped her envision the costume, bearing, and gesture of her Grecian heroine. Overemphasizing the "sculpturesque," however, could tempt her into "*poses plastiques*," like those assumed by acrobatic artists who turned themselves into living statues. Certain of these performers, notably Andrew Ducrow, were genuinely artistic, but an actress of the high poetic drama would not court comparison with them.[2] Helen Faucit was tactful in her use of "classical" poses, making them part of a fluid succession of attitudes and movements.

As at Covent Garden, an "ancient Greek stage" was constructed in the Theatre Royal, Dublin, which fortunately was large enough to accommodate it effectively. According to the *Evening Packet* (25 February), the action took place before the palace, on the proscenium, or elevated stage; there were five splendidly-draped doors, one at each side and three in front, the one in the centre being reserved for the King. The choruses, grouped in front and on each side of the stage, rarely changed position until the final act. Classical costumes were used but no masks.

All the principal Dublin performers – Calcraft as King Creon, Harcourt Bland as his son Haemon (betrothed to Antigone), Miss Chalmers as Antigone's sister Ismene, and H. Cooke as the blind prophet Tiresias – were well received, and the choruses, which had been augmented by specially-hired singers, were described as "most efficient" (*Packet*). But it was Helen Faucit's Antigone, a classical heroine haloed with romance, that translated success into triumph.

The Grecian draperies were particularly becoming to Helen, as one sees in Sir Frederick Burton's watercolour portrait of her as "The Greek Muse": soft and flowing, they suggested the lines of her figure more faithfully than most other costumes could do. Yet this feminine physique was displayed with a statuesque nobility that encouraged lofty thoughts. A full-length sepia drawing of a classically-robed Helen Faucit with bound wrists, also by Burton, shows her wearing a large mantle, which is flung back to reveal a clinging garment moulded to heroically proportioned limbs.[3] It has a more dynamic look than "The Greek Muse," yet there is a monumental quality about it, too, which suggests, just as the more formal portrait does, Helen Faucit's potent combination of physical and spiritual appeal.[4] Burton paid tribute to her special beauty not only in his portraits but also in an eloquent word-picture:

> … Miss Faucit was endowed with pre-eminent physical advantages. Her height; a length of limb surpassing the common proportions of the female form … lent a natural dignity to her gait, and an inborn grace to every movement and gesture … Her head was nobly balanced on a pillar-like neck. Seen in profile, the remarkable expanse between the front of the face and the finely set ear, the length from the chin to the throat, the beautiful outward curve of the full and pliant lip, all called vividly to mind the Greek ideal known to us in sculpture and in designs on the finer Athenian vases.[5]

A youthful diarist who was also captivated by this Antigone gives some additional details:

> When the curtain drew up and showed the classic background and pillars of the Greek Theatre, even then I began to have a sense of mystery and awe … But when she came forth, looking a very Grecian maid, her slow and graceful walk, the classical marbleness of her features, her hair gathered to perfection in the Grecian knot by a fillet, this completed the enchantment. … Her dress, too, the pure white under-robe edged with gold and the crimson-and-gold embroidered

pallium [mantle], which she would disperse [i.e.dispose?] at times in graceful attitudes, one time resting it on the back of her head like a mantilla, another time letting it droop down at her feet![6]

Some of Helen Faucit's poses as Antigone, from Sir Frederick William Burton's sketchbook (by courtesy of the Harvard Theatre Collection, Houghton Library)

In acting, as in costume and demeanour, Helen Faucit reconciled the formal with the dynamic, the classical ideal with human emotion. This harmonious duality, which is evident from reviews of her performances, is strikingly illustrated in a series of small sketches by Burton. They depict her as Antigone in a variety of attitudes – imploring heaven, with arms flung high; agonizing, with dishevelled hair and open mouth (like the tragic mask); stoically submitting to her fate, with head bowed and arms crossed over her breast; proudly and coldly erect, with one arm outstretched as if in denunciation. The sketchbook containing these fascinating pictures (now in the Harvard Theatre Collection) records the artist's attempts to capture with his pencil some of the salient moments in Miss Faucit's performance. Burton tells of his delight in the "plastic beauty of her movements and attitudes, and their marvellous expressiveness," but he also recalls the chagrin he experienced because of her reliance upon momentary impulse rather than predetermined pattern. Having failed to reconstruct some fleeting pose he had wished to perpetuate, he would attend the next performance, hoping to see it again, but that picture would have vanished, giving place to a new one.[7]

Helen Faucit's Antigone emphasized two themes: the fate that inexorably followed her family and the human love that motivated her actions. Thus in her first scene, when she declared her determination to bury her brother's body despite Creon's prohibition, her face reflected "sad thoughts of the destiny that hung upon her race" but her voice was full of "earnest tenderness."[8] When brought before Creon for accusation, she "formed a study for the sculptor" with her arms folded over her bosom and "her classic head drooping," but she soon overcame her sense of helplessness. During the guard's damning story her form was "averted in scorn," and when Creon commanded her to speak, the "instant uplifting of the head, the slow turning of the form, the fixing of that proud calm eye" gave weight to the simple answer, "All he asserts I do confess I did." When Creon angrily demanded why she had disobeyed his decree, she "looked all the queen" as she declared with impressive dignity, "Because thy mandate was opposed to Jove's ..." Then, softened by the thought of her brother, she awaited her sentence with a resigned smile.[9] Most memorable, however, was Antigone's last scene, when Creon had condemned her to be walled up, alive, in a cave. The love that had sustained her before was now "absorbed in the contemplation" of her own approaching doom. Antigone's long lament beginning "Oh, dreadful tomb! – oh, dreary bridal bed!" was spoken as if in recitative, accompanied by the orchestra. Here the rich, deep tones of Helen Faucit's voice and its "heart-stirring quality of sincerity" produced a thrilling effect.[10] Antigone's human emotions, though eloquently depicted, were somewhat formalized in expression by the musical chant and statuesque attitudes; and her sufferings as an individual, though poignantly felt, were kept in perspective, as part of a larger fate.

"The Greek Muse" (Helen Faucit as Antigone), by Sir Frederick William Burton (by courtesy of the Scottish National Portrait Gallery)

Viewers marvelled at Helen Faucit's ability to project the Greek ideal. Frederick Burton thought that, despite her dependence on Bartholomew's feeble version, she had divined the essence of Sophocles' tragedy "intuitively." Theodore Martin declared that her manner of speaking the words redeemed any loss the "sublime thought" had suffered in translation, and he rejoiced in her "opening of a new world, or more truly … the vivifying of a dead but familiar one." More than fifty years later Percy Fitzgerald wrote: "That classical vision haunted my boyish dreams for weeks, and does still … It seemed some supernatural figure lent temporarily to this base earth. Never since have I understood in the same way the solemnity of the Greek play."[11]

This Antigone had an astonishing impact upon the intellectual and cultural life of Dublin. An unprecedented tribute was paid to Helen Faucit by a group of thirty-five distinguished men, mostly members of the Royal Irish Academy and the Society of Ancient Art. In a formal visit to her they presented a complimentary address and a large golden fibula, or brooch, enhanced with emeralds, designed by Frederick Burton. The address declared that her "noble representation of Antigone" had "greatly advanced" the study of classical literature and art in Dublin "by creating a love and admiration of the beauty and grandeur of ancient Greece."[12]

Hardly less complimentary in its way was the response to Helen Faucit's Antigone by the "Young Ireland" coterie who published *The Nation.* Though they had sneered at Dublin's scholars as dull and "puritanical," they now congratulated them for rising out of their stupefied condition long enough to recognize Helen Faucit's genius. *The Nation,* founded in 1841 by a group of young men who believed that the Irish people "had not a sufficient understanding of their 'nationhood,'" put much emphasis upon the "ancient glories of the race" and the deplorable state of culture under English domination. Not simply an organ of propaganda, the journal included foreign news, court and society news, a "poet's corner," and so on,[13] but it had hitherto ignored the theatre. Now, in a glowing article, "Miss Faucit's Antigone" (1 March: 345), one of its writers – evidently the flamboyant "Speranza," Jane Francesca Elgee[14] – explained why:

> We habitually disregard the Dublin Theatres, not because we think little of the teaching and enjoyment of the drama, but because it is here so miserable. Now, however, we see the exception – a drama breathing of the virtue and genius of Greece, represented by one whose grandeur, tenderness, and consummate grace fit her to have received the applause of Athens.

After a eulogistic review Speranza concluded wistfully, "We wish but one change in Miss FAUCIT – we wish her an Irishwoman." Once its silence had been broken, *The Nation* paid tribute to Helen Faucit's Pauline, Rosalind, and other characters during this and subsequent engagements.

During this visit Helen broadened and deepened her friendships in Dublin. She became especially intimate with the family of Dr. William Stokes, an eminent physician with many scholarly and cultural interests, who became in 1845 Regius Professor of Medicine at the University of Dublin.[15] They had previously met at Mrs. Hutton's, but a closer relationship began with a letter she brought from Archibald Alison of Glasgow. No recommendation could have been more effective: Mrs. Stokes was from Glasgow originally, and Dr. Stokes was a close friend of Alison's brother, under whom he had studied medicine at the University of Edinburgh. From now on Helen was like a member of the family. Two of the children later wrote of her place in their home. As Sir

William Stokes recalled, she "found herself … in her natural atmosphere" with them, "and her genius warmed and expanded among those who grew to love her there." Under her influence Dr. Stokes further developed his ideas about dramatic poetry, which had been a "passion" since boyhood. And, as Margaret Stokes said, her father, a student of human nature in his own profession, "recognised in her [its] true painter."[16] He, in turn, had a strong influence on Helen. Though only ten years her senior, he took a fatherly interest in her, understanding her physical and nervous problems; but his sympathy, balanced by wit, was bracingly expressed – a talk with him was, as Helen said, "like a walk on the Downs."[17]

Dr. William Wilde, left, and Dr. William Stokes, right, sketch from a photograph made in the 1850s by Lord Fitzgibbon, (from T. G. Wilson's *Victorian Doctor*)

During Helen Faucit's early triumphs in Dublin the Stokes family were among her most ardent fans. Night after night she would look out from the stage and see Dr. and Mrs. Stokes with "half a box full of children,"[18] including fifteen-year-old Whitley and twelve-year-old Margaret, with whom she would have ties in later years. Every Saturday the Stokeses kept an "open evening" at their spacious home on fashionable Merrion Square. Since Dr. Stokes was a classical scholar and a patron of the arts, the cultural elite of Dublin were usually present, and often there would be distinguished foreign visitors as well.[19] At such gatherings Helen was the centre of interest for several young men. Her admirer from earlier visits to Dublin, Dr. William Wilde, would certainly have been present, for he was a former student and close friend of Dr. Stokes. Another frequent visitor was the young artist Frederick Burton, who was among Dr. Stokes's favourite protégés – his "Grecian Muse" was first owned by Stokes.[20] According to a biographer of Wilde, he and Burton had been good friends until now but they came to the parting of the ways over Helen Faucit: both had fallen in love with her.[21] Burton was the more prepossessing by far: unlike Wilde, he was extraordinarily handsome, with his brown, copper-tinged hair, grey-blue eyes, and aristocratic features; his charm of manner contrasted favourably with his rival's restless, erratic personality; and he was certainly superior in personal morals.[22] On the other hand, there was something fascinating about the homely, monkeylike Wilde. (A picture of him, in a convivial pose with Dr. Stokes, gives some hint of his appeal: he has the look, half quizzical, half sensual, of a partially-civilized faun.)[23] A third – and most persistent – competitor for Helen's attention, Theodore Martin, also frequented the Stokes home during her 1845 engagement.[24]

Sir Frederick William Burton, by George F. Mulvany
(by courtesy of the National Gallery of Ireland)

Dr. Wilde reportedly proposed marriage to Helen but was refused.[25] Apparently the gossip-mongers got wind of this incident but thought the proposal had been accepted, for the *Theatrical Journal* (30 January 1847: 38) carried the news that Miss Faucit would soon marry "an eminent physician in Dublin." It is interesting that Wilde did not marry until December 1851, several months after Helen's wedding to Theodore Martin – and that his bride was "Speranza," the young woman who had eulogized Helen Faucit in *The Nation*. As for Frederick Burton, he never married. A few months after Helen's marriage he left Ireland for a seven-year stay in Germany; later, living in London, he was a valued friend of both Martins. In the spring of 1845, however, when all Dublin was at Helen's feet, no one, not even the dazzling (and bedazzled) young woman herself, knew which, if any, of her suitors would be successful.

Going from Dublin to Edinburgh that year was like making another stage in a royal progress. News of Helen Faucit's spectacular success as Antigone had preceded her, with Theodore Martin as an enthusiastic witness. The elegant fibula, too, bore its mute testimony to her honours. At an evening party given by Sir William Allan it was the centre of fun as well as admiration: when several people expressed curiosity about its Greek inscription (meaning "To Helen, who captured the spirit of Antigone, in commemoration"), Theodore Martin gravely challenged William Aytoun to demonstrate his classical scholarship, and Aytoun just as gravely declined to translate such words in the presence of ladies.[26] Queen Helen had acquired a court jester.

During her eighteen-night engagement at the Theatre Royal, Edinburgh Helen Faucit appeared in twelve characters, most of which were now familiar here. A notable exception was Beatrice, which she had never before acted as a star. It proved a valuable addition to the few comic roles in her repertory[27]. According to the *Caledonian Mercury* (21 April), her engagement was unusually brilliant. On the final night, when she acted Juliet for her benefit, the house was "crammed" and people had to be turned away.

The Glasgow engagement that followed was virtually a repetition of the Edinburgh one except for the inferior quality of the supporting actors. On Helen Faucit's last night, though her Juliet was wildly applauded, the play had its farcical moments: Tybalt refused to die in the duel and Romeo finally had to chase him from the stage.[28] The most noteworthy criticism, because of its novelty, was published in the *Glasgow Dramatic Review* (30 April 1845: 125-26). The writer declared that Helen Faucit was "a successful actress, rather than an original one," that her fame was mostly provincial, that she had not gained a reputation in a single character equal to that of Miss O'Neill or Miss F. H. Kelly (a low blow!), and that she was not so exciting as Charlotte Cushman. How, then, could one account for the adulation heaped on her by the presses of Edinburgh, Glasgow, and Dublin? the portraits of her for sale in the print-shops? the number of would-be poets racking their brains for sonnets in her praise? The secret lay in her "peculiar power of pleasing":

> … few have been able to render a character more interesting to an audience … For much of this … she is indebted to her fine voice, the tones of which fall so mellifluously on the ear, that one could listen for hours, and when she ceases to speak, we feel an almost irresistible wish to hear her again. Her person is not strictly beautiful, nor are her attitudes particularly graceful, yet these seem to heighten, rather than diminish, the effect of her acting … [She is] the most charming actress on the stage.

In denying Helen Faucit's originality and gracefulness this critic was certainly swimming against the tide, but for anyone who has read the hundreds of hyperbolic tributes that gushed from the presses at the height of her popularity, any attempt at judicious criticism is a welcome relief. Yet even this reviewer, while taking away from her with one hand, gave generously with the other. Having declined to deify her like his colleagues, he went on to praise in the highest terms her Juliet and, in later articles, her Beatrice, Mrs. Haller, and other characters. Of Mrs. Haller, for instance, he wrote:

> Miss Faucit made more of the character than we have ever seen. In her penitence she was superior to her author. The display of emotion in the last scene was absolutely painful. So powerful was the interest felt by the audience, that for many minutes breathing seemed to be suspended; and, with the exception of her own sweet voice, half stifled by sobs, the theatre was as silent as the city of the dead. (7 May: 133)

At this time Helen's friendship with the Alisons ripened into greater intimacy. She visited them at Possil House "for several days together" and accepted an invitation to join them later for a summer holiday.[29]

Meanwhile, in late May and early June, she had short engagements in Perth, Dundee, and Aberdeen. The theatre at Perth was built on the foundation of the old Blackfriars Monastery, which had been levelled by zealots after John Knox preached his fiery sermon against idolatry in that city. It held only five hundred people, but theatrical interest had so declined that even this many were hard to attract. While Helen Faucit was there, however, there were always crowded houses. According to Robb Lawson, chronicler of the Scottish stage, she was regarded as the "greatest dramatic female star that ever walked the boards of Perth."[30] At Dundee, where she acted at the Theatre Royal, Castle-Street, her patience was tried by the inferior actors in Adam's company (Barry Sullivan and Mrs. Ryder excepted), who also accompanied her to Aberdeen. Although Helen had never visited Aberdeen before, she would have heard frequently about Marischal College (now a part of Aberdeen University): Archibald Alison had recently been installed as its Rector, having defeated Thomas Babington Macaulay for this honorary post, and Theodore Martin's close friend John

Stuart Blackie was a member of the faculty. The strongly literary review of her performances in the *Aberdeen Herald* (14 June) may well have been written by someone at the college. The description of her final scene as Belvidera reflects the increasingly strong pictorial element in her acting:

> There are looks sometimes ... that engrave themselves upon memory forever. Hers was one of these, so fixed and frozen in its vacant lunacy, by the intensity of unsufferable anguish, that not even the smiles of delusive joy could relax it. It would have almost made a painter's fame to have transferred it exactly to the canvas.

On her return to Glasgow in mid-June Helen was met by Archibald Alison, who escorted her by steamboat to his family's summer retreat on the Isle of Arran. Later he would look back on her two weeks there as a time of idyllic enchantment. She enthralled his family with readings from Milton, Shakespeare, Sophocles, and Schiller; she was a lively participant in conversation-filled walks to picturesque spots; she inspired him with the nobility of her conceptions, the loftiness of her ambition (he compared her to Schiller's Joan of Arc), but she also charmed him with her "Female fascination, perhaps not unmixed with coquetry." Their most ambitious excursion was the climbing of Goatfell, a rocky mountain in the northern part of the island. This was no undertaking for the fainthearted – half a mile from the summit one had to clamber over "huge masses of loose granite, on the top of a narrow ridge, between deep ravines" – but Helen, despite her delicate health, was an energetic sportswoman. The magnificent prospect from the top of Goatfell was worth the climb: the ocean spread out like a girdle below, and the view opened out for miles in every direction, with the Hebrides visible far to the west, the Highland mountains to the north, and the faint outline of the Giant's Causeway in Ireland to the southwest.

During their talks "on almost every imaginable subject of poetry, the drama, and the fine arts," the historian was astonished to find in this young, superficially-educated woman such acute understanding of artistic principles, such intelligent appreciation of the world's great dramas. Some of her suggestions so inspired him that he later worked them out in his essays.[31]

With her holiday over, Helen travelled to Carlisle for a three-night engagement (2-4 July) at the oddly-constructed, cramped little Theatre Royal there. Macready's father had built it some thirty years earlier with the purpose of getting "the greatest number within the smallest space." There was no greenroom – the actors used a lane alongside the theatre for this purpose – and the "star dressing room" was a cubbyhole five feet by six.[32] The manager, John Daly, having enjoyed the first profitable season in his four years, now catered to the new interest by bringing "the most Popular and celebrated Actress of the Age" to Carlisle for Race Week.[33] Supported by Mun Noble Paumier, Helen Faucit was so successful that the *Carlisle Journal* (12 July) suggested additional "experiments" of this kind.

After another brief engagement, at the comparatively palatial Theatre Royal, Newcastle-upon-Tyne, Helen made her initial visit to Manchester. At first sight the city, girdled with cotton mills, dye-works, machine shops, and foundries, was not prepossessing. Yet it was impressive in its way. "Factories, seven stories in height, rear their lofty fronts along the banks of the Irwell, and along the borders of the canals, which penetrating into the town, form an interior navigation": so, in effect, wrote a French observer, Léon Fauchet, just a year earlier. Despite its great volume of commerce and industry, Manchester had not the bustle of London or Glasgow. During most of the day it was seemingly deserted, and its prevailing sound was "the breathing of the vast machines"; only at certain hours did the city come alive, its streets filling suddenly with thousands of workers as they changed shifts. One of Fauchet's passages sounds much like Dickens's description of Coketown in *Hard Times*: "Amid the fogs which exhale from this marshy district, and the clouds of smoke vomited forth from the numberless chimneys, Labour presents a mysterious activity, somewhat akin to the subterranean action of a volcano."[34]

The volcano had erupted several times already, for Manchester was a centre of working-class agitation, and it had provided many enthusiastic supporters for the Chartist Movement, with its attempts to secure universal male suffrage. Manchester was also a centre for free-trade ideas, held by the lords of industry as well as by "intelligent workingmen," for large amounts of raw cotton were imported for the spinning mills and a regular supply of agricultural products was needed to feed the rapidly-expanding population. The Anti-Corn-Law League had its headquarters here.[35]

Another side to Manchester life could be seen in institutions for cultural activities and self-improvement: literary societies for the elite, "people's parks" for the working classes, the Royal Institution where lectures were held. The annual Manchester Festival included concerts, plays, and masquerade balls.[36] And there was the theatre. Fauchet complained that the Manchester theatre did "nothing to purify and elevate" the taste of the people,[37] but the performances here were much like those in Liverpool, Birmingham, and other British cities – something for every taste. A casual visitor saw only the tip of Manchester's cultural and social life, however. As in Edinburgh and Dublin, much of it was found only in private homes, where there was the same kind of intellectual discussion and witty banter that Helen had enjoyed at the homes of Sir William Allan and Dr. and Mrs. Stokes.[38]

Although Helen's initiation into the inner circle occurred later in Manchester than in other major cities, in time she would find many friends among the elite here. As an actress she would have strong supporters in all classes. Manchester, in fact, would play a prominent role in her later career.

Her first engagement here was at the Queen's Theatre, Spring Gardens, where she acted for twelve nights in Juliet, Pauline, Lady Mabel, Julia, Mrs.

Haller, Belvidera, and Rosalind. As always, she impressed critics with her feminine charm and even, as some insisted, with her ideal embodiment of femininity itself. Edouard Thierry's "*Elle est femme*" found an English echo in the *Manchester Times*, whose reviewer declared that her nature was "that of WOMAN" and in "every embodiment she seem[ed] to raise the veil from a shrined feeling in her individual heart."[39]

The play that evoked the most interesting response during Helen's early visits to Manchester was *The Patrician's Daughter*. Not that it was her most successful vehicle here, but that Manchester was the city in which it was best liked. Here something more than Mabel's sufferings attracted sympathy: Mordaunt's egalitarian principles were appreciated, even if his cruelty to Mabel was deplored. Helen Faucit would bring the play back for her second and third engagements, each time to large audiences and enthusiastic reviews (*Manchester Guardian*, 6 May 1846 and 8 May 1847).

Her leading man at the Queen's Theatre was Gustavus Vaughan Brooke, a gifted actor with whom she would be paired on a number of future occasions. He was a handsome blond giant with a beautiful voice, a magnetic personality, and the ability to express emotions with apparent spontaneity; yet he was an uneven performer because of indolence, carelessness, and occasional dissipation. One of Helen Faucit's strongest criticisms of him was his refusal to think through his characters; he would eagerly accept any suggestion she made but would not bother to work things out for himself. Although Brooke had been acting for twelve years, since his debut at age fourteen, he was yet to experience the greatest successes – and failures – of his erratic career.[40]

Helen's first Manchester visit would be remembered later as the last time she saw her "darling Harry." Harriet and Humphrey Bland, determined to try their fortunes in America, had accepted engagements at the Park Theatre in New York, to begin on 30 August. On their way to Liverpool, from which they would sail, they stopped at Manchester to say goodbye. Harriet spent the evening in her sister's dressing room so that the two could visit during Helen's offstage moments. They laughed and cried together, and, since Helen was acting Juliet that night, they recalled the September evening in 1833 when she had first attempted this role.[41] In parting next morning they meant only *au revoir*, but, as things turned out, it was farewell indeed.

After leaving Manchester Helen acted Pauline in the resort town of Buxton one night to the Claude of her brother John, who had taken the theatre there for a short summer season; then she went on to Sheffield, where she and Brooke repeated some of their Manchester roles in a five-night engagement. At last, after six months in the provinces, she was able to return to London, the city she always regarded as home.

Sadly, she no longer had a theatrical home there. The Theatres Regulation Act of 1843 had taken away the exclusive rights of the patent houses, and these two giants were no longer even token representatives of the "national" drama. Covent Garden would soon be transformed into an opera house; Drury Lane under Bunn was mostly that already. Although all the numerous London theatres were now free to produce the best available plays, the dramatic renaissance that reformers had hoped for had not taken place. For consistently fine productions one had to go out to Sadler's Wells Theatre in Islington, where for the past year Samuel Phelps and Mrs. Warner had been astonishingly successful in gripping their working-class audiences with such plays as *Macbeth* and *The Fatal Dowry*.[42] But of course there was no place for Helen Faucit with Phelps and Warner, both of whom cordially disliked her. The best she could hope for was an occasional engagement as a star at one of the other houses.

The situation was the same for Macready. He had been considering an offer from Maddox at the Princess's Theatre when he received feelers from Webster at the Haymarket, a theatre he would have preferred despite the weakening of old distinctions. Replying, via John Forster, to Webster's query about fellow players, Macready suggested Charlotte Cushman and remarked pointedly that he did not wish to "*over-weight* the theatre" with prominent actors. Later he asked Forster not to give his name "*officially* to Mr. Webster as recommending Miss Cushman, which might seem unkind to Helen Faucit," but clearly he wanted no repetition of the Parisian situation. As it turned out, Macready engaged with Maddox, after all, because of his more advantageous terms.[43]

When Webster found this out, he determined to "take the wind out of Mac's sails." Apparently he had already been in touch with Helen Faucit, hoping to pair her and Macready; now he invited James Anderson to act with her. Anderson had to cancel one of his provincial engagements (for a "pecuniary consideration") but he was willing to do so if he were given equal billing with Helen Faucit. She seems to have fallen in eagerly with Webster's plan.[44] Still smarting from Macready's attitude in Paris, she was on her mettle.

Macready had been playing in London for a week when Helen Faucit and James Anderson began their Haymarket engagement on 20 October. *The Lady of Lyons*, their opening play, was still, as the *Times* noted (21 October), "as great a favourite as ever"; people retained their interest in the story, still shed tears and applauded in all the right places. The *Theatrical Journal* declared that Bulwer had "done more for the stage in this one play than the whole catalogue of most of our bygone dramatists."[45] Attacks on the play's subject matter had faded by now – except in one instance. Never, before or since, was there such a diatribe against *The Lady of Lyons* as appeared in the *Observer* on 26 October 1845. The play is a "garnished mass of immorality," fumed the critic; it is composed of "fetid, pestiferous, mental trash" which never should have been permitted to "pollute the stage with its seductive vices"; Claude has the "heart … as well as the horny skin of a peasant," and Pauline is a spineless creature who, spaniel-like, "licks the hand that has smote her." Yet, despite all this, he was so enthralled by Helen Faucit's performance that he wrote the most detailed analysis it ever received.

When the first-night curtain drew up and discovered a "handsome" Pauline reclining elegantly on a sofa, the audience broke into spontaneous applause, which continued for some time. They were welcoming back an old favourite whom they had not seen (except in a single benefit performance) for more than two years. Anderson, who had been absent from London for the same period, was also cordially received. Miss Faucit's performance was applauded throughout, and at the end, after repeated calls, she was led onstage by Farren to be rewarded with renewed applause, handkerchief-waving, and a shower of bouquets.[46] It was a happy homecoming for her. Anderson's fine voice, "gallant bearing," ardour, and "manly pathos" won him applause in the first three acts, but in the fourth act, for some reason, he broke into a furious style of ranting that caused some laughter and even a little hissing. He was given a curtain call at the end, however, and critics agreed that he would make an excellent Claude if he would moderate his excesses and give up his imitations of Macready.[47]

Helen Faucit's portrayal of Pauline was enthusiastically praised; the only complaints worth noting concerned some distracting attempts at realistic speaking – unduly long pauses and an occasional sinking of the voice to inaudibility, as if with emotion.[48] Her long absence from London had raised questions about possible changes in style. Critics disagreed about this, one saying that she displayed the same merits as before but "excelled her former efforts" (*Morning Chronicle* 21 October), another declaring that, with Macready's dominating influence removed, "such is the change in style that, with the same person, she is another actress" (*Athenaeum* 25 October). Even if the *Athenaeum* overstated its case, Helen Faucit might well have shown signs of a growing tendency "to think, to feel, to act for herself." Macready, of course, deplored any departure from his methods. After watching two acts of *The Lady of Lyons* he decided that Anderson had "deteriorated" but that Helen Faucit had "in some respects improved, in some fallen off" (*Diaries* II: 310).

The Faucit-Anderson engagement ran for fourteen nights, from 20 October to 18 November (three nights a week, plus a benefit for each of the stars). There was so much demand for *The Lady of Lyons* that it was acted on ten of the nights, thus severely limiting the number of other plays. *The Hunchback* was given twice, *The Stranger* once, and *As You Like It* once. The most consistently full and interesting reviews of Helen Faucit's performances were those in the *Observer*. They were written, obviously, by someone of strong Tory principles, unyielding notions about morality in women, and a literary approach to Shakespeare[49] – decidedly not a journalist. Helen Faucit had so impressed him as the Ideal Woman that he found her Mrs. Haller unconvincing: he could not believe for one moment, however she might groan and swoon in confessing her guilt, that this woman could ever have been an unfaithful wife. Her Julia and Rosalind, however, struck him as "masterpieces": in Julia, she spoke "Do it! …" magnificently, looking like "a Pythoness of yore"; in Rosalind, she gave "breadth and intensity" to the "tender" and "impassioned" parts and unmistakable "sharpness" to the "salient points" of wit, veiling any "licentiousness" with a "modest bearing."[50] Whatever this critic's identity, he was among those who responded most ardently to the poetic element in Helen Faucit's acting.

The Haymarket rivals did not "take the wind out of *Mac's* sails": Macready acted on eighteen nights, repeatedly appearing in just three characters – Hamlet, Othello, and Lear – and the Princess's Theatre was continually crowded with Shakespeare-starved Londoners, eager to see the finest tragedian of his age.[51] The *Spectator* remarked superciliously that the "two asteroids" did not "counterbalance the preponderating force of the greater planet." One might add that Bulwer did not eclipse Shakespeare. As a deliberate counter-attraction to Macready, Helen Faucit and James Anderson did not deserve to succeed; but, as attractions in their own right, they (especially she) were a decided success.

Helen Faucit left for the North immediately after concluding her Haymarket engagement, for she was to open in Edinburgh the following Monday (24 November). On the way she paused in Derby to act Mrs. Haller on one night for her brother John. (He had been managing the Nottingham and Derby theatres since the previous year.) Her appearances in Edinburgh were limited to nine, but she arranged to return there following an engagement in Glasgow, at which time a long-awaited production of *Antigone* would be ready. The novelty was well timed, for Charlotte Cushman, the dynamic American actress, had just finished her first Edinburgh visit. She had been electrifying her audiences with her forceful Lady Macbeth and her weird, witch-like Meg Merrilies in another "Scottish play." In Glasgow, too, Miss Cushman was triumphant. When Helen Faucit appeared in that city, on the heels of her new rival, the critic for the *Glasgow Dramatic Review* wrote an interesting comparison of the two actresses, each of whom he considered admirable in her way: Miss Faucit was a "seducer," he thought; Miss Cushman, a "conquerer."[52] Theodore Martin must have gnashed his teeth. During the following year he would help to spread a scandalous rumour about Miss Cushman's sister Susan, who travelled with her. Although the originator, apparently, was Edwin Forrest, Martin's "warning" to the Cushmans' Edinburgh friends sounds like an attempt to discredit Helen's only powerful rival.[53]

Antigone, which was performed in Edinburgh for seven nights in late December, was a success, but probably not the overwhelming one recollected by John Coleman: "The new Antigone set all hearts on fire, and modern Athens well-nigh went mad over her."[54] Coleman's memory was coloured by his own emotions: that season, as a young actor in Edinburgh, he had acted for the first time with Helen Faucit, whom he had long adored from afar. A report opposite to his was given in the *Caledonian Mercury* (25 December): namely, that, despite its "imposing spectacle," *Antigone* seemed "too remote" to move the audience to anything more than "cold studious gravity," and even Helen Faucit could not "make bricks out of straw." But this account, like Coleman's, must be taken with a grain of salt: when a possible production of *Antigone* had first been discussed in Edinburgh, the *Mercury* critic had warned that it would be caviar to the general (3 April 1845); perhaps he now wished to justify his prophecy.

Whatever coldness *Antigone* may have encountered in some quarters, Helen Faucit's performance inspired two of the most extravagant passages of praise ever written: one by the enraptured Coleman, the other by Thomas De Quincey. As Antigone, Coleman wrote, Miss Faucit was a "goddess":

> Beauty of face and form were combined with those rarer gifts – beauty of mind and purity of soul … "More than common tall," and perfectly balanced from head to heel, the short waist and long and superbly molded lower limbs which go with the Grecian type of beauty, harmonised perfectly with the sloping and majestic shoulders, the virginal bust, and the arms lost to the Venus of Milo. Then her face was the face of Artemis herself, while her eyes of Aphrodisian grey varied in colour and expression with every mood as they glittered through their long dark lashes. Her voice, with its infinite varieties of tremulous minors and full flushed resonant crescendoes, was "an alarm to love!"[55]

De Quincey, though he was less than delighted with the Caledonian version of the ancient tragedy, was in ecstasies over its heroine:

> Then, suddenly, – oh, heavens! what a revelation of beauty! – forth stepped, walking in brightness, the most faultless of Grecian marbles … What perfection of Athenian sculpture! the noble figure, the lovely arms, the fluent drapery! What an unveiling of the ideal statuesque!

Despite her husky voice (she had a cold), Helen's Antigone was, for him, the "redeeming jewel of the performance." His concluding tribute is a fine bit of hyperbole: "To see *Helen*, Helen of Greece, was the chief prayer of Marlowe's Dr. Faustus; the chief gift which he exacted from the fiend. To see Helen of Greece? Dr. Faustus, we *have* seen her …"[56]

Helen Faucit's engagements in Edinburgh and Glasgow were as successful as ever, despite the excitement aroused by Charlotte Cushman's recent visits. In both cities there were the usual crowded houses, the usual storms of applause and rains of flowers, the usual superlative praise in the journals.[57] Theodore Martin need not have worried: no actress, however admired, would ever be more beloved in Scotland than Helen Faucit.

Martin's concern for himself was better justified. His hopeless devotion had become a joke among the actors in Edinburgh. Coleman recalls hearing Edmund Glover, who was friendly with the young lawyer, express the opinion that Miss Faucit never gave him a thought. But Miss Cleaver, who played parts like Lady Capulet and Widow Melnotte, was not so sure. "Bide a wee, Mr. Glover," she admonished him, smiling benignly; "bide a wee."[58] It was patience and persistence, finally, that won the day.

Sometimes, though, it was hard to be patient. When his frustration needed an outlet, Theodore would seek out John Brown, a singularly gentle, sympathetic young physician whom he had known intimately for years. The two friends would often go for a walk, "round and round the Calton Hill," while poor Theodore "poured out" his "fervour and utter love."[59]

Helen may have said something during her Christmas visit of 1845 that made Theodore believe she would marry him, after all, for on 8 January 1846 Dr. John Brown wrote to a cousin of his, "Miss H. Faucit is to be married to Theodore Martin in June for certain."[60] Actually the courtship would have to go on for five more years. Did Helen, under the pressure of Theodore's ardour, give a half-promise which she thought better of later? She obviously encouraged his friendship, and she corresponded with him regularly – he was one person who never tired of hearing about her thoughts and emotions, her trials and her triumphs. She was probably fond of him. But she could not bring herself to marry him. Not yet.

Only a grand passion could have persuaded Helen to change her way of life at this time, and she never found another Macready. Unlike most "unprotected" women of that period, she did not need to marry for practical reasons. She loved acting for itself as well as for its very substantial rewards; having spent years in developing her talent, she found her greatest satisfaction in exercising it well. Theodore might protest that she need not give up her art, but to marry anyone except an actor would inevitably limit her professional life. Another consideration must have influenced her, if only subconsciously. Despite her winsome air of demure coquetry, she had a determined spirit and, as she had recently discovered, a love of independence. No longer subject to the dictates of a theatrical manager, why should she submit to management of another kind?

Chapter 10

Harvest Time

IN 1845 Helen Faucit filled at least 16 engagements and acted on at least 131 nights. This unusually demanding year was also unusually significant: it set the seal on her high reputation, and it determined the final stage in the development of her acting style. The combined influences from classical sculpture, *Antigone*, and conversations with Archibald Alison resulted in an increasingly strong inspiration from the fine arts. Similar experiences in 1846 confirmed her in this tendency. In the next year or two she perfected her individual style by using artistic techniques more purposefully and by amplifying her already-remarkable revelations of a character's inner life through "silent acting." Afterwards there would be little change except for further refinements.

Some early admirers wished Helen Faucit had been content with less elaboration. Thus a reviewer for the *Liverpool Albion* (20 April 1846) said that her "bursts of startling passion" were introduced "more discreetly" now and her portrayals were "more substantial," "finish[ed]" and "consisten[t]," yet he had admired her too much "in the exuberance of a genius that scarcely needed culture" to believe that the change was for the better. Later critics, too, while appreciating her "exquisite" artistry, would sometimes wish for more simplicity, less subtlety. At its best, though, her mature style delicately balanced spontaneity and artifice.

Although 1845 was a landmark year for Helen Faucit, most of its accomplishments grew naturally out of the preceding ones. Except for her Parisian performances the broad pattern of her career was much the same throughout her period of full-time starring, from mid-June 1843 until late August 1851. Her steps toward the professional heights have already been closely followed; similar footprints lead across a high plateau, her remaining five and a half years before marriage. Easily recognised by now, the individual steps are less important than the terrain they cover. What follows is a mosaic of the British theatrical world at mid-century as experienced by a major Victorian actress.

Engagements

An overview of Helen Faucit's engagements for her whole period of full-time starring shows that an average year was at least as demanding as an average London season under Macready's management. Counting only fully documented performances, the minimum annual average of acting nights is 103+ for the seven complete years, 1844-50 (or 108 for the eight years, 1843-51, if the partial years are amalgamated). Only 1847 and 1849 show significantly fewer nights than Helen Faucit's last Drury Lane season (illness and a recuperative vacation being responsible, respectively), and these are balanced by three unusually busy years – 1845, 1846, and 1848.

In 1846-51 the staples of her career were engagements with major provincial theatres where she had already won most acclaim (Dublin, Glasgow, Edinburgh, Liverpool, Manchester). These were supplemented by less frequent engagements with other previously-visited theatres (Brighton, Bristol, Bath, Newcastle, Cork, Dundee, Perth, Aberdeen) and by occasional ones at a number of new places. She sometimes acted for her brother John, especially at Nottingham, where he and his family had their longest, most important association, but also at Derby, Chesterfield, Leicester, and Sheffield. Places that she tried once or twice included Exeter, Plymouth, Cambridge, York, Hull, Norwich, North Shields, Yarmouth, and Greenock. She also returned to London for several benefits and three starring engagements – at the Haymarket (15 nights in 1847) and the Olympic (29 nights in 1850, 12 in 1851).

If the emotional strain was less in her starring years than in her London period, the physical strain was much greater. Besides the hardships of travel there were the discomforts of many theatrical lodgings. A dresser who travelled with her recalled later "how your poor brain used to throb when you returned home, & the sleepless nights you had – and the unkind noisy people in some houses, with no consideration or feeling … and the bumpy beds & very hard pillows…"[1]

Earnings

Although it is impossible to compute Helen Faucit's earnings for an average year of stardom, there are isolated hints of her financial success. At Newcastle, for example, two engagements in her first starring season (1843-44) included 16 performances (spread over 22 days), for which she received 262 pounds, 17 shillings, averaging more than 16 pounds per night; thus she was compensated for her time in Newcastle at more than 86 pounds per week. The figures are nothing like as high as the 400 pounds Macready would receive in 1845 for 8 nights at the same theatre, but much higher than Helen Faucit's previous earnings in London. Although Newcastle was not an important centre for her, she was the best paid of the six stars engaged there that season, earning four times as much as her nearest competitor.[2] With her increasing renown she undoubtedly increased her demands. In cities like Edinburgh, Glasgow, and Dublin her earnings were much higher. According to theatrical gossip, she made 700 pounds during a 10-night engagement in Glasgow in 1847. Notoriously unreliable as such rumours are, this one may have been true.[3] Helen Faucit's most successful series of performances comprised her double engagement at the Theatre Royal, Dublin in 1846, when she acted on 41 nights between 24 October and 23 December. Unfortunately a significant portion of her earnings was "on paper": according to a report in the *Theatrical Journal* (29 May 1847: 389), when Calcraft became insolvent in the spring of 1847 he still owed Helen Faucit 500 pounds – more, by far, than any other actor. Losses on such a scale must have been rare, however.

Starring actors often stipulated a particular fraction of the profits, or even the gross receipts.[4] According to the *Theatrical Times*, Miss Faucit split all the profits equally with the manager during the lucrative Glasgow engagement of 1847 – a liberal arrangement when applied to the entire engagement, not just the benefit. In 1848 she accepted the following terms from J. V. Davenport: "thirds & half at Norwich for one week [that is, one-third each night except her benefit, one-half that night] … three nights the week following in Yarmouth, sharing the house [i.e. gross receipts] – a clear half on each night and one night in Cambridge the same week, terms a clear third."[5] For a popular star, such an arrangement was more profitable than a flat salary.

Helen Faucit's highest salary during her London period was 30 pounds a week; in the provinces she made, in her best engagements, considerably more in a single night. Her expenses were much higher, of course: in addition to travel and lodgings for herself, she had to pay these, plus wages, for a maid or dresser who accompanied her. (Starring actors might, if they wished, rely on the services of a local dresser, but since women rarely travelled alone, an unmarried female star took her own.) Even so, provincial starring was far more lucrative than the usual London engagement. Hence Helen's refusal of offers in London during the busiest provincial season: as she wrote to Alfred Bunn (probably in 1847), "From Christmas to the end of April is my harvest time in the provinces, and to give up this I must have such an equivalent as I fear would be beyond your power to meet."[6] Until after her marriage she always preserved that "harvest time" for provincial engagements. In other periods she would accept comparatively modest salaries for the sake of acting in London. She drew the line, however, at insulting offers like one made by Bunn in 1848. Under fire for neglecting legitimate drama at Drury Lane, he proposed engagements of "one or two months" to Helen Faucit, Louisa Nisbett, and James Anderson, offering

25 pounds a week to each actress and 20 to Anderson. All turned him down. In an indignant letter to the *Morning Post* (3 October) Bunn declared that the salaries he had offered were as much as Miss O'Neill, Mrs. Jordan, and Edmund Kean had received in their prime, yet the modern actors had unreasonably demanded more – Helen Faucit had insisted on 15 pounds a night, which would amount to 90 a week. All three actors replied through the *Post*. Miss Faucit's letter, dated 6 October, argued that terms were always higher for limited engagements than for extended ones and that payment for three nights (her expected number per week) would be, at her terms, only 45 pounds.[7]

"I *must work* while I am young & my sun is shining," Helen Faucit had written to Mme. Colmache. She knew that to insure her future independence she must build up a substantial estate during the years of greatest popularity, which, for an actress, were usually limited to the prime of her physical attractiveness. By the time she finally decided to marry, she had undoubtedly accumulated a small fortune.

Public Relations

By becoming an actress Helen Faucit had egregiously defied her society's prescription of a sheltered life for women, flaunting herself before the public and even, occasionally, showing her legs in a breeches part. She had convinced her admirers, however, that she had sacrificed a lesser womanly role for a greater one, thereby inspiring thousands of spectators. Yet practically speaking, how could she maintain an offstage image in keeping with the ideal woman she supposedly represented – modest, unselfish, noble-spirited – and at the same time win the professional rewards she craved? She handled the problem adroitly.

In business matters she let no womanly modesty stand in her way: she could drive a good bargain, and she could refuse an unsatisfactory proposal in the coldest and tersest of terms.[8] According to Theodore Martin (249), she unselfishly insisted that a manager "should reap as much profit by her performance as she did" and she objected to the raising of prices during her visits since this caused a decline in regular receipts later. Actually, prices were often raised for her engagements, even at her brother's theatres. Perhaps the system was as much to blame as the star, but Helen Faucit was neither bashful nor unusually altruistic in her demands.[9]

But theatre managers had no illusions, anyway. It was in public relations that skill and tact were needed to avoid the appearance of unfeminine boasting. Fortunately Helen had influential friends in major cities who promoted her reputation. Indeed James Anderson explained her great success by her cultivation of prominent people:

> But to make money as an actor you must become "a lion," the pet of some city party, and be continually acting *off* the stage as well as *on* … you must breakfast, dine, sup, and sometimes sleep with your patrons

> [i.e. stay at their homes], if you wish to become a wooden god and be worshipped. Charles Kean did it for years; so did Helen Faucit ... (*An Actor's Life* 161)

This is unfair, but friends undoubtedly did much of the advertising for her. She herself often provided them with copy. She sent eulogistic reviews to George Fletcher in London (from which he quoted passages as "postscripts" to his essays in *Studies of Shakespeare*), and reviews of the Dublin Iphigenia to Peter Fraser in Edinburgh, hoping to stir up interest in producing the play there. She evidently gave Theodore Martin a copy of Fletcher's article praising her Rosalind, for he inserted an extract from it in a "Bon Gaultier" colloquy of *Tait's Magazine*.[10] And in her letters to him she reported her successes, half-humorously deprecating the excessive praise she was receiving. He in turn broadcast her latest triumphs and reported how modest she had remained.

Helen Faucit in classical costume, by Sir Frederick William Burton (Private Collection)

Theatrical Conditions

The great differences among provincial theatre buildings become apparent in accounts of Helen Faucit's early years of starring. Her new playing venues simply increased the variety. The same was true of the stock companies: they ranged from very good, like the one in Edinburgh, where even William in *As You Like It* was excellently portrayed, to wretchedly inept, like the one at Sheffield, where (if James Anderson is believed) the wardrobe keeper was the best actor of the lot.[11]

Particularly trying variations in theatrical conditions were the unpredictable differences in temperature. In the days before air conditioning and efficient systems of central heating, theatre managers fought an unequal battle with the weather. Sometimes, to combat stifling warmth, they resorted to ingenious devices, like the large silver star in the dome of the Theatre Royal Exeter, "so contrived that it acted as a ventilator."[12] In winter the large London theatres could be unpleasantly cold for the audience, the dressing rooms even colder for the actors: at Covent Garden, Queen Victoria had kept her fur cloak on throughout the performance of *Richelieu*, and Helen Faucit, during the run of *The Tempest*, had been "chilled to the heart" between her infrequent stage appearances.[13] As a star Helen had no long periods of waiting, but she still faced the hazard of cold, draughty theatres. Strategically-placed stoves may have ensured the warmth of smaller theatres during performances, but there was probably less attention to comfort during rehearsals. At the relatively large Theatre Royal, Glasgow, she required a large chair on stage for rehearsals in case she grew tired, with a screen behind it to keep off draughts.[14] The stock-company actors, jealous of her special treatment, considered her delicacy an affectation. Actually she needed protection against colds because of potential hoarseness and "chest affection."

Rowdiness in theatres could be a problem anywhere, but it was much worse in some provincial theatres than in any of the London "royals" where Helen Faucit had acted. The ruder deities in the gallery liked to throw orange peels or pour beer on the spectators below; some even practised long-distance spitting. Fighting or rough clowning could lead to violent mishaps, as when a man tumbled from the gallery at the Exeter theatre and broke the back of a seat in the pit. There were periodic efforts to control the situation – by hiring a police officer to arrest offenders (in Carlisle), by offering rewards for information about culprits, and, on occasion, admitting only a limited number to the gallery (in Sheffield) – but the problem remained perennial.[15] It was compounded sometimes by the presence of infants and small children. At Derby, Saville forbade children in arms, but, unless his rules was better enforced than Alexander's at Glasgow, babies were smuggled in anyway: just a year earlier, when Helen Faucit was acting Juliet there, a "squalling child in the gallery" had caused "universal dissatisfaction."[16] At some theatres, such as the Theatre Royal,

Edinburgh, uncouth behaviour was relatively rare, and at others there was more hurling of jests than of missiles. Even at the quieter ones, however, holding the attention of the gods was a challenge.

Perhaps the greatest cause of dismay for a professional-minded actress was the inadequate rehearsals and indifferent supporting actors at many provincial theatres. Like Macready, Helen Faucit was impatient with such conditions, though she was likely to freeze rather than explode in response. According to Walter Baynham, she was unpopular with the actors at Glasgow because of her "coldness, disdain, exacting habits and want of consideration." Since Baynham himself was an actor there during her later years, his report cannot be discounted. It is hard, however, to accept his assertion that she was habitually late for rehearsals, sometimes as much as two hours;[17] considering her serious attitude toward her work, stories from other sources about her extreme regard for punctuality[18] seem more probable. The actors were reportedly annoyed by the "minute" preparations made for her rehearsals. They probably resented, even more, the care with which Helen Faucit conducted the rehearsals, for she often took these over herself. Her painstaking efforts to bring out the best in each actor sometimes exhausted her more than the actual performances did.[19] But the unaccustomed labour was hard on the others, too. Provincial actors played an enormous number of roles – often several in an evening with frequent changes of bill and occasional pre-dawn sessions for memorising unfamiliar parts.[20] No wonder they became sullen when an officious star, scorning the usual perfunctory rehearsal, insisted on a long, meticulous one.

Some actors, however, appreciated Helen Faucit's efforts to improve their performances. Lester Wallack, who was young and inexperienced when he first acted with her (at Manchester, in 1845), gratefully testifies:

> She was one of the gentlest and sweetest actresses I ever met. She gave me more encouragement than I had ever received before, and the patience with which she rehearsed … was remarkable. She … went over our scenes again and again with me, until I got my part in some kind of shape; and it was through her kindness that I made something of a hit with the audience.[21]

Even Baynham admitted (137) that Miss Faucit was "delightful, affable, and forbearing" with actors on whom she knew she could rely.

According to a story by Arthur Mursell, she could be extraordinarily forbearing even when there were lapses in reliability. Young Mursell, who was teaching at a private school in Glasgow, often helped behind the scenes at the Theatre Royal there. One evening, when Helen Faucit was acting Juliet, he was operating the lights and attempting at the same time to coach a nervous young debutante in a small part for the afterpiece. During the potion scene he became so interested in the debutante that he "'over-regulated' the gas effects, and put the house as well as the stage in darkness." In an "agony of panic" he groped his way to the star and sobbed out his contrition, expecting to receive a box on the ear if nothing worse. But she "whispered quite composedly, and very kindly, 'Don't mind, or take it to heart; it is quite a mistake.'" Then, "in a relighted house, she gave such a rendering of the scene as lifted the people off their seats."[22] Responsive associates felt the warmth of her kindness; indifferent and uncooperative ones received her chilly disdain.

Rivalries

Despite many triumphs during these years, Helen Faucit did not enjoy an uncontested reign. Three rivals are particularly noteworthy. Mrs. Charles Kean (formerly Ellen Tree) had long had a faithful following; she and her husband, a popular pair, usually drew good houses wherever they went. By the time Helen married, in 1851, they would be firmly based in their own London theatre, the Princess's, and well into Kean's famous series of "historically-correct" Shakespearean revivals. A more exciting actress than the "womanly" Mrs. Kean, but also a more erratic one, was Mrs. Butler (still thought of as Fanny Kemble). In February, 1847, having separated from her American husband, she reappeared on the British stage, where she had not been seen since 1832. Her engagements, beginning with one at Manchester, were very successful, and in February, 1848, she was Macready's leading lady at the Princess's Theatre in London. By the summer of that year, however, she was back in America, and she never again performed on the English stage. Despite the brevity of her comeback, she made a lasting impression on the minds of some spectators. Articles in the theatrical journals would continue for years to compare her with Helen Faucit, often awarding the palm to Mrs. Butler.

But the rival who most directly confronted Helen Faucit in 1846-51 was Charlotte Cushman. The two had never had simultaneous engagements until April, 1846, when both appeared in Liverpool, Miss Faucit at the Theatre Royal with William Creswick as leading man, Miss Cushman and her sister Susan at the Adelphi. Both began with *Romeo and Juliet.* The Royal staged a sumptuous revival, with, reportedly, the best scenery and costumes ever seen in Liverpool; yet the production, despite its visual beauty and Helen Faucit's "exquisite" acting, aroused no such excitement as the one at the Adelphi, where spectators were falling over themselves to see Charlotte Cushman as Romeo. Everyone was talking about the fire, the headlong passion that this American actress threw into her masculine role. True, she threw some exaggeration in as well, but in this she showed "an appreciation of the taste of the age, which require[d] to have everything painted … a shade beyond nature." At the Royal, Creswick's Romeo was earnest and competent but not very dashing, and Helen Faucit's Juliet was too subtly shaded to give the production the competitive brilliance it needed.[23] Later in their Liverpool engagements both actresses played Lady Macbeth, and once again Miss Cushman's strong, rather melodramatic interpretation attracted full houses, whereas Miss Faucit's more "womanly" Lady, though it won critical approval, drew a "shamefully scanty" attendance in the dress boxes.[24] Charlotte Cushman was Liverpool's darling that season, and Helen Faucit was forced into the unusual position of "also ran."

Popularity with Audiences

It *was* unusual, for there are numerous testimonies to her enormous popularity. Some are obviously hyperbolic: at Dublin (1846) the theatre had been "all but deserted" until she came, when it was "crowded to the ceiling every night"; at Glasgow (1847) there were "crowded tiers" of spectators and "deafening bursts of applause" throughout her engagement, but afterwards all was "desolate emptiness and silence."[25] But there are also practical indications of Helen Faucit's drawing power, like the special trains that took theatregoers from neighbouring towns to cities where she acted.[26]

It is surprising to read of her effectiveness with the gallery gods, despite the increasing subtlety of her style. The *Manchester Guardian* (13 May 1846) noted, for example, their fine attentiveness during her performance of Nina Sforza – a performance praised for its "picturesque attitudes" and its psychological and imaginative qualities. In Dublin, as Margaret Stokes recalls, the audience were "very noisy upon occasion, and the Lord Lieutenant's nights or the manager's benefit, were always seized on for a free expression of native wit and boisterous spirits." On one such night little of the play was heard, "but the moment Miss Faucit came on the stage stillness reigned, and the gallery, like the rest of the house, listened like a three years' child."[27] Sometimes the gallery folk seemed more appreciative than the fashionable patrons of the boxes. The *Bristol Mercury* (10 October 1846) sneered that when society people flocked to see some French or Italian dancer yet stayed away from a performance by the "most intellectual actress of the day," one was "led to doubt that the 'upper' were the 'educated' classes."

As a rule, though, Helen Faucit fared very well in attracting elite spectators – that is, culturally as well as financially privileged ones. Provincial theatrical announcements were often headed: "To the Nobility, Gentry, and Inhabitants ...". This was, in many cases, an overly-optimistic formula, if not a completely outmoded one. Yet, practically speaking, the term "Gentry" might well have been stretched to include many of the "inhabitants." One should not overlook such gentry-in-the-making as wealthy provincial merchants – undereducated, some of them, but with sons who were receiving the best educations money could buy. Particularly one should not overlook the professional and artistic people. Among Helen Faucit's most ardent supporters, both in London and in the provinces, were lawyers, physicians, university professors, writers, artists. These often sat in the pit, but often, too, in the boxes when accompanied by their wives. The local "aristocracy" varied from city to city; it might include theatrically-inclined nobility and landed gentry (if there were any), but it was certainly not limited to them.

The Search for New Roles

A star who visited the same theatres at regular intervals was obliged to expand the repertoire whenever possible. Starring roles were especially difficult for a woman to find: an actor might win fame in Hamlet and Othello; an actress could not risk her reputation with frequent performances of Ophelia or Desdemona. Hence the occasional female Romeos and Hamlets. But male roles, even idealised ones like Ellen Kean's Ion, were not for Helen Faucit.

1. Antigone in London

Antigone was the one famous character in her repertoire that had not been seen repeatedly in most of her cities. Since her original success in Dublin she had introduced it nowhere else except Edinburgh, but on 3 August 1846 she finally acted it in London, for William Farren's benefit. Her performance, at the Haymarket, was received with fervid appreciation by a large, constantly-applauding audience.[28] The critics, too, were impressed – *The Times* (4 August) declared that both the "elegant classic mind" and the "deep genuine feeling" were admirably portrayed – but some considered intense passion incompatible with Greek tragedy.[29]

Requests for Helen Faucit to repeat her Antigone in London could not be honoured. Except for her own performance, the Haymarket production had been ridiculously inadequate. Either Covent Garden or Drury Lane would have housed the "Greek" stage more effectively, but neither was now functioning as a legitimate theatre. Nor did this Antigone appear in any new provincial theatres. Calls for it in Glasgow and Manchester[30] were evidently ignored. Helen Faucit could offer no double attraction in *Antigone* as the Vandenhoffs did, for none of her leading men had a reputation in classical roles. Since she could draw good audiences in plays requiring no special preparation, managers understandably baulked at producing one with obvious problems and uncertain profits. All her later performances of Antigone, except for three in Edinburgh (April, 1847), took place in Dublin. Frustrating as it must have been, this role, which kindled her imagination and inspired some of her finest acting, was seen only thirty-five times in all, mostly in a single city.

2. Iphigenia in Dublin

The Dublin manager, Calcraft (or Cole, his real name), was so impressed by the furore over *Antigone* that he produced another classical drama. Euripides' *Iphigenia at Aulis*. He used his own translation, which relied partially on previous ones and, in the "lyrical portions," on assistance from a literary gentleman of Edinburgh (Martin?).[31] The composer was Levey, the theatre's musical director, who modified Euripides' chorus of women to include both sexes. The cast was very competent: besides Helen Faucit as Iphigenia, there were Calcraft as Agamemnon; Gustavus Vaughan Brooke, Achilles; H. Cooke, Menelaus; Mrs. Ternan, Clytemnestra; and little Ellen Ternan, the child Orestes. On the opening night, 28 November 1846, the theatre was packed to its limits, and the elite of Dublin were there in force. They were not disappointed. No expense had been spared for a lavish entertainment.[32]

Agamemnon's great purple tent formed a striking background for the action. The audience gasped in admiration as a chariot pulled by four white horses drew up before it, and the virginal Iphigenia, wearing a white gown shot with silver and a wreath of blush roses, alighted, with her mother Clytemnestra and little brother Orestes. Her joyous air and light, youthful voice here contrasted strongly with the shuddering horror of look and speech after she learned the true purpose of her arrival – not to marry Achilles, but to be sacrificed to Diana to ensure favourable winds for Agamemnon's fleet. In Iphigenia's long, pleading speech to her father, with its changing moods and styles (rhetorical, lyrical, familiarly emotional), Helen Faucit's bravura performance amazed the audience, and when she twined herself around his knees, reminding him of his former affection, while Orestes, though uncomprehending, lifted his little arms in sympathy, the "domestic tragedy" touched (as the *Freeman* said) all home-loving hearts. Her passionate conclusion, "Life! Grant me life! – all is compris'd in that ..." drew "unbounded" applause.[33] Left alone, Iphigenia, like Antigone, bewailed her fate in an aria-like passage, accompanied by music. Achilles now entered, offering to rescue Iphigenia, but as he talked with Clytemnestra, the maiden herself underwent a transformation. Accepting her fate, she declared her determination to suffer death willingly as a religious and patriotic duty. The incantatory couplets – "Farewell beauteous orb of day!/ Farewell, bright ethereal ray! . . . Freely I go – by death to crown,/ Of Greece, the glory and renown!" – were spoken in "measured" tones but with exalted attitude, "head erect and proud, and arms stretched to heaven," which powerfully impressed the imagination.[34] After Iphigena was led off to the sacrifice, a messenger brought word that Diana had miraculously substituted a milk-white hind for the intended victim. As the play ended, the tent scene was replaced by a panoramic spectacle of the Grecian ships "wafted" from the bay of Aulis, while the chorus sang a prayer for their safe return.[35]

After Helen Faucit had received a standing ovation and a "shower of flowers," Calcraft and Levey were also called and vigorously applauded. The actor-manager-translator, in euphoric mood, called the occasion a "national triumph." That became the keynote for ecstatic reviews of this first *original* production of a Greek tragedy in Ireland. Never since the days of Sophocles and Euripides, wrote the *Freeman* critic, and "perhaps not even then," had *Antigone* and *Iphigenia at Aulis* been "performed with the same power" or produced with the "same effect" as they had been on the Dublin stage. He rejoiced in Dublin's dramatic renaissance: men who had deserted the theatre were returning, scholars were discussing theatrical matters, and periodicals were teeming with articles on the drama. All this was owing to "the genius of … Miss Helen Faucit," "the greatest actress of our own or perhaps any other time."[36] Dubliners always felt a proprietary interest in Helen: it seemed to them that her "genius" inspired and glorified their own – that *it* was somehow Irish, even if she herself was, regrettably, English.

Iphigenia at Aulis, with its strong domestic appeal, its patriotic speech of self-sacrifice, and its "happy ending" after a thorough harrowing of the emotions (the typical pattern of melodrama), would seem to have been more suited to the temper of a Victorian audience than *Antigone* was. (Its ironies were simply ignored.) [37] Yet it proved, after all, only a nine days' wonder – almost literally so. It was performed seven or eight times during Helen Faucit's engagement of November-December 1846 and was repeated twice during her engagement of April-May 1848; it had no other revivals.

Although *Iphigenia* was never acted outside of Dublin – Murray's tentative promise to produce it in Edinburgh was not fulfilled,[38] – the role was important to Helen Faucit as an actress. Her additional proficiency in sculpturesque effects and her further development of stylistic flexibility, gained in acting *Iphigenia*, influenced her performances of several other roles. The most immediate example was Hermione in *The Winter's Tale*, a part she had not acted since her last season under Macready. Now, during the same Dublin engagement as *Iphigenia*, she revived the play with such success that she used its last two acts as an afterpiece on two later nights.[39] Hermione remained in her repertoire for several years, and it was revived at least twice after her marriage. Her statue scene was strangely moving. Remote at first, the white-robed "statue" stood atop a crimson-curtained dais at the back of the stage, sharply defined against the brilliant colour. The head was turned slightly to the side and one hand rested on a marble pedestal, as in Burton's "The Grecian Muse." Standing immobile while Leontes poured out his admiration and remorse, Helen Faucit used that time to imagine Hermione's thoughts: as she listened to his voice, feelings for him that she had supposed long dead re-awakened.[40] Thus a marble-like Hermione really did come to life at Paulina's command. Spectators were spellbound:

> The turning of the head and the earnest gaze of the full eyes … [which] breaks the transition from repose to motion … made the suspended blood to throb. And when she descended from the [dais] with a slow and gliding motion, and wearing the look of a being consecrated by long years of prayer and seclusion, it seemed … as if we looked upon a being almost too pure to be gazed on with unveiled eyes. (*Caledonian Mercury* 8 March 1847)

The reconciliation of statuesque formality and human emotion which Helen Faucit had learned in Antigone and Iphigenia once more proved its power.

But acting these classical heroines also fixed in her mind a pattern that profoundly affected her imagination. Their combined thematic influence – an influence all the greater for her lifelong admiration of noble, self-sacrificing heroines – had its most striking result in a new interpretation of *Romeo and Juliet*. Believing that the innocent lovers served as "sacrifices" to expiate their relatives' guilt and effect their reconciliation,[41] she adopted Shakespeare's version of the tomb scene instead of Garrick's and gave Juliet a calmer portrayal in that scene.

3. Isabella

A character new to Helen Faucit, though old to the theatre, was the heroine in Garrick's *Isabella: or, The Fatal Marriage*, a part that had challenged actresses ever since it gave Mrs. Siddons her first London triumph in 1782. (Southerne's tragedy, of which Garrick's was an adaptation, went back to 1694.) Isabella, after mourning seven years for her husband (reportedly a battle casualty), finally marries the faithful Villeroy, who has rescued her and her child from poverty. The next day Biron, her first husband, "returns from the dead." Her emotions swing wildly from ecstatic happiness at his return to horror at her own "adultery" until she goes mad and, after her husband has been killed by his treacherous brother, commits suicide. The old-fashioned play, though deplored by critics as "painful and embarrassing," "over-strained and unnatural,"[42] gave Helen Faucit a chance to harrow the emotions, as she had done effectively in Belvidera and Lady Mabel. After introducing the character in Dublin on 10 November 1846, she kept it in her repertoire for more than eight years. She aroused great enthusiasm by her portrayal of diverse emotions, culminating in the "frenzy produced by unbearable grief." A Glasgow critic typically wrote: "we do not hesitate to give the closing scene – when she is dragged off the stage – still holding with convulsive tenacity to her dead husband, and *dragging him after her* – the preference to any representation of manic grief we have ever witnessed."[43] That bizarre business did not originate with her – it went back to Mrs. Siddons – but it never failed to thrill her audiences.[44]

4. Florence Delmar

The first original play written for Helen Faucit during her starring days was a failure. It was Westland Marston's *The Heart and the World*, produced by Webster at the Haymarket on 20 October 1847, with Helen Faucit and William Creswick in major roles. This romantic blank-verse drama, set in the seventeenth century, depicts the vacillations of the newly-wealthy Vivian Temple between love for Florence Delmar, his old sweetheart, and enthralment with fashionable new friends, especially the coquettish Lady Laura Hallerton. Florence becomes disillusioned by his inconstancy but regains her faith after he fights a duel to defend her character. Marston's new play preserved the worst feature of *The Patrician's Daughter*, its pseudo-Elizabethan language, but none of its merits. The *Morning Chronicle* remarked (21 October) that too much of the action took place in the minds of the characters and what did occur overtly was hard to follow. As *The Times* (21 October) stated with devastating succinctness, "Never … was so little incident enveloped in so much obscurity." Only one passage stirred the audience's interest: when Florence said that just one "pang" would wreck a woman's future, the "*fall from worth*" by the man she loves, Helen Faucit's poignant expression of woman's generous love and her consequent vulnerability aroused an outburst of enthusiasm. The play was acted only four times. The reviewers' warm praise of Miss Faucit was poor compensation for her disappointment in the new role.[45]

5. Anne Bracegirdle

A successful novelty for Helen Faucit was John Oxenford's petite comedy *The Tragedy Queen*, adapted from a French *vaudeville* by Marc Fournier. The plot was slight: a charming actress (Anne Bracegirdle in the English version) is adored by a poetic young man, David Standfast; in response to a plea from David's father, she cures the youth of his infatuation by pretending a complete lack of refinement in everyday life; then to save her disillusioned admirer from suicide, she must once more convince him of her worthiness. The play was still new when Helen Faucit tried it out at the Theatre Royal, Edinburgh on 4 March 1848, as an afterpiece following *Much Ado about Nothing*. (It had been introduced at the Lyceum that season with Mrs. Stirling as Anne.) It drew such a favourable response that she kept it in her bills, often as a tasty morsel after heavier fare.

Although afraid at first of encouraging a derogatory view of actresses, she was able to suggest Anne Bracegirdle's basic worthiness without losing the fun of the comedy.[46] In fact, the *Manchester Examiner and Times* (5 June 1850) said the "subtle perception of character" and the "elegance and refinement of manner" in the early scenes "made the humour the more telling. Her laugh was catching, and the broad sketchy style of the [purposely vulgar scene] was as true to nature as the finer touch of sentiment…"

6. Evadne

Seeking a strongly dramatic new part, Helen Faucit decided to revive Richard Lalor Sheil's *Evadne* (based on a seventeenth-century play, *The Traitor*, by James Shirley), which had originally been performed in 1819 with Eliza O'Neill in the title role. The plot is full of intrigue and sensational incidents, but the chief interest is in Evadne, who is betrothed to Vicentio but lustfully desired by the King of Naples. Vicentio, convinced by a villain that Evadne has become the King's mistress, leaves her for another woman. The great scene for the actress is between Evadne and the King: in a hall filled with statues of her ancestors, she flings her arms around a statue of her father, who had died saving the young prince (now the King) in battle, and dares her would-be seducer to "reward" his rescuer by bringing shame to his daughter. At the end of the play Vicentio, who proves to be alive after his reported death, will now marry the virtuous – and forgiving – Evadne.

Helen Faucit first performed Evadne in Dublin on 22 November 1848. Judging by the next day's review in the *Freeman's Journal*, she made the most of her opportunities, running the gamut from "confiding love to indignant vindication of her honour" to the "force and power" of the "crowning scene" in the hall of statues. She repeated the part several times before leaving Dublin and later acted it successfully in Edinburgh and Newcastle.[47] Her portrayal aroused particular enthusiasm at Manchester. A writer who remembered Miss O'Neill in this role declared that even her "dignity and pathos … did not impress the audience with so truthful a picture of the woman as Miss Faucit."[48]

Theodore Martin (207) says she abandoned the play after a few years because she lacked rapport with a woman who would "restore to her affections a weak, impulsive lover" like Vicentio. Doubtless those were her sentiments, but she had a more compelling reason for abandoning Evadne: audiences soon tired of the complicated, old-fashioned play. Even while the success of its first Manchester revival was fresh, the critic for the *Courier* (1 June 1850) had second thoughts, calling it a thing of "shreds and patches" which only Miss Faucit's acting was keeping alive. When she last performed it, the *Guardian* (28 April 1852) not only denounced the play's "revolting … incidents, clumsy … construction" and "bombastic diction" but even censured Miss Faucit's acting for overstepping the line "which separates … distraught anguish from a tiger-like ferocity." *Evadne* was allowed, after that, to slide back into oblivion.

7. Iolanthe

An important addition to Helen Faucit's repertoire was the blind princess Iolanthe in Theodore Martin's version of *King René's Daughter*, a "dramatic poem" by the Danish writer Henrik Hertz. Strangely enough, this brief and delicate play, with little story and no striking effects, reached the British stage in two translations and enhanced the reputations of three fine actresses. For Helen Faucit it became a permanent favourite.

Princess Iolanthe of Provence, blinded in infancy by a traumatic fall, has been reared privately in the beautiful Valley of Vaucluse. Her blindness has been kept secret for political reasons, and, since she has never been told about sight, even she is not aware of any handicap. Having reached sixteen, an age propitious for a cure, she has been put into a trancelike sleep by the Moorish physician Ibn Jahia. Sir Tristan de Vaudemont, roaming in the valley with a companion, stumbles upon Iolanthe's Eden and is enchanted by the sleeper's ethereal beauty. When he takes the sleep-inducing amulet from her breast as a memento, Iolanthe awakes. She entertains the strangers hospitably, and her blindness does not become apparent until she fails to distinguish between red and white roses. The men leave, but, after Iolanthe has been put to sleep again, they return with armed retainers, thinking to rescue her from the enchanter who, they suppose, is keeping her captive. Tristan learns with astonishment that she is King René's daughter, to whom he has been betrothed since childhood. Suddenly Iolanthe awakes, fully cured. Though at first terror-stricken by the strange new world of sight, she learns to accept it thankfully, and she finds Tristan's appearance a match for the voice and personality she already loves. In Martin's version, the play is a dreamlike idyll, whose graceful poetry is far superior to his usual verse. Its parallels with Shakespeare's *Tempest* and the fairytale of the Sleeping Beauty are obvious. Iolanthe's role, though not conventionally dramatic, has a psychological and symbolic interest, linked to the related awakenings to love and sight, that could be subtly exploited by a suggestive actress.

Helen Faucit's original intention, to introduce the play in Dublin during the 1848-49 season, fell through, possibly because of illness; and, before she could renew her plan, Charles and Ellen Kean brought it out there in Edward Phipps' translation. The response was ecstatic, but the Keans reaped the glory.[49] Never willing to appear anticlimactic, Helen waited more than a year before showing Dubliners her own Iolanthe. Meanwhile, having just returned from a convalescent stay at the German spas, she allowed her stepfather, now managing the Strand, to use Martin's version for the play's London premiere (11 December 1849), with Mrs. Stirling as Iolanthe. A week later the Keans presented their version at the Haymarket. Both productions were favourably received.[50]

Helen Faucit's debut in Iolanthe took place, at last, on 17 January 1850 at her brother John's theatre in Sheffield, where she stopped briefly on her way to Scotland. According to a local critic, her portrayal "took hold upon the audience with quiet power" and would long be remembered as "beautiful" and "holy".[51] (The word "holy," odd as it seems, was an index to future reviews.) Her first real test of the role, however, was on 23 January at the Prince's Theatre, Glasgow. The manager, Edmund Glover (formerly leading man at Edinburgh) staged the play attractively and played Sir Tristan himself. Helen Faucit's Iolanthe thrilled her audiences, inspired her critics, and delighted her manager.[52] A long review in the *Glasgow Herald* (25 January 1850) declared that no part could have been "more peculiarly adapted" to her powers, for, varied though her talents were, she was "pre-eminently at home" in "the region of the elevated and romantically poetical." She repeated Iolanthe several times during this engagement, always to large and appreciative audiences.[53] Perhaps the best testimony to the play's popularity in Glasgow was a production here several months later (7 June): *King Zany's Daughter, or The Princess That Was Blind of One*

Eye and Could Not See Out of the Other, featuring Miss Fielding's imitation of Helen Faucit and Mr. Cockrill's imitation of Charles Kean. (The Keans had been in Glasgow that spring.) Even the parodies of burlesque could be a sincere form of flattery. Meanwhile Helen Faucit had performed Iolanthe in Edinburgh and Liverpool in March, Dublin and Belfast in April, Manchester in May and June.

She would continue to act this role of a childlike sixteen-year-old throughout her career. One can only marvel at her foolhardiness – and at the witchcraft that helped her get by with it as long as she did. Magic of some kind there must have been. Many critics testified to her "enchantment": the spectators were spellbound, too intent to applaud until the end; they saw a new phase of life opening up, found themselves dreaming of Iolanthe as "the radiant inhabitant of a fancy world"; they were "struck ... with the force of heavenly revelation," as "some divine effusion seemed to emanate from [the actress's] whole person."[54]

The depiction of Iolanthe's blindness was endlessly fascinating to spectators. Some friends of Helen's explained the singular attraction of the play for the "middle and working classes" of Manchester by the fact that blindness was so common there (because of industrial accidents?) that Iolanthe's situation "touched their hearts to the quick." Reviewers in Manchester, Glasgow, and Dublin praised Miss Faucit's skill in conveying an impression of unconscious blindness. Eschewing the stereotyped "stage blindness," they said, and even the more artistic methods of her two rivals (uncertainty of motion and a frequent resort to touch), her Iolanthe moved about in "unembarrassed freedom," yet suggested in many small ways that she trusted to sound and touch. The Irish novelist William Carleton, who had studied blind people that "never remembered sight" when preparing to write *The Clarionet*, was impressed by the truthfulness of her portrayal, both in her "beautiful serenity of aspect" and in her slight deviation from a straight line when approaching someone – so slight that most spectators were probably not consciously aware of it.[55] Years later a London oculist inquired how she had learned the tones and movements of persons born blind. According to Martin, she simply trusted to intuition:

> ... she imagined herself to be blind; her eyes, though open as usual, saw nothing, and if she moved, acted, spoke like a blind person, this was wholly due to the fact that for the time she was practically blind. ... She always, however, suffered a certain amount of pain in the eyes after playing Iolanthe. (217-18)

Helen Faucit's portrayal, however convincing, made the blindness more poetic than distressing. Victorian drama is full of handicapped people –deaf, dumb, blind, lame, hunchbacked, mentally retarded – all designed to arouse the audience's pity, though this would be tinged sometimes with the fascinated revulsion associated with flagrantly abnormal characters like madmen and vampires. Although Iolanthe, who is joyously happy while blind, hardly resembles these, the reviewers' occasional references to "the poor blind girl" show the power of stereotyped responses. Much of the play's attraction for refined audiences lay in the idealised treatment of Iolanthe's blindness, which poignantly reminded them of her vulnerability but avoided any melodramatic element of fear or disgust. The *Manchester Guardian* (30 October 1867), though averse to physical defects as dramatic subjects, admitted that in seeing Helen Faucit's portrayal the audience almost lost the sense that blindness was a "physically-painful phenomenon."

Different as *King René's Daughter* is from *Antigone* and *Iphigenia at Aulis*, some techniques developed for the Greek tragedies were used again for this play, perhaps to suggest an air of legendary remoteness. Thus, according to a critic, Iolanthe's "classical beauty of attitude" created the illusion that Flaxman's sculptures had "taken motion" or that viewers had been transported to "the golden age of art."[56] In turn, skills used for Iolanthe's blindness may have carried over into Lady Macbeth's sleepwalking scene – witness descriptions of the open yet unseeing eyes.

Helen Faucit, later Lady Martin, by Sir Frederick Burton
(by courtesy of the Manchester City Art Galleries)

8. Marie de Meranie

On 4 November 1850, at the Olympic Theatre, Helen Faucit made her second attempt as a star to introduce a new play in London. *Philip of France and Marie de Meranie*, a blank-verse tragedy, was by Westland Marston, whose *The Heart and the World* had failed so miserably several years before. In the meantime, however, Marston had proved himself with a tragedy, *Strathmore*, which the Keans had acted with great success. *Philip of France*, too, became a tremendous hit.

The play concerns the politically-bedevilled love of Philip Augustus (the French King in Shakespeare's *King John*) and Marie, daughter of the Duc de Meranie (a historical person, usually called Agnes, about whom little is known). Marston's Marie is an exalted representative of his ideal woman – pure, loving, unselfish, inspirational (she encourages Philip, despite his nobles' displeasure, to redress his poor subjects' wrongs). Marston's Philip, as much fictional as historical,[57] is endearingly impulsive and generous, but he vacillates between weak suggestibility and arrogant stubbornness. Though virtually engaged to Marie, he succumbs to political advice and weds Ingerburge, sister of the King of Denmark; then in revulsion, he has the marriage annulled by his pliant bishops and marries his real love Marie. He defies the Pope's command to reinstate Ingerburge as Queen, continuing his resistance despite a threat of interdiction. Finally, to save him and the country from the papal curse, Marie resigns her crown but asks that the question of her marriage be referred to the Council of Bishops. When they delay, Philip, anticipating the worst, reinstates Ingerburge to avoid coercion. (Actually Rome would have upheld Marie's marriage.) Marie, indignantly rejecting Philip's plan to live with her despite his official marriage to another woman, retires to a castle and wastes away. In the last act Philip, fresh from a victory in battle, receives word that Ingerburge, who is now in a convent, wishes a divorce. Free to restore Marie to heart and throne, he rushes to see her – just in time for her to die in his arms.

Marston, though without much of a plot, had several strong situations, which he worked up well; his protagonists gave good opportunities to the players; and his verse was among the best in neo-Elizabethan dramas. Marie's lofty speeches, if unappealing today, probably seemed uplifting in 1850. *Philip of France* is not tragedy, rigorously defined: Philip's errors result in Marie's "fall," not his own; his final bitter words, "And this is fame!" suggest a theme that is pertinent but not central to the play. It is, nevertheless, an interesting example of the later poetic drama.

The Olympic Theatre was managed at that time by William Farren, Helen Faucit's stepfather, whose company included her two half brothers and her uncle, Charles Diddear; all were in the new play. Gustavus Vaughan Brooke, who had now gained a London reputation, played Philip. Farren staged the play impressively, with splendid scenery and costumes.[58] On its opening night, an audience "crowded to suffocation" welcomed Helen Faucit to London, after a three-year absence, with "an "enthusiasm such as is seldom … witnessed within the walls of a theatre." The excitement remained intense, and when the curtain fell she was "vociferously called for." Afterwards Brooke was honoured, then the author.[59]

The play pleased most of the critics: several said it was Marston's best so far, and one rated it among the finest English plays "since the golden age of the drama." The production, too, was highly praised, particularly the climactic scene at the end of the third act: "The King on his throne hurling defiance at the prelates opposite, the nobles wavering between the two contending powers, Marie imploringly clinging to her husband … and the accompaniment of the whole scene by the dismal bell tolling forth the interdict…"[60] Brooke's usually beautiful voice was, unfortunately, plagued with hoarseness, but it improved as the engagement proceeded. The *Sunday Times* described his Philip as "full of grandeur and simplicity, exhibiting the fiery courage and untameable pride of the young monarch," but some other reviewers accused Brooke of boisterousness and rant.[61] Helen Faucit felt frustrated by his acting: "I am obliged to make [my Philip] for myself," she wrote to a friend, "… and this is a great drawback to all one's responsive and impulsive feeling."[62] This hardly interfered with her own portrayal, however, which critics euphorically described as "soul-stirring," "delicate, impassioned, and full of psychological suggestion." Miss Faucit, they wrote, caught the lightest nuance and gave a world of meaning to simple words; her melodious voice enhanced the poetry; she expressed the varied passions truthfully, yet exalted them by her "fine intellectuality."[63] They particularly admired her "insulted, yet still loving" response to Philip's unworthy proposal and her "poetical and profound pathos" in the death scene.[64] Marston dedicated the play to her and later wrote some high praise of her portrayal.[65]

Philip of France continued to draw overflow houses night after night.[66] Helen Faucit, who performed four nights a week, acted Marie on 17 nights before interrupting the run for another part; in all, she devoted 21 of her 29 nights to Marie. The whole Olympic engagement was remarkably successful, especially in view of the unusual competition: in December 1850, as W. J. Lawrence points out, Macready was acting at the Haymarket,the Keans at the Princess's, James Anderson at Drury Lane (which he had recently taken over), Phelps and Miss Glyn at Sadler's Wells. Creswick at the Surrey[67] – an astonishing rain of activity after a seven-year-old drought of serious theatre in London.

Triumphant as Helen Faucit's Marie was in its original run, the role did not remain permanently in her repertoire. She did repeat it fairly often in 1851, in Liverpool, Glasgow, Edinburgh, and Manchester (not in Dublin because of the play's anti-papal sentiment),[68] but after her marriage in August she never revived it. Even amidst the initial excitement she had realised its limitations. As she wrote to a friend: "Marie is sweet, noble, womanly, and carries my sympathies with her more almost than any character out of Shakespeare. She is *great* only in her self denial and endurance, therefore not so effective a character on the stage as many others."[69]

Lady Macbeth in London

Except for Isabella in *Measure for Measure*, acted just once as a benefit novelty, there were no further additions to Helen Faucit's repertoire in this period. She continued, however, to find new life in "old" characters, notably Lady Macbeth. Her innovative portrayal, much applauded in Paris, had also been winning influential converts in the British provinces. Professor John Wilson ("Christopher North") exclaimed, after seeing it in Edinburgh (1845), "This is the true Lady Macbeth! Mrs. Siddons has misled us"; later, in one of his *Blackwood* papers, he elaborated on his new conception.[70] And in Dublin (1846) the novelist William Carleton felt, as he watched the play, that he had "never seen or understood Lady Macbeth's true character before." Helen Faucit's portrayal of a loving wife who wanted to gratify her husband's ambition gave the role more complexity, kept it within the pale of humanity, and lent a "beautiful and significant moral to the closing scenes of the Queen's life."[71]

In London, however, this Lady Macbeth remained unknown. Not once had Helen Faucit attempted the part there since the night in 1843 when she temporarily replaced Mrs. Warner. During a short engagement at the Olympic, on 4 August 1851, she finally tested her mature portrayal before a London audience, with J. W. Wallack as her Macbeth; she repeated it four days later. The experiment, though brief, was particularly interesting, for audiences had the opportunity of comparing her with two prominent London actresses of Lady Macbeth, Mary Amelia Warner and Isabella Glyn. Both rivals were seen at Sadler's Wells: Mrs. Warner, long familiar in the part, acted it before going to America; then Miss Glyn took it over. Although the latter's calculating, materialistic Lady Macbeth differed in some important points from Mrs. Warner's dignified, majestic one (and, of course, from Mrs. Siddons's awesome impersonation), both actresses were strongly influenced by the Siddons tradition.[72]

Helen Faucit's significant differences from other interpreters were noticed by several critics. The *Morning Post* (5 August) said her Lady Macbeth "was not the conventional stage portrait but the *Lady Macbeth* of Shakespeare and nature." George Fletcher, delighted at last to see his favourite actress giving the interpretation he had been preaching, wrote an enthusiastic review of this "truer and more spiritual reading of the part" (*Literary Gazette* 16 August: 565). Predictably, some critics preferred the actresses in the Siddons tradition, mainly because of their superior "power and energy,' their "grandeur of outline and largeness of execution."[73] At least one, however, credited Helen Faucit's portrayal with an impressive amount of intellectual, if not physical, power. Even a devotee of Siddonian grandeur found parts of her early scenes "unsurpassable," her sleepwalking scene "beautiful and touching," and her portrayal as a whole, "if not the most powerful, one of the [theatre's] most intellectually perfect assumptions..."[74]

Personal Life

In the summer of 1846, while in Brighton for a brief rest, Helen was "prostrated by a severe inflammatory attack" whose "consequences ... affected her health for many years."[75] She was too ill in September to keep her engagements at John's theatres in Derby and Leicester,[76] and she had barely recovered when she went to Dublin in late October for the first part of what proved to be an unusually successful double engagement; indeed she succumbed to a fresh attack while there. Renewed bouts of illness interrupted an engagement in Cork (early January 1847) and caused postponements at Belfast and Glasgow in the following weeks.[77] As late as 5 May the *Manchester Guardian* noted some "marks of delicate health, if not suffering," which gave "additional interest to a very interesting face."

That summer, travelling with friends, she took her first long vacation (July to September) on the Continent, enjoying the art galleries in Amsterdam and The Hague, a boat trip on the Rhine, and visits to Germany and Switzerland. While in Homburg she met Henry Edward Manning (the future Cardinal), and, more important, his friend John Moultrie, rector of the parish church at Rugby. Despite Moultrie's anti-theatrical bias, he and Helen soon developed a warm friendship.[78] It proved a timely one for her.

The autumn started propitiously, with noticeably improved health.[79] Then misfortunes began to strike. First came the failure of *The Heart and the World*, but she recovered from that with the resiliency she had always shown professionally. It was the next blow that found her defenceless: the sudden loss of "darling Harry," who died in Boston, Massachusetts, of typhus fever, on 5 November 1847.[80] Helen's grief was numbing. She lost interest in everything, felt incapable of continuing her work.

One prior commitment she was obliged to honour: to perform Act 4 of *Romeo and Juliet* in a monster Covent Garden benefit for the purchase of the Shakespeare House at Stratford. No play could have been more difficult than this, so closely associated with memories of Harriet. On the night of the benefit (7 December) Helen shut herself up in her dressing room and refused to see anyone – even Macready, whose very voice, heard at her door, was "all but too much." Her greatest trial was in acting the potion scene. As she later wrote, when the Nurse left Juliet alone,

> her desolation, her loneliness, became mine, and the rushing tears would have way ... the fearful images presented to Juliet's mind ... soon sent softer feelings away; but how glad I was when the fancied sight of Tybalt's ghost allowed the grief that was in my heart to find vent in a wild cry of anguish as well as horror![81]

That was not the first time, or the last, when a player, feeling great emotion while acting, has had a totally false idea of the effect on the audience. Helen Faucit was not aware that "venting" her personal grief made Juliet's emotions seem, paradoxically, less genuine rather than more so. One or two critics, ignorant of the circumstances, gave her the worst censure of her mature career. Thus the *Morning Chronicle*, long her faithful supporter, denounced her acting as "painfully overdone, the passion amounting … to most indubitable rant."[82]

After the ordeal of the Shakespeare Night, Helen went home to her bed and remained there, ill, for some time.[83] As she grew stronger, though, she became increasingly aware of a need to rouse herself. For all her highly strung, emotional nature, she had a strong will, a strong sense of duty, and a strong respect for practical reality. These estimable Victorian qualities now came to her rescue. She tried to console herself with poetry, she exhorted herself with maxims. In her memorandum book she dutifully copied out a passage from a biography which she was reading: "He only rescued himself from the grief that had laid hold on his life by the most strenuous exertions of mind and body." This, she determined, was what she would do. Yet the firmest of resolutions was not sufficient. To Dr. Stokes, who had written as comfortingly as he could, she replied:

> If you had ever seen us together, known what we had been to each other, you would understand why all now appears a cheerless blank before me. I know such feelings are wrong and wicked to indulge in, and, believe me, I strive with all my might to conquer them … but you did not know her, – so good, devoted, loving, generous a heart I never knew – never shall again. … Her poor husband wrings my heart with his letters, and, because of her great love for me, clings to me for comfort. Alas! I cannot yet find any for myself.

In the same letter, however, she told of her decision to return to work, seeking "support" against destructive emotions in "active duties."[84]

After resuming her engagements, Helen wrote from Edinburgh (10 February 1848) to Theodore Martin, who was now living in London: "I knew I had to meet a trial in coming here, but oh, I could not guess how terrible it was to be? [sic]. … The battle is hardest in my comedy parts. I have … been in constant fear lest a shriek should come in place of a laugh."[85] The sights and sounds of Edinburgh were forever associated with Harriet, for Helen had first seen and heard them with her. Oddly enough, the comic roles, which seemed so difficult, formed an unusually large proportion of this engagement. However uncongenial, they were better for her state of mind – and for her acting – than the tragic ones.

Acting, even against the grain, did more than anything else to help Helen overcome the corrosive effects of her grief. But friends helped, too. One was the Reverend John Moultrie, whom she had visited at Rugby shortly before she received word of Harriet's death. She turned to him now for counsel, and he helped to "tranquillise her mind."[86] In April, after completing an engagement in Glasgow, the fatigued and nervous young woman had a soothing visit with her friends the Armstrongs in their home near Newcastle. Her hosts were so gracious, there was such "exquisite order and perfection" in the house and all its appointments, that she found her spirits refreshed by a much-needed sense of peace and harmony.[87] Still later, after acting in Dublin, she remained for some time among her friends there and sat to Frederick Burton for another full-length portrait.[88]

Her health continued precarious, however. In 1849 engagements at Manchester and Liverpool had to be turned down on this account. Finally, in August, she travelled to Germany for a protracted rest at spas like Kreutznach and Schwalbach; she did not return until November. Since she accepted no engagements between May, 1849, and January, 1850, she was away from the stage for a longer period than at any other time since her London debut. While in Germany she was constantly in the company of Dr. Bruce Joy and his wife Arumella, an idealistic but acutely observant woman – a good companion in this time of spiritual as well as physical convalescence.[89]

By that time Helen had become more reconciled to her loss, partly through a positive act of her own. In the summer of 1849 she had erected, with Moultrie's help, a memorial tablet to Harriet in Rugby church, "near a spot intimately associated with the remembrance of her loss." Idealist though she was, Helen was never satisfied with abstractions. The visible and enduring memorial put a formal seal on her grief.[90]

The following year was much better for her. According to Martin, her leisurely visit to Ireland in the summer of 1850 was intended to begin a "year's rest." She did not make this plan because of ill health, for she readily cancelled it in order to act Marie de Meranie that autumn. Perhaps poor Theodore had to suffer another postponement.

This faithful adorer "never faltered" in his "worship," as Mrs. Sellar of Edinburgh later wrote,[91] never lost a chance to sing his idol's praises. In 1849, when Helen was about to visit Aberdeen, he hoped that John Stuart Blackie and his wife would meet her. Mrs. Blackie's fear that the awe-inspiring actress would not be a comfortable personal acquaintance drew an eloquent letter from Martin:

> You must be under no fears of my friend Miss Faucit. She is one of the gentlest, most unaffected & most winning of women – You must know her well before you see … how much latent power there is under that soft and quiet exterior. She is a heroine in embryo – and … in the finest things I have seen her express in embodying Shakespeare, she was only giving expression to qualities & faculties in her own nature. Every woman, I think, ought to love her and be proud of her.[92]

Whether Mrs. Blackie was reassured by this is hard to say.

But when would so much faithfulness have its reward? Sometimes Theodore tried to relieve his feelings through love poetry – and typically, he published it. The *Dublin University Magazine* of May 1849 (608-11) contains a "Bouquet of Ballads. By Bon Gaultier," several of whose poems seem to reflect personal thoughts and emotions. "Love in Absence," for example, expresses the poet's attempt to rise above a need for the beloved's physical presence – an exercise in neo-platonic rationalisation with which Theodore was only too familiar. "A Sea-Side Musing" reveals the lover as less capable of sublimating his longing: "Roll on, bright waters, roll,/ And to my loved one bear/ An echo from my soul/ Of the tempest surging there –/ Of the voice that *will* be heard,/ Howe'er, where'er I be –/ 'Where, where is thy sweet bird,/ That she nesteth not with thee?" Even Helen's early nickname "Bird" may have been used deliberately.

Perhaps the long delay in Helen's marriage stemmed from something more than a love of independence and a determination to harvest the golden crop while her sun was shining. Is it fanciful to suppose that even so late as 1850 she still needed to exorcise the giant phantom of Macready? It is a good guess that, after recovering from her outrage over his behaviour in Paris, she hoped to act with him again. The public would have responded enthusiastically. Theatrical journals occasionally suggested a renewed pairing or deplored the stars' inability to move in one sphere. Macready, however, kept his distance, and now the prospect of a Macready-Faucit revival was rapidly diminishing. In 1849-50 Helen would have heard often of his imminent retirement: from her sister-in-law, Marianne Saville, who frequently accompanied the great actor on his last rounds of provincial theatres, and from friends in London, who could report the crowds that filled the Haymarket during the first series of his farewell performances. In the excitement, any remaining shreds of pride and resentment were blown away. On 14 March 1850 she wrote to him, offering her services "*in any way*" for his final performance. Macready"s reply was stiff and indefinite:

> Whether I may have the power of availing myself of your valuable services must depend upon the play selected for my close. . . . I shall be happy to bear in mind what you have so kindly communicated, and furnish you with the earliest notice, if I should be enabled to add your name to the list of those performers, who grace with their assistance my last theatrical appearance.[93]

Actually Benjamin Webster had hoped to bring the two stars together at the Haymarket before Macready's final night, not in the same plays but during the same period of time. In replying to his proposal, Helen Faucit wrote, in October 1850: "If you could afford to produce a new play on Mr. Macready's off nights & bring it out with all the effect you could give it I might then have some little chance of serving you & myself. I need not point out ... how little the public feel inclined to follow two attractions at one Theatre unless there should be something singularly new & good in both."[94] Although the Olympic's production of *Philip of France and Marie de Meranie* was surely in preparation at the time, she would have contrived its postponement either to co-star with Macready or to appear as his formidable rival. But she would not play second fiddle.

Macready's "Last Farewell Forever" occurred on 26 February 1851, almost a year after Helen Faucit's offer to act for him. Her name did not "grace" the occasion. Meanwhile Macready had heard rumours of her "abuse" of him, and Mrs. Warner had reported the Foleys' opinion that Miss Faucit's offer to act for him "showed an amiable nature as forgiving or forgetting injuries."[95] Thus the offer served not to reconcile but to irritate. To be fair, however, the choice of a farewell play – *Macbeth* – did determine, as he had predicted, the choice of fellow players. He would not have selected Helen Faucit, whatever their relationship, for he preferred a more forceful, less sympathetic "partner in greatness." On his farewell night, before a brilliant Drury Lane audience, Macready acted Macbeth "as never, never before,"[96] and the loyal Mrs. Warner was her usual majestic Lady Macbeth. Helen Faucit was not even present. She was in Liverpool, playing Marie to Barry Sullivan's Philip.

With Macready's departure the most powerful force in Helen's life disappeared. Her early career had been determined to a great extent by his influence; his retirement from management in 1843 had brought the first phase of that career to an end and propelled her into stardom. Although she had thenceforth developed in her own way, her art and her intellectual life had retained his permanent impress. His heroic figure was always present somewhere on the scene – to challenge her emulation if not to invite dreams of joint conquest. Perhaps there was no connection between the two events, but just six months after Macready's Farewell, Helen Faucit ended the second phase of her career and became Mrs. Theodore Martin.

PART III: "The End Is the Renown"

All's Well That Ends Well, 4.4.36

Chapter 11

Marriage at Last

On Monday, 25 August 1851 – little more than two weeks after completing her engagement at the Olympic – Helena Faucit Saville, aged thirty-six, became the wife of Theodore Martin. True to her early promise, she was married by her friend Henry Wagner in his Church of St. Nicholas of Myra, Brighton. This square-towered church of grey Sussex flint, which dates from the fourteenth century, stands near the top of a steep hill, looking out over the buildings of Brighton to the sea. At the time of Helen's wedding the interior, which was later remodelled, still had the dark and cluttered look it had acquired late in the previous century from the addition of galleries over the box-pews; redeeming features were the gracefully carved rood screen and the massive Norman font, carved from a single Caen stone with scenes from the lives of Jesus and St. Nicholas.

The wedding party, arriving at ten in the morning, were greeted by the joyous pealing of bells in the church tower. Helen, almost obsessively determined to keep her personal life separate from her professional one, had wanted a small, very private wedding; she must have been dismayed, on alighting from her carriage, to see a crowd of eager spectators in the churchyard and, on entering the church, to find it full. News of her plans had leaked out, and a great many uninvited guests "had the satisfaction of being accidentally present." One hopes she never saw the *Theatrical Journal*'s remark that the bride "might have walked straight from the last act of *The Lady of Lyons*."[1]

The curiosity-seekers found little spectacle, for Helen had only two bridesmaids, her teen-aged niece Kate Saville and a Dublin friend, Eliza Bruce. But the miniature picture they did see was properly romantic – the girls in their pastel dresses and flowered hats, the bride in a lace-trimmed white silk gown and a "rich veil" suspended from a wreath of orange blossoms.[2] Helen was not conventionally radiant, however: "pale and agitated" throughout, she "shed tears abundantly during the reading of the prayers."[3] The conflicting emotions she felt at the weddings of friends were even stronger at her own. As she once wrote in her diary, "What a dreadful leap this into marriage always seems! 'Til death do us part!"[4]

Helen Faucit, later Lady Martin, by an unknown artist
(by courtesy of the National Portrait Gallery, London)

A cheerier occasion was the "elegant *déjeuner*" at the Pier Hotel. Among the party were Helen's eldest brother, John Saville, who had given the bride away, his wife, Marianne, and probably all three daughters; her second brother, Edmund, and his wife, Clementina; her two half-brothers, William and Henry Farren; her uncle, Charles Diddear; and her mother, Mrs. Faucit. (The elder William Farren had the good sense to stay away.) Aside from the family, the guests were mainly actors, writers, and artists. Among them was Zouch Troughton, author of *Nina Sforza*, who had served as a witness to the marriage[5]. During the festivities one of the bridesmaids jested that Theodore was an old ogre for carrying off such a bride. The phrase struck Helen's fancy, and forever afterwards her husband was nicknamed "my Ogre."[6]

The next day bride and groom left on their honeymoon journey, which took them to Paris, then to the historic and artistic centres of Italy that Helen had long dreamed of seeing, and, eventually, to parts of scenic Switzerland. While in Florence they visited Casa Guidi, hoping to see the Brownings, but were disappointed to find them away. They returned to London early in November.[7]

As Helen had anticipated, marriage made a radical change in her life. Although she would continue her professional career on a limited basis, from now on acting would take second place to her domestic and social activities. The kind of world she had fleetingly inhabited in visits to the Alisons, the Stokeses, and other well-to-do, cultivated friends, now became her own. Not that the theatre ever lost its importance for her, or that her theatrical influence died with her marriage – far from it! The distinct but mutually influential aspects of her public world, professional and social, will be discussed in the next two chapters. For the moment, though, the focus must be on the private world of her marriage.

Most of the Martins' income came from Theodore's work as a Parliamentary agent, in which he had been engaged for some five years, ever since leaving his legal practice in Edinburgh and moving to London. This consisted of representing individuals or corporate groups that wished either to promote or to oppose private bills and other legislation of "local application."[8] He would remain in this work for the rest of his life, well known as an able, energetic, and highly successful agent.[9] His greatest pleasure and widest reputation, however, came from his literary work: new editions of the Bon Gaultier ballads; translations of poetic and dramatic works from German, Latin, and other languages; a drama of his own, *Madonna Pia*;[10] a monograph on his favourite poet, Horace; numerous essays, published mainly in *Blackwood's* and *Fraser's* (some on dramatic subjects were later collected in volumes); and several biographies – one of which would dramatically affect the Martins' lives.

The Martins' first home was at 24 James Street, Buckingham Gate, in Westminster, where Theodore himself had been living for some time.[11] In 1852 they bought a house in fashionable Onslow Square, Brompton, in the South

Kensington vicinity, newly built on the grounds of a former "lunatic asylum" by C.J. (later Sir Charles) Freake. The tall, handsome white town-houses stood in unbroken rows, each having a small porch with two columns topped by an ornate entablature, and, above this, a balcony enclosed with iron railing. They fronted on a small private park, protected by a spiky fence to whose gate only residents had keys. During the Martins' early years in the square a church, St. Paul's, was built at one end of it; but, convenient as it was, its "low" services might have discouraged their regular attendance. In later years they were communicants of St. Peter's in nearby Cranley Gardens.[12]

No. 36 Onslow Square: Thackeray's former house, near the site where the Martins' similar house stood (photograph taken in 1967)

Inside, the new house was like many others designed for upper-middleclass families: the basement would include kitchen and other service rooms; the ground floor (or first floor in American parlance) would have a large entrance hall with dining room and parlour opening into it and a library at the back; the first floor would be devoted to the reception rooms, the second and third to the main bedrooms; the housekeeper and butler would have quarters in the basement, where the servants' hall was, and the maids would sleep either on the top floor or in the garret. Behind the houses were rows of two-storeyed mews with coach-houses and stables below and coachmen's quarters above.[13]

The Martins' house was not ready for occupancy until 1853,[14] but meanwhile Helen had the congenial task of choosing its furniture and decorations. As later descriptions by her guests indicate, this went far beyond selecting carpets and draperies. After a visit in 1855 Sir Archibald Alison wrote glowingly to her of "that beautiful dwelling where so much that is exquisite in art is presided over by all that is attractive in genius"; and in 1862 Arthur Munby, who considered the Martins' house "one of the most charming in London," recorded in his diary: "It has a lofty spacious hall, made more beautiful by pictures & statues; and a noble staircase sloping up round three sides of it, leads to a suite of drawing rooms furnished with costly and most fastidious elegance. The whole interior of the house, I believe, is due to the taste and the professional genius of Mrs. Martin herself." Helen evidently did enjoy spending some of her hard-earned money on works of art, but both Martins were ardent and discriminating collectors.

In the 1860s the Martins acquired a country home in the Vale of Llangollen, North Wales (near the small town for which the area is named), which would become their favourite retreat for more than three decades. During their first visit to that region, in the summer and early autumn of 1861, they fell permanently under its spell – a serene but potent enchantment deriving from the wine-like air, the harmoniously contrasted landscape, the ancient monuments rich in romantic associations. No visitor is immune to that magic. A sea of verdant fields, dotted with hillocks like rounded waves, is rimmed by loftier hills with variegated foliage; the tall Eliseg Rocks appear now pink, now beige or silver, according to the light; the tree-shadowed stillness of the Welsh Canal contrasts with the rushing white water of the nearby River Dee. On one of the grassy knolls stands Eliseg's Pillar, erected by Concenn, King of Powys, in memory of his great-grandfather, who saved the old Welsh kingdom from the English; not far away looms the roofless shell of Valle Crucis Abbey, home of Cistercian monks from the early thirteenth century until the time of Henry VIII; and, crowning a demi-mountain seen for miles around, are the black ruins of Dinas Bran, a castle evoking dreams of bygone rulers like Madoc ap Gruffydd, ancestor of Owen Glendower.[15]

The cottage rented by the Martins clung to a spur, or rounded protuberance, of Bryntysilio, a large hill rising from the banks of the River Dee. Their bit of the hill – and perhaps the cottage itself – was sometimes known as Braich-y-Gwynt (the Elbow of the Wind) because of its exposed position in stormy weather, but its situation, looking out southward over a broad, spreading landscape and westward onto Bryntysilio's great neighbouring hills, was one of the prettiest in the region. The Martins were so charmed with this spot, and with the countryside around it, that they determined to buy the property if it ever came on the market. In May, 1866 they were able to get the cottage and the land belonging to it. (Later purchases greatly expanded Martin's Welsh property; eventually he owned about a thousand acres of land in the Glyn Valley, most of which was evidently tilled by tenant farmers.)[16] The house, which they named Bryntysilio after the hill, was extensively enlarged and modified before it suited their wishes. When the remodelling was complete, the small Georgian cottage had become a moderately spacious Italian villa. A verandah had been added, with cast-iron railings and arches (painted white), extending across the front of the house from the point where a new west wing began and turning the corner to the east side of the house – that is, the side one approached when coming up the hill by the carriage drive. The effect was especially attractive after the verandah became "overhung with rose and jasmine, clematis and honeysuckle." The whole setting was a blend of the formal and the natural, from the velvet lawn in front, with its abrupt edge from which the Horseshoe Falls could be heard below, to the "pleasure grounds," with their shrubberies and statues, and the gardens, with their fruits and flowers, west of the house and on the upward slope behind it.[17]

Bryntsilio, seen from the drive (photograph taken in 1969)

The main entrance of the house had been moved from the front to the east side for ease of entry from one's carriage. On the ground floor were a sitting room for Helen, a small study, a larger library, an "inner hall," and, in the new wing, a drawing-room and a dining room; there was also a large service area at the back. The inner hall, a particularly interesting feature of the house, rose through two stories and was lighted from above, probably by a small stained-glass dome in light shades of amber and green: it was separated from the stairs by arches on the ground floor and by columns above. With a fine sense of drama – and a cheerful adaptation of Italian design to Welsh custom – the Martins had the "ceremony of kettledrum" performed here. Upstairs were the bedrooms, including Theodore's "den" – a spacious "compound of bedroom, sitting-room, and library." Like the London house but on a smaller scale, Bryntysilio was filled with drawings, paintings, and sculptures.[18]

As Mrs. Theodore Martin, Helen found herself in control of a miniature domestic kingdom. In the era before modern plumbing and central heat, a house like the one on Onslow Square required a sizable staff. (For a start, the hot water for washing and shaving had to be carried up three flights of stairs.)[19] The number of servants employed here may have varied from time to time, but in later years there were a housekeeper, a butler, and perhaps eight or ten others (not counting a groom or coachman). Bryntysilio, though more modest in its demands, had a resident housekeeper and gardener; the Martins also took some of their London staff with them when they went to Wales.[20] According to her admiring husband, Helen was an efficient administrator, and, though new to such duties, she soon created a "model household." Not that she was without servant problems. "*Sobriety* is a grand matter," she wrote when inquiring about a Scottish lass who had been recommended to her. "I have suffered so much in my maids, I grieve to say, from the other thing." Actually one is rather sorry for the servants who "learned to fulfil their duties" under her "observing eye," for her rule was to slight nothing, however trivial, which "could either make or mar completeness."[21] But, despite her gimlet-eyed perfectionism, Helen could respond warmly to conscientious servants, just as she had done to young actors, however clumsy, who accepted her suggestions for improvement – and she could inspire loyalty and affection in them. A particularly devoted attendant in later years was Jane Anne Williams, who first caught the Martins' interest as a child living near Bryntysilio. When she left school, at age fourteen, Jane joined their service and was trained by Helen to be her personal maid; she remained, in an association of mutual regard, for nearly twenty years, and, even after she married, Mrs. Jones (as she then was) would return in cases of special need.[22]

The Martins obviously had a life of domestic comfort, but what of the more intimate relationship of husband and wife? Would not Theodore have been rather like Thackeray's faithful Dobbin when at last he had his Amelia? And would not Helen have tired sometimes of the idealised role he had assigned her?

If there was the slightest disappointment on Theodore's part he never let it be seen: as far as anyone could tell, his devotion was as great as ever and his new felicity brought the kind of contentment he had craved. He never lost his pride in Helen as an actress; not only had he agreed before marriage that she would be "free to continue the practice of her art," but he encouraged her in her occasional engagements and sometimes accompanied her. As he later wrote, "One might as justly say to Tennyson, Do not write ... as have said to her, Do not act!"[23] Theodore remained, as before, Helen Faucit's chief fan and public relations man. His reverential attitude toward his wife's "genius" was proverbial: according to one story, "when she came on stage for the first time in the evening he used to rise in his stall and bow to her."[24]

Not only as an actress but also as a critic – of art and literature, as well as of theatrical performance – Helen commanded her husband's admiration. In letters to friends he spoke proudly of her taste and acumen, and he quoted her criticisms freely. He often wrote to John (and later William) Blackwood to give his reactions to articles and stories in *Blackwood's Magazine*. Sometimes he would report Helen's agreement with him, but at least once, having committed himself to praising a story before Helen had read it, he later backed down, chastened, after hearing her criticisms.[25] He often read his own works to her as he was composing them and asked for advice. When he paid tribute, in her biography, to the "fine judgment and tact" with which she had helped him over difficulties in his writing and to the "severely critical eye" that had caught any "flaw in composition, great or small," he was simply echoing what he had been saying to friends for years.[26] And when Edward Russell wrote that Helen Faucit's "literary and critical consciousness," so much "more definite and more delicately cultivated" than that of most actors, was probably due in part to her husband's influence, Theodore hastened to set him straight: "it is not I," he wrote, "who have helped to develop her literary taste & insight, but she who has done that for me."[27]

Theodore was proud of his wife's fashionable appearance, and he took a smug satisfaction in visits to the famous Charles Worth in Paris, who designed dresses for her.[28] Arthur Munby, a young friend of the Martins, mentions her "very elegant toilette" in one of his diary entries and remarks that "her taste in dress is admirable."[29] Advancing age did nothing to diminish Helen's interest in beautiful clothes or Theodore's pride in the way she looked. Mrs. Margaret Oliphant describes the ageing husband and wife in a vivid but patronizing way, tinged perhaps with envy:

> There used to be Lady Martin ... in a large Rubens hat and a long sweeping feather, though long past the age of such vanities ... with all the old world graces, and the consciousness of having been more admired than any woman of her day, which gives an ineffable air to an old beauty. Her husband ... was so evidently and so constantly the first

> of all her admirers, leading the band, that the group was always interesting and touching … . There was the twinkle of Bon Gaultier in Sir Theodore's eye on other matters, but never where his wife was concerned.[30]

In his biography of his wife Theodore Martin never tires of extolling her principles, especially her ideals for the theatrical profession. He approvingly quotes from her letter thanking the Bishop of Manchester for his speech defending the stage: "I have ever found my art a most purifying and ennobling one and the aim of all my life has been to educate and elevate myself *up to it*."[31] That Helen's life had been a model of nobility was an article of faith with her husband. When a correspondent asked her whether a stage career did not present many temptations to immorality, Theodore was outraged: "a strange question to put to my wife of all women." Her reply was amusingly disingenuous: any such temptations would have to come from "defects of character" and from allowing "personal vanity" to outweigh a pursuit of "art for its own sake, and as an instrument of good."[32] One must remember, however, the detraction constantly suffered by the acting profession from stern religious doctrines, snobbish social ideas, and loose popular gossip –to say nothing of harsh comments by luminaries of its own like Macready and Fanny Kemble. Ardent in defending her profession, Helen resolutely forgot her family's irregularities, her own early "temptations." The sincerest devotion in her life was to her art, and she justified it, in the best way possible at that time, by arguments that the theatre was a powerful force for good. It is no wonder that Theodore, seeing the light of mission in her eyes, mistook it for the light of holiness.

Luckily for her husband, Helen was not always in the heroic vein. As an actress she had often been praised for the captivating charm of her love scenes. "Her expression of love," wrote George Vandenhoff, "is the most beautifully confiding, trustful, self-abandoning in its tone, that I have ever witnessed in any actress; it is intensely fascinating."[33] Her Rosalind's unreserved expression of love had enchanted Theodore in 1843, and he had never stopped dreaming of being the real-life lover who would inspire that radiant look, those rapturous tones. Let us hope he got his wish. Being a gentleman, he would not have mentioned this aspect of his personal life. Instead he emphasized the inspiration he had received, so he said, from his wife's sweetness, modesty, and quiet charm. In the tenth year of their marriage he published his translation of Dante's *Vita Nuova*, which, he reported, had grown out of "a magazine article written in 1845, – the result, in great measure, of the impression made upon me by Miss Faucit … . She had indeed opened up to me `a new life' … ." He dedicated it to her, with a sonnet comparing her to Dante's Beatrice.[34]

The picture is so perfect that one looks for a flaw. What of the "Meek, unpretending" spirit that Martin attributes to his wife? Surely the woman who ordered her household so expertly and expressed her views on the arts with such assurance was more like Shakespeare's Beatrice than like Dante's, as envisioned by Martin. A "self-distrustful" tendency had once existed, truly enough, along with the ambition and pride that made it the more painful, but would it not have vanished with the independence and fame of stardom? Theodore, however, believed it permanently ingrained, and there is evidence that the self-protective habits of earlier days were never quite overcome. Although modest and unassuming among friends and admirers, the mature Helen, when she suspected hostility or indifference, became the most formidable of *grande dames*. Madge Kendal, for example, found her manner "rather alarming" at first, but when the veteran actress realized the younger one's genuine pleasure in meeting her the ice melted in smiles, revealing a "beautiful character."[35]

Any such conflicts in Helen's personality would have been sympathetically understood by her husband, for she had told him about her early unhappiness – all except the sufferings over her love for Macready and the sordid gossip that arose from it. "Life had much to make up to her," he believed, and he had long since vowed to take the burden of compensation upon himself. When Helen had written him, after Harriet's death, about the soothing effect the Armstrongs' "pattern house" had on her spirits, and had added sadly that her "passion for order and fitness" was a disadvantage, "considering how small is one's regulating power through life," he had inevitably determined to provide her with a model home of her own.[36] In order to afford the luxuries of their life together, he worked very hard at his profession – "grinding at the mill," as he put it wryly. Sometimes, at the end of the day, he was too tired even to read, much less do any literary work.[37] Fortunately his profession was seasonal; several months of the year could usually be devoted to travel, recreation, and writing.

Knowing of Helen's past illnesses, Theodore was unremittingly attentive to her well-being. When London weather was "trying," he arranged for a visit to Bath, Brighton or some other resort; when the Martins travelled, he planned the journey in easy stages so as not to overtire her; when she became ill, he looked after her assiduously. He rarely grumbled when her health caused a change in his plans: just once, in scores of his letters, does one find a slight touch of annoyance on this subject.[38] His solicitude for her peace of mind was equally great. Touching evidence of this is his official (and, no doubt, embarrassed) presence at her mother's second marriage ceremony. Helen's father died on 31 October 1853; on 16 November, her mother and William Farren, after living together for more than three decades, were married in Holy Trinity Church, Brompton. Theodore Martin signed his name as a witness.[39] One can imagine Helen waiting at home with nervous impatience until her husband returned with the reassuring news that all was now legal. What this belated respectability meant to her may be guessed from her letter, written many years later, to correct some mistakes in Charles E.L. Wingate's article "Some Famous Hermiones of the Past." At the end she wrote of her mother, "Perhaps you knew that she made a second marriage with the famous comedian Mr Wm Farren – by whom she had two sons …"[40] If the careful wording conveyed a misleading notion of chronology, who could blame her? Certainly not her sympathetic husband.

As for Helen, she obviously enjoyed her new role in society, and she liked being cherished and deferred to by her husband. If she grew tired of his constant solicitude, no sign of her impatience remains. She seems to have been genuinely fond of him and to have enjoyed his companionship – as in the winter evenings when he read aloud from Scott's novels, his "Scotch tongue" giving "the right meaning and accent" to the passages in dialect.[41]

Although Theodore clearly idolised his wife, one does wonder whether, as a self-respecting Victorian husband, he did not sometimes insist upon the obedience she had vowed at marriage. He certainly subscribed to the conventional belief that the man is head of the household. When a friend deplored Prince Albert's presumption in advising Queen Victoria on matters of state, Theodore replied sharply: "When [the sovereign] is a woman, unless you are to suppose a divorce of *mind*, while there is a union of *body*, she must take counsel with her husband. … While, therefore, *queens are permitted*, we must accept the facts of human nature, & make Queen and Consort as nearly *one* as we can."[42] (This in spite of his great respect for Queen Victoria!) Yet, for all his belief in the natural leadership of men, Theodore also esteemed strength of mind and personality in women. In reading Harriet Martineau's autobiography, for example, he found that, even when he disagreed with her ideas, it was "impossible not to admire the many fine qualities of the Woman, both of brain and heart, & above all her splendid courage in giving expression to her Convictions."[43] For exceptional women he would bend the rules – and no woman was more exceptional than that "heroine" to whom he was married. Certainly he did not try to dominate her financially: long before the Married Women's Property Act, she retained control of her professional earnings and wrote cheques on her account as she pleased.[44] As to Helen's demeanour toward her husband, she was a woman of tact, with an actress's sense of timing. She knew when to insist and when to defer, so that no impasse was allowed to develop. And, though she minced no words when her opinions were requested, she obviously respected her husband. Theodore's chivalry and Helen's "womanliness" seem antiquated and artificial today, and the notions of men and women on which they were based are suffocatingly restrictive; yet, practically speaking, the Martins may have achieved a nearer approach to equality than many couples have done in an age with more enlightened views.

The Martins never had any children. This was a disappointment to Theodore, as he occasionally let slip to old friends.[45] Perhaps Helen felt the same way. At any rate, she was fond of other people's children. During the early years of her marriage one of her maids had a four-year-old daughter who could "sing like a little angel." Helen liked to have the child brought to see her, and she never forgot hearing her sing "Where the bee sucks," the "thrilling sweet upper notes" coming out in an unselfconscious and birdlike way.[46] Later there were the "fresh, bright" Dalrymple sisters, Theodore's second cousins, who sometimes came to stay with the Martins. Other special young friends were the Elias girls, Dora, Annette, and Eleanor, protégées of Helen's who remained lifelong friends.[47] And there was a teenaged cousin of hers (probably a Diddear or a Saville) who spent several Christmas vacations with her and Theodore. Helen liked to take her friends' daughters to the theatre, and, even as an elderly lady, "Victorianly clad … in sweeping skirts and shawls," she had the neighbourhood children over for tea.[48]

Some young friends looked to the Martins' marriage as an ideal. During an "animated conversation" about "the ways of married folks, their pettiness & little mutual cruelties of word & look," Annie Thackeray exclaimed ardently, "Oh, dearest Mrs. Martin! I often think if it were not for you & Mr. Martin I could not bear it – it makes me so unhappy, seeing all this among so *many* people one knows!"[49]

As Helen looked back on the emotional turmoil of her first love, it was not in regret over what she had missed but in commiseration with her earlier self – "Poor young thing!" When she thought of Macready now, it was mostly with tenderness and gratitude. Yet sometimes, even after many years, she could receive a sudden, poignant reminder of the old emotions – as on 2 March 1868, when she realized that the next day was Macready's birthday. "How long ago," she wrote in her diary, "and yet how near, it looks since he told me it was his birthday. I remember it well – even his very words." Under pressure of this memory she wrote to him, breaking the long silence of their estrangement. A few days later a sale was announced of Macready's "fine collection of line engravings," and Helen was eager to have one "as a memorial of the old times." She bid for and obtained Raphael's "Sunoatore di Violino," engraved by Felsing, which used to hang in Macready's London house – and used to remind people of her. As Theodore reported, though without realizing the full significance, "The sight of the once familiar engravings seems to have awakened recollections of 'old unhappy times,'" for in the diary entry telling of them she wrote: "Why do people sigh, and look back, and think youth means happiness … I would not go through that time again for anything that life has, that I see, to offer."[50] And yet she wanted Macready's engraving to hang in her boudoir. It was a little like Harriet's memorial tablet on the wall of Rugby church.

After this Helen wrote to Macready for each birthday. Occasionally she corresponded with Mrs. Macready (his second wife), who wrote on behalf of her ailing husband. The birthday letter of 1870, which begins "Will you accept, my very dear friend, my heartiest greetings" and ends "Your very affectionate friend," reveals that the friendship had been reestablished – and on the level that

Macready had hoped for in the early days. In it Helen recalls his introducing her to Tennyson's poetry with a gift volume, and she adds, "… I have many [other acts of kindness] to remind me … how good you were in putting things before me to help me work upwards!"[51]

In the summer of 1871, when Macready, now very frail, was in London for medical treatment, Helen went to visit him. She found him "changed, and yet not changed – like a great ship, past its work but grand in its ruin." She was so touched by his "tender, gentle, affectionate greeting" that she could not trust herself to stay long, but she returned the next day, bringing Theodore with her. Macready was asleep on a couch when they arrived. When his eyes opened, to see Helen watching him, he "gazed at [her] with a pleased surprise" – very like that of King Lear, she thought, when he awakened to see his long-estranged daughter restored to him.[52] Less than two years later he was dead. But the reconciliation had been complete, the old ghosts laid peacefully to rest.

Chapter 12

Mrs. Martin as Helen Faucit

THE BRIDE lost no time in proving that marriage had not ended her career. Early in 1852, barely two months after returning from her honeymoon, she began some occasional appearances at Drury Lane, and later the same year she had three provincial engagements. But, although she continued to act professionally for two decades longer, this period of her career differed drastically from the eight years of stardom before her marriage. Instead of more than a hundred performances annually, the average now varied erratically, from forty-nine in her busiest year to none at all (barring a single benefit) in four of the years. The decline in acting venues was just as striking. Instead of thirty-three cities there were only nine, four of which were of predominant importance – London, Manchester, Glasgow, and Edinburgh. No wonder reviewers sometimes said she had "come out of retirement" to act for a few nights. But, though she no longer gave priority to her career, she kept a firm hold on it. By retaining the name Helen Faucit for the stage she not only marked off her professional from her private life but also stressed the continuity of her career.

Her first engagement, at Drury Lane, included just seven performances, devoted to three characters – Juliet, Pauline, and Julia – and spread over about four weeks. Reviewers praised all the portrayals, especially the passionate and poetic Juliet.[1] They complained, however, that deficiencies in the productions were the more glaring when contrasted with Helen Faucit's fine acting. Alfred Bunn, who had taken over Drury Lane again after Anderson's bankruptcy, was up to his old tricks, spending money on opera, ballet, and pantomime but skimping on legitimate drama. In *Romeo and Juliet* the "miscellaneous and inconsistent scenery," the "dingy dresses of no particular age or nation," and, worst of all, the "poor, flat, and meagre interpretation of the tragedy, when its heroine is not upon the stage" were denounced by the *Morning Chronicle* (29

January 1852). The *Spectator* agreed: Helen Faucit was surrounded by "such a troop of inanities" that her "really impassioned acting barely suffice[d]" to make the play "endurable."[2]

In mid-April, to inaugurate an eighteen-night engagement at Manchester, Helen Faucit introduced a new role, the heroine in *Adrienne Lecouvreur*, translated by her husband from the French of Eugène Scribe and Ernest Legouvé. The original play had premiered at the Comedie Française in April 1849, with Rachel as Adrienne, and later that year John Oxenford's English version, *The Reigning Favourite*, had appeared at the New Strand, London, with Mrs. Stirling; in 1850 both productions had played in London.[3] No version had yet been seen in Manchester, however. In this drama, Adrienne Lecouvreur, a favourite eighteenth-century actress, meets at a party the Princess de Bouillon, a married woman who is attempting to carry on an affair with Adrienne's beloved, the Count de Saxe. When asked to give a dramatic reading, Adrienne delivers with bitter vehemence a speech from *Phèdre* about guilty passion, pointing it obviously at her rival. The Princess, in revenge for the insult, sends her a poisoned bouquet, and Adrienne inhales its deadly fragrance. Before realizing her danger she becomes reconciled to de Saxe, who promises to marry her; the poison acts, and she dies in his arms. Although love intrigue, jealousy, and revenge rarely featured in Faucit vehicles, the strong situations must have tempted "the English Rachel" to demonstrate her power.

Helen Faucit's Adrienne was very successful; the *Examiner and Times* (21 April 1852) even called it "one of her greatest triumphs." The reviewer admitted, however, that Rachel's interpretation, though less beautiful, was nearer the authors' intention: she had emphasized an artist's distinctive emotions, whereas Helen Faucit had portrayed simple human love as only a woman can feel it. So successfully did the latter bring out Adrienne's womanly qualities that her "tigress-like exultation" over the Princess's discomfiture was considered "foreign and repugnant" to her "noble-minded, pure-hearted" character (*Guardian* 21 April). She was predictably triumphant in the death scene, which gave rein to her talent for depicting morbid physical and mental states.[4] Although Swinbourne, as de Saxe, was ill at ease in eighteenth-century costume and deficient as tender lover, the play was popular enough to be performed on six successive nights of the engagement. Despite her success, however, Helen Faucit never acted Adrienne again: Martin had begged her never to repeat its devastating death scene;[5] and, besides, the Manchester critics, much as they admired her acting, did not care for this "Gallican" play, so "repugnant to English tastes, habits, and feelings."[6]

On 8 June Helen Faucit was in Manchester again to act Iolanthe for one night of the annual Festival, and on 1 November she returned for a second full engagement. This time her novelty was Imogen in *Cymbeline*, which she had never acted here before. Here was an ideal woman, the kind audiences loved to see her portray. Unfortunately, Paumier, especially engaged to act Posthumus, proved unfamiliar with the play; he amused but offended the audience by not responding to cues, then had the audacity to lead the star onstage for her curtain call and to remain there for a speech of self-defence. Although he redeemed himself in a second appearance, his initial difficulty suggests why Imogen, a personal favourite of Helen's, was not more often acted.[7]

On 20 November Helen Faucit began a short engagement at the Theatre Royal, Edinburgh. Murray had retired in 1851, but the new manager, Robert Wyndham (no longer the raw young actor of Parisian days), was struggling to maintain this theatre's high standards. Helen Faucit had lost none of her popularity here: enthusiastic audiences overflowed the house; "pittites" who could not get their accustomed seats let dignity go and sat in the six-penny gallery.[8] Critics called her "queen of the British stage" and "unrivalled representative of Shakespeare's women."[9] Their only complaint – that she wasted her talents on plays by Knowles and Bulwer-Lytton[10] – was contradicted by the playgoers, who remained faithful to Julia and Pauline.

In 1853 Helen Faucit, hoping to bring out Robert Browning's lyrical drama *Colombe's Birthday*, accepted a brief engagement at the Haymarket under J.B. Buckstone, Webster's successor as manager.[11] Browning, writing from his home in Italy, gave her *carte blanche* in cutting the play for the stage; as he wrote John Forster, he expected her to do "just what she liked," adding, "I always liked her."[12] In slightness of plot *Colombe* resembles *King René's Daughter*. Colombe of Ravestein, Duchess of Juliers and Cleves, has her right to Cleves contested on the basis of Salic law by her cousin, Prince Berthold, who, however, chivalrously offers marriage. Valence, the Advocate, who has come to argue for redress of the poor people's sufferings, is deputed to present Berthold's letter to the Duchess. The two fall in love, and, after much soul-searching, Colombe decides to give up the duchy and marry Valence. Helen Faucit could have expected to make no strong effects in Colombe, but she probably hoped, as with Iolanthe, to exploit its delicate beauty.

Buckstone mounted the production attractively and cast the parts as strongly as possible, giving Valence to Barry Sullivan, who had recently made a successful London debut, and Prince Berthold to Henry Howe, a sterling player of the old school. The theatre was full on the opening night, 25 April 1853, and, as *The Times* noted the next day (perhaps ironically), there were all the usual signs of success. Some critics were enthusiastic about the play – the *Morning Post*'s reviewer (26 April) called it one of the best he had seen "for many a day"[13] – but most did not believe the public taste would respond to what was essentially a dramatic poem.[14] *The Times* stated uncompromisingly that there was "scarcely a poem less fitted for stage representation." In Florence Mrs.Browning, who had waited anxiously for the English newspapers, was jubilant over the "satisfactory & flattering" review in the *Post* and, despite the "snarling" tone of *The Times*, indications of "a 'succès d'estime' & something more."[15]

Most reviewers, whether they liked *Colombe* or not, admired Helen Faucit's performance, and some credited it with whatever success the play had enjoyed. She had spoken undistinguished passages with impressive effect, they said, and had made a potentially unintelligible play clear to an audience of mixed cultural backgrounds. Although a few critics thought her sensitivity savoured of affectation or sentimentality,[16] most agreed that her graceful, imaginative acting had demonstrated once more her superlative talents in dramas of a "lofty poetical cast."[17] Interest in her performance kept *Colombe* in the bills for seven of her ten nights, but it was not the new hit she needed.[18] Later, in Manchester, where *King René's Daughter* was so beloved, *Colombe's Birthday* proved even more disappointing. The critics praised Helen Faucit's acting, but they considered the drama too "occult" for the average playgoer.[19] After one repetition she never acted Colombe again.

Her final engagement of 1853, late in the year, was at Liverpool – the last one here until shortly before her retirement.

In 1854 Helen Faucit's theatrical activity fell off sharply because of travels with her husband.[20] Her only engagement, at the Theatre Royal, Manchester, in July, was short and unsuccessful. She was unlucky both in her leading man, John Coleman, who was repeatedly damned by the critics,[21] and in the timing of her appearances. Gustavus Vaughan Brooke, once a favourite stock-company actor in Manchester, had returned to star at the Queen's, and the town rallied to welcome back its own. If the Theatre Royal really did take in only 35 pounds on Helen Faucit's opening night, as Brooke gloatingly reported, while the Queen's was "jammed," her pride suffered a severe blow.[22] She did not act in Manchester again for almost twelve years.

The year 1855 was one of Helen Faucit's busiest theatrical years in this period. It marked a geographical expansion, too: for the first time since her marriage she returned to two cities where she had been a favourite star, Glasgow in February and Dublin in April. At Glasgow, where Edmund Glover now managed the Theatre Royal, she found a much better company than during Alexander's tenure. Her roles were mostly old favourites like Pauline and Rosalind, but her inclusion of Constance in *King John* (rarely acted in her starring days) indicates a continued search for novelty. As always, she was warmly welcomed; from now on, Glasgow would be, next to London, the city where she appeared most often. Her appearances at Dublin signalled a change in policy at the Theatre Royal: John Harris, who succeeded Calcraft as manager in late 1851, had devoted his early years to building as strong a stock company as possible, relying solely on the local actors except in opera; Helen Faucit's engagement in April 1855 broke this practice, unlocking the door for other stars.[23]

This year was notable, too, for her last creation of a dramatic character: Margaret in *Love's Martyrdom* by John Saunders. Despite the enthusiasm of Charles Dickens and Walter Savage Landor, she had been sceptical of the play's chances; but, spurred by sympathy for its young author – and, no doubt, by desperation for a new poetic role – she had agreed to act in it.[24] Her reservations are easy to understand. *Love's Martyrdom* was inspired by Sheridan Knowles's *The Hunchback*, which, maugre its faithful adherents, was outdated as a dramatic model: there were similarities in character types, dramatic situation, and even style of writing. Franklyn, a hunchback, is a country squire, well-to-do, brilliant, and idealistic, but jealous and embittered. He loves his ward, Margaret, a high-spirited, stubborn, but warm-hearted girl, who returns his love. When his younger brother, Clarence, returns after a long absence and renews an old interest in Margaret, Franklyn leaps to the conclusion that she is inconstant and denounces her. He wounds Clarence in a duel but immediately repents and is ready to bless the marriage he believes both young people want. Margaret's pride is so hurt by his lack of faith that she accepts Clarence's proposal. In a dramatic scene her cousin Laneham explains to her the effect her guardian's deformity has had on his personality and convinces her that Franklyn still loves her. Belatedly she realizes the depth of her own love, but honour demands that she keep her engagement. Fortunately Clarence repents of having "ruined" Laneham's sister Julia and determines to marry her, leaving Margaret free to marry Franklyn. That is the main plot; a secondary one is equally trite. *Love's Martyrdom* is, however, more interesting than a summary suggests. In an acute analysis the *Spectator* (16 June 1855) theorised that Saunders had intended to go beyond Knowles in exploring a handicap's influence on "an essentially virtuous disposition" but that he had "stumbled between" two kinds of plays – a conventional "drama of action" and a modern psychological study. Sustained emphasis on the hunchback, rather than on Margaret, might have resulted in a "powerful and original play." Exactly. But without Helen Faucit in the cast.

Buckstone introduced *Love's Martyrdom* at the Haymarket on 11 June 1855 during Helen Faucit's engagement there. The *mise en scène* was appropriate, and the cast included proficient actors like Barry Sullivan as Franklyn and William Farren, Jr. (Helen's half-brother) as Clarence. Reviewers agreed on the play's success, but, judging by a detailed account of audience response (*The Times*, 12 June), it was partial at best. Sullivan was disappointing as Franklyn, frustrated by a character who, though described as admirable, shows mainly his darker side in action.[25] Helen Faucit, luckier in Margaret, was entirely successful. The *Globe* gushed that, for passion, pathos, and exquisitely shaded depiction of "womanly love," she was beyond compare with "any actress we know, French, English, or German."[26] The *Morning Chronicle* credited the play's success, not to its own merit, but to her acting, especially in the "wild outbreak of tumultuous emotion" when she avowed to Laneham her great passion for Franklyn, now apparently lost to her. That "sensation," said the *Theatrical Journal*, "probably saved the piece."

But it was "saved" for only six nights. The *Sunday Times* (17 June) called its production a "respectable mistake" since the "blasé public" demanded some amusement "beyond literature." From now on Helen Faucit would venture on a new play only if it had unmistakable theatrical potentialities as well as literary merit. In the years ahead, hopes for such a paragon would arise, time after time, but would always come to nothing.

On 16 July, ten days after concluding her own engagement, Helen performed Iolanthe, also at the Haymarket, as part of a lengthy programme celebrating William Farren's farewell to the stage. The aftermath, with its prolonged cheering and handkerchief-waving, its stageful of well-wishing friends,[27] was a vivid reminder of Charles Kemble's farewell, some nineteen years before, in which she as a young actress had weepingly participated.

Having found her way back to Ireland, Helen Faucit returned there in May 1856 for an engagement at the Theatre Royal, Dublin (notable for a special production of *Cymbeline* with much-admired scenery and costumes), followed, after a visit with the Stokeses, by several nights at the Theatre Royal, Belfast, in early June. Both engagements were very successful. A recurring theme in the Dublin reviews was Miss Faucit's retention of her youthful charms.[28] In her early forties, she was hardly in danger of decrepitude, but there was such demand for youth and beauty in a romantic actress that much was made of her agelessness. In later years such assertions would seem like whistling in the dark.

Helen had accepted engagments in Glasgow and Edinburgh in November 1856, but a serious illness, which struck the day after her arrival in Glasgow, forced her to cancel them and even prevented her from travelling home for a month.[29] In 1857, however, she did act in these cities (in March) as well as in Belfast and Dublin (in April). In Edinburgh she first met young Henry Irving, who acted Pisanio to her Imogen. Edmund Glover, actor-manager at Glasgow, also travelled to Belfast as her leading man. In all four engagements she reintroduced Lady Mabel in *The Patrician's Daughter*, which had not been seen since her marriage. As in the past, critics praised her acting but found fault with the play. In Belfast, though, Mordaunt's ringingly democratic lines, in the much-condemned rejection scene, won "acclamation" both for Glover's effective delivery and for the "local appropriateness of the words."[30] Helen did not act Lady Mabel after this year. Its brief revival, the inclusion of the rarely-acted Desdemona at Glasgow and the long-ignored Kate the Shrew at Dublin – all speak of the difficult search for variety.

Early in 1858 Helen was caught up in the excitement over the Princess Royal's approaching marriage to Prince Frederick William of Prussia. Among the celebrations planned were four Festival Performances, to be held at Her Majesty's Theatre and devoted, respectively, to tragedy, comedy, English opera, and Italian opera. Charles Kean, who had been producing Shakespeare impressively at the Princess's Theatre and also managing the Windsor theatricals, was widely expected to direct the Festival Performances. When John Mitchell of St. James's Theatre was chosen instead, Kean indignantly refused an invitation to have his company perform *Macbeth* on the "tragic" evening. After repeated appeals had failed, Mitchell recruited Phelps and Helen Faucit, who acted the Macbeths on 19 January. The awkward circumstances put Phelps out of favour with Kean's supporters and encouraged a tendency to belittle the performances, particularly *Macbeth*.[31]

The guests of honour contributed to the awkwardness. The theatre had been elegantly decorated for them, with lacy draperies hanging over the panels of the boxes, festooned at the top with blue silk, and wreaths of flowers suspended in the spaces between the tiers. Eight boxes had been thrown together to accommodate the royal party and their attendants – enough people to fill sixteen carriages. By 7:30, the announced curtain time, everyone was eagerly awaiting the entrance of this glittering company. When half an hour had passed without their arrival, the director tried to appease the restless audience by beginning the play, but the performance moved too slowly to keep attention from the empty box. Finally, at nine o'clock, in the midst of Macbeth's dagger soliloquy, the royal party arrived – the Queen "magnificently attired" and decked with a "profusion of diamonds," the Princess Royal appropriately gowned in white, with a wreath of red roses on her head. After the audience had risen and applauded, the performance was resumed, but any momentum had been lost. Although the two stars received curtain calls, Helen Faucit did not acknowledge hers. As for the Queen, she fidgeted and longed to be freed from this singularly gloomy form of festivity. Even the Keeleys in the farce *Twice Killed* did not erase her bad humour. No wonder: it was nearly one o'clock when the final curtain closed. Home at last, she fumed to her diary: "The performance of 'Macbeth' perfectly atrocious. Phelps and Miss Helen Faucit indescribably bad and slow… Much too long." A German visitor, Theodor Fontane, in his entertaining account of the event, calls it "little better than a fiasco," not because of the acting – "Both leading roles … were played masterfully" – but because of the "tactless choice" of a play for the occasion.[32]

Reviewers were embarrassed because the illustrious foreigners had not been treated to a sumptuous production in Kean's style. Their criticisms of the major actors were mixed. If the visitors considered English acting below the standard of Rachel and Talma, said the *Morning Herald*, they were right. Some critics remarked that Phelps was not at his best in Macbeth, that he was a careful elocutionist rather than an effective impersonator of the character.[33] Helen Faucit fared somewhat better. The *Sunday Times* praised her "thrilling power" and declared, hyperbolically, that she had "never in her life played better." The *Examiner*, in Whiggish denial of the public's "flunkeyism" toward the Court, asserted that she never for a moment lost her power over the audience; but the *Spectator*, exaggerating on the other side, declared that the Court was everything and the tragedy "nothing."

Barely a month later Helen Faucit's Lady Macbeth was seen in more favourable circumstances. During an engagement at Charles Dillon's Lyceum (between 18 February and 15 March) she devoted the first four of nine performances to *Macbeth.* For the past two years Dillon, now in his late forties, had been trying to duplicate in London the popularity he had won in the provinces, meanwhile fighting a losing battle as a manager.[34] An effective emotional actor, he depicted Macbeth as more spirited and less cowardly than usual, but at the same time eloquently expressed his agitation, superstitious fancies, and "tenderly pensive" reflections.[35] Helen Faucit's Lady Macbeth was "rapturously" applauded by a "brilliant" audience, and it received warm praise from reviewers. Nowhere in Europe, boasted the *Literary Gazette*, could the stage produce a "finer masterpiece of art" (20 February: 187). Other critics, slightly more restrained, ranked Lady Macbeth among Miss Faucit's best characters and declared that she was "unrivalled" in the part.[36] Her "brilliantly imaginative" performance won praise for its intelligence and artistry, its skilful balancing of the character's contrasting qualities. Most lauded were her early passages, with their "fearful steeling" of the woman against her own nature, and her banquet scene, with its "subtlety and refinement."[37]

Helen Faucit, however, could not convert everyone to her complex interpretation. Her portrayal was too sympathetic to please traditional critics: the *Daily Telegraph*, though admitting her artistry, declared that an actress who tried to impart anything but a "savage temperament" to this character undertook a thankless task.[38] Yet it was sufficiently wicked and painful to horrify spectators who idealised Helen Faucit. One who signed herself "E.de C." wrote to the actress on 27 February:

> … we cannot love Lady Macbeth. We admire with a sublime horror; we pity, hate, and dread. The more perfect the impersonation, the stronger the impression … I … cannot divest myself of the image of the [sleepwalking] queen … a fearful vision, a triumph of the histrionic art, but not Miss Helen Faucit. If ever face were formed to feel all that is most tender, most noble, most lovable in woman, it is surely [hers].[39]

Such responses may reflect some influence beyond stage tradition and type-casting. Lady Macbeth – ambitious, assertive, destructive, yet grand and impressive – was the opposite of the womanly ideal. It seemed shockingly inappropriate to endow her with feminine grace and wifely passion.

When acting Lady Macbeth in London in 1851, Helen Faucit had been pitted against two strong rivals. Now Mrs. Warner was dead, and Miss Glyn was devoting herself primarily to Shakespearean readings. Thus the critics, rather than making comparisons, were mostly content to consider Miss Faucit's portrayal on its own merits. Her 1858 performances of Lady Macbeth, though few, brought her successfully before Londoners in a role they had not usually associated with her.

In the next few years she devoted very little time to her profession. Her only engagement in 1859 was at Glasgow, where she reintroduced *Nina Sforza* after years of dormancy – a futile attempt at variety with a play that had never been popular there.[40] After no engagements at all in 1860, she had two in 1861. At Glasgow, where the recently widowed Mrs. Edmund Glover was valiantly keeping the Theatre Royal going, she acted with brilliant success in late February and early March. Her lavishly praised performances were enhanced by T. Swinbourne's fine cooperation, especially in *Macbeth*.[41] At the Theatre Royal, Edinburgh, however, where Wyndham's company had lowered its standards until it lacked the aggregate talent for Shakespeare, she had a disappointing engagement late in the year.[42] Her Portia, dispirited by a Bassanio who emoted in "turgid tragic style," was understandably less "lively" than usual.[43]

Two years passed with no professional engagements, though she did participate in a fund-raising benefit for a national Shakespeare monument (Drury Lane, 30 June 1863). Mrs. Glover, who had lost the Theatre Royal, Glasgow, by fire but started over in January 1863 at the Prince's Theatre, hoped to include Glasgow's favourite actress in her new season, but apparently the plan fell through.[44] Helen Faucit did have a short engagement there, however, in the spring, 1864, and also one at Edinburgh. This time she aroused excitement in both cities.[45] A review in the *Caledonian Mercury* (15 April), which declared Lady Macbeth one of her finest parts, gave approving emphasis to her "wickedness, and power, and pride" but deplored the traditional omission of the "fainting (or affected faint)." Helen agreed the faint was important but thought it genuine.[46] When next she acted in *Macbeth*, the Lady fainted.

The most important theatrical events of 1864, celebrations of Shakespeare's Tercentenary, revealed Helen Faucit (like many others) in a discreditable light. Since Richard Foulkes, in his excellent book on the Tercentenary, has already told the sorry but amusing story of its planning stages,[47] there is no need to discuss subjects like the rival committees in London and Stratford (Theodore Martin belonged to both), but only to touch on salient theatrical problems. The Keans, being in Australia, were unavailable. Both Phelps and Helen Faucit agreed to act in the "birthday week" performances at Stratford, but both withdrew: Phelps because, having expected to perform a tragic hero, he was cast as Posthumus to Helen Faucit's Imogen, while Charles Fechter, the innovative French actor, was announced for Hamlet; Helen Faucit because, having accepted Rosalind when plans for *Cymbeline* fell through, she was shocked by the substitution of *Romeo and Juliet* for *Hamlet*, with Stella Colas, a new French actress, as Juliet. (Rosalind had to be taken by Mrs. Hermann Vezin.) As Robert E. Hunter, quondam paid secretary to the Stratford Committee, remarked, "the Siddons of the age" could not appear in comedy after "a French lady had played *Juliet*."[48] The *London Review* remarked cynically:

> Mr. Phelps was jealous of Mr. Fechter, Miss Faucit of Miss Stella Colas, and Miss Glyn would not act for either party – London or Stratford – because her husband, Mr. Dallas [a journalist], had written down one side and written up the other. This is called honouring Shakespeare. (7 May 1864: 490)

Helen Faucit's behaviour was, in part, a response to events of the preceding year. On 24 June 1863 young Stella Colas had burst upon the London scene in Juliet at the Princess's Theatre. Although her heavy accent and her manner of chopping up the lines made her unintelligible at times, her beauty and fire took the public by storm. Some critics were unimpressed,[49] but others were as enthusiastic as the audiences that filled the theatre each night. The *Sunday Times* (28 June) exclaimed rapturously: "for the first time since Miss O'Neill's day, the character has been sustained by a lady who possesses the almost impossible characteristics of the part – extreme youth and brilliant and accomplished histrionic powers." Helen must have seethed, for Juliet was *her* character, the one with the strongest hold on her memories and emotions. Theodore did what he could to dethrone the impostor: in an anonymous article deploring modern theatrical and critical trends, he declared that Stella Colas had made Juliet a mere vehicle for "displaying the attractions of a pretty face, the coquetry of a French *ingénue*, and the rodomontade of a Boulevard theatre."[50] But it was all in vain. When the Gallic Juliet was chosen for Stratford, Helen was understandably affronted.

When Stella Colas returned to the Princess's in May, 1864, Henry Morley of the *Examiner* wrote that, although her Juliet was not "quite so bad" as before, it was still "abominable." Several months later he attacked this actress as "obtrusively self-conscious, showy, jerky, artificial as a puppet," even in French melodrama. "To name Mlle. Colas in the same line with Mrs. Hermann Vezin," he declared, "would be preposterous enough; but she simply is not an actress at all in the sense in which an English Helen Faucit or an Italian Ristori is an actress."[51] Here was balm for Helen's wounded pride.

Better still was her own triumphant return to the London stage a few months later. She had received no London offer since 1858, despite letters and articles in the press urging her return; but now, in the Tercentenary year, her services were again in demand – and at Drury Lane, where she had not acted in twelve years. Despite its vicissitudes since 1843, Drury Lane's reputation as the elder of the great "national" theatres had not been forgotten. The theatres that had best deserved the title of "national" in the 1850s could claim it no longer: Kean had left the Princess's in 1859 and Phelps had given up Sadler's Wells in 1862. But Drury Lane, under Edmund Falconer and F.B. Chatterton, gave promise of becoming once more the home of poetic drama: having offered two impressive productions during their second season (1863-64), the managers were now planning a series of Shakespearean revivals. Although

Phelps, their principal actor and director, was the staple attraction, Helen Faucit joined them as a visiting star for two productions in the autumn (1864) and returned for two additional ones in the spring (1865), usually acting four nights a week; she had a final engagement at Drury Lane in the autumn of 1866.[52] These engagements, the longest and most intensive in London since her Macready years, were among the great successes of her career – astonishingly so for an actress past her physical prime who played romantic heroines in a style no longer in vogue.

Her first role was Imogen in *Cymbeline*, which opened on 17 October 1864 with Samuel Phelps as Posthumus and William Creswick as Iachimo. Despite critical admiration of Imogen's character, the play itself had been relatively unpopular, but this production was very favourably received. Its visual beauty reminded several critics of Macready's staging – aptly enough, since the scenery *was* Macready's, still in good condition after twenty years in storage and freshly touched up by William Beverley.[53] Imogen's tent-shaped bed made its appearance again with a lacy new canopy.[54] The "angel-like" beauty that her unknown brothers saw in "Fidele" was suggested by the delicacy and grace of her white pageboy tunic, edged in blue. In short, the decor was, like the play itself, more romantic and symbolic than realistic or historical. The acting was "altogether exceedingly creditable," said *The Times*, and most of the other journals agreed. Phelps was praised for his "manly earnestness," his tenderness, his rapid emotional transitions, and his "passionate outburst" when reunited with Imogen. Creswick's Iachimo was notable for its "easy audacity," and Walter Lacy's Cloten, rather than the usual buffoon, was a "gentleman" struggling with a "boor." As the reviews show, however, the star was clearly Helen Faucit.[55]

The excitement over her reappearance was tremendous. The expectations, both from old admirers and from playgoers who had only heard of her, were so great, said the *Morning Herald*, that a "less consummate actress" would have been doomed to disaster, yet everyone who saw her was convinced that "a great actress stood before him." An enormous first-night audience welcomed her tumultuously, and as the play progressed the applause increased – not just "a tribute to established fame but a fresh appreciation of artistic excellence" (*The Times* 18 October). Gratifyingly (for she had just passed her fiftieth birthday), several writers maintained that Miss Faucit's voice, figure, and bearing were still as charming as in her heyday and her art was as masterful; the only difference was that her acting now seemed "more elaborated and finished."[56] Her portrayal's artistic completeness was what impressed critics most. *The Times* (20 October) emphasized her "voice-and-gesture painting," which was so expressive that "the slightest thought or feeling" seemed to have "its reflex in a plastic frame."[57] Several reviewers contrasted her "true art" with the "vulgar and sensational performances" of ordinary London actresses.[58]

Helen Faucit as Imogen, by an unknown artist
(by courtesy of the Folger Shakespeare Library)

An apologist for the newer school of acting, however, argued on the basis of changing political and social attitudes that her style, grounded in "dramatic idealism," was no longer in tune with the times. He maintained that, despite *Cymbeline*'s admitted incongruity with modern realism, and despite Imogen's airy ideality in some passages, an infusion of human weakness was needed for a greater sense of reality (*Spectator*). Some critics who approved of Miss Faucit's idealising tendency disliked certain techniques associated with it: for example, her excessive care (as Henry Morley thought) "to make every gesture an embodiment of thought … as when after the cry, 'What ho, Pisanio!' she remain[ed] with upraised arm throughout half the speech of Iachimo" (*Examiner*). It was the hint of stylization, perhaps, that annoyed him, not merely the use of gesture to suggest thought. Like some other critics, he noticed that Miss Faucit had not always "the art to conceal art."[59] Even so, Morley was among her warmest admirers. Noting her "quick and refined perception of the poetry she is interpreting," he wrote later (11 Mar. 1865: 152), "She can realize line by line, with tone and gesture, more of the spiritual grace and beauty of true poetry than any lady who now acts upon the English stage."

After eight performances *Cymbeline* was halted and the theatre closed for two nights while "Immense Preparations" were made for a grand revival of *Macbeth*. The production, which opened on 3 November, was full of striking pictures – like the eerily beautiful cauldron scene, whose rocky, moonlit landscape was cut by a large chasm, strangely lit by the bluish glare of the cauldron; and the impressive denouement at Dunsinane Castle, where a breach made by battering rams in apparently solid stonework was filled with an "endless succession of assailants swarm[ing] beneath the protecting smoke of the conflagration."[60] This was the most spectacular production in which Helen Faucit ever acted.

It was enormously popular. On the first night the theatre was besieged long before curtain time, and even after all seats and standing room were filled, a disappointed crowd still remained outside. Reviewers were jubilant: the public taste for great drama had been revived; Drury Lane's regained prestige had the "practical value of a patent."[61] Night after night crowds flocked to the theatre. When John Oxenford, who had already reviewed the production for *The Times*, returned to see it again, he had to stand the whole evening; so did Theodore Martin, the husband of "Lady Macbeth."[62] During the run of *Cymbeline*, other plays had been performed on Helen Faucit's free nights, but *Macbeth* had to be given continuously, with Creswick and Miss Atkinson as the Macbeths on the off-nights. (Phelps and Faucit performed 27 times.) The audiences apparently remained large until 17 December, when the run was ended so that *Cymbeline* could be seen twice more before the holidays.[63] Shakespeare might eventually "spell ruin" for the Drury Lane management, but at the moment - judging by attendance, at least – he spelled success in capital letters.

Although spectacle undoubtedly made the production a hit, the major performances also attracted unusual interest. Despite some complaints about distracting mannerisms and other minor flaws,[64] Phelps was widely esteemed for his intelligence, dignity, and versatility. His Macbeth was a weak and suggestible character in most of the play – "subdued … by the stronger will of his wife," mentally "subjugated" to the Weird Sisters, sunk by guilt into enervating misery – but at the end he triumphed over his weakness.[65]

Helen Faucit's Lady Macbeth, though it was well known in the provinces and had received much attention from London reviewers in 1858, was still considered an innovation.[66] As often before, many critics thought Miss Faucit less suited to this character than to others like Imogen, since she was too fragile in physique and "too essentially feminine" in temperament for the "fiend-like queen."[67] Others, however, either conceded no lack of grandeur or declared that, as one put it, "her intellect tower[ed] above all physical deficiencies."[68] The *Sunday Times* even insisted that "tragic dignity and grandeur" were "precisely the qualities" she was able to represent most satisfactorily, that her Lady Macbeth was, in fact, superior to her admirable but "too perfect" Imogen. The disagreement about "grandeur" arose in part from varying responses to Helen Faucit's devices for gaining this effect without benefit of physical power: her regal bearing was sufficiently impressive for some spectators, like John Doran, but in addition she occasionally used statuesque poses to set the tone of a scene or to endow a high moment with poetic significance (see Afterpiece). John Oxenford found these very effective, but some critics considered them too artificial.[69] For others nothing could replace the imposing form and easy power of more robust actresses. As usual, however, the crux of Helen Faucit's controversial Lady Macbeth was its strong "feminine" element. The critic for the *Daily News* remarked that her "womanly grace" was "often out of tune with the words," but the one for the *Sunday Times*, who praised the portrayal for originality of conception as well as "power, subtlety, and finish," found its femininity profoundly moving. Although the latter, after restudying the play, relinquished the "sympathetic" view as invalid, he could not forget the attraction of the portrayal.[70] Its sympathetic quality was, however, only relative. Indeed for some viewers the womanly traits, rather than mitigating the character's wickedness, subtly emphasized it: illustrating her own precept, this Lady Macbeth looked like the innocent flower but was the serpent under it (*Daily Telegraph*).

Helen Faucit's performance was uneven at first, but it grew in strength and consistency as the run of the play continued. The challenge of making herself heard in huge Drury Lane after an absence of twelve years had produced difficulties, even in Imogen,[71] and in Lady Macbeth these were compounded many times. Henry Morley, the critic who stressed the problem most, wrote in the *Examiner* (3 December) that Helen Faucit's chief defect, over-exertion to compensate for lack of physical strength, was most evident in the scenes prior to Duncan's murder, where she was "far too demonstrative and noisy." Helen, profiting by his unsparing criticism, relearned the lesson taught her by Constance many years before: to substitute emotional intensity for strenuous attempts at physical volume. In his second review of *Macbeth*, 17 December, Morley reported that her change in technique had resulted in "a most harmonious interpretation of the part" and that some passages in the early scenes were now "among the gems of the performance." Her greatest acting, however, was in the "second phase" of the character; here, he said, particularly in the banquet scene, her performance was one that no other English actress could approach (*Examiner* 3 December). There was an odd disagreement about her sleepwalking scene: several critics thought artistry more evident than real feeling, but others were deeply moved by her pathos and "poetical imagining of the character."[72] The *Morning Post*'s summary probably spoke for many viewers: "There may have been a more majestic, but there has rarely, if ever, been a more truthful or a more impassioned representation of Lady Macbeth."

In their "intellectuality" Helen Faucit and Samuel Phelps were compatible, but in personalities and interpretations they were not. Neither had much use for the other: Phelps thought Miss Faucit "gave herself airs," and she looked down on him as an "inadequate successor" to Macready. Later, when recalling their performance in *Macbeth*, she accused him of invariably attempting to upstage her.[73] Phelps, on the other hand, was frustrated as director by her refusal to adopt his suggestions. Accustomed to the "Siddonian" interpretations of Mrs. Warner and Miss Glyn, he probably found the "feminine" Lady Macbeth disconcerting; his hag-ridden Macbeth required a dominant Lady.[74] The wonder is that, with so much discord, the production fared as well as it did.

On 6 March 1865 Helen Faucit began a new series of performances, three nights a week for five weeks, in Imogen, Rosalind, and Juliet. This time there was little reason for a feud: Phelps acted in none of her plays but appeared in such well-known characters of his as Richelieu and Sir Peter Teazle. Walter Montgomery replaced him as Posthumus and also acted Orlando and Romeo. James R. Anderson took over Iachimo from Creswick (not for the better)[75] and also acted Jaques. The plays, which alternated in repertory style, were attractively but not lavishly staged.

The revival of *As You Like It*, which opened on 8 March, proved that the middle-aged Helen Faucit could still delight a London audience in her ever-popular Rosalind. Critics vied with one another in praising her performance. Not even the blarney-specialists of Cork had expressed more enthusiasm for her acting than did the *Sunday Times* of 12 March 1865, and no reviewer anywhere had described a performance in more loving detail. Critics for other journals joined in praising her Rosalind for its grace, subtlety, and refinement balanced with humour, spirit, and "vibrating vivacity."[76] The few adverse comments were usually outweighed by the praise with which they were mixed. G.H. Lewes wrote, for example, in the *Pall Mall Gazette* that the performance was "freckled occasionally" by an over-elaboration of detail and an unnecessary slackening of tempo that marred the otherwise beautiful delivery; yet he described the portrayal as "a diamond with many facets, remarkable for the variety and delicacy of its effects," and he declared that no one who had seen "such a Rosalind" could read *As You Like It* without finding it "illuminated."

The production of *Romeo and Juliet*, first seen on 20 March, was notable for the use of the Shakespearean conclusion and, still more unusual, the original prologue. Both were important to Helen Faucit's mature interpretation of the play as a "Greek tragedy." Since no other actor would learn the additional speech, she spoke the prologue herself, wearing a silk domino over Juliet's costume.[77] Her Juliet was less satisfactory than her Rosalind, mainly because, as the *Morning Post* said (21 March), "Youth, not comparative but absolute and undeniable," was, for many people, an essential qualification. Some critics did gallantly assert that her appearance belied her years and that her manner had lost no "delicacy, grace, or even juvenility." A more honest admirer simply advised spectators to ignore superficial matters and thus discover "a performance as ideal, as intellectual, and as suggestive as the modern stage [was] capable of offering."[78] For some playgoers, however, poetic suggestiveness was not enough. One was John Ranken Towse, a Cambridge student barely twenty years old at this time, who would later become a well-known drama critic in the United States. In his old age Towse recalled seeing Helen Faucit only once, as Juliet, when she "made no effort to conceal the signs of middle age":

> … there was nothing in her face or person to suggest the fascinating and impassioned Juliet. Nor was there much apparent endeavor to simulate either youth or passion. … But, nevertheless, [the performance] had some notable qualities. It had the large, free, significant gesture and the fine diction of the old school. She recited rather than acted, the balcony scene, but her reading of the lines was delicious… In the potion scene she exhibited impressive declamatory power, giving each word and clause its value, and artfully saving her voice for the climaxes, when she poured it forth in magnificent volume, without degenerating into shrieking … vehemence. It was … thoroughly intelligent and artistic, but not inspired. She did not thrill me with a sense of clairvoyant horror, as did Stella Colas. But she had not the spell of youth and beauty to aid her.[79]

As in her preceding engagement, Helen Faucit was held up by some critics as superior to the usual London actors; this time the comparisons were more objectionable because more specific. The most egregious examples were by G.H. Lewes, in the *Pall Mall Gazette*. In *As You Like It*, he declared, none of the acting except Helen Faucit's reflected the "airy, fantastic humour of the piece." Even more damaging was his criticism (8 April) of Phelps, Montgomery, and Anderson in *Julius Caesar* (not a Faucit play), which censured them not only for bad acting but for lacking any "settled *style*." Two styles were open to the Shakespearean actor, he explained, the "ideal," used by John Kemble in the past and by Adelaide Ristori at present, and the now-popular "natural." The latter's most common mistake was "confounding vulgar realism with poetic naturalness." Helen Faucit's style combined the ideal and the natural, her "happiest effects" being in the "poetically natural."

In 1866, prior to her final Drury Lane series, Helen Faucit had three provincial engagements (two in Manchester, one in Birmingham) and gave a dramatic reading in London, 8 June, in aid of the Brompton Consumption Hospital (François Ponsard's *Ulysses* as translated by H.B. Farnie, with Gounod's music).[80] Her last twelve performances at Drury Lane were spread over four weeks (19 November-14 December). This time she repeated Rosalind and added two non-Shakespearean characters, Pauline in *The Lady of Lyons* and Julia in *The Hunchback*. No more appropriate choices could have been made for her last professional appearances in London, as these proved to be: Julia was the first role she had acted here; Pauline was the most famous of her original creations; and Rosalind was the most popular of her Shakespearean characters. Her appearances cut into the run of a spectacular version of *Faust*, with Phelps as Mephistopheles, which could now be seen only on her free nights. But, if reports of packed houses for all her performances are true, Chatterton (now the sole lessee) lost no money by the interruptions.[81]

It had been fourteen years since Helen Faucit had made any London appearances in *The Hunchback*, which was generally considered *passé*. *The Times* observed (3 December) that Julia's incongruities would repel Miss Faucit, who insisted on developing "some definite idea" in each impersonation, but that the passionate scenes in the later acts would attract her; she had fully demonstrated their value, and her "fine performance" deserved careful study. That could be called a "careful" criticism. The *Daily Telegraph* (1 December), which also stressed her effectiveness in the later, more emotional scenes, said – not surprisingly – that the early ones lacked some of the "natural girlish simplicity" and "happy levity" of her former portrayals.

After more than twenty-eight years *The Lady of Lyons* was still holding its own in the theatre, and audiences were still responding emotionally to Helen Faucit's Pauline. Annie Thackeray, now Mrs. Ritchie, wrote to Helen after seeing it: "What a sight that great enthusiastic house was! Why didn't you come when we clapped and clapped and cried!" (Miss Faucit seems to have refused, on principle, an inter-act call.) Geraldine Jewsbury, though not enthusiastic about the play, considered Pauline one of Helen Faucit's "very best pieces of acting."[82] *The Times* (15 December) praised the performance and described it in some detail. Capping the compliments, the *Observer* (25 November) noted the "remarkable" fact that after so long a time Miss Faucit was still "unquestionably the best representative of the part she created."

The Lady of Lyons had many years of life in it yet. Critics might scoff, but there would still be actresses winning success in Pauline and audiences weeping and rejoicing with them. For example, there were highly successful revivals by the Kendals in 1875, by Henry Irving (with Ellen Terry as Pauline) in 1878, and by Mary Anderson in 1883.[83] But, though many actresses played Pauline effectively, both during and after Helen Faucit's career, none ever excelled her portrayal. The *Observer* critic's judgment of 1866 was echoed at various times over the years by other writers – including Bulwer-Lytton's son, Robert, first Earl of Lytton. In respect to the "genuine note of passion," he wrote in 1885, Mary Anderson's Pauline was "altogether inferior to Mrs. Kendal's; still more inferior to Miss Helen Faucit's – the best I have ever seen."[84]

During Helen Faucit's 1866 engagement several critics continued to hold her performances up as models. As before, one or two went further and insulted her fellow players, as in this passage: "it is something when an actor consistently sustains the illusion that she is … Rosalind … but how much … greater the testimony to her skill, when she contrives to maintain the illusion in the face of half a dozen people whose every word mocks it!" (*Pall Mall Gazette*, 24 November).

Although her colleagues received some compensatory praise, the extraordinary eulogies given her at their expense provoked some reactions against her. Most shocking in his defection was the critic for the *Sunday Times*, whose earlier reviews were among the most enthusiastic of her career. Now, in criticising her Julia (9 December), he let loose a counterblast, indignantly protesting against the denigration of other actors and declaring that excessive adulation was ruining Helen Faucit's acting. Her recent performance had been marred by two great defects: a smirking self-consciousness that was "inexpressibly sad to witness" and an outpouring of energy that made the gods applaud but "the judicious stare." The writer added, with a disillusioned lover's mixture of anger, sadness, and reluctant admiration:

> This exhibition is all the more painful as it is obviously insincere and against her own better judgment… Underlying an ugly and evil impersonation were a fine and intellectual conception. Glimpses of true and remarkable power reveal themselves. So strangely blended are beauty and deformity we scarcely know where to look for a parallel.

This about-face is so emotionally expressed and so much at variance with other reviews that it seems more astonishing than convincing. Yet *something* must have been behind it – not only disgust at the disparagement of other actors but something in Helen Faucit's demeanour. Perhaps, after being so frequently held up as a model, she was smugly, if unconsciously, exaggerating those qualities the critics had applauded.

In the following year, 1867, Helen Faucit had four provincial engagements: in Manchester, where her popularity had recently been renewed; in her favourite old haunts, Edinburgh and Glasgow; in Newcastle-upon-Tyne, which she had not visited since her marriage. Everywhere the audiences were large and enthusiastic, and the critics were full of praise – all but one or two. Interestingly, the strongest dissent was in Glasgow, where she had enjoyed the most continuous support. In reviewing her Portia the *North British Daily Mail* declared that her casket scene was "painful," its "gushing tenderness …

bordering under the circumstances on the ridiculous." The meaning was made mercilessly clear:

> Portia was never one of Miss Faucit's best characters, and she is now more than ever past looking the part… . those who have seen her in her more palmy days cannot now look upon her without a strong feeling of regret mingling with their admiration – regret that she had not thought proper to withdraw from the scene of her many victories while her laurels were at their freshest.

Oddly enough, the same journal praised Helen Faucit in the childlike Iolanthe (27 November); declared that her Rosalind showed "the very slightest if any falling off" from its "prime of excellence" (30 November); and, while remarking that her Lady Macbeth was more Miss Faucit's than Shakespeare's, admired its "power and grandeur" (3 December).

Though welcomed, entertained, and praised by old friends wherever she went, Helen Faucit must have realized that she could not much longer maintain her supremacy in the kinds of heroines with which her reputation was associated. Critics had rarely been quite so blunt as the one in Glasgow (though one London writer had jested that Claude was young enough to be Pauline's son),[85] but even some who complimented her youthfulness had let her know that certain characters were no longer so appropriately represented as before. She had no interest in "character parts"; one cannot imagine her acting the Nurse in *Romeo and Juliet* or Mistress Page in *The Merry Wives of Windsor*, as Ellen Terry later did. Helen Faucit must be a star or nothing, and there were few starring parts for mature women. After no acting at all in 1868, she began, late the next year, to make some highly selective farewell appearances.

Her engagements in Glasgow and Edinburgh in November 1869 were announced as farewells to those two great centers of her popularity. In each city she acted at the Theatre Royal for eight nights, appearing in Iolanthe, Rosalind, Pauline (twice), Lady Macbeth, Beatrice and Portia. For her final night in Glasgow she added Julia, but for the one in Edinburgh she repeated Rosalind. Remembering, perhaps, the *Sunday Times* review of her most recent Julia, she had not intended to act the role at all, but she was persuaded by a disappointed letter to the *North British Daily Mail* (16 November) signed "An Old Royalist." The performances drew overflow houses in both cities. In Glasgow, on the night when Miss Faucit played Lady Macbeth, there was a great crush at the pit door, and after the seats had all been filled people continued to push forward in "tremendous and unavailing struggle." The *Evening Citizen* (16 November), which had received a number of complaining letters, suggested that on such occasions tickets for the pit (normally unreserved) should be sold in advance. A letter to the *North British Daily Mail* (17 November), signed "A New Royalist," spoke of "hundreds who were turned away – crushed, wearied, and disappointed" and expressed the hope that Miss Faucit would prolong her engagement; repeating Lady Macbeth and adding Imogen and Constance would "fittingly conclude the most brilliant and successful series of farewell performances ever witnessed in Glasgow."

Helen Faucit did not extend her engagement, but she did make a brief return visit to Glasgow a year later as a "postscript" to her farewell. She began with Lady Macbeth and went on to Pauline, Rosalind, Julia, and Beatrice. Once more the theatre was crowded each night, and most of the reviews were laudatory. But once more the *North British Daily Mail* spoke of Miss Faucit's deterioration, this time in Pauline: her voice had lost its "old rich ring," and her acting was "stiff and laboured." For her Lady Macbeth and even her Beatrice, however, the *Daily Mail* had nothing but praise.[86]

Immediately after this engagement Helen Faucit went to Liverpool for four nights at the Royal Amphitheatre, where she acted the same roles as at Glasgow except for Julia. It was during this farewell visit that her Lady Macbeth received, in the *Liverpool Daily Post* (13 December 1870), one of the most detailed and interesting reviews of her career, written by Edward (later Sir Edward) Russell.

Her final farewell to the professional stage took place at the Theatre Royal, Manchester, in the two-week period beginning Monday, 13 November 1871. The roles were well chosen to display her versatility: Lady Macbeth, Rosalind, Juliet, Pauline, Beatrice, and, for the valedictory performance, Iolanthe followed by Portia's trial scene. The choice of Iolanthe was a compliment both to her husband, who had translated the play, and to her Manchester audience, who had always peculiarly loved it.

Conditions at the Theatre Royal, Manchester were hardly ideal. Since each of Miss Faucit's plays was to be given only once, stock scenery and costumes were relied on. These varied considerably in quality, as did other aspects of the staging: the scenery and appointments in *Romeo and Juliet* were tawdry and sometimes inappropriate, whereas D'Avenant's extra witches and spirits in *Macbeth* were impressively costumed and grouped; the "Locke" music in *Macbeth* was respectably performed, but the incompetently-rendered songs in *As You Like It* "convulsed the house with laughter."[87] More effort had been made for the acting, with several additions to the regular company. T. Swinbourne, who had acted as Miss Faucit's leading man in each of her farewell engagements, was a very competent actor, rather "slow" as Romeo but jovial as Benedick, and dignified, often forceful as Macbeth; beside Helen Faucit, however, he seemed merely conventional. Perhaps, as one critic suggested, he was simply overawed, for her brilliance was obviously dazzling during this final round of performances. E. Emery, another recruit, pleased the "gods" by his noisy Macduff but had little voice left when he tried to portray Touchstone. Miss Annie Ness, however, was a happy acquisition: as Celia she played up well to Miss Faucit's Rosalind. Even so, reviewers emphasized the wide gap between the acting of the star and that of her supporters. *Macbeth* seemed like a mere dress rehearsal, wrote one, until Helen Faucit entered and changed everything. *The Lady of Lyons* hardly revealed its flaws as a play, said another, while she was on the stage, but when she was absent the performance was "commonplace" to the point of "weariness."[88] And so on.

The mediocrity of the company must have been frustrating to Helen Faucit, but the excitement of the occasion and the enthusiasm of the audiences were heady compensations. Despite her ambitiousness and pride as an actress, she had always taken pains to "play to" her fellow actors and had sometimes even softened her interpretation in order to keep up the illusion. During this farewell series, however, she let her high spirits run away with her. Thus her Beatrice ran circles around her "harmless" Benedick and seemed, by comparison, almost alarmingly vital and energetic.[89] One gets the impression that during this last professional engagement Helen Faucit gloried in her comic gaiety, her tragic power, and that she let herself go in an uninhibited fashion, sometimes even to the point of undermining some cherished interpretation of her own. It is curious to read in the *Guardian* (15 November) that her Lady Macbeth, except in certain passages (notably the sleepwalking scene), was a "one-sided" interpretation, over-emphasizing her wild ferocity. The critic, in expounding his own view of the character – that of a complex human being, capable of deceit and cruelty but also capable of "a woman's tenderness and the passion of a wife's devotion" – was describing precisely the interpretation that Helen Faucit had been advocating and portraying for years, often in the face of critical disagreement. Had she been so successful in her campaign for a womanly Lady Macbeth that even her own portrayal did not now seem sympathetic enough? Perhaps, but more likely she was so wrought up by the excitement of this last performance of the character that she allowed its savage passions more scope than she intended.[90] Even her Rosalind, which was evidently closest to its normal interpretation, sounds in reviewers' descriptions bolder and more flamboyant than usual – "the maiden adventurer, aghast at no extravagance till it has been committed."[91] Despite the physical fatigue and emotional stress of these farewell performances, Helen enjoyed herself hugely.

The public response was extraordinary. The theatre was thronged every night, and *The Lady of Lyons* attracted such an overflowing audience that hundreds had to be turned away. All the reserved seats for the final night, scheduled for Friday, 24 November, were taken well in advance, and the demand was stll so great that Miss Faucit agreed to repeat the same bill on Saturday, the 25th. So she said her "last farewell" twice.

The valedictory strain running through the reviews of her performances gave them an oddly mixed tone of enthusiasm and melancholy. Hyperbole was the language of the day: there was no other actress who even aimed at, much less achieved "such self-abandonment," such complete identification with her character; Miss Faucit was the "last fine English actress of romantic comedy";

it seemed vain to hope for another Juliet of such tenderness, dignity, and tragic intensity.[92]

An atmosphere of excitement and emotion enveloped the concluding performances. After Helen Faucit's "delicate and spiritual" impersonation of Iolanthe and her "fine acting and grand declamation" in Portia's trial scene, she surprised her audience by turning to them, rather than to Antonio, and using Portia's words as her own farewell: "I wish you well, and so I take my leave." The effect was "electrical." The whole audience rose to its feet, waving handkerchiefs and cheering. The stage was soon covered wth bouquets. Again and again Helen Faucit was recalled and applauded. The scene was repeated the next night, when her second "final appearance" took place. Even after the cheering crowd permitted her to leave the theatre, she found another throng gathered outside, waiting patiently in the rain to bid her goodbye.[93]

In the wake of the Manchester triumph Helen had some wistful thoughts about one more farewell – a grand metropolitan one befitting the first lady of the English theatre – but she feared that the London stage was too "degraded" for this at present.[94] By the autumn of 1873, when she declined an engagement at Drury Lane, she had given up all such dreams and decided to make no further professional appearances.

Yet it was hard to adjust to the idea that her art, once the centre of her life, would no longer have even an occasional outlet. Though the transition from full-time career to complete retirement had been long and gradual, her periodic returns to the stage had been Antaean experiences, putting her in touch with something primitive and sustaining in her own nature. As her husband remarked, acting, however fatiguing, seemed to "quicken the blood and enliven the spirits" as nothing else did.[95]

Luckily there were still occasions when a dowager queen of the stage might fittingly appear. Helen had earlier refused to act for either of the actors' benevolent organizations: the Royal General Theatrical Fund, which paid annuities to retired or incapacitated members of the contributing group, or the Royal Dramatic College, which aimed to provide housing for indigent retirees and, ultimately, to educate the children of poor actors. While still active professionally, she had feared that performing for one charity would bring demands from numerous others.[96] Now she began to look more favourably on requests to appear. In fact, she did not always wait to be asked.

Late in 1873, having learned of increased claims upon the Royal General Theatrical Fund, she offered to help raise additional money for it. A production of *As You Like It* was decided upon, with Helen Faucit as Rosalind, John Ryder as Jaques, Henry Compton as Touchstone, and Henrietta Hodson as Celia. When Helen requested "that young American Hamlet" for her Orlando, Steele Mackaye accepted the invitation with alacrity and meekly obeyed the summons to 31 Onslow Square for private rehearsals.[97] The performance, at the

Haymarket Theatre on the afternoon of 20 December, was an immense success, both for the Fund and for Helen Faucit. The audience greeted her with a "shout of welcome," and critics commented on her "nearly" undiminished looks, her "capacity to delight an audience as much as ever." Frank Archer, a young actor who was seeing her for the first time, found it hard "to realise that she was fifty-six years old" (actually fifty-nine).[98] Her portrayal of Rosalind, praised for its grace and refinement, its "fine, sympathetic intelligence," must have been quieter than the one at Manchester, though it retained some "'merrier' parts."[99]

In 1874 Helen Faucit appeared on the stage twice. On 2 March, at Drury Lane, she acted Lady Teazle to Samuel Phelps's Sir Peter in a star-studded benefit for Benjamin Webster on his retirement; and on 12 December, at the Haymarket, she played Beatrice to the surprisingly lively Benedick of William Creswick in a benefit for the Theatrical Fund. Again she had the satisfaction of drawing a "storm of applause" – the audience tried to give her an inter-act call – and of seeing her performance described in the *Daily News* (14 December) as a "model and a masterpiece."

The following year, 1875, brought two more performances. At Drury Lane, on 23 April, she acted Rosalind, for the last time in London, in a benefit to raise funds for a Shakespeare Memorial Theatre in Stratford. Unfortunately she found Charles Warner's Orlando unpoetic and the whole production "unsatisfactory." On 9 December, at the Haymarket, she acted Iolanthe for the Theatrical Fund – a character ill-chosen for London, however popular elsewhere. The only time she had appeared in it here before, she had been complimented for making Iolanthe seem "real" despite an undramatic play (*Daily News* 9 July 1855). Now, twenty years later, it was hardly surprising that *The Times* (10 December) described *King René's Daughter* as "obsolete" and its heroine as adapted to the "peculiarities" of the "old school" of acting. Less predictable was the sympathetic review in the *Era* (17 December), which attributed a "soft atmosphere of enchantment" to this "deeply poetic" play and declared that Helen Faucit, "banish[ing] the years as if by witchcraft," made the audience feel "all the charm of ethereal girlhood." Here was a voice from the past – or from Manchester.

In 1876 Helen made the mistake of declining to act in a farewell benefit for John Baldwin Buckstone, long-time friend of the Farrens as well as prominent dramatist, comic actor, and manager. "Oh that he had asked me to do anything but that tiresome Lady Teazle!" she wrote to her old provincial acquaintance Henry Irving, now a successful actor-manager at the Lyceum.Still uneasy over discreditable gossip about her motives for declining, she was disturbed by a fresh rumour that she would not appear with Irving. When she offered to act with him for his benefit, Irving readily accepted but proposed *The Lady of Lyons* instead of *King René's Daughter* (her choice). She demurred, holding firm against his repeated pleas: she would be "hoarse and speechless before the end of the 3d act" in

Pauline, she argued, whereas Iolanthe, "or any character without much passion or emotion," would be "safe" for her. At last Irving capitulated – against his better judgment.[100] One sees here a striking change in Helen Faucit. In the old days she would never have looked for a "safe" character or one without much emotion. And she would have had a better sense of the theatrical climate.

Irving did all he could to make the production a success: his "pretty" scenery met Helen Faucit's exacting requirements, and he himself acted Sir Tristan. There was a "great house" for the occasion (Lyceum, 23 June 1876), but, despite the applause, Helen did not feel that "people's hearts were in the play and going along with [her]" as when she had acted Iolanthe in Glasgow and Manchester.[101] She was right, and not only because this was London. One member of her audience was Percy Fitzgerald, who as a teenager in Dublin had been "enraptured" by Helen Faucit's Antigone; now living in London, he eagerly attended the theatre to "see the fine old school of acting revived" and his "old vision of beauty" renewed. "But," as he recalled later, "what a shock! An ancient dame, with a hard and tuneless voice, and such superannuated methods, almost grotesque! … The old Helen had gone for ever, long since. This was but an attempted copy."[102] Even allowing for exaggeration provoked by a painful surprise, Helen Faucit's acting had obviously deteriorated, not only since her Dublin triumph in the 1840s, but since her London performances in the 1860s. Long out of practice, calling mechanically upon methods that had once been animated by spirit, passion, and a sense of identification with her character, she now seemed, at times, a caricature of her former self. She was aware of this possibility: "it is hard," she later wrote in her diary, "to fear that one's past self may condemn the present." Yet, ignoring this truth, the ageing actress lingered in the wings, awaiting her cue to appear onstage once more.[103]

Early in 1877 her pride suffered a hard blow. When the fine comedian Henry Compton, whom she had known for years, left the stage because of illness, he particularly wished her to participate in his benefit. Her consequent letter to the planners, proposing a Shakespearean act or scene with Henry Irving, was ignored, however. "My services are not wanted," she wrote bitterly to Irving, "& not worthy of a reply."[104]

She made no further appearances until 1879, but that last year of her theatrical life was an important one. On 23 April she had the honour of playing Beatrice in *Much Ado about Nothing* at Stratford-upon-Avon, the inaugural production of the new Shakespeare Memorial Theatre. Benedick was acted by Barry Sullivan, who also directed the production.[105] The Shakespeare Festival, which began on the birthday itself (a Wednesday) and lasted through the Saturday of the following week, included a number of other performances, both theatrical and musical. Stratford was *en fête*: houses were hung with wreaths and banners; Shakespearean mottoes and coats-of-arms were everywhere; unofficial festivities were planned, like athletic events, fireworks, and marching bands. Tourists came from all parts of Britain and some from America. Unfortunately the weather was as uncooperative as it had been during Garrick's famous Jubilee of 1769 (newspaper writers made jocose comparisons): at the beginning and for several days afterwards rain drenched the crowds of determined sightseers and merrymakers.[106] Nothing, however, could dampen Helen Faucit's spirits on the historic first night.

The new theatre, built of red brick with stone dressings, held about eight hundred spectators in its auditorium, which was brilliantly lighted by a "sunburner" in the roof. Clusters of columns flanked the proscenium, and, when the maroon curtain was withdrawn at the beginning of the evening's program, a handsome drop-scene was revealed, in which was depicted – splendidly if unhistorically – a visit of Queen Elizabeth to the Globe Theatre.[107] Despite the abnormally high prices, the theatre was well filled on the opening night. After a poetic address, written by Westland Marston and recited by Kate Field, the "richly mounted" production of *Much Ado* took place. All the principal players were warmly applauded, Helen Faucit in particular: she was greeted with cheers at the beginning, was "frequently recalled, and at the end received a shower of bouquets."[108] Turning to John Ryder, a long-time acquaintance who had played Leonato, she said, "I suppose we shall never meet on the stage again," then, handing him a rose from her bouquet, "Take this rose for remembrance, and may God bless you." The "tears in her voice" found a response, no doubt, in the eyes of many spectators as her touching epilogue brought the evening to a close.[109]

For Helen the experience was one of the high points in her career. "The characters were well supported," she later wrote, "and the [place and occasion] seemed to inspire us all. I found my own delight doubled by the sensitive sympathy of my audience. Every turn of playful humour, every flash of wit, every burst of strong feeling told…"[110] Perhaps the excitement of the occasion, as well as the lively character of Beatrice spurred her to a better performance than her last one as the quietly lyrical Iolanthe.

Critical responses varied, though most were polite. Some American journalists were amusingly ambivalent, describing Helen Faucit's performance as "marvellous" in view of her age (they believed she was nearly seventy). But one of these, Moncure Conway, after smiling over the appropriateness of Benedick's "What, my dear Lady Disdain, are you yet living?" found this Beatrice "very much alive," after all – indeed "on her mettle" and, in the "Kill Claudio" sequence, "quite electrical."[111] Not everyone was so pleasant, however. A particularly hostile writer for the *Era* (27 April) complained that it would be difficult to find a more artificial Beatrice – whenever she moved, "she was a picture, her attitudes were elegant in the extreme, but her style [was] foreign to the natural acting of the present day."

Whatever the critics said, the audience's response had been so reassuring that Helen Faucit decided to repeat Beatrice in London if Irving would act with her. He told her that he was "not ready"[112] in Benedick, but he evidently agreed to act another role in a benefit for the Theatrical Fund. The plan came to nothing, however. "After nearly a month's silence," she wrote him on 25 June, "the directors ... have written me word that they can get no Theatre ... ." Irving may have replied with some suggestion, for two days later Theodore Martin wrote him on Helen's behalf, "As we shall be leaving town in a few days, all thought of a performance ... has been put aside till the autumn." There the matter rested, for – to everyone's relief, perhaps – quite a different plan developed for the autumn.[113] Sad to say, the most admired actress of her day had become an embarrassment for the London stage.

Happily, her single remaining performance would be an unalloyed triumph. A production of *As You Like It* was planned for 1 and 2 October 1879 at the Theatre Royal, Manchester, as a memorial to the late Charles Calvert, actor-manager of the Prince's Theatre, and a benefit for Mrs. Calvert, who had acted with him in a series of splendid Shakespearean revivals.[114] The women's roles, except for the silent "ladies of the Court," would be taken by professional actresses (Kate Pattison was Celia), but the men's would be played by amateurs. Normally Helen Faucit avoided amateur theatricals, but since these were distinguished men with a worthy cause, she agreed to act Rosalind on the second (more desirable) night. Miss Wallis, who had played Hero to her Beatrice at Stratford, took the part on the first night. The only male actor who had ever played professionally was the Orlando, Hon. Lewis Wingfield, son of the Sixth Viscount Powerscourt; this talented dilettante-adventurer had traveled in the Orient, nursed the wounded in Paris, and tried his hand at literature and art as well as acting. Touchstone was acted by Herman Merivale, a lawyer-turned-dramatist (later novelist), and Jaques by Alfred Darbyshire, a prominent architect specializing in theatre design; even small parts were taken by such well-known men as the dramatist Tom Taylor.[115]

As Merivale recalls, the actors' first response to their Rosalind, "in clothes of another tradition, speaking the lines after a half-forgotten convention, gradually merged into wonder and finally into intense admiration."[116] Helen, though not quite recovered from an attack of neuralgia, worked tirelessly with her fellow players, helping them with their parts and making them – the men, at least – her adoring slaves. Derbyshire later called her the "Goddess of my idolatry," and Merivale declared outrageously that "Shakespeare wrote the part of Rosalind, in a prophetic dream, for Helen Faucit." Her acting at rehearsals drew spontaneous applause from the amateurs, but it sometimes "bewitched" them into forgetting their lines.[117]

On the day of performance Helen had a fresh attack of her illness, but that evening she rose above the pain, as she had often done in the past.[118] When she first appeared onstage, the audience rose *en masse*, and such a "thunderclap of applause" came from both before and behind the curtain that she was stunned. Recovering from her momentary stagefright, however, she acted with an authority and vivacity rarely shown in her recent years. The other actors had moments of confusion because of the different interpretations and stage business used by the two Rosalinds, and once Wingfield, as Orlando, "became so fascinated with the Faucit acting that he forgot to go on to his cue." But they quick-wittedly covered for each other's errors, so the audience had little idea of the strain they were under.[119] The "Holbein" costumes worn by most of the

Helen Faucit as Rosalind in the Calvert Memorial Performance, Manchester, 2 October 1879: her last appearance on the stage, sketch by J. D. Watson (published in the *Graphic*, 18 October 1879)

actors added a picturesque interest to the production and inspired much journalistic sketching. During the performance the artist J.D. Watson, who had the bit part of First Lord, put an Inverness cape over his costume and "coolly went into the stalls to draw Rosalind." The result, our only known picture of Helen Faucit in her best character, was a full-length figure of her, looking trim but flagrantly feminine in her "boy's dress" (not exactly Holbein), which was later published in the *Graphic*.[120] Although the Rosalind of this last performance was more dignified than ever and less mischievous – a great lady who "never forgot her royalty for a moment in the lovely garnish of a boy,"[121] – Watson's sketch shows a *panache* of attitude and a sardonic curl of lip that suggest, in spite of everything else, the presence of an impudent "boy." In the fourth act Helen, feeling her strength flag, was terrified lest she could not get through; but somehow, drawing on her reserves, she finished the performance with her usual liveliness. She even "felt quite a keen regret" when it was over.[122]

Afterwards, though, her forced energy deserted her, the neuralgia renewed its attack, and she spent several days of illness at the home of Mrs. Willert, her Manchester hostess.[123] Then Mrs. Theodore Martin, having left Helen Faucit behind her at last, went to Wales with her husband to recuperate – and to celebrate her sixty-fifth birthday.

Chapter 13

Mrs. Martin's Social World

DURING THE years when Helena Faucit Martin occasionally resumed the persona of Helen Faucit , she devoted most of her time to the role of Mrs. Theodore Martin, not just in the home (as already seen) but in public. No picture of her – no theatre-related picture, even – is complete without the context of her social world. For the society she lived in very likely encouraged her increasingly refined acting (despite a contrary theatrical trend), and she in turn, through a potent combination of Helena Faucit and Mrs. Martin, undoubtedly influenced that society.

The Martins' Friends

Like most other distinguished Londoners, the Martins had close acquaintances among accomplished people in every field of endeavour. Although particularly drawn to those in the theatre, art, literature, and scholarship, they had good friends, too, in the clergy, industry, the military, medicine, law, government, and the landed aristocracy.

They hospitably entertained theatrical "lions" from abroad, like Charles Fechter and, in later years, Tommaso Salvini, Lawrence Barrett, and Edwin Booth;[1] but they also welcomed Helen's less eminent colleagues from the old days as well as some talented newcomers. Even after her retirement in 1871, Helen kept up her strong catholic interest in the stage. According to Justin McCarthy, the "animation and sympathy" with which she spoke of "[e]very new play, every new actor or actress … showed that her heart was still with" her old profession.[2] She took a special interest in Henry Irving, who first became famous at this time: having known him as a struggling young actor in the provinces, she followed his London successes with pleasure, even when she disagreed with his interpretations. He, though amusingly cast as her protégé, was always friendly and respectful.

Among artists, the Martins had cordial relations with painters like John (later Sir John) Millais and Dante Gabriel Rossetti, as well as Helen's early admirer from Dublin, Frederick (later Sir Frederick) Burton, who in 1874 became Director of the National Gallery; also with sculptors like Helen's old friends the Foley brothers and a younger one, Susan Durant, who, with her Parisian master Baron Triqueti, was patronised by the royal family.

Many eminent writers were pleasant acquaintances – Tennyson, Ruskin, Carlyle, Arnold, George Eliot – and some, like Thackeray and Browning, were more intimate friends. Browning, who had known Helen since her early years with Macready, was often a guest of the Martins after he returned to England following his wife's death. The Martins were particularly close to Thackeray and his daughters, Anne Isabella (Annie) and Harriet Marion (Minnie), who were for some time their near neighbours in Onslow Square. The families exchanged frequent visits, and, between times, many hand-carried notes; even after Thackeray moved to Palace Green and had to communicate by penny post, he would still begin a note to Helen "Dear Neighbouress." Often, while his daughters were with their grandmother in France, he joined the Martins at their breakfast table, talking with voluble frankness, and they readily responded to his need for sympathy – a little-known side of this supposed cynic. He gratefully praised Helen's sweetness to family and friends.[3]

After Thackeray's death Annie and Minnie lived in Onslow Gardens, not far from their old home on the Square. In 1867, during preparations for Minnie's marriage to Leslie (later Sir Leslie) Stephen, Helen was present for the fitting of the bridal gown, and early on a June morning she and Theodore were at the church on Onslow Square for the wedding.[4] Unfortunately the bride died young; it was by his second wife that Stephen became the father of Virginia Woolf. In 1877, Annie, the older sister, married her second cousin, Richmond (later Sir Richmond) Ritchie, and on 28 June 1878 Helena Faucit Martin stood as godmother to their infant daughter, Hester Helena Makepeace Thackeray Ritchie, when she was christened at Kensington Church.[5] Annie, a novelist and memoir-writer, dedicated her *Records of Tennyson, Ruskin and Browning* (1892) to the Martins "with old affection and remembrance."

Both Matthew Arnold and George Eliot became friendly with the Martins because of Helen Faucit's acting. In 1858, after her successful engagement at the Lyceum, Arnold wrote her, asking whether she would consider acting the heroine in his *Merope*; without her, he said, he would not try to have the drama performed, for she was the only actress now on the English stage with the necessary "nobleness, seriousness, and powers of feeling." After reading the play, Helen regretfully replied that it had little chance of theatrical success. Arnold called on her to thank her for her trouble, and the meeting resulted in a permanent friendship.[6] George Eliot had "fallen in love with" Helen Faucit because of her "poetic" quality when the two met at a soirée in 1853, but their friendship did not develop until 1864. George Henry Lewes, the novelist's husband in all but name, had conceived the idea of a play for Helen Faucit, to be written by George Eliot. Shortly afterwards, when Helen had an engagement in Glasgow, the "Leweses" went there to see her act, then talked over the projected play with her. Although Helen, after hearing the plot, reluctantly advised against it, the experience on the whole was pleasant for both couples. Lewes wrote that they had enjoyed Helen Faucit's acting and had seen a great deal of the Martins (who were staying in the same hotel), "liking them more the more we saw of them."[7] After that, the Theodore Martins appeared rather often among the visitors listed in Lewes's journals. George Eliot and G. H. Lewes attracted many interesting people to their home, the Priory, where they received friends on Sundays. Since society did not condone the irregular union, however, it took courage and self-assurance to be one of the comparatively few women visitors.[8] Friendship may partially account for Lewes's praise of Helen Faucit in his reviews (1864-66) – but, then, admiration of her acting had first led to that friendship.

Several successful but less eminent writers were on affectionate terms with Helen – particularly her longtime friends the Halls and her equally ardent, though more recent one, the odd but gifted Geraldine Jewsbury. The latter, an energetic little redhead, author of six novels and innumerable articles and reviews for periodicals, was constantly flouting convention: she was an admirer of George Sand; she smoked cigarettes openly; she enjoyed throwing out innocent-sounding but shockingly indecorous remarks. An intense person, she was "always being carried away in whirlwinds of emotion, 'swearing eternal friendship' with one woman or another, from Charlotte Cushman [in the 1840s] to Helena Faucit [in the 1860s and 70s]" or "casting a vehement personal devotion at the feet of some astonished man."[9] Like Anna Maria Hall, she wrote letters of appreciation after Helen's performances, and she passed on compliments she had heard from others. In a letter of 25 May 1865, for example, she reported Thomas Henry Huxley's facetiously flattering remark that the "*exquisite graciousness*" with which Helen Faucit's Lady Macbeth received Duncan at her castle "made a man feel *quite willing* to have his throat cut at the price," and she also called attention to a novel, *Once and Again*, which contained a "genuine tribute" to Helen. (In the novel, when a French equivalent of *The Patrician's Daughter* is about to be performed, a member of the audience remarks: "I once saw an English lady in this part, Miss Helen Faucit – the only Englishwoman I ever saw on the stage who thoroughly pleased me. To an elegant appearance she joined an unaffected pathos that went to the heart ...") Miss Jewsbury, originally a resident of Manchester, was a friend of Mrs. Willert (later Lady Heron) of that city, at whose home she and Helen were guests when the latter acted for the Calvert benefit in 1879.[10]

Helen Faucit's acting had always had a special attraction for clergymen – those who allowed themselves to attend the theatre. (One had to use the royal box, with private entrance, at Drury Lane so as to see her Lady Macbeth without "unpleasant publicity.")[11] She exercised the same fascination on them in person. A particular favourite of the Martins was Charles Kingsley, the noted clergyman, novelist, and advocate of social reform. Helen first met him about the same time she met Arnold and for a similar reason: he wished to write a drama for her. They had almost settled on a subject when some friends of Kingsley's, fearing that his authorship of an *acted* play would "injure his influence as a clergyman," persuaded him to give up the project. By this time, however, he and Helen had discovered an affinity, and Kingsley became a frequent visitor in Onslow Square.[12] A clergyman with whom Helen shared a mutual admiration was Alfred Ainger, who was for many years reader at the Temple (the church for the inns of court) and later, after a period as canon of Bristol, Master of the Temple; he was a wit, a man of letters, and a fine dramatic reader as well as an influential preacher. Other friends of the Martins were the Hon. and Rev. Francis Byng (later Lord Stafford), their own clergyman, and Arthur Penrhyn Stanley, Dean of Westminster, whose wife, Lady Augusta (née Bruce) Helen had met long ago in Paris.

Both Helen and Theodore had long had scholarly friends; some of them died during this period (Sir Archibald Alison, for example, in 1867), but others remained a valued part of the Martins' lives. Theodore's youthful companion John Stuart Blackie, by this time Professor of Greek at Edinburgh – a fluent speaker of ancient Greek (with, as he maintained, the "correct" Gaelic accent) and a lively, irreverent translator of classical verse – frequently visited the Martins during his annual pilgrimages to London. Though eccentric and aggressive, he was relatively genial among friends. Helen found him "like a rough day in summer, full of breezes, but somewhat fatiguing to the nerves."[13] Her special favourite was Margaret Stokes, daughter of "dear Dr. Stokes" of Dublin, who in her later years was a recognised authority in Celtic art and archaeology;[14] despite the difference in age, the two women were intimate friends, keeping in touch over the years through letters and visits. A more recent acquaintance was the historian Anthony Froude, who lived near the Martins (in Onslow Gardens) for many years, and was a frequent visitor at their house. Although he could assume a cynical attitude at times, he was charmed by Helena Martin, whom he described to a mutual friend as having "the most beautiful mind he ever met with."[15]

Among the scientists, the Martins' closest friend was John Couch Adams, Professor of Astronomy and Geometry at Cambridge and Director of the Cambridge Observatory, who in 1863 married Helen's bridesmaid Eliza Bruce. In his early twenties he had deduced the existence of the planet Neptune, but the papers demonstrating his theory were so tardily acted upon that the actual discovery of the planet was not made in England. Personal fame meant little to him, however; later he refused the position of Astronomer Royal at Greenwich.[16]

The Martins had several friends who were highly successful in applying scientific knowledge to industrial development. Charles William (later Sir William) Siemens, whom they knew through his wife, the former Anne Gordon of Edinburgh, was a physicist and engineer who made a fortune with his versatile and prolific inventions in the field of applied electricity. Henry Robertson, a Scotsman like Theodore, was a civil engineer who made his reputation in railroad construction (for example, the impressive viaduct across the River Dee) and also acquired lucrative interests in the related industries of coal and iron production and locomotive manufacturing. He built a "magnificent chateau" in North Wales, about sixteen miles up the Dee from Bryntysilio, the place the Martins chose for their summer home. Their first visit to that area was probably made on Robertson's recommendation.[17]

An important military friend was Edward (later Sir Edward) Hamley, a colonel in the Army who had served with distinction in the Crimean War (1854-56); later he became a lieutenant-general and participated in the successful Egyptian Campaign of 1882. Though reputedly "autocratic, and of a violent and vindictive temper," this handsome and brilliant man could be a pleasant companion among people he liked. Listening to his tales of "hairbreadth scapes i' th' imminent deadly breach," Helen must have felt she was playing Desdemona to his Othello.[18]

A physician, Dr. William Stokes, was, of course, one of Helen's closest friends. Her last verifiable engagement in Dublin was in 1857, but she may have visited there later. Dr. Stokes certainly visited the Martins at Bryntysilio, if not in London, and the friends remained in touch until his death in 1878. In Dublin the Martins also saw Helen's old admirer Dr. William Wilde (Sir William after 1864), whose handsome wife, the former Jane Francesca Elgee, had once written inflammatory articles in *The Nation*; an Amazon with dark, flashing eyes, she now ruled, exotically dressed, over a crowded, rather bohemian salon. When Lady Wilde moved to London in 1880, several years after her husband's death, she valiantly attempted to revive her salon there, despite her cramped quarters and straitened circumstances. And Helen, loyal to her old friendship, sometimes attended. One wonders what she made of young Oscar Wilde, whom she met there.[19]

Theodore Martin knew many lawyers, of course. One of his oldest friends among these was Robert Horn of Edinburgh, a prominent member of the Faculty of Advocates and later its Dean. But the lawyers whom Helen knew best were two younger men: Whitley Stokes (Dr. Stokes's son) and a friend of his, Arthur Munby. Stokes, who had moved from Dublin to London, was a barrister in the Inner Temple until 1862, when he left for India and a successful legal career there;

twenty years later he would return as a member of the Governor-General's Council.[20] Munby, a lawyer who had become a civil servant in the office of the Ecclesiastical Commissioner, was probably the strangest of the Martins' friends. Almost no one realised the extent to which this pleasant, well-mannered young man typified the contradictions and tensions of his society. Though a gentleman of good family, he was fascinated by working-class women; he fell in love with a house-maid and eventually married her, but he kept the union a secret from almost everyone. His detailed diary tells, on the one hand, of his literary and artistic friends and his fashionable social life and, on the other, of interviews with amazonian fisherwomen, brick-makers, and ballast-diggers and of simple, quiet visits with his dear Hannah. As this astonishing document reveals, Munby was strongly attracted to Helena Martin in a platonic way. He found her "charming & spirituelle." "The grace of all her movements," he wrote, "has once, perhaps, been studied, but is now habitual and instinctive, and the expression of her mouth and eyes in conversation is, from long tragic habit, so intense, that it requires some selfpossession to speak to such a listener. I never saw a face that seemed, as it were, to come so close in upon one's own soul." Derek Hudson, who in 1972 edited selections from the previously unpublished diary, remarks that "Munby's taste in women was for the highest or the lowest," never for the "affected and ineffective" young lady of the "conventionally eligible" sort.[21]

Munby had difficulty bringing his two ideals of womanhood together because for him they were tied to separate social classes. When he saw a well-bred woman, like the sculptress Susan Durant, displaying the kind of "self-asserting strength" that he admired as "heroic" in working-class women, he found it "masculine and out of place" – though Miss Durant, whatever her class, was certainly a working woman. And when he saw actresses, who had made public exhibitions of themselves, mingling with good society, he was both shocked and puzzled. (The elegant Mrs. Martin, whom he had seen only in the drawing-room, clearly belonged there, but why was she so undiscriminating in inviting theatrical people to her parties?) Munby found it hard to believe that two "tall, ladylike, & quietly beautiful" young women whom he met at the Martins' were the daughters of Mrs. German Reed, who, as Priscilla Horton, had displayed her legs rather freely when she danced and sang on the stage. He was even more astonished to find that Mrs. Reed herself was "a pleasant elderly lady" who "might have been a Bishop's wife." Did this prove the versatility of women, he wondered, or did it not show, rather, that they kept their purity "in many cases where fools allow it not"?

Despite his enlightening experience, Munby was apprehensive about seeing Helen Faucit as Rosalind during her last London engagement (1866). Although he had known her for ten years, he had never been to any of her performances, evidently for fear of spoiling his image of her. When he finally saw her on the stage he was agreeably surprised:

> … I expected that it would be a shock … to see one whom you know as a highbred accomplished lady, moving in good society & mistress of a fine house, … appear in public as an actress, and in men's clothing. But her Rosalind is so graceful and natural, so pure and transporting, and withal so like her own self off the stage, that one forgets the publicity and indeed everything but the part. And Helen Faucit plus Rosalind makes a delightful compound result, for those who know both Shakespeare and Mrs. Martin.[22]

The Martins' most intimate friend among government people was Arthur (later Sir Arthur) Helps, Clerk of the Privy Council and an informal but influential advisor to the Queen; he was also a writer, with novels, dramas, and historical works to his credit. Helps lived up to his name: through his royal connection he was instrumental in giving Theodore's career its biggest boost (more of that in a moment), and in his novel *Realmah* he contrived a graceful public compliment to Helen's acting. The scene of the novel is a country estate, where guests, who are thinly disguised portrayals of actual statesmen, are attending a houseparty. In the relevant passage there is a discussion of the importance of seeing great plays acted rather than merely reading them. Milverton, the host, remarks: "If there is anything in the world that I think I know well, it is *Macbeth* … but when I came to see a great actress in Lady Macbeth's part – Helen Faucit – new lights burst in upon me, and I saw what a delicate and refined fiend Lady Macbeth could be." Admiration for Helen Faucit underlies the following discussion, but there is disagreement about her best role – Lady Macbeth, Rosalind, or Pauline. [23]

Beginning in the late 1860s, the Martins made many acquaintances among the landed aristocracy, people whom they saw at court and visited in the country. Helen's closest friend among them was the "highly educated & charming" Lady Abercromby (née Julia Janet Georgianna Duncan-Haldane), one of the Queen's ladies-in-waiting. When they met, early in 1877, the two women found themselves instantly *en rapport*, and they soon developed a warm relationship. Later the Martins would visit Lady Abercromby's mother, the Countess of Camperdown, and would, in fact, enjoy an enduring friendship with the whole family.[24]

Their personal acquaintance with such people – and with Queen Victoria herself – came about as a result of Theodore's most important literary project, writing Prince Albert's official biography. General Charles Gray, the Queen's Private Secretary, had been designated for this task but had given it up after completing only one volume; the Queen then (in 1866), acting on Arthur Helps's recommendation, appointed Theodore Martin as Gray's replacement.[25] Martin soon decided that he could not simply pick up the Prince's life where Gray's volume left off but would have to start over in his own way; eventually the book, which he had intended for three volumes, stretched out to five and (partly because of his Parliamentary work) took more than twelve years to complete.

While working on the biography. Theodore was occasionally summoned to conferences with the Queen. On 10 January 1868, while staying (supposedly for a few days) at Osborne, the royal residence on the Isle of Wight, he fell on the ice of the skating pond, painfully injuring one knee. When the Queen realised that he could not be moved for several weeks, she sent for his wife to come and take care of him. Meanwhile she herself visited "poor Mr Martin" and made what arrangements she could for his comfort. Helen arrived on the 12th, having been met at Portsmouth by one of the royal yachts, and got her first intimate look at palazzo-like Osborne House, with its tall campaniles, its first-storey loggia, and its Italian Garden, which was to be her home for the next three weeks. That night Her Majesty described Mrs. Martin in her journal as "very pleasing" and added that it seemed "strange to meet her again, at her husband's bedside, not having seen her, since many years, when she was on the stage." For several days afterwards, the Queen sat with the Martins for a while each day, talking "most agreeably with these charming people."[26] By a nice coincidence, Helen arrived just as the royal children were practising for three *tableaux vivants*, all illustrating the legend of "The Finding of the True Cross by the Empress Helena," which they planned to present in honour of Prince Christian's birthday. She proved "invaluable," as the Queen said, in helping to place the performers, arrange their costumes, and so on.[27] On three other occasions she gave, at the Queen's command, some readings from poetry and drama, doing the scenes from *As You Like It* "remarkably well." (Disraeli was present twice.) She was not treated like a professional entertainer, however: she and Theodore were twice invited to dine with the Queen. Indeed their royal hostess wrote to Arthur Helps that she was "selfishly glad" Mr. Martin had to stay on at Osborne and that she thought Mrs. Martin "most pleasing, clever, and distinguished – really very charming." When the Martins left on 3 February, she sent a messenger after them with a gracious note and a diamond and ruby necklace for Mrs. Martin.[28] In 1869 and 1870 the Martins were invited to Osborne for what might be called anniversary visits, each time in February. They also attended a garden party at Buckingham palace, where all the royal family "noticed" them "most graciously" and the Prince of Wales talked pleasantly of Helen Faucit's Rosalind at Drury Lane. In later years they were both invited occasionally to spend the day at Windsor. Helen received further gifts from the Queen: a cashmere shawl and a *Shakespeare's Birthday Book* inscribed in Her Majesty's hand (eventually all members of the royal family signed at the appropriate dates). Theodore was among the select few who were invited to Princess Louise's wedding in April 1871. Each of the Martins sent a gift, and Helen was especially fastidious about finding one that was appropriate without being ostentatious. Later that year, when the Prince of Wales recovered from a critical illness that had kept all London in suspense, the Martins received tickets for the grand service of thanksgiving at St. Paul's. (Helen was attacked by her old demon of claustrophobia in the crowded cathedral and spent several sleepless nights afterwards, but she would not have missed this splendid occasion.)[29] With the Queen herself setting the example, the Martins became, of course, favoured persons in aristocratic society.

Carte de Visite photograph of Helena Martin
(by courtesy of the Toronto Reference Library)

The Martins as Hosts and Guests

In common with other Victorian hostesses, Helen frequently chose the evening party (sometimes the musical evening) as a form of entertainment. Occasionally, especially when there was a young houseguest, she invited both "grown and growing children."[30] Most parties began about 9.30 or 10.00 p.m. and ended, usually, between 1.00 and 2.00 a.m.; those that included children followed a similar pattern except for slightly earlier hours. A tea room was arranged on the ground floor, where arriving guests could refresh themselves before going upstairs to the drawing-rooms. Later in the evening everyone went down to the dining room for supper. For a musical evening a formal programme was planned, usually featuring a well-known performer such as Jules Lefort.[31] Any evening party was likely to include some music, however, Theodore himself would sometimes sing his Scottish songs.[32] Once Helen, with the aid of a male guest, gave some readings from *The School for Scandal* and *Romeo and Juliet.*[33] Sometimes there was dancing – often, probably, for Helen loved it.

The Martins' parties were elegant affairs, glittering with the presence of "men wearing stars and orders; a Bishop in purple coat and silver buckles"; "gorgeous women old and young, in fluff and feathers and brilliant silk or gauze"; Stanley "in full costume as Dean of Westminster."[34] Many of the guests were excellent talkers. There was dapper little Browning, for instance, with his "crisp grizzled beard" and "keen restless … face," who had an amusing anecdote or a bit of doggerel for any occasion. There was big, white-haired Thackeray, who "lounged about the room in an easy smiling way," stopping now and then before some friend and "with raised forefinger and head on one side gravely giving out one of his irresistible little jokes." There was Froude, with his large head of thick black hair, his "glowing eyes" and "strange romantic appearance," who could talk eloquently on some occasions, sneeringly on others, but always interestingly.[35]

The Martins frequently entertained at dinner, sometimes "quietly" with half a dozen intimate friends, sometimes formally with many more guests – Helen's diary mentions seventeen on one occasion.[36] The Victorian dinner party was notoriously lavish and ceremonious. Although fashionable hostesses, following the French mode, divided a dinner into only two main courses, or "services," plus the dessert, each course, with its successive kinds of dishes and its appropriate wines, was equivalent to two or more dinners for the average modern diner. There were always at least two varieties of each dish and each wine so as to provide a choice, and fashion decreed a much larger variety for certain dishes – for example, at least six kinds of *entrées* and eight kinds of *entremets* for eighteen diners, according to one formula. No wonder a character in Helps's *Realmah* cited the dinner party, with its endless choices, as an illustration of the needless complexity of modern life.[37]

Helena Martin, with her meticulous attention to details and her gracious manner, must have been an ideal hostess – except for one breach of etiquette. After dessert and coffee, instead of rising and leading the other ladies to the drawing room, she often lingered at the table. If the gentlemen grew impatient for their cigars and port, the proud husband did not notice. Later, in fact, he revelled in "many memories" of evenings when a group of distinguished men sat round the Martins' dinner table "talking their best under the encouragement of the hostess, who shared and delighted in their conversation, and was always on such occasions as slow to retire with the ladies … as her male guests were prompt to follow her ..."(257). Helen cannot have been the only woman who talked animatedly of matters more interesting than the fashion in hats – not when the eager, outspoken Geraldine Jewsbury was present, or the brilliantly articulate Anna Swanwick.[38] Even so, it is good to have this glimpse of her blithely ignoring a gender-based convention and getting by with it.

In 1877 Helena Martin inaugurated a new kind of entertainment: drawing-room readings of Shakespeare. The first was a reading of *The Merchant of Venice*, given on two different afternoons, 27 June and 2 July, so as to accommodate those who wished to come without crowding the room too much. Fifty-six attended on the first day, seventy on the next. The later readings were evidently confined to a single day, with eighty-odd invited guests attending. They were generally held in the Martins' own house, but one took place at the mansion of the Baroness Burdett-Coutts (on 5 June 1878), and the last two (on 30 June 1886 and on a later, unspecified, date) were given at Miss Anna Swanwick's house in Regent's Park. After the first few, the readings usually featured scenes from several plays: the one at the Baroness's home, for example, comprised scenes from *Romeo and Juliet*, *Macbeth* and *The Lady of Lyons* (the only time a non-Shakespearean play was included).

Except for the hostess, all participants in the first two readings were amateurs, with two clergymen – Ainger and Byng – in the most important male roles. These two took part in later readings as well, and other clergymen joined them from time to time, including a bishop on one occasion. Among the non-clerical readers were a lecturer in elocution (Charles John Plumptre) and a publisher (Kegan Paul).[39] After the initial readings Helen gained a valuable ally in Henry Irving. On 16 February 1878 she wrote to him saying she had received many requests to repeat *The Merchant of Venice* and asking whether he would help her with it. With the superb confidence of an old star writing to an up-and-coming new one, she offered him the role of – Bassanio. "My Shylock on this occasion", she wrote, "is to be Mr. Moritz [a Hungarian actor], who was introduced to me some few days back. As a foreigner & a stranger I have, of course, assigned to him the most important character." Apparently Irving meekly assented. After this he was a regular participant. The only other professional player was Kate Saville, who once read Celia to her aunt's Rosalind.[40]

Audiences always included old friends like Mrs. Bruce Joy and, until her fatal illness, Geraldine Jewsbury. Among the occasional guests were Mrs. Holman Hunt, wife of the artist; Mrs. Grote, widow of the historian; and Mrs. Baird Smith (De Quincey's daughter), who had often seen Helen Faucit on the Edinburgh stage in earlier years. A number of eminent men attended at least once, some more often – among them Froude, Huxley, Tennyson, Max Muller (the Oxford philologist and Orientalist). The distinguished American actor Edwin Booth, who was in England in 1882, came to hear Helen Faucit and

Henry Irving in Beatrice and Benedick. There were always guests prominent in courtly circles: Lady Essex, Lady Ducie, Lady Wolsley, Viscountess Combermere; even Princess Louise came once.[41] The readings were, in fact, as much social attractions as cultural events. Not everyone was impressed by the readings themselves. Gaythorne Hardy, First Earl of Cranbrook, found Mrs. Martin very different from the Helen Faucit he had often seen on the stage; and Augustus Hare, though he admitted her "fine illuminative face," thought there was "too much manner" in her readings.[42] Many guests responded enthusiastically, however – at least, in their letters to Lady Martin.

The hospitable Martins, in their turn, dined out, attended soirées, and listened to music at their friends' houses. Being a gregarious couple, they probably enjoyed themselves. Only during the "season" (from Easter through July), when there was no respite from the giddy pace of entertaining and being entertained, did they tire of what Helen called the "hard work of pleasure." "Even one's mornings are not safe," Theodore once complained – "with these hateful things called breakfast parties."[43]

Afterwards they would take refuge at Bryntysilio, recovering their spirits in the serene but invigorating life there. They were entranced by the shifting lights and colours of the panorama seen from their hillside vantage. As Theodore wrote one August, "gleams of sunshine bring out in charming contrast the purple heather, the gold of the gorse, & the vivid verdure of the bracken, & the shadows of the flying clouds are always producing some new phase of beauty in the landscape." Helen could watch the scene for hours, fascinated by the subtle transformations of the sky, just as she had always been by the motions of the every-changing sea.[44] But the Martins also enjoyed tramping about the nearby hills, for they were both good walkers. A London journalist who arrived in 1878 to write an article on their country home saw Helen as she returned from a windblown "mountain stroll," carrying a walking stick and wearing a "very wear-and-tear looking hat," her face protected by an "immense blue veil" that hid her features from view. Though tall and graceful, she "hardly recall[ed] the elegant hostess of Onslow-square."[45] Beautiful as the house and its furnishings were, life at Bryntysilio was always informal as compared with life in London. One of the pleasantest pictures of Helen that we have is a drawing by Annette Elias made in 1881: it shows her looking by no means shabby but somewhat more casual than usual; her hat is loosely draped with a veil, which has been pushed back from her face, and her scarf is carelessly knotted at the neck. Perhaps the artist, a frequent visitor at Bryntysilio, had caught her hostess in walking costume.

Bryntysilio would not accommodate more than two guests at a time, but in some years there was a long succession of them – people like Dr. Stokes, Reginald Cholmondeley, Fitzjames Stephen and his wife, the Anthony Froudes. Among the Martins' favourite guests were Eliza and John ("Hans") Adams. The eminent astronomer, who combined scientific curiosity with a love of fun, reportedly carried a clumsy aneroid barometer about with him so as to know how high he was climbing on his Welsh rambles.[46]

Even during the relaxing periods at Bryntysilio, however, Helen neglected no opportunity to use her dramatic talents. Twice, in September 1877 and a year later, she gave Shakespearean readings as part of public entertainments for the benefit of the Llangollen Cottage Hospital: scenes from *Romeo and Juliet* the first time, most of *The Merchant of Venice* the second. A special train was run from Corwen on these occasions to accommodate visitors.[47]

The Martins were often houseguests at the homes of friends. They made a good many visits, over the years, to Lord and Lady Egerton at Tatton Park (putting up with their hostess's sharp tongue for the sake of her interesting personality) and to Reginald Cholmondeley at Condover Hall, "a charming old Elizabethan place on a grand scale", they were guests of Lord and Lady Ducie at Sarsden; they spent a few days now and then at Wynnstay, the estate of Sir Watkin Wynn at Rhuabon in North Wales; they were members of a houseparty at New Lodge in Windsor Forest, home of M. Silvain van de Weyer (a friend of the late Prince Consort).[48] When they attended the concerts during Festival Week at Birmingham in 1873, they were fellow guests with Arthur (later Sir Arthur) Sullivan at the home of Mr. and Mrs. James Beale at Edgbaston. Helen set her maid to making a laurel wreath, and after the supper following the evening's performance she crowned Sullivan with it.[49]

After Helen Faucit's retirement in 1871, the Martins no longer went regularly to Scotland, but they made some memorable visits for special occasions. One was for Helen's public reading in Glasgow on 21 March 1879, in which she took all the parts in scenes from *Romeo and Juliet* and *The Merchant of Venice*, earning 500 pounds for victims of the Bank failure. This was a thoroughly happy visit: the large attendance, the appreciation of critics ("Not in our lifetime shall be seen her like upon the English stage"), and the hospitality of friends made the Martins forget the "slush, drizzle, din & lacerating east wind outside."[50]

Travel and Recreation

In the early years of their marriage the Martins often went to the Continent in the summer or early autumn. Usually they visited one of the spas – Homburg, Kissingen, Spa (in Belgium), Ems, Baden-Baden – for a month or so of "penance," as Helen called it, then left "all this bathing & water drinking" in search of "more agreeable occupations" elsewhere.[51] In 1867 they spent some time in the Thüringen forest, among other places in Germany, and enjoyed the trip, despite the grimy, malodorous hotel at Gotha – "Napoleon occupied the same rooms after the battle of Leipzig," Helen wrote in her diary, "so a tablet on the walls tells you. Poor man! The beginning of the end!" Among its high points for her was some unexpectedly delightful theatre-going in Coburg, where she was pleased by the excellent acting of Herr Haaser and was reminded a little of William Farren.[52] The Martins always remained awhile in Paris before returning home.

Friends enlivened some of these holiday journeys. At Homburg in 1852 the Martins met a newly-married Scottish couple, Professor William Sellar (a classical scholar) and his bride Eleanor (née Denistoun), who became their permanent friends. Mrs. Sellar had often seen Helen Faucit on the Edinburgh stage, and "often and often" had prepared bouquets for her brother Alexander to throw to her, but the two women had never met before. In a later year, during a stay at Spa, the Martins met Thackeray; at the Rouge-et-Noir he pointed out to Theodore a seedy-looking gambler who was the original of his character Deuceace in *Memoirs of Mr. C. J. Yellowplush*. In 1867 they met George Eliot and G. H. Lewes at Calais and travelled with them to Brussels, where they dined and played whilst together before embarking on separate itineraries.[53]

In Paris they often saw old friends, including always Marcellin de Fresne. After a dinner at his house in 1859, Helen gave some dramatic readings in his salon for two hundred distinguished and brilliantly dressed guests. At their request, remembering her Parisian performances fourteen years before, she gave Lady Macbeth"s sleepwalking scene and Juliet's balcony scene (with de Fresne) and potion scene. No costumes or props were used – only a white scarf thrown over her evening gown for the sleepwalking scene. Her naive, passionate, and dreamy Juliet was enthusiastically applauded, but, according to Henry de Riancey's review, published in the next day's *Union*, the Lady Macbeth scene was her greatest triumph. It was a chilling performance: her eyes were open and fixed, her gestures feverish; her features and attitude conveyed a torture of soul that bordered on madness.[54]

In 1870 the Franco-German War put an end to the Martins' annual visits to the Continent. M. de Fresne had died the year before, but Helen, who received news from beleaguered Paris by carrier pigeon, was concerned for the safety of her remaining friends there. One of the closest, Mme. Colmache, fled to England that year and remained in London from then on.[55] Not until 1878 did the Martins make another trip abroad. In the meantime, they patronised English spas like Scarborough, Buxton and Harrogate.

From the beginning they enjoyed brief holiday visits to Helen's old seaside haunts. Brighton and Hastings. During the Easter holidays of 1856, when they were staying at St. Leonards, near Hastings, their friend Francis Bennoch (a lawyer) brought the American writer Nathaniel Hawthorne to call on them. It was one of those happy occasions when strangers immediately feel at home with one another. Hawthorne, a reserved New Englander, had been taken aback while in England by the unexpected effusiveness of certain new acquaintances (Carter Hall in particular), and he found relief in the quiet friendliness of the Martins. As he later wrote:

> [Mr. Martin's] face and manners suited me at once; a simple, refined, sincere, not too demonstrative person. His wife, too, I liked: a tall, dark, even sallow, but fine and ladylike woman, with the simplest manners, that give no trouble at all, so must be perfect. With these two persons I felt myself, almost in a moment, on friendly terms, and in fine accord...[56]

It is pleasant to have this glimpse of Helen at ease and informal (as at Bryntysilio), with her fair skin tanned by the seaside sun.

New Roles

Meanwhile Theodore Martin's work on the biography of Prince Albert had become increasingly burdensome. The early excitement had faded; industry had turned to laboriousness and laboriousness to drudgery. Overwork brought on headaches, and at one time his doctor forbade him to write anything for several weeks – thus bringing on frustration of another kind.[57] He would take refuge at Bryntysilio, away from clients and friends' "spinning" away (as he called it) at the fabric of his current volume. John Blackwood's prophecy that Martin would come to "hate the memory of the Sainted Albert" came close to fulfilment. Helen, who read with a critical eye everything her husband wrote and responded sensitively to all his worries, had her share of the burden. "Pray God it were done!" she once exclaimed to Geraldine Jewsbury.[58]

Then, finally, it *was* done – the last volume was completed in December 1879 and published early the next year. In March, 1880, reborn in spirit if fatigued in body, the Martins set out for a carefree holiday in Italy. It was like a second honeymoon journey – except that they did not go, this time, as Mr. and Mrs Martin. Shortly before their departure the Queen rewarded Theodore for his years of conscientious work by creating him Knight Commander of the Bath.[59] Sir Theodore and Lady Martin returned from six weeks on the Continent bearing with them from Paris the latest creation of the famous couturier Worth. This Court Dress, to be worn on 11 May when Helen made her curtsy at the Queen's Drawing-Room, was a confection of cream-coloured satin with a train of pale blue silk damask, richly embroidered. On the great day, elegantly attired in her new costume, her hair elaborately dressed with feathers and jewels, Lady Martin performed with all the dignity and charm of Helen Faucit; Sir Theodore was courtly and sure-footed (she had worried that he might tread on her train). The atmosphere of cordiality, with the Queen smiling "sweetly" at Helen and the Prince of Wales and several Princesses shaking hands with her, banished all her twinges of stagefright. The next day Sir Theodore received a letter from Lady Ely bearing Her Majesty's wish that the Martins come to Windsor for an overnight visit; it added that the Queen had admired Lady Martin's grace at the Drawing-Room and had thought her beautifully dressed.[60] The Martins had passed inspection in their new roles.

The miraculous year, 1880, had more benefits in store. Among the red-letter events was the Martins' visit to Braemar, near Balmoral, in the Scottish Highlands, where they received the attention due to *protégés* of the Queen. They arrived at the Fife Arms Hotel on 18 September 1880, intending to stay only eight days, but they remained a week longer to take the excursions suggested by the Queen and Lord Fife[61] – notably, a visit to the Glassalt Shiel, a lodge built by Victoria at the head of Loch Muick. In her letter of thanks for the day's enjoyment, Lady Martin dwelt with pleasure on the "lights & shadows in the mountains," their "wild beauty," and the "drive home through pine woods, with red setting sun seen through the trees & colouring all things…"[62] Another pleasing event, in November, was the election of Sir Theodore to the Lord Rectorship of St. Andrews University, an honorary post with a four-year term. He took particular satisfaction in defeating the rival candidate, Edward Freeman, who was a harsh critic of the Martins' friend Anthony Froude.[63] In 1880, too, Lady Martin assumed a new role as a Shakespearean critic – but her literary career must be saved for the next chapter.

Helen Faucit/Helena Martin as a Social Catalyst

Lady St. Helier, speaking of Society in its most exalted form (that is, the aristocracy and those whom they recognised as worthy associates), recalled that at one time "Every door was closed against the dramatic profession, though Mr. and Mrs. Alfred Wigan and Miss Helen Faucit … were exceptions to this universal rule," but she added that suddenly (in the 1870s, apparently) "the conventional rules were swept away, and those who had the courage … to open their houses to everyone who was interesting and distinguished found an ideally delightful society…"(180). Although Lady St. Helier surely exaggerated Helen Faucit's almost exclusive acceptability to the elite prior to 1870, she was correct in seeing her as unusually favoured. What she did not see was that the social change that seemed so sudden to her had been gradually prepared for and that Helen was among the most effective agents of that change during the transitional period. By continuing to act professionally while successfully filling her place in a privileged society; by enthusiastically conversing with her genteel guests about acting as an art; by entertaining actors along with prominent people from other circles; and by making dramatic readings into elegant social occasions – in all these ways Helen did much to bring her two worlds together.

Chapter 14

Lady Martin, Critic

LESS THAN a year intervened between Helen Faucit's last appearance as a theatrical interpreter and Lady Martin's debut as a literary interpreter. Over the years Helen had confidently made known her literary and artistic views in conversations and letters, and she had jotted down occasional critical comments in her diaries. Never until 1880, however, had she attempted anything approaching formal essays. Even her essays on Shakespeare's heroines, which were begun that year, are not exactly formal in organization or style, but they contain some comprehensive and thoughtful discussions. Consideration of her critical views must be based mainly on these, her only published writings. But her informally expressed opinions about the modern stage and about literature, art, and music must not be neglected, for they reveal the interrelatedness of her theatrical ideals and her critical thinking on other subjects.

Essays on Shakespeare's Heroines

Her career as a literary critic was begun at the insistence of Geraldine Jewsbury, who had often urged her to write down her interpretations of Shakespeare's heroines. Helen had objected that her ideas could not be adequately conveyed except through acting, but, now that her friend was mortally ill with cancer, she determined to fulfil her request. So in the summer of 1880 the new Lady Martin, ensconced at Bryntysilio, hastily composed essays, or "letters," as she called them, on two of the characters in which Miss Jewsbury had expressed particular interest – Ophelia, then Portia – and sent each by post as soon as it was completed. The second was finished by 9 September, just two weeks before her friend died. She immediately began a "letter" on Desdemona but abandoned it after learning that Miss Jewsbury had sunk into a coma. Meanwhile Theodore, impressed as always by anything his wife did, had arranged for Blackwood to print the two completed essays in "elegant brochures" for friends. William Blackwood then asked permission to publish them in *Blackwood's Magazine*.[1] Those on Ophelia and Portia came out, respectively, in the January and February numbers (1881), and the finally-completed one on Desdemona (also addressed to Miss Jewsbury, though most of it was written after her death) was published in March. That last one gave Helen twice as much trouble as the first two, for she was acutely conscious of writing for publication. Never again would she write with such speed and facility as before.

Friends now began urging her to record her interpretations of other heroines. Anna Maria Hall, her earliest admirer, naturally suggested Juliet, the character in which she had seen "A Young Lady" at her debut in Richmond. Helen did begin a "letter" to Mrs. Hall, but she put it aside upon her old friend's sudden death shortly afterwards. Blackwood wanted an essay for the October number of his magazine, but she replied (on 4 August 1881), "I have not the same impulse upon me as last year."[2] When she resumed work on Juliet, at his urging, she was so overwhelmed by memories of personal experiences that she broke her "letter" into two parts, the first devoted largely to reminiscences connected with Juliet and the second to critical discussion. These, dedicated to Mrs. Hall's memory, were published in *Blackwood's Magazine* early in 1882 (January and February, respectively).

In the next few years Martin kept his wife to the task of writing, hoping it would serve as both a substitute for her acting and a distraction from her neuralgic pains, which were often severe in the later years. The results were essays on Imogen (addressed to Anna Swanwick), Rosalind (to Robert Browning), and Beatrice (to John Ruskin), each of which was privately printed, then published in *Blackwood's*.[3] In 1885 the essays were collected in a volume, *On Some of Shakespeare's Female Characters*, published by Blackwood, with a dedication to Queen Victoria. The book went through six more editions, the last in 1904. The only substantial change made in Lady Martin's lifetime was an added "letter" on Hermione (addressed to Tennyson) in the fourth (1891) and subsequent editions. The last two editions, published posthumously, added a preface which, according to Sir Theodore, she had written for the fifth edition but decided not to use.[4]

Despite initial misgivings about putting her interpretations into writing, Helen believed she had valuable knowledge about Shakespeare's heroines: she had enjoyed "the great advantage of throwing [her] nature into theirs, of becoming moved by their emotions," and she had sometimes found in performance a sudden clarification of meaning that could have been gained in no other way (viii, 108).[5] The problem was in communicating what she had learned. Chafing at the difficulty of organizing her material,[6] which was aggravated by her excursions into personal reminiscence, she took refuge in the loose, informal style of the letter. But the greatest difficulties lay in trying to translate stage experience into words at all. On the stage Helen Faucit, though aware of the intricate connections among performances, had been directly responsible for her character alone; in trying to capture the complex experience on paper, however, she had the responsibility for everything. How could she take advantage of her special identification with Desdemona, for example, yet do justice to Othello? "The woman *will* come out so much finer than the man," she complained – "noble & heroic as he is represented." Even more frustrating was the inadequacy of any language to transmit the thoughts and emotions felt and conveyed in her portrayals; sometimes she would throw aside her writing in despair of finding "words eloquent enough" to express them.[7] On the stage she could have suggested everything by a tone, a look, a gesture.

The autobiographical passages with which Lady Martin sprinkled her essays are interesting, not only for vivid evocations of episodes in her life, but also for occasional digressions on roles other than those of her primary concern: especially Lady Macbeth and Pauline (see Afterpiece). Aside from these, a typical essay gives a detailed interpretation of the subject heroine, tracing her through all her scenes, discussing her relationships with other characters (and incidentally discussing those characters too), and explaining the thoughts and emotions that presumably underlie her speeches and actions. A notable feature is the inclusion of imagined bits of the character's extra-dramatic life, evidently with the intention of illuminating her psychology or explaining some situation in the play. Typical, too, are her attempts to help the reader visualize a character in action by references to her facial expressions, tones of voice, attitudes and movements. Recollections of the actress's own emotions experienced in certain parts of a performance – "I felt my pulse beat quicker; my very feet seemed to dance under me" (162), or "The tears at this point always welled up in my eyes, and my whole body trembled" (256) – seem to suggest that Rosalind or Juliet or Beatrice would have experienced those identical emotions at those very moments.

Lady Martin's book was generally received sympathetically.[8] Several reviewers compared it favorably with other criticism, much of which was said to be "empty and pretentious" (*Athenaeum*). Some noted the fresh illumination she had shed on Shakespeare's creations, her revelations of the "marvellously fertile resources" of his dramatic power (*The Times*). One remarked that only two preceding critics (Mrs. Jameson and Fanny Kemble) had said anything worthwhile about Shakespeare's women; now one could add Helen Faucit, whose writing reflected her experience of interpreting these characters "with a force, a delicacy, and an intelligence which no actress of her generation [had] compassed" (*St. James's Gazette*). Several other writers, however, rejected the idea that an actress was particularly well equipped to interpret a play critically. Edward Dowden, the Shakespearean scholar, observed (as, indeed, Helen had done herself) that an actor-turned-critic may have "the same intention and meaning" as in stage performance, yet "the touch of inspiration … may refuse to be transferred from eye, and voice, and gesture to the written page." William Archer went further and declared that the best actor cannot be the best critic since the actor's task is synthetic whereas the critic's is analytical. He considered Lady Martin's method of interpretation fine for an actress but dangerous for the Shakespearean critic in general since the "habit of treating fictitious characters as actual personages lies at the root of half the pseudo-criticism of Shakespeare."[9] Even these critics granted, however, that much of what she said was "right, and true, and graceful" (Dowden) and that the value of her essays lay in "the light they throw on the workings of an artist's mind in approaching the great problems of the master-poet" (Archer). Some mainly favourable critics pointed out certain weaknesses in the essays – for example, the "curious feminine partisanship" that allowed her to tell "home truths" about the hero but made her defend the heroine (*Pall Mall Gazette*); also, of course, her fanciful notions about the offstage experiences of her characters. A few, however, even accepted the latter: "What charms us most," said the *St. James's Gazette*, "is the delicacy of perception which enables her to bring out every *nuance* of the character, and the sympathy which has availed her to grasp the whole 'life-history' of her heroines." And Alan Japp, in the *Gentleman's Magazine*, insisted that her subjective approach would have a great attraction for "those who … believe that life's riddles and therefore also the riddles of the drama, admit of an imaginative and human, rather than of a critical and logical solution."

Among the greatest admirers of Lady Martin's essays in their own day was the American scholar Horace Howard Furness, editor of the New Shakespeare Variorum. Not only did he include extracts in some volumes of the Variorum, but he told his sister in 1897 that Lady Martin's book was, in his opinion, "the finest that [had] ever been written on Shakespeare."[10] Furness developed a warm friendship with both Martins through correspondence with them.

Today, I suspect, Lady Martin's essays are often considered as curiosities rather than as critical writings to be taken seriously: sentimental descriptions of Victorian gentlewomen masquerading as Shakespearean heroines. They are considerably more than this, but it is easy to see why their value may be overlooked. The sentimentality is there, truly enough, in many of the ideas but more particularly in a general tone that mistily enwraps even some stimulating and original ideas. The chief problem is the style of writing, which, charming as it might have seemed at one time, strikes the modern reader as quaint if not ridiculous. (It may have been considered, even in Lady Martin's time, the "antiquated," if "elegant," style of a "graceful feminine enthusiast.")[11] The too-numerous exclamations are wearisome, the "pretty" phrases embarrassing. But it is a mistake to suppose that these peccadillos of style are true indications of what the essays have to offer. One must remember, too, that the exclamations and hyperboles cannot be attributed entirely to either Victorian extravagance or natural gushiness. Lady Martin could write as crisp, no-nonsense prose as anyone when she wished, but it would have been too flat and prosaic for her attempt to express in words the emotions conveyed in performance. It is not really surprising that in trying to do the impossible she occasionally came out with such exclamations as "Oh happiness beyond belief, oh rapture irrepressible!" (256). Readers who understand this will find their patient tolerance repaid.

Lady Martin's interpretations of characters and plays, though influenced by the ideas of her period, are not mere Victorian stereotypes. They have grown out of repeated and thoughtful readings of the text and, in most cases, numerous performances over many years.[12] Thus they are based on a combination of theory and practice – including, admittedly, influential practice in non-Shakespearean plays. Some of these interpretations are unusual for their time: for example, that Desdemona is not "a pretty piece of yielding amiability" but "a woman of the true, heroic mould" (56, 60) and that Iago is a petty trickster, with no satanic grandeur and no great intellect (64-65). The actress's identification with the heroine does sometimes distort her view of other characters, yet some of the things she sees from her special perspective cause the reader to look freshly at these characters and to question too-easily-accepted assumptions. Because she read a play as if seeing it in performance, Lady Martin could point out the dramatic value of "unnecessary" scenes or bits of scenes that were often omitted on the stage – for example, the brief scene in *The Winter's Tale* in which Cleomenes and Dion describe their awesome experience at Delphi (358-59). One of the most valuable features of the essays, in fact, is their discussions of numerous individual scenes. Sometimes these are mere summaries with quotations and appreciative comments, but often they include graphic details which help one to visualize the scene in action. Lady Martin's creations are in no sense synonymous with Shakespeare's – they are extensions of the originals (or of salient aspects of them), imaginatively developed by an actress with a psychological bent and a lofty ideal of womanhood, – but they offer fresh insights into the potentialities and the dramatic workings of Shakespeare's plays.

The greatest importance of these essays, however, is in helping us to understand Helen Faucit's methods as an actress and to envision her stage interpretations. They are particularly valuable when studied in conjunction with her promptbooks and the reviews of her performances. (See Afterpiece.) The promptbooks, though important for text and suggestive annotations, give no evidence of the detailed characterizations implied in some of her reviews; the essays, however, show how carefully worked out these characterizations were – there one sees the *rationale* for the details described by reviewers.[13] Some autobiographical passages obviously illustrate Helen Faucit's approach to her acting: the comment that her claustrophobic tendency had helped her, as Desdemona, to fight for her life in the murder scene is one of many indications that she drew on recollections of her own emotional experiences to enhance the realism of character and situation.

Even the reconstructions of the characters' extra-dramatic experiences, which, for the casual reader, are the most antiquated parts of Lady Martin's essays, are interesting evidences of the methods she had used in thinking herself into her characters. Being a conscientious interpreter, a close reader of the plays in their entirety, she generally kept her imaginative reconstructions subservient to the "facts" of the dramatic text: these passages occupy only a small part of their respective essays and they are usually tied directly to something in the play. For example, Ophelia's childhood is reconstructed, not for its own sake, but to explain portions of the mad scenes as arising from recollections of early life;[14] Portia's youthful studies with her learned cousin are imagined to explain her quick detection of the flaw in the bond (even before leaving Belmont, according to Lady Martin), her understanding of the law when consulting Bellario for confirmation, and her confident presentation to the court. In some of the essays the imaginative material has been woven into the fabric of the interpretation by so many fine threads from the play as to be almost indistinguishable from the rest. Thus Lady Martin's description of Desdemona's pre-dramatic relationship with her father, though it reflects, I believe, some early experiences of her own, is allowable to an actress, if not to a literary critic. (For imagined off-stage experiences within plays see Afterpiece.)

The extra-dramatic passages that have the least justification, even for an actress, are the post-dramatic ones. For example, there is the epilogue to the essay on Imogen, with its notion that the sensitive and delicate Imogen has suffered too much, both physically and psychologically, to live long after her joyful reunion with the repentant Posthumus.[15] Superficially one is reminded of such heroines as Lady Mabel and Marie de Meranie, who go into a decline and die after being mistreated by the men they love. Lady Martin's sentimental language encourages this comparison. But, without discounting the influences from Victorian literature (especially the dramas in which Helen Faucit had acted), I suggest two others. First, although she greatly admired the virtues of forgiveness and loyal devotion, Helen seems to have been unable, personally, to empathize with a woman who could live happily with a man who had injured her; she disliked the ending of *Evadne* for this reason. She might go into raptures over Imogen's transcendently forgiving and loving nature, but something in her own nature rebelled. And, second, although she had finely evoked the atmosphere of romance in some of her acting, especially in *Cymbeline*, she had always grounded her interpretations in a sense of real persons and events. Thus, having thrown herself fully into the imagined horrors of Imogen's trials, she must have found it difficult to accept the quick shift (typical of romance) from shock and suffering to "happy ever after." The happy ending of *The Winter's Tale* seems to have been more acceptable because Leontes has suffered sixteen years of repentance and sorrow before Hermione – to her own surprise, according to Lady Martin – finds her old love for him reawakened (386). Readers of Lady Martin's "Imogen" were not all of her mind. Tennyson, who knew how a fairytale should end, wrote to her, "I don't and won't believe that she died of consumption."[16]

The most egregious example of Lady Martin's post-dramatic reconstructions is her "dream" ending the essay on Portia. Portia is described as leaving the comforts of Belmont for repeated visits to the sick and broken Shylock, bringing him food and wine, cheering him with her winsome presence until, by embodying the quality of mercy, she eventually causes him to value it (39-44). The reason for Lady Martin's including this passage is not far to seek. When she was composing the essay, Henry Irving's sympathetic Shylock was a great and recent success. Although she herself felt a certain compassion for Shylock after his daughter's elopement and at the very end, she had no sympathy for him while he was demanding his pound of flesh; and she utterly rejected certain critical notions that Irving's Shylock seemed to encourage – that the Christians were the true villains, that Portia's legal quibble was merely frivolous, that the decision of the court was a travesty on justice. (Uncomfortable as she was with the requirement that Shylock change his religion, she suggested that Antonio had seen Shylock ruining people's lives with his extortionate practices and perhaps he thought, "in the spirit of his age," that even enforced Christianity might "work some miraculous change in his heart.") Portia was a great lady of the Renaissance, intellectual, charming, gracious, and, above all, generous. Such a character, Lady Martin thought (in the spirit of *her* age), could not have lived happily if she left her defeated enemy to suffer. The after-events predicted in the essay, however, could hardly have been suggested on the stage.

After reading the privately-printed essay on Portia, both Browning and Ruskin remonstrated with the author about this "dream" of post-dramatic events. As Lady Martin wrote to Blackwood, "Mr Ruskin thought it was not in the spirit of the age [i.e. the Renaissance] – & Mr Browning said the whole party would be more likely to rejoice over the discomfiture of the Jew." Although she "could never agree" with them, she wondered whether she should omit the passage when the essay was published in *Blackwood's*. Anthony Froude, however, encouraged her to leave it in, and Sir Theodore naturally supported her.[17] So it stayed, in defiance of objection by friends and possible derision by critics. It stayed, too, when the essay was later published in Lady Martin's book. The "dream" was obviously important to her. In this case, however, I do not believe it was a legacy from her acting days, as was the "dream" of Ophelia's childhood; it was, rather, a response on Portia's behalf to Irving's portrayal of Shylock.

The reaction of some reviewers to Lady Martin's "afterpiece" for Portia kept her on the defensive about it. One reviewer objected to it on the ground that, had Portia really been mercifully inclined, she had plenty of opportunity during the trial scene to effect a compromise.[18] For Lady Martin, however, any compromise would have undercut Shakespeare's purpose of having Shylock condemn himself by insisting upon the letter of the law without regard for mercy. Her problem was in trying to reconcile this thematic necessity with the demands of Portia's character, which was obviously meant to be sympathetic. The need to justify her actions in the trial scene underlies a passage she wrote in a long letter to H. H. Furness (5 October 1889), which constitutes a kind of addendum to her essay:

> I think the modern way of making [Shylock] appear wronged & interesting is a mistake. The only sympathy he excites in me is by … his great endurance at the last under the un-Christian sneers of Gratiano. The mockery of turning Christian is a drop in the cup too much.
>
> I cannot see, as many of our modern critics say, that Shylock is defeated by a mere quibble. He is defeated because under the cover of a quibble in the phrase "a pound of flesh" he has sought to compass the life of a Venetian citizen.
>
> It is only when Shylock's conduct has put this beyond a doubt that Portia uses the weapon which her own quick wit & the legal knowledge of Bellario have supplied her. In a case of this kind where Shylock insists upon the strict letter of his bond the Court was surely justified in construing the bond according to the strict letter.
>
> But to me it seems that the true point on which Portia's judgment rests was the demonstration by Shylock's own demeanour that he meant to kill … . She has thoroughly tested his deadly purpose before she pronounces judgment.
>
> Holding this view I was always careful, soon after entering the scene as the Doctor of Laws, to go up to the Clerk's table where Nerissa sat, send for the Statute book, & after referring to my notes cause her to keep it open at the point marked in my notes.
>
> To explain further Portia's position & function I also made a point, while Antonio's farewell to Bassanio was proceeding, of going up to the Duke & *quietly* indicating by my manner that I was informing him of the judgment I was prepared to pronounce and of obtaining the Court's sanction of it. This is necessary to show that Portia is merely the mouthpiece of the Court, and I always slightly turned to the Duke when I said "The Court awards it and the law allows it" so as to emphasize this fact.[19]

Critical Attitudes Toward the Modern Theatre

In her later years Lady Martin, though still very much interested in the theatre, was disappointed by the turn it had taken: she deplored the loss of the poetic drama and its too-frequent replacement (as she thought) by trivial, commonplace plays; and she saw a similar deterioration in acting and staging. Spectacle had become too elaborate, she said, too important as an end in itself; Macready, her ideal as a manager, had made the scenic illustration serve the drama rather than dominate it. She was concerned, too, about the growing use of such theatrical customs as inter-act (or even inter-scene) calls, which interfered with illusion and character-identification, and long runs, which prevented the staging of less popular plays with a potential appeal to discerning audiences.[20]

As for modern actors, Lady Martin agreed with Jenny Lind that they had become "extremely *off-handed and unartistical*": they no longer learned to sit, stand, and walk with grace and dignity, to articulate their words clearly, and to cultivate a musical and resonant voice. She herself thought that the greatest need was to educate "actors of all grades" in the correct speaking of blank verse: they should "know the laws of its construction" and should learn "while giving the meaning, to give the music of it also." She was saddened by the "level of feebleness and commonplace" to which Shakespearean performance had been reduced by "that nerveless and colourless thing, mistakenly called 'natural acting.'"[21] Another charge she made against modern acting was its lack of "breadth, dignity and above all *repose*," its emphasis upon action for its own sake rather than for the revelation of character. As she wrote to H.H. Furness:

> The study of character seems to be from the *outside* & to result in a multiplicity of trivial details and bits of "stage business." Such as sitting down here, getting up there ... in this way the words become of secondary importance. All this is most distracting to the auditor. The impersonation becomes "a thing of shreds and patches" & no real impression is left on the mind, of the man or woman whom the poet meant to portray.[22]

Helen Faucit, whose own use of "by-play" had become legendary, certainly did not object to stage business in general, only to the frittering away of its interpretive possibilities by too much meaningless action.

The kind of business she approved was well illustrated by Edwin Booth's use of a handful of straws in portraying King Lear's madness. According to Theodore Martin's description, "At one time it became the bow to 'draw me a clothier's yard' ... at another, each separate straw seemed to be to the poor mad king a living creature, against whom he launched the shafts of his sarcasm and railing." Martin's comment that such acting is "a living commentary on the text"[23] reflects the ideal of fine acting subscribed to by both Macready and Helen Faucit. After seeing that same performance by the distinguished American tragedian, Helen wrote in her diary (18 February 1881): "Very much pleased; it is quite his best bit of acting. The Fourth Act, mad scene, was very fine."[24] Rarely in these latter times did she express such enthusiasm. She once told Mary Anderson that "since Macready, few actors had approached Mr. Booth in intellectuality, perfect elocution, grace, personal magnetism, or the power of complete identification with his characters."[25]

Both Martins were very much interested in Henry Irving, pre-eminent British actor of the day, and made a point of seeing each of his productions if possible. Helen was concerned about him personally: she warned him in several letters about the dangers of overtasking his strength.[26] (Theodore believed that Helen's neuralgia was a belated result of her own overwork in her youth.) She obviously considered Irving a gifted actor, but she did not always approve of either his acting or his directing. After congratulating him on the success of his first London *Hamlet*, she remarked: "If it were not ungracious I would speak of some drawbacks to my enjoyment. But this never grateful task I could not undertake without much encouragement and in any case not now with … the pleasure I enjoyed uppermost in my mind." Evidently the "encouragement" was not forthcoming, for her later letters include little criticism. She certainly considered his production of *Becket* a remarkable achievement, both in his characterization of the hero and in his turning a work she had considered undramatic into effective theatre.[27]

The old actress's objections to modern methods could hardly be surprising. Nor could those of her husband, who was convinced that the great age of the British theatre had passed with his famous wife's retirement; seeing new actresses applauded in her roles was painful to him. Sir Theodore vented his displeasure in two essays, published anonymously in *Blackwood's Magazine*. In the first, "Theatrical Reform: The 'Merchant of Venice' at the Lyceum" (December, 1879), he censured Ellen Terry for her forwardness toward Bassanio *before* his choice of the right casket; although his ostensible point was that uncritical applause was ruining some potentially good actors, readers could guess that his real protest was against any young upstart who dared replace the one great actress of the century. In the later essay, "'As You Like It' à l'Americaine" (September, 1890), he attacked another young actress whom London had taken to its heart: Ada Rehan, leading lady of the American company under Augustin Daly's management. The public's applause of this impudent, hoydenish wench as if she were the true Rosalind was too galling to accept without a fight; accordingly he blasted the whole production, with special attention to Miss Rehan. Unfortunately the article had an effect opposite to the one he intended. Since Lady Martin had now become known as a writer on Shakespearean subjects, some readers were convinced that *she*, a great Rosalind in her day but now passée, had written the essay to discredit her young supplanter.[28] Nothing about the episode is creditable, but it is one more indication of Theodore's fierce, unswerving loyalty to his wife. As in the old days, when he had fought against Macready because he was holding Helen Faucit back and against Charlotte

Cushman because she threatened to become a serious rival, so now he buckled on his rusty armour and took to the field again.

Although Helen was certainly not immune to feelings of jealousy, she occasionally took a special interest in one of the young actresses. Among her favourites was Mary Anderson, the beautiful young American. Though sometimes censured for her coldness, Miss Anderson had won a considerable reputation in her own country, and she was very successful in her first visit to London (1883). It was during her second visit, in 1885, that the two women became friends. On 28 March Helen saw Mary Anderson as Julia in *The Hunchback*, and a few days later (3 April) she had her as a guest for afternoon tea. The young actress won her heart by requesting that the distinguished creator of Pauline read some of the scenes from *The Lady of Lyons*. (She herself, already considered a successful Pauline, would be playing the part at the Lyceum three days later.) Helen gladly assented, and, as Miss Anderson later reported:

> Neither in costume nor in looks did she in the least suggest Bulwer's heroine; yet she had not turned the second page before I felt myself in the presence of an ideal Pauline. I have seen the part played by many young and beautiful women, but Lady Martin, book in hand, spectacles on nose, seated by her tea-table, with no audience but Sir Theodore and myself, produced greater effects than any of the others with all their stage accessories. She had … a power of saturating herself with the vital essence of what she read, and infusing it into her listeners.[29]

Critical Attitudes toward Literature and the Arts

Helen was a typical "cultivated" woman of her time, an eclectic reader, but she had one strong individual interest: the poetic drama. Her admiration extended not only to the classics she acknowledged as greatest (like those of Sophocles and Shakespeare) but to some works of her own day. Prominent among the latter were several long closet dramas: Charles Kingsley's *The Saint's Tragedy*, George Eliot's *The Spanish Gypsy*, and Robert Browning's *The Ring and the Book*. Other kinds of literature might interest or entertain her, but this was what gripped her emotions and stirred her imagination.

Her letter to Browning, written on 6 March 1869, shortly after reading *The Ring and the Book*, reveals the ecstatic mood induced in her by such works and also shows the kinds of qualities she valued in them. Browning's poem was a "tragic Greek-like drama," she thought, in which the "sins of the fathers" were "visited upon the children":

> How else should this "white lamb" be called upon to bear the weight of such sorrow, such humiliation! The fine old Pope, though, makes us feel that the expiation was accepted, & complete… . the unconscious purity of the "child woman" … becomes a light to lighten all the hidden best within him, & reveals to him of what his nature is capable.

She was enthusiastic about Browning's characterization. His villain appealed to her imagination, just as Milton's Satan had done in her adolescence:

> Loathe this monster as we will … still we must own how the very strength of his badness wrings something like respect out of us – "Then I rose up like fire, and fire-like roared." What masses of rude Titan like images of speech he … blurts out continually!

And, on the other side, she praised the "simple" but "grand" depiction of the Pope, a man who "looks back through his life's experience" from the higher ground he has progressively attained "& is thus enabled to see motives, as well as acts, & so arrive at the real truth of things." She saw these characters vividly, as in a fantastic picture:

> ah that I could *paint*, as I *feel* them! Sometimes I dream of that loathsome Franceschini coming before me as "Comus" … with his unholy household of wicked women, & savage men making up the "rabble rout," with all the rude noise, but without the "jollity" – and in the midst I see "A 'Lady,' young, tall, beautiful, strange & sad." In the far distance, for my comfort, & my bit of brightness, I can just discern the "Elder Brother" – the "Warrior Priest."[30]

In responding to Browning's dramatic poem Helen was imaginatively reliving some of her "noblest" theatrical roles: Pompilia was a "sacrifice" – like Antigone, Iphigenia, and Juliet; she was Virtue, untouched by the evils and temptations around her – like the Lady in *Comus*. And the setting she envisioned for Browning's vigorously-drawn characters was inspired, not by anything in *The Ring and the Book*, but by her memory of Macready's exciting and mysterious stage-picture more than a quarter of a century before.

In the best art and music, as in the best literature, Helen looked for some appeal to the emotions, the imagination, even the soul. The viewer or listener must not only admire the design and execution but also be drawn into participation, must experience a catharsis of some kind or find a satisfying relationship between the ideal in his or her own mind – perhaps one not hitherto realized – and its objectification in picture, statue, or musical performance. This effect could not be achieved through exaggerated emotion in the work itself – something she deplored; rather (to state definitely the ideas she often implied), it depended on such qualities as verisimilitude and *élan* – that is, a life-affirming spirit that she looked for in depictions of both joy and grief, good and evil. Her favourite word for the finest in artistic achievement was "noble," an adjective that might seem oddly chosen in some instances unless one realized its peculiar implications for her.[31]

Millais and Rossetti fell short of her ideal in their paintings. She admired Millais for his technical achievements, but his works did not move her: she could look even at "Jephtha's Daughter," with its grief accurately depicted, and remain "hard-hearted." Rossetti's use of colour was "masterly," she thought,

Helena Faucit Martin, by Rudolf Lehmann (platinotype copy sent to T. Edgar Pemberton by Sir Theodore Martin, now in possession of the author)

and his composition was admirable, but his women were too languid and morbid-looking: there was no "upward" movement in these pictures.[32] Among the paintings that moved her most deeply was Titian's "Sacred and Profane Love" – "so composed, lovely, and satisfying." Both figures, she thought, were meant to be the same woman, the intention being to show "how noble and chaste she could look under any aspect"; the "profane" love was just as "sacred" as the other.[33] Why was it, she asked herself once, that the Old Masters always satisfied one best? "Is it the harmony, with a certain retiring reticence about them … a self-respecting reserve, so that the fancy can play over them?"[34] For this "psychological" actress, who in some of her best moments depended on subtle suggestion rather than explicit portrayal, the answer was undoubtedly "yes." Her comments about musical performances show similar tendencies: she loved grandeur but disliked showiness. Christine Nillson sang well but "without soul or fire"; Viardot, on the other hand, fatigued her listeners with power, making them long for "a little simplicity and respose."[35]

It was no accident that the principles by which Helen judged poetry, painting, and music were the same ones she had taken for her guides in acting. "My art," she called it – and she used the term proudly, seriously, without embarrassment.

Chapter 15

Final Stages

WRITING HER essays helped Lady Martin relive her theatrical experiences, but it was hardly a substitute for acting itself. Her nearest approaches to the theatre in the 1880s were in occasional dramatic readings, not only those in her own drawing-room but others both public and private.

One was held unexpectedly in October 1881 when the Martins visited St. Andrews for Sir Theodore to deliver his inaugural address as Rector. After liberal entertainments by faculty and students and after Sir Theodore's well-received address, Lady Martin was visited by a student delegation requesting a Shakespearean reading. She presented the trial scene from *The Merchant of Venice* and parts of *As You Like It*, taking on the identities of all the characters. The reading proved effective despite the "fearful" sounds of wind and rain and the flickering of a gas lamp that caused her to lose her place several times. But, after all these years, the old actress still chafed at the coldness of a Scottish audience: these well-behaved students were "silent as mice, except at the end of scenes, when applause was vociferous."[1]

Occasionally Lady Martin's talents were called on for dramatic readings at other people's houses, especially at Kinlochluichart, the Ross-shire lodge of Louisa, Lady Ashburton. This darkly handsome woman, widow of William, Second Lord Ashburton, was an enthusiastic deviser of charades, recitations, and musical performances during her house-parties. Accounts of two such entertainments show Helen on her worst and her best behaviour, respectively. Once, according to James Lowther, Viscount Ullswater, Lady Ashburton decided to stage a dramatic reading of the trial scene from *The Merchant of Venice*, with Lady Martin as Portia, Sir Theodore as the Duke, Lord Ullswater as Shylock, and several other guests as minor characters. The performance was barely underway, however, when the leading lady "jibbed and declined altogether to proceed." It was not clear whether she was offended because of the inadequacy of the Shylock or the "incongruous appearance of Charles Drummond in a kilt reading the part of a Venetian nobleman."[2] But, knowing what Helen was like, one may make a shrewd guess. Very likely the "actors" were clowning their parts, and Helen, though not without a sense of fun, could not tolerate an insult (as she would perceive it) to Shakespeare – and to her own "art." On another occasion, however (probably in September, 1882), when asked on the spur of the moment to give the sleepwalking scene from *Macbeth*, she was more cooperative. After only a brief interval to call her imagination into play, she miraculously transformed herself from modish gentlewoman to "vision-haunted somnambulist," speaking in a "half-hushed voice, in which there was a wail of heart-searching pathos," and transported her awestruck listeners from Lady Ashburton's spacious drawing-room to the gloomy corridors of Macbeth's castle.[3] Perhaps the wildly beautiful scenery of the Scottish highlands had already put actress and audience in a suggestible state. Helen never enacted the sleepwalking scene again; she left the spectre of Lady Macbeth to haunt her native Scotland.

Her last public reading – all of Portia's scenes in *The Merchant of Venice* through the trial scene – occurred on 23 August 1888 at the Town Hall, Llangollen, for the benefit of the new public library there. Strange as it seems, she was nervous and apprehensive for some time beforehand, and she experienced a little of the old "heart-sinking" as performance time arrived; once she began to read, however, all was well. "Am so *thankful* that it is so well over!" she wrote in her diary that night. "Should not have thought, after all I have gone through, I should have nerve enough left to be … in such full possession of myself."[4] "*Thank God it is over*!" – so the young Helen Faucit had written after her London debut more than half a century before. And now the veteran actress, almost seventy-four years old, was writing in much the same strain.

In the early 1880s the Martins continued their busy social life, both in London and at their friends' houses in the country. They kept up their foreign travels, too, visiting Italy in 1881 and Monte Carlo in 1882. All such pleasures were abruptly halted, however, in the spring of 1883, by Helen's severe neuralgic attacks, which recurred intermittently for many months. During her illness she was consoled by the frequent inquiries, advice, and good wishes of the royal family.[5] Gradually she regained her health: by mid-1884 she could "move about a little in society again," but it was 1885 before the Martins resumed their usual round of activities.

Their last visit abroad, spent mostly at Cannes on the French Riviera, December 1886 to March 1887, proved unusually eventful. While there they made a pilgrimage to see the Villa Sardou, where Rachel had died. Helen, her mind full of the young Rachel she had known, hoped that the great actress had not suffered too much, here in this "out-of-the-way, dismal, unfinished-looking

Lady Martin in 1881, drawing by Annette Elias, from Sir Theodore Martin's *Helena Faucit (Lady Martin)*

place." At Cannes, too, the Martins established a warm friendship with the Goldschmidts (Jenny Lind and her husband), whom they had evidently known earlier but never so well as now. The women found each other particularly sympathetic. (Jenny Lind-Goldschmidt died later that year, but Theodore and Helen continued a fond relationship with her husband, Otto.) The most vivid memories of Cannes that the Martins, like everyone else, carried away were those of the earthquake which struck on 25 February 1887. They congratulated themselves on their intrepidity during this experience, when panic reigned among multitudes of other vacationers.[6] Despite Martin's complaints of insalubrious weather, the holiday had been so bracing that Helen kept up her strength throughout June and July for many festivities in honour of Queen Victoria's fifty-year Jubilee.

There were two events in the 1880s, however, both at Bryntysilio, that stood out above all others in these later years: the visits of Robert Browning and his sister Sarianna in 1886 and of Queen Victoria in 1889.

In the summer of 1886, when the Brownings could not take their usual holiday abroad (Sarianna was still convalescing from a serious illness), the Martins invited them to visit Bryntysilio instead. Both Brownings replied cordially. As Miss Browning said, they could not be houseguests since she must be quiet and keep early hours, but they would like to stay in nearby Llangollen. Accordingly the Martins arranged accommodations at the attractive Hand Hotel, in the centre of town, directly across the street from the curving river, with its picturesque bridge, its bankside gardens and public promenade. Browning was delighted: "We shall be most pleasantly near you," he wrote, "and if my sister's feet have not lost their old cunning, a two-mile walk [to Bryntysilio] will be no impediment …"[7]

The Brownings arrived in the second week of August and stayed unitl 19 October, well pleased with their "excellent" hotel and its amenities.[8] (Sir Theodore had put a word in the hostess's ear.) Almost every day they visited the Martins. After a vigorous tramp from Llangollen, Browning would burst upon the peace of Bryntysilio, his "elastic spirits" on the stretch and his spring of racy talk ready to spill over. One day, as Helen's diary records, she was sitting on the verandah with her two houseguests of the moment, Anna Swanwick and Annette Elias, reading aloud *The Flight of the Duchess*, when Browning and his sister "broke in" upon them. "No more reading. His talk stops all … ." On another day the Brownings came to lunch, and Helen commented afterwards: "What a fund of anecdote he has, and how well he tells his stories! Conversation there is none, but one is only too glad to listen." Helen often wondered how he could seem so little like a poet in his manner and conversation – his "outside" was "so cordially kind and sympathetic," his "inner man so above you and profound."[9]

On Sundays the Brownings usually met their hosts for the afternoon service at Llantysilio, the little church just beyond Bryntysilio's garden gate. Afterwards they would all go to the Martins' house, usually bringing the vicar with them, where they would have tea in the garden and remain there, talking, until the stars came out. Browning seemed to take pleasure in "bringing out" the vicar, who had been rather in awe of him at first. As Sir Theodore remarks, these Sundays were remarkable since Browning, though deeply religious in his own way, was not a church-goer by habit. Browning himself remembered the occasions in a graciously nostalgic way: two years later, in replying to the Martins' invitation for another visit, he wrote that, if he and his sister had not made plans for Italy, they could have enjoyed "another term of delightful weeks – each tipped with a sweet starry Sunday at the little church leading to the House Beautiful … ."[10]

Helen had known Robert Browning for more than fifty years, and for the last twenty-five she and Theodore had seen him often in a pleasant, social way. But the informal, day-to-day visits at Bryntysilio brought their friendship to an intimate and affectionate stage that it had not reached before.

A more exalted friendship was also prospering – one of long standing and warmth, though never of intimacy or informality. Theodore Martin's assiduity in serving Queen Victoria was not diminished after he completed the biography of Prince Albert. He was conscientious and sympathetic when she consulted him on literary and other matters, and he occasionally made some unsolicited suggestions. (When he miscalculated, she quickly set him right – his proposal that a Shakespearean scholar come and lecture to her received the terse reply, "The Queen dislikes lectures.")[11] He began writing her a poem each year for a Christmas or New Year greeting, and he went on to compose an occasional sonnet to commemorate some other special occasion, such as the Empress Frederick's visit to England in 1888 and the death of Prince Alexander of Bulgaria in 1893. Often, with the Queen's approval, he sent a copy to *Blackwood's* for publication and distribution to members of the royal family. In fact, Sir Theodore had constituted himself a minor poet laureate.[12] The Queen rewarded the Martins with many tokens of her appreciation: she kept them informed of royal news, sent them invitations to Windsor, showed concern for their health. And, to cap these favours, she allowed them to entertain her in their own drawing-room.

When Queen Victoria decided in 1889 to pay a long-intended visit to Wales, Henry Robertson (son of Theodore's old friend) put his estate of Palé at her disposal. Bryntysilio being not far away, she wished to honour the Martins by calling there. She would come for afternoon tea on 26 August.

As soon as the plan became known, numerous people offered to lend or hire their treasures for the occasion, but Helen always declined. "Our little home," she wrote in her diary, "will be as it always is."[13] Well – not quite. The one change was the Martins' transfer of all their royal mementos from London to Bryntysilio. In the entrance hall, replacing the bust of Helen Faucit (which had just been shipped to Blackwood's for their collection of authors' portraits), was a bust of Victoria at age eight; the corridor boasted a statuette of the Queen by Boehm, which had been presented to Lady Martin by Her Majesty; the principal object on the drawing-room wall was a handsome silver plaque that the Queen had given Sir Theodore.[14] Helen did adhere to her rule of simplicity, however. With admirable if rather self-conscious taste, she resisted any temptation to concoct elaborate bouquets in the Queen's honour. No doubt there were bowls of flowers here and there, but, especially for the Queen, there was a small nosegay of "pretty pink heather, with a centre of white heather," placed on a table near her chair. As with the decor, so with the refreshments: they must be both simple and appropriate. Buttered Welsh lightcakes gave the right local touch.[15]

Queen Victoria, dressed in black with a light feather in her bonnet, arrived at Llangollen by train and was met at the festively-decorated station by a delegation of railway officials, including Captain Best, the Martins' neighbour across the Dee. She was followed by Prince and Princess Henry of Battenberg (i.e. Princess Beatrice and her husband) and Princess Alice of Hesse. A guard of honour presented arms, a band played the National Anthem, there were loud acclamations from the crowd assembled in the street.

The Queen and her entourage travelled to Brynstysilio in a small but impressive procession. Leading the way rode a local dignitary, Major Leadbetter, followed by two scarlet-coated outriders. Then came the Queen's carriage, with the Scottish gillies seated behind it; it was drawn by four greys, the near horses being mounted by postilions in blue and gold. At its rear rode Col. Cornwallis West, M.P., and, behind him, the equerries with a pair of outriders. A second carriage contained Henry Ponsonby, the Queen's Private Secretary, and several of her attendants; a third carried her Indian attendants. The road from Llangollen to Bryntysilio was bright with flags, mottoes, and festoons of colourful bunting. A choir of twelve hundred children, stationed on a platform opposite the Cottage Hospital, burst into the strains of "God Save the Queen" as the royal carriage passed. Spectators lined the road all the way, cheering and waving hats and handkerchiefs.[16]

At Bryntysilio the Martins' household staff gathered at the window above the main entrance and watched the brilliant cavalcade as it wound its way up the hillside drive.[17] The Queen was met by Sir Theodore and Lady Martin and Miss Alice Helps, who was staying with them. She allowed Lady Martin to take her upstairs, where she enjoyed the views from the windows and saw, with particular interest, the room where Sir Theodore had written the biography of Prince Albert. After tea, everyone except the Queen and her hostess went out through the drawing-room window to the terrace, where the suite were walking about. Inside, the two women talked together as they listened to some Welsh songs sung by a small, hand-picked choir that had gathered on the lawn. Later Her Majesty went to the window and graciously accepted a bouquet presented by one of the girls on behalf of the choir. Afterwards, at the Martins' request, she signed her name on a sheet of Bryntysilio stationery; as she wrote the date, she looked up and said, "The dear Prince's birthday!" (She had actually planned her visit for that day, her hosts realized, to show her appreciation for the work done under this roof.) When she stepped into her carriage to leave, Helen was gratified to see that she was holding the nosegay of heather. The royal visitors returned with stately procession to Llangollen, where a public ceremony was to take place at the Assembly Rooms.[18] The Martins, however, could relax at last and congratulate themselves that all had gone well. Perhaps they had time now to recall that yesterday had been their own thirty-eighth wedding anniversary.

On 30 August, after the Queen had gone from Palé to Balmoral, Lady Martin wrote to her, expressing the Martins' gratitude for the royal visit. Despite the stiff third-person style, the conclusion of the letter glows with delight: "It will be like a fairy dream to look back upon in the future life that may be spared to them. But, happily, it will be unlike a dream, in that the great honour and happiness have been real, and can never pass away from them."[19] Later she received a gift that had been left for her at Palé and, even more pleasing, a letter from the Queen, written 15 September, speaking with pleasure of her visit, the beauty of the scenery, and the kindness and loyalty of the Welsh people. Helen's letter had not exaggerated in the least. The memories of that day never did "pass away." Even the tea set and linens became holy relics: they were never used by the Martins again, but "treasured" the rest of their lives.[20]

From the euphoria of August, 1889, Helen and Theodore were plunged into gloom in December by Browning's serious illness, which quickly ended in death on the 12th. "Quite ill all the day," Helen wrote on the night of the 13th, having heard the news that morning. "… How memory will go back to the early days, when I had to act in his plays and received such full kindness and more than appreciation … ." Browning was to be buried in Westminster Abbey on 29 December, but in the meantime his body lay, its coffin draped with a purple pall and footed by "great Italian wreaths," in a ground-floor room of the house he had shared with his sister. On Christmas Day Anne Thackeray Ritchie, on her way to the Browning house, stopped impulsively at the Martins'. As she wrote to her sister-in-law, "one has a hankering after one's old friends at such times." Anthony Froude was there when she arrived, and afterwards "dear old Sir Theodore came in, very pale and sad," from the Brownings' house. He was to be one of the pall-bearers. Although Annie and Helen arranged to sit together at the funeral, Theodore, thinking of the inevitable claustrophobia and headaches, persuaded his wife – much against her will – not to go.[21]

After all, though Westminster Abbey was the right place for the poet's tomb, it was not the church that Helen associated with her friend. When the Martins next returned to Wales, she arranged for a memorial tablet to Browning on the wall of little Llantysilio. On the first Sunday after it was put up, she could hardly keep her mind on the service because of a "curious feeling that he was beside [her]." If Browning's spirit did haunt Bryntysilio, it was a cheerful, beneficent spirit. In her diary Helen wrote this private tribute: "His very presence brought with it a feeling of contentment and large-heartedness. I never heard him, even in joking … say an unkind or cynical word of any person or thing, and yet how angry and indignant he could be!"[22]

Helen was at the age when old memories came crowding back but many of the friends who had shared them were gone.[23] Two family ties were particularly important to her now: her favourite among the Farrens was her nephew Percy (known on the stage as "William Farren jun."), son of her halfbrother William and namesake of her "dear master" of long ago; but closest of all in her affections was Kate Saville Thorpe, daughter of her eldest brother John, who had long been like a younger sister to her. The Thorpes and the Martins would sometimes spend the Christmas season together, either at Onslow Square or the Thorpes' home in Kettering (near Nottingham).[24] Occasionally Helen would renew acquaintance with an old friend, like Westland Marston,[25] with whom she had lost touch.[26] Sometimes she would be heartened by a stranger's recollection of what her acting had meant to him in his youth. Professor James Dewar (later Sir James), the eminent scientist, told her that he had been one of her devotees in Scotland (during her later years of acting) and had been present in pit or gallery every night when she was in town. J.O. Halliwell-Phillips, the Shakespearean scholar, wrote to say that it was her performance of Imogen in Macready's production of *Cymbeline* that had first sent him to the study of Shakespeare. At such moments the dreamlike past sharpened into reality anew.

In the 1890s Helen was so often incapacitated that she had to give up much of her former social life, but she still "received" on Sundays and, when she could manage it, she still liked to see what was new at the theatres and museums. In 1896, on Theodore's eightieth birthday, she rejoiced with him over the latest mark of the Queen's favour – a letter awarding him the Victoria Order. The following year, when the Queen was celebrating her sixty-year Jubilee, the Martins were invited by Lady Burdett-Coutts to watch the procession from her balcony, but the prospect of trying to get to and from her mansion through the thronged streets dampened their enthusiasm. The fifty-year Jubilee had been splendid, but this one seemed rather wearisome to them, with its scaffoldings obstructing the streets everywhere one turned.[27] The procession that meant the most to the elderly Martins was the small but unmistakably royal one that was still present to their mind's eye, winding its way up their drive at Bryntysilio.

The neuralgia which had afflicted Helen so severely in 1883-84 returned periodically to plague her, and in 1895-96 there was another protracted siege. Although she gradually recovered her strength, the enemy was never far away. Her new definition of happiness was a day when the pains were moderate. At such times she would converse with so much of her old vivacity that friends did not realize she was once more "onstage," playing the most difficult role of her career. On her bad days, though, the mere click of a teaspoon in a saucer was excruciating to her nerves.[28] Although her husband later insisted that she had borne her long "martyrdom" without murmuring, the gossip among their neighbours in Wales (probably retailed by servants) was that she was sensitive, peevish, autocratic, and hard to please. Sir Theodore, on the other hand, was devotedly kind and chivalrous, whatever her moods.[29] The severe headaches of neuralgia would have moved even the saints to murmur, and Helen, as much as she had always admired those lofty souls, had never had the patience and self-abnegation demanded of a martyr. What she did have were fortitude, determination, and self-respect. These characteristic virtues had carried her through illness, rejection, and criticism in her youth, and they were her best weapons now against her last, most implacable enemy.

On 1 January 1898 Sir Henry Irving brought out a new play at the Lyceum, *Peter the Great*, written by his son Laurence. The Martins had tickets for the matinee on 2 February, but at the last moment Helen suffered a relapse of her latest illness and had to send her husband and a party of friends off to the theatre without her. The flowers sent by Sir Henry cheered her, but, as she wrote to him, she felt very sorry for herself when everyone came in chattering happily about the excellence of his "Great Peter." "Oh I *must* grow well enough to see it next Wednesday!" she exclaimed.[30] If she did see that production, it was probably the last of her many experiences in the theatre.

In July the journey to Wales had to be postponed because of illness, but at last the Martins were reëstablished in their summer home and Theodore was hoping that Bryntysilio would exert its usual beneficent influence. This time, however, there was no rallying of forces. By late September it was clear, even to him, that recovery was impossible. October came, bringing Helen's birthday on the 11th (her eighty-fourth), but no one felt like celebrating. Her only pleasure was in looking out the window to the hills, with their autumn foliage. At night she would lie awake, with nothing to distract her from her pain, and remember how even as a child she had suffered from insomnia. "What a long sleep is owing to me!" she wrote one night.[31]

During this last illness the Queen was constant in her inquiries and expressions of sympathetic concern. Late in the evening of Sunday, the 30th, a solicitous telegram arrived from her, which Helen, "with her humble duty," tried to acknowledge in her own hand. She could not do it, and Theodore had to manage for her. In the early morning she could sleep at last, and she did not awake.[32]

On Monday, 31 October 1898, Queen Victoria wrote in her journal: "Heard with great regret that Ly Martin died this morning … It will be a dreadful blow to poor Sir Theodore." Two days later she wrote to the bereaved husband, addressing him, in her kindness, with unusual simplicity and directness: "What your grief, your loneliness must be, I can but too well understand … I was most anxious to pay my respect to dear Lady Martin's memory for her own sake & for yours – for I can never forget all you have done for me."[33]

On Wednesday, after a brief service in the inner hall at Bryntysilio, conducted by the Vicar of Llantysilio, Lady Martin's body, in its oak coffin, was transported by horse-drawn hearse to the Llangollen railway station for a last journey to London. It was accompanied by friends and neighbours in their carriages, some of whom (like Captain Best, one of the pall bearers) would go with Sir Theodore to attend the funeral. Groups of sympathetic Welsh people lined the way, and a large assembly waited at the station to pay their last respects.[34] At noon on Friday, 4 November, Helen's body, which had spent Thursday night at the Martins' London house, was placed in another hearse for the drive to St. Peter's Church, Cranley-gardens. So many flowers had been sent that they filled an open carriage, which preceded the hearse; among them were a large wreath of white chrysanthemums and lilies from Queen Victoria (who also sent a personal representative to the funeral) and a cross of pink immortelles from Princess Beatrice. The pall bearers included, among others, Sir Frederick Burton, Otto Goldschmidt, and Percy Farren ("William Farren, jun."). Kate Thorpe and her surviving sister, Eliza Helena Saville, were among the chief mourners. Arthur Munby, long an admirer of Helen's, was present. During the services, the Rev. Dr. Frederic Ridgeway, Vicar of St. Peter's, praised Lady Martin for having nobly used her opportunity to "make the stage what it was meant to be … a pulpit streaming forth … wondrous influence upon the lives and characters of men …"[35] As the coffin was about to be carried from the church, the sun, which had previously been obscured by clouds, suddenly broke forth for one golden moment. Munby's romantic heart was touched by this symbolic transfiguration, but Sir Theodore, bowed with grief, did not see it. One last procession took the body to Brompton Cemetery for interment at a site near the north gate. As the coffin was lowered into the grave, the sun burst once more through its veil of cloud, and this time it dazzled Sir Theodore's tear-dimmed eyes. It was a message from Helen, he thought: she was happy now, and he must not grieve.[36]

He did grieve, of course. "We were all in all to each other," he wrote to William Blackwood, "& my life is cut in twain …" But Helen had wished him to "seek relief … in work," and since his Parliamentary duties were heavy that season he was obliged to take her prescription. He found the best outlet for his grief, however, in establishing memorials to his wife, designed not only to express his own devotion but also to keep her reputation alive for future generations. The tombstone erected in Brompton Cemetery was only the first of a series of monuments that he planned and, in all but one case, carried out. It bears, in addition to her name and death date, a quotation from Anne Thackeray Ritchie's tribute to Lady Martin in her preface to a volume of Thackeray's works – "Her gracious gift of genius belonged to the world; the charm of her goodness was for her home, and for the friends that loved her" – followed by a passage from Shakespeare's *The Winter's Tale* – "the sweet'st companion, that e'er man / Bred his hopes out of." In the year following his wife's death, Sir Theodore put up on the wall of Llantysilio a handsome memorial sculpture, an alto relievo designed some years earlier by J.H. Foley (who had since died) and now reproduced in white marble from his plaster model by a young Irish sculptor named Hughes. It shows Lady Martin seated, in profile, holding a partially-opened book; a medallion of Shakespeare's head rests against her chair, and the masks of Tragedy and Comedy are seen, respectively, at the upper left and right corners of the entablature. Engraved on the base are the words, "In memory of / Helena Faucit – Lady Martin / Who died at Bryntysilio / 31st October 1898," followed by the same quotation from Lady Ritchie that appears on the tombstone.[37]

Sir Theodore was particularly eager to keep his wife's name alive in Stratford-upon-Avon – alive and forever associated with Shakespeare's. Perhaps the most valuable "monuments" he could have devised were the collection of Helen Faucit's promptbooks that he presented to the Shakespeare Memorial Library (now the Shakespeare Centre Library) and her portrait by Rudolf Lehmann that he later left to the Gallery of the Theatre. But Sir Theodore envisioned something more striking. The scene was to be Shakespeare's church, Holy Trinity, and there would be two memorials. The first was a new pulpit, designed by G.F. Bodley, which Sir Theodore presented to the church in memory of his wife. It was made of green marble and decorated with full-length figures of five saints sculptured in white marble. (Many people thought the figure of St. Helena bore a remarkable resemblance to Helen Faucit in her prime.) The Bishop of Worcester dedicated it on 18 October 1900, and Helen's old friend Canon Ainger preached an "eloquent sermon" on the occasion.[38] Sir Theodore's dramatic *coup* was meant to follow immediately: a copy of the Llantysilio sculpture was to be placed on the chancel wall, opposite the tomb and bust of Shakespeare.

Sculpture of St. Helena on a marble pulpit designed by G. F. Bodley, given by Sir Theodore Martin to Holy Trinity Church, Stratford-upon-Avon (photograph by Michael Baker, in possession of the author)

Sir Theodore, who had served on the Committee of the Shakespeare Memorial Library and had been, since 1889, a trustee of Shakespeare's Birthplace, had built up considerable influence in Stratford. For this reason, perhaps, he came close to achieving his wish about his wife's memorial. The Bishop of Worcester even gave his permission to remove a tablet in memory of a former vicar so as to make room for the new sculpture. But Sir Theodore had reckoned without the opposition of Marie Corelli, best-selling novelist and determined crusader for the preservation of the national heritage represented by Stratford. When she heard of Martin's intentions she was outraged. She wrote letters and gave interviews denouncing his plan, accused Martin of "buying" the church's complicity by promising a substantial contribution, and declared that, if the church would oppose Martin, she would lead a campaign to raise the full sum of nine hundred pounds that it needed. The vicar told her that he could not stop Martin in view of the permission already given by the Bishop, but when she found that the widow of the vicar whose memorial was to be moved had not been consulted, she had ammunition for a further battle. Eventually Sir Theodore, dismayed by the controversy, withdrew his offer of the sculpture. He was crushed, for he could never understand why anyone would consider the pairing of Helen Faucit's sculpture with William Shakespeare's an incongruity, much less a desecration of a national monument.[39] Balked of his first intention, he finally presented the sculpture to the Gallery of the Shakespeare Memorial Theatre. The poor man would have been horrified had he known that the gift meant to keep his wife's name in perpetual memory would later be lost from sight for two decades and, when rediscovered in the 1970s, the finder's first thought would be that this Victorian lady in the "Whistler's Mother pose" would make a nice bit of marble for his bathroom.[40]

The most important of Martin's "monuments," of course, was his biography of his wife. Barely a month after her death he was assembling his materials to write a "Memorial Life," as he called it,[41] and from that time on he worked on the book whenever possible; his manuscript was finished in August, 1900, and the book was published by Blackwood in November of that year.

The reviews seem to have been, as Sir Theodore himself remarked, "on the whole, very fair." There were some high compliments: for example, *The Times* (28 January 1901) described the book as "not merely an interesting record of the career of a really great actress, but a picture of the mind of a really great woman." There were, on the other hand, some protests against Sir Theodore's "extravagant homage to his wife." The reviewer for the *Illustrated London News* (26 January 1901) was unusually blunt: "The pity of it is that a work which might have been an interesting chronicle of the stage is merely an exercise in conjugal idolatry that few people will have the patience to read." More typical was the recognition that the book, though understandably biased, contained much that was valuable. W.L. Courtney called it a "chaplet of laurel laid upon

[Lady Martin's] tomb, not a cold, analytical dissection of her qualities," but he advised every actress to read it; he himself praised Helen Faucit as "the most completely equipped interpreter of Shakespeare's heroines which this century has seen" (*Daily Telegraph*, 30 November 1900).

Memorial tablet, with alto relievo of Helena Faucit Martin, designed by J. H. Foley. Now on the wall of Llantysilio Church; copy in the Royal Shakespeare Gallery, Stratford-upon-Avon
(published copy of engraving by J. Brown in possession of the author)

Eventually Martin re-established his normal life, and, though he might not have admitted it, with a freedom he had not enjoyed in his wife's last years. In the summer of 1899 he had dreaded returning to Bryntysilio for the first time after her death, but there in particular he became again his old genial self. He would entertain houseguests once more and sometimes he would sing them the old Scottish songs, his voice quavering a little but still surprisingly strong. He would attend the Sheep Dog Trials, an annual event at Llangollen, and would even bring along a lady companion – a different lady each time, it was observed – handing her out of the carriage and escorting her about like a gallant if ancient beau. With his servants, as with his peers, he was a courtly old gentleman, and with the family of one former servant he was more like a friend than an employer or patron. This was Jane Anne Jones (née Williams), who had served Helen as personal maid for many years. When Mrs. Jones's husband died early, leaving her with two little daughters, Martin built her an attractive house, which they named "Helenfa" for the woman to whom they had both been devoted. On Sundays he frequently had the Jones girls come to Bryntysilio, attend church with him, and stay for lunch; and often the mother and daughters would spend their holidays in his London house.[42] Helenfa was the most practical of his memorials.

Sir Theodore died on 18 August 1909, shortly before his ninety-third birthday, and was buried beside his wife in Brompton Cemetery. A memorial tablet was erected by a nephew in the little church of Llantysilio; so here, too, the Martins were remembered together.[43]

Until the end Martin had continued to preach the gospel of Helen Faucit. When Reginald, Viscount Esher, called on him in March 1908, the two talked for an hour about the late Queen's recently-published letters and other royal matters; then Sir Theodore, a white-haired but agile old man, "perfectly hale and hearty," took his guest upstairs – actually running ahead – to show him a bust of his wife. "Not a bit like an actress, was she?" he said. "She was an *Artist*, and not an actress."[44] Helen Faucit would have preferred him to say, "She was what a good actress *should* be – an artist."

PART IV: “A Crown’s Worth of Good Interpretation”
2 Henry IV 2.2.92

Afterpiece

As THE scenes of Helen Faucit's life have unrolled, they have presented many brief glimpses of her dramatic characters – but no full views. Now that the chronological sequence is complete, however,it is possible to take a more comprehensive look at some of these. Five portrayals with special significance for her career will be described: Shakespeare's Juliet, Rosalind, and Lady Macbeth, Pauline in Bulwer's *The Lady of Lyons*, and Antigone in Bartholomew's English version of Sophocles' tragedy. Although word-pictures can never recapture lost realities, those presented here, being based on hints from Helen Faucit's essays, her promptbooks, and eyewitness descriptions of her performances, can at least suggest what the originals were like.

Some introductory paragraphs will summarize the salient characteristics of Helen Faucit's acting style and will comment generally on her handling of dramatic texts. Then, for every role except Antigone, there will be a reconstruction of her portrayal, including, for Shakespearean roles, comments on the textual changes most relevant to performance. Since her Antigone has already been described rather fully (see Chapter 9), the discussion here will focus, not on the details of her acting, but on her basic approach to the character. The reconstructions must be composite ones since the evidence for them comes from different parts of her career. Even so, they can show both the special strengths and the more dubious idiosyncrasies of her acting as viewed by her contemporaries. They will demonstrate, I believe, how her interpretive skill and acting style resulted in some of the most remarkable portrayals of her day.

Young Helen Faucit's inclination toward the dynamic acting associated with Kean was tamed by her own limited resources and by strong influences from her mentors. The latter pointed in two different directions: the "ideal" method of the Kembles and the "psychological" style of Macready. Her mature acting reflected both influences: fundamentally she was a psychological actress, hence dedicated to the portrayal of individualized characters; yet, by her interpretive emphasis on "womanly" traits and by her artistic and poetic techniques, she often created an effect of ideality. Critics disagreed about whether her acting was "studied" or "impulsive." The sense of study, which was strongest in her later years, came, paradoxically, from a meticulous effort to create a "real" person by revealing the character's inner life, as well as from her use of artistic techniques which, after the advent of "natural" acting, often seemed unduly artificial.[1] Yet many of her admirers never stopped thinking of her acting as spontaneous. This was because they felt a real passion beneath all she did and because they found a freshness in each new portrayal of the same role: the main conception might not vary, but there were "particular touches – new felicities" each time.[2]

The psychological emphasis accorded with her natural inclination to identify with her characters. From the beginning she had entered imaginatively into their experiences, relating them to some of her own. As a maturing actress, she built up more detailed conceptions of her characters' lives and personalities. For each role she tried to understand the thoughts and emotions that might underlie every speech, action, or silence, and to make audiences aware of these by vocal tone, facial expression, attitude, and gesture. To explain possible influences and motives, she made a minute study of the text, extrapolating from whatever hints she could find in it. As her essays show, sometimes she fell back on imagined events that occurred prior to the play or between its scenes. Her resulting conception of a heroine's life enabled her to give a sense of unity to her performances, to make receptive audiences feel that they were witnessing only part of a reality that existed beyond the scene of the moment. Using this approach, she gave unusually complex pesonalities to some characters, and she showed even the simpler ones in the process of developing.

The impression of wholeness in Helen Faucit's portrayals was due not only to her imaginative identification with her characters but also to the artistry of her acting. In her most emotional speeches she worked up to – and down from – a climax, prolonging the "sentiment and impressions" by expression and attitude after she had finished speaking, "like the murmurs of a wave breaking on a long echoing shore."[3] She was so adept at shaping scenes, orchestrating their different effects into a single composition, that some of them seemed like dramas within themselves.[4] In a play as a whole, she was sensitive to artistic and interpretive patterns and to such contributing effects as parallels, analogies, and contrasts. Her performances, which reflected this interest, were sometimes compared to well-composed paintings. Her pictorial and statuesque effects have been mentioned several times in the biography. In their most noticeable form – that is, in the momentary creation of a "picture" or "statue" – these were used for Shakespearean plays sparingly and purposefully. In working them out Helen

Faucit was influenced in part by certain stage conventions of her early years: for example, "dilation," a traditional technique of tragic acting that created the impression of a majestic swelling of the figure, appropriate to transcendent moments of fury, exultation, noble declamation, and so on. It consisted of rising on the toes and letting the head "tower," and it was often accompanied by lifted or extended arm (or arms) and thrilling voice. (In later years, the use of this technique, by then no longer popular, may have struck a note of old-fashioned melodrama.) A more potent influence, the acting of Antigone and Iphigenia, increased Helen Faucit's respect for stylized effects, which she then used emblematically to punctuate her largely natural performances.

Her acting was described in terms of poetry as well as picture, sometimes as if the arts were interchangeable – as when her "poetic" impersonations were compared to "the charming paintings of Claude Lorraine."[5] "Poetic" was occasionally applied to a suggestive bit of stage business that charmed the eye and stirred the imagination; more often it denoted a brief, unexpected change in facial and vocal expression that endowed some simple word or phrase with delicate shades of irony or pathos – even with a subtle hint of universal significance. The poetic effect was intensified by the "marked musical rhythm" of her more emotional speeches: "The charms of the iambic, the sapphic, the hexameter, [were] all borrowed, as if unconsciously, and used in the same speech" with a power whose source was not easily detected. Such effects contributed to the ideal quality in her acting, which, at certain moments, could transport suggestible spectators into the realm of "the beautiful." This quality was nourished by her psychological methods as well as by her artistic principles: appeals to subconscious memories and semi-conscious trains of thought made possible a sympathetic explanation of dubious speeches and actions; and the use of selection, composition, and perspective resulted in a view of human reality that was "nature itself, but nature as it appears to a poet's eye."[6]

The basic characteristics of Helen Faucit's acting were the same for her new roles as for her Shakespearean ones. The most obvious differences were in degree: a sense of psychological complexity characterized all her portrayals but it was strongest in the Shakespearean ones simply because there was more to work with there; her emotionally harrowing scenes were more likely to seem melodramatic (excessive for the occasion and unsupported by the language) in some new plays than in any of Shakespeare's – or so a modern reader would suppose. Such considerations aside, there must have been a great deal of "cross-fertilization" between Shakespearean and non-Shakespearean portrayals by Helen Faucit and other actors of romantic drama. Arthur Colby Sprague, in his provocative essay "Shakespeare and Melodrama" remarks that Pauline could have shown Imogen how to speak in denouncing Iachimo.[7] In Helen Faucit's case, Imogen could have shown Pauline a thing or two as well, for Pauline had her moments of pathos. Such "cross-fertilization" occurred among the new roles, too. For example, the formal containment of intense emotion in the classical heroines probably encouraged less painful performances of Lady Mabel's dying scene in *The Patrician's Daughter*.[8] Helen Faucit did, of course, vary the finer details and even the stylistic modes of her portrayals to suit the period and genre of each play and the personality of each heroine.

Despite her respect for Shakespeare's artistry and her critical appreciation of scenes often considered "unnecessary" in the theatre, she did not mind making large cuts in the text to serve some special purpose, such as condensing a play for use in a double bill of mainpieces. In a few instances she even used a slice of a Shakespearean play (such as the trial scene in *The Merchant of Venice*) as an afterpiece.[9] More often, however, she simply edited a play in the usual way: to suit her conception of theatrical effectiveness, especially the effectiveness of her own role. Even a scene she admired artistically might be sacrificed if it detracted from the latter. She was, after all, a star. Yet she did make a good many Shakespearean restorations when using a conventional acting text. And, regardless of her cuts for *performance*, she based her *interpretation* on a thorough study of the whole play.[10] In those ways she was unusual.

Her treatment of text is less significant in her new plays than in her Shakespearean ones since these dramas were already designed for a contemporary audience and since there were no previous adaptations or stage traditions to be considered. In some plays, too, it is impossible to know whether her cuts are the same as those made originally by Macready. Those she undoubtedly made generally helped to quicken the dramatic pace or to give her role better histrionic opportunities. A passage in *King René's Daughter* was obviously cut on both accounts. In the original text young Iolanthe, newly cured of her blindness, was advised by Ibn Jahia to thank God; when she asked him to teach her how, he replied, "Then kneel thee down, my darling child, and say, 'Mysterious Being …'" and so on; Iolanthe obediently knelt and repeated his words. Helen Faucit omitted all this, down to Iolanthe's voicing of the prayer, which thus became her own words.[11] Her radiant, otherworld Iolanthe would speak this prayer from her heart – and the actress, delivering it with impressive reverence, would add to the sense of mystical inspiration she gave to this portrayal. Helen Faucit's verbal substitutions in her promptbook texts usually improved the rhythm or made the lines sound more natural. Even in her classical dramas, where formality and artifice were expected, she often moderated the stiffness of the rhetoric to produce a more convincing emotional tone. In *Iphigenia in Aulis*, for example, when Iphigenia was pleading with her father not to sacrifice her, Calcraft had her say, after reminding him of their mutual words of love in former times: "Thou hast forgotten thine and would'st destroy me./ By Pelops I entreat thee! by they sire/ Atreus! …" Helen Faucit's Iphigenia said instead: "Thou hast forgotten thine, ay, & would'st kill me./ Oh no! By Pelops thy dread grandsire, no!/ No, by thy father Atreus! …"[12] The simple directness of "kill" and "no" (repeated) charged the lines with greater emotion and thus gave the actress more scope.

Juliet

Helen Faucit based her first interpretation of *Romeo and Juliet* on a stage version of the play; she began revising it, however, after reading the original text, and she was confirmed in her new ideas by experiences in the classical drama. Though delayed by managerial opposition,[13] she eventually made an acting version based on the genuine text.

Her experimentation is reflected in two promptbooks of *Romeo and Juliet.* The basic text for the earlier one is a Cumberland acting edition using Garrick's version of the play.[14] In addition to changes common to many theatrical texts (omissions for the sake of propriety or compactness, verbal substitutions, added "curtain lines" for some scenes, spectacular and musical embellishments), it had two notable substantive alterations: at the beginning, instead of pining for Rosaline, Romeo secretly loves Juliet from afar; and, in the tomb scene, Juliet awakes while Romeo still lives and the lovers have a tragic reunion before death claims them both. Helen Faucit left these adaptations intact. In addition, she cut some Shakespearean passages that were retained in the conventional text: for example, Romeo's extravagant bewailing of his banishment. But she also restored a number of Shakespearean words and lines, and she struck out an intrusive funeral procession and chorus. She used this promptbook until 1846, possibly longer; but, before giving it up, she finally excised Garrick's interpolations in the tomb scene and restored some Shakespearean lines. She was not yet ready, however, to relinquish the "curtain lines" added to the potion scene.

The second promptbook, based on Charles Knight's Cabinet Edition of Shakespeare's *Romeo and Juliet* (1843), was probably used by Helen Faucit from about 1847.[15] Virtually all of her textual changes are cuts: nearly 600 lines, not counting some passages that were omitted at one time and restored at another.[16] Many cuts are traditional, and others, though new, are the kind that any dramatic editor might have made to sharpen the dialogue and accelerate the action. A few, however, are more interesting.

In Shakespeare's text, the bantering dialogue between Romeo and Juliet at the Capulets' ball (1.5.93-106) forms a "sonnet," ending with a kiss. The theatrical version spoiled this effect by omitting eight lines (two in each quatrain and the final couplet), then inserting a new line that led to the kiss, an arrangement that Helen Faucit had retained in her first promptbook. In her second one she omitted the same lines as before but did not insert the adaptor's line – and, this time, she did not even allow a kiss. Her most significant cuts in other scenes were those eliminating Shakespeare's complicating factors so as to focus more directly on Juliet or on the two lovers together. In her arrangement, for example, Juliet's first scene (with her mother and the Nurse) was omitted; thus the audience first saw Juliet at the same time Romeo did, at the masquerade. Later, when Juliet, secretly married to Romeo but promised by her father to Paris, encountered Paris at Friar Lawrence's cell, her forced attempt at badinage was cut out so that her mood of desperate resolution could be sustained without distractions. In the tomb scene, Romeo's poignant "Forgive me, cousin," upon seeing Tybalt's corpse, was omitted so as to keep his attention fixed on Juliet and the audience's on these two alone.

Cuts notwithstanding, however, Helen Faucit's second version of *Romeo and Juliet* has important elements of a "restoration": her choice of a complete Shakespearean text as its basis, her discarding of the adaptor's added lines, and her retention of certain Shakespearean passages that were customarily omitted in acting. Some of those retained passages were important to her mature interpretation of the play.

According to her essay on Juliet,[17] *Romeo and Juliet* has a scope and significance beyond that of its love story, beautiful though that is: in it, as in certain Greek tragedies, "the young and innocent" are doomed to suffer for "the guilt of kindred whose 'bloody feuds' [are] to be expiated and ended by the death of their posterity." The keynote is struck in the Prologue to the play, which should always be spoken in performance. It is omitted from the first promptbook but retained in the second.[18] Helen Faucit points out the workings of "Destiny" in the lives of the lovers, and she stresses the importance of Shakespeare's "elaborate close" to the tomb scene, in which their sacrifice is recognized and the families are reconciled. This denouement, though severely cut at one time, even in the second promptbook, was largely restored later.

When studying Shakespeare's text Helen Faucit noticed that Romeo, as well as Juliet, makes a sudden transition from juvenility to adulthood. In his initial lovesickness for the "fair but icy" Rosaline he shows "that vague yearning of the fancy, that idle listlessness" which issues in exaggerated sighs and artificial poetry; all this gives way immediately to genuine, passionate love when he meets Juliet (110, 114, 124). In the second promptbook Romeo's infatuation with Rosaline is retained, and so is his passionate lament over his banishment.

Despite unsympathetic parents and a foolish, vulgar nurse, Juliet was at the beginning of the play a girl with a romantic imagination and a "boundless capacity for self-devotion." Her dreams of an ideal hero and an all-absorbing love were, however, insubstantial as yet (essay 112-13).[19]

At the Capulets' ball (1.5) Juliet, "heartwhole and coy," conducted herself with "grace and maidenly modesty" and spoke with the "bird-like silver voice" of a child – a tone never quite echoed until the end of the play.[20] When

Romeo, dressed in pilgrim's costume, took her hand and initiated his wordplay on "pilgrim" and "saint," Juliet playfully joined in. But Romeo (in Helen Faucit's conception) took the game of saint-worship more seriously: his few words were eloquently amplified by "beseeching eyes" and "tremulous voice full of adoration and humility" (essay 115). Eliminating the kiss preserved Juliet's delicacy and also emphasized Romeo's unassuaged longing. A kiss between these two must be something more than the prize for "a set of wit well played."

In the balcony scene (2.2) Juliet's demeanour had radically changed,[21] for her brief encounter with Romeo had brought her dreams of love to sudden reality. "What a new life [had] opened to her! … The invincible and unknown Eros [had] come upon her … in all his terror and in all his beauty" (essay 116-17). The allusion to the *Vita Nuova*, with its memorable visitation from Eros, is significant, for, like Dante's work, Helen Faucit's portrayal of Juliet combined the erotic and the ideal. Erotic emotion was given a freer rein than was normally expected on the Victorian stage. This Juliet expressed her emotion with "unconventional" fervour, completely abandoning herself to the "raptures … portrayed in the voluptuous language." "Her eager passion, unrestrained by the boundaries of fashion or etiquette, beam[ed] out of her sparkling eyes, [spoke] itself in the heaving bosom, could even make itself known by her most eloquent gestures alone." But, unmistakable as her passion was, she infused its words with the "delicacy … fondness and gushing spirit of womanhood." Helen Faucit's skill in combining passion with delicacy and "purity of … devotion" enabled her to exceed the bounds of conventional modesty without censure – indeed with enthusiastic approval.[22]

Her richly-textured balcony scene contained many contrasting effects. For example, there was an "air of childlike simplicity, yet deep and absorbing impulse." This was well illustrated in "Dost thou love me? I know thou wilt say 'Ay,'": Juliet "asked the question anxiously and slowly, and before Romeo could reply she answered it quickly herself." In other passages, ardour was mingled with bashfulness or "tempered … with a slight touch of raillery." The artistry of the scene was as notable as its variety. Sometimes this was purely visual, as in a gracefully "picturesque" use of a scarf as part of the byplay.[23] Basically, however, it was shown in subtle transitions from one mood to another, each shading into the next. For example, in "My ears have not yet drunk a hundred words/ Of thy tongue's uttering …" this Juliet "charmingly blended" several emotions: love was evident, but so was a lingering hint of the "startled terror" from which she had "not quite recovered" (originally expressed in "What man art thou …?") and also "a half apologetic air" arising from her fear that Romeo might misjudge words she had not intended for his ear (an anticipation of "Thou know'st the mask of night …"). "O swear not by the moon" was spoken with a touch of raillery, but the thought of inconstancy brought a "slight shadow of mistrust" which developed into "a presentiment of evil" in "I have no joy of this contract tonight."[24] Near the end of the balcony scene, Juliet, after going inside in response to the Nurse's call, returned and abruptly brought up the subject of marriage – something the lovers had not mentioned before. Helen Faucit explained the "marked" change (and the apparent forwardness?) by imagining an offstage scene in which the Nurse had questioned Juliet on "what she thought of Paris and of her approaching marriage with him"; then Juliet, dreading the possibility of being forced into such a union, hastily asked Romeo about their own plans (121-22).

The coaxing scene (2.5) was full of by-play: Juliet leaned, cheek to cheek, against the Nurse, knelt before her, cupped her chin in her hands, rocked her on her chair, cajoled, flattered, and petted her – all the while impatient for news of Romeo. Helen Faucit charmed her early audiences with these childish arts, but, as she continued to act Juliet in her later years, she found it difficult to assume them without seeming "self-conscious … and affected."[25]

In the second scene of Act 3 Juliet's ardent soliloquy, "Gallop apace, you fiery-footed steeds," was conventionally deprived of references to lovers' "amorous rites," losing "a winning match," and so on. Helen Faucit also omitted the obliquely sexual lines "O, I have bought the mansion of a love,/ but not possess'd it." Thus her passionate Juliet had to express her longing through look and tone while speaking only the most general and poetic words.

The Nurse's incoherently-told news of the fatal duel made Juliet think at first that Romeo was dead, then that both he and Tybalt were dead. Finally understanding the truth, she denounced Romeo as an angel-faced fiend. But when the Nurse exclaimed, "Shame come to Romeo!" this Juliet turned on her with startlingly sudden effect, shouting in a "rapt," inspired voice, "Blister'd be thy tongue/ for such a word!" Audiences responded to the Siddons-like vehemence with deafening applause. This sounds like an "effect" for its own sake, but at least one viewer interpreted it as the first indication of the "heroine" to come. In later years Helen Faucit rejected her former vehemence and showed that a deep, inward emotion "predominated over the indignation." She reserved her climactic effect for a frenzied joy in "My Romeo lives that Tybalt would have slain," followed by a "shower of sorrow" over Romeo's banishment.[26]

The lovers' sorrowful farewell after their wedding night (3.5.1-59) took place, as Helen Faucit described it, on the same balcony from which Juliet had confessed her love, and Romeo, after descending the rope ladder, stood looking up at her as he had done before (essay 134-36). The *Literary Gazette*, noticing the ironic parallel, spoke of the "depth of tragic pathos" in this scene. Looking down, Helen Faucit's Juliet expressed her "melancholy prevision" of Romeo "dead in the bottom of a tomb" in such "hushed and plaintive tones" that listeners seemed to hear the lovers' knell. She followed her husband's disappearing figure with her eyes, even while reluctantly turning her steps away to answer her mother's summons.[27]

In the following sequence of interviews (lines 64-234), first with the mother, then with both parents, and finally with the Nurse, this Juliet found herself increasingly isolated. While her parents were insisting on an immediate marriage with Paris, she "hurrie[d] from one to the other … with appeals truly pitiable, and finding no response, she seize[d] on the hand of the nurse, and retain[ed] a nervous clutch upon it, for some human support." When her parents had left, Juliet begged the Nurse for a word of comfort and was shocked by her advice to forget Romeo and marry Paris. One can imagine Helen Faucit releasing her clutch and withdrawing from the old woman in horror. In her reminiscent words:

> All my blood seemed to be forced back upon my heart as I listened to these words. I grew as stone … I have often been startled at the sad solemnity of my own tones as I put the question, "Speakest thou from thy heart?" and in the very significant "Amen!" which follows [the Nurse's] reply – "From my soul too; or else beshrew them both." (138-39)

"Amen" was sometimes spoken in a half-whisper, at other times, apparently, in a deeper tone. The "pale cheek, fixed eye," sorrowfully resolute look, and "rigid muscles" as Juliet listened to the Nurse were the outward signs of "turning to stone." After the Nurse's exit, Juliet was left alone, forsaken. As she stood, dry-eyed and "erect in her desolation," her childlike "trust in others [fell] from her … She [was] henceforth the determined woman" (essay 139). On a blank page of her first Juliet promptbook is this quotation in Helen Faucit's hand: "– rose from her seat & stood erect, pale, inactively, in the touching majesty of a misery too great for consolation." Whatever its source, it describes the effect she aimed to create at Juliet's turning-point. The "cold, clear, concentrated passion" with which she spoke the following soliloquy suggested the disillusioned but determined adult.[28]

Originally Helen Faucit's Juliet spoke to Friar Lawrence in a trembling voice when describing the horrors she would undergo rather than be false to Romeo (4.1.77-88),[29] but in later performances she was more self-possessed. Her "slender form covered with a long black veil," she spoke of fearful ordeals with quiet intensity. She was "a very type of calm resolve and heroic fortitude."[30]

In kneeling to her father, ostensibly to beg forgiveness for her disobedience and agree to marry Paris (4.2), Helen Faucit's Juliet "mutely" took leave of him by kissing his hand, for she knew she would soon be drinking the potion and might never see him again (essay, 143). In the next scene (4.3), bidding her mother goodnight with the word "Farewell" had the same significance. Sometimes she dropped to her knees as Lady Capulet and the Nurse turned to leave and kissed her hand to her mother's retreating figure.[31] Speaking as if she were Juliet indeed, the actress later recalled:

> This breaking up of all the natural ties of youth and home, the heart-sick feeling of desolation, overpowered me, and sobs came against my will. The very room looked strange, larger, darker [she helped to create this effect by having the lights "a little down"] ... I used to lift the lamp from the table and peer into the shadows, to try to take away their terror. Already I could fancy I had descended into the vault. (143)

In the following soliloquy (lines 24-58), using pantomime and the "rapid transformations" of her expressive face, this Juliet powerfully conjured up a "sequence of horrible and strange visions" as she imagined a too-early awakening in the ancestral vault. The image of "bloody Tybalt, yet but green in earth" always drew from her "an exclamation of ... disgust" (essay 144) and a shudder that a longtime playgoer remembered as one of the most thrilling points in his experience. Juliet's panic, as if pursued by unseen, fearful things, was expressed (to use the old playgoer's absurd but graphic phrase) in a "terrified look *over both shoulders at the same moment.*" Reviewers wrote that her horror became "almost too horrible for stage representation." Audiences were "held fascinated," and when the scene ended "it seemed as though some terrible incubus had been removed from every breast."[32]

As oblique "stage directions" for the potion scene, Helen Faucit wrote in the margins of her first Juliet promptbook (pp. 55, 57) two quotations from the Psalms: "My heart is disquieted within me and the fear of death has fallen upon me"; "Fearfulness and trembling are come upon me and an horrible dread hath overwhelmed me." In her second promptbook, also at the potion scene (p. 201), she wrote a line from Shakespeare's Prologue: "The fearful passage of their death-marked love!–" These evocative phrases were in her mind as she studied the scene, and, by working on her imagination, they must have helped her produce the effects of morbid horror so vividly described by her critics.

Suddenly a dramatic change came over Juliet. During the soliloquy fear had temporarily overcome love and all had seemed madness, but as the frenzied girl seemed to see Tybalt rise from his grave and pursue Romeo, the thought of Romeo brought love back into power. At this point, wrote Helen Faucit, "I used to feel all my resolution return... . [Juliet] will pass through the horror of hell itself to reach what lies beyond; and she swallows the potion with his name upon her lips" (145). Descriptions of her acting, as far apart as Paris in 1845 and London in 1865, emphasized the invincible resolution that overcame her horrified imaginings.[33]

Over the years Helen Faucit changed the way she acted after drinking the potion. While using her first promptbook she spoke these non-Shakespearean lines before falling on the bed: "O, potent draught, thou hast chill'd me to the heart! –/ My head turns round; my senses fail me. –/ O, Romeo! Romeo!" She acted accordingly: "the expression she gave to the paralyzing effect of the potion was most harrowing."[34] Later, having adopted the Shakespearean text, she realized that the soliloquy had been "harrowing" enough and that Juliet's "toast" to Romeo – "I drink to thee" – was the right conclusion to her renewed resolution, not to be spoiled by further excitement. Now she simply retired to bed, exhausted. As Westland Marston wrote admiringly, other parts of her potion scene showed what she "could *do*," but its ending showed what she "could *refrain from doing*."[35]

Helen Faucit sometimes ended Act 4 with the potion scene, thereby omitting both the vignette of wedding preparations, whose ironic juxtaposition to the potion scene she professedly appreciated, and the discovery of Juliet's "death," which, as the *Caledonian Mercury* pointed out, is necessary to the plot.[36] The star's sense of theatre seems to have been warring with the imaginative critic's artistic perceptions.

The tomb scene (5.3), while Helen Faucit was using the Garrick version, had a strong gothic appeal to many spectators. Scottish audiences were particularly thrilled by the "painful effect[s]" she created in Juliet's "return from stupor to consciousness – her dismay at Romeo's inevitable fate – her dispair [sic] at finding the fatal phial exhausted – and the eager satisfaction with which she places the dagger in its vital sheath." Young Theodore Martin was wildly excited by "that fearful starting from the tomb – the Lazarus look – the frantic clinging to the dead head of her dear lord! It was Isabella with her pot of basil…"[37] These shocking analogies – Lazarus, still in his cerements, "starting" from the dead; Isabella cherishing the pot of herbs containing her lover's severed head – speak of acting with a powerful mixture of the marvellous and the grotesque. Helen Faucit's unusually quiet tomb scene in her Parisian performance[38] was probably an isolated experiment inspired by her French audience's response to subtle effects. In Edinburgh, not long afterwards, she was once more clinging to Romeo's dead body, throwing herself into the "agonies" and "despairs" of the scene with "an abandonment that [swept] every thing before it."[39]

By May, 1847, when her tomb scene had become relatively subdued (since she had rejected Garrick's version), it was described as "more effective" than a rival actress's "because more simple and less strained." Later, when her version was more thoroughly Shakespearean, a Scottish reviewer reported that her dying scene was "brief and comparatively quiet" but explained (apologetically?) that this was "in strict keeping with the text."[40] A more perceptive critic noticed a subtle artistic effect made possible by Shakespeare's text: Having awakened but not yet learned of Romeo's death, Juliet, as if reborn, greeted the Friar in the same clear, childish treble she had used in her first scene but not since; the repetition of this keynote, heard before on the threshold of love and now on the threshold of death, was full of pathos, but pathos calmed by the sense of a completed symphonic pattern.

Although Helen Faucit no longer thrilled her audiences with a gothic spectacle, she did leave them with a picture: "She … burie[d] the dagger in her own heart. Then, laying her face upon her husband's bosom, she raised his nerveless arms and folded them above her head."[41] This image was central to a larger picture, in which Montague and Capulet looked sadly upon the result of their feud and learned too late the "lesson of amity and brotherly love" (essay 153).

Rosalind

Helen Faucit's only known promptbook of *As You Like It* is based on John Philip Kemble's popular acting edition.[42] Perhaps, as Charles H. Shattuck suggests, it was used for Macready's Drury Lane production of 1842, but, if so, it served on other occasions as well. (Many passages are marked for cutting, then for restoring.) Actually, despite considerable similarity to Macready's text, there are some interesting differences. Macready's promptbook, though based on a Shakespearean text, shows frequent cuts that bring his version into conformity with Kemble's; thus his innovations are especially notable.[43] Helen Faucit's version has two significant instances of agreement with Macready as opposed to Kemble: omission of the "Cuckoo Song," traditionally interpolated in *As You Like It* from *Love's Labour's Lost*, and restoration of the Rosalind-Jaques dialogue that introduces the first scene of Shakespeare's Act 4.[44] On the other hand, it retains (or cuts, then restores) some passages kept by Kemble but not by Macready, and it restores some omitted by both.

Particularly striking is the retention of lines, cut by Macready, that relate to physical traits: Rosalind's height (1.3.115), the colour of Orlando's hair (3.37-38, 10-12), the sparseness of Orlando's beard (3.2.376-78), and Phebe's "inky brows … black-silk hair," and so on (3.5.46-48). Helen Faucit appreciated such details, no doubt, for the colourful, realistic tone they gave the dialogue; besides, she knew she could use the lines with humorous effect – as indeed she did. Other notable restorations function structurally besides adding spice to Rosalind's badinage. The one beginning "Troilus had his brains dashed out by a Grecian club" (4.1.97-106) tells of men whose deaths have been blamed on love but were actually due to more mundane misfortunes; these examples of romantic "lies" lead up to the aphoristic "men have died from time to time, and worms have eaten them, but not for love." Macready kept the aphorism but cut the introductory examples; Helen Faucit kept the whole passage. Her most significant difference from Macready is the retention of Rosalind's "Come, woo me," etc. (4.1.68-69), which was one of the key passages in her portrayal. Strangely enough, her promptbook shows no restoration of the climactic passage to which this one leads: "I do take thee, Orlando, for my husband." Its importance to her is clear from her own essay and from various eyewitnesses of her performances. Although not in her basic text (Kemble as well as Macready omitted it), her restoration would normally have been written into her promptbook. This is an instance in which a promptbook "tell[s] lies,"[45] as Shattuck puts it. Was there another Rosalind promptbook, now lost? Or did the actress simply insert the crucial line from memory? Who can tell?

There was a "sad and subdued beauty" about Helen Faucit's Rosalind[46] as she listened, in her first scene (1.2.1-42), to Celia's plea to "be merry." She was brooding on her precarious position at her uncle's court as well as on her father's banishment, but, to spare Celia's feelings, she mentioned only the latter. When Celia insisted that she look on her father as her own, Rosalind smiled sadly, but she quickly assumed an air of gaiety and joined in her cousin's bright chatter.[47]

In the meeting with Orlando (1.2.149-156) her conflicting emotions – fears for his safety, respect for his courage, empathy with his feeling of friendlessness – united in an overwhelmingly sudden experience of love. This complex emotional state was suggested through subtle indications of "admiring interest, tender solicitude, and bashful self-consciousness." As she and Celia tried to dissuade Orlando from fighting, Rosalind's attention was "riveted" on him. Her varying facial expressions were so suggestive that the "almost instantantaneous" change from pity to love seemed "prolonged," allowing an imaginative viewer to detect every stage in the process. As she watched the wrestling match, each slight movement, each shift in expression spoke eloquently of her mounting interest. Afterwards, when she heard that Orlando was the son of her father's loyal supporter, she showed a still stronger sense of a bond with him. In congratulating the young victor, she stealthily kissed the chain she had taken from her neck before saying in a "tremulous" voice, "Wear this for me"– adding with sad gentleness, "One out of suits with fortune,/ That could give more, but that her hand lacks means." Orlando remaining silent, she turned away, but "subtly and delicately" showed that love was warring with girlish modesty: though barely looking back, she seemed on tiptoe to hear his faintest word. Then, giving way to an irresistible urge, she turned suddenly round, as if hearing him speak, and said, "semi-apologetically" to Celia, "My pride fell with my fortunes." Her "half-enigmatical" confession to Orlando – "Sir, you have wrestled well,/ And overthrown more than your enemies" – was usually spoken with unmistakable clarity, but in later years it was sometimes murmured softly, as though not meant to reach Orlando's ears.[48]

In the banishment scene (1.3.40-90), as Helen Faucit conceived it, the Duke's sudden decree fired the spirited "princess" with indignation, but she controlled herself and asked in "a tone of entreaty" for what fault she was being banished. The Duke's "Thus do all traitors" aroused her royal blood: "gentleness [gave] place to righteous remonstrance" as she demanded his evidence. His reply, "Thou art thy father's daughter; there's enough" brought her pungent answer,

"What's that to me? My father was no traitor." The last words were spoken to the traitorous Duke with a slight emphasis (essay 248-49). In Helen Faucit's performance the emotional transitions were impressively managed: "the gradations from amazement and incredulity … to defiant indignation," the instant rise from a niece's suppliant pose to a daughter's "native dignity," and the decline once more to entreaty as Rosalind thought of separation from Celia.[49]

When Rosalind appeared as Ganymede in the forest scenes (beginning with 2.4), her "nature expand[ing] in the enjoyment of her new-born liberty," she charmed everyone with her graceful appearance and manner:

> What a series of pictures passed before us as she moved to and fro, in a page's dress of lavender cashmere, edged with emerald green velvet, that set off her symmetrical form to the greatest advantage, her hair falling in natural loose curls upon her shoulders, from under a broad felt hat, with a hawthorne spray or some stray wild flower twisted into its band!

The costume was not always the same – another time it had "a light mixture of grey and green, air and flowers" – but, despite the traditional boar-spear, it was always romantic, never the coarse wear of a forest-dwelling shepherd boy. There was no attempt to make Rosalind look convincingly male: her "mannish disguise" was "like a cockade upon a woman's hat, a saucy symbol of the masculine type, which makes you the more conscious of her absent masculinity." Although literal-minded viewers might have wondered at Orlando's blindness, the ambivalent costume was appropriate to Helen Faucit's portrayal. Her Rosalind was always a dual character.[50]

After roaming the forest and dreaming of Orlando, Rosalind could hardly suppress her excitement when she first discovered the tree-borne verses extolling her name; she reminded herself, however, that there were many Rosalinds in the world and that Orlando was undoubtedly far away. All this took place in offstage events which, in Helen Faucit's imagination, led up to Rosalind's eager questioning of Celia (3.2.123-250). When Celia mischievously hinted at the identity of the versifier, yet kept up the suspense as to the truth of her insinuations, Rosalind used every weapon in her armoury to make her give up the sober truth: she assailed her "now in terms of the most abject and persuasive entreaty, and anon in the hot language of rising anger"; she "seized `Celia' in her arms, and endearingly importuned her to tell all she knew," and "the seducing tones of her voice, the warm pressure, the gaze with which she seemed to read [in her cousin's face] what she wished the tongue to speak was witchery itself." Finally, when Celia's meaning was beyond doubt, Rosalind's "burst of uncontrollable joy … [found] vent in a thousand mad transports and fond endearments." In the excitement of the scene, her hat slipped back from her head and, "suspended at her back by its ribbon add[ed] to her grace at the moment when she seem[ed] most beside herself."[51]

Orlando then came in view, talking with Jaques (3.2.251-294). Rosalind, invisible to them but not to the audience, listened with pleasure while Orlando "more than held his own" against misanthropic jests about love. When she heard that she was indeed the subject of his poems, she was so delighted that she forgot her earlier fears about his seeing her in doublet and hose. "Speak to [him] she must at any hazard." Jaques having gone, she accosted Orlando in a "rough and saucy" manner so as to keep up her disguise (3.2.295-435), assuming a "swagger" and a "defiant air." According to a prompter's notes, "Miss Faucit calls after Orlando 'Who, – whoo – whoop!' and beckons him insolently back with her spear. He returns abruptly – she ½ recoils back recovers herself and says with bravado – 'Do you – hear, forester?'" This boisterous behaviour established (despite any feminine look) the bold boyishness of Ganymede.[52]

In Helen Faucit's interpretation, Orlando found himself intrigued by the "pretty youth," but Rosalind, by immediately engaging him in "brilliant talk," allowed him no time to examine her appearance or analyze his own feelings too closely. When he confessed to having written the love poems, Rosalind pretended disbelief so as to hear him declare his love; then, when he earnestly protested, she was so amused by the situation that she teased him further (essay 258-60). In all this dialogue Helen Faucit's Rosalind moved deftly from one passage to another, matching her vocal tones to the constantly varied moods. For the witty discourse on time she assumed a spirit of light raillery until she reached the reference to time's galloping with "the thief at the gallows"; then "a shadow [came] over the face that [had] been wreathed with smiles," creating (as one viewer thought) a moment of pure poetry. In "considering Orlando's paucity of beard," she "attained the very quintessence of mock solemnity" as "she gravely said, 'I pardon you for that.'" She used a sharply "incisive" tone for the line "That's one of the points in which women still give the lie to their consciences"; but, seeing that Orlando was "rather dashed" by this sarcasm, she asked, with a "softened" voice, "But in good sooth, are you he that hangs the verses on the trees …?" Then, standing slightly in front of him with her face turned away so that her expression might not betray her, she assumed "the affectation of a bright-eyed ease."

> Her attitude is that of manly *insouciance*, such as might be chosen by one accustomed to exchange such confidences, as that to which her question leads; but her face, which he cannot see, is radiant with content and happiness. In her hand, crumpled up and pressed with loving earnestness, is one of the very sonnets of which she speaks so cavalierly, and while she waits for his answer it is furtively pressed to her lips… He who has seen, or can realize this scene, with its blending of the two parts of Ganymede and Rosalind, has the whole lovely conception before him.[53]

When Rosalind-as-Ganymede told of curing a love-sick man by playing the role of his mistress, she illustrated each of the adjectives applied to women – "proud, fantastical, apish, shallow, inconstant" – with suitable tone and expression. The "playfulness, the wit, the sarcasm bubble[d] up … with bewildering rapidity." The proposal to cure Orlando by pretending to be his Rosalind was made with a lingering on the name Rosalind (essay 261) and, according to the *Scotsman* (1845), as a "half-urged," hesitating request, reflecting a fear of denial. Such tentativeness, following upon the previous effervescence, was typical of Helen Faucit's transitions. Her manner may have changed later, however. In her essay she attributes "an air of unhesitating confidence" to the "imperious youth."

Rosalind's scenes with Silvius and Phebe (3.5 and 4.3) were important to Helen Faucit for the light they shed on the heroine's character: she explained Phebe's infatuation with Ganymede, not simply by the "boy's" physical beauty, but also by his distinguished bearing and by the "strange tenderness that tempers the severity" of his rebukes (267). In her acting, however, she must have varied Ganymede's manner toward Phebe from time to time. On some occasions it was much in line with her written interpretation: although she preserved all the fun of the "equivoque," she also showed a real interest in reconciling Phebe to Sivius and even seemed "touched by the hopeless devotion of the shepherdess to herself." Less sympathetic at other times, however, she either reproved "the disdainful Phoebe and her chicken-hearted suitor" with "indignant vigour and irony" or amused the audience with her pretended gravity in advising them.[54]

Helen Faucit saw in Rosalind's brief encounter with Jaques (4.1.1-38) a demonstration of her "healthy common-sense": the "princess" finds Jaques' "patronising address" disagreeable, and she recoils from "a man who has exhausted the zest for life in … sensual indulgence, and who sees only the dark side of human nature" (267). Although she intended to restore this passage, which was usually omitted in performance, she probably encountered a good many actors of Jaques who balked at memorizing the unfamiliar lines at short notice.[55]

In the mock wooing (4.1.38-200) the actress continued her portrayal of a dual role: on the surface, the sprightly boy; underneath, the deeply loving woman. She "mingled the greatest modesty and passion with archness and intense love of fun. A daring soft mockery in her voice and lip, were joined to a womanly tenderness and changeful grace." Chameleonlike, she assumed the shifting moods of a "mischievous Cupid": "coy solicitations, brave masquerade, even the arts of burlesque … succeed[ed] each other … like the fitful transformations of an April day." The audience caught the contagion of her "buoyant merriment." Indeed, according to an unusual complaint, her undue emphasis on Shakespeare's indelicate passages won laughter and "bravos" from pit and gallery.[56]

In the passage leading to the mock marriage she acted the ironic jester, yet made the audience sense an undercurrent of emotion. Both her inward happiness and her sense of humour came through as she exclaimed to Orlando, "Come, woo me!" Then, as "he hung back, half amazed, half shy," she said with "deepened emphasis" and "radiant" face, "Woo me, for now I am in a holiday humour, and like enough to consent!" As she asked, "Am I not your Rosalind?" her voice "vibrate[d]" with hardly-concealed feeling, but in order to curb this "dangerous" tendency, she "dash[ed] off again into her playful mocking mood, with the words, 'Well, in her person I say I will not have you.'" Her jesting was by turns sarcastic, genial, and wistful; sometimes it seemed an indistinguishable blend. She fenced with "buttoned foils" and curbed her "bitterest mockery" with "loving courtesy." Ironic as her tone was in "men have died from time to time … but not for love," one felt she did not really believe in the cynicism she was expressing. When Orlando said that Rosalind's frown might kill him, her reply, "By this hand, it will not kill a fly," was spoken with a change of tone that disclosed a "vein of tenderness" underlying the "wild raillery."[57]

As played by Helen Faucit, the mock marriage allowed Rosalind's genuine feelings to triumph for a moment. When she gave her hand to Orlando, she seemed magically transformed from "impudent gallant" to "bashful maiden." She stood with "head slightly averted as Orlando said, 'I do take thee, Rosalind, for wife' … [her] voice deepening almost to pathos, as she said, 'I do take thee, Orlando, for my husband!'" Instead of giving a "comic grimace to the audience" as another Rosalind did at this point, she "flushed up" and suggested by the "deep and true emotion" in her voice that she "was indeed giving herself to Orlando." Helen Faucit prolonged the magical moment by throwing Rosalind "into a state of dreamy abstraction, as if half inclined to believe in the reality of the rite," but she soon broke the silence with a "merry laugh," followed by the "flashes of mingled wit, sarcasm, raillery, and pathos, in which Rosalind hides the emotions of perfect happiness."[58]

In the fainting scene (4.3.74-182), her changing facial expressions, as she listened to Oliver's story, and her slight hints of physical weakness, quickly suppressed in favour of "mock masculinity," suggested the turmoil in Rosalind's mind – pride in Orlando's courage and magnanimity, vivid images of the lion and the serpent, a shocking sense of near-loss. Her sudden swoon showed how intense the half-hidden emotions had been.[59]

As the play approached its denouement, this Rosalind showed (in 5.2) a "contagious eagerness and exuberance of spirits" in "collect[ing] all the threads of the plot together." In the final scene (5.3), though she had dropped Ganymede's "witty volubility," she spoke her few words with deep feeling, and she continued to throw a "film of glamour" over her lover – it was she, "of course," who arranged the masque of Hymen. According to Helen Faucit, however, this musical spectacle, though both beautiful and appropriate, "delays the action too much." (She was thinking of Macready's elaborate production.) In her promptbook she retained the figure of Hymen to lead Rosalind forward, dressed in women's clothes, but she cut out even his song and wrote in simply "*A Dance.*"[60]

According to her own statement (285), she felt a "shrinking distaste" when she had to deliver the epilogue: addressing the audience "as one's own very self" undercut the illusion that she had really become Rosalind while representing her. Since tradition obliged her to include the speech (with "If I were a woman" changed to "If I were among you"), she used it to illustrate the reassertion of the "high-toned winning woman" after doublet and hose had been laid aside. Reluctant or not, she made the most of her opportunities. She appeared onstage with her veil "down," perhaps to symbolize a hidden identity, but she could not have kept her expressive face covered long. Critics were captivated by her "witching grace," "winning archness," and "quiet eloquence." The epilogue confirmed what many had sensed throughout the play, a special affinity between herself and Rosalind.[61]

Lady Macbeth

The promptbook of *Macbeth* that Helen Faucit probably used throughout her career is based on an edition of the play as revived at Drury Lane in November 1814.[62] This is a conventional acting version with such notable differences from Shakespeare's text as omission of characters (the Drunken Porter, the Old Man, the Third Murderer, Lady Macduff and her son), additions to the witch material, and insertion of a dying speech for Macbeth. The only important changes affecting Lady Macbeth are her exclusion from two scenes: 2.3 (in which she faints as Macbeth is describing Duncan's body), and 3.1 (in which Macbeth hypocritically urges Banquo not to miss the feast). In her promptbook Helen Faucit restored Lady Macbeth to the latter scene but not to the former; on stage, however, she acted in both scenes – at least on some occasions.

Helen Faucit's Lady Macbeth[63] swept grandly downstage in her first scene (1.5), her head and shoulders softly draped in a white veil and her dark, fur-lined robe swirling about her in heavy waves. When she paused to read the letter, she created an imposing tableau with her "majestic, menacing" figure and her statuesque manner of holding the scroll. As she read, she became "transfixed" by the account of the Weird Sisters, and when she came to the words "Hail, King that shalt be!" her figure seemed to "dilate" with the great conception of her husband's majesty. "A strange, equivocal fire played in the eyes"; her expression and attitude conveyed a sense of evil desires, only "half formed" as yet, and "a foreshadowing of horror from which she half shrank." Then, her better nature vanquished by supernatural excitement, she succumbed to an "ecstasy almost painfully intense." Like a character in Greek tragedy, she seemed suddenly "impelled by an irresistible destiny to a deed of blood."[64]

Her soliloquy, "Glamis thou art, and Cawdor, and shalt be/ What thou art promis'd," was declaimed slowly but with such power that each syllable seemed to be "charged with meaning." Yet, despite the deliberate style, there was a sense of terrible urgency: "Nothing shall stand between Macbeth and his greatness." The description of Macbeth's character was given with "clear, unmistakable emphasis." Though passionately devoted to her husband, Lady Macbeth was perfectly aware of his weaknesses. Having determined to win him the glory he craved, she saw his "milk of human kindness" as "slight and unworthy." For one thoughtful viewer, Helen Faucit's "vivid rendering" of the soliloquy brought home as never before the "dual character of Lady Macbeth" – a woman strong in her directness of purpose and freedom from sentimentality but potentially weak in her attraction to supernatural influences and her inability to endure their unforeseen effect on her husband.[65]

Conscious that the "fearful change" in herself must be sustained by "more than human firmness," this Lady Macbeth resorted to a marrow-chilling invocation to the spirits of evil. Though she spoke quietly and stood firmly "plant[ed]" at first, her "anxious thrilling accents and mistily wandering eyes" carried a weird suggestiveness. At the lines "You murd'ring ministers,/ Wherever in your sightless substances/ You wait on Nature's mischief!" imaginative spectators "could see the very air peopling" with forms. As she continued, her voice increased in volume and "the swelling exultation and keen sense of triumph which seem[ed] to dilate her and take possession of all her faculties" had "the sublimity of wild impassionment." From anxious supplication she had risen to an exalted attitude of command – a "Medea conscious of her power over the preternatural world."[66]

"Great Glamis! worthy Cawdor!/ Greater than both, by the all-hail hereafter!" – Lady Macbeth's "ecstatic" greeting upon her husband's arrival continued the mood of the previous invocation. Her acceptance of the Weird Sisters' forecasts as inevitable led naturally to the suggestion of murder: she herself seemed less a "tempter" than a "prophetess." Although Helen Faucit believed the idea of murder had originated with Macbeth, her insinuating manner of asking "And when goes – hence?" must have encouraged the assumption that Lady Macbeth was initiating the suggestion. Throughout this scene Lady Macbeth watched her husband's face intently, evidently to see what effect her words were having. In advising him to "bear welcome in your eye,/ Your hand, your tongue," she playfully curtseyed about – giving a parodic preview of her welcome to Duncan. If the incongruous levity was intended as relief from abnormal emotion, its effect was brief. For the last words of her speech – "and you shall put/ This night's great business into my dispatch;/

Which shall to all our nights and days to come/ Give solely sovereign sway and masterdom" – she used "an exultant tone very loud at the close."[67]

In her gracious welcome of Duncan (1.6.10-30), Helen Faucit showed the womanly charm that had once been natural to Lady Macbeth but now, with the perversion of her nature, had to be forced. "The courtesy was obviously overdone and though the King [could not] see through the mask the audience [could] detect the difficulty with which it was worn."[68]

When Macbeth told his wife (in 1.7.27-82), "We will proceed no further in this business," she saw all their hopes threatened. She had keyed herself up to a deed which violated her own nature but which had taken on an aura of greatness: her husband's attempt to renege made her almost hysterical. Attacking him at every vulnerable point, she showed more desperation than dominating power. Critics who preferred a stronger Lady Macbeth thought Helen Faucit's vixenish tone beneath the dignity of the character. One declared that the famous passage in which Mrs. Siddons had "transformed herself into a she-fiend" ("I have given suck …") was "poured out" by Helen Faucit in the termagant manner of "the scold at the door of the gin-shop" – genuine passion, perhaps, but not "the self-possessed determination" Lady Macbeth ought to have. For another, however, the shrewish tone was the right one: the "spitefulness" with which this Lady Macbeth accused her husband of cowardice "[told] with immense force" because it was "perfectly truthful." In the passage about dashing the infant's brains out, she was frantic, not fiendish. As she spoke the terrible words, her manner subtly betrayed her basic humanity, "not with any faltering of pity … but with a spasm of pain caused by the passing conflict of emotions."[69]

After this her manner grew calmer and more confident. In answer to Macbeth's "If we should fail?" she spoke the equally-weighted words "*We fail*" in the Siddons manner, not with any "exclamation of surprise" but as a "concession that failure is failure and ruin to them both … but changing at once into words of encouragement." Macbeth's admiring "Bring forth men children only!" was Helen Faucit's cue for resuming some of her earlier "sublimity." In answer to Macbeth's "Will it not be received … That they have done't?" she drew herself up, her right arm uplifted in menacing fashion, "with out-spread fingers all abroad," and replied in a "voice pitched to its highest key," "Who dares receive it other,/ As we shall make our griefs and clamour roar/ Upon his death?" This stylized conclusion, doubly striking after some unusually realistic acting, pictured Lady Macbeth's triumph over her husband's vacillation.[70]

In the murder scene (2.2), Lady Macbeth, dressed in white, rushed onstage, showing by "the dilated eyes, the flushed cheek, the flurried gestures, the short, quick drawings of her breath … that she [had] been at the wine cup" – this before she said, "That which hath made them drunk hath made me bold." Her claim to boldness was contradicted by her agitation as she listened for sounds from Duncan's chamber. Both here and in the fragmentary dialogue with

Macbeth as he came in from the murder, Lady Macbeth "by the intonation of a phrase, by a slight shiver, or a momentary look of superstitious terror convey[ed] … a mysterious sense of horror, as if the spirit of murder … were hovering in the chamber." She mastered herself with an effort, however, to keep her fears from her husband, and a "slight pallor and a voice deeper and more guttural" were the only remaining signs of her emotion." At "Why did you bring these daggers from the place?" she reverted to the shrewish tone of her earlier scene, "spitting out at him the word painted" in "'tis the eye of childhood/ That fears a painted devil." She was fighting furiously against her own weakness as well as her husband's. After returning the daggers herself, however, she could no longer maintain the courage and resolution to which she had forced herself. Unlike some other Lady Macbeths, who led Macbeth forcefully from the room, she gave way to a "sudden access of terror" and clung nervously to the husband "whom a moment before she had upbraided for lack of resolution." As Marvin Rosenberg rightly remarks, here was a "foreshadowing of disintegration."[71]

When the alarm bell, following the discovery of Duncan's murder, brings Lady Macbeth upon the scene (2.3.81-125), she faces a difficult test. As her husband, to justify his killing of the grooms (the supposed murderers), describes the King's bloody corpse, she faints – that is, in Shakespeare's text. In acting versions since the eighteenth century, however, Lady Macbeth was absent from this scene, the theory being that her obvious hypocrisy would produce inappropriate laughter. Helen Faucit was, as far as I know, the first English actress to reintroduce the faint. (A few foreign actresses anticipated her.) She evidently waited until late in her career to do so, perhaps for fear the audience would not understand her interpretation (a genuine collapse rather than a strategic diversion), but she certainly included the faint at Drury Lane in November and December, 1864.[72] As she later explained, Lady Macbeth had been in an "agony of anxiety" ever since the murder "lest her husband in his wild ravings should betray himself"; now, to her "amazement" and "horror," he began describing with "fearful minuteness of detail" the "gashed and gory" Duncan, whom she had seen when replacing the daggers. "[To] have the whole scene thus vividly brought again before her was too great a strain upon her nerves. No wonder that she faints" (232). Her success in conveying this idea was mixed: for example, Henry Morley, a major London critic, did understand, though he supposed Lady Macbeth was overcome by the memory of Duncan's resemblance to her father (*Examiner*, 17 December 1864), but a Manchester reviewer simply assumed that she was a consummate hypocrite (*Guardian*, 16 April 1866).

Helen Faucit was particularly successful in the second part of the play, beginning with Act 3. Here she showed Lady Macbeth, having accomplished her purpose, "gradually sinking her spirit" and allowing her natural womanliness to reassert itself. In her first appearance as queen (3.1.11-43), her "stately composure of visage and deportment" contrasted strongly with her hectic behaviour in the murder scene; she seemed designed by nature for the regal dignity to which she had aspired. But, as the actress suggested in subtle ways, she never found joy in it. While Macbeth was asking Banquo about the journey he and little Fleance were to take, Lady Macbeth gently caressed the boy's hair – a gesture that was generally appreciated but sometimes misinterpreted. This was no repetition of her hypocritical graciousness to Duncan (Macbeth had not, as yet, even hinted at his new plot), but an unconscious reassertion of her natural tenderness. Perhaps it had a further significance: "The fingers of the woman who has been a mother, and who has murder on her soul, wander sadly and tenderly over the type of her lost innocence." In this scene, once more, Helen Faucit suggested two Lady Macbeths: one consonant with her natural inclinations, the other reflecting the evil influences with which she had allied herself:

> When Miss Faucit's Lady Macbeth caressed the little son of Banquo, she fairly looked a lovable person, above all suspicion; but when she passed silently from the stage, and no human eye was supposed to be on her, the whole woman was transformed – all the fiend, cruel and perplexed, was there; yet not a vulgar, but a well-bred fiend, the very sweep of her admirable drapery helping the illusion.[73]

Early in the following scene (3.2), Lady Macbeth's brief soliloquy "Naught's had, all's spent …"), spoken "in the tones of heartbroken musical wail," allowed Helen Faucit to put into words her "disappointment and hidden suffering." In her written comments she emphasized the importance of these lines, "pointing, as they do, to the beginning of that mental unrest brought on by the recurrence of images and thoughts which will not 'die with them they think on,' and which culminates in the 'slumbery agitation' of the troubled nights that were quickly followed by her death." When Macbeth, in response to her attempts to comfort him, spoke of the "affliction of these terrible dreams/ That shake us nightly," Helen Faucit's Lady Macbeth gave an "involuntary" shudder that revealed her own silent suffering from their terrors. When Macbeth hinted at a new crime, her response – "What's to be done?" – was spoken in a "tone of weariness of wonder and of dread." And when he replied, "Be innocent of the knowledge, dearest chuck,/ Till thou applaud the deed," she stood, averted, as he crossed the stage (evidently to speak "Come, seeling night" as a soliloquy, apart), then (at "So prithee go with me") she "mechanically" followed his lead. In the murder of Banquo she was no accomplice.[74]

In the banquet scene (3.4) Lady Macbeth must once again play two roles at once – the wife trying to overcome the fears of her distraught husband and the hostess anxious to salvage both entertainment and reputation. Helen Faucit's complexity as an actress was particularly evident here as she maintained a façade of composure for the guests during much of the scene, yet, at the same time, conveyed to the audience by gesture and facial expression the "passion of fear" with which she struggled in playing her dual game. Perhaps her agitation was less evident on some occasions than on others, for a generally sensitive critic saw "no sign of wincing" until the latter stage of Macbeth's disordered behaviour: "perfectly equal to the part," she "gracefully suppresse[d] the rising turmoil and curiosity amongst the guests" and "recall[ed] Macbeth by a sharp appeal to his wits." But at Macbeth's second outbreak a change came over her. During his speech "What man dare, I dare," she revealed through her byplay that a dreadful new light had broken upon her. She made a last effort to reclaim Macbeth, but she knew it was hopeless.

> With a sudden frenzy she begs the guests to depart. Then fearing she has been too brusque, the troubled queen bows low and bids a kind goodnight to all.
>
> For a moment or two she remains in that position, and when she rises she is a broken woman… She has seen that her husband's malady is incurable …[75]

After the guests had departed, leaving "the guilty pair … alone in their vast hall," the "excitement subside[d] into a deep mournfulness" as Lady Macbeth collapsed with weariness. Sometimes there was a "touch of melancholy tenderness" as husband and wife, leaning despairingly upon each other, made futile efforts at giving and receiving comfort. Sometimes Lady Macbeth's love for her husband shone briefly in the tender pity with which she said "you lack the season of all natures, sleep." But at other times her attempts at consoling him were given "mechanically, and as if in sleep." All was hopeless: "the bent spring ha[d] snapped in twain."[76]

At the end of the scene, Lady Macbeth tottered to one of the tables and sat down, resting her forehead on her hand. In doing so she touched the crown. She took it off with "a melancholy, not quite absent air," and, as she rose to follow her husband from the room, she let it hang "listlessly in her hand." The slow and halting manner in which she followed Macbeth was "full of mute eloquence": as she lingered, moving slowly, she suddenly stopped and uttered "a half-smothered sound of anguish" – the "prelude to the prolonged sigh in the sleep-walking scene." Macbeth had already gone out when she finally made her exit: "her magnificent mantle drag[ged] heavily on the ground after her … . She [was] visibly in a dream."[77]

When next the audience saw Lady Macbeth (5.1), her deterioration was complete. No longer regal, she looked slight and vulnerable in her white nightdress, and the "firm, dignified countenance" had changed to "the thin, shrunken-eyed, pale-cheeked face of a wasted invalid." Gone was her usual grace of movement: she walked with the "heavy and unelastic" tread of the somnambulist. Her voice had at times a "muffled" quality, at times the "sharp, metallic husky ring of illness." Her vacantly staring eyes were "fixed on empty space" – or on "some horrible vision, and sightless to all else."[78]

Advancing toward the audience with "wandering and uncertain steps," Lady Macbeth began to speak in a "low, moaning tone." Some of the words were "scarcely more than breathed," yet they were heard with ease in the spellbound silence. In trying to wash the blood from her hands, there was none of Mrs. Siddons's "feverish action"; yet references to her "earnestness" and "struggles," her lapses into "shrill testiness," suggest greater energy and variety than are popularly associated with sleepwalking.[79]

As Lady Macbeth imaginatively relived past events, her white nightdress, reminiscent of the white garment she had worn in the murder scene, helped to create the illusion of a flashback. The recapitulation had a nightmarish quality: "The sleeper's face was itself a tragedy," and her words were "surcharged with … the contending emotions of a chequered lifetime compressed into the … compass of a dream." The brief, ballad-like passage "The Thane of Fife had a wife: where is she now?" was given with a "touching tenderness which suggested a sad story." "Here's the smell of the blood still" brought the murder scene forcibly to mind, with its contemptuous assurance, "A little water clears us of this deed." Lady Macbeth's sad, white face and the "dreamy pathos" of her voice aroused the compassion of many spectators as she lamented "the corruption of the little hand." Moved by a "strange power of suggestiveness," they entered imaginatively into Lady Macbeth's thoughts: her "tender womanly pride in a point of beauty," her nostalgic return to "days of childhood and innocence."[80] Her exit was "weird and startling": "the concluding scared whisper, half suffocated by horror, 'To bed, to bed, to bed,' as she disappeared" might have caused even the "wickedest" husband to shudder at the invitation. One spectator, dismayed by the "phantom" Helen Faucit had called up, could not "divest [herself] of the image of the Queen, ever vanishing, ever beckoning, a fearful vision."[81]

Helen Faucit's sleepwalking scene was an "appalling" picture of a soul in torment: "the parched mouth … told of the burning tortures within," and "those eyes, those corpse-like hands telling their unconscious tale of crime" could excite some soul-searching among spectators. "It [was] a thing to haunt the imagination for ever."[82] The horror was softened, however, by the "beautiful and touching" glimpses of Lady Macbeth's former tenderness and grace, which produced "an infinite feeling of sorrow … more akin to forgiveness … than condemnation."[83] An awe-inspiring solemnity reconciled the disparate emotions and made the whole scene "grand," "profound," "sublime," "only less awful … than a real visitation from the grave itself."[84]

Pauline

When Helen Faucit first acted Pauline, most reviewers emphasized her energy and passion, especially in the third act; even then, however, some gave equal stress to her sweet, touching, and tender moments.[85] As her portrayal matured, its subtler aspects became more important: the poetic "heightening" of the dialogue; the fine touches in the acting, which, "like those of a great painter … escape the vulgar eye, but fascinate the close observer"; and, especially, the "shadowing forth of suppressed emotion … letting the audience feel instinctively … what she feels herself."[86] Such qualities contributed to her best achievement in this role, the gradual revelation of Pauline's essential character.[87]

The curtain rose to discover Pauline elegantly reclining on a sofa, becomingly attired in "the quaint costume of the last century" and somehow communicating to the audience that ineffable charm which, according to Madame Deschappelles, made "young and old, rich and poor, do homage to the Beauty of Lyons." A "magnificent bouquet" she was holding repeatedly distracted her from her conversation with "her coarse and hard mamma." A love of beauty, suggested by her delicately stressed admiration of the flowers, raised her above the level of her mother's mercenary advice: "You are born to make a great marriage, – Beauty is valuable or worthless, according as you invest the property to the best advantage." Viewers sensed that Pauline's vain and frivolous manner was the product of social convention, not an expression of her true nature; yet they saw nothing "stagey" in it, only a "sprightly, wayward girlishness." Here, they felt, was a woman of "deep feeling … which had never been called forth."[88]

Pauline's romantic speculations about the sender of flowers were rudely shattered when he proved to be only Claude Melnotte, a gardener's son. Contemptuously she rejected his message of love (an incident reported but not staged). While smarting from her cruelty, Claude agreed to a scheme, financed by the wealthy Beauseant (another rejected suitor), to trap and humiliate her.

The garden scene in the second act, between Pauline and the Prince of Como (that is, Claude in disguise), was romantically appealing. When the Prince wittily evaded her uncle Damas's attempt to trap him, a "radiant smile … play[ed] around [Pauline's] mouth at the victory gained by her lover." In the later passages, when the two were alone, Pauline revelled in a "warm abandon" to love. As she listened to the Prince's description of the ideal home on Lake Como to which he would like to take her, she seemed "almost dissolved in languid rapture"; so intense was the emotion reflected in her face that a spectator could imagine the "glowing words" visibly "stealing into [her] soul." Her "absorbing love" was expressed in a voice "by turns languishing, earnest, and passionate." When, at one point, she declined her head "as if too much happiness had wrought a trembling modesty of feeling," this slight motion was "a poem in itself." The "gush of eloquent feeling" with which she assured the Prince of her constancy, even in the event of poverty, revealed a passion whose depth was inconsistent with mercenary concerns.[89]

In the climactic cottage scene (3.2), Pauline, just married to her "Prince" and beginning, as she thought, the first part of their honeymoon journey, was puzzled by the disappearance of their retinue and the choice of a poor cottage for their wedding night. Her first emotion upon arriving there was "a feeling of blank surprise, shown by the way in which she scrutinize[d] the humble objects around her." She realized there was something wrong. Unable to confess the shameful trick himself, Claude begged the Widow Melnotte to explain. She replied reproachfully that she had thought Pauline was to be told "all" before the marriage took place. At Pauline's "All! what – My blood freezes in my veins!" the Widow frankly identified the "Prince" as her son. Pauline could not believe it. "Is this a jest?" she asked Claude, in quiet but anguished tones, walking about in her suspense, "is it? I know it is: only speak – one word – one look – one smile. I cannot believe that thou art such a – no, I will not wrong thee by a harsh word."[90] Her tones, her "picturesque action … eloquent pauses" and all the "mutations" of her facial expressions "thrilled the brain and rent the heart." Recognition of the truth sent her into hysterical laughter and a tirade of grief and fury, all the more shocking because of the quiet intensity she had maintained before.[91] She was "carried away by the most absolute frenzy. It [was] as if the shock had maddened her." The "heedless violence" was like the tantrum of a spoiled child, yet there was "something uncanny" in her "great ironical speech" which mockingly echoed the Prince's earlier description of the home to which he wished to take her. So said one witness. Others saw nothing childish but did see much that was uncanny. Her "passion was so appalling," wrote one, "as for the moment to make the scene as frightfully unreal as the ghost scene in 'Hamlet' or the incantation in 'Macbeth.'" Yet, as witnesses agreed, even in the midst of her terrible indignation, one could tell that a "deep affection … lay clouded and concealed beneath it." Helen Faucit's own comment (in her prompt part) is simply "mocking misery." The hysterical mockery must have subsided somewhat, leaving the misery uppermost, when she asked, "This is my bridal home, and thou my bridegroom?" The agony in her tone "told how sadly she was betrayed, and yet how dear was the betrayer"; other actresses might speak these words with scorn, but for Helen Faucit "the wrong was too deep for sarcasm." Testing her hope that this was "some horrid dream," Pauline took Claude's hand, then quickly let it drop, saying "it is too real." Spectators were both thrilled and touched as she asked, reproachfully but with queenly dignity, "What have I done to thee? how sinn'd against thee,/ that thou shoulds't crush me thus?" They felt that a "wounded spirit," not the "immolation" of mere vanity, was what "crushed Pauline."[92]

Claude replied at length, telling of his long-cherished love for her, his efforts at self-improvement by study and cultivation of the arts to make himself worthy of her, and his suffering from her scorn when he had finally declared his love in a signed poem. During most of his account Pauline had nothing to do except listen, but Helen Faucit "fill[ed] up the outline of the situation" with suggestive byplay. Pauline had not given the slightest external sign of forgiveness, yet the "calm interest with which, though with averted face, she heard Claude's confession was an earnest of the love which she afterwards displayed." When she was reminded of the "indignity she had shown to the peasant," she hid her face in her hands in "momentary remorse." Pride was obviously struggling with sympathy; it still predominated, but her "growing softness" showed that its influence was waning. Although Claude's power to fascinate her held sway only while he was speaking – when he paused she was "ready with an indignant answer" – it was clear that he would ultimately be pardoned. Ultimately, but not yet. When Claude, in his emotion, tried to take her hand, she exclaimed, "No, touch me not! … Let my wrongs make me sacred." One can imagine the appeal of those words to Helen Faucit (like Constance's "Here I and sorrow sit"); her "utterance" of them, wrote a reviewer, would "long be remembered." Claude promised to take no advantage of her: she would sleep alone tonight; tomorrow he would send for her father and agree to a divorce. The act ended as Pauline slowly mounted the stairs, escorted by the Widow Melnotte, and, turning her "faded countenance" toward Claude, "'cast one longing, lingering look behind.'"[93]

In the fourth act, which began the following morning, Helen Faucit continued to show Pauline's contradictory feelings, but here she had more opportunities than before for a sympathetic emphasis on her "strongly lingering affection for Claude." A significant turning-point came in her scene with the Widow Melnotte while Claude was away sending word to M. Deschappelles. Pauline's reluctance about the divorce was suggested in her comment that Claude would remarry afterwards – her added words, "I am sure I hope so," being capable of an opposite implication. The Widow replied, breaking into sobs, "he could have married the richest girl in the province … but … he could think of nothing but you." Pauline, trying to comfort her, said impulsively, "Don't weep, mother" – which Helen Faucit spoke with "an exquisite touch of genuine nature." The audience could "plainly see … that the compassion (charmingly pourtrayed) for the Widow Melnotte [would] soon expand into an avowal of love for Claude."[94]

In the interview with the villainous Beauseant, who had sent the Widow off by a pretended message from Claude, Helen Faucit's Pauline was "scornful" and "withering … yet most affecting." Her repulse of this rejected suitor resonated with a long-standing contempt for him and a bitter awareness of her present vulnerability. But when she came to the words "A husband's roof, be it ever so humble, is the temple of his wife's honour," she spoke them with "majestic pride," showing "a spirit imbued in virtue impregnable, and dignity that no circumstances could subdue."[95]

Shortly before her parents arrived to take her away, Pauline murmured to herself, in an "irrespressible longing to pour out a sea of generosity," "If he would but ask me to forgive him!" – then, turning to Claude she declared "in tones that purposely belie[d] her words," "I never can forgive you, sir!" But Claude, too conscience-stricken to take the hint, merely replied, "I never dared to hope it."

One of Helen Faucit's greatest successes came during the following scene with her indignant parents. Upon her father's refusing her suggestion that Claude live with them as his son, Pauline exclaimed, "And you would have a wife enjoy luxury while a husband toils! Claude, take me … ." Her "exquisite tenderness" in speaking these words brought tears to many eyes. Tears were, in fact, a common response in both cottage scenes, from men as well as women. Julia Ward Howe, the American writer and reformer, tells of the experience she and her party had when they saw Macready's production of the play at Drury Lane in 1843: "The pathetic moments … moved me to tears, which I tried to hide. I soon saw that my companions [her husband, Samuel Gridley Howe, and two prominent male friends] were affected the same way and were making the same effort."[96]

After Act 3 Helen Faucit's acting had grown progressively quieter. In Act 5 it was considered "a perfect triumph of delicate art, – no noisy appeals – no playing for applause; but pure, quiet nature" (*Buxton Herald*). During the two and a half years that supposedly elapsed between the fourth act and this one, Pauline, though she had heard nothing from her husband, had remained true to him. Now, however, just as General Damas and Morier, a famous hero (actually Claude), had returned, she was on the verge of signing an agreement to divorce Claude and marry the wealthy Beauseant – this being the latter's price for saving her father from bankruptcy.

In the play's final scene, Pauline's father thanked her for saving him, then, seeing her despair, said, "Come, let us hope that Beauseant's love –." "His love!" she interrupted, "talk not of love … *He* knows not love… ." But when Deschappelles offered to annul the contract, she replied: "No – no – forgive me! You, my honour'd father, – You, who so lov'd, so cherish'd me … You see I am prepared – no tears – all calm,/ But, father, *talk no more of love*." Helen Faucit's acting had its "crowning triumph" here because of the agonizing emotions evoked by the contest between love for husband and love for father (*The Nation*).

Damas and Morier (unrecognizable as Claude because of his bronzed complexion, moustache, and enveloping cloak) now entered. Damas, not knowing the reason for Pauline's supposed faithlessness, ironically congratulated her on her prospective marriage, saying, "You ought to be excessively happy!" When Helen Faucit first acted in Edinburgh, her tone and look in speaking Pauline's one-word response, "Happy!," were so effective that William Murray, as Damas, felt his breath taken away. After explaining her plight, Pauline begged Damas to pay her father's debts and save her from Beauseant, but the spendthrift general admitted he had not the means. Helen Faucit's acting in this passage was notable for the "affecting truthfulness" with which she portrayed Pauline's "imploring anxiety" as she awaited her uncle's response and "her despair and touching resignation when this hope failed her."[97]

When Damas told Pauline that Morier was Claude's closest friend and could take him any message she might send to "soften the blow," she diffidently approached the cloaked hero. According to one witness, Helen Faucit suggested Pauline's intuitive but unrealized sense of Claude's presence by "a tremor of unconscious consciousness with which she approach[ed] him, half averted from his presence." In the interview that followed,

> Pauline's spasmodic struggle to justify her conduct to the soldier whom she thought only the comrade of … her husband – the working of her features – the heaving of her breast – and, when she did speak, the tremor of her tones, so fraught with sadness and despairing attachment … cannot be adequately described.

Finally, when Morier tore up the nuptial agreement, paid Deschappelles' debt, and spoke in a voice that Pauline recognized, the "mute rapture" expressed by Helen Faucit "beggar'd description."[98]

The Lady of Lyons was indeed, as hostile critics said, full of "claptraps," some more conventionally sentimental than others, but they were cleverly worked up, and they gave the actress of Pauline many opportunities for appealing to the spectators' natural feelings (that is, those within their actual experience). In Act 3, where she must display a constantly changing variety of emotions, Helen Faucit, with her skilful use of contrasting techniques (ranging from silent byplay to stormy abandon) was equal to all challenges; not only could she shift convincingly from one emotion to another, but she could convey the impression of two emotions at once, genuine love beneath the scornful fury occasioned by its betrayal, wistfulness beneath a seemingly unforgiving repulsion. In Act 4, notable for passages intrinsically appealing to Victorian audiences (those glorifying the domestic virtues and emotions), she gave each of them with proper pathos, nobility, or tenderness. The last scene of Act 5, with its further domestic emphasis, had, for sensitive Victorian spectators, a "painful interest" of which today's reader, finding it merely melodramatic, is hardly aware – a reminder of the many women in everyday life whose unhappy marriages were dictated by economic necessity or family pressure. Helen Faucit's acting brought the parallel forcefully home. As a woman critic ("Speranza" of Dublin) wrote:

> Who can witness Helen Faucit in that bitterest of moments, when, after vainly summoning up all the fortitude of her nature, she falls on the old man's bosom with that heart-crushed sentence –
>
> 'never speak of love again,'[sic]
>
> and not think of how many a silent tragedy the heart performs, while the looker-on hears only … ringing laughter, and sees only … beaming smiles? (*The Nation*)

Helen Faucit did exploit, with great artistry, the opportunities given her by Bulwer's play, but her superiority to other actresses of Pauline was due to something more subtle and profound in her acting. On page 6 of her prompt part she wrote a quotation from Madame de Stael: "We cannot too often repeat that imagination, far from being an enemy to truth, brings it out more than any faculty of the mind." Throughout each performance she appealed to the imaginations of the spectators, thereby creating for them a dramatic "truth"; not only did she excite them – "playing" on their "pulses"[99] – but she made them believe in Pauline as a person, one whom they came to know well as her best potentialities developed through love and suffering, and whose emotions became, for a time, their own.

Antigone

Sir Frederick Burton, recalling Helen Faucit as Antigone (Dublin, 1845), wrote that she recreated Sophocles' "heroic figure" in a genuinely classical spirit, with "reserved force" and "restrained passion," elevating her audience into an "ideal region."[100] The emphasis on nobility and restraint in her performance was very common. But the furore of enthusiasm it aroused was a response to something more than the "ennobling dream" it inspired. For Helen Faucit's portrayal was not only an awesome recreation of a great mythical heroine: it was also the depiction of a young woman with very human affections and fears. This Antigone loved her brother and was willing to sacrifice herself for his peace in the afterworld, yet she bewailed her imminent fate with a passion which, despite its formalized expression, deeply engaged her audience's own feelings. Two enthusiastic viewers, "Speranza" (Jane Francesca Elgee) and Theodore Martin, were so caught up in the emotions of the last scene that they could hardly distinguish between Antigone and Helen Faucit – or indeed between Antigone and themselves. Speranza was "savage at her fate rather than astonished at her skill." Entering sympathetically into Antigone's experiences, she heard the wings of death beating in her ears and felt the poignant regret of "unwed love." Martin, envisioning the streams and meadows, the golden sunlight of Greece, exclaimed fervently, "we share the passionate ecstacy [sic] with which the young girl … gazes on them for the last time."[101]

When Helen Faucit acted the part in London in 1846, the *Morning Chronicle* (4 August) said that in the impassioned speech in the last scene she "[carried] the feelings of the audience entirely with her, and [rose] into tremendous eloquence as she described the terrors of her untimely and unpitied doom." Yet this reviewer, though he had obviously felt the same sympathy as the audience in general, considered so much human passion incompatible with Greek tragedy. The *Daily News* (4 August) was more adamant: Greek tragedy should produce awe, not sympathy; rather than bemoaning her fate, Antigone should have shown that in conjuring up the horrors ahead she was simply rejoicing in "the strength which [enabled her] to look them, by anticipation, in the face."

Helen Faucit could not have accepted that austere interpretation. Although Antigone was even more idealized than her other heroines and the emotions were less realistically expressed, her approach to the character was basically the same for this role as for the others. Antigone, for all her nobility, was no archetypal figure to her but a "real" woman, one with whose thoughts and feelings she identified her own and through whose eyes she viewed the rest of the play. This attitude is clear from a letter she wrote to Professor John Stuart Blackie. When he questioned whether the Chorus diminishes the audience's sympathy for Antigone, she replied no, quite the opposite: the Chorus represents "the large body of wiseacres in the world who are always ready to moralise and condemn when a wrong has been irretrievably done, but who never put forth a finger to prevent it."

> The perfect isolation of the devoted girl in thought, feeling, and purpose, even where she most might have expected sympathy, –as in her sister, and in her countrymen who compose the Chorus, – deepens the pathos of her position, & brings into stronger light the energy and dignity of her character. Had her devoted deed been *recognised* she would have met death … with the serenity, and perhaps the elation of heroism, but she is doubly a martyr – "Cut off ere nature's period!" … and with no hope … *beyond* the tomb. Surely higher or more generous sacrifice than this it is scarcely possible to imagine! To secure repose to her brother's shade she devotes her own spirit to the doom from which she rescues him…

Rather than "weakening our admiration for Antigone," the "cowardly vacillation, and merely prudential motives of the Chorus, are admirable foils" for her steadfastness and self-sacrifice.[102]

No one could have shed more light on Helen Faucit's approach to character than she herself does here. Let the actress have the last word.

Notes

Prologue

1. Lowe's description, in the headnote to the entries for her works in *A Bibliographical Account of English Theatrical Literature* (London, 1888), is reprinted in James Fullerton Arnott and John William Robinson's revision of this work, *English Theatrical Literature 1559-1900* (London, 1970) 261. Knight's praise is found in his article "Faucit, Helena Saville," DNB Supplement (1901).
2. See Martin's letter to Miss Aytoun, 12 Jan. 1866, MS. 4934, ff. 7-8, NLS.
3. Corbett, *Representing Femininity* (New York and Oxford, 1992) 107-8; Hankey, essay in *Cross-Cultural Performances: Differences in Women's Re-Visions of Shakespeare*, ed. Marianne Novy (Urbana, Ill., 1993) 50-69.
4. For a modern view of the volatile, almost accidental element in performance see Michael Pennington, "Hamlet," *Players of Shakespeare: Essays in Shakespearean Performance by Twelve Players with the Royal Shakespeare Company*, ed. Philip Brockbank (Cambridge, 1985) 127.
5. Janet Suzman reportedly did this in Cleopatra after only a few weeks. See Richard David, *Shakespeare in the Theatre* (Cambridge, 1978) 18-19.
6. For the political orientations of various newspapers during Helen Faucit's period see Charles Mitchell, *The Newspaper Press Directory*, 3rd ed., rev. (London, 1851); also Stephen Koss, *The Rise and Fall of the Political Press in Britain*, Vol. I: *The Nineteenth Century* (London, 1981).
7. For example, see Koss 40-45 (*Morning Post, Observer*, and *Globe*); also Mitchell, entry on the *Morning Chronicle.*
8. Alan S. Downer, *The Eminent Tragedian: William Charles Macready* (Cambridge, Mass., 1966) 166.
9. Harold Hobson, Phillip Knightley, and Leonard Russell, *The Pearl of Days: An Intimate Memoir of The Sunday Times 1822-1972* (London, 1972) 25, 36, 40-41. See also William Beach Thomas, *The Story of the Spectator, 1828-1928* (London, 1928) 211-13, for the moralistic and utilitarian slant given to reviews of literature and drama in the *Spectator*'s early years.
10. Alan S.Downer 167-68.

11. John Hollingshead, *My Lifetime*, 2 vols. (London, 1895) I: 181. For more on the *Daily News* see Joseph Hatton, *Journalistic London, Being a Series of Sketches of Famous Pens and Papers of the Day* (London, 1882) 49-54. A number of other newpapers and their reviewers are discussed in this book and in Stanley Morison's *The English Newspaper: Some Account of the Physical Development of Journals Printed in London between 1822 and the Present Day* (Cambridge, 1932).
12. Leslie A. Marchand, *The Athenaeum: A Mirror of Victorian Culture* (Chapel Hill, N.C., 1941) 56, 227; [Members of *The Times* Staff], *The History of The Times*, 2 vols. (New York, 1935) I: 90; II: 440-43.
13. Simon Brett, *Star Trap* (New York, 1986) 159.

Chapter 1

1 For example, Clara Lane's letter of congratulation, dated 22 Mar. [1880] and signed only "Clara," begins "Dearest Lady-bird" and says that Helen's new title "has long instinctively foreshadowed itself" in all her "pet-names." RA Z 507/46.
2. Helena F. Martin 101. Death certificates in St. Catherine's House give John Diddear's death date as 19 Feb. 1841 and his age as 80, Elizabeth Diddear's death date as 14 May 1838 and her age as 75; but the burial register of St. Alphege Church, Greenwich (checked for me by Mr. J.V. Stacey) gives Elizabeth Diddear's age as 77.
3. The earliest account of Diddear's youthful career that I know is in "Mrs. Faucit," *Authentic Memoirs of the Green-room* (London, 1814): 48. Some theatre historians give his Christian name as Charles, obviously confusing him with his son.
4. DIDDEAR'S EARLY CAREER: Statements that he first acted at Bath, then in Ireland cannot be confirmed. Two playbills for the Penzance Theatre, on the Exeter circuit (for 20 June 1787, in the Morab Library, Penzance, and for 9 July 1787, in BL Playbills 298) show him acting in after-pieces. HIS MANAGEMENTS: (1) Margate, Dover, and Deal: see Malcolm Morley, *Margate and Its Theatres* (London, 1966) 42-43, 45, and the table opp. Index; also Philip Highfill, Jr., Kalman A. Burnim, and Edward A. Langhans, *Biographical Dictionary of Actors*, 16 vols. (Carbondale, Ill., 1973-93) IV: 392 (note Copeland's letter to Winston). (2) Brighton: see theatre news and reviews in the "Lewes" column, *Sussex Weekly Advertiser* 1796-98 (late June to early or mid-October each year). (3) Richmond (1800-1802): playbills and press-cuttings in the Richmond Public Library.
5. SUCCESS AS MANAGER: (1) At Brighton: Reviews offer repeated evidence of this. (2) At Richmond: An unidentified clipping in the Richmond Public Library (handwritten date 14 Aug. 1800) praises him, as does the *New Monthly Mirror* (1801), cited by Highfill et al. IV: 392. COPELAND'S MANIPULATIVENESS: For example, in 1803, after Diddear had served as principal manager of the Richmond theatre for three seasons, living in the dwelling-house adjoining the theatre,

Copeland took over the theatre and moved into the dwelling-house. (See his advertisement in the playbill for 20 June.) On 14 Jan. 1804 Charles Mate, an actor in the company, wrote to James Winston that Diddear had been "jockeyed out of the concern" by his partner. Highfill et al., though they quote this letter (IV: 392), assert that Diddear "remained in the management … until 1805." He did perform at Richmond occasionally in 1803 and 1804, and he may have been a silent partner, but he was no longer an active manager.

6. See Helena F. Martin 101 (account of her London debut); also her diary entry of 5 Jan. 1836, quoted by Sir Theodore Martin 13.
7. Helena F. Martin 101; also diary entry of 5 Jan. 1836, quoted by Sir Theodore Martin 13. By the Friends' rules at that time Elizabeth would have been expelled from her church when she married a non-Quaker. A benefit was given for Mrs. Diddear at the T.R. Brighton on 16 Oct. 1798 (see "Lewes" column of *Sussex Weekly Advertiser*, 15 Oct. 1798). Richmond playbills of 29 Sept. 1800 and 3 Aug. 1801 say that tickets may be bought from "Mrs. Diddear, at the Dwelling-House adjoining the Theatre."
8. She was baptized at Falmouth on 25 Dec. 1789 (International Genealogical Index, Church of Jesus Christ of Latter-Day Saints, Columbia, S.C.). She was the eldest of the known children. Elizabeth was younger than Harriet, for she was billed as "Miss E. Diddear" until mid-season, 1805, when Harriet, previously "Miss Diddear," became "Mrs. Faucit"; Elizabeth was then known as "Miss Diddear" until her marriage to Thomas Sheppard in 1819. Theatre historians sometimes confuse Elizabeth with Harriet: e.g. Mary Theresa Odell in *Mr. Trotter of Worthing* (Aylesbury, 1944) 29. Martha Louise's birthdate is given as 8 Aug. 1797 in the record of her baptism, 24 Aug. 1797 (Brighthelmston Register Book Christenings and Burials, 1791-99: 48. Public Record Office, Lewes, PAR 255/1/1/6). Charles was probably born about 1800 or 1801.
9. *Sussex Weekly Advertiser*, 11 and 18 July 1796, 5 Sept. 1796.
10. The surname is given as "Savill" or "Saville" in the official records of his marriage, his death, the baptisms of all but one of his children and the marriages of all of them. Although he generally spelled it "Savill," his children, including Helen Faucit, used "Saville." I have adopted the latter.
11. For an early account of Richardson and his fairground theatre, based on the old showman's recollections in interviews, see Pierce Egan, *The Life of an Actor* (1825; London, 1892) 194-206. Most of the same material is repeated in Egan's *The Pilgrims of the Thames* (London, 1839) 91-119. For a good modern discussion see Sybil Rosenfeld, "Muster Richardson – 'The Great Showman,'" *Western Popular Theatre*, ed. David Mayer and Kenneth Richards (London, 1977) 105-21.
12. JOHN'S SIZE: "Memoir of Mrs. Faucit," *Oxberry's Dramatic Biography*, 5 vols. (London, 1825) III: 131. MARRIAGE; Record in the Bishop's Transcript (Parish of St. George, Southwark) p. 252, item 752, London County Record Office. The marriage was "by Banns." John gave his name as "John Savill" only. (Since this is the earliest official record I have seen for him, it may be, after all, that his real name was John Savill[e] Faucit and that, having dropped "Faucit" to prevent possible recognition when the banns were read, he was stuck with "Savill[e]" as his children's surname.) THEATRICAL COMPANY: Sir Theodore Martin (1) says that Faucit was in the Margate company when the couple eloped, as does Malcolm Morley (44); but I accept the information in earlier publications: *Authentic Memoirs of*

the Green-room (49) and *Oxberry* (III: 128). The Margate playbill for 7 Aug. 1805 lists Miss Diddear but not Mr. Faucit; those for 11 Oct. and 18 Oct. 1805 list both Mr. and Mrs.Faucit.

13. For the Norwich circuit see James Winston, *The Theatric Tourist* (London, 1805) 72. For the Faucits' connection with it see *Authentic Memoirs* 49; "Mrs. Faucit," *La Belle Assemblée* Aug. 1817: [51]; *Oxberry* III: 126-29. According to *Oxberry* (129), they left the circuit in 1810 because of a dispute with the acting manager but returned after three months with M'Cready at Newcastle.
14. Baptismal records, in the Parish Register, All Saint's Church, Norwich (now in the Norwich Public Record Office, PD 74/75 and PD 74/76) give exact birthdates for all except Harriet. Births and baptisms are as follows: John, 30 Mar. 1807, 24 Apr. 1807; Harriet, Dec. 1808, 23 Apr. 1809; Edmund Henry, 17 Mar. 1811, 24 Mar. 1811; Alfred, 28 Nov. 1812, 7 Feb. 1813.
15. "Mrs. Faucit," in "The Dramatic Gallery," a section of an unidentified periodical (probably published about 1828 or shortly thereafter), V: 31-34, in the Library of the Performing Arts, New York Public Library, Lincoln Center. The reference to sewing is on p. 33.
16. For the Faucits' lines of parts see BL Playbills 274 (Bury, 1806) and 296 (Norwich, 1807); playbills in the Local History Library, Central Public Library, Norwich; and John Faucit's letters. The letters, all in the HTC, are as follows: 25 Oct. 1808, to Mr. Ward, Secretary to the Board of Management, Drury Lane; 18 June 1809, to Charles Reynolds of Drury Lane; an undated letter (but with 1811 written in by someone), to Mr. Ward; 10 Mar. 1812, to Mr. Ward; 10 Mar. 1812, to the Committee of the Drury Lane Theatre; 20 Jan. 1813, to Mr. Winston of the Haymarket.
17. COVENT GARDEN DEBUT: *Theatrical Inquisitor and Monthly Mirror* Nov. 1813: 253-54; *The Scourge* Nov. 1813: 431; *The Satirist* Nov. 1813: 466. ROLES AND STYLE: Cleopatra brought her most attention in her first season: see Martin Holmes, "A Regency Cleopatra," *Theatre Notebook* XVIII (1954): 46-47. LATER ROLES: Among the best was Celia in a revival of Beaumont and Fletcher's comedy *The Humorous Lieutenant*: see Thomas Kenrick, ed., *The British Stage and Literary Cabinet* 1 Jan. 1817: 29-30. She excelled in the suffering wives and mothers of domestic melodrama (*Theatrical Inquisitor* 12 Feb. 1818: 128) and also in wilder, more chilling parts like Meg Merrilies in *Guy Mannering* ("Mrs. Faucit," in "The Dramatic Gallery" [n. 15, above] V: 34). Her "tragedy queen" style as Volumnia in *Coriolanus* is amusingly described in *Examiner* 5 Dec. 1819; rpt. in *Leigh Hunt's Dramatic Criticism*, ed. Lawrence and Carolyn W. Hutton (New York, 1949) 223-25. Her arrogant manner as Cora in *Pizarro* provoked a scathing attack (unidentified clipping pasted on the back of the Covent Garden playbill for 17 June 1816, in the Theatre Museum).
18. The dwelling-house is mentioned as part of the theatre property in the Rate Books of that period, now in the Local History Library at Greenwich. For praise of John Faucit's character by the Greenwich Magistrates see *Morning Post* (London) 1 Nov. 1817. Mrs. Faucit's popularity among the "most elevated families" is asserted, perhaps hyperbolically, in *Oxberry* III: 131.
19. The anonymous statement is written at the bottom of a portrait of Helen Faucit engraved by Heaphy. For the evidence concerning Helen Faucit's birthdate see Carol J. Carlisle, "Two Notes on Helen Faucit," *Theatre Notebook* XXX (1976): 99-102. The Parish Register of St. Martin-in-the-Fields is now in the City of

Westminster Library.

20. Charles Faucit Saville was born on 16 Sept. 1816 and baptized at St. Alphege Church, Greenwich, on 8 Oct. 1816. (The parish register, still with the incumbent, was checked for me by Mr. J.V. Stacey.) Theodore Martin (2) does not give Charles's name, but his comments are obviously meant for him. (He incorrectly says that Helena was the youngest of the Faucit children.) Edmund's medical training is mentioned in "Mr. Edward [sic] Faucit Saville," *Theatrical Journal* 11 Mar. 1843: 79, and in "Memoir of Mr. E.F. Saville," *Theatrical Times* 29 Aug. 1846: cover and 90. Charles Faucit's appearance in Sydney is discussed by Eric Irvin in "From the London Theatres," *Theatre Notebook* XXII (1968): 171-72. When I inquired whether he might have continued a stage career under the name Saville, Mr. Irvin replied in a letter (1 Jan. 1983) that a "Mr. Saville" acted at the Royal Victoria Theatre, Sydney "up to at least 1845" and that a "Mr. Saville" was a member of George Darrell's company in Dunedin, New Zealand in the 1870s. I have no further information.
21. FAMILY SUCCESSES AT MARGATE: *Morning Post* (London) 19 Sept. and 20 Oct. 1817; playbills for T.R. Margate in the Folger Library, the Margate Public Library, and BL Playbills 294. DIDDEAR AT THE BOX-OFFICE: announcements in several playbills for 1817-20. DECLINE IN MRS. FAUCIT'S APPEARANCES: T.R. Margate playbill. 30 Aug. 1819 (B.L. 294); starring instead – playbill for T.R. Birmingham, 11 Aug. 1819, in the volume of *Cymbeline* playbills, Shakespeare Library, Birmingham Reference Library.
22. MRS. FAUCIT: My description is based on hints from a number of sources – e.g. Sir Theodore Martin; theatrical reviews and trivia; Helena F. Martin (never direct indictments of her mother, but one may read between the lines) – which, along with known facts about her behaviour, cohere into a pattern. MR. FAUCIT: I am less confident here, but both his letters (see n. 16) and the description of him after his wife left him (see n. 26) give the impression of a naive and uxorious husband. LONG SEPARATIONS: *Oxberry* III: 131.
23. FARREN FAMILY: Highfill et al. V: 175-82. WILLIAM FARREN'S ACTING: *Theatrical Journal* 28 Dec. 1870: 410-11; David Rinear, "From the Artificial towards the Real: The Acting of William Farren," *Theatre Notebook* XXXI (1977): 21-28.
24. Alfred Bunn, *The Stage*, 2 vols. (London, 1840) I: 225-28 (autocratic pronouncements, love of money, good nature when hoaxed, gentlemanliness); "Chit-Chat," *The Idler* 2 Sept. 1837: 128 (cock-salmon story, one of Farren's hard bargains); "Our Actors: And Their Originally Intended Trades, Crafts, and Callings. By Asmodeus Pry" [4th part of a multi-part article], *Metropolitan Magazine* XVIII (Jan. 1837): 85-91 (cock-salmon, love of money, fooled by a hoax, handsome style of living); letter, dated 15 Sept. 1839, from W.H. Phillips (a Brighton actor) to George Gitton (MS in a Grangerized copy of Erredge's *History of Brighthelmston*, Brighton Public Library) ("very pleasant & chatty – not an Aristocratic Star at all").

25 FARREN'S APPEARANCE: "Memoir of William Farren," *Oxberry* III: 37 (Faucit more attractive than Farren); J. Westland Marston, *Our Recent Actors* (London, 1890) 109. Portrais of Farren confirm the descriptions. I have found no portrait of John Faucit Saville. MRS. FARREN: "Our Actors ... By Asmodeus Pry" [4th part] (Jan. 1837): 90. FARREN AND BELATED "PHILOPROGENESIS": "Our Actors ..." [4th part] (Jan. 1837): 91 and [5th part] (Feb. 1837): 138. The earlier part (74-91) includes a satirical biographical sketch of Farren (85-91), ending with his

dissatisfaction with his childless marriage; the later part (130-44) includes, in a discussion of theatrical immorality, an obvious reference to Farren and Mrs. Faucit (though not by name), including Farren's jest (138).

26. A playbill for the T.R. Margate, 2 Sept. 1820 (Margate Public Library) has an advance announcement of Farren's performance. Otherwise my account of these events draws heavily on *Oxberry* III: 42-44. The description of Faucit's reaction is reportedly taken from a letter written by a Margate friend. Although *Oxberry*'s account cannot be accepted without question, it is consonant with all the known facts about the Faucits' separation except the date (*Oxberry*'s 1822 is too late).
27. Assignation Book 1820: DL/C/129, pp. 313, 328, 344, 362, 376, 377, 378, 382, 414, 428. London County Record Office. Witnesses called to support Harriet's "libel" were John and Elizabeth Diddear (her parents), Elizabeth Isabella Sheppard (her sister), Richard Hust (a witness of her marriage), and John Seton (unidentified). There are no extant copies of the "libel" presented by Harriet's lawyer, Pott, the testimonies of witnesses, or the counter-allegation made by John's representative. *Oxberry* (III: 133) reports that annulment proceedings have been taken "on the score of informality, the parties being both under age." Only Harriet had been underage at marriage, but the alleged ground for annulment was probably correct.
28 See O.B. McGregor, *Divorce in England* (London, 1957) 11. For Farren's parents see Highfill et al. V: 175-82.
29. Mrs. Farren's new home may have been in Everton, a suburb of Liverpool. According to a romantic, first-person account purportedly by an Irish-born actress now living in England, when she visited a childhood friend in Everton (date unspecified), she saw a pale, melancholy woman who lived next door. This, it transpired, was Farren's abandoned wife. Though in comfortable circumstances physically, she was broken-hearted. The account, subheaded "The Fair Victim," is the last section of a rambling, satirical biographical sketch of Farren in Folger Library MS. T.b.12, which is catalogued as four essays on the drama by Thomas Campbell. The earlier sections (written in the third person), which give a fair amount of information about Farren's career in Dublin – possibly correct in the basic facts though hostile in interpretation – overlaps in part with "Our Actors" [4th part]: 85-91. (See n. 25, above.)
30. NO. 26: advertisement, *Morning Herald* 27 Sept. 1838. THEATRICAL NEIGHBOURS: Harold F. Clun, *The Face of London* (London, 1932) 332. SERVANTS: The 1851 census lists three servants as living with the Farrens (PRO 107/1469, Book I, District 3, p. 9). In earlier days there would have been a nanny as well. CARRIAGE: see a passage quoted by Mrs. Anne Mathews in *Memoirs of Charles Mathews, Comedian*, 4 vols. (London, 1838) IV: 165; also "Our Actors..." [5th part] in *Metropolitan Magazine* (Feb. 1837), which sneers that the adulterers now revel in every luxury and are "splendidly vehicular."
31. Mrs. Faucit's regard for the sacraments is suggested by the second baptism of her son Edmund: he had been baptized privately at Norwich when only a week old (probably because of illness), but was baptized again at St. Alphege Church, Greenwich, at age nine, on 23 Apr. 1820 (parish register, reported by J.V. Stacey). The two baptismal records refer to the same child, for each gives the birthdate as 11 Mar. 1811. Both Farren sons were baptized in the Church of St. Mary Abbot, Kensington: William on 16 Oct. 1825, and Henry on 17 Oct. 1827 (parish register, still with the incumbent.) The parents were named as William and Harriet Farren. For Mrs. Faucit's marriage with William Farren, see Ch. 11.

32. OBITUARY: unidentified clipping in the Library of the Performing Arts, New York Public Library, Lincoln Center. DIVORCE PROCEDURE AND EXPENSE: McGregor 15-17.
33. "WIVES": obituary (See n. 32). CHILDREN: Saville's daughter Ann, a minor actress, married John Henry Wilkins, actor and dramatist. Their marriage certificate names Phoebe Faucit Saville as a witness. In 1851 Saville's "youngest daughter" (possibly Phoebe or some third daughter) died suddenly, evidently by an accidental dose of laudanum. See "Our Little Chatter Box," *Theatrical Journal* 13 Aug. 1851: 265, and "The Late Miss Saville," *Nottingham Journal* 19 Sept. 1851. SAVILLE'S DEATH: 31 Oct. 1853 (death certificate, St. Catherine's House), at the home of a widowed daughter (probably Ann Wilkins, whose husband had died young). See "Sudden Death of a Veteran Actor," *Sunday Times* 6 Nov. 1853.
34. A letter in the HTC from Farren to "My dear Sir" asks to be remembered to "John Saville and Wife" – i.e. John, Jr. (It was written at the Hen and Chickens, Birmingham, and dated only "Wednesday.") *Theatrical Journal*, 6 Oct. 1843: 317-18 tells of Alfred's imitation of Farren.
35. For additional information see my essay "The Faucit Saville Brothers; or, Theatre and Family," in *Scenes from Provincial Stages: Essays in Honour of Kathleen Barker*, ed. Richard Foulkes (London, 1994) 114-26.
36. The anonymous statement referred to in n. 19 says Helen was educated at this school. Although this is now unverifiable, I believe it is correct. Both Sir Theodore Martin (2) and Helena F. Martin (89) refer to Helen's school in Greenwich. Miss Kimbell certainly had a school in King St. during the relevant period: the location is confirmed by a Greenwich Hospital estate plan of 1826 and by *Pigot & Co.'s London and Provincial Directory* for 1827 (p. 434). The latter gives Miss Kimbell's first name as Elizabeth. The Rate Books list the house in Sarah Kimbell's name from 1800 to 1823 and in Elizabeth Kimbell's name from that time through 1828. (One may guess that Miss Kimbell began keeping her school in the family home before her mother's death.) The house was demolished in 1837 to make way for Nelson Road. Mr. J. Watson, Local History Librarian, Greenwich, provided most of this information.
37. Samuel Phelps's daughter was sent home from her expensive school because the father of three schoolmates had objected to his daughters' being "educated with an actor's." See Wendy Trewin, *The Royal General Theatrical Fund: A History 1838-1988* (London, 1989) 27-28.
38. Sir Theodore Martin 2-3 (quoted passages); Martin's letter, dated 12 Apr. 1899, to Sir Edward Russell, NLS Acc. 8641 (holidays with grandparents). Martin had been told by his wife about her childhood sorrows.
39. Helena F. Martin 47-48 (early experiences with claustrophobia); Sir Theodore Martin 330 (passage from her 1871 diary, recalling her childhood insomnia).
40. Helena F. Martin 6 ("too fond of fun"), 38 ("birdie" – one of several references to this nickname).
41. See G.A. Sala's description of his mother's school, in *The Life and Adventures of George Augustus Sala*, 3rd ed., 2 vols. (London, 1895) I: 5. According to Deborah Gorham, the average middle-class girl of this period who attended boarding school (instead of being taught entirely at home as most daughters of upper-class families were) did so for only two or three years in her early teens; only an orphan or a child whose family circumstances made it difficult to live at home would attend a boarding school from childhood through adolescence. See *The Victorian Girl and the Feminine Ideal* (London

and Canberra, c.1982) 22. The Faucit girls would fit the latter category.

42. MISS KIMBELL'S CHARGES: No statement is available, but they were probably the same as those advertised by two other Greenwich schools, Mrs. Hartnoll's Maize Hill Establishment for girls and Mr. Goodale's Churchfields Academy for boys, in the *Greenwich, Woolwich, and Deptford Gazette* in 1834. (There was no earlier newspaper for Greenwich.) MORE EXPENSIVE SCHOOLS: An exclusive boarding school for girls in Brighton had the nominal charge of 120 to 130 pounds per year, but this represented "scarcely a fourth of the charges for 'extras'" (Gorham 34, n. 32). For various types of private schools, see Brian Simon, *Studies in the History of Education 1780-1870* (London, 1960) 110-13; also Gorham 19-26.
43. In a letter to the editor of the *Glasgow Herald*, dated 18 Nov. 1869 (rpt. in the *Glasgow Morning Journal* and partly quoted by Sir Theodore Martin 304), Helen Faucit mentions "Mrs. Marcet's histories" among the books she studied at school. Since Mrs. Jane Marcet's history of England had not yet been published when Helen was in school, she was probably telescoping someone else's history with one or more of Mrs. Marcet's earlier books – a series of simplified but highly regarded introductions to advanced subjects like chemistry and political economy. See "Marcet, Mrs. Jane," *DNB* (1893); also Mrs. E.H. Field, *The Child and His Book*, 2nd ed. (London, 1892; rpt. Detroit, 1968) 344-46. Mrs. Hartnoll (see n. 42), who wrote a scathing indictment of the usual education for women, boasted that geography, astronomy, and geometry were taught in her school.
44. Helena F. Martin 5 (note).
45. Sala I: 58-59; Sir Theodore Martin 80-81, 142.
46. Helena F. Martin 89 (mentions the dancing master); Sir Theodore Martin 58 (Helen's diary entry of 4 Jan. 1839), 284 (Scottish dances).
47. MUSICAL TRAINING: Her letter to the Glasgow editor (see n. 43) recalls "struggling" with Cramer's *Lessons* for the piano. See also Sir Theodore Martin 10 (vocal training) and 61 (Helen's diary entry for 20 [Jan.] 1839, mentioning an air she had composed). COMPARISON WITH HARRIET: Harriet often had roles that required singing; occasionally she appeared in opera. Helen rarely had to sing on the stage; once when she did, the *Sunday Times* critic (24 Apr.1842) "devoutly" hoped she would never do so again.
48. The drawing is in Harriet Faucit's Autograph Book, Folger MS. Y.d.3.
49. H.C. Barnard, *A History of English Education from 1760* (London, 1961) 157.
50. Letter from Macready to Helen Faucit, 3 Apr. [1840], quoted by Sir Theodore Martin 71. The original is in an extra-illustrated copy of Lady Martin's *On Some of Shakespeare's Female Characters*, NLS, MS. 16443, opp. 202.
51. Sir Archibald Alison, *Some Account of My Life and Writings ... Edited by His Daughter-in-Law Lady Alison*, 2 vols. (Edinburgh, 1883) I: 533.
52. Helena F. Martin 159.
53. Helena F. Martin 87. For descriptions of Greenwich Park and Blackheath Common see Mrs. Arthur G. [Nancy R.E.] Bell, *The Historical Outskirts of London* (London, 1907) 112, 114-15.
54. Information about the church and graveyard, with pictures, was sent me by Mr. R.A. Greenhill of the Lewisham Library in a letter dated 6 Dec. 1978. The church Helen knew was later demolished and the old cemetery closed; a third church was built across the road, with a new churchyard.

55. Helena F. Martin 89. She describes here as actual what I interpret as only imagined – the slimy steps, the massive door, etc. Mr. Greenhill (see n. 54) wrote that "none of the vaults are now accessible, by steps or any other means and none of the earlier views show vaults open below ground level." I assume that the schoolgirl fancies evoked by "Juliet's Tomb" had come to seem, in Lady Martin's memory, something that had actually been seen.
56. Mrs. C. Baron Wilson, *Our Actresses* (London, 1844) 7; letter to Helena Faucit Martin from Ellen Braysher, written in Dec. 1882, quoted by Sir Theodore Martin (73). Much of Mrs. Wilson's sketch of Helen Faucit was later copied verbatim in *The Theatre* 1 Dec. 1851 and 1 Jan. 1852.
57. Helena F. Martin 4. Helen's early removal from school may have been due not only to delicate health but also to Miss Kimbell's moving, or possibly disbanding, her school some time before Helen's fifteenth birthday (in Oct. 1829). See Rate Book reference in n. 36.
58. Helena Faucit Martin 4 ("kind but busy"); Sir Theodore Martin 12 (Kate).
59. JOHN'S ACTING AT BRIGHTON: Playbills, T.R. Brighton, in BL Playbills 202 and in the Brighton Public Library. HIS MARRIAGE: Brighthelmston Parish Register of Marriages, Oct. 1828-Mar. 1831, p. 259, Public Record Office, Lewes. PAR 255/1/3/6. MARIANNE'S AGE: She was underage at marriage (the consent of her widowed mother was recorded). Her age at death, 31 Mar. 1889, was given as 77 (death certificate, St. Catherine's House).
60. A.F. Day gives an interesting description of Wagner and his controversies in *The Church of St. Nicolas of Myra, Dyke Road, Brighton: A History with Some Deviations* (Brighton, n.d. [ca. 1974]) 16-18. For Helen's friendship with him see Sir Theodore Martin 202, 229, 298.
61. Helena F. Martin 89 (dog), 4-5 (Satan, her books); Letter of Helena F. Martin to Horace Howard Furness, 1 July 1892, Furness Library (love of sea from childhood).
62. Helena F. Martin 4, 107.
63. Helena F. Martin 4 (Ophelia), 47 (Desdemona).
64. Helena F. Martin 54-55 (Desdemona's father), 47-48 (manner of her death).
65. Helena F. Martin 86; Sir Theodore Martin 5.
66. "Death of an Old Inhabitant," *Thames Valley Times* 10 Apr. 1889.
67. The Rate Books are now in the Central Reference Library, Richmond. Information about the later additions to the house is from Miss Diana Howard of that library (letter of 19 Dec. 1973).
68. Helena F. Martin 86, 87.

Chapter 2

1. This belief became current rather early (see Mrs. C. Baron Wilson, *Our Actresses* II: 4), and it was stated authoritatively after her death by Sir Theodore Martin (4). She herself implied it when she wrote that she had never seen any of Shakespeare's heroines before acting them (Helena F. Martin 49).

2. Walter Donaldson, *Recollections of an Actor* (London, 1865) 245-46. By the time his book was published (late in Helen Faucit's career), some London shops had women as assistants, but they were underpaid in comparison with the men. See Derek Hudson, *Munby Man of Two Worlds* (London, [1972]) 98-99.
3. Despite long hours and low wages, factory jobs had advantages over domestic service. See Milton Briggs and Percy Jordan, *Economic History of England*, 10th ed. (London, 1962) 216. In the latter part of the century, as Tracy C. Davis has shown, the average woman industrial worker would be better off financially than the average actress (broadly defined), considering the latter's professional expenses and relatively short working year. See the section on "Theatrical and Industrial Wage Rates for Women" in her *Actresses as Working Women* (London, 1991): 32-36. But, even if this had been true in Helen Faucit's youth, a factory job would not have been considered for her.
4. Donaldson, 246-47. This was especially true of talented "mainline" actresses. There was great diversity, of course, among women of the theatre. Tracy Davis, in her fine study (see n.3), includes dancers, singers, and other performers of all ranks, talents, and affiliations.
5. For the professional status of acting see Michael Baker, *The Rise of the Victorian Actor* (London and Totowa, 1978) 20-27 et passim. For an actress's vulnerability see Tracy Davis, Part II, passim.
6. This ideal is reflected in many advice books for women, as well as in the imaginative literature of the late eighteenth and nineteenth centuries. Its importance to the rearing of a middle-class girl is interestingly discussed in Deborah Gorham's *The Victorian Girl and the Feminine Ideal* passim.
7. See Wendy Trewin, *The Royal General Theatrical Fund* 15-16, 34, 39-40, 44, 47, 57, 67, 68-69, 70, 72. Ellen Terry was among the 40 ladies segregated from the 300 gentlemen diners in 1884 (67).
8. For a detailed study of Harriet Faucit's career see Carol J. Carlisle, "The Other Miss Faucit," *Nineteenth Century Theatre Research* VI (1978): 71-88.
9. This complaint was made of Mrs. Faucit's Lady Macbeth in *Theatrical Observer* IV, No. 130(16Apr. 1822).
10. Helena F. Martin (3) deplores the tradition of a weak Ophelia. Harriet's relatively strong interpretation is noted in the *Liverpool Albion* 4 July 1836.
11. William Charles Macready mentions the "constitutional asthma" that obliged John Philip Kemble "for the sake of distinction to adopt an elaborate mode of utterance, enunciating every letter in every word." Actors without Kemble's problem sometimes imitated his deliberate style of elocution. See *Macready's Reminiscences and Selections from His Diaries*, ed. Sir Frederick Pollock, 2 vols. (London, 1875)1:149.
12. Macready contrasts J.P. Kemble and Mrs. Siddons in *Macready's Reminiscences* 149. Fanny Kemble contrasts the refined style of her father, Charles Kemble, with the dynamic one of Edmund Kean and suggests that Mrs. Siddons "united the excellencies" of both. See Frances Anne Butler, *Journal*, 2 vols. (Philadelphia, 1835)1:143-49.
13. Pierce Egan, *Life of an Actor* 197-201. Richardson said that Kean's mother, Anne Carey, had acted in the company with her sons Edmund and Henry. The latter would have been Kean's half-brother, Henry Darnley. See Harold N. Hillebrand, *Edmund Kean* (New York, 1933) 6, 10, 319, 321. Mark Sorrell, in "Edmund Kean and Richardson's Theatre," *Theatre Notebook* L (1996) 29-38, supports the essential

truthfulness of this account as reported by Egan. Note that Edmund Henry Faucit Saville, named before Edmund Kean became famous, was the only child of "Saville Faucit" who was given a double Christian name.

14. Hillebrand 316-18; Carlisle, "The Other Miss Faucit" 73-74.
15. Hillebrand 319.
16. Helena F. Martin 86-87. I give an edited version of Lady Martin's account, which is almost certainly correct in its essentials but not in some details. Representing herself as "quite a child," she describes appropriately immature behaviour and implies that she was still a boarding-school student. Kean did not take up residence in Richmond, however, until 1831, when Helen was 16. A younger age was in line with her alleged birthdate (1817).
17. Helena F. Martin 88-89, 90.
18. Helena F. Martin 90-93. A reference to the broken phial was made many years before Lady Martin's own account by someone who had seen her act at Richmond in 1833. See the letter to the editor, headed "Miss Helen Faucit" and signed "A Friend to Dramatic Reminiscences," *Hiscoke and Son's Richmond Notes A Monthly Record of Local Information for Richmond and Its Neighborhood* (April 1865): 41.
19. "Miss Helen Faucit," *Our Actresses* 2: 8. The "most cordial" response is also reported by Mrs. Wilson.
20. MRS. HALL AND HELEN FAUCIT: S.C. Hall, *Restrospect of a Long Life* 2 vols. (London, 1883)11: 460. DESCRIPTION OF THE HALLS: "Hall, Samuel Carter" and "Hall, Anna Maria" in the DNB (1890); Hall, *Retrospect* 2: 298, 421-78 et passim; William Bell Scott, *Autobiographical Notes*, ed. W. Minto, 2 vols. (London, 1892)1:108; Mrs. [Margaret O. Wilson] Oliphant, *Autobiography and Letters*, ed. Mrs. Harry Coghill (Edinburgh, 1899) 35-38; Nathaniel Hawthorne, *The English Notebooks*, ed. E. Randall Stewart (1941; rpt. New York, 1962) 311, 313.
21. Helena F. Martin 93.
22. The playbill for Harriet's benefit, 6 Nov. 1833 (BL Playbills 299), gives her address as Miss Jeffcott's house in Hill Street. The house was in what is now the Petersham Road, a continuation of Hill Street (information from the Rate Books, sent me by Diana Howard of the Richmond Reference Library in a letter of 19 Dec. 1973).
23. Frances Anne Kemble, *Records of a Girlhood*, 2nd ed. (New York, 1879) 377.
24. The playbill for 25 Nov. 1833 announces that the theatre will open every Monday until further notice, but later playbills for that season are lacking.
25. Helena F. Martin 93-94. Her account leaves the erroneous impression that Juliet was the only character she acted in her first trial at Richmond and that she did not act again until her London debut.
26. Among them, possibly, were Portia in *The Merchant of Venice* and Belvidera in *Venice Preserved*. In Jan. 1836 an American journalist (quoted by Theodore Martin 16) recalled seeing Helen Faucit's "exquisite" Portia at Richmond "eighteen months ago"; and, when she first acted Belvidera in London, the *Morning Chronicle* (23 Jan. 1836) said that her friends had been talking about her Belvidera "for the last two years."
27. In his *Reminiscences* (I: 55-56) Macready vividly describes Mrs. Siddons's performance of Mrs. Beverley.
28. CRITICAL AUDIENCES: see two letters written by a Brighton actor, W.H. Phillips, to his friend George Gitton, 15 Sept. and 7 Nov. 1839 (MSS in a Grangerized copy of J. Ackerson Erredge's *The History of Bricihthelmston* in the

Brighton Public Library). UNPOPULARITY OF TRAGEDY: Even Mrs. Siddons could not fill the theatre during a 1798 engagement at Brighton. See Henry C. Porter, *History of the Theatres of Brighton* (Brighton, 1886) 20. Judging by newspaper reviews in later periods, the preference for lighter forms of entertainment persisted. BRIGHTON THEATRE IN THE MID-CENTURY: Kathleen Barker, "The Decline and Rise of the Brighton Theatre 1840-1860," *Nineteenth Century Theatre Research* VIII (Spring 1980): 29-51.

29. *Brighton Herald* 27 Dec. 1834 (advertisement for the T. R. Brighton).
30. Henry Saxe Wyndham, *The Annals of Covent Garden Theatre*, 2 vols. (London: Chatto and Windus, 1906)11: 97-103.
31. The Covent Garden playbill for 29 Dec. 1835 announced that on 5 Jan. Juliet would be acted by "a young lady, her first appearance." But the playbill of 31 Dec., which announced Julia instead, gave Helen Faucit's name.
32. Helena F. Martin 97-98; Sir Theodore Martin 11.

Chapter 3

1. Frances Anne Butler, *Journal* II: 156 (note). Many years later she pointed out the shortcomings of the play, but she still praised its powerful dramatic effects, much of its dialogue, and its two major characters. See Frances Anne Kemble, *Records of a Girlhood* 378.
2. Theodore Martin 17. In later years she changed her mind and called the role a "piece of taskwork" requiring the actress to "veil" its inconsistencies and "so animate it with feeling … as to make the audience forget the improbabilities." See Helena F. Martin 99, n.1.
3. Diary entries for 1, 2, 3, and 4 Jan. 1836, quoted by Sir Theodore Martin 12; Helena F. Martin 98 (Miss Taylor's help at rehearsals). A number of pictures show the hair style. The *Morning Chronicle* (6 Jan. 1836) said it made her head look too small, but she continued to use it.
4. Alan S. Downer, in *The Eminent Tragedian* 20-21, gives a fuller description of Covent Garden as it was in 1809. The building was the same in 1836, but the wax candles had been superseded by gas in 1817.
5. For more on the democratization of theatre audiences and possible reasons for it, see Ernest Bradlee Watson's classic study, *Sheridan to Robertson: A Study of the Nineteenth-Century London Stage* (1926; rpt. New York, 1963) 6-19; also Joseph Donohue, *Theatre in the Age of Kean*. Drama and Theatre Studies (Totowa, 1975) 149-51. Donohue cautions, however, that too little is known about these audiences, thus the "conventional generalizations … in some cases obscure our view of the complex and inconsistent realities of theatrical attendance in the age." This caveat, though written of the early nineteenth century, also applies to the later 1830s and 1840s. For private boxes see Donohue; also Alan Downer 21.
6. *Theatrical Journal* 17 July 1841.

7. The classic study is Richard Southern's *Changeable Scenery: Its Origin and Development* (London, 1952). See pp. 249-81 for an extensive discussion of flat scene and set scene. Charles H. Shattuck gives a brief and admirably clear explanation of the flat-wing-border system in the introduction to his *William Charles Macready's* King John: *A Facsimile Prompt-Book* (Urbana, 1962) 14-17. See also Sybil Rosenfeld *A Short History of Scene Design in Great Britain.* Drama and Theatre Studies (Totowa, 1973) 103-10, which describes specific scene painters and special effects. The advantages of gaslight are discussed on pp. 104-5.
8. LARGE ATTENDANCE, LITTLE PUFFERY: *Spectator* (9 Jan. 1836: 39). FASHIONABLE AUDIENCE: *Times* 6 Jan.; *Sunday Times,* 10 Jan. CONFUSION WITH HARRIET: *Spectator* (expected to see the familiar Miss Faucit, pleasantly surprised); *Morning Post* 6 Jan. and *Sunday Times* (thought they had seen her but she was better than ever). REVIEWS OF DEBUT: In addition to the journals cited above, *Morning Chronicle* 6 Jan.; *Athenaeum* 9 Jan.: 36; *Observer* 10 Jan.; *John Bull* 10 Jan.: 14; *Literary Gazette* 9 Jan.: 27-28; *New Monthly Magazine* XLVI (Feb. 1836): 245-46; a London correspondent for an American journal, quoted by Sir Theodore Martin 16-17.
9. Helena F. Martin 101.
10. Helena F. Martin 98-99 (entrance, Harriet Taylor), 100 (unable to see her "master"); *Morning Chronicle* ("indistinctly," etc.).
11. SAD INTERVAL, RECOVERY: Helena F. Martin 99-101. SALARY: The *Observer* reported (10 Jan. 1836) that Osbaldiston had engaged Helen Faucit at terms "such as have never before been given under similar circumstances with one only exception" –an allusion to the 30 guineas a week paid to Fanny Kemble after her exciting debut in 1829. See Frances Ann Kemble, *Records of a Girlhood* 226. J.C. Trewin, in *Mr. Macready: A Nineteenth-Century Tragedian and His Theatre* (London, 1955) 130, says that Macready, when preparing for his Covent Garden management (1837), signed an agreement to pay Helen Faucit £15 a week "instead of her previous thirty."
12. *Morning Herald* ("deeply affected"); *Morning Post* ("deafening" applause); journalist quoted by Sir Theodore Martin 17 (backstage tears).
13. *Morning Chronicle, Spectator, Observer,* American journalist quoted by Sir Theodore Martin 16. The last said the applause had been greater at Miss Faucit's debut than at Miss O'Neill's. Mrs. C. Baron Wilson, who claimed to have been present at both debuts, said the same thing in *Our Actresses* II: 9.
14. *Times, Morning Chronicle, Spectator, Observer, Athenaeum, Morning Herald, Morning Post, John Bull.*
15. *Morning Herald, Observer New Monthly Magazine. The Times* was more admonitory about her "extravagance," however.
16. *The Times, Morning Chronicle, Spectator, Athenaeum.*
17. *Morning Chronicle, Spectator.* The *Observer* said, however, that the interview between Julia and Walter produced such excitement that the wave of enthusiasm carried the audience through the "flat and tame" conclusion with no sense of anticlimax.
18. "Dramatic Intelligence" column, 10 Jan. and 24 Jan. 1836.
19. The *London Metropolitan Magazine* (Feb. 1836: 54) actually said Miss Faucit had the air of a "tragedy queen" in this passage.
20. *Diaries of William Charles Macready 1833-1851,* ed. William Toynbee, 2 vols. (London, 1912)1: 268.

21. Quoted by Sir Theodore Martin 25.
22. Diary entry of 18 Jan. 1836, quoted by Sir Theodore Martin 18.
23. HER ACCOUNT: diary entry for 27 Jan. 1836, quoted by Sir Theodore Martin 19. CROWDED THEATRE, APPLAUSE, STANDING OVATION: *Morning Chronicle* 28 Jan. CRITICISM OF HER BELVIDERA: *Morning Chronicle; The Times* 28 Jan.; *Morning Herald* 28 Jan.; *Morning Post* 28 Jan., 2 Feb. and 8 Apr.; *Athenaeum* 30 Jan.: 92; *Literary Gazette* 30 Jan.: 76; *Sunday Times* 31 Jan. *Examiner* 31 Jan.: 69 New York *Spirit of the Times* 12 Mar.; *Metropolitan Magazine* May 1836: 22-23. Note that the *Sun* 29 Jan. and *Bell's Life in London* 31 Jan. repeat *verbatim* parts of the review in the *Morning Chronicle* and that the *Observer* reprints the whole in its "Theatre" column. The "Dramatic Intelligence" column in the *Observer* 31 Jan. is original, however.
24. *Morning Chronicle* (monotony); *Times* (abrupt transitions).
25. FACE: *Morning Post.* O'NEILL: *Morning Post, The Times.* STYLE AND TUTELAGE: *Examiner, Sunday Times.*
26. There were also highly favourable reviews in the *Literary Gazette* and the New York *Spirit of the Times.* The London correspondent for *Spirit* was particularly ecstatic.
27. Diary entry of 28 Jan. 1836, quoted by Sir Theodore Martin 21-22.
28. Sir Archibald Alison, "The British Theatre," *Essays: Political Historical and Miscellaneous,* 3 vols. (Edinburgh, 1850) III: 569-70 (note); Sir Theodore Martin 23 (diary entry of 6 Feb. 1836).
29. Excerpt from her diary, quoted by Sir Theodore Martin 23. I base my discussion of her portrayal on reviews in *The Times* 9 Feb. 1836; *Morning Chronicle* 9 Feb.; *Morning Herald* 9 Feb.; *Morning Post* 9 Feb.; *Bell's Life in London* 14 Feb.; *Sunday Times* 14 Feb.; *Spectator* 13 Feb.: 151; *Metropolitan Magazine* (May 1836): 22-23.
30. Sir Theodore Martin 23.
31. Margaret S. Carhart, *The Life and Works of Joanna Baillie.* Yale Studies in English 64 (New Haven, 1923) III: 54-55, 109-42. Of the 38 plays that Miss Baillie published, only 7 were ever professionally acted.
32. *Fraser's Magazine* (Feb. 1836): 240; "Dramatic Intelligence" column, *Observer* 28 Feb. 1836; *Fraser's Literary Chronicle* 26 Mar. 1836: 269 (quoted by Carhart 161); *Morning Chronicle* 26 Feb. 1836.
33. *Henriguez* had its only performance at Drury Lane on 19 May 1836. According to Carhart (164-65), the production was "set" to reappear in Easter Week but there were no further notices about it during the spring. Alfred Bunn, manager of Drury Lane, admits that he preferred a money-making opera to the relatively unremunerative *Henriguez*. See *The Stage* II: 17-19.
34. Diary entry of 25 Feb. 1836, quoted by Sir Theodore Martin 27. My discussion of the critical reception is based on reviews in *The Times* 26 Feb.; *Morning Post* 26 and 29 Feb.; *Morning Chronicle* 26 Feb.; *Morning Herald* 26 Feb.; *Athenaeum* 27 Feb.: 164; *Literary Gazette* 27 Feb.: 140-41; *Examiner* 28 Feb.: 133; *Sunday Times* 28 Feb. Most criticisms of the play are very similar.
35. Helena F. Martin 297; Sir Theodore Martin 28-30 (extract from letter on p.30).
36. *Morning Post* 11 Mar. 1836 (quotation); Helena F. Martin 98.
37. Diary entries quoted by Sir Theodore Martin 32-33; *Morning Herald* 18 Apr. 1836; *Morning Post* 18 Apr. *Don Juan of Austria* was translated by Mrs. Charles Gore from the French of Casimir Delavigne.
38. Downer, *The Eminent Tragedian* 145-50; Sir Theodore Martin 38 (from Helen Faucit's diary).

39. Sir Theodore Martin 36. See also *Diaries of Macready* I: 316.
40. Sir Theodore Martin 37.
41. Sir Theodore Martin 38; *Diaries of Macready* I: 322.
42. Brief commendations of Helen Faucit's performances in Cork, especially Juliet and Julia, are in *Cork Evening Herald* 27 July and 3 Aug. 1836; *Constitutional* 28 July; *Southern Reporter* 28 July. My information about the Galway engagement is in a letter of 14 Aug. 1836, written at Galway by Charles Kean to his mother: "William Farren and his daughter commence here on Monday next (tomorrow), but I think *I* have reaped all the Harvest Galway can afford before their arrival." (MS. 1737-38 in the National Library of Ireland)
43. Rice worked by day at the British Museum, but at night he sometimes sang comic songs at taverns, and he frequently attended the theatre. His notebooks, a series entitled "Dramatic Register of the Patent Theatres, &c.," are in the HTC. His comment on Helen Faucit's Portia, dated 25 Sept. 1836, is on some detached pages (44-45, originally in Vol. V), now belonging to Mr. Jack Reading, who has kindly allowed me to quote from them. The comment on Helen Faucit's Kate is from the entry for 9 Apr. 1837, in Vol. VII, pp. 23-25 (MS in the HTC).
44. The exceptionally strong cast drew, on the second night, an overflowing audience whose uproar over seating delayed the performance. See *Morning Herald* 26 Oct. 1836.
45. Entry for 5 June 1837, in Vol. VII, pp. 172-73 (MS in the HTC).
46. Entry for 18 Dec. 1836, originally pp. 253-54 of Vol. V (detached pages, pasted on playbills in the Theatre Museum, but copies are inserted in Vol. V, HTC). The comments on Kate, Desdemona, Imogen, and Juliet are published, with slight changes in punctuation, in *The London Theatres in the Eighteen-Thirties*, ed. Arthur Colby Sprague and Bertram Shuttleworth (London, 1950) 38, 53-54, 48-49, 79-80. All my quotations, however, follow the original text.
47. Unidentified journal, quoted by Sir Theodore Martin 41 ("fragile and delicate," etc.); *John Bull* 9 Oct. 1836 ("raw girl,' etc.).
48. NEGATIVE CRITICISM: *Spectator* 8 Oct. 1836; *Examiner* 9 Oct. PRAISE: *John Bull* ("conception … credit," "proved … hoped for"); *Observer* 16 Oct. ("decided originality"). See also the enthusiastic passage from an unidentified journal, quoted by Sir Theodore Martin 41.
49. *The Times*, 24 Dec. ("fire," "archness"); *Morning Chronicle*, 24 Dec. ("point" without "shrewishness").
50. For an excellent account of the evening, including a detailed description of Kemble's Benedick, see Jane Williamson, *Charles Kemble, Man of the Theatre* (Lincoln, Neb, 1964) 218-29.
51. Helena F. Martin 294. Later Theodore Martin presented these promptbooks to the Shakespeare Memorial Library (now the Shakespeare Centre Library), Stratford-upon-Avon. I quote the inscription directly from one of the volumes of promptbooks.
52. Helena F. Martin 295. A note from Charles Kemble to Helen Faucit, dated only "Monday Evening" but evidently written in Jan. 1838 (during the rehearsals for Macready's *King Lear*), begins "My dear little Friend" and says "I shall be delighted to receive you in Park Place, when your rehearsal of Cordelia is concluded … ." (MS inserted in the extra-illustrated copy of Helena F. Martin's book, NLS MS. 16443). He may well have been helping her prepare for acting Cordelia.

53. *Brian Boroihme*, though new to London, had been written more than 10 years earlier and had been acted in Dublin, Belfast, New York, Philadelphia, and Glasgow. London critics agreed it was unworthy of Knowles in his maturity. Fitzball's *Walter Tyrrel* was described by *The Times* (17 May 1837) as a "tissue of absurdities." Helen Faucit was successful in both of these unsatisfactory dramas.
54. Diary of Ann Mathews (MS. Thr. 54, HTC), entry for 5 Jan. [1837]. For the background of the production see *Diaries of Macready* I: 278-80, 282-83, 285, 355, 363, 365-66, 369-70; Charles H. Shattuck, ed., *Bulwer and Macready: A Chronicle of Early Victorian Theatre* (Urbana, 1958) 17-55, esp. 27, 29, 31, 47-55.
55. Ann Mathews records in her Diary (5 Jan. [1837]):".. . William Brade jr called & told me of the partial failure of M: Bulwer's Play…" (HTC). Both *The Times* (5 Jan.) and the *Spectator* (7 Jan.: 10) call its success "equivocal." Other journals speak of "moderate" or "incomplete" success. My discussion of the play and the acting is based on the journals named above and the following: *Morning Chronicle* 5 Jan.; *Observer* 8 Jan.; *Athenaeum* 7 Jan.: 15; *Morning Herald* 5 Jan.; *Morning Post* 5 Jan.; *Sunday Times* 8 Jan.; *John Bull* 8 Jan.
56. On 10 Jan. Helen Faucit, who was acting in spite of "severe indisposition," asked the indulgence of the audience for any deficiencies; after that she succumbed to her illness and could act no more that week. See *Morning Post* 11 Jan. 1837; *John Bull* 16 Jan.
57. DEPLORABLE MATTER: *The Times, Athenaeum, Spectator, John Bull.* WEAK CONSTRUCTION, ETC.: *Morning Herald* (among others). LACHRYMOSE CHARACTER: *The Times, Spectator.* PRAISE FOR HELEN FAUCIT: *Morning Post* (among others).
58. Macready had described *Paracelsus* as a poem "of great merit" before he ever met Browning. The meeting occurred in the chambers of the Rev. William Fox ("an original and profound thinker") on 27 Nov. 1835. See *Diaries of Macready*, ed. Toynbee, I: 247 (*Paracelsus*), 264 (meeting). Other friends of Macready, like Talfourd and Forster, were also highly impressed by Browning.
59. *Autobiographical Notes of the Life of William Bell Scott*, ed. W. Minto, 2 vols. (London, 1892)1:124-25.
60. *Times* 2 May 1837; *Athenaeum* 6 May: 331; *Spectator* 6 May: 423.
61. VAN DYKE COSTUMES: Macready's – *Examiner* 7 May 1837; *John Bull* 7 May. Both – Lady Martin's letter to Anne Thackeray Ritchie, dated 30 Apr. 1891, giving her memories of the production; quoted in Mrs. Ritchie's *Records of Tennyson, Ruskin and Browning* (London, 1892) 177-80, and (with slight variations) by Sir Theodore Martin 242-44. Such meticulousness was typical of Macready but not of Osbaldiston's management. The *Examiner* complained that most of the characters were "a barn's wonder to look at."
62. Copy of Browning's Notes on Macready's Diary (Ashley MS. 5755, BL); *Literary Gazette* 6 May: 292; Sun 2 May; *John Bull* 7 May. The *Morning Chronicle* reported that Helen Faucit's soliloquy beginning "The king – ever the king!" was much applauded.
63. Ritchie 178.
64. *Diaries* I: 350, 356, 363.
65. *The Eminent Tragedian* 151-52.
66. J. Westland Marston, *Our Recent Actors* (London, 1890) 37-38; John Coleman, *Fifty Years of an Actor's Life*, 2 vols. (London, 1904)11: 341. For Miss Huddart see Alan Downer 128, 195.

67. Shattuck, *Bulwer and Macready* 4. Macready's self-reproaches for jealousy and loss of temper are scattered through his diaries.
68. *Diaries* I: 364, 397, 370.
69. One senses this both in reports of her acting and in her eager forwardness as reflected in Macready's diary records, something very unlike her tremulous, diffident behaviour in the past.
70. George Rowell, *Queen Victoria Goes to the Theatre* (London, 1978) 16.
71. Helen Faucit's MS letter is in the Mander and Mitchenson Collection.
72. Helena F. Martin 297, note 1.
73. *Diaries of Macready* I: 405.
74. *Diaries of Macready* I: 408. Alan Downer, evidently misled by the heading "Birmingham" for Macready's diary entry of 10 Sept. 1837, says Macready "went to act for his step-mother in Birmingham" at this time (163). The playbill evidence of the Macready-Faucit engagement at Liverpool is conclusive, however. Perhaps Macready stopped in Birmingham en route to Liverpool and forgot to give a new heading to the next day's diary entry.
75. *Diaries* I: 409.

Chapter 4

1. *Theatrical Observer* 18 June 1825 ("tried to look big"); "Our Actors" (Feb. 1837): 138 ("fat lady").
2. *Actors by Daylight* 12 May 1838: 87. For examples of jests about the Farrens see the same journal, 14 Apr. 1838: 55 (a facetious "programme" for a concert) and 17 Nov. 1838: 304 (a list of "benefit performances").
3. G.A. Sala, *Life and Adventures* I: 59.
4. *Diaries* I: 464 (entry for 15 June 1838).
5. On 10 Oct. she said something that made him doubt her "constancy" (see *Diaries* I: 416). His diary is silent on the subject on 11 Oct. and for two weeks afterwards.
6. See *Morning Post* 6 Apr. 1836.
7. *Diaries* I: 419 (Virginia), 421 (contract not altered).
8. *The Times* 2 Oct. 1837; *Observer* 1 Oct.; Alan Downer, *The Eminent Tragedian* 164.
9. Helena F. Martin 51.
10. *Spectator* 7 Oct. 1837: 945. See also *John Bull* 1 Oct. and *Examiner* 8 Oct.: 646.
11. P. 25 of the detached pages from Vol. V of Rice's "Dramatic Register," owned by Mr. Jack Reading.
12. SCENERY: "enchanted wood," Helena F. Martin 328-31; "beautiful gardens," Sir Theodore Martin 296 (Helen's diary entry of 2 Mar. 1868). DESPOTISM: Helena F. Martin 390; James R. Anderson, *An Actor's Life* (London, 1902) 70. Macready reportedly told Anderson, "I must be a despot, or no manager."
13. Helena F. Martin 52. Macready's diaries show that rehearsals for *Lear* began three weeks before the first night of performance, but those for *Woman's Wit* only six days

before. During the next season, Bulwer's *Richelieu* was rehearsed over a period of a month or more.

14. Macready reports that Sheridan Knowles, in visiting a rehearsal of *Woman's Wit*, was "very much struck with the mode of putting the play upon the stage, drilling the actors, and teaching them their business" (*Diaries* I: 457-58).
15. Helena F. Martin 51, 296.
16. *Morning Post* 2 Oct. 1837; *Times* 2 Oct. The *Post*'s account is full of praise. *The Times* says that Macready's acting in the statue scene was "sometimes admirably natural, sometimes exaggerated to the last degree." Helena F. Martin (389-90) gives a detailed description of Macready's acting and her own response.
17. *Morning Post.* See also *The Times; Morning Chronicle* 2 Oct.; *John Bull* 1 Oct.; *Literary Gazette* 7 Oct.: 645. The *Spectator* (7 Oct.: 946), though unfavourable to Helen Faucit, said that if her "personation of the woman had been as real as that of the statue," it would have been a triumph indeed.
18. *Diaries of Macready* I: 436-38.
19. For a less positive view of Macready's "restoration" see Adele Seeff, "Charles Kean's *King Lear* and the Pageant of History," in *Shakespeare, Man of the Theatre*, ed. Kenneth Muir, Jay L. Halio, and D.J. Palmer (Newark, Del, 1983) 232-33.
20. PRAISE: *English Chronicle* 27 Jan. 1838: 43; *Court Journal* 27 Jan.: 58; *Atlas* 3 Feb.: 75; *Metropolitan Conservative Journal* 27 Jan.: 65. COMPLAINT OF INAUDIBILITY: *Literary Gazette* 27 Jan.: 59; *Sunday Times* 28 Jan.; *The Town* 3 Feb.: 287.
21. MACREADY'S PORTRAYAL: Anderson, *An Actor's Life* 75-76. HIS "VOW": *Diaries* I: 455.
22. *Bulwer and Macready* 71.
23. *Diaries* I: 443. Some of Bulwer's early suggestions for a title – "Nobility," "The Adventurer," "The Ambitious Lover," and simply "Melnotte" – indicate the direction of his original plan. See Shattuck 61, 65, 67, 68.
24. Shattuck, *Bulwer and Macready* 58, 60, 70.
25. Helena F. Martin 165.
26. Westland Marston, *Our Recent Actors* (London, 1890) 39; Helena F. Martin 50-51. Macready told Marston he had played *The Lady of Lyons* "to a serious loss" for the first two or three weeks. Actually, the author's identity was announced at the end of the second week, but the play had opened on a Thursday and was acted only three times in each week.
27. Victor Alexander George Robert Bulwer-Lytton, Second Earl of Lytton, *The Life of Edward Bulwer First Lord Lytton*, 2 vols. (London, 1913) I: 538-39.
28. In discussing the criticism I refer to reviews in *The Times* 16 Feb. 1838; *Morning Chronicle* 16 Feb.; *Morning Post* 16 Feb.; *Morning Herald* 16 Feb.; *Spectator* 17 Feb.: 160; *Examiner* 18 Feb.: 101; *Sunday Times* 18 Feb.; *Idler* 24 Feb.: 63.
29. Helena F. Martin 161-62. Helen Faucit wears such a costume in Myra Drummond's portrait of her as Pauline (Sir Theodore Martin opp. 50). Both M.S. [Martha Sara] Rolls and George Scharf sketched some of Macready's scenes; the former, focusing on characters, shows the costumes more clearly; the latter, offering broader views, gives more details of scenery. See George Rowell, "Another View of Macready," *Theatre Notebook* XLVIII, No. 2 [1994]: 63-76.) See the contrasting treatments of the "Prince of Como" scene: Scharf's, Plate 5 in Charles H. Shattuck, *Bulwer and Macready*; Rolls's, Plate 8 in Rowell's essay.

30. Helena F. Martin 162 (incl. note); also Sir Theodore Martin 59 (diary entry for 9 Jan. 1839 and note).
31. Diary entry for 2 Mar. 1868, quoted by Sir Theodore Martin 296. In speaking of love scenes I do not include the bashful, tentative love passages in *Ion* or expressions of love between husband and wife.
32. Helena F. Martin 161-62, 164. An unintentional "effect" in the cottage scene caused the actress some embarrassment (see 163-64). Carried away by the emotions of the scene, she tore her handkerchief to shreds without realizing it. The *Spectator* critic, thinking this an unworthy trick, sneeringly noted the "waste of muslin."
33. The most derogatory criticism of Helen Faucit's acting was in the *Sunday Times.*
34. *Morning Chronicle, Morning Herald.* For a detailed description of Helen Faucit's portrayal see the Afterpiece.
35. *An Actor's Life* 71-72.
36. My discussion of the criticism is based on reviews in *The Times* 24 May 1838; *Morning Post* 24 May; *Morning Chronicle* 24 May; *Morning Herald* 24 May; *Literary Gazette* 26 May: 351-52; *Examiner* 27 May: 325; *Athenaeum* 26 May: 379-80 ("most delightful"); *Idler* 26 May: 165; *Sunday Times* 27 May; *Spectator* 2 June: 510; *The Age*, as quoted in *Spirit of the Times* (New York), 23 June 1838: 145.
37. The sketch, along with nine others (mostly in sepia tones) showing scenes for *Woman's Wit*, are in Anderson's promptbook of the play, now in the HTC. They were probably copied from sketches of scenes used for Macready's production.
38. "Seven Decades of an Actor's Life," installment in the *Newcastle Weekly Chronicle* 5 Mar. 1887. Most of Anderson's discussion of *Woman's Wit* was reprinted in *An Actor's Life* (76) but not the passage referred to here. *Woman's Wit* was occasionally acted in the provinces and in America: for example, at the T.R. Liverpool in Aug. 1838, with Harriet Faucit as Hero, and, the same month, at the Park Theatre, New York, with Charlotte Cushman.
39. Anna Maria Hall, who considered Hero the "greatest" of Helen Faucit's "triumphs" thus far, wrote in a congratulatory note, dated 24 May 1838, that Carter, her husband, had been "surrounded by critics" at the theatre and "they were all delighted." (See Sir Theodore Martin 55.)
40. *Morning Post.* See also *Morning Chronicle.*
41. *Diaries of Macready* I: 457.
42. MACREADY'S ANNOUNCEMENT, CURTAIN CALLS: *Morning Herald* and *Morning Post.* HELEN'S RUDE BEHAVIOUR: *Diaries of Macready* I: 458. Macready reprimanded her the next day and she promised to apologize to Anderson.
43. The death certificate gives "decay of nature" as the cause of Mrs. Diddear's death. She was buried at the Church of St. Alphege, Greenwich. (information from the Parish Register, via Mr. J.V. Stacey). Mr. and Mrs. Diddear had been living in a house in Upper George St., Greenwich. (letter of 7 July 1978 from Mr. J. Watson, Local History Librarian, Greenwich).
44. *Diaries of Macready* I: 439-41, 448-49, 453-54; Thomas Noon Talfourd, *The Athenian Captive. A Tragedy. In Five Acts* (London, 1838) ix-x. The title page of Talfourd's play bears the information (which, like the cast, proved incorrect): "First acted at Covent Garden Theatre, April 28, 1838."
45. Alan Downer 177-78. Downer, who had evidently not seen the cast and preface in the play's first edition, assumed, inaccurately, that Helen Faucit had at first refused

the part of Ismene, which had then been given to Mrs. Warner (174-76). Sir Theodore Martin, who had seen this edition but did not know what had actually happened, assumed Helen Faucit had acted Creusa (54).

46. [Sydney Owenson, Lady Morgan], *Lady Morgan's Memoirs*, [ed. W. Hepworth Dixon], 2 vols. (London, 1862) II: 441.
47. Charles C.F. Greville, *The Greville Memoirs: A Journal of the Reigns of King George IV. King William IV. and Queen Victoria*, ed. Henry Reeve, new ed., 8 vols. (London, 1888), IV: 109.
48. DESCRIPTION OF SCARBOROUGH: Thomas Baines, *Yorkshire, Past and Present*, Vol. II, Pt. 2 (London, [1877]} 547-59. HORSEBACK RIDING: Sir Theodore Martin 58; also "Scarborough" in his Index.
49. *Diaries of Macready* I: 463, 465, 467.
50. *Diaries* I: 474-76 (events between 31 Oct. and 13 Nov. 1838).
51. *Diaries of Macready* I: 500 (entry of 5 Mar. 1839).
52. Helena F. Martin 160. Mrs. Siddons had also worn a long garment as a breeches costume; so had the American actress Nancy Hallam, but hers had an oriental look. See the frontispiece in Charles H. Shattuck's *Shakespeare on the American Stage: From the Hallams to Edwin Booth* (Washington, D.C., 1976).
53. *Diaries of Macready* I: 472 (Imogen); II: 4 (Rosalind).
54. *Diaries of Macready* I: 490. 491, 494-95; Shattuck 119. According to *The Life and Times of Frederick Reynolds. Written by Himself*, 2 vols. (London, 1846) II: 399, Eliza O'Neill (an idol of Macready's) had refused to act Imogen: "nothing could induce [her] to appear in boy's clothes."
55. James Laver, *Taste and Fashion* (New York, 1938) 53-54, 218. (Bathing costumes would become more daring by the 1870s.) C. Willett Cunnington and Phyllis Cunnington give a picture of a riding habit of the 1830s in *Handbook of English Costume in the Nineteenth Century*, 3rd ed. (London, 1970) 409.
56. See Tracy C. Davis, "The Actress in Victorian Pornography," *Theatre Journal* XLI (Oct. 1989): 294-315; also her *Actresses as Working Women* 105-8 et seq.
57. [Margaret Stokes, with contribution from Georgianne Colmache, ed by Theodore Martin], "Helen Faucit." *Blackwood's Edinburgh Magazine* CXXXVIII (Dec. 1885): 474 (costume); *Manchester Guardian* 17 Nov. 1871 (costume; also "daydream"); *Cork Examiner* 12 Aug. 1844 (poem referring to her "pleasing shapes" in boy's costume).
58. Statistics, exclusive of Helen Faucit's, are from Alan Downer 185.
59. SCENERY: *Morning Chronicle* 15 Oct. 1838; *Morning Post* 15 Oct.; *Athenaeum* 20 Oct.: 763-64. CHARACTERIZATION: *Morning Chronicle.* HELEN FAUCIT: Besides the *Post*, the *Idler* (20 Oct.: 18-19) deplores her affectation; the *Examiner* (21 Oct.) defends her.
60. Diary entry for 22 Jan. 1839, quoted by Sir Theodore Martin 61.
61. *Diaries of Macready* I: 496, 497, 499; *Morning Post* 9 Mar. 1839 (unusually even performance). See also Denis Salter, "A Picturesque Interpretation of History: William Charles Macready's *Richelieu*, 1839-1850," *When They Weren't Doing Shakespeare*, ed. Judith L. Fisher and Stephen Watt (Athens, Georgia, 1989) 39-63.
62. *Diaries of Macready* I: 498.
63. Shattuck, *Bulwer and Macready* 179-80.
64. *Our Recent Actors* 25-35.
65. GENERAL DESCRIPTIONS: *Morning Chronicle* 8 Mar. 1839; *Examiner* 10 Mar.: 150; *Spectator* 9 Mar.: 225. INSULTED VIRTUE: *Morning Post* 9 Mar. FILIAL AIR:

Times 8 Mar. For a detailed description of her performance on a later occasion, see "Miss Helen Faucit in *Richelieu*," *Theatrical Journal* 16 Jan. 1841: 17-19, 23 Jan. 1841: 25-26.

66. RA Queen Victoria's Journal, 9 Mar. 1839.
67. MS letter, E.L. Bulwer to Helen Faucit, dated 8 Mar. 1839; in extra-illustrated copy of Helena Faucit Martin's *On Some of Shakespeare's Female Characters* (following 206), NLS.
68. *Examiner* 16 Dec. 1838: 790 (rpt. from *Courier*).
69. Alfred Bunn, *The Stage* III: 117-19, 121-22.
70. RA Queen Victoria's Journal, 1 Feb. 1839.
71. Quoted from her Journal of 6 Mar. 1838, in George Rowell, *Queen Victoria Goes to the Theatre* 23.
72. Helena F. Martin 229-30.
73. Vandenhoff's Diary, Folger MS. W.a.z., entries for 18 Apr. [1839] and 6 May [1839].
74. Helena F. Martin 229-30.
75. Diary entry for 4 Jan. 1839, quoted by Sir Theodore Martin 58.
76. Henry Vizetelly, *Glances Back through Seventy Years*, 2 vols.(London, 1893) I: 305-6.
77. Rupert Gunnis, "Foley, John Henry, R.A.," *Dictionary of British Sculptors 1660-1851* (Cambridge, Mass., 1954) 153-54.
78. Christopher Wood, *Dictionary of Victorian Painters.* Antique Collectors Club (Woodbridge, Suffolk, c. 1971) 95; S.C. Hall, *Retrospect of a Long Life* II: 268-70. For "oldest professional friend" see M'Ian's letter to Helen Faucit, quoted by Sir Theodore Martin 102.
79. Diary entry for 1 Jan. 1839, quoted by Sir Theodore Martin 58.
80. Shattuck, *Bulwer and Macready* 129.
81. *Diaries of Macready* I: 509-11, II: 14.
82. MS letter of Helen Faucit to Macready, dated 15 July [1839], in Mander and Mitchenson.
83. *Diaries of Macready* I: 503, 507; II: 3, 4, 6, 9, 11.

Chapter 5

1. *Theatrical Journal* 17 July 1841: 230 (dimensions of theatres); *Diaries of Macready* II: 22 ("dog-hole"); Westland Marston, *Our Recent Actors* 154 (Webster).
2. MACREADY ON KEAN'S ENGAGEMENT: Diaries I: 507. ELLEN TREE'S AMERICAN SUCCESS: John William Cole, *The Life and Theatrical Times of Charles Kean*, F.S.A., 2 vols. (London, 1859) 1: 332-33.
3. *Diaries* II: 23-24. Six years earlier Macready had said Ellen Tree had "the *matériel* of the best actress on the stage" (*Diaries* I: 45).
4. DESCRIPTIONS: John Coleman, *Fifty Years of an Actor's Life*, 2 vols. (London, 1904) I: 188; Marston 151. LACK OF POWER: *Theatrical Journal* 1 Aug. 1850: 344-45; 30 Jan. 1851:[33].

5. FAVOURABLE: *Morning Chronicle* 20 Aug. 1839. UNFAVOURABLE: *Morning Herald* 20 Aug. (lacked pathos); *Satirist* 25 Aug.: 270 (scream).
6. Helena F. Martin 77. Fanny Kemble, who also gave an unusually spirited portrayal, remarked that most Desdemonas on the English stage "acquiesce with wonderful equanimity in their own deaths." See Frances Anne Kemble, *Records of Later Life* (New York, 1882) 630-31.
7. CARLYLE: Sir Theodore Martin 101; Helena F. Martin 77, note 1. ELTON: Helena F. Martin 50.
8. MS letter from Helen Faucit to Mrs. Hall, dated only "Saturday" (but possibly written on 26 Oct. 1839), opp. p. 14 in an extra-illustrated copy of Edwina Booth Grossmann's *Edwin Booth: Recollections by His Daughter … and Letters to Her and to His Friends* (New York, 1894), Folger W.b.511.
9. *Morning Herald* 1 Nov.1839. The *Era* (3 Nov.: 63) called Violet "the most stupid and silly heroine upon the stage" and said she would not be tolerated except in the hands of Helen Faucit.
10. *Diaries of Macready* II: 30 (1 Nov. 1839), 31 (18 Nov.).
11. *Diaries of Macready* II: 23 (25 Sept. 1839), 26 (12 Oct.).
12. *Diaries* II: 26 (7 and 9 Oct. 1839).
13. *Diaries of Macready* II: 31-33.
14. *Diaries* II: 32 (23 Nov. 1839), 34 (12 Dec.), 37-38 (26 and 28 Dec.).
15. *Diaries of Macready* II: 37-38 (28 and 30 Dec. 1839).
16. She also missed a brief engagement at Drury Lane, which Macready had arranged for her between the Haymarket's closing on 15 January 1840 and its reopening in mid-March. Fortunately so, for the manager, W.J. Hammond, got into difficulties and decamped, leaving the actors to their own devices. See *Diaries of Macready* II: 31, 36-37, 38; Downer, *Eminent Tragedian* 196.
17. These physicians' diagnoses were later published in the *Observer*, 15 Mar. 1840.
18. So far I rely mostly on Mark S. Micale, "A Short History of Hysteria," in his *Approaching Hysteria: Disease and Its Interpretations* (Princeton, 1995) 19-29 (see also "The Major Interpretive Traditions," 33-107). For my discussion as a whole, I use, in addition, Ilza Veith, *Hysteria: The History of a Disease* (Chicago, 1965) passim (Ch. 9 deals with the Victorian period); and Elaine Showalter, *The Female Malady: Women, Madness, and English Culture, 1830-1980* (New York, 1985) passim (esp. Ch. 5, but also much material in Chs. 2 and 3). Recent scholarship shows that Veith's book, previously considered the definitive work on hysteria, must be used with caution. See, for example, Sander Gilman et al. *Hysteria Beyond Freud* (Berkeley, 1993), especially the essays by Helen King and Roy Porter; also Micale 38-39. Even so, her substantial study offers much valuable information.
19. Veith 141, 143. On the other hand, Micale (24) tells of a "neuro-uterine model" favoured by gynecologists that located the "pathogenesis of hysteria" in diseases and irregularities of the reproductive system, carried through the body by the nerves.
20. Showalter 122-27. Ironically but not surprisingly, the most vehement arguments against "brain work" and higher education for women were published in the 1870s, just as opportunities were opening up for women.
21. SEXUAL REPRESSION: Veith 201; Showalter 131-32. SOCIAL CONSTRICTION: Showalter 56-57, 61-66, 131.

22. Shakespeare's King Lear, 2.3.56-58, experiencing this sensation and fighting to regain control of his surging emotions, figuratively exclaims, "O how this mother swells up toward my heart! / *Hysterica passio*, down, thou climbing sorrow,/ Thy element's below."
23. Sir Theodore Martin 142, quoting from a letter written by Helen Faucit on 13 Jan. 1845.
24. Letter of 26 Jan. 1990, from Professor Gerald N. Olsen, M.D., Director, Division of Pulmonary and Critical Care Medicine, Department of Medicine, University of South Carolina School of Medicine.
25. Letter of 16 Feb. 1990 from Professor Thomas McCullough, M.D.,of the Department of Neuropsychiatry and Behavioral Science, University of South Carolina School of Medicine. Dr. McCullough says that both he and Dr. Lebert Harris, a psychoanalyst in his department, reviewed the materials about Helen Faucit and were similarly struck by her losses as a young child.
26. *Scotch Reformer's Gazette* 4 May 1844 ("sensibility, vibrating"); *Manchester Advertiser and Chronicle* (nerves "vibrate").
27. *Diaries* II: 40.
28. *Diaries* II: 39 (1 Jan. 1840), 48 (3 Mar. 1840). He was chagrined to find that his name had been scandalously linked with Priscilla Horton's and Emmeline Montague's as well as with Helen Faucit's.
29. *Diaries* II: 40 (12 Jan. 1840).
30. For the riding-whip see the diary entry of 1 Jan. 1840, quoted by Sir Theodore Martin 58. The books were later donated by Sir Theodore to the Shakespeare Memorial Library (now Shakespeare Centre Library), Stratford-upon-Avon. They are copies of Knowles's *Love* (inscribed "To my most dear Helen from her affectionate and true Friend – E.B. Decr 7 – 1839"), Bulwer's *The Sea-Captain* (inscribed "To my dearest Helen from her affectionate and steady friend Ellen Braysher April 30th – 1840"), and Bulwer's *The Duchess de la Vallière* (perhaps an earlier gift – there is no inscription, but its similar binding and decorations indicate the same donor).
31. RA Z 507/32 – MS letter from Ellen Drew Braysher to Mrs. Theodore Martin, congratulating her on her husband's completion of his biography of Prince Albert.
32. Letter dated only "Friday Evening" but certainly written in 1858, quoted by Sir Theodore Martin 255-56.
33. Showalter 139-44.
34. Helena F. Martin 53.
35. Helena F. Martin 52-53. Sir Theodore Martin (71) quotes most of Macready's letter of 3 April [1840] telling Helen Faucit how sorely she is missed. The original letter, whose derogatory references to other actresses are omitted by Martin, is inserted in the extra-illustrated copy of Lady Martin's book, NLS MS. 16443.
36. From a letter of 26 Mar. 1840, quoted by Sir Theodore Martin 70.
37. *Diaries* II: 51-52 (12 Mar. 1840).
38. *Diaries of Macready* II: 44 (4 Feb. 1840), 48 (3 Mar.), 49 (4 and 7 Mar.).
39. Sir Theodore Martin 70 (see Macready's reference to horseback riding in his letter); *Diaries of Macready* II: 55 (1 Apr. 1840), 56 (11 Apr.).
40. *Morning Chronicle* 27 Apr. 1840; *Observer* 26 Apr. 1840.
41. *Diaries* II: 63 (26 May 1840), 64 (2 June).
42. *Diaries of Macready* II: 66 (26 June 1840), 67 (2 July), 68-69 (9 and 10 July), 70-71 (11 and 16 July).

43. Macready tells of an essay and a two-hour lecture (at Mrs. Braysher's house) in *Diaries* II: 70 (13 and 15 July 1840).
44. These principles are nos. 1, 2, 4, and 7 in a list of nine rules of good acting, headed "Remember," which Sir Theodore Martin found among his wife's papers after her death. (See *Helena Faucit* 75-76). They were written in her hand and dated 20 Apr.1840 (shortly before she returned to the stage after her illness). The last two rules on the list, which emphasize precise articulation, sound like Percy Farren's instructions; the rest are very much in line with Macready's ideas and practices, though at least two would have been approved by Charles Kemble as well. Christopher Murray argues in "Macready, Helen Faucit, and Acting Style," *Theatre Notebook* XXIII (1968): 21-25, that the list is the one Macready drew up for Helen to study while at Hastings (see *Diaries* II: 40). I believe it is based largely on that list but may include precepts from earlier mentors.
45. *Diaries* II: 73 (12 Aug. 1840).
46. M'IAN'S FANATICISM: S.C. Hall, *Retrospect of a Long Life* II: 269. HELP WITH COSTUMES: *Diaries of Macready* II: 60.
47. DISLIKE OF THE ROLE: Sir Theodore Martin 77. PRAISE OF HER ACTING: *Morning Post*, 25 May 1840; *Morning Chronicle*, 25 May; *Examiner*, 31 May: 341; *Literary Gazette*, 6 June: 365.
48. FAVOURABLE TO PERFORMANCE BUT NOT TO ROLE: *Literary Gazette*, 3 Oct. 1840: 645; *Morning Chronicle*, 28 Sept. FAVOURABLE TO BOTH: *Observer*, 27 Sept.; *Examiner*, 4 Oct.: 629; *Era*, 4 Oct. UNFAVOURABLE TO PERFORMANCE: *Athenaeum*, 3 Oct.: 781-82; *Morning Herald*, 28 Sept.; *Satirist*, 4 Oct.: 314; *Sunday Times*, 27 Sept. ("robustly rejoiceful").
49. For Macready's work on the production see Charles H. Shattuck, ed. *Bulwer and Macready* 150-87, passim.
50. Bulwer wrote to a friend, "It is so common for a young woman of a generous and romantic temper to think there is something very noble in an imprudent marriage, that I wished to show that there were two sides to think of." Quoted by Victor A.G.R. Bulwer-Lytton I: 553.
51. According to Lester Wallack, in *Memories of Fifty Years* (New York, 1889) 124, Macready described his character, Alfred Evelyn, as a "damned walking gentleman."
52. Letter of Dickens to Bulwer, 12 Dec. 1840, published in Victor A.G.R. Bulwer-Lytton's *Life of Edward Bulwer* I: 554.
53. 12 Dec. 1840: 803-804. OTHER PRAISE OF *MONEY*: *Morning Chronicle*, 9 Dec. and *Observer*, 13 Dec. ADVERSE COMMENTS: *Morning Post*, 9 Dec.; *Athenaeum*, 12 Dec.: 993; *Bell's Life in London*, 13 Dec.; *Satirist*, 13 Dec.: 304; *Sunday Times*, 13 Dec.
54. Wallack 123-24. Oddly enough, one of the most amusing scenes in the play, well acted by Benjamin Webster and Mrs. Glover, was hissed; later it was much appreciated. Westland Marston (160) describes Webster's performance.
55. *Theatrical Journal*, 9 Jan. 1841: 13 (doggerel verse).
56. Marie and Squire Bancroft, *The Bancrofts* (New York, 1909) 126-34; Shattuck, *Bulwer and Macready* 184; J.S. Bratton, "Down to Brass Tacks," *TLS*, 27 Nov. 1981: 1403 (review of the RSC production, which also includes an interesting discussion of the play).
57. *Spectator* 12 Dec. 1840: 1187-88; *Morning Herald* 9 Dec. See also *Morning Chronicle* 9 Dec.; *Athenaeum* 12 Dec.: 993; *Times* 9 Dec.

58. *Spectator* 23 Jan. 1841: 82. MACREADY'S COMMENT: *Diaries* II: 114 (7 Jan. 1841).
59. Downer, *Eminent Tragedian* 203; *Diaries of Macready* II: 108, 111.
60. *Diaries of Macready* II: 92 (28 Oct. 1840), 128 (16 Mar. 1841); MS letter of Helen Faucit to Macready, dated 19 Mar. [obviously 1841], in Mander and Mitchenson. Although she mentions her brother without naming him, it was most likely John. He had been acting at the Adelphi for two seasons, and he made his last appearances there in the week of 22 March 1841; he would be at the Strand in May and early June. The period between his engagements coincides with much of Helen's vacation from the Haymarket.
61. Sir Theodore Martin 80 ("best society"), 80-81 (Rachel).
62. Marvin Carlson, *The French Stage in the Nineteenth Century* (Metuchen, N.J., 1972) 96-98.
63. Rees Howell Gronow, *Reminiscences and Recollections of Captain Gronow*, abridged, introd. John Raymond (New York, 1964) 161; Sir Theodore Martin 81.
64. Sir Theodore Martin 80, 143. The undated letter was written to Martin himself shortly after Helen's second visit to the Louvre, on Christmas day, 1844.
65. Description in the *Sunday Times* 18 Apr. 1841.
66. *Diaries of Macready* II: 135 (9 May 1841); Bernard Falk, *Rachel the Immortal* (London, n.d.) 93-94 (quotation from *Satirist*), 159 (thimble). Falk got the information about the thimble directly from Mme. de Navarro (Mary Anderson). According to him, Rachel also gave Helen Faucit, on some occasion, a "cast of her hand, taken as she grasped 'Roxane's' dagger."
67. *Athenaeum* 22 May 1841: 412, 17 July: 542; *Examiner* 30 May: 340, 17 July: 454.
68. *Diaries of Macready* II: 485-86 (10 Jan. 1851). Mrs. Warner reported to Macready that Helen Faucit had told the Foleys he had "stopped the run of *Nina Sforza*." He did stop the run by leaving the Haymarket, but his managerial plans required this. Her resentment suggests that she had expected the "run" to be resumed at Drury Lane.
69. The phrase is from a telegram that Lady Martin sent to William Blackwood (undated, but probably late in 1881), verifying a reference she had made to Zouch Troughton in the first part of her two-part essay on Juliet (MS. 4423, f. 188, NLS).
70. CRITICISM OF PLAY AND PRODUCTION: Reviews in *Times* 2 Nov. 1841; *Morning Post* 2 Nov.; *Morning Herald* 2 Nov.; *Morning Chronicle* 2 Nov.; *Examiner* 6 Nov.: 710; *Athenaeum* 6 Nov.: 860; *Spectator* 6 Nov.: 1072; *Theatrical Journal* 6 Nov.: 355; *Bell's Life in London* 7 Nov. SHAKESPEAREAN ELEMENTS: *Times; Athenaeum; Morning Chronicle.* MACREADY'S SPINOLA AS SERPENT: *Examiner; Athenaeum.*
71. *Athenaeum.* See also Westland Marston 67-68.
72. RECUPERATIVE HOLIDAY: Ellen Braysher's letter to "My dear Sir" (obviously Webster), dated 5 Sept. 1841, tells of Helen Faucit's illness and her plan to go to the seashore (Folger MS. 116.Y.c.417 1). Dr. Babington's certificate of the same date, which originally accompanied the letter, is now in the HTC. J.F. SAVILLE, JR.'S BRIGHTON MANAGEMENT: Kathleen Barker, "The Decline and Rise of the Brighton Theatre": 35. BLANDS AT COVENT GARDEN: Carol J. Carlisle, "The Other Miss Faucit" 79.
73. *Diaries* II: 108 (9 Dec. 1840 – Helen Faucit's terms at Haymarket), 136 (15 May 1841 – Macready's agreement to the same terms).

Chapter 6

1. Advertisements in the *Brighton Herald* on 15 Jan. and 29 Jan. 1842 announced, respectively, that she would appear on the 18th and the 31st.; she did not act here, however, until 22 and 24 March. (J.F. Saville had closed his theatre on 17 Mar. but reopened it for her.) See review in the *Herald*, 26 Mar. 1842.
2. "Police Intelligence," *Brighton Herald* 22 Jan. 1842; *Examiner* (London) 22 Jan. 1842: 51. See also "Church Rates," *A Dictionary of English Church History*, ed. S.L. Ollard, Gordon Crosse, and Maurice F. Bond, 3rd ed., rev. (London, 1948) 118-19.
3. Raymond Mander and Joe Mitchenson, *The Theatres of London* (London, 1963) 67-68; Downer 209. According to Downer, the management had no legal right to refuse money at the door, but Macready made the situation so unpleasant for prostitutes that he virtually excluded them.
4. *Diaries of Macready* II: 113 (29 Dec. 1840), 114-15 (8 and 9 Jan. 1841), 130 (26 Mar. 1841); letter of Macready to Serle, 26 Mar. 1841, Folger MS. Y.c.411. (160).
5. *Theatrical Journal* 29 Jan. 1842: 33. The role, new to Helen Faucit, was Bertha in Charles Kemble's *The Point of Honour*. In the event, she never acted it; her replacement, Miss Ellis, retained it.
6. *Theatrical Journal* (19 Feb. 1842: 59).
7. *Sunday Times*, 27 Feb. 1842; *Morning Herald*, 24 February. See also *Theatrical Journal* 5 Mar. 1842: 75.
8. PRODUCTION AND AUDIENCE RESPONSE: *Times* 21 Apr. 1842 (audience gleeful in murder scene); *Morning Herald* 21 Apr.; *Sunday Times* 24 Apr. (satirical account of everything); James R. Anderson, *An Actor's Life* 111 (ludicrous account of the murder scene, which should be taken with a grain of salt). HELEN FAUCIT'S ACTING: *Sunday Times; Morning Post* 21 Apr.(commiserates with her in the "agony of giving embodiment to the outrageous conceptions").
9. See *Diaries of Macready* II: 171-72.
10. CALCRAFT'S HELP: Letter of Helen Faucit to Mrs. Hall, 18 May 1842, Folger MS. Y.c.902.(8). MRS. HATTON: Sir Theodore Martin 89.
11. Maurice Craig, *Dublin 1660-1860* (London, 1952) 298; G.N. Wright, *An Historical Guide to the City of Dublin*, 2nd ed. (London, 1825) 147. The quotation is from the latter, which also has an engraving of the Theatre Royal. For descriptions of Trinity College and the Bank of Ireland, see David Alfred Chart's *The Story of Dublin*, rev. ed. (London, 1932) 158-63, 167, opp. 174 (picture of the Bank).
12. "Characters of Shakespeare's Plays," *Complete Works of William Hazlitt*, Centenary Edition, ed. P.P. Howe, 21 vols. (London, 1930-34) IV: 188-90.
13. Helena F. Martin 230. Six years earlier she had refused Osbaldiston's request that she act Lady Macbeth to Macready's Macbeth. She wrote in her diary (8 May 1836): "I always look upon that part as hallowed ground, upon which I dare not tread. I must have a great deal more confidence than I now have, if I ever attempt it." Quoted by Sir Theodore Martin 36.

14. *Diaries of Macready* II: 172, 174; Helena F. Martin 230-31.
15. Helena F. Martin 231.
16. Helena F. Martin 231. Sir Theodore Martin (90) names the "friend" as Mrs. Hutton.
17. *Diaries of Macready* II: 173-75.
18. *Diaries* II: 176 (22 June 1842).
19. Sir Theodore Martin 91 and index entry for "Scarborough"; Register of Baptisms, Brighthelmston Parish, 1840-1851, Public Record Office, Lewes, PAR 255/1/2/12a.
20. The Drury Lane statistics are from Alan Downer's *The Eminent Tragedian* 224.
21. Juliet Creed, Lady Pollock, *Macready as I Knew Him* (London, 1884) 20-22.
22. *Athenaeum* 8 Oct. 1842: 876; *Theatrical Journal* 8 Oct.: 321-23. For a study of the whole production see Charles H. Shattuck, *Mr. Macready Produces AS YOU LIKE IT* (Urbana, Ill., 1962).
23. *Theatrical Journal* 24 Sept. 1842: 307.
24. *Diaries of Macready* II: 73 (12 Aug. 1840), 77 (2 Sept. 1840). For his admiration of Mrs. Jordan see *Macready's Reminiscences* I: 62-63.
25. Lady Pollock 21-22.
26. *Mr. Macready Produces AS YOU LIKE IT* 55-57.
27. See Charles H. Shattuck, *William Charles Macready's "King John"* (Urbana, 1962) 11-12, 17-30.
28. My discussion is based on reviews in the following journals: *Times* 25 Oct. 1842; *Morning Herald* 25 Oct.; *Morning Advertiser* 25 Oct.; *Morning Chronicle* 26 Oct.; *Evening Star* 29 Oct.: 346; *British Statesman* 27 Oct.; *Court Journal* 29 Oct.: 793; *Athenaeum* 29 Oct.: 933; *Examiner* 29 Oct.: 693; *Spectator* 29 Oct.: 1046; *Theatrical Journal* 29 Oct.: 346; *John Bull* 29 Oct.: 524-25; *Weekly Chronicle* 29 Oct.: 5; *Conservative Journal* 29 Oct.: 8; *Literary Gazette* 29 Oct.: 749; *Court Gazette* 29 Oct.: 1572; *Argus* 29 Oct.: 11; *Bell's Weekly Message* 29 Oct.: 353; *Era* 30 Oct.; *The Age* 30 Oct.; *Bell's Life in London* 30 Oct.; *The Satirist* 30 Oct.: 350; *The Planet* 30 Oct.: 5.
29. *Morning Post, John Bull, Spectator, Satirist, Bell's Weekly Message.* Bell's said that the character itself was unsympathetic.
30. *Era, Weekly Chronicle, Morning Advertiser.* See also the praise for Miss Faucit's tender and pathetic passages in *Court Journal, Conservative Journal,* and *Morning Herald.*
31. See *Britannia* 29 Oct. 1842: 719.
32. *Diaries of Macready* II: 186 (24 and 25 Oct. 1842).
33. "Female Characters in 'King John.' Present Acting of the Lady Constance ...," *Athenaeum* 18 Feb. 1843: 161-63; later republished in *Studies of Shakespeare* (London, 1847) 27-35.
34. Extract, "In the Pit of a Theatre," from an unnamed book or journal, 282-87, pasted in a volume of reviews of Helena Faucit, Lady Martin's *On Some of Shakespeare's Female Characters*, NLS MS. 16442.
35. Henry Turner, "Recollections of Ryder," *The Theatre* 1 May 1885: 224. For a more detailed description of Helen Faucit's Constance see Carol J. Carlisle, "Constance: A Theatrical Trinity," *King John: New Perspectives*, ed. Deborah Curren-Aquino (Newark, London and Toronto, c. 1989) 149-54.
36. Sir Theodore Martin 92-93. Helen Faucit and Fletcher actually became acquainted earlier than Martin reports here, however.
37. *Diaries of Macready* II: 128.

38. See Carol J. Carlisle, " Macready's Production of *Cymbeline," Shakespeare on the Victorian Stage*, ed. Richard Foulkes (Cambridge, 1986) 138-52. *Times* (23 Jan. 1843) and *Spectator* (28 Jan.: 81) are especially good on the banquet scene and Macready's acting. For comments on the various performances see, in addition, *Observer* 22 Jan.; *Morning Chronicle* 23 Jan.; *Morning Post* 23 Jan.; *Morning Herald* 23 Jan.; *Athenaeum* 28 Jan.: 92; *Literary Gazette* 28 Jan.: 59; *Theatrical Journal* 4 Feb.: 34; also the final portion of George Fletcher's four-part essay "Characters in *Cymbeline*," in the *Athenaeum* 15 Apr. 1843: 366-68 (republished in *Studies of Shakespeare* 95-108).
39. *Times, Morning Chronicle, Literary Gazette, Observer, Theatrical Journal.*
40. *Diaries of Macready* II: 202-4 (7, 12, 14, 16, 17, 18 Apr. 1843). The playbill for 19 Apr. 1843 advertises *Othello* for that night, with Helen Faucit as Desdemona, but a copy of this bill in the Shakespeare Library, Central Reference Library, Birmingham, has a handwritten note saying that Hamlet was substituted because of Helen Faucit's illness.
41. Quoted by Sir Theodore Martin 109.
42. *Diaries of Macready* II: 206-7 (5 and 8 May 1843).
43. MACREADY'S *LOVE FOR LOVE*: Alan S. Downer, "Mr. Congreve Comes to Judgment," *Humanities Association Bulletin* XXVII, No. 2 (Autumn 1966): 5-12. HELEN FAUCIT'S ANGELICA: *Times* 21 Nov. 1842; *Morning Post* 21 Nov.; *Examiner* 26 Nov.: 758; *Spectator* 26 Nov.: 1142; *Observer* 20 Nov.; *Morning Herald* 21 Nov. The part for which Helen gave up Angelica was Lady Mabel in *The Patrician's Daughter.*
44. The *Sunday Times* (26 Feb. 1843) estimated that there were 150 bacchanals. For a study of the whole production see Charles H. Shattuck, "Macready's *Comus*: A Prompt-Book Study," *Milton Studies in Honor of Harris Francis Fletcher*, ed. G. Blakemore Evans et al. (Urbana, 1961) 731-48.
45. Helena F. Martin 329-30.
46. See Macready's letter to Lady Pollock, 20 June 1856, published in *Macready's Reminiscences* II: 441.
47. Helena F. Martin 330-31.
48. *Examiner* 25 Feb. 1843: 118; *Times* 25 Feb.; *Sunday Times* 26 Feb.; *Theatrical Journal* 4 Mar.: 65. *The Morning Post* (25 Feb.) said, however, that the scene was overdone.
49. Quoted by George Henry Lewes, in "Article IV," *Westminster Review* XXXVII (Jan.-Apr. 1842): 340. The statement is said to be in Marston's preface to the first edition of *The Patrician's Daughter* (London, 1841). The first edition is not available to me. Although both of the editions I have seen (second, 1842, and third, 1843) include the "Preface to the First Edition," both omit the statement about the conflict between aristocratic and democratic pride. It was later repeated, however, in Marston's *Dramatic and Poetical Works*, 1876.
50. CRITIQUES OF THE PLAY: *Times* 8 Nov. 1841 (highly favourable); G.H. Lewes's review, cited in n. 49 (adverse but very interesting). THE PLAY AS TRAGEDY: Carol J. Carlisle, "Lofty Tragedy for Mundane Audiences: John Westland Marston's *The Patrician's Daughter* and *Stathmore," When They Weren't Doing Shakespeare* 152-62; Fred C. Thompson, "A Crisis in Early Victorian Drama: John Westland Marston and the Syncretics," *Victorian Studies* 9 (1966): 375-98. REVIEWS OF THE PRODUCTION: *Observer* 11 Dec. 1842; *Times* 12 Dec.; *Morning Chronicle* 12 Dec.; *Morning Post* 12 Dec.; *Morning Herald* 12 Dec.; *Spectator* 17 Dec.: 1209; *Examiner* 17 Dec.: 806; *Athenaeum* 17 Dec.: 1091-92; *Literary Gazette* 17 Dec.: 866-67; *Illustrated*

London News 17 Dec.: 512; *Theatrical Chronicle* 3, No. 36 (17 Dec. 1842): 274; *Bell's Life in London* 18 Dec.; *Theatrical Journal* 24 Dec.: 410.

51. *Morning Chronicle* (charm); *Athenaeum* (vivacity); *Morning Herald* (renunciation scene); *Times* ("shattered frame"); *Theatrical Chronicle* ("painfully thrilling"); *Examiner* (the best of her original characters); *Theatrical Journal* 24 Dec. (one of her most effective roles).
52. They resumed their friendly relationship when Macready wrote a letter of consolation to Browning after Mrs. Browning's death. Browning's cordial letter in reply, dated 18 July 1861, is in the BL, Ashley MS. A.2547.
53. Letter to Alfred Domett, written in May 1843, quoted by W. Hall Griffin and Harry Christopher Minchin, in *The Life of Robert Browning* (New York, 1912) 116-18.
54. Helena F. Martin 50-51, 395; Griffin and Minchin 118.
55. My discussion of the play and its production is based on reviews in the *Observer* 12 Feb. 1842; *Times* 13 Feb.; *Morning Post* 13 Feb.; G.H. Lewes, "Poetry and the Drama," *Westminster Review* XXXIX, Pt. 2 (Feb.-May 1843): 603-4; *Examiner* 18 Feb.; *Spectator* 18 Feb.: 160; *Literary Gazette* 18 Feb.: 107-8; *Theatrical Journal* 18 Feb.: 51.
56. *Diaries of Macready* II: 196 (11 Feb. 1843).
57. *Our Recent Actors* 199-200. Marston's admiration was not inspired solely by Phelps's 1843 performance, however. Phelps revived *Blot* at Sadler's Wells in the 1848-49 season for eight performances. See Shirley S. Allen, *Samuel Phelps and the Sadler's Wells Theatre* (Middleton, Conn., 1971) 279-80.
58. Quotations are from the *Literary Gazette* (confession scene) and the *Morning Post* (final scene).
59. *Diaries of Macready* II: 204 (22 Apr. 1843).
60. This doctrine was advocated in advice books for women, like Dr. John Gregory's *A Father's Legacy to His Daughters* (first published in 1774) and Mrs. Sarah Ellis's *The Daughters of England* (1843); it was also reflected in 19th-century novels, from Jane Austen's *Sense and Sensibility* (1811) to Anthony Trollope's *The Small House at Allington* (1864). For a real-life illustration see Duncan Crow, *The Victorian Woman* (London, 1971) 38-39.
61. 25 Apr. 1843. See also *Morning Herald* 25 Apr.
62. *Atlas* review, quoted by Sir Theodore Martin 110; *Examiner* 29 Apr. 1843: 262; *Bell's Life in London* 30 Apr.
63. *Diaries of Macready* II: 208 (18 May 1843); Sir Theodore Martin 112, note 1.
64. The *Examiner* deplored Helen Faucit's tendency, "perhaps unconsciously," to imitate Rachel, and the *Sunday Times* spoke truculently of her "Parisian action." But the *Theatrical Journal* praised her as "the English Rachel, imperial in high genius."
65. "Shakespeare's Female Characters and Their Present Representatives on the Stage," *Athenaeum* 4 Feb. 1843: 111. Fletcher's chief point is that only an actress with a "great variety of powers" could do justice to Shakespeare's complex, often idealized heroines. See also his "Characters in 'As You Like It' – III," *Athenaeum* 27 July 1844: 697.
66. *Theatrical Journal* 17 June 1843: 185-87; *Illustrated London News* 17 June: 421-22.
67. RA Queen Victoria's Journal – 12 June 1843.
68. Helena F. Martin 94-95. Despite Helen Faucit's difficulty in memorizing her speech, she evidently spoke it very effectively. See Julia Ward Howe, *Reminiscences 1819-1899* (Boston, 1899) 104.

69. *Diaries of Macready* II: 208 (25 May 1843), 209 (28 May), 210 (1 and 2 June); Downer, *The Eminent Tragedian* 253.

Chapter 7

1 Helena F. Martin 95.

2 Her letter to "My dear Sir," dated 10 July 1843, Folger MS. Y.c.902.(1), is a first response to the Drury Lane proposal, doubtful but inquiring about salary. For other offers see Helena F. Martin 95-96.

3 *An Actor's Life* 118.

4 *Evening Packet*, 4 July 1843; *World*, 8 July. According to testimony at the inquest, the man, Sillery, though always violent-tempered, had never been considered deranged; it was suggested that the "love powders" he had recently bought contained some drug that set him off.

5 "Seven Decades of an Actor's Life," serial instalment of 9 Apr. 1887 in the *Newcastle Chronicle* (not included in *An Actor's Life*).

6 T. G. Wilson, *Victorian Doctor, Being the Life of Sir William Wilde* (New York, 1946) 16; Patrick Byrne, *The Wildes of Merrion Square* (London and New York, 1953) 27-36 et passim.

7 *Midland Counties Herald, Birmingham and General Advertiser* 27 July 1843; Anderson, *An Actor's Life* 119.

8 *Bristol Times and Bath Advocate* 2 Sept. 1843.

9 *Brighton Herald* 23 Sept. 1843.

10 *Theatrical Journal* 28 Oct. 1843: 342-43 (Farren) and 4 Nov. 1843: 352 (Helen Faucit).

11 "Chit Chat," *Theatrical Journal* 4 Nov. 1843: 352. According to the Birmingham correspondent for this journal (11 Nov. 1843), Helen Faucit had created a "sensation" in *The Wife* – a difficult feat for any actress.

12 The address on St. David St. appears in several of Helen Faucit's letters. My observations about this part of Edinburgh are based on personal visits. For a description of the Calton Hill and its structures (all of which were completed before Helen Faucit's first visit) see A. J. Youngson's *The Making of Classical Edinburgh* (Edinburgh, [1967]) 158-60.

13 For a good picture of the theatre see John Britton's *Modern Athens Displayed in a Series of Views ... from Original Drawings by Thomas Shepherd ...* (1831; rpt. New York, 1969) opp. 70. For descriptions see Robert Chambers, *Walks in Edinburgh*, 2nd ed. (Edinburgh, 1829) 28, and Youngson 249-50. "Mephistopheles," in a letter to the *Caledonian Mercury* 21 Dec. 1843, mentions 1200 spectators, a considerable increase over the theatre's capacity in the 1770s (see Youngson 250).

14 John Coleman, *Fifty Years of an Actor's Life*, 2 vols. (London: Hutchinson, 1904) I: 24, 193, 201 (descriptions of Sullivan, Glover, and Lloyd); Helena F. Martin 96, 284-85 (tributes to Murray's acting).

15 Helena F. Martin (96) says she had a "sufficiently cold reception from a house far from full." Edinburgh audiences were notoriously unresponsive. See *Diaries of Macready* I: 22. For applause see *Edinburgh Observer* 17 Nov. 1843.

16 Helena F. Martin 96; *Edinburgh Observer* 24 Nov. 1843.

17 *Caledonian Mercury* 27 Nov. 1843.

18 The quotations come, respectively, from *The Scotsman* 18 Nov. 1843; the *Evening Post*, excerpt reprinted in the T. R. Edinburgh playbill for 21 Nov.; and the *Edinburgh Observer* 28 Nov.

19 Sir Theodore Martin 120.

20 1 Dec. 1843. The article published on 28 Nov. also emphasised the audience's involvement in Helen Faucit's last two scenes, whose "awful truth" caused a "choking and higging at the heart." Sir Theodore Martin, 122-23, quotes a long passage from this review but omits some figurative language and changes the Scottish word "higging" to "tugging."

21 NLS, MS. 590, No. 1589 (Watson Coll.). The signature, "Helena Faucit," is the one used for personal rather than professional letters at this time. In earlier years she had signed all her letters "Helen Faucit," but after leaving London, she generally used "Helena" except professionally and in writing to old friends.

22 The *Theatrical Journal*, whose provincial news was rarely up-to-date, reported (16 Dec. 1843: 399) that Helen Faucit's illness had prevented her playing at Glasgow for "upwards of a week" (evidently between 5 Dec., when she finished her Edinburgh engagement and 11 Dec. when she began acting at Glasgow).

23 Sir Theodore Martin 117. The original letter from Dickens, which Martin later bought at a sale at Sotheby's, is now in an extra-illustrated copy of Lady Martin's *On Some of Shakespeare's Female Characters* in the NLS, MS. 16443, between p. 160 and p. 161.

24 David and Francina Irwin, *Scottish Painters* (London, 1975) 204-13.

25 Sir Theodore Martin 117.

26 Rosalie Orme Masson, "William Edmonstoune Aytoun," in *Pollok and Aytoun*. Famous Scots Series (Edinburgh, 1898) 110. (Mrs. David Ogilvy [née Dick] tells of charades in reminiscences she contributed.) See also Theodore Martin, *Memoir of William Edmonstoune Aytoun* (Edinburgh, 1867).

27 "Martin, Sir Theodore," *DNB* Second Supplement (1912). My description of Martin is based on a large collection of his correspondence in the NLS, letters in other collections (published and unpublished), articles that he published anonymously, statements about him in memoirs of people who knew him, and several portraits and photographs.

28 The Writers to the Signet derived their title from their exclusive right of signing writs of summons and arrestment, which were "expedited through their hands from the signet of the king[or, at this time, the queen], who, in the Scottish supreme courts, is supposed to be the chief moving cause and instigator of all the proceedings." See Chambers 103-6.

29 Sir Theodore Martin 119.

30 [John G. Lockhart], *Peter's Letters to His Kinsfolk*, 2nd ed.(Edinburgh, 1819) III: 147-48, 150-51. "Peter Morris" is Lockhart's fictitious letter-writer, but he describes actual places and conditions.

31 Sir Archibald Alison. *Some Account of My Life and Writings* I: 344-48, 357-59.

32 "Alison, Sir Archibald," *DNB* (1885); Alison I: 294-336.

33 Alison I: 342-43 (Possil House), 531 (meeting Helen); Alison's letter to Helen Faucit, dated 5 Apr. 1848 (copy made by Theodore Martin), NLS, MS. 16444, f. 80 ("lambs playing round the trees").

34 THE THEATRE: Robb Lawson, *The Story of the Scots Stage* (Paisley, 1917) 199-201, 231; Walter Baynham, *The Glasgow Stage* (Glasgow, 1892) 120, 195. ALEXANDER: Baynham 168. BAD ACTING: Baynham 124; James R. Anderson, "Theatrical Eng[agements] & Memda"(MS in the HTC) entry for Glasgow engagement beginning 18 Dec. 1848.

35 ROMEO: Baynham 150-52 (story repeated by various other writers). "Lilt": Coleman I: 231-32. VEGETABLE SHOWER: *Theatrical Observer and Daily bills of the Play* 15 May 1844, rpt. from the *Glasgow Argus; Glasgow Constitutional* 8 May 1844 (mentions Alexander's "dastardly reception" without giving details).

36 Coleman I: 241-43. I think we can trust Coleman's physical description, but his stories about the lengths to which Paumier would go to punish rudeness sound like exaggeration at best. My comments on Paumier's acting are based on many reviews, both in Glasgow and elsewhere. There was considerable disagreement about it.

37 Letter to the editor, signed "Mephistopheles," *Caledonian Mercury* 21 Dec. 1843. (Although Helen Faucit is not named, the reference is obviously to her). The clergyman, named Begg, had denounced the theatre during a religious meeting and had been cheered by his colleagues.

38 Quoted by Sir Theodore Martin 371.

39 Sir Theodore Martin 126.

40 See, for example, the passage beginning "The rich thrilling notes of her voice," quoted by Sir Theodore Martin (125) from an unnamed Glasgow journal.

41 "The British Stage," in *Essays, Political, Historical and Miscellaneous*, 3 vols.(Edinburgh, 1850) III: 585. The essay was originally published in two parts in the *Dublin University Magazine* Nov. and Dec. 1846. Besides giving his own description, Alison quotes a passage from Chateaubriand's *The Martyrs* describing the lovely Cymodoce, priestess of the Muses, and says that "what genius has ascribed to ideal beauty" can be "truly applied" to Helen Faucit.

42 See especially the review of her second performance of Juliet, *Glasgow Herald* 18 Dec. 1843.

43 Sir Theodore Martin 127-28.

44 *Theatrical Journal* 6 Jan. 1844: 6 ("Glasgow"), 13 Jan. 1844: 15 ("Chit Chat"); Baynham 134.

45 Harold Oswald, *The Theatres Royal in Newcastle upon Tyne Tyne* (Newcastle-upon-Tyne, 1936) 84-87.

46 "Armstrong of Cragside," *The Complete Peerage of England, Scotland, Ireland , Great Britain and the United Kingdom ... by G[eorge] E[dward] C[okayne]*, new ed., rev. and enl.,ed. the Hon. Vicary Gibbs (London, 1910-59) I: 218-19. Cragside was the country estate. Helen Faucit visited the Armstrongs at Jesmond Dene, near Newcastle (Sir Theodore Martin 201).

47 MS in the HTC.

48 Sir Theodore Martin 128-129.

49 *Caledonian Mercury* 7 Mar. 1844.

50 Folger promptbook CYMB 2 (Shattuck, Cymbeline No. 14). Prof. Shattuck's guess that the promptbook was used in Helen Faucit's touring days in the 1840s and 50s is surely right. Its cuts differ considerably from those in the text used for Macready's

Drury Lane productions (see Folger Promptbook CYMB 17 [Shattuck No. 10]). Helen Faucit's performances of Imogen at Edinburgh on 7 and 16 Mar. 1844 were her first since leaving Drury Lane

51 Another rival, "R.M.," wooed Helen with a poem learnedly referring to "Siene's well" and "Eratosthenes." On the back of the poem is a note, dated 4 Feb. 1849, expressing R.M.'s hope that he has convinced Miss Faucit of his sincerity and that he has outstripped his "competitors" in winning her "good will." See NLS MS.16437.

52 *Dundee Courier* 26 Mar. and 12 Apr. 1844.

53 Sir Theodore Martin , 129, n. 1, tells of meeting this girl (by then an elderly woman) 55 years later, when he was in the vicinity of Dundee.

54 *Scotch Reformer's Gazette* 13 Apr. 1844; *Glasgow Chronicle* 12 Apr.; *Glasgow Argus* 18 Apr.; *Glasgow Courier* 23 Apr.; *Glasgow Constitutional* 24 Apr. and 8 May.

55 This is the address to which Archibald Alison directed John Blackwood to send his *History* as a gift for Helen Faucit. See his letter dated 3 June 1844, NLS, MS. 4068, f. 40.

56 *Theatrical Journal* 15 June 1844: 187.

57 Arrangements for the Paris venture are discussed in Chapter 8. Hints in her letter to Mme. Colmache suggest an earlier approach.

58 J. W. Flynn, *Random Recollections of an Old Play-Goer* (Cork, 1890) 10-11; Robert M. Sillard, *Barry Sullivan and His Contemporaries* (London, 1901) I: 26-27. The story of the Seymour-Alexander rivalry is told by Baynham 115-17. James Anderson wrote an angry diary note about some tricks he had detected in the book-keeping methods of this "great rascal" (Seymour). See the entry for his Cork engagement beginning 14 Feb. 1849 in his Eng & Memda (MS in the HTC).

59 Deficiencies: *Cork Examiner* 23 Aug. 1844 (in theatre); Flynn 17-18 (in actors). The company evidently varied from time to time in both size and quality. James Anderson, in the diary note referred to in n.58, wrote: "There are 6 men (?) and 3 women engaged as performers – & 4 Musicians in the orchestra! and all apparently in the most wretched raggedness and ignorance. Had I not brought Mr Barry from Dublin we could not have played at all." When he and Mrs. Warner returned to Cork for a "re-engagement," however, he reported that Seymour had "improved his company much."

60 Flynn 12-14; *Southern Reporter* 1 Aug. 1844.

61 Quoted by Sir Theodore Martin 130. Martin gives the date of the letter as 13 July 1844, but that is impossible. Helen Faucit did not begin her engagement at Cork until 29 July. In the letter she says she acted Ophelia "last night," which means she was writing on 11 Aug. 1844.

62 *Cork Examiner* 5 Aug. 1844. My discussion of the newspaper criticism in Cork is based principally on the reviews in the *Cork Examiner* (31 July, 1 Aug., 5 Aug., 12 Aug., 23 Aug.) and in the *Southern Reporter* (30 July, 1 Aug., 9 Aug., 13 Aug.).

63 *Cork Examiner* 2 Aug. See also 23 Aug.

64 *Limerick Chronicle* 7 Sept. 1844, 2nd ed. This conservative journal calls the demonstration a "disgraceful uproar."

65 *Limerick Chronicle* 11 Sept. 1844.

Chapter 8

1. Letter to Serle, 17 Mar. 1844, Folger MS. Y.c.411.(264).
2. Letter to Serle, 14 May 1844, Folger MS. Y.c.411.(264).
3. Helena F. Martin 233; Sir Theodore Martin 131, 140.
4. Letter dated 20 Aug. 1844, Folger MS. Y.c.411.(268).
5. B. Juden and J. Richer, "Le Théâtre anglais à Paris. Saison de 1844-1845," *La Revue des lettres modernes*, Nos. 74-75 (1962/63): 9.
6. Letter to his wife, Folger MS. Y.c.411.(105).
7. Joseph Leach, *Bright Particular Star: The Life and Times of Charlotte Cushman* (New Haven, 1970) 136; Emma Stebbins, *Charlotte Cushman: Her Letters and Memories of Her Life* (Boston, 1878) 44-45, 47-48.
8. HELEN'S ILLNESS: Sir Theodore Martin 133. MACREADY'S ACCIDENT: Victor Leathers, *British Entertainers in France* (Toronto, c. 1959) 104; Juden and Richer 9. WILLIAM: A reference to him in Helen Faucit's letter of 26 Feb. 1844 to Mme. Colmache (HTC MS. Thr 32) suggests that he had been seeing this friend in person. William was evidently the "Mr. Farren" who was included among the guests in a breakfast at M. de Fresne's on 15 Dec. 1844. See *Diaries of Macready* II: 278. REQUEST FOR ADVANCE: Helen Faucit's letter to Mitchell, dated 2 Dec., Folger MS.Y.c.902.(27).
9. Juden and Richer 4-5.
10. Juden and Richer 4-5; T.E.B. Howarth, *Citizen-King: The Life of Louis-Philippe King of the French* (London, 1961) 295-96.
11. Sir Theodore Martin 133, quoting from a letter Helen had written to him at that time.
12. Helena F. Martin 233; Sir Theodore Martin 140.
13. The *Sunday Times* (London), 22 Dec. 1844, tells of the brilliantly filled house. The description of the auditorium is from Albert Soubies' *Le Théâtre italien de 1801 à 1913* (Paris: Libraire Fischbacher, 1913) 121-22 (including the picture). It was Théophile Gautier who compared the first gallery to a basket.
14. *Diaries of Macready* II: 278-279.
15. Helena F. Martin 6.
16. *Sunday Times* (London), 22 Dec.1844. According to the Parisian correspondent, *Othello* was "barbarously" interpreted except in the two main roles, but *Hamlet*, on the second night, was "infinitely better acted."
17. Gautier's reviews of the 1844-45 performances were later republished in his *Histoire de l'art dramatique en France depuis vingt-cinq ans*, 6 vols. (Leipzig, 1858-59; rpt. Geneva, 1965). For the review of *Othello* see III: 318-24. The comments on costume and makeup are on pp. 321-22.
18. Sir Theodore Martin 135. He quotes from a passage Mme. Colmache contributed to Margaret Stokes's "Helen Faucit," published anonymously in *Blackwood's Magazine* (Dec. 1885), an article that he himself edited.

19. "Feuilleton du Journal des débats," 22 Dec. 1844, signed "J.L." Juden and Richer (67) conjecture that the author is either Janin or Jules Lacroix. There is good reason, however, to accept the statement in the *Sunday Times* (22 Dec. 1844) that on this occasion it is "M. Lemoine." John Lemoinne was a regular contributor to the *Journal des débats*. According to a table of "collaborateurs" in *Le Livre du centenaire du Journal des débats 1789-1889* (Paris, 1889) 615, Lemoinne began writing for this journal in 1840; he was in charge of the English correspondence, and, among other things, contributed many "Varietées littéraires." Although his usual signature was "John L.," he was most likely the "J.L." of the reviews during the English actors' visit.
20. Their self-restraint did give way, however, in the production of *Macbeth* when Banquo's ghost and the apparitions in the cauldron scene produced some titters. See "Feuilleton," *Journal des débats*, 12 Jan. 1845.
21. "Les Acteurs anglais" 264-65. Throughout the present chapter I use my own translations of the French reviews except in the case of the brief quotations documented in n.26 below, which are given in the translation provided by Leathers. I use quotation marks to indicate passages meant as precise translations rather than summaries or paraphrases.
22. For the reactions during the 1827-28 visits of the English actors see Leathers 69-92, esp. 77.
23. Théophile Gautier found him more romantically exciting than did some of his colleagues. See his descriptions of Macready's performances in Othello and Hamlet, *La Presse*, 23 Dec. 1844; reprinted in *Histoire de l'art dramatique* III: 322, 326.
24. Thierry's article, which covers all of Helen Faucit's performances in France, was originally published on 20 Jan. 1845. It was republished in the appendix to Helena F. Martin's book, pp. 405-10. The part on Desdemona is on pp. 405-6.
25. *Histoire de l'art tragique* III: 322-23.
26. Comments from *La France théâtrale* and *Courrier des spectacles* are from Leathers 104.
27. Juden and Richer 11. The critic was a writer for the *Globe.*
28. Quoted by Sir Theodore Martin 135
29. Helena F. Martin 6.
30. *Illustrated London News*, 28 Dec. 1844.
31. Quoted by Sir Theodore Martin 135.
32. Helena F. Martin 19-20.
33. Helena F. Martin 7-8.
34. Miss Smithson was now dead, but Hector Berlioz, who had married her, was still living and was the music critic for the *Journal des débats.*
35. See also the warm praise by correspondents for the London journals: the *Sunday Times* (22 Dec.) and the *Illustrated London News* (28 Dec.).
36. Quoted, in the original French, by Sir Theodore Martin 137.
37. Literally, the first bracketed passage would read "which no longer controlled the will"; the second would read "is."
38. *Diaries of Macready* II: 278 (16 and 18 Dec.1844), 279 (23 Dec.).
39. Reprinted in Helena F. Martin 407-8.
40. Juden and Richer 22.
41 Sir Theodore Martin 142, 143.
42. *Diaries of Macready* II: 281.
43. Quoted by Sir Theodore Martin 138.

44. *Diaries of Macready* II: 281.
45. Helena F. Martin 232-33, 401-3.
46. Nerval, "Les Acteurs anglais," *La France musicale*, 19 Jan. 1845; republished in *La Revue théatrale*, No. 29 (1er Trimestre 1955): 7. Thierry, republished in Helena F. Martin 408. Lucas and Merle, quoted by Juden and Richer 23.
47. Quoted by Juden and Richer 23.
48. Mme. Girardin, reported in "Helen Faucit," *Blackwood's*: 743, as part of Mme. Colmache's contribution to the article (see n.18, above); Gautier, *La Presse*, 13 Jan. 1845. See also Thierry on the sleepwalking scene, republished in Helena F. Martin 408.
49. *Diaries of Macready* II:282.
50. "Helen Faucit," *Blackwood's*: 744; Sir Theodore Martin 138. In the former, however, Mme. Colmache incorrectly reports that Jules Janin spoke of "ce grand paravent de Macready" in his review of *Othello* for *Débats*. The quoted phrase does not appear in that review, which, in any case, was evidently written by Lemoinne.
51. *Diaries* II: 283.
52. *Diaries of Macready* II: 282; *Sunday Times*, 19 Jan. 1845.
53. Helena F. Martin 234, 404.
54. *Diaries of Macready* II: 283-84; *Sunday Times*, 26 Jan. 1845.
55. *La Presse*, 20 Jan. 1845; republished in *Histoire* IV: 30.
56. Quoted by Sir Theodore Martin 141.
57. *Histoire* IV: 28-29.
58. Helena F. Martin 408-9.
59. Nerval, "Les Acteurs anglais," republished in *La Revue théatrale*: 8. Oddly, Nerval calls *Romeo and Juliet* a double triumph for Helen Faucit and Macready; Juden and Richer, too, seem to assume that Macready acted Romeo, for they attribute the clumsy behaviour at the curtain call to him (24-25).
60. Helena F. Martin 410 (Thierry); Gautier, *Histoire* IV: 29-30.
61. Gautier, *Histoire* IV: 28; [Colmache], "Helen Faucit": 744.
62. For example, Robert M. Sillard, in telling of Barry Sullivan's refusal of a "tempting offer" from the Salle Ventadour (June, 1872), recalls that "Macready and Helen Faucit visited Paris in 1840 [sic] to undertake a similar engagement, and failure was the result." See *Barry Sullivan* II: 129.
63. It is true that the English performances of 1844-45 had less impact on French culture than those of 1827-28 (they came at a less critical time in literary history and they covered a period of barely five weeks as compared with eleven months of the earlier performances), but they probably had a much greater influence than they are often credited with. See Juden and Richer 3-4, 28-35; also Eric Partridge, *The French Romantics' Knowledge of English Literature (1820-1848)* (Paris, 1924) 206-7.
64. On 14 January 1845, the day after the series of twelve performances had ended, Macready recorded that their receipts had "exceeded those of any theatre in Paris!" See *Diaries* II: 283.
65. Richard Moody, *Edwin Forrest: First Star of the American Stage* (New York, 1960) 213-15. Forrest arrived in France on 14 January. (The last of the twelve officially-sanctioned performances had taken place on the 13th.) Moody blames Macready for prejudicing Mitchell against Forrest, as does James Rees in *The Life of Edwin Forrest with Reminiscences and Personal Recollections* (Philadelphia, c. 1874) 228-29. But neither biographer mentions the twelve-night limitation placed on the English performances.

66. William Gilmore Simms, in a letter to James Lawson, 27 Feb. [1845], remarked, "I am sorry for Forrest's sake that the English Theatre in Paris proved a failure. I had no expectations from it. I suppose the Letter in the Post [i.e. the New York *Evening Post*] is Forrest's." See *The Letters of William Gilmore Simms*, ed. Mary C. Simms Oliphant, Alfred Taylor Odell and T.C. Duncan Eaves (Columbia, S.C., 1953) II: 38-40 (Letter # 240).
67. "Helen Faucit": 742. Mme. Ancelot was the wife of Jacques-Arsene-François Ancelot, dramatist and man of letters.
68. Bernard Falk, *Rachel the Immortal* 158-59; Rachel Brownstein, *Tragic Muse: Rachel of the Comédie-Française* (New York: Alfred A. Knopf, 1993) 148-51. The latter is misleading, however, in saying that "as the respectable wife of Sir Theodore Martin, she could visit a 'fallen' Rachel no more than she could be visited by George Eliot." Helen Faucit had not yet married Theodore Martin at the time when she reluctantly declined Rachel's overtures, and it would be many years after her marriage before she became Lady Martin. For her relationship with George Eliot, see Chapter 13.
69. Quoted by Sir Theodore Martin 133-34.
70. *Diaries* II: 293 (20 Apr. 1845), 299 (22 July 1845), 319 (13 Jan. 1846), 331 (28 and 29 Mar. 1846), 485-86 (10 Jan. 1851).
71. Martin so describes Helen Faucit's feeling for Macready (133).

Chapter 9

1. Sir Theodore Martin 145, 153.
2. According to Macready (*Diaries* II: 288-89), the director of the orchestra and chorus for the Covent Garden *Antigone* had made this mistake. For the best in such art see A.H. Saxon, *The Life and Art of Andrew Ducrow and the Romantic Age of the English Circus* (Hamden, Conn., 1978) 226-32.
3. For "The Greek Muse" see p.147; for the sepia drawing, p.165. A replica of the former, "apparently retained by the artist as a memento," is now in the National Gallery of Ireland. See Richard and Leonée Ormond's article, "Helen Faucit as Antigone," *Country Life* 7 Dec. 1967: 1507-8, a well-illustrated description and concise history of Burton's portraits and other artwork inspired by Helen Faucit.
4. Tracy Davis, discussing female *poses plastiques* and *tableaux vivants* in taverns and variety theatres (second half of the century), writes: "The objective of living pictures such as *Diana Preparing for the Chase* ... was to provide a narrative of ideal female beauty while the paradigmatic male erotic fantasy of voyeurism was legitimized by the pretense of classical mythology" (125). Helen Faucit, acting in a Theatre Royal – and in an actual Greek tragedy – was protected from the crassest kind of response. The ideal effect was surely dominant, but the erotic, sublimated or not, must have been involved to some extent. Rachel Brownstein, discussing the frequent comparisons of Rachel to a statue, gives some fascinating suggestions about the implications of this conceit. See *Tragic Muse*, esp. 172-81.

5. Sir Theodore Martin 151, quoted from notes Burton gave him after Lady Martin's death. For the notes in full see 150-52.
6. [Percy Fitzgerald], *Recollections of Dublin Castle and Dublin Society* (New York, 1902) 27-28. Fitzgerald quotes a "youthful critique" of Helen Faucit's performance that he "lately found in an old diary" of his. He gives no date, but it may have been 18 Apr. 1850 (the only night, as far as I know, when Helen Faucit acted both Antigone and Anne Bracegirdle, as he says). Fitzgerald would have been about sixteen.
7. Quoted by Sir Theodore Martin 151.
8. [Theodore Martin], "The Drama in Connexion with the Fine Arts," *Dublin University Magazine* July 1846: 105.
9. *Evening Packet* 25 Feb. 1845 ("study for the sculptor … arms folded … classic head drooping"); *Dublin Times* Feb. 1846 [when Helen Faucit repeated Antigone], as quoted by Sir Theodore Martin 149 ("averted in scorn," "instant uplifting … all the queen"); *Recollections of Dublin Castle* 28 (resigned smile).
10. "The Drama in Connexion with the Fine Arts" 105 ("absorbed"); Frederick Burton, quoted by Sir Theodore Martin 151 ("heart-stirring sincerity"); *Evening Packet* 25 Feb. 1845 ("thrilling effect").
11. Burton, quoted by Sir Theodore Martin 151; Martin, "The Drama in Connexion with the Fine Arts" 105; Fitzgerald, *Recollections of Dublin Castle* 26-27. See also the reference to an "ennobling dream," *The Nation* 1 Mar. 1845.
12. *The Nation* 29 Mar. 1845: 409; Sir Theodore Martin 157-58.
13. Byrne, *The Wildes of Merrion Square* 17-18.
14. Terence De Vere White, *The Parents of Oscar Wilde: Sir William and Lady Wilde* (London, 1967) 117.
15. Sir William Stokes, *William Stokes His Life and Work (1804-1878).* Masters of Medicine (London, 1898) passim.
16. Sir William Stokes 81-82; Margaret Stokes, quoted by Sir Theodore Martin 156. For Dr. Stokes's relationship with Alison see Sir William Stokes 31-33; for Mrs. Stokes see 47-48.
17. Diary entry of 4 June 1867, quoted by Sir Theodore Martin 287.
18. Reminiscence in Helen's letter to Margaret Stokes, written in 1880, after Dr. Stokes's death; quoted by Sir William Stokes 82-84; also (with slight differences in wording) by Sir Theodore Martin 156-57. Helen's affection for Dr. Stokes and her dependence on him for encouragement and guidance are strongly reflected in this letter.
19. Sir William Stokes 87-88.
20. "The Drama in Connexion with the Fine Arts" 105, note.
21. T.G. Wilson, *Victorian Doctor* 144-45. Mr. Terence De Vere White suggested to me, in a letter of 25 Dec. 1982, that Wilson, a Dublin physician, got the information about the rivalry of Wilde and Burton from a member of the Stokes family.
22. CONTRASTS BETWEEN THE TWO: T.G. Wilson 145. BURTON: Walter G. Strickland, *A Dictionary of Irish Artists* (Dublin, 1913; rpt. New York, c. 1968) 135 (also illustrations opp. 130 and 140); portraits in the National Gallery of Ireland (by George Francis Mulvany and by Burton himself). Information about his colouring, based on the Mulvany portrait, was sent me by Miss Barbara Dawson of the National Gallery. WILDE'S SEXUAL LAPSES: already flagrant, they later received notoriety during a law suit: see White, *The Parents of Oscar Wilde* 184-204.
23. According to Wilson (232-33), the photograph was taken in the late 1850s by Lord Fitzgibbon; Wilson gives his own drawing of it (232).

24. It was Stokes who encouraged Martin to write his article showing the relation between Miss Faucit's acting and the fine arts. See Sir Theodore Martin 153.
25. Horace Wyndham, *Speranza: A Biography of Lady Wilde* (New York, 1951) 45-46.
26. Rosaline Masson, *Pollok and Aytoun* 151-52. I borrowed the translation of the Greek inscription from Richard and Leonée Ormond.
27. Other characters introduced in Edinburgh were Belvidera and Mrs. Beverley.
28. *Glasgow Dramatic Review* 21 May 1845: 147-48.
29. Alison, *Some Account of My Life and Writings* I: 530-32.
30. *The Story of the Scots Stage* 186.
31. Alison, *Some Account of My Life* I: 531-37 (Helen Faucit's visit, including Goatfell excursion and conversations); Alison, "The British Theatre," in *Essays: Political, Historical, and Miscellaneous* III: 586 ("Female fascination" – mentioned in connection with her acting, but obviously exercised offstage as well).
32. *Macready's Reminiscences* I: 80. The building was converted into small tenements a few years after Helen Faucit's engagement (*Carlisle Patriot* 1 Sept. 1848). In 1971 a remnant of the old theatre was discovered as part of a building owned by Binns, a department store (clippings of two articles from the *Carlisle News*, Record Office, The Castle, Carlisle).
33. See the report of Daly's speech on the last night of the season, *Carlisle Journal* 14 June 1845, and the advertisement for the T.R. Carlisle in the *Carlisle Journal* 29 June 1845. Clippings of these items are in the Carlisle Museum Files, Museum and Art Gallery, Tullie House, Carlisle.
34. Léon Fauchet, *Manchester in 1844: Its Present Condition and Future Prospects*. Trans. with notes by a Member of the Manchester Athenaeum (1844; rpt. London, 1969) 16-20.
35. [British Association for the Advancement of Science], *Manchester and Its Region: A Survey Prepared for the Meeting Held in Manchester August 29 to September 5, 1962* (Manchester, 1962) 137-38.
36. For a good description of Peel Park, an unusually fine "people's park," see *Selections from the Letters of Geraldine Endsor Jewsbury to Jane Welsh Carlyle*, ed. Mrs. Alexander Ireland [Annie Elizabeth Nicholson Ireland] (London, 1892) 238-39. In a letter to Mrs.Hemans the older Jewsbury sister, Maria Jane, colourfully describes the preparations for the Manchester Festival. See *Maria Jane Jewsbury: Occasional Papers, Selected with a Memoir by Eric Gillett* (London, 1932) xliv.
37. *Manchester in 1844* 21.
38. Geraldine Jewsbury's accounts of Manchester dinner parties and "swarries" reflect this kind of atmosphere. See, for example, *Selection from the Letters* 219-20.
39. Quoted by Sir Theodore Martin 161.
40. John Coleman, *Fifty Years of an Actor's Life* II: 438; Robert M. Sillard, *Barry Sullivan and his Contemporaries* 168-69; W.J. Lawrence, *The Life of Gustavus Vaughan Brooke, Tragedian* (Belfast, 1892) 59-60 et passim. Lady Martin's letter to Lawrence, giving her opinions about Brooke (dated 9 Jan. 1890), is in the HTC.
41. Helena Faucit Martin 103. She does not give the date or place of this visit, but the last time she acted Juliet before the Blands left England was at Manchester on 14 July 1845.
42. For an excellent study of such productions see Shirley S. Allen, *Samuel Phelps* 111-63. There is a misstatement, however, on p. 87. In arguing that Mrs. Warner had been held back by Macready because of his preference for Helen Faucit, Professor Allen writes: "he had even refused to allow her Lady Macbeth in his last season at

Drury Lane, until Helen Faucit's obvious failure in the role forced him to recast it." In fact, Macready *always* cast Mrs. Warner as Lady Macbeth (it was one of her "heavy" parts); only on one occasion, when she was unable to play, did he request Helen Faucit to take the role.

43. Macready, *Diaries* II: 299-301. To his chagrin Macready heard that Charlotte Cushman had refused an offer at the Princess's Theatre if it entailed acting with him. Apparently Maddox had made overtures to Helen Faucit as well. When Miss Cushman refused his offer she wrote to a friend, "Miss Faucit I am told won't go." See Leach, *Bright Particular Star* 164.
44. Anderson, *An Actor's Life* 132-33. Anderson says that he and Helen Faucit played for 24 nights to fine houses. Actually it was 14 nights.
45. 25 Oct. 1845: 338-39; 1 Nov. 1845: 347.
46. *Observer* 26 Oct. 1845; *Morning Chronicle* 21 Oct.; *Sunday Times* 26 Oct.; *Theatrical Journal* 25 Oct.: 339.
47. ANDERSON'S CLAUDE: *Examiner* 25 Oct. 1845: 677; *Morning Herald* 21 Oct., Supplement; *Times* 21 Oct.; *Illustrated London News* 25 Oct.: 267; *Sunday Times* 26 Oct.; *Observer* 26 Oct. (The *Examiner*, which denies that Anderson imitated Macready, is particularly favourable.) SIZE OF AUDIENCE: Reports differ dramatically. The *Morning Herald*'s (21 Oct.) is perhaps correct: "Although the house was not extremely well filled, the reception … was animated and fervent." During the rest of the engagement the audiences seem to have been excellent.
48. HIGH PRAISE: *Morning Herald* 21 Oct.; *Sunday Times* 26 Oct.; *Theatrical Journal* 25 Oct.: 339. COMPLAINT MIXED WITH PRAISE: *Examiner* (25 Oct.: 677).
49. He quotes from commentaries by Knight and Hallam, for instance.
50. 3 Nov. 1845 (Mrs. Haller); 26 Oct. (Julia); 9 Nov. (Rosalind).
51. The *Theatrical Journal*, 29 Nov. 1845: 381, lists the dates and performances of the Macready engagement as compared with those of the Faucit-Anderson engagement and says both series were highly successful.
52. 17 Dec. 1845: 289-91.
53. Leach 173-74.
54. *Fifty Years of an Actor's Life* I: 331. Coleman is confused about some of his other facts. For example, he implies that the production of *Antigone* in Edinburgh preceded the one in Dublin.
55. *Fifty Years Of an Actor's Life* I: 328-29.
56. "The Antigone of Sophocles, as Represented on the Edinburgh Stage in December 1845," *Tait's Edinburgh Magazine* Mar. 1846: 160, 162. (The two-part article, originally published in the Feb. and Mar. numbers of *Tait's*, 1846, has been republished in the various editions of De Quincey's collected works. I use the spelling and punctuation of the original.) Sir Theodore Martin (155) explains Helen Faucit's husky voice.
57. See, for example, the *Scotsman* 29 Nov. and 3 Dec. 1845; the *Caledonian Mercury* 4 Dec.; the *Glasgow Courier* 16 and 18 Dec. The reviews in the *Courier* are probably by Archibald Alison.
58. *Fifty Years* I: 328, 332.
59. The quotation is from a reminiscent passage in Brown's letter to Theodore Martin, dated only "Sunday Evening" (probably written in 1861), in *Letters of Dr. John Brown. With Letters from Ruskin, Thackeray and Others*, ed. John Brown, Jr. and D.W. Forrest, introd. Elizabeth M'Laren (London, 1907) 147. See also

Alexander Peddie, *Recollections of Dr. John Brown Author of "Rab and His Friends," etc. With a Selection from His Correspondence* (London, 1893) 25, 55-59 et passim.; and E.M. [Eleanor May] Sellar, *Recollections and Impressions* (Edinburgh, 1907) 92-95.

60. Letter to John Taylor Brown, *Letters of Dr. John Brown* 61.

Chapter 10

1. Extract by Sir Theodore Martin from a letter to his wife, dated 5 Oct. 1884, NLS, MS. 16444, f. 33. Martin says the latter is from "one of Lady Martin's dressers" but does not give her name.
2. This was Fanny Ternan, the child star. James Anderson, T. P. Cooke, and Charles Mackay (the great favourite in Scottish parts) had also starred there. See James Munro's report of expenses for the Newcastle theatre (June, 1844) in Harold Oswald, *The Theatre Royal in Newcastle upon Tyne* 104-5.
3. "Gossip of the Week," *Theatrical Times* 27 Feb. 1847: 61. According to this, her nightly average of 70 pounds is "not much less than Mrs. Butler, in the first flush of novelty, gains at Manchester." The allusion to the salary of Fanny Kemble Butler was based on an earlier report, which, however, was corrected elsewhere in the present issue (40 pounds, not 80). Although the "Gossip" was just as likely to be wrong about Helen Faucit, my impression is that stars could usually make much more money in Glasgow than in Manchester. See, for example, the extremely high earnings of Charles Kean at Glasgow, as reported by Cole in *The Life and Theatrical Times of Charles Kean, F.S.A.* I: 223.
4. James Anderson's record book, "Theatrical Eng & Memda – 1848 to 18[57]," now in the HTC, tells of many such arrangements.
5. Folger MS. Y.c.902.(4). The letter is dated only 31 Aug, but it has a notation in another hand, presumably Davenport's: "31st Augt 1848 Miss Faucit."
6. MS letter dated only 10 Nov., in the Shakespeare Centre Library, Stratford-upon-Avon. Since the letter was written in London, the only possible years are 1845, 1847, and 1849; the likeliest is 1847. The *Dramatic Mirror*, 17 Dec, 1847: 224, reports: "Bunn has offered Miss Helen Faucit and James Wallack an engagement at the Surrey, but they very prudently declined."
7. James R. Anderson, in *An Actor's Life* 152-155, gives an account of the affair, with the texts of all the letters. For Helen Faucit's, see 153.
8. An example is her letter to the managers of the Southampton Theatre, dated 6 Aug. [probably 1845]: "Miss Helen Faucit presents her Compts … & … begs to say that it will not suit her arrangements to visit Southampton this season." MS in the Theatre Museum.
9. See, for example, the playbills for the T. R. Perth, 19 Feb. [1849] (BL Playbills 298) and the T. R. Edinburgh, for 2 Mar, 1850 (Central Public Library, Edinburgh).

10. See Helen Faucit's letter to Mme. Colmache, 26 Feb. 1844 (MS in the HTC); "Bon Gaultier and His Friends," *Tait's Magazine* Feb. 1844; George Fletcher, *Studies of Shakespeare*; and Helen Faucit's letter to Peter Fraser, dated 1 Dec. 1846, NLS MS. 3873, p. 9.
11. Helena F. Martin 284-85 (Murray's portrayal of William); James Anderson, "Theatrical Eng & Mema," entry for an engagement at Sheffield beginning on 8 Jan. 1849.
12. Eric R. Delderfield, *Cavalcade by Candlelight: The Story of Exeter's Fine Theatres 1725-1950* (Exmouth, [1950]) 61.
13. RA, Queen Victoria's Journal, 9 Mar. 1839; Sir Theodore Martin 61 (passage from Helen Faucit's diary).
14. Baynham, *The Glasgow Stage* 136.
15. EXETER: Delderfield 65. CARLISLE: Playbill of 29 Dec. 1845, in the Folger. SHEFFIELD: Playbills of 25 Oct. 1841 and 4 May 1849, in BL Playbills 396.
16. DERBY: playbill of 22 May 1846, BL Playbills 278. GLASGOW: *Glasgow Dramatic Review* (21 May 1845) 148.
17. *The Glasgow Stage* 136. Baynham was an actor at the T. R. Glasgow beginning in Feb. 1861.
18. For example, the "Old Playgoer" in J. W. Flynn's *Random Recollections of an Old Playgoer* 17, is quoted as saying that G. V. Brooke "was very unpunctual, and Helen Faucit was quite the contrary."

19 Sir Theodore Martin 130. See Helena F. Martin 284 for Miss Faucit's own comments about her attempts to help others at rehearsals.

20. See, for example, James H. Stoddart's description of his parents' experience at Glasgow in the 1830s and 40s, in *Recollections of a Player* (New York, 1902) 31-33.
21. *Memories of Fifty Years* (New York, 1889) 56.
22. *Memories of My Life* (London, 1913) 62-63.
23. CUSHMAN'S EXAGGERATON DEFENDED: Liverpool *Albion*, 20 April 1846. FAUCIT-CRESWICK PERFORMANCE: *Liverpool Chronicle*, 18 April 1846 (lukewarm review). A notable feature of the Cushman performance was the restoration of the Shakespearean ending. Helen Faucit, though privately favouring this, would wait another year before abandoning Garrick's tomb scene.
24. *Liverpool Chronicle* 25 Apr. 1846.

25 "Dublin T. R.," *Theatrical Journal* 5 Dec. 1846: 390; "Miss Helen Faucit," *Glasgow Theatrical Review* 24 Feb. 1847: 106-7. In fairness it should be mentioned that G. V. Brooke, who was very popular in Ireland, was acting with Helen Faucit in Dublin.

26. Special trains are advertised in playbills for the T. R. Newcastle-upon-Tyne, 27 Apr. [1847] (BL Playbills 262) and 27 Apr. 1849 (in my personal collection), and for the Theatre, Sheffield, 3 May 1849 (BL Playbills 396). Sir Theodore Martin (293) says that when Miss Faucit acted at Glasgow (evidently in 1867) special trains were run "for more than thirty miles round."
27. "Helen Faucit," *Blackwood's Magazine* (Dec. 1885): 745. See also the *Evening Packet* (24 December 1846).
28. *Theatrical Journal* 8 Aug. 1846: 250; *Illustrated London News* 8 Aug. 1846: 90.
29. *Morning Chronicle* 4 Aug. (which, despite the reservation, is enthusiastic) and *Daily News* 4 Aug. See Afterpiece for more discussion.
30. "The Antient Drama – Antigone," *Glasgow Theatrical Review* 10 Mar, 1847: 122; "Theatre Royal," *Manchester Courier* 8 May 1847.

31. *Evening Packet* 1 Dec. 1846; *Evening Freeman* 1 Dec. 1846. Calcraft's version of the play was published by James M'Glashan of Dublin and was dedicated to Helen Faucit "whose genius suggested the revival."
32. *Evening Packet* 1 Dec. 1846; *Theatrical Times* 12 Dec. 1846: 246; *Evening Freeman* 1 Dec.: *Theatrical Times* 5 Dec.: 230, and 12 Dec.: 247.
33. *Evening Packet* 1 Dec., including quotations from *Saunders's News Letter* and *Evening Mail.*
34. *Evening Mail,* as quoted by *Evening Packet.*
35. *Evening Freeman.*
36. For Macready's reaction to the "terms of laudation" used of Helen Faucit in several letters and papers he had received about the production see *Diaries* II: 351 (5 Dec. 1846).
37. Classically-educated spectators could scarcely have ignored the irony in the concluding chorus, but few would have admitted the larger ironies that modern critics sometimes see in Euripides' play. (For an extreme example see Prof. Dimock's discussion in *Iphigenia at Aulis,* trans. W. S. Merwin and George E. Dimock, Jr. *The Greek Tragedy in New Translations,* ed. William Arrowsmith [New York, 1978] introd., 3-21). Certainly they would not have questioned the value of Iphigenia's patriotic self-sacrifice.
38. See her letter to Peter Fraser, 1 Dec. 1846, NLS MS. 3873, p. 9.
39. The reviewer for the *Evening Mail,* as quoted by Sir Theodore Martin (173-74) said he had never seen an audience "so struck with admiration."
40. Helena F. Martin 385-6; *Glasgow Courier* 23 Mar. 1848, 2nd. ed.
41. Helena F. Martin 107-9, 153. Romeo and Juliet are even compared to the "spotless Iphigenia" (109).
42. *Manchester Guardian* 8 May 1847 ("painful and embarrassing"); *Newcastle Chronicle* 30 Apr. 1847 ("overstrained and unnatural"). See also *Manchester Express* 4 May 1847 ("gloomy and depressing") and *Edinburgh Evening Courant* 25 Feb. 1847 ("trash," "worthless," "Satanic school of tragedy").
43. *Glasgow Courier* 11 Feb. 1847, 2nd. ed. See other descriptions in *Evening Freeman* (Dublin) 12 Nov. 1846; *Evening Packet* (Dublin) 12 Nov. 1846; and *Manchester Express* 4 May 1847.
44. Isabella Glyn, trained by Charles Kemble, also used this "stroke of Siddonian business" when she acted Isabella – and, according to John Coleman, effected "the most thrilling tour de force" he had ever seen in a theatre. See his *Fifty Years of an Actor's Life* II: 573.
45. The review most favourable to the play is a two-part article in the *Theatrical Times* 30 Oct. 1847; 341-42 and 13 Nov.: 359-60. *The Morning Chronicle* 21 Oct. and the *Literary Gazette* 25 Oct.: 756 said that Helen Faucit's scenes were the only interesting ones, that she saved the play. For other reviews see *Morning Post* 21 Oct.; *Morning Herald* 21 Oct.; *Spectator* 23 Oct.: 1017; *Illustrated London News* 26 Oct.: 267; *Dramatic Mirror* 28 Oct.: 180-181.
46. Sir Theodore Martin 195-96; *Dublin Evening Post* 16 Apr. 1850.
47. *Edinburgh Evening Courant* 27 Jan. 1849; *Caledonian Mercury* 29 Jan. 1849, *Newcastle Chronicle* 27 Apr. 1849.
48. *Examiner and Times,* 25 May 1850, as quoted by Sir Theodore Martin 207. See also *Manchester Guardian*) 25 May 1850, which calls the production a "brilliant success" and says Helen Faucit's acting was "of the highest order,' her third act being "one of the most perfect histrionic displays" the writer had ever witnessed.

49 TWO VERSIONS OF THE PLAY; Apparently Martin's was finished well before Phipps's (in 1846), but its appearance in the *Dublin University Magazine* (June 1848: 671-96) was slightly anticipated by the London publication of Phipps's version. See Sir Theodore Martin 209 and the Dublin editor's note to Martin's play. HELEN FAUCIT'S ABORTIVE PLAN: *Sheffield and Rotherham Independent.* 12 Jan. 1850, which quotes from Martin's preface to his work when published as a separate volume. ADULATION OF KEANS' DUBLIN PRODUCTION: Percy Allen, *The Stage Life of Mrs. Stirling* (London, [1922]) 114n. The date he gives (28 Nov. 1848) cannot be correct. Helen Faucit was acting Pauline at the T. R. Dublin that night.

50. MRS. STIRLING: Allen 114. (Allen was Mrs. Stirling's grandson.) MRS. KEAN: *Sunday Times* 23 Dec. 1849.
51. *Sheffield and Rotherham Independent* 19 Jan. 1850.
52. The next day's playbill (24 January) blazingly headlined her "touching and exquisite performance" before "the most splendid audience of the season." This "puff" had more substance than most, for, the following November, Glover boasted that *Love's Sacrifice*, with Laura Addison starring, had been "successful beyond any Play ever acted in this Theatre (with the exception of 'King René's Daughter')". See the playbills in the Mitchell Library.
53. See *Theatrical Journal* 31 Jan. 1850: 40 ("Chatter Box").
54. The quotations are from *Manchester Guardian* 30 Oct. 1867 ("radiant inhabitant"); an unidentified Glasgow paper in the Saville Scrapbooks, vol. 1, f.5, Nottingham Public Library ("heavenly revelation"); and William Carleton's letter to the *Dublin Daily Express*, quoted by Sir Theodore Martin 216 ("divine effusion"). See also *Dublin Evening Post* 6 Apr. 1850; *Manchester Guardian* 26 Apr. 1851, 23 Oct. 1866; *Manchester Courier* 8 July 1854, 23 Oct. 1866; *Manchester Examiner and Times* 23 Oct. 1866, 25 Nov. 1871; *North British Daily Mail* (Glasgow) 27 Nov. 1867.
55. BLINDNESS IN MANCHESTER: Sir Theodore Martin 214-215. NO "STAGE BLINDNESS": *Manchester Examiner and Times* 23 Oct. 1866 and 30 Oct. 1867; *Glasgow Herald* 25 Jan. 1850; *Manchester Courier* 18 Apr. 1866 and 23 Oct. 1866. CARLETON: quoted by Martin 215-216.
56. *Glasgow Herald* 25 Jan. 1850; *Manchester Examiner and Times* 29 May 1850.
57. For a historian's account of the story see Ch. Petit-Dutaillis., *The Feudal Monarchy in France and England from the Tenth to the Thirteenth Century* (London, [1949]) 209.
58. *Theatrical Journal* 7 Nov. 1850: 453-54; *Morning Chronicle* 13 Nov. 1850. My discussion of *Philip of France* and its premiere production is based on these and the following: *Times* 5 Nov.; *Morning Post* 5 Nov.; *Morning Herald* 5 Nov.; *Examiner* 9 Nov.: 720; *Literary Gazette* 9 Nov.: 842; *Spectator* 9 Nov.: 1066; *Sunday Times* 10 Nov.; *Theatrical Journal* 14 Nov.: 446; *Tallis's Dramatic Magazine* Dec. 1850: 53-54.
59. CROWDED THEATRE: *Times, Sunday Times.* WELCOME: *Morning Post.* CURTAIN CALLS: *Times.*
60. *Times; Tallis.*
61. VOICE: *Theatrical Journal* 7 and 14 Nov. BOISTEROUSNESS: *Morning Chronicle; Examiner; Morning Herald.*
62. Quoted by Sir Theodore Martin 223. Martin gives the date of the letter as 14 Nov. 1850 but gives the place as Glasgow. Actually, Helen Faucit was acting Marie in London in Nov. 1850.
63. *Theatrical Journal* 7 Nov.; *Tallis; Morning Chronicle; Literary Gazette.*

64. RESPONSE TO PROPOSAL: *Sunday Times*. DEATH SCENE: *Theatrical Journal* 7 Nov. See also *Morning Post, Morning Herald*, and *Times*.
65. *Our Recent Actors* 307.
66. *Theatrical Journal* 14 Nov.
67 *Gustavus Vaughan Brooke* 112.
68. Sir Theodore Martin 223.
69. Quoted by Sir Theodore Martin 223.
70. Sir Theodore Martin 159. For Wilson's new interpretation see "Dies Borealis, Christopher under Canvas." *Blackwood's Magazine* (Nov. 1849): 620-54. This is a Platonic dialogue, but the main tendency is to decry the glorification of Macbeth and to show that Lady Macbeth (a "bold, bad woman – not a fiend") is superior to him in character.
71. Carleton wrote his appreciative description in a letter to Dr. Stokes, an extract from which was quoted in a review by another critic in *Freeman's Journal* 18 Dec. 1846, reprinted in *Evening Freeman* 19 Dec. The writer was identified only as "one of the greatest ornaments of Irish literature," but his name is given in Helena F. Martin (401-3) and the whole text of the letter published, with slight variations from the newspapers' text. My quotation is from the *Freeman's Journal.*
72. For descriptions of Lady Macbeth as portrayed by these two actresses see Dennis Bartholomeusz, *Macbeth and the Players* (Cambridge, 1969) 171 (Mrs. Warner), 188-89 (Miss Glyn).
73. *Theatrical Journal* 13 Aug. 1851: 260 ("energy and power" – this critic considered Miss Glyn best); *Sunday Times* 10 Aug. ("grandeur").
74. *Illustrated London News* 9 Aug. 1851: 183 ("power"); *Sunday Times* 10 Aug. ("unsurpassable," etc.).
75. Sir Theodore Martin 169.
76. According to the *Derby and Chesterfield Reporter* (28 Aug. 1846), J. F. Saville was to have Helen Faucit at Derby for two nights in September; there is no indication that this engagement took place. According to the *Theatrical Times* (12 September 1846: 112), Miss Faucit had been seriously ill in Leicester; the same journal (19 Sept.: 120) reported that her illness had prevented her entering upon her engagement in Leicester.
77. *Evening Packet* (Dublin) 7 Nov. and 10 Nov. 1846; *Evening Freeman* (Dublin) 12 Nov.; *Cork Examiner* 6 Jan. 1847; *Belfast Commercial Chronicle* 18 Jan. (advertisement, including a statement from Dr. Stokes): *Glasgow Theatrical Review* 27 Jan.: 75.
78. Sir Theodore Martin 185.
79. When she was acting at the Haymarket *Bell's Life in London* (10 Oct. 1847) remarked that she "seemed thinner, but otherwise looked extremely well."
80. Death certificate, Health Department – Registry Division, City of Boston. Date of record: 7 Nov. 1847.
81. Helena F. Martin 103-4.
82. 8 Dec. 1847. This criticism was repeated, word for word, in the *Dramatic Mirror* the next day.
83. Helena F. Martin 104.
84. Quoted by Sir Theodore Martin 192-93.
85. Quoted by Martin 194-95.
86. Sir Theodore Martin 190-91, 208.
87. Quoted by Sir Theodore Martin 201.

88. Sir Theodore Martin 201. The portrait, is shown on p.178, now in the Manchester Art Gallery.
89. Sir Theodore Martin 208-9, 224-6. Mrs. Joy's Christian name is signed to a letter of congratulation on Theodore's knighthood, written 6 Apr. 1880 (RA Z 507/47).
90. RUGBY MEMORIAL: Sir Theodore Martin 208-9. VIEW OF ABSTRACTIONS: See her letter of 11 Jan. 1851 to Mrs. Bruce Joy, quoted by Sir Theodore Martin 224-26, esp. 225. IMPORTANCE OF VISIBLE MEMORIAL: She had contributed earlier to a monument in Mount Auburn Cemetery, Boston, whose inscription reads in part: "erected by the united affection of her husband, Humphrey Bland, and her only sister, Helen Faucit" (unidentified clipping in HTC). Since she had never seen it, however, it could not have had the significance of one she erected.
91. E. M. [Eleanor May] Sellar, *Recollections and Impressions* 36-37. In her youth, as Eleanor Denistoun, she used to hear about Martin's following Helen Faucit about from place to place.
92. Letter dated 20 Feb. 1849, NLS MS. 2622, ff. 104-7.
93 MS letter of Helen Faucit to Macready and draft of Macready's letter on the back of it, in Mander and Mitchenson. Macready's beloved daughter Nina had recently died (on 24 February); his grief at this time possibly affected the tone of his letter.
94. Letter dated "Brompton Square Oct 14th" in my personal collection.
95. *Diaries of Macready* II: 485-86 (10 Jan. 1851).
96. *Diaries of Macready* II: 496. For descriptions of the occasion see Alan Downer 317-18, and Shirley Allen 129.

Chapter 11

1. CHURCH: A.F. Day, *The Church of St. Nicolas of Myra* 3, 8, 13. Illustrations, 6-7, 12. WISH FOR PRIVACY: Sir Theodore Martin 229. "ACCIDENTALLY PRESENT": A writer for the *Illustrated London News* (30 Aug. 1851) says this of his own attendance. CROWD AT CHURCH: "Marriage of Miss Helen Faucit," *Brighton Gazette* 28 Aug. *LADY OF LYONS*: "Our Little Chatter Box," *Theatrical Journal* 3 Sept.: 269.
2. Sir Theodore Martin (229) names the bridesmaids. For typical bridesmaids' costumes see George Augustus Sala, *Twice Round the Clock; or the Hours of the Day and Night in London* (London,1859) 115. Helen's bridal costume is described in *Illustrated London News* (30 Aug. 1851). A wedding dress at that period was a "white day dress," which typically had a closely-fitted bodice, full skirt, and open sleeves revealing frilled or lace-trimmed under-sleeves. See Cunnington and Cunnington, *Handbook of English Costume in the Nineteenth Century* 443-45, 451, 453.
3. *Illustrated London News.* Both *Observer* and *Theatrical Journal* describe her as "charming" but also mention her tears.

4. Diary entry of 18 June 1867 (after she had watched Minnie Thackeray try on her wedding dress), quoted by Sir Theodore Martin 287.
5. GUESTS: *Brighton Gazette.* FAMILY MEMBERS: *Illustrated London News* (followed by the *Theatrical Journal* and the London *Observer*). Helen's brother Alfred is not named; Charles had already gone to Australia; Kate Saville's sisters, Maria and Eliza, though not named, were probably present. WITNESSES: Zouch Troughton, John Saville, Eliza Bruce, and Kate Saville. See Register of Marriages in St. Nicholas Church, Brighton, June 1851 – May 1852 (PAR 255/1/3/23), p. 49, item 97, in the Record Office, Lewes, Sussex.
6. Sir Theodore Martin 287, note 1. Helena Martin frequently mentions "my Ogre" in diary and letters, and Mrs. Adams (Eliza Bruce) mentions the nickname in a letter to her many years later.
7. Sir Theodore Martin 230. For the unsuccessful visit to Casa Guidi see Helen's letter to Robert Browning, dated 22 Jan. 1853, in "Holograph Correspondence to Robert Browning," f. 48, Baylor Univ.
8. A bill affecting private interests is not introduced directly by a Member of Parliament; instead, its sponsors present a petition, with a copy of the proposed bill attached, "praying leave" for the bill to be brought in. A Parliamentary agent advises the sponsors, drafts all necessary documents, and guides his clients' bill through the appropriate Parliamentary committee. See L.A. Abraham and S.C. Hawtry, A *Parliamentary Dictionary* (London, 1956) 24-29 ("Bill, Private") and 131-32 ("Parliamentary Agent"); also Frederick Clifford, *A History of Private Bill Legislation.* Reprints of Economic Classics, 2 vols. (1887; rpt. New York, 1968) II: 878-81.
9. "Martin, Sir Theodore," *DNB* (1912). Martin's first partner was Hugh Innes Cameron, who was already established in the practice when Martin joined him. His longest partnership was with William Leslie (1862-97).
10. Never acted, as far as I know, though Helen strongly hinted to Henry Irving that it should be. See her letter of 31 May [1876], in the Theatre Museum.
11. Theodore Martin gives this address in a letter of 20 Feb. 1849 (NLS, MS. 2622, ff. 104-7). Helena F. Martin gives the same address in a letter of 1 Dec. [1851] (NLS, MS. 2643, ff. 87A-87B). Both letters are to Mrs. John Stuart Blackie. The year of the latter may be deduced from the content, which is evidently concerned with Martin's using his influence for Blackie's appointment at the University of Edinburgh. Blackie became Professor of Greek there in 1852.
12. FREAKE'S WORK: *The Museums Area of South Kensington and Westminster*, Vol. XXXVIII of *Survey of London*, ed. F.H.W. Sheppare (London, 1975) 263, 288, 316. THE MARTINS' HOUSE (NO. 31): It no longer exists, though some other houses in Onslow Square are still standing. NO.36 (ONCE THACKERAY'S HOME): F. Hopkinson Smith, *In Thackeray's London: Pictures and Text* (London, 1913) 71 (sketch made early in the 20th century). No. 31, would have looked the same way. CHURCHES: See *Museums Area* 349. *The Times* 5 Nov. 1898, in describing Helena Martin's funeral, says the Martins had worshipped at St. Peter's for many years.
13. *The Museums Area* 316-17.
14. According to Helen's letter to Robert Browning dated 22 Jan. 1853 (see n.7, above), the Martins were still living at 24 James St. at that time. Alison's letter of 31 May [1855] is quoted by Sir Theodore Martin 246. For Munby's diary entry see Derek Hudson, *Munby, Man of Two Worlds* 125.

15. A brief history of Dinas Bran, Eliseg's Pillar, and Valle Crucis Abbey is found in Sara Pugh Jones's *A Hurried History of Llangollen.* Llangollen Blue Guide Sheets (Bala, 1961) 5-8, 10-11. My descriptions of landscape are based on my own observations during a number of visits.
16. WELSH PROPERTY: Theodore Martin (263-64) says he bought the house in 1865, but Mr. Edward Hubbard of *The Buildings of Wales* told me (in a letter of 26 Sept. 1978) that the initial purchase was made in 1866 and that additions to the property were made in 1870, 1871, and 1888. The later purchases may have been for Martin's Glyn Valley property, which he refers to in a letter to Robert Rawlinson, 21 Aug. 1874, MS in "Correspondence between R. Rawlinson Esqre C.B. and Sir Theodore Martin," National Library of Wales; also in a letter to William Blackwood, 29 Jan. 1888, NLS, MS. 4520, ff. 198-99. BRAICH-Y-GWYNT: The "spur" of Bryntysilio hill is so named in "Mr. and Mrs. Theodore Martin at Braich-y-Gwynt," in No. 120 of the series "Celebrities at Home," *The World* 4 Dec. 1878: 4-5. The author uses the same name for the house, but the Martins called it Bryntysilio. Theodore Martin does refer to "the Arm of the Winds," however, in a letter to Robert Browning, 27 Dec. 1886 (MS in "Holograph. Correspondence to Robert Browning," f. 64, Baylor Univ.
17. In a letter to me, dated 29 Nov. 1978, Mr. Edward Hubbard described the probable changes in the house made by the Martins and provided a sketch of the ground-floor plan as he had reconstructed it. All the architectural details in my description are from this letter. The quoted phrase "overhung with roses ..." is from "Mr. and Mrs. Theodore Martin at Braich-y-Gwynt" 4. The location of the drive, the gardens and "pleasure grounds" (a phrase from Sir Theodore's Will) are from my own observations.
18. When I visited Bryntysilio in the summer of 1969, there was a small stained-glass window above the staircase landing in the colours I mention. Miss Sara Pugh Jones of Llangollen told me there had once been a small dome in those colours. Mr. Hubbard suggested its probable location above the inner hall since that room is known to have been two storeys high and top-lit. According to the *World* article, the "light and airy" colour scheme of the inner hall set the motif for the whole house. See that article also for kettledrum, "den," and objects of art. Bryntysilio is still standing, but it has undergone drastic changes, including the demolishing of the west wing and the modification of the interior, which, among other things, has eliminated the inner hall. Even so, when I first saw the house, the view as one came up the drive gave much the same impression as in pictures from the Martins' time, and the well-tended shrubbery (though minus most of the sculptures) suggested what the grounds were once like. Since then there has been a deterioration. When I saw Bryntysilio in 1990, it was used as a holiday camp and "Outdoor Education Centre." The verandah posts were painted black, and the grounds had a barren, neglected look.
19. Marion Lochhead, in *The Victorian Household* (London, 1964) 42-43, discusses the duties of the various servants and their routines for the day. See also Elizabeth Burton's discussion of baths in *The Early Victorians at Home 1837-1861* (London, 1972) 108-12.
20. In a letter to me dated 3 Aug. [1967], Miss Gwyneth Jones, daughter of Jane Anne Williams Jones (see p. 194), wrote that when the Martins went to Wales the butler and six servants moved with them from London; these were in addition to

the housekeeper and three gardeners permanently employed at Bryntysilio. The London housekeeper remained at Onslow Square, for there are references in Martin's letters to her forwarding the mail. Other servants must have remained in London also, for Bryntysilio was smaller than the house on Onslow Square.

21. Sir Theodore Martin 231-32 ("model household," "observing eye"); Letter from Helen Faucit Martin to Mrs. Robert Wyndham, dated only "April 24th" (about the Scottish lass), Folger MS. Y.d.3.(92). The letter is in an album that once belonged to Harriet Faucit Bland.
22. Information from Miss Gwyneth Jones during an interview, Aug. 1981, at her home in Llangollen.
23. Sir Theodore Martin 230-31. There is no substance to the stories that she had agreed to marry on condition that she would do some acting each year to help support a family member, or members. She did give financial help, however, to her brother Edmund (E.F. Saville) and his family. Several letters of Helena F. Martin to William Cullenford, Secretary of the Royal General Theatrical Fund, mention cheques she is sending on their behalf. See, for example, her letter dated "Nov. 25th"in the Theatre Museum, and one dated "March 5th" (probably written after Saville's death in 1857), Folger MS. Y.d.3.[94].
24. *Dame Madge Kendal. By Herself* (London, 1933) 5.
25. HER THEATRICAL CRITICISMS: Theodore Martin 366-67. HER ARTISTIC CRITICISMS: Martin's letter to Robert Horn, 9 Feb. 1871, NLS MS. 3706, ff. 36-37 (Samuel Bough's drawing of Iona Cathedral); Martin's letter to Robert Horn, 28 May 1876, NLS MS. 3706, ff. 176-77 (wants his wife to see portrait by Robert Herdman before the final sitting so she can make suggestions – "There is no better critic"). HER LITERARY CRITICISM INFLUENCES MARTIN: Martin's letters to William Blackwood, 28 Jan. and 31 Jan. 1897, NLS MS. 4663, ff. 75-76 and 77-78.
26. Sir Theodore Martin 364. He speaks here of his wife's assistance with his biography of Prince Albert, but he makes similar statements elsewhere about other works. In a letter to William Blackwood, 15 Nov. 1894, he called his wife a "merciless critic" (NLS MS. 4620, ff. 127-28). See also his letter of 17 June 1895, MS. 4634, ff. 11-12.
27. Russell's statement was made in a review of Helena F. Martin's book on Shakespeare's heroines, in the *Liverpool Daily Post*, 24 June 1885. Theodore Martin's letter to Russell, dated 26 June 1885, is in NLS Acc. 8641 [Letters of Theodore Martin, 4th letter].
28. Sir Theodore Martin 364.
29. Hudson, *Munby* 128.
30. *Autobiography and Letters* 135.
31. Letter of 8 Oct. 1878, quoted by Sir Theodore Martin 349-51. The quoted passage is on p. 350.
32. Quoted by Sir Theodore Martin, 345-46.
33. *Leaves from an Actor's Note-Book* (New York, 1860) 42.
34. Sir Theodore Martin 264.
35. *Dame Madge Kendal* 5.
36. Sir Theodore Martin 201 (her "passion for order"), 297 ("much to make up").
37. Many of his letters mention heavy professional work. Examples: to Robert Horn, 14 May 1869, NLS MS. 3706, ff. 22-23 ("grinding at the mill"); to "Dear Sir"

(probably the Rev. Lucas Collins), 13 Apr. 1870, NLS MS. 4265, f. 152 (no time for literary work); and to William Blackwood, 18 June 1897, NLS MS. 4663, ff. 83-84 (too tired to read).

38. A number of Martin's letters in the NLS mention these subjects; a few examples follow. FLIGHTS FROM LONDON WEATHER: Letters to William Blackwood, 15 Nov. 1883, MS. 4448, ff. 122-23 and 2 May 1885, MS. 4475, ff. 160-61; and to John Stuart Blackie, 18 May 1887, MS. 2637, f. 56). TRAVEL BY EASY STAGES: Letters to Robert Horn, 1 Nov. 1869, MS. 3706, ff. 28-29; and to William Blackwood, 9 Jan. 1887, MS. 4504, ff. 218-19). ONLY COMPLAINT: Letter to Robert Horn, July 1877, MS. 3706, ff. 214-15.
39. Marriage record in St. Catherine's House, Kingsway.
40. Letter dated 3 Jan. 1891, MS in the HTC.
41. Diary entry of 26 Mar. 1886, quoted by Sir Theodore Martin 386.
42. Letter to Robert Horn, 4 Nov. 1873, NLS MS. 3706, ff. 71-72.
43. Letter to John Blackwood, 2 Apr. 1877, NLS MS. 4363, ff. 113-14.
44. HER BANK ACCOUNT: There are various references to purchases she made and cheques she wrote after marriage. Checks to the Theatrical Fund (see n. 23, above) are examples. When she wanted an engraving in a collection to be auctioned, her husband accompanied her to the dealer's rooms, but she put in her own order, or bid, for it (see n. 50, below). And when Robert Horn let her buy a drawing in his own collection as a wedding gift for Princess Louise, Theodore wrote and thanked him on her behalf, enclosing her cheque for £17, 10 s. to pay for it. See his letter to Horn, dated 15 Mar. 1871, NLS, MS. 3706, ff. 45-46. ESTATE AT DEATH: After all her expenditures, she still left an estate of £20, 059/8 (Probate, 1898).
45. Letters of Theodore Martin to Robert Horn, 19 Apr. 1871 and 1 July 1874, NLS MS. 3706, ff. 48-49, 103-4.
46. Helena F. Martin's letter to Horace Howard Furness, 25 Feb. 1892, Furness Library.
47. The Dalrymples are described by Arthur Munby (Hudson 128). Helen's early interest in the Elias girls is seen in a letter of 16 Sept. 1869 that she wrote to Dora, obviously intended for her sisters as well, giving advice about their reading. Theodore Martin's copy from the letter is in NLS MS. 16444, f.45. "Miss Elias" was a houseguest at Bryntysilio in 1886 (see Sir Theodore Martin 388). For Annette's picture of Helen, see p.261.
48. Helena Martin's letters to Henry Irving, 19 Jan. and 21 Jan. [1880], in the Theatre Museum, refer to her young cousin's holiday visit. Her note to a friend's daughter, Florence Tottenham [or Nettenbum?],dated only "June 26th," Folger MS. Y.c.902.(19), proposes some alternative excursions, including one to Drury Lane to see Salvini. In a letter to me, dated 10 July 1967, Mrs. M.H. Stephenson, whose family lived near the Martins when she was a child, recalls being taken by her sister to tea at Lady Martin's.
49. Reported in Arthur Munby's diary. See Hudson 231.
50. Quoted by Sir Theodore Martin 296-97.
51. Letter of 2 Mar. 1870, MS in Mander and Mitchenson.
52. She made three visits in all: on 2 and 3 June and a few days afterwards. See Sir Theodore Martin 316 (the "great ship" passage, from Helen's diary entry of 2 June 1871) and 317 (analogy with King Lear); also Helena Faucit Martin's letter to

Robert Browning, mentioning Macready's "tender ... greeting" ("Holograph Correspondence to Browning," f. 52, item 6, Baylor Univ.).

Chapter 12

1. See especially *Sunday Times* 1 Feb. 1852. The same review was published in *The Theatre* (1 Feb.: 139-40) and in the *Theatrical Journal* (4 Feb.: 33-34). Although embarrassingly hyperbolic, it is in line with other reviews in its essentials.
2. 31 January: 100-101. The *Sunday Times* said much the same thing. See also the article "On the Establishment of a Central Legitimate Company" in *Theatrical Journal* 17 Mar. 1852: 83-84.
3. Percy Allen, *The Stage Life of Mrs. Stirling* 106-8, 112.
4. *Courier* 24 Apr. 1852; *Examiner and Times* 21 Apr.
5. Sir Theodore Martin 233-34.
6. *Guardian* 21 Apr. 1852. See also *Courier* 24 Apr. and 1 May.
7. *Guardian* 10 Nov. and 13 Nov.; *Examiner and Times* 10 Nov.; *Courier* 13 Nov. Another possible reason why *Cymbeline* was not performed more often: despite approval of Helen Faucit's "exquisite" Imogen, one critic thought the play too "gross in its details of plot and incidents" to be fit for contemporary representation (*Manchester Courier* 13 Nov. 1852). I suspect, however, that practical considerations were more important.
8. *Weekly Review and Dramatic Critic* 26 Nov. 1852: 427. See also *Caledonian Mercury* 25 Nov.; *Edinburgh Evening Courant* 23 Nov.
9. "QUEEN": *Weekly Review*. "UNRIVALLED": *Scotsman* 24 Nov. See also *Edinburgh Evening Courant* 23 Nov. and *Caledonian Mercury* 22 Nov.
10. *Scotsman* 24 Nov. 1852. The same review praises Helen Faucit's Juliet.
11. This play had been published first in 1844, as part of Browning's series *Bells and Pomegranates*, then in 1846 in a collected edition of this series. It had never been acted.
12. Helen Faucit's letter of 22 Jan. 1853, requesting permission, is in "Holograph Correspondence to Robert Browning," f. 48, Baylor Univ.; Browning's reply, dated 31 Jan. 1853, is quoted by Sir Theodore Martin 237-38. Browning's letter to Forster, dated 12 Apr. 1853, is published in *New Letters of Robert Browning*, ed. William Clyde De Vane and Kenneth Leslie Knickerbocker (New Haven, 1950) 60-62.
13. *Daily News* 26 Apr.; *Literary Gazette* 20 Apr.: 435; *Illustrated London News* 30 Apr.: 327; *Athenaeum* 30 Apr.: 537.
14. *Times* 26 Apr.; *Examiner* 30 Apr.: 278; *Spectator* 30 Apr.: 414; *Morning Herald* 27 Apr.; *Morning Chronicle* 26 Apr.
15. Letter to her brother George, dated 2 May [1853], in *Letters of the Brownings to George Barrett*, ed. Paul Landis with Ronald E. Freeman (Urbana, 1958) 183-85 (Letter 44).
16. For example, *Examiner* and *Morning Chronicle.*
17. *Morning Herald* ("lofty poetical"); also *Morning Post; Daily News; Illustrated London News; Times; Athenaeum; Literary Gazette.*

18. Sir Theodore Martin (239) blamed the mildness of the play's success on mediocre performances by his wife's colleagues. Barry Sullivan did get mixed reviews, but the basic problem was the play's lack of dramatic substance.
19. *Examiner and Times* and *Guardian* ("occult"), both 1 June 1853.
20. Sir Theodore Martin 244.
21. *Examiner and Times* 5 July and 8 July 1855; *Guardian* 8 July.
22. See Brooke's letter of 4 July 1854 to his friend James Morris, quoted by W. J. Lawrence in *Gustavus Vaughan Brooke* 144.
23. After Helen Faucit's engagement in April 1855, Charles Mathews and Samuel Phelps came in May, Isabella Glyn in June, Ira Aldridge in December, and various other stars in the following year. See the playbills for the T.R. Dublin in the HTC: both the unbound ones covering the period 1851-57 and the bound ones covering 1854-55. These amply contradict the statement, in an obituary of Harris (*Irish Times*, 16 Mar. 1874), that he did not break his "steadfast rule of opposition to the 'starring system'" until Charles Kean's visit of 1859.
24. Sir Theodore Martin 244-46.
25. For Sullivan's performance see *Theatrical Journal* 20 June 1855: 196; *Globe*, quoted by Sir Theodore Martin 247; *Examiner* 16 June: 374; *Morning Herald* 13 June. For Franklyn's "dark side" see *Morning Chronicle* 12 June.
26. Quoted by Sir Theodore Martin 247-48.
27. *Observer* 22 July 1855.
28. DUBLIN: *Evening Packet* 13, 17, and 22 May 1856; *Evening Freeman* 19 May. BELFAST: The enthusiastic reviews of her Juliet, Pauline, and Rosalind in the *Daily Mercury* (3, 5, and 6 June 1856, respectively) are so detailed as to suggest that the writer has not seen her before.
29. Letters of Theodore Martin to John Stuart Blackie, NLS MS. 2624, ff. 167-70 (26 Oct. 1856), ff. 221-22 (11 Jan. 1857).
30. *Belfast Daily Mercury* 7 Apr. 1857. For reviews of Helen Faucit's last performances of Lady Mabel in Edinburgh and Dublin, see *The Scotsman* (11 Mar.1857) and the *Evening Freeman* (20 Apr.), respectively.
31. John Cole, in his *Life and Theatrical Times of Charles Kean* II: 232-47, gives an account of the Festival Performances, taking, of course, Kean's point of view. A number of articles deal with the supposed mistreatment of Kean and the various squabbles that allegedly plagued the performances. The account in *The Times*, 20 Jan. 1858, seems to be a reasonably balanced one; the most violently biased one, on the side of Kean, is in the *Theatrical Journal* 2 Feb. 1858: 35 (signed B.W.W.).
32. RA Queen Victoria's Journal, 19 Jan. 1858. My description of the evening is based on accounts in *The Times* 20 Jan 1858; *Morning Chronicle* 20 Jan.; *Morning Herald* 20 Jan.; *Daily News* 20 Jan.; *Daily Telegraph* 20 Jan.; *Theatrical Journal* 20 Jan.: 20; *Examiner* 23 Jan.: 53; *Spectator* 23 Jan.: 88; *Sunday Times* 24 Jan.; *Observer* 24 Jan.; and Theodore Martin 250-51. (One must discount, however, the long passage allegedly quoted from the *Art Journal*. See Prologue.) Fontane's account: see his *Shakespeare in the London Theatre 1855-58*, trans. and ed. Russell Jackson (London,1999) 108-11.
33. See, for example, the *Morning Herald, Morning Chronicle, Examiner.*
34. For an excellent survey of Dillon's career see Kathleen Barker, "Charles Dillon: A Provincial Tragedian," *Shakespeare and the Victorian Stage*, ed. Richard Foulkes 283-94.
35. See especially *Athenaeum*, 27 February 1858; also *Morning Post* and *Daily News*, both of 19 Feb. Although Dillon's vigour is emphasized by these and other periodicals,

the *Spectator* (20 Feb.: 202) says he gave a "steady well-considered impersonation" rather than a startlingly effective one, and the *Daily Telegraph* (19 Feb.) reports that his best scenes were "those in which pathos predominates over passion." Even if not exciting, however, Dillon's interpretation was evidently stronger than usual at that time.

36. *Daily News* 19 Feb.; *Sunday Times* 21 Feb.
37. CONTRASTS: *Morning Post* 19 Feb.; *Sun* 19 Feb. INTELLIGENCE AND ARTISTRY: *Morning Post; Sunday Times.* Both the early passages and the banquet scene were praised by the *Daily News* and the *Morning Post*; the latter also praised Miss Faucit's manner of persuading Macbeth to murder Duncan (though the *Sun* thought her too shrewish here) and her sleepwalking scene – the same two scenes the *Morning Chronicle* had singled out in reviewing the Festival Performance (20 Feb.).
38. 19 Feb. 1858. The *Observer*, which often stole reviews from other journals at this time, concocted a review (21 Feb.) combining some praise from the *Daily News* and some blame from the *Daily Telegraph.* The *Spectator* (20 Feb.: 202) damned with faint praise, saying the whole production reflected the "genius of carefulness."
39. Quoted by Sir Theodore Martin 254-55.
40. I have not seen a review of this performance, but Baynham (189) says it was "not pronounced a success." His date for the performance, 21 Apr. 1859, is incorrect, however. According to my records, the play was acted on 1 Apr., the last day of Miss Faucit's engagement. She stayed in Glasgow, "at great inconveniece to herself" (*Glasgow Daily Herald* 5 Apr.), to act Beatrice for Glover's benefit, but left after that.
41. A particularly interesting review from the *Citizen* makes this clear. See the undated clipping in the Saville Scrapbooks, vol. 5, f. 5 (recto), Central Public Library, Nottingham. See also the *Courier* 21 Feb., which defends Helen Faucit's conception of Lady Macbeth.
42. *Edinburgh Evening Courant*, 12 Nov.
43. *Evening Courant*, 12 Nov. The Bassanio was J.F. Cathcart.
44. Mrs. Glover's ad in the *Glasgow Daily Herald* 6 Feb. 1863 listed Helen Faucit among those she had engaged for the new season, but I can find no evidence that she acted there. Sir Theodore Martin (265), says she had engagements at Glasgow and Edinburgh in March and April 1863, 6 nights each, but I am certain she was not in Edinburgh at that time. He was evidently thinking of her engagements at those two cities in *1864*; the roles he names are the ones she acted that year, and one of the passages he quotes from unnamed reviews is from the *Caledonian Mercury* of 8 Apr. 1864.
45. Her acting partner, Swinbourne, however, was less appreciated in Edinburgh than he had been in Glasgow. He was accused of artificial elocution in Macbeth (*Caledonian Mercury* 15 Apr. 1864) and tameness in Romeo (*Scotsman* 12 Apr.).
46. Helena F. Martin 232. I do not know wheter she had temporarily abandoned the faint in Apr. 1864 or had not yet begun to use it.
47. *The Shakespeare Tercentenary of 1864* (London, 1984) 1-26.
48. Hunter, *Shakespeare and Stratford-upon-Avon, a "Chronicle of the Time": Comprising the Salient Facts and Traditions … together with a Full Record of the Tercentenary Celebration* (London, 1864) 159.
49. G.H. Lewes considered her Juliet "wholly without distinction." See *On Actors and the Art of Acting* (Leipzig, 1875) 151-53.

50. "Plays, Players, and Critics," *Fraser's Magazine* LXVIII (Dec. 1863): 767-76; the quotation is from 770. The article was republished under Martin's name in his *Essays on the Drama* [1st ser.] (London, 1874).
51. *The Journal of a London Playgoer* (London, 1891) 277-80 (Juliet), 283-84 (French melodrama). The reviews were first published in the *Examiner* on 14 May and 6 Aug.1864, respectively.
52. For a good critical survey of Shakespearean productions at Drury Lane in this period and a well-balanced assessment of Chatterton as a Shakespearean producer, see Daniel Barrett, "'Shakespeare Spelt Ruin and Byron Bankruptcy': Shakespeare at Chatterton's Drury Lane, 1864-1878," *Theatre Survey* XXIX (Nov. 1988): 155-73. As Barrett points out, the notorious phrase in his title was actually coined by Boucicault.
53. *Times* 20 Oct. 1864.
54. Derided by E.W. Godwin in "Theatrical Jottings," *Western Daily Press* (Bristol) 2 Nov. 1864. The bedroom furnishings were, however, appreciatively mentioned in *Morning Post* 19 Oct.
55. FIDELE COSTUME: *Art Journal* Dec. 1864: 373. PHELPS: *Morning Post*; *Sunday Times* 23 Oct. CRESWICK: *The Times* 20 Oct. LACY: *Morning Post*; *Sunday Times.* My discussion of HELEN FAUCIT'S IMOGEN will be based on the reviews already mentioned and those in *The Times* 18 October; *Morning Herald* 19 Oct.; *Athenaeum* 22 Oct.: 537; *Observer* 23 Oct.; *Spectator* 29 Oct.: 1237-38; and *Examiner* 5 Nov.: 712. The only critique I have seen that disparaged the production as a whole is the one by Godwin (see n.54, above), and even he admitted that Helen Faucit's acting was "undoubtedly a treat."
56. *Morning Post* (voice, figure, etc.); *Morning Herald* (same art but more finished).
57. The *Sunday Times* made much the same point but with greater emphasis on the harmoniousness and "poetic suggestiveness" of her acting.
58. *Observer.* See also *Morning Herald* and *Athenaeum.*
59. For another such criticism see the *London Review* IX (July - Dec. 1864): 455-56.
60. All the scenes are described in detail in the *Daily Telegraph* (5 Nov. 1864). See also *Observer* (6 Nov.) and *The Times* (7 Nov.) for the banquet scene and *Sunday Times* (6 Nov.) for the final scene. I base my discussion of the production on these sources and the following: *Daily News* 4 Nov.; *Sun* 4 Nov.; *Morning Post* 5 Nov.; *Morning Herald* 7 Nov.; *Examiner* 5 Nov.: 712, and 3 Dec.: 776; *Athenaeum* 12 Nov.: 643; *Illustrated London News* 12 Nov.: 498; *Bell's Life in London* 26 Nov.; *London Review* 9 (July-Dec. 1864): 534-35.
61. *Sun; Sunday Times; Times.* See also *Observer.*
62. Sir Theodore Martin 275-76.
63. The production was still very popular at the end of November (see *Bell's Life in London* 26 Nov. 1864), and presumably it continued to be well attended.
64. Other complaints were that he was not poetic enough and that his actions did not always bear out his words. See *Observer; London Review; Examiner; Illustrated London News.*
65. WEAK CHARACTER: *Daily News; Observer; Daily Telegraph; The Times.* STRONG AT THE END: *Examiner* 3 December.
66. For a reconstruction of her portrayal see Afterpiece.
67. NO "SIDDONIAN GRANDEUR": *Daily Telegraph.* TOO FEMININE: *Examiner* 3 Dec. See also *Daily News, The Sun, London Review.*
68. See *The Times; Sunday Times; Morning Herald* ("intellect towered"); *Observer.*

69. DORAN: Sir Theodore Martin 277. OXENFORD: *Times*. ARTIFICIALITY: *Illustrated London News* and *Athenaeum*. (The last two reviews, which are very similar in ideas, may have had a single author.)
70. His detailed and enthusiastic review of the performance was published on 6 Nov. 1864. On 27 Nov. was published an article, "The Character of Lady Macbeth," in which the critic, having reread the play, set forth the evidence for his own interpretation.
71. See *Examiner* 5 Nov.: 712.
72. LESS FAVOURABLE: *Illustrated London News, Athenaeum*, and *Examiner* (3 Dec.). PATHOS: *Sunday Times and Daily News* (see also *Morning Post* and *Observer*.) "POETICAL IMAGINING": *Morning Herald*, which says Miss Faucit was "transcendent" here.
73. PHELPS ON FAUCIT: John Coleman and Edward Coleman, *Memoirs of Samuel Phelps* (London, 1886) 188. FAUCIT ON PHELPS: Helena F. Martin 234-35.
74. Shirley Allen says that Helen Faucit, having "learned from Macready ... how to make effective points," was unwilling to accept the "tutelage" of an actor to whom Macready had assigned minor roles (*Samuel Phelps* 297-98). Actually Helen Faucit had long since departed radically from Macready's conception, but, after years as a star, she undoubtedly considered Phelps's suggestions impertinent.
75. See *Examiner* 11 Mar. 1865.
76. See especially *Daily News* 9 Mar. 1865; *Sun* 9 Mar.; *Athenaeum* 18 Mar.: 392-93; *Observer* 12 Mar.; *Pall Mall Gazette* 10 Mar.; *Times* 22 Mar.
77. Helena F. Martin 108-9 (including note), 153-54. (The date in the note should be 1865 rather than 1869.) *The Times* mentions both of the departures from stage convention, and the *Morning Post* says Miss Faucit spoke the prologue very impressively.
78. *Observer* 26 March ("delicacy, grace"); *Sunday Times* 26 May ("ideal ... intellectual"). *Daily Telegraph* (22 March) said that her "fair face and slim figure" gave little clue to the calendar but also admitted that she no longer had all her former qualifications for Juliet. As in the past, her Juliet was praised for such contrasting qualities as fervour and refinement. See *Morning Post* 21 Mar. 1865; *Times* 22 Mar.; *Illustrated London News* 25 Mar.: 279.
79. *Sixty Years of the Theatre: An Old Critic's Memories* (New York, 1916) 60-61. Towse says Miss Faucit came out of retirement at the age of 53 to give a single performance of Juliet for "some charitable object." Since, as far as I know, there was no such occasion, I assume he saw her during her Drury Lane engagement of 1865, when she was 50. According to my records, she acted Juliet only twice after this (in regular engagements at Manchester, 1866 and 1871). Towse left England in 1869.
80. Sir Theodore Martin 281-82.
81. INTERRUPTIONS OF *FAUST*: *Daily News* 20 Nov. 1866; *Daily Telegraph* 20 Nov.; *Times* 23 Nov. PACKED HOUSES: *Morning Post* 24 Nov. and 1 Dec. 1866; *Times* 3 Dec.; Edward Stirling, *Old Drury Lane: Fifty Years' Recollections of Author, Actor, and Manager*, 2 vols. (London, 1881) I: 275.
82. *The Morning Post* (24 Nov.) tells of an overflowing audience and "fervid applause." See Sir Theodore Martin 283 for Mrs. Ritchie's letter and 284 for Miss Jewsbury's.

83. *Dame Madge Kendal* 37; Bram Stoker, *Personal Recollections of Henry Irving*, 2 vols. (New York, 1906) I: 156; Ellen Terry, *The Story of My Life* (London, 1908) 109; Letters of Mary Anderson to William Winter, Folger MS. Y.c.61 (46 and 49). Both Madge Kendal and Ellen Terry defend the play.
84. "Miss Anderson's Juliet," *Shakespeariana*, 10 vols. (1883-93; New York, 1965) II: 6.
85. *London Review* XIII (1 Dec. 1866): 605.
86. Pauline: 30 Nov. 1870. Lady Macbeth: 29 Nov. Beatrice: 6 Dec.
87. *Examiner and Times* 18 Nov. 1871 (*Romeo and Juliet*); *Guardian* 15 Nov. (*Macbeth*); *Courier* 17 Nov. (*As You Lke It*).
88. *Examiner and Times* 14 Nov. (*Macbeth*); *Courier* 22 Nov. (*The Lady of Lyons*). The review praising Miss Ness's Celia is in the *Courier* 17 Nov.
89. *Guardian* 24 Nov. 1871.
90. *The Examiner and Times* (14 Nov.) agreed with the *Guardian* that the "true womanly side" of Lady Macbeth made itself felt only in the sleepwalking scene.
91. *Manchester Guardian* 17 Nov. 1871.
92. *Courier* 15 Nov. ("self-abandonment"); *Guardian* 17 Nov. (romantic comedy); *Examiner and Times* 18 Nov. (Juliet). Theodore Martin (318) incorrectly attributes the *Courier* review to the *Guardian.*
93. Sir Theodore Martin 327-28; *Examiner and Times* 25 Nov. 1871. See also Arthur Munby's record of Mrs.Martin's exuberant comments about the appreciative Manchester audiences, in Hudson, *Munby* 301.
94. Hudson, *Munby* 301. Zouch Troughton wrote to Sir Theodore on 6 Dec. 1871, "Of course London must be the scene of her actual farewell to the Stage" (NLS MS. 16437), and other admirers felt the same.
95. Letter to Miss Aytoun, dated 25 Dec. 1867, NLS MS. 4934, ff. 111-14. See also Helen Faucit's diary entry of 7 May 1871, quoted by Sir Theodore Martin (316).
96. For Helen Faucit's letter of 29 Jan. 1870, explaining her position, see Wendy Trewin, *The Royal General Theatrical Fund* 43. Although she had not acted for the Fund, however, she had made gifts to it (Trewin 12), as well as contributions on her brother Edmund's behalf.
97. Percy Mackaye, *Epoch: The Life of Steele Mackaye, Genius of the Theatre, ... A Memoir by His Son Percy Mackaye* (New York, c. 1927) 218.
98. Unidentified clipping in the Saville Scrapbooks, f.2 (verso), Nottingham Public Library, same article quoted by Sir Theodore Martin 334 ("shout of welcome" and "capacity to delight"); *Observer* 21 December ("nearly" undiminished looks); Frank Archer, *An Actor's Notebooks* (London, 1912) 153.
99. Archer 153 (grace and refinement); *Pall Mall Gazette* 23 Dec. 1873 ("fine ... intelligence"); Anna Maria Hall's note to Helen Faucit, quoted by Sir Theodore Martin 334 ("merrier parts").
100. See Helena F. Martin's letters to Henry Irving, 27 Apr. and 19 May 1876 (about the Webster benefit); 19 May, 22 May, and 27 May 1876 (about the proposed benefit for Irving), all in the Theatre Museum. See also Sir Theodore Martin 341.
101. See her letter to Irving, dated 7 June 1876, in the Library of the Ransom Research Center, Unversity of Texas, Austin (instructions about the scene) and her diary entries, quoted by Sir Theodore Martin 341.
102. *Recollections of Dublin Castle and Dublin Society* 29-30.
103. Diary entry of 18 Sept. 1879, quoted by Sir Theodore Martin 361. See also Rudolf Lehmann, *An Artist's Reminiscences* (London, 1894) 305.

104. Letter of 17 Jan. 1877, in the Theatre Museum.
105. Playblll in the Saville Scrapbooks, Vol. I, f. 6 (verso), Nottingham Public Library. See also Robert M. Sillard, *Barry Sullivan* II: 219-20. When the play was repeated, Ellen Wallis, who first played Hero, took over Beatrice.
106. Detailed articles on the Stratford Festival appeared in the *Daily News* (24, 25, and 26 Apr. 1879) and the *Sunday Times* (27 Apr.). In addition to these I used a review in the *Daily Telegraph* 25 Apr. and cuttings from a number of newspapers in Vol. I of "Theatre Records," Shakespeare Centre Library, Stratford-upon-Avon.
107. *Daily News* 24 Apr.; *Sunday Times.*
108. *Illustrated Sporting and Dramatic News* 3 May 1879: 22; *New York Herald* 5 May (among cuttings, see note 106). The quotation is from the *Herald.*
109. *Daily Telegraph; Sunday Times.*
110. Helena F. Martin 327.
111. "Letter from Stratford-on-Avon," *Boston Daily Commercial* 26 Apr. 1879. See also *New York Herald* 5 May (among cuttings, note 106).
112. Irving's response is mentioned in Helena F. Martin's letter to him, dated 15 May, in the Theatre Museum. No year is given, but it was undoubtedly 1879. See note 113, below.
113. Helena F. Martin's letters are dated only 15 May and 25 June, respectively, but Theodore Martin's letter, obviously written the same summer, is fully dated, 27 June 1879. All are in the Theatre Museum.
114. See Richard Foulkes, *The Calverts: Actors of Some Importance* (London, 1992) 55-75 (the Calverts' Shakespearean productions); 92-95 (the Memorial Performances).
115. For the cast see Alfred Darbyshire, *The Art of the Victorian Stage* (1907; New York, 1969) 65-66. This list, taken from the printed programme, gives Sambourne's name for Corin, but on p. 64 Darbyshire tells of the last-moment substitution. Information about the men who played the chief parts is from the *DNB*: Wingfield (1900), Merivale and Darbyshire (1912); and from Foulkes, *The Calverts,* which emphasizes their work with Calvert (see esp. 66 and 68).
116. Reported by Violet Vanbrugh in *Dare to be Wise* (London, 1925) 39, quoted by Foulkes 94.
117. Sir Theodore Martin 361-62 (he quotes Merivale on 362); Darbyshire 61 (rehearsals), 68 ("Goddess").
118. Sir Theodore Martin 361.
119. ILLNESS: Sir Theodore Martin 361. APPLAUSE BY AUDIENCE AND ACTORS: Darbyshire 67; Helena F. Martin 283; Merivale, quoted by Sir Theodore Martin 362. CONFUSION CAUSED BY TWO ROSALINDS: Darbyshire 67. For a critical response to the production see *Examiner and Times* 3 Oct. 1879.
120. Darbyshire 69-70.
121. Herman Merivale, quoted by Sir Theodore Martin 362. See also *Examiner and Times* 3 Oct. 1879.
122. Letter from Helena F. Martin to Lewis Wingfeld, dated 6 Oct. 1879, Folger MS. Y.c.902.(25); Helena F. Martin 283-84 ("keen regret").
123. Sir Theodore Martin 363.

Chapter 13

1. SALVINI: See Helena F. Martin's letter to Robert Browning, 12 June 1875, asking his help in inviting Salvini to dinner (ms in "Holograph Correspondence to Robert Browning," f.53, item 7, Baylor Univ.). BARRETT AND BOOTH: Sir Theodore Martin 372, 374.
2. *Reminiscences*, 2 vols. (London, 1899) II: 245-46.
3. *The Letters and Private Papers of William Makepeace Thackeray*, ed. Gordon N. Ray, 4 vols. (Cambridge, Mass., 1946) IV: 284, 338 (examples of Thackeray's notes to the Martins), 121-22 (letter to his daughters praising Mrs. Martin); Sir Theodore Martin 258 (Thackeray at the breakfast table, his note to Lady Knighton praising Mrs. Martin).
4. Sir Theodore Martin 287.
5. Sir Theodore Martin 348.
6. Sir Theodore Martin 256-57.
7. *The George Eliot Letters*, ed. Gordon S. Haight, 9 vols. (New Haven, 1954-55) II: 97-98 (letter to Mrs. Charles Bray, about Helen Faucit at soirée); IV: 139 (note 4), 144 (Lewes's journal entry of 4 Apr. 1864). See also Sir Theodore Martin 265.
8. Rudolf Lehmann, *An Artist's Reminiscences* (London, 1894) 235.
9. Susanne Howe, *Geraldine Jewsbury. Her Life and Errors* (London, 1935) 44 et passim; *Selections from the Letters of Geraldine Endsor Jewsbury* ed. Mrs. Ireland, Introd., v-xviii, esp. xii-xiv. The quotation is from Howe.
10. Geraldine Jewsbury's autograph letter is in my personal collection. For the pertinent passage in the novel, see *Once and Again A Novel, By the author of "Cousin Stella"* ... *etc. etc.* 3 vols. (London, 1865) III: 163. The author was a Mrs. C. Jenkin. For Miss Jewsbury at Mrs. Willert's see Sir Theodore Martin 361.
11. John Hollingshead, *My Lifetime*: 178-79. The clergyman was Dr. Norman Macleod, who was later Queen Victoria's chaplain.
12. Sir Theodore Martin 257; "Kingsley, Charles," *DNB* (1892-93).
13. Diary entry of 12 May 1867, quoted by Sir Theodore Martin 286. For Blackie's personality see Introd. to *The Letters of John Stuart Blackie to His Wife*, ed. Archibald Stodart Walker (Edinburgh, 1909); also Anna M. Stoddart, *John Stuart Blackie: A Biography*, 2 vols. (Edinburgh, 1895) I: passim. For Blackie's Gaelic-style Greek see Arthur Mursell, *Memories of My Life* 48-50. In letters to his wife Blackie makes numerous references to visits with the Martins.
14. "Stokes, Margaret McNair," *DNB* (1901).
15. "Froude, James Anthony," *DNB* (1901): Sir Theodore Martin 401. It was Lady Ducie to whom Froude expressed his admiration of Helena Martin.
16. "Adams, John Couch," *DNB* (1901).
17. Letter of Theodore Martin to Robert Horn, 15 June 1873, NLS, MS. 3706, ff. 65-66; George G. Lerry, *Henry Robertson, Pioneer of Railways into Wales* (Oswestry, 1949) passim; E. T. MacDermot, *History of the Great Western Railway*, 2 vols. (London, 1927)

I, Part I: 343-45. At least two other "railroad aristocrats" had houses near the Martins': Mr. Beyer, Robertson's partner in a Manchester locomotive firm, who built a "chateau," Llantysilio, behind the Martins' property; and William Wagstaff, who owned the imposing Plas-y-Vivod on Benwyn Hill, across the Dee from Bryntysilio.

18. "Hamley, Sir Edward Bruce," *DNB* (1901); M. J. Williams, "The Egyptian Campaign of 1882," *Victorian Military Campaigns*, ed. Brian Bond (New York and Washington, 1967) 254 ("autocratic," etc.); letter of Theodore Martin to William Blackwood, 16 Aug. 1893, NLS, MS.4604, ff. 33-34 (Hamley's narrow escapes in battle).
19. Patrick Byrne, *The Wildes of Merrion Square* 55-59 (salon in Dublin), 149-51 (salon in London); Horace Wyndham, *Speranza* 77; Terence De Vere White, *The Parents of Oscar Wilde* 126 (salon in Dublin), 243-50 (salon in London, descriptions of her and her sons, etc.). Wyndham (113-14) names Helen Faucit among those who attended Lady Wilde's London salon. Both Martins refer to Lady Wilde in letters: e.g. in Theodore Martin's letter to John Blackwood, 16 Oct. 1870 (NLS, MS. 4265, ff. 204-5); and in Helena F. Martin's letter to Lady Wilde, dated only 17 Apr. (probably 1879) about the latter's prospective move to London (Folger MS Y.c.902 [21]). See also Helena F. Martin's letter to Oscar Wilde, dated only 4 Feb., regretfully declining, on account of illness, his invitation to "meet" his mother at his home on Friday (Library of the Henry Ransom Humanities Research Centre, University of Texas).
20. Hudson, *Munby, Man of Two Worlds* 126, 128. See also "Stokes, Whitley," *DNB* (1912).
21. Hudson, *Munby* 124-25.
22. Hudson, *Munby* 227, 232 (diary entries of 6 July and 19 Nov. 1866).
23. "Helps, Sir Arthur," *DNB* (1891); *Realmah. By the Author of "Friends in Council,"* new ed. (London, 1869) 475-76.
24. Sir Theodore Martin 342, 385. The quoted phrase is from Helena F. Martin's letter to Henry Irving, written 17 Jan. [1880?], in the Theatre Museum.
25. Sir Theodore Martin, *Queen Victoria as I Knew Her*, 3rd impression (Edinburgh, 1908) 3-11.
26. RA Queen Victoria's Journal, 10-17 Jan. 1868; Martin, *Queen Victoria* 22-24; Elizabeth Burton, *Early Victorians at Home* 71-72 (description of Osborne House). Although the Martins were first-time guests at Osborne House, they had visited the Isle of Wight before. A letter from Helena Martin to Mme. Sala, dated 31 May, was written at a hotel there. Mme. Sala died on 11 Apr. 1860. (MS in my collection.)
27. RA Queen Victoria's Journal, 20-22 Jan. 1868; Sir Theodore Martin, 295-96.
28. RA Queen Victoria's Journal, 23 Jan.-3 Feb. 1868; Martin, *Queen Victoria* 25, 32.
29. Sir Theodore Martin 301-2, 306 (Osborne visits, garden party, shawl), 341-42 (Birthday Book – it is now in the Shakespeare Centre Library, Stratford-upon-Avon) 2 Mar., 328-30 (Prince's illness, services at Westminster Abbey and St. Paul's); also letters of Theodore Martin to Robert Horn, 9 Feb., 13 Feb., 1 Mar., 2 Mar., 6 Mar., 19 Apr. 1871, NLS, MS. 3706, ff. 36-49 (Helen's wedding gift to Princess Louise). Public rejoicing over the Prince's recovery: *Munby*, ed. Hudson 304-5, and Charles L. E. Brookfield, *Random Reminiscences* (London, 1902) 18-19.
30. See her letter of 6 Jan. 1879, inviting Henry Irving to such a party. MS in the Theatre museum.

31. See Helena F. Martin's letter to Robert Browning, undated but obviously in the early 1870s, in "Holograph Correspondence to Robert Browning,' f.59, item 20, Baylor University. (The published version of this letter inaccurately gives the name "Lefect" instead of "Lefort" and silently omits "room" from the phrase "room singing" (i.e. drawing-room singing as contrasted with public concerts).
32. According to Munby's diary entry of 6 July 1869 (Hudson 273), there had been some "good singing" that night, "with Benedict at the piano. Martin himself sang with great feeling." Scottish songs were Martin's speciality.
33. Helen's diary entry, 17 July 1881, quoted by Martin 374.
34. Hudson, *Munby* 335, 284-85, 273 (entries for 11 July 1873, 30 May 1870, and 6 July 1869, respectively).
35. BROWNING: Hudson, Munby 126; E. M. Sellar, *Recollections and Impressions* 215-17, 304-7, esp. 306. THACKERAY: *Munby* 126. FROUDE: "Froude, James Anthony," *DNB* (1901); Sellar 123); *Munby* 176-77.
36. Diary entry of 11 July 1867, quoted by Martin 287 (17 guests). Numerous references to dinners, large and small, occur in letters to Browning, Blackie, Irving, and other friends.
37. VICTORIAN DINNERS: Elizabeth Burton, *Early Victorians at Home* 154-59; Marion Lochhead, *The Victorian Household* 37-38; Charles André Francatelli, *Francatelli's The Modern Cook (1846): 1462 Recipes by Queen Victoria's Chef,* new introd. Daniel V. Thompson (New York, c.1973) 507-54 et passim. COMPLEXITY: Helps 307.
38. GERALDINE JEWSBURY: p.231, above. ANNA SWANWICK: Sir Theodore Martin 388.
39. Sir Theodore Martin 344, 347-48, 357-60, 377, 387.
40. IRVING: A number of the Martins' letters to him in the Theatre museum (including the one I quoted) deal with the readings. KATE SAVILLE: A letter of Theodore Martin's to Irving, 27 June 1879, mentions her prospective reading of Celia.
41. See the references in n.39, above; also Edwina Booth Grossman, Edwin Booth 14.
42. Hon. Alfred E. Gathorne Hardy, ed. *Gathorne Hardy, First Earl of Cranbrook. A Memoir, with Extracts from His Diary and Correspondence,* 2 vols. (London, 1910) II: 71 (diary entry of 6 June 188); Augustus J. C. Hare, *The Story of My Life,* 4 vols. (London, 1901) III: 252.
43. Letter of Helena F. Martin to Henry Irving, 8 July [1882], in the Theatre Museum, Letter of Theodore Martin to William Blackwood, 26 May 1870, NLS, MS. 4265, f.165.
44. See Theodore Martin's letter to Horace Howard Furness, 24 Aug. 1892, and Helena F. Martin's letter, also to Furness, 1 July 1892, both in the Furness Library.
45. "Mr. and Mrs. Theodore Martin at Braich-y-Gwynt," *The World* 4 Dec. 1878: 4.
46. Helena F. Martin, letter of 21 Jan. 1876 to Geraldine Jewsbury (two guests at a time, succession of visitors), published in Howe's *Geraldine Jewsbury* 208-9. A good many guests are named in various of the Martins' letters. Adams's barometer is mentioned in an obituary, "Death of Helen Faucit," unidentified newspaper clipping dated 1 Nov. 1898, in the Extra-Illustrated *Actors and Actresses,* HTC.
47. Sir Theodore Martin 345, 348; "Grand Entertainment in Aid of the Cottage Hospital," newspaper clipping (unidentified but with 7 Sept. 1877 handwritten) in the Saville Scrapbooks, Vol. I, p.3 (Nottingham Public Library); "Llangollen

Hospital – Entertainment. Reading by Mrs. Theodore Martin," *Oswestry Advertiser*, 25 Sept. 1878.

48. Lady St. Helier, *Memories of Fifty Years* (London, 1909) 79-80 (Lady Egerton's personality); letters of Theodore Martin to Robert Horn, 17 Oct. 1874, NLS, MS. 3706, ff. 124-25 (Condover Hall), and to William Blackwood, 11 Dec. 1877, NLS, MS. 4363, ff. 141-42 (New Lodge); Martin, *Queen Victoria* 20-21 (identity of Van de Wayer). The Martins' visits to other friends are mentioned in various letters. Helena F. Martin's letter to Gerlading Jewsbury, 21 Jan. 1876, published in the appendix of *Geraldine Jewsbury* (208-9), includes several place names that Susanne Howe could not read: "Tat–Park" and "A–Hall" should be "Tatton Park" and "Condover Hall" (which often looks like "Andover" in Helen's handwriting).
49. Sir Theodore Martin 332.
50. CRITICAL PRAISE: quoted phrase from Sir Theodore Martin 354 (he gives the wrong year; 1878); see also the detailed and enthusiastic review in the *Glasgow News* 22 Mar. 1879. WEATHER: Letter of Theodore Martin to Mr. [John?] Blackwood, dated 20 Mar. 1879, NLS, MS. 4395, ff. 74-75.
51. Helena F. Martin to "My dear Sir" [Robert Wyndham], 22 Aug. [1864], Folger MS. Y.c.902 (26).
52. Sir Theodore Martin 289-90. The quotation is from his wife's diary entry of 5 Sept 1867.
53. E. M. Sellar, *Recollections and Impressions* 36-37; Herman Merivale and Frank T. Marzials, *Life of W. M. Thackeray*. Great Writers Series (London, 1891) 235-36; letter from G. H. Lewes to Mrs. Charles Lee Lewes, 8 Aug. 1867, in *The George Eliot Letters*, ed. Haigh, IV: 383.
54. Sir Theodore Martin 260-61. He quotes the review in the original French.
55. Sir Theodore Martin 308; letter of Theodore Martin to John Blackwood, 8 Oct. 1870, NLS, MS. 4265, ff. 202-3. For a description of conditions in Paris at that time see Frank Archer, *An Actor's Notebooks* Ch. 3.
56. Hawthorne, *The English Notebooks* 310.
57. Theodore Martin's letter to Robert Horn, 21 Sept. 1875, NLS, MS. 3706, ff. 153-54.
58. See Theodore Martin's letters of 29 Mar. 1877 ("spinning") and 19 Aug. 1877 (Bryntysilio, eight hours a day at his desk), to Robert Horn, NLS, MS. 3706, ff. 205-6 and f. 220, respectively. Blackwood's "Sainted Albert" letter was written to Martin on 26 Apr. 1870; it is now in the NLS, MS. 30363, pp. 304-5. Helena F. Martin's letter to Geraldine Jewsbury, dated 21 Jan. 1876, is published in Howe 208-9.
59. She had already honoured him with the Companionship of the Bath in 1875. For a description and picture of Sir Theodore's coat of arms see Arthur Charles Fox-Davies, *Armorial Families: A Directory of Some Gentlemen of Coat-Armour*, 3rd ed. (Edinburgh, 1899) 569-70.
60. Sir Theodore Martin 364-65.
61. Letter of Theodore Martin to William Blackwood, 28 Sept. 1880, NLS, MS. 4409, ff. 260-61. Lord Fife was the 6th Earl of Fife, later created Duke, a member of the Duff family and, through his mother, grandson of William IV and the actress Dorothy Jordan.
62. Letter of 30 Sept. 1880, RA S 12/51.
63. Theodore Martin to William Blackwood, 20 Oct., 26 Oct., 26 Nov., and 11 Dec 1880, NLS, MS. 4409, ff. 262-65, 268-71.

Chapter 14

1. Sir Theodore Martin 368-70; Martin's letters to William Blackwood about private printings, 30 August 1880 (Ophelia), 9 Sept. 1880 (Portia), and 31 Oct. 1880 ("brochure looks very elegant"), NLS, MS. 4409, ff. 246-47, 250-51, and 266-67; copy of William Blackwood's letter to Theodore Martin, 23 Nov. 1880 (pleased that Lady Martin agrees to publication in "Maga"), NLS, MS. 30368, p. 167.
2. Letter of Helena F. Martin to William Blackwood, 4 Aug. 1881, NLS, MS. 4423, ff. 186-87; William Blackwood to Theodore Martin, 8 Sept. 1881, NLS, MS. 30368, pp. 458-9.
3. Offprints of the *Blackwood* publications were also provided, with blank flyleaves for inscriptions. Hence the fairly numerous "pamphlets" of the individual essays still to be found.
4. There was also a German edition (1890). My references are to the fourth edition (1891), which contains all the essays but not the preface that Lady Martin herself had discarded. An extract from the latter is published in Sir Theodore Martin's biography of his wife, 403-5.
5. Helena F. Martin viii, 108.
6. In a letter of 4 Aug. 1881 to William Blackwood (see n.2, above), Lady Martin confessed that she had "no power of composition." She would sometimes jot down passages, as they came to her and later try to fit them in where they seemed to go best. See also Sir Theodore Martin's letter to William Blackwood , 1 Feb. 1881, NLS MS. 4423, ff. 197-98.
7. Letters of Helena F. Martin to William Blackwood, 28 Jan. 1881, 7 Feb. [1881], and 4 Aug. 1881, NLS, MS. 4423, ff. 180-83, 186-87.
8. Discussion will be based on articles in the *Athenaeum*, 12 Sept. 1885: 345; *Times*, 26 Nov. 1885: 16; *St. James's Gazette* (undated clipping in the Saville Scrapbooks, Vol. I, p. 8, Nottingham Public Library); *Academy*, 27 June 1885: 447-48 (review by Edward Dowden); *The Theatre*, n.s. VI1 (July 1885): 17-27 (William Archer, "Ophelia and Portia: A Fable for Critics"); *Pall Mall Gazette*, 13 June 1885: 5; *Gentleman's Magazine*, CCLX (May 1886): 451-62 (Alex Japp, "Lady Martin's Female Characters of Shakespeare").
9. Archer's article, though not intended as a review of Lady Martin's book, is more interesting than W.E. Waller's approving but perfunctory review, which directly follows it in the same number of *The Theatre*, pp. 28-34.
10. Letter to Mrs. Wister, 24 Oct. 1897, in *Letters of Horace Howard Furness*, ed. H.H.F. Jayne, 2 vols. (Boston, 1922) I: 338-39. Extracts from Lady Martin's comments on Portia, Rosalind, Beatrice, Lady Macbeth (from her Rosalind essay), and Leontes (in *The Winter's Tale*) are included in the relevant volumes of the Variorum.
11. Margaret Oliphant later described it so. She added that, at Lady Martin's age, this was "so touching as to make one ashamed of [a] smile." See *Autobiography and Letters* 135.

12. As far as I know, Helen Faucit acted Ophelia only six times in her career, four being in Paris. She acted Desdemona fairly often during her London period (1836-43) but very few times in her starring days. The other characters discussed in her essays were acted throughout her career.
13. Discussions of Helen Faucit's portrayals in the Afterpiece show how passages in the essays relate to her performances as described by reviewers and other eyewitnesses.
14. See my discussion of her Ophelia as acted in Paris, Ch. 8.
15. Helena F. Martin 219-23. Some of Helen Faucit's admirers expressed pleasure in her essay because it reminded them of her portrayal of Imogen – "the only absolutely perfect one" of his age, Halliwell-Phillips wrote to Sir Theodore (6 Dec. 1882); the Shakespearean character that most resembled her representative, Lady Wilde assured Lady Martin (24 Jan. 1883). Extracts of these letters, copied by Theodore Martin, are in NLS MS. 16444, ff. 31-32.
16. Theodore Martin's copy of a passage from Tennyson's letter to Lady Martin (13 Jan. 1883), NLS, MS. 16444, f. 32.
17. Letters of Helena F. Martin to William Blackwood, 14 Jan. [1881], and Theodore Martin to William Blackwood, 19 Jan. 1881, NLS, MS. 4423, ff. 178-79, 193-94.
18. *Athenaeum*, 12 Sept. 1885: 345.
19. MS in the Furness Library. Georgianna Ziegler, in her fine essay "The Actress as Shakespearean Critic: Three Nineteenth-Century Portias," *Theatre Survey* XXX (1989): 98, suggests that, by showing Portia as "merely a mouthpiece of the Court," Lady Martin was "passing the burden of this harsh judgment off from Portia" and also "submerging Portia's 'own quick wit' under the accepted judgment of a masculine court." I suggest a different explanation of Helen Faucit's byplay. Bellario had been appealed to by the Duke for his legal opinion, but neither he nor his representative should have the authority to pronounce judgment independently of the Court. Theodore Martin, trained in the law, was probably uneasy about Shakespeare's cavalier treatment of courtroom procedure, and Helen Faucit invented some business to make the situation seem more regular.
20. Sir Theodore Martin 402-3 (decline in drama, staging, acting); Helena F. Martin 328-31 (misuse of scenery; good use by Macready), 332-33 (inter-act calls): Letter of Helena F. Martin to Henry Irving, 31 May [1876], MS in the Theatre Museum (long runs).
21. Sir Theodore Martin 391 (Jenny Lind's letter); Helena F. Martin 331.
22. Letter of 5 Aug. 1889, MS in the Furness Library.
23. "The Meiningen Company and the London Stage," published anonymously in *Blackwood's Magazine* CXXX (Aug. 1881): 253; rpt.in Martin's *Essays on the Drama*, 2nd ser. (London, 1889).
24. Quoted by Sir Theodore Martin 372.
25. Mary Anderson (Mme. De Navarro), *A Few Memories* (London, 1896) 30, note.
26. For example, she wrote on 9 June 1882: "With all my enthusiastic love of my art at no time could I have borne such a strain upon my brain & strength. I hope you will not tax them too far" (MS, Theatre Museum).
27. Letters of Helena F. Martin to Henry Irving, in the Theatre Museum: 27 Jan. 1875 (*Hamlet*); 20 May 1893 (*Becket*).
28. Letter of Theodore Martin to William Blackwood, 8 Sept. 1890, NLS, MS. 4556, ff. 198-99. ("It is rather too bad to be giving Lady Martin the blame for it. Nothing could induce her to write a line of criticism of any living actor or actress.") A

periodical called *The Illustrated American* published a reproduction of Kenneth Macleay's portrait of Helen Faucit on 25 Oct. 1890, with a caption reading, in part: "It is she who is credited with a fierce attack on Ada Rehan's Rosalind, which recently appeared in 'Blackwood's.'" A clipping of this is in a scrapbook devoted to Ada Rehan in the Robinson Locke Collection, Library of the Performing Arts, New York Public Library, Lincoln Center.

29. Mary Anderson 242. Another time Lady Martin read the last three acts of *As You Like It* to Mary Anderson. It is not clear whether this was before or after the latter's production of the play at Stratford. See Sir Theodore Martin's letter to William Blackwood, 18 Sept. 1885, NLS, MS. 4475, ff. 175-76.
30. "Holograph Correspondence to Robert Browning," Baylor Univ. Helen's praise was as sincere as it was enthusiastic. In a letter to Macready, 2 Mar. 1870 (MS in Mander and Mitchenson) she reported that Queen Victoria admired Mrs. Browning's poems but did not care for Browning's. "I wish the Queen had time to read for herself 'The Ring and the Book,'"she wrote. "How she would change her opinion!" For Helen's love of *The Saint's Tragedy* and *The Spanish Gypsy* see Sir Theodore Martin 257 and 299, respectively. Of the latter she wrote, "It is a wonderful book, so deep, so tender, and yet so sad, as all great things must be ... I think only a woman could have written it."
31. For example, see her comment on Sir Thomas Lawrence's portrait of Elizabeth Farren (Sir Theodore Martin 288). She had never cared for Lawrence's work until she saw this picture, which charmed her with its grace, life, and elegance. On this work of his, but no other, she bestowed the accolade "noble."
32. Diary entries of 7 Apr. 1867 (Millais) and 6 Nov. 1870 (Rossetti), quoted by Sir Theodore Martin 285-86 and 308-9.
33. Diary entry of 2 May 1881, quoted by Sir Theodore Martin 372-73.
34. Diary entry of 21 Dec. 1883, quoted by Sir Theodore Martin 379.
35. Diary entries of 20 July 1867 and 23 Sept. 1867, quoted by Sir Theodore Martin 288, 291.

Chapter 15

1. Sir Theodore Martin 375-76.
2. Rt. Hon. James William Lowther, Viscount Ullswater, A *Speaker's Commentaries*, 2 vols. (London, 1925) I: 149. Judging by the context, he is referring to a visit to Lady Ashburton in either 1881 or 1882. The Martins were there in the first week of Jan. 1881 (letter of Helena F. Martin to William Blackwood, 31 Dec. 1880, NLS 4409, ff. 227-28) and in Sept. 1882 (Sir Theodore Martin, 378).
3. Sir Theodore Martin 360. No date is given, but the incident must have occurred after 20 June 1882, the probable date of Lady Martin's last sleepwalking scene at one of her own drawing-room readings (she added it to the scheduled readings from *Much Ado*).

4. Quoted by Sir Theodore Martin, 393-94.
5. Sir Theodore Martin 379-82. When Lady Martin gave a small dinner party in Nov. 1884, she told Browning it was the first she had been able to give in more than two years. See her letter of 24 Nov, [1884], in "Holograph Correspondence to Robert Browning," f. 55, item 12, Baylor Univ.
6. Sir Theodore Martin 390-93; Theodore Martin's letter to Arthur Munby, written at the Hôtel de Provence, Cannes, 2 Mar. 1887, MS. in the Osborn Collection, Beinecke Library, Yale University (one of several letters describing the experience).
7. Helena F. Martin's letter to Robert Browning, 24 July 1886, "Holograph Correspondence to Robert Browning," f. 56, item 13, Baylor Univ.; Robert Browning's letters to Lady Martin, 28 July 1886, and Sir Theodore Martin, 2 Aug. 1886, MS. 12816 and MS. 12818, respectively, in the Huntington Library (quotation from the latter, which is also published in *New Letters of Robert Browning*, ed. William Clyde De Vane and Kenneth Knickerbocker [New Haven, 1950] 331-32); Sir Theodore Martin 388 (quotes from Sarianna Browning's letter).
8. See Browning's letter to Mrs. Charles Skirrow, 30 Aug. 1886, *New Letters* 333-34.
9. Sir Theodore Martin 388-89 (diary entries of 10 Sept. and 14 Oct. 1886). A number of Browning's friends attempted to describe his talk. An especially vivid description is quoted by Edmund Gosse in *Robert Browning, Personalia* (Boston, 1890) 81-82.
10. Letter of Robert Browning to Lady Martin, 12 Aug. 1887, MS. 12825 in the Huntington Library. Sir Theodore Martin (389-90) quotes from it, inexactly.
11. Arthur Ponsonby, *Henry Ponsonby: Queen Victoria's Private Secretary* (New York, 1943) 46.
12. *Blackwood's Magazine*, Dec. 1888 (poem on Empress Frederick); *Blackwood's*, Jan. 1894 (on Prince Alexander). Martin refers to such poems in a number of letters to William Blackwood.
13. Sir Theodore Martin 394.
14. "The Queen's Visit to Denbighshire," *Oswestry and Border Counties Advertizer*, 28 Aug. 1889, 7-8. This is a continuation, in the newspaper proper, of its *Royal Visit Supplement.*
15. Sir Theodore Martin (395) quotes a diary entry telling of the nosegay; Miss Gwyneth Jones, whose mother told her about the Queen's visit, mentions the lightcakes in a letter to me, dated 3 Aug. [1967].
16. *Oswestry Advertizer*, 28 Aug. 1889, 7-8.
17. Letter to me from Miss Gwyneth Jones, 3 Aug. [1967].
18. Sir Theodore Martin 394-95; *Oswestry Advertizer.*
19. RA L 27/72b.
20. Sir Theodore Martin 395-96 (Queen's letter); Gwyneth Jones, letter to me (teaset).
21. Sir Theodore Martin 398-99; *Letters of Anne Thackeray Ritchie. With Forty-two Additional Letters from Her Father William Makepeace Thackeray*, ed. Hester Ritchie (London, 1924) 210.
22. Quoted by Sir Theodore Martin 399.
23. Diary entry of 11 Jan. 1886, quoted by Sir Theodore Martin 386.
24. PERCY FARREN: A copy of Lady Martin's book, with an inscription to Percy Farren, is in the Shakespeare Centre Library; pasted in it are a letter to him (written 27 Sept. 1895) and two Christmas cards from Lady Martin, also a small photograph of her. The Folger has a series of letters to Augustin Daly about a

possible position for William Farren, jun. (Percy) in his company, including a letter of recommendation from Helena F. Martin. KATE SAVILLE THORPE: Kate had left the stage in 1872 and married William Roby Thorpe, a wealthy merchant of Nottingham.

25. Letter from Marston to Frank Archer, written 5 Dec. 1888, quoted in Archer's *An Actor's Notebooks* 233. See also the extract from Marston's letter to Lady Martin, written 13 Dec. 1888, copied by Sir Theodore, in NLS, MS. 16444, ff. 18-19.
26. Sir Theodore Martin 401-2.
27. VICTORIAN ORDER: In a letter to his sister, dated 22 Nov. 1896, Furness tells of Lady Martin's news about this. See *Letters of Horace Howard Furness*, ed. Jayne I: 309. JUBILEE: See Theodore Martin's letter to William Blackwood, 18 June 1897, NLS, MS. 4663, ff. 83-84.
28. Sir Theodore Martin 381, 401, 406. Martin's letters to William Blackwood contain many references to his wife's poor health.
29. Mrs. Catherine Gedge, whose father had been a steward on one of the estates at Berwyn (across the Dee from Bryntysilio), told me this in an interview at her hotel in Worthing on 16 July 1967. She said that she had lived on Berwyn hill until she was 17 or 18 years old, had often seen Lady Martin in her pony cart, and had heard much talk of the Martins.
30. Helena F. Martin, letter to Henry Irving, 2 Feb. 1898, MS in the Theatre Museum.
31. Sir Theodore Martin 406. Martin's letter to William Blackwood, 27 Sept. 1898 (NLS, MS. 4678, ff. 115-16), expresses his fears for his wife: she has not been able to leave her room since they arrived at Bryntysilio.
32. Sir Theodore Martin 406.
33. RA Queen Victoria's Journal, 31 Oct. 1898; RA Y 165/6.
34. *The Times*, 4 Nov. 1898.
35. *The Times*, 5 Nov. 1898; *Times*, 7 Nov.1898 (includes report of sermon); "Funeral of Helen Faucit," unidentified clipping in the Extra-illustrated *Actors and Actresses*, HTC. This last article says, incorrectly, that the service included no address.
36. Letter of Theodore Martin to Arthur Munby, 29 Nov. 1898, MS in the Osborn Collection, Beinecke Library, Yale University. This was written in reply to Munby's letter of condolence, which had mentioned the burst of sunshine at the end of the church service. Martin said the sun did not come out then but did so as the coffin was lowered into the grave. Munby annotated Sir Theodore's letter: "There were two bursts of sunshine; and the first and most striking was in the church. But he was too much stricken to notice."
37. Letter of Theodore Martin to William Blackwood, 13 Nov. 1898, NLS, MS. 4678, ff. 117-18; Sir Theodore Martin 407; "Memorial to Helen Faucit," *Illustrated London News*, 21 Oct. 1899; my own viewing of the memorial at Llantysilio.
38. Sir Theodore Martin 407. Ainger had also been one of the officiating clergymen at Lady Martin's funeral.
39. See the numerous newspaper cuttings about the controversy, Shakespeare Centre Library, Stratford-upon-Avon, P.83.6; also George Bullock, *The Life and Death of a Best-Seller* (London, 1940) 137-38; and Eileen Bigland, *Marie Corelli: The Woman and the Legend* (London, 1955) 192-93. Sir Theodore's chagrin over this matter is reflected in his letter to William Blackwood, 10 Nov. 1900, NLS, MS. 4703, ff. 200-201. He does not mention Miss Corelli's interference, however.

40. John Bott, "Looking for answers, found questions about original Shakespeare Memorial Theatre," *Stratford-upon-Avon Herald*, undated clipping sent me by Miss Dorothy Withy. Needless to say, the sculpture was cleaned and restored to its rightful place in what is now the Royal Shakespeare Company Collection.
41. Letter to William Blackwood, 30 Nov. 1898, NLS, MS. 4678, ff. 121-22.
42. Recollections of Sir Theodore's singing, atttending Sheep Dog Trials, etc. were given me by Mrs. R.H. Jones of Llangollen on 10 Aug. 1969. Mrs. Jones, whose maiden name was also Jones, was the daughter of Sir Theodore's head gardener, who was engaged shortly after Lady Martin's death. Information about Jane Anne (Williams) Jones and her little daughters was given me by Miss Gwyneth Jones (one of the daughters) at her home in Llangollen in Aug. 1981. Miss Sara Pugh Jones (not related) took me to see the house, "Helenfa."
43. The nephew, James Martin Macadam of Sydney, Australia, inherited the bulk of Sir Theodore's estate. Sir Theodore left sizable legacies or, in some cases, annuities, to Helen's nephew Percy (or Percival) Farren and her niece Kate Saville Thorpe; to his nieces Mary Milligan, Mary Pooley, and Hannah Macadam; to his second cousins Katherine and Mary Jane Dalrymple; to Miss Alice Helps; and to Misses Annette, Dora, and Eleanor Elias. He also left bequests to his housekeeper, Mrs. Honor Forte, and his manservant, Horatio Stephens.
44. *Journals and Letters of Reginald Viscount Esher*, ed. Maurice V. Brett, 4 vols. (London, 1934-38) II: 291-92.

Afterpiece

1. See, for example, *Manchester Guardian* 29 Apr. 1851.
2. Sir Arthur Helps, *Realmah* 475-76 ("new felicities").
3. *Buxton Herald* 9 Aug. 1845.
4. Her potion scene in *Romeo and Juliet* was "comme un drame complete," according to Thierry, *Le Messager* 20 Jan. 1845; rpt. in Helena f. Martin 409. William Smith, in a letter to Sir Theodore Martin, 22 Nov. 1864, declared that her sleepwalking scene in *Macbeth* was a "striking exemplification of the truth of Aristotle's definition of tragedy." See Martin's extract from this letter, NLS, MS. 16444, f. 15.
5. Sir Archibald Alison, "The British Theatre," in *Essays* III: 589.
6. *Manchester Guardian* 14 Apr. 1866 ("musical rhythm," etc.); Theodore Martin, "The Drama in Connexion with the Fine Arts" 104 ("poet's eye").
7. *Essays and Studies* n.s. XVIII (1965): 1-12 (Pauline and Imogen, p.4).
8. The *Theatrical Journal* (17 Dec. 1843: 402-3) described it as "painfully though truthfully harrowing"; the *Newcastle Chronicle* (25 Apr. 1846) said it was full of "tragic grandeur."
9. On one occasion the *Manchester Guardian* (29 Oct. 1866) censured her for condensing and rearranging *The Merchant of Venice*, but on another the *North British*

Daily Mail (26 Nov. 1867} reproached her for retaining too full a text in Act 5 of the same play, including dialogue which was "to say the least, equivocal."

10. The *Manchester Guardian* (17 Nov. 1871) said that the basis for her artistry was her understanding of her character as a whole and the play as a whole.
11. See Helen Faucit's promptbook of *King René's Daughter*, now in the library of the Garrick Club. The basic text is *King René's Daughter. A Danish Lyrical Drama by Henrik Hertz*. Translated by Theodore Martin, 2nd ed. (Edinburgh and London, 1864). The promptbook, is inscribed by Helena Faucit Martin to Percy Farren ("William Farren"). Obviously there was an earlier promptbook, but I have not seen it. There is a MS part of Iolanthe in the Shakespeare Centre Library, Stratford-upon-Avon, bound in the document "Miss Helen Faucit. Stage Parts."
12. MS part of Iphigenia (see note 11). The changes are made in Helen Faucit's hand.
13. See George Fletcher, *Studies of Shakespeare* 377-78. Evidently he did not know Helen Faucit had abandoned the Garrick version by 1847.
14. PROMPT *Rom* 8, Folger (Shattuck, *Romeo and Juliet* #14). It is marked, in her hand: "1st book Helen Faucit." Shattuck dates it Covent Garden, 10 Mar. 1836, the date when Helen Faucit first acted Juliet in London. At the end of Act 1, she has written "Jany 17th /45," the date when she acted Juliet in Paris, but this seems to have no significance for the text. Both this promptbook and the later one show that her text did not remain constant during the respective periods of their use: some passages marked through for omission have "in" written beside them; some evidently spoken previously have "out." One cannot tell when the restored Shakespearean lines were written in, except that those in the tomb scene were obviously inserted at the time Garrick's interpolations were cut.
15. PROMPT *Rom* 9, Folger (Shattuck, *Romeo and Juliet* #21). "Helen Faucit Prompt copy" is written in her hand on a blank leaf at the beginning of the book. Shattuck dates the promptbook from about 1845, but I think 1847 more likely – possibly even later since Garrick's version of the tomb scene was abandoned while ROM 8 was still in use.
16. This is approximate. It is difficult to tell, in some cases, exactly where Helen Faucit's cuts are meant to begin and end: she often simply draws a careless line down the middle of the part to be omitted, in some cases obviously needing to retain some words at the beginning or end of the marked-through passage; rarely does she block off a passage with unmistakable clarity. The *Manchester Guardian* (22 May 1850) censured her for excessive cuts in this play.
17. Helena F. Martin 107-54.
18. The chorus-like introduction to Act 2 is also intact. As far as I know, however, it was never spoken in any production involving Helen Faucit. The Prologue to the play was used at Drury Lane in 1865. See Chapter 12.
19. Despite her omission of Juliet's first scene for acting, she studied it for clues in forming her conception of the youthful Juliet. In describing this portrayal I use her two promptbooks, her essay, several sources to be cited later, and (most important) reviews and other articles in the following journals: *Glasgow Herald* 18 Dec. 1843; *Newcastle Chronicle* 27 Jan. 1844; [Theodore Martin], "Bon Gaultier and His Friends," *Tait's Edinburgh Magazine* (Feb. 1844): 122-23; *La Presse* (Paris) 20 Jan. 1845, rpt. in Theophile Gautier, *Histoire de l'art dramatique en France* 4: 28-29; Edouard Thierry, *Le Messager* (Paris) 20 Jan. 1845, rpt. in Helena F. Martin 408-10 (appendix); *Evening Packet* (Dublin) 4 Mar. 1845; *Scotsman* (Edinburgh) 26 Apr. 1845;

Liverpool Chronicle 18 Apr. 1846; *Derby and Chesterfield Reporter* 29 May 1846; *Glasgow Courier* 13 Feb. 1847, 2nd ed.; *Express* (Manchester) 11 May 1847; *Manchester Examiner and Times* 22 May 1850; *Morning Post* (London) 17 July 1851; *Morning Chronicle* (London) 29 Jan. 1852; *Literary Gazette* (London) 31 Jan. 1852: 117; *Sunday Times* (London) 1 Feb. 1852 and 26 Mar. 1865; *Belfast Daily Mercury* 3 June 1856; *Caledonian Mercury* (Edinburgh) 12 Apr. 1864; *Times* (London) 22 Mar. 1865; *Manchester Daily Examiner and Times* 17 Apr. 1866 and 18 Nov. 1871; [Margaret Stokes, ed. Theodore Martin], "Helen Faucit": 755-57, 760; T.A.C., "Helen Faucit. Recollections of a Great Actress. By an Old Theatrical Hand," *News and Post* 24 May 1889. See also my article "Passion Framed by Art: Helen Faucit's Juliet," *Theatre Survey* XXV (1984): 177-92.

20. *Manchester Daily Examiner and Times* 1871 ("heartwhole," "grace and maidenly modesty"); [Stokes] 760 ("birdlike silver voice").
21. *Manchester Daily Examiner and Times* 1871.
22. *Belfast Daily Mercury* ("unconventional"); *Glasgow Herald* ("complete abandonment"); *Sunday Times*, 1852 (long quotation); *Evening Packet* ("fervour" and "purity"). See also *Scotsman, Liverpool Chronicle*, and *Morning Post.*
23. *Dame Madge Kendal by Herself* 4 ("Dost thou love me?"); *Morning Chronicle* ("childlike simplicity ... absorbing impulse"); *Times* ("passion ... raillery"); *Manchester Examiner and Times,* 1850 (scarf).
24. These examples of "blended" emotions are all from the *Sunday Times* except for the reference to raillery in "O swear not by the moon," which is from *The Times.* Since both reviews deal with the same production, I believe their differing reports of this speech can be taken together as a typical example of Helen Faucit's subtle transitions.
25. Thierry, *Messager*, rpt. Helena F. Martin 409 (early audience response); John Ranken Towse, *Sixty Years of the Theatre* 60-61 ("self-conscious").
26. *Express* ("rapt"); *Belfast Daily Mercury* ("tone and vehemence"); *Morning Post* ("heroine"); *Sunday Times*, 1865 ("deep emotion," "frenzy," "shower of sorrow").
27. *Sunday Times*, 1865 ("hushed and plaintive"); *Literary Gazette* ("knell"). Helen Faucit omitted Juliet's "O Fortune, Fortune ..." (ll. 60-64a), thus ending this "scene" with Romeo's "Adieu, adieu!"
28. *Scotsman* ("half-whispered," "pale cheek"); *Express* ("sorrowful resolution"); *Literary Gazette* ("rigid muscles"); ROM 8, blank page opposite the cast of characters ("–rose from her seat"); *Manchester Daily Examiner and Times*, 1866 ("cold, clear, concentrated passion").
29. Charles Rice, "Dramatic Register of the Patent Theatres, &c," HTC, entry for 18 Dec, 1836, originally pp. 253-54 of Vol. V (detached pages, pasted on playbills in the Theatre Museum, but copies are inserted in Vol. V, HTC. Rice tells about the trembling delivery and defends it against a reviewer's objection.
30. [Stokes], "Helen Faucit": 755.
31. *Messager*, rpt. in Helena F. Martin 409 (farewell to father, knelt and kissed her hand to mother); ROM 9, p. 200 (stage direction for dimmed lights, written in pencil in the left margin).
32. *Messager*, rpt. in Helena F. Martin 410 (pantomime, facial expressions, "sequence of ... visions"); *Glasgow Courier*, 1847 ("rapid transformations," "singularly expressive"); *Evening News and Post* (shudder, "*both shoulders*"); *Belfast Daily Mercury* (powerfully, "almost too horrible," "held fascinated," "terrible incubus"). See also *Derby and Chesterfield Reporter* ("deathlike silence" of the audience) and *Sunday Times* 1865.

33. *La Presse*, 1845, rpt. in Gautier's *Histoire* IV: 28-29; *Sunday Times*, 1865.
34. *Newcastle Chronicle.*
35. Marston's letter of 31 Jan. 1852, quoted by Sir Theodore Martin 232.
36. The second promptbook, by giving directions for soft music and slow curtain after both the potion scene and the discovery scene, indicates alternative endings for Act 4. See ROM 9, pp. 201, 206.
37. *Glasgow Herald* ("painful effect[s]"); "Bon Gaultier," *Tait's Edinburgh Magazine* ("Lazarus look").
38. *Le Messager*, rpt. Helena F. Martin 410.
39. *Scotsman.*
40. *Manchester Express* ("more effective" – the other actress was Fanny Kemble Butler); *Caledonian Mercury* ("in strict keeping").
41. [Stokes], "Helen Faucit: 760 (repeated keynote, symphonic pattern); 757 (description of final picture).
42. PROMPT *AYL* 40, Folger. (Shattuck *As You Like It* #15).
43. Macready's promptbook text is reproduced in Charles H. Shattuck's *Mr. Macready Produces AS YOU LIKE IT.*
44. The relevant scene in Kemble's arrangement is 4.3. Although Helen Faucit did not copy the text of the Rosalind-Jaques passage into her promptbook, she signalled her intention of including it by writing this heading for the scene: "Introduction enter with Jaques"; she also cut from an earlier scene (Shakespeare's 2.5) some lines Kemble had taken from the Rosalind-Jaques colloquy, presumably intending to restore them to their proper place.
45. *The Shakespeare Promptbooks: A Descriptive Catalogue* (Urbana, 1965) 3.
46. My reconstruction is based on Helen Faucit's promptbook, her essay on Rosalind (Helena F. Martin 227-85), several sources to be cited later, but, most important, Margaret Stokes's anonymous "Helen Faucit": 746-48 and reviews in the following journals: *Brighton Herald* 1 Oct. 1842; *Caledonian Mercury* (Edinburgh) 19 Feb. 1844 and 7 Apr. 1845; *Southern Reporter* (Cork) 1 Aug. 1844; *Cork Examiner* 12 Aug. 1844; *Nation* (Dublin) 15 Mar. 1845: 377; *Scotsman* (Edinburgh) 12 Apr. 1845; *Aberdeen Herald* 14 June 1845; *Dramatic Review* (Glasgow) 17 Dec. 1845: 29; *Evening Freeman* (Dublin) 29 Oct. 1846; *Glasgow Courier* 6 Feb. 1847, 2nd ed.; *Greenock Advertiser* 2 Apr. 1847; *Glasgow Theatrical Review* 17 Feb. 1847: 99; *Manchester Courier* 8 May 1847 and 17 Nov. 1871; *Manchester Examiner* 8 May 1847; *Hull Advertiser* 9 June 1848; *Manchester Guardian* 28 May 1850; *Manchester Examiner and Times* 23 Apr. 1851 and 4 June 1853; *Belfast Daily Mercury* 6 June 1856; *Pall Mall Gazette* (London) 10 Mar. 1865: 10 and 24 Nov. 1866: 12; *Sunday Times* (London) 12 Mar. 1865; *Examiner* (London) 11 Mar. 1865: 151; *Manchester Daily Examiner and Times* 13 Apr. 1866 and 16 Nov. 1871; *Birmingham Journal* 28 Apr. 1866; *North British Daily Mail* (Glasgow) 30 Nov. 1867; *Edinburgh Evening Courant* 2 Dec. 1869; *Manchester Examiner and Times* 3 Oct. 1879. For a more general description see pp. 65-74 of my essay "Helen Faucit's Rosalind," *Shakespeare Studies*, 12 (1979): 65-94; the rest includes much the same material as the present account. (Because of mislabelling in a scrapbook of press cuttings, the 1866 review documented as *Manchester Courier* 16 Apr. in the article is incorrect; the correct reference is *Manchester Daily Examiner and Times* 13 Apr. 1866.)
47. [Stokes], "Helen Faucit": 746 "sad and subdued"; Helena F. Martin 242-43 (explanation of melancholy). See also *Brighton Herald.*

48. *Birmingham Journal* (subtle indications of "self-consciousness, etc.; [Stokes]: 746 ("riveted," followed the speakers, kissed the chain, "tremulous" voice, unmistakable clarity – "penetrating" tone); Helena F. Martin 243-44 (admires courage, identifies with friendlessness, feels bond strengthened); *Sunday Times* (suggestive facial expressions, "almost instantaneous" but seemed "prolonged,"etc., not intended for Orlando's ears); *Belfast Daily Mercury* (movements and expressions during wrestling match – see also *Manchester Examiner and Times*, 1879).
49. *Manchester Examiner and Times*, 1879 ("gradations ... indignation"); *Caledonian Mercury* (rose to "native dignity"); *Sunday Times* (condescended to the entreaty, etc.).
50. [Stokes]: 746 (long quotation); *Manchester Guardian*, 1871 ("grey and green, air and flowers"); *Cork Examiner* ("pleasing shapes"); *Pall Mall Gazette* (G.H. Lewes's comments on the "mannish disguise"). Note the sketch of Helen Faucit in Ganymede costume drawn by J.D. Watson (see Ch.12). See also *Belfast Daily Mercury* (slight awkwardness beneath the "superficial ease" in her male disguise).
51. Helena F. Martin 255 (dreaming of Orlando, etc.); *Birmingham Journal* ("abject and persuasive,"etc., "burst of uncontrollable joy"); *Glasgow Dramatic Review* ("seized 'Celia,'" "seducing tone ... witchery itself"); *Pall Mall Gazette*, 1866 (hat slipped back, etc.).
52. Helena F. Martin 257-58 (Rosalind listening to Orlando and Jaques, greeting Orlando); John Moore's promptbook, Folger Library AYLI 23 (Shattuck, *As You Like It* #37). Moore often included in his promptbooks, as he does in this case, bits of business used by various actors whom he had seen.
53. *Theatrical Times* ("shadow [came] over the face," pure poetry); *Manchester Daily Examiner and Times*, 1866 ("mock solemnity," "incisive"); *Scotsman* ("a little in front," "bright-eyed ease"); *Sunday Times* (long quotation).
54. *Manchester Examiner* 1847 ("real interest," "touched"); *Birmingham Journal* ("indignant vigour"); *Manchester Daily Examiner and Times*, 1866 ("grave advice").
55. Alfred Darbyshire did undertake the scene in the Calvert Memorial production of 1879. See his account in *The Art of the Victorian Stage* (1907; rpt. New York, 1969) 67-68.
56. *Nation* ("modesty and passion," "daring soft mockery"); *Manchester Daily Examiner and Times* 1871 ("mischievous Cupid," etc.); *Hull Advertiser* ("buoyant merriment"); *Manchester Guardian* (indelicate passages). It is hard to know which passages in Helen Faucit's promptbook text could have been considered indelicate. The *Guardian* critic, an admirer of Ellen Kean, may have been exaggerating any possible flaw in her competitor, but even he commended Helen Faucit's "fine flow of spirits."
57. [Stokes] 747 ("Come, woo me!"); Helena F. Martin 270 ("vibrate[d]," "dangerous," etc., "marked change of intonation," etc.); *Birmingham Journal* ("hardest thrusts," "buttoned foils," "vein of tenderness," etc.); *Manchester Courier* 1847 (despite cynical tone, believed her own generation *would* die for love).
58. *Sunday Times* ("transition," "almost magical"); [Stokes] 747 ("head slightly averted," "deepening almost to pathos," "marvellous series"); Ellen Terry, *The Story of My Life* (London, 1908) 189 ("flushed up"); *Manchester Courier* 17 Nov. 1871 ("dreamy abstraction," "merry laugh"). For another account of the difference between Helen Faucit's and some other Rosalinds in this scene see *Edinburgh Evening Courant* 2 Dec. 1869.

59. The general description is based on Helen Faucit's essay (275-77), but reviews of her performances also emphasize her silent acting while listening to Orlando's narrative. See, for example, *Caledonian Mercury*; also *Manchester Courier* 1871. The quotation "mock masculinity" is from *Manchester Daily Examiner and Times* 1866; "painful intensity" from *Birmingham Journal.*
60. *Birmingham Journal* ("contagious eageress"); Helena F. Martin 281 ("witty volubility," comments on masque); promptbook 73; Shattuck, *Mr. Macready Produces AS YOU LIKE IT* opp. 100 (Macready's elaborate masque).
61. EPILOGUE: Promptbook 75 ("Veil down")Promptbook 75 ("Veil down"); *Greenock Advertiser* ("witching grace"); Unnamed and undated clipping (review of the benefit performance at the Haymarket, Dec. 1873), Saville Notebooks, Vol. 1, p.2 (verso), Nottingham Public Library ("winning archness"); *Aberdeen Herald* ("quiet eloquence"). See also *Evening Freeman* and *North British Daily Mail.* AFFINITY: *Glasgow Courier; Manchester Examiner and Times,* 1851; Hudson, Munby 232 (diary entry of 19 Nov. 1866).
62. Shakespeare Centre Library, S.R./P.72.19 (Acc. 4010) (Shattuck, *Macbeth* #28).
63. My reconstruction is based on Helen Faucit's promptbook, the comments on Lady Macbeth interpolated in her essay on Rosalind (Helena F. Martin 230-35), several sources to be cited individually, and (most important) reviews and other articles in the following journals: *Edinburgh Observer* 5 Dec. 1843; *Newcastle Chronicle* 25 May 1844; *La Presse* (Paris) 13 Jan. 1845, rpt. in Gautier's *Histoire* 4: 18-26; *Scotsman* (Edinburgh) 26 Apr. 1845; *Liverpool Chronicle* 25 Apr. 1846; *Freeman's Journal* (Dublin) 18 Dec. 1846; *Morning Post* (London) 5 Aug. 1851 and 19 Feb. 1858; *Sunday Times* 10 Aug. 1851 and 6 Nov. 1864; *Examiner* (London) 23 Jan. 1858: 53, 3 Dec. 1864: 776, and 17 Dec, 1864: ; *Glasgow Citizen* 23 Feb. 1861; *Caledonian Mercury* 15 Apr. 1864; *London Review* 9 (July - Dec. 1864): 534-35; *Observer* (London) 6 Nov. 1864; *Times* (London) 7 Nov. 1864; *Athenaeum* (London) 12 Nov. 1864: 643; *Dublin Evening Mail* 23 Dec. 1864, quoted by Sir Theodore Martin 277; *Manchester Courier* 16 Apr. 1866 and 15 Nov. 1871; *Manchester Guardian* 16 Apr. 1866 and 15 Nov. 1871; *Manchester Daily Examiner and Times* 17 Apr. 1866 and 14 Nov. 1871; *North British Daily Mail* (Glasgow) 29 Nov. 1870; *Liverpool Daily Post* 13 Dec. 1870; [Margaret Stokes] 758; T.A.C., "Helen Faucit...," *Evening News and Post* 24 May 1889. For a somewhat fuller discussion see my essay "Helen Faucit's Lady Macbeth," *Shakespeare Studies* XVI (1983): 205-33. (The page number for Sir Theodore Martin in Note 81 should be 228, not 225.) The present account includes most of the material on pp. 212-26 of that essay.
64. [Stokes]: 758 (costume); *Times* ("majestic, menacing," manner of holding the scroll); *Athenaeum* (also notes sculturesque effect); *Edinburgh Observer* (figure seemed to "dilate"); *Sunday Times,* 1864 ("strange equivocal fire," evil desires, "foreshadowing of horror," better nature vanquished); *Liverpool Daily Post* ("transfixed," "ecstasy ... painfully intense"); *Sunday Times,* 1851 (Greek tragedy, "irresistible destiny").
65. DELIBERATE BUT POWERFUL SPEECH: *Manchester Daily Examiner and Times,* 1871. See also *Sunday Times,* 1864; and Helen Faucit's promptbook, which, with unusual heaviness, marks this whole scene for phrasing and emphasis. IMPETUOSITY AND RESOLUTION: *North British Daily Mail.* DESCRIPTION OF MACBETH'S CHARACTER: *Examiner,* 1864 ("unmistakable emphasis"); *Liverpool Daily Post* ("milk" seen as "unworthy," "dual character").
66. *Sunday Times,* 1851 ("fearful change," "more than human firmness," marrow-chilling ["thrills to the very marrow"]); promptbook (directs herself to "begin

quietly" and to "plant poise the figure"); *Liverpool Daily Post* ("thrilling accents," "air peopling"); *Morning Post*, 1858 ("swelling exultation"); *Times*, 1864 (Medea).

67. *Times*, 1864 (same conception as in invocation, "prophetess"); *Manchester Courier*, 1871 (letter introduced "ecstatic" greeting and "led naturally" to suggestion of murder, plotting revealed in "And when goes – hence?"); Helena F. Martin 232 (Lady Macbeth "falls into his design"); promptbook (directs herself to "Mind his face"); *Examiner*, 3 Dec. 1864 ("curtseying about," "exultant tone").
68. *Times*, 1864 (quoted passage). *Examiner*, 3 Dec. 1864, objected to the "want of subtlety," but *Manchester Daily Examiner and Times*, 1871, reported that there was "an indefinable something, a fine suggestion of true genius, which indicated treachery."
69. AGAINST SHREWISHNESS: *Examiner*, 3 Dec. 1864 ("gin-shop"); see also *London Review*. FOR SHREWISHNESS: *Times*, 1864 ("perfectly truthful"). CONFLICTING EMOTIONS: *Manchester Guardian*, 1871 ("spasm").
70. "WE FAIL": *Sunday Times*, 1864 ("failure is failure"); but see *Caledonian Mercury* (disapproves the reading). CONCLUSION OF SCENE: *Examiner*, 3 Dec. 1864; see also *Times*, 1864.
71. Sir Theodore Martin (dressed in white); *Edinburgh Observer* ("at the wine-cup"); *Manchester Daily Examiner and Times*, 1871 ("mysterious sense of horror"); *Examiner*, 3 Dec. 1864 ("spitting … the word painted"); Marvin Rosenberg, *The Masks of Macbeth* (Berkeley, 1978) 350 ("sudden access of terror," etc.).
72. For Helen Faucit's evident delay in using the faint see Ch. 12, p. 209 and note 46. Rosenberg (368) says that Adelaide Ristori used a feigned swoon in London as early as 1857 and that some years later she made the faint genuine.
73. *Newcastle Chronicle* ("gradually sinking her spirit"); *Edinburgh Observer* ("stately composure"); Doran's review in *Dublin Evening Mail*, quoted by Sir Theodore Martin 277 ("fashioned by nature," "looked a lovable person … well-bred fiend"); *Times*, 1864 (hypocritical graciousness); *Examiner*, 3 Dec. 1864 ("fingers … wander sadly").
74. Sir Theodore Martin's extract from a letter to his wife, written by Westland Marston on 13 Dec. 1888, NLS, MS. 16444, ff. 18-19 (reminiscence of her "heartbroken musical wail"); *Examiner*, 3 Dec. 1864 ("disappointment and hidden suffering," "tone of weariness," stood averted, "mechanically" followed); Helena F. Martin 232-33 ("mental unrest," "involuntary" shudder); *Scotsman* (also mentions her shudder).
75. *Times*, 1864 (two roles); *Sunday Times*, 1864 ("passion of fear"); Liverpool *Daily Post* (long quotation). See also *Examiner*, 3 Dec. 1864, for praise of her byplay during "What man dare …"
76. *Times*, 1864 ("guilty pair"); *Examiner*, 3 Dec. 1864 ("deep mournfulness"); *Glasgow Citizen* ("inexpressible despair"); *Morning Post*, 1851 (tenderness and pity); *Liverpool Daily Post* ("mechanically"); *Manchester Guardian* 1866 ("bent spring").
77. Liverpool *Daily Post* ("totters … touches the crown," "magnificent mantle"); *Times*, 1864 ("mute eloquence"); *Manchester Daily Examiner and Times*, 1866 ("lingers … suddenly stops … half-smothered sound … prelude").
78. *Manchester Daily Examiner and Times*, 1866 (from "firm" to "shrunken-eyed"); Helena F. Martin ("unelastic," "muffled"); [Stokes]: 758-59 ("fixed on empty space," "horrible vision" – the last quoted from a letter of 5 Nov. 1864, writer unnamed).
79. Sir Theodore Martin 228 ("wandering and uncertain," "low, moaning tone," quoted from an unnamed journal); *Examiner*, 1858 ('scarcely more than breathed"); *Sunday Times*, 1864 (no "feverish action"); Helena F. Martin 231 (no violence that

would awaken sleeper); *North British Daily Mail* ("earnestness"); *Freeman's Journal* ("struggles"); Liverpool *Daily Post* ("shrill testiness").

80. *Manchester Examiner and Times*, 1871 (face a "tragedy," words "surcharged," "Thane of Fife," "strange power of suggestiveness," "womanly pride"); *North British Daily Mail* ("smell of blood"); *Manchester Courier*, 1866 (white face, "corruption" of hand); *Sunday Times* ("dreamy pathos," carried back to childhood).
81. *Liverpool Daily Post* ("weird and startling"); [Stokes] (quoting from letter): 759 ("concluding scared whisper"); *Dublin Evening Mail*, quoted by Sir Theodore Martin 277 ("wickedest of … husbands"); "E. de C.," letter of 29 Feb. 1858 to Helen Faucit, quoted by Sir Theodore Martin 254. Gautier in *La Presse* said that the impatient and unquiet gesture with which Lady Macbeth summoned her husband to bed would be remembered always.
82. *Morning Post*, 1851 ("appalling"); *Freeman's Journal*, 1846, quoting William Carleton's letter ("parched lips" … heart-searching); *Edinburgh Observer* (haunt the imagination"). See also *Liverpool Chronicle* ("inroads" of crime, "painful"); *Morning Post*, 1858 (heart "riven with remorse," "distressing").
83. *Sunday Times*, 1851 ("beautiful and touching"); *Glasgow Citizen* ("akin to forgiveness"). See also *Observer* ("deep pathos").
84. *Morning Post*, 1851 (solemnity); *North British Daily Mail*, 1870 ("profound impression"); *Manchester Courier*, 1871 ("grand," "sublime" – also *La Presse*, "sublime"); *Glasgow Citizen*, 1861 ("visitation from the grave").
85. See *Morning Herald*, 1838 ("passionate and touching"); *Literary Gazette* (played "sweetly" but with "power"; *Idler* ("alike effective in … tenderness and … a powerful display of energy"). For a reminder of the plot see the discussion of Helen Faucit's first performance of Pauline (Ch. 4, above). My present description of her portrayal is based on her promptbook in the Shakespeare Centre Library, the MS part of Pauline bound with it, the remarks about *The Lady of Lyons* interpolated in her essay on Imogen (Helena F. Martin 160-65), a few other sources to be cited later, and (most important) reviews in the following journals: *Morning Herald* (London) 16 Feb. 1838 and 29 May 1855; *Literary Gazette* (London) 17 Feb. 1838: 108; *Idler* (London) 24 Feb. 1838: 63; *Constitutional and Perthshire Agricultural and General Advertiser* 28 May 1845; *Aberdeen Herald* 14 June 1845; *Buxton Herald* 9 Aug. 1845; *Times* (London) 21 Oct. 1845 and 15 Dec. 1866; *Observer* (London) 26 Oct. 1845; *Nation* (Dublin) 24 Jan. 1846: 233; *Manchester Advertiser and Chronicle* 8 May 1847; *Morning Post* (London) 5 Oct. 1847; *Belfast Daily Mercury* 5 June 1856; *Evening Freeman* (Dublin) 15 Apr. 1857; *Morning Chronicle* (London) 5 Mar. 1858; *Bell's Life in London* 7 Mar. 1858; *Manchester Daily Examiner and Times* 27 Oct. 1866; *Manchester Guardian* 4 Nov. 1867 and 22 Nov. 1871; *Edinburgh Evening Courant* 15 Nov. 1867; *Daily Post* (Liverpool) 15 Dec. 1870; *Manchester Courier* 22 Nov. 1871. All quotations from the play are from the text in the promptbook.
86. SUGGESTIVENESS: *Morning Chronicle*. POETRY: *Daily Post* ("marvellous heightening"); *Bell's Life in London* (fine points). The *Manchester Guardian*, though declaring Bulwer's "vulgar" sentiments irredeemable, described Helen Faucit's portrayal as "a creation bathed in poetry."
87. *Edinburgh Evening Courant* (revelation by "gradual development"). The character the actress "revealed" was one with that she herself largely created. She remarked that Claude and Pauline are "commonplace people" unless "dealt with poetically and romantically" (essay on Imogen 162).

88. *Observer* ("handsome"); *Belfast Daily Mercury* (ineffable charm – "*je ne sais quoi,*" quoted from the play; also "magnificent bouquet"); *Daily Post* ("hard mamma," delicately stressed, "girlishness"); *Morning Chronicle* (convention, not nature; "deep feeling … never called forth").
89. *Morning Post* ("radiant smile"); *Daily Post* ("warm abandon," "languid rapture," "convincing earnestness," "depth and spirituality"); *Manchester Daily Examiner and Times* ("glowing words," etc.); Sir Theodore Martin 164, quoting Westland Marston's note to Helen Faucit, 8 Nov. 1845 (poem in itself); *Observer* ("gush of eloquent feeling").
90. The marks for emphasis are Helen Faucit's, in her prompt part, p. 4, and the directions "quiet – anguish of suspense" and "walk about" are opp. p.4.
91. Prompt Part, opp. 5 ("quiet till this").
92. *Times*, 1845 ("blank surprise"); *Buxton Herald* ("thrilled the brain"); *Daily Post* ("spoilt child," "uncanny"); *Observer* ("unreal as the ghost scene"); *Morning Chronicle* ("deep affection … concealed"); *Manchester Advertiser and Chronicle* ("betrayed," "too deep for sarcasm," thrilled and touched); prompt part, opp. p.5, across from wild laugh ("mocking misery"); promptbook, opp. p. 45 ("takes his hand & drops it"); *Buxton Herald* ("queenly … dignity and … reproach"); *Morning Herald*, 1855 ("wounded spirit"). A description of this climactic passage in *Manchester Chronicle* (1871) – i.e. the suggestion of sustained excitement concluding in hysterical weeping – differs from all others I have seen. Helen Faucit usually gave the passage a very different "shape": a quiet beginning, a stormy middle, and a quiet ending. But note other unusual portrayals in the farewell performances (Ch. 12).
93. *Times*, 1845 (byplay during Claude's explanation, struggle of pride and sympathy); *Manchester Guardian* 1871 ("growing softness"); *Times*, 1866 ("fascination" only in speaking, ultimate pardon certain); *Idler* ("long be remembered"); *Observer* ("lingering look behind").
94. *Observer* ("contradictory"); *Daily Post* ("strongly lingering"); *Idler* ("exquisite touch"); *Times*, 1866 ("expand into an avowal").
95. *Aberdeen Herald*. In 1870, during her farewell performances in Liverpool, the *Daily Post* used the phrase "serene majesty" of her whole scene with Beauseant.
96. *Belfast Daily Mercury* ("exquisite tenderness"); Julia Ward Howe, *Reminiscences* 104. The *Constitutional and Perthshire … Advertiser* also mentions both men and women in tears.
97. Sir Theodore Martin 118 (reporting Murray's anecdote); *Evening Freeman* ("despair and touching resignation").
98. *Manchester Guardian* 1867 ("unconscious consciousness"); *Belfast Daily Mercury* ("spasmodic struggle," "mute rapture"). See also *Manchester Guardian* 1871 ("incredulous delight," "reckless abandonment of joy").
99. *Buxton Herald* ("pulses"). See also *Manchester Advertiser and Chronicle*.
100. Quoted by Sir Theodore Martin 151.
101. The *Nation* 1 Mar. 1845: 345 (unsigned review by "Speranza"); [Martin], "The Drama in Connexion with the Fine Arts": 105. Both emphasize the nobility as well as the deeply-engaging emotion. The phrase "ennobling dream" is from *Nation*.
102. NLS, MS. 2643, ff. 83-86. The letter is dated only "July 29th." Both the signature and the address indicate that it was written before Miss Faucit's marriage. The probable year is either 1849 (she had not yet met Blackie when she visited Aberdeen in March of that year) or 1850.

Bibliography

1. Books

Alison, Archibald. *Essays: Political, Historical, and Miscellaneous.* 3 vols. Edinburgh: Blackwood, 1850.

--- *Some Account of My Life and Writings … Edited by His Daughter-in-Law Lady Alison.* 2 vols. Edinburgh: Blackwood, 1883.

Allen, Percy. *The Stage Life of Mrs. Stirling.* London: T. Fisher Unwin, 1922.

Allen, Shirley S. *Samuel Phelps and the Sadler's Wells Theatre.* Middleton, Conn.: Wesleyan University Press, 1971.

Anderson, James R. "Seven Decades of an Actor's Life." *Newcastle Weekly Chronicle, Supplement,* 1 Jan. 1887-21 April 1888. All instalments are bound in one volume in the Harvard Theatre Collection, Thr 471.4.2 PF.

--- *An Actor's Life.* London: Walter Scott Pub Co., 1902.

Anderson, Mary (Mme. de Navarro) *A Few Memories.* London: Osgood, McIlvaine and Co., 1896.

Archer, Frank. *An Actor's Notebooks: Being Some Memories, Friendships, Criticisms and Experiences of Frank Archer.* London: Stanley Paul, 1912.

Arnott, James Fullerton and John William Robinson, eds. *English Theatrical Literature 1559-1900: A Bibliography, incorporating Robert W. Lowe's* A Bibliographical Account of English Theatrical Literature, *published in 1888.* London: Society for Theatre Research, 1970.

Austen, Jane. *Sense and Sensibility.* 2nd ed., 1813. Signet Book. Introd. Margaret Drabble. New York: Signet-Penguin, [1995?].

Baines, Thomas. *Yorkshire, Past and Present: A History and a Description of the Three Ridings ... from the Earliest Ages to the Year 1870...* [Vol. II, Pt. 2 says to 1875]. 2 vols. in 4. London: William Mackenzie, [1871-77].

Baker, Michael. *The Rise of the Victorian Actor.* London: Croom Helm; Totowa, N.J.: Rowman and Littlefield, 1978.

Bancroft, Marie and Squire. *The Bancrofts*, New York: E. P. Dutton, 1909.

Barnard, H. C. *A History of English Education from 1760.* London: University of London Press, 1961.

Bartholomeusz, Dennis. *Macbeth and the Players.* Cambridge: Cambridge University Press, 1969.

Baynham, Walter. *The Glasgow Stage.* Glasgow: Robert Forrester, 1892.

Bell, Mrs. Arthur G. [Nancy R. E.]. *The Historical Outskirts of London.* London: Methuen, 1907.

Bigland, Eileen. *Marie Corelli: The Woman and the Legend.* London: Jarrolds, 1955.

Brett, Simon. *Star Trap.* New York: Dell, 1986.

Briggs, Milton and Percy Jordan. *Economic History of England*, 10th ed. London: University Tutorial Press, 1962.

[British Association for the Advancement of Science]. *Manchester and Its Regions: A Survey Prepared for the Meeting held in Manchester, August 29 to September 5, 1962.* Manchester: Published for the Association by the Manchester University Press, 1962.

[Britton, John and Thomas Shepherd]. *Modern Athens Displayed in a Series of Views; or Edinburgh in the Nineteenth Century. Illustrated by a Series of Views from Original Drawings by Thomas Shepherd. With Historical, Topographical & Critical Illustrations by John Britton*, Edinburgh, 1831; rpt. New York: Benjamin Blom, 1969.

Brookfield, Charles L. E. *Random Reminiscences.* London: Edwin Arnold, 1902.

Brown, John, Jr. and D. W. Forrest, eds. *Letters of Dr. John Brown. With Letters from Ruskin, Thackeray and Others.* Introd. Elizabeth M'Laren. London: Adam and Charles Black, 1907.

Browning, Elizabeth Barrett and Robert. *Letters of the Brownings to George Barrett.* Ed. Paul Landis with Ronald E. Freeman. Urbana: University of Illinois Press, 1958.

Browning, Robert. *New Letters of Robert Browning.* Ed. William Clyde De Vane and Kenneth Leslie Knickerbocker. New Haven: Yale University Press, 1950.

Brownstein, Rachel. *Tragic Muse: Rachel of the Comédie-Française.* New York: Alfred A. Knopf, 1993.

Bullock, George. *Marie Corelli: The Life and Death of a Best-Seller*. London: Constable, 1940.

Bulwer, E. L. *The Duchess de la Vallière*. 2nd ed. London, 1836. (Bound in blue watered silk, with gold lettering and gilt-edged pages. Helen Faucit's signature is on the flyleaf with the date 15 July 1840. There is no inscription, but the book is probably a gift from Ellen Braysher. Shakespeare Centre Library.)

--- *The Sea-Captain*. 4th ed. London, 1839. (Bound in blue watered silk, with the gold emblem of a ship on the cover, and with gilt-edged pages. Inscription on the flyleaf: To my dearest Helen from her affectionate and steady friend Ellen Braysher April 30th – 1840." Shakespeare Centre Library.)

Bulwer-Lytton, Victor Alexander George Robert, Second Earl of Lytton. *The Life of Edward Bulwer First Lord Lytton*. 2 vols. London: Macmillan, 1913.

Bunn, Alfred. *The Stage: Both Before and Behind the Curtain*. 3 vols. London: Richard Bentley, 1840.

Burton, Elizabeth. *The Early Victorians at Home 1837-1861*. London: Longman, 1972.

Butler, Frances Anne. *Journal of a Residence in America*. 2 vols. Philadelphia: Carey, Lea, and Blanchard, 1835.

Byrne, Patrick. *The Wildes of Merrion Square*. London and New York: Staples Press, 1953.

Calcraft, John [pseud. for John William Cole], trans. *Iphigenia in Aulis*. By Euripides. Dublin: James McGlashan, 1847

Carhart, Margaret S. *The Life and Works of Joanna Baillie*. Yale Studies in English LXIV. New Haven: Yale University Press, 1923.

Carlson, Marvin. *The French Stage in the Nineteenth Century*. Metuchen, N. J.: Scarecrow Press, 1972.

Chambers, Robert. *Walks in Edinburgh: A Guide to the Scottish Capital*. 2nd ed. Edinburgh: William Hunter, 1829.

Chart, David Alfred. *The Story of Dublin*. Rev. ed. London: J. M. Dent, 1932..

Clifford, Frederick. *A History of Private Bill Legislation*. Reprints of Economic Classics. 2 vols. London: Butterworth, 1887; rpt. New York: Augustus M. Kelley, 1968.

Clun, Harold F. *The Face of London: The Record of a Century's Changes and Developments*. London: Simpkin Marshall, 1932.

Cole, John William. *The Life and Theatrical Times of Charles Kean, F.S.A.* 2 vols. London: R. Bentley, 1859.

Coleman, John. *Fifty Years of an Actor's Life*. 2 vols. London: Hutchinson, 1904.

--- and Edward Coleman. *Memoirs of Samuel Phelps*. London: Remington, 1886.

Corbett, Mary Jean. *Representing Femininity: Middle-Class Subjectivity in Victorian and Edwardian Women's Autobiographies*. New York and Oxford: Oxford University Press, 1992.

Craig, Maurice. *Dublin 1660-1860*. London: Cresset Press, 1952.

Crow, Duncan. *The Victorian Woman*. London: George Allen & Unwin, 1971.

Cunnington, C. Willett and Phyllis Cunnington. *Handbook of English Costume in the Nineteenth Century*. 3rd ed. London: Faber and Faber, 1970.

Darbyshire, Alfred. *The Art of the Victorian Stage*. London: Sherratt and Hughes, 1907; rpt. New York: Benjamin Blom, 1969.

Davis, Tracy. *Actresses as Working Women: Their Social Identity in Victorian Culture*. London: Routledge, 1991.

Day, A. F. *The Church of St. Nicolas of Myra, Dyke Road, Brighton: A History with Some Deviations*. Brighton: FotoDIRECT, n.d. [ca. 1974].

Delderfield, Eric R. *Cavalcade by Candlelight: The story of Exeter's Fine Theatres 1725-1950*. Exmouth: Raleigh Press. [1950].

Donaldson, Walter. *Recollections of an Actor*. London: John Maxwell, 1865.

Donohue, Joseph. *Theatre in the Age of Kean*. Drama and Theatre Studies. Totowa, N.J.: Rowman and Littlefield, 1975.

Downer, Alan S. *The Eminent Tragedian: William Charles Macready*. Cambridge, Mass.: Harvard University Press, 1966.

Egan, Pierce. *The Life of an Actor*. 1825; London: Pickering and Chatto, 1892

---. *The Pilgrims of the Thames in Search of the National*. London: Thomas Tegg, 1839.

Ellis, Mrs. [Sarah Stickney]. *The Daughters of England: Their Position in Society, Character and Responsibilities*. London: Fisher, 1842.

Esher, Reginald. Viscount. *Letters and Journals of Reginald Viscount Esher*. Ed. Maurice V. Brett, 4 vols. London: Ivor Nicholson and Watson, 1934-38.

Falk, Bernard. *Rachel the Immortal: Stage-Queen: Grande Amoureuse: Street Urchin: Fine Lady*. London: Hutchinson, n.d.

Fauchet, Léon. *Manchester in 1844: Its Present Condition and Future Prospects.* Trans. by a Member of the Manchester Athenaeum. 1844. London: Frank Cass, 1969.

Field, Mrs. E. H. *The Child and His Book.* 2nd ed. 1892; rpt. Detroit: Singing Tree Press, 1968.

[Fitzgerald, Percy]. *Recollections of Dublin Castle and Dublin Society. By a Native.* New York: Brentano's, 1902.

Fletcher, George. *Studies of Shakespeare in the Plays of* King John, Macbeth, As You Like It, Much Ado About Nothing, Cymbeline, Romeo and Juliet: *with Observations on the Criticism and the Acting of Those Plays.* London: Longman, Brown, Green & Longmans, 1847.

Flynn, J. W. *Random Recollections of an Old Play-Goer: A Sketch of Some Old Cork Theatres.* Cork: Guy, 1890.

Fontane, Theodor. *Shakespeare in the London Theatre, 1855-1858.* Translated with an introduction and notes by Russell Jackson. London: Society for Theatre Research, 1999.

Foulkes, Richard. *The Calverts: Actors of Some Importance.* London: Society for Theatre Research, 1992.

---. *The Shakespeare Tercentenary of 1864.* London: Society for Theatre Research, 1984.

Francatelli, Charles André. *Francatelli's The Modern Cook (1846): 1462 Recipes by Queen Victoria's Chef.* New introd. Daniel V. Thompson. New York: Dover, c.1973.

Furness, Horace Howard. *Letters of Horace Howard Furness.* Ed. H. H. F. Jayne. 2 vols. Boston: Riverside-Houghton Mifflin, 1922.

Gautier, Théophile. *Histoire de l'art dramatique en France depuis vingt-cinq ans.* 6 vols. Leipzig, 1858-59. Geneva: Slatkine Reprints, 1965.

Gilman, Sander L., Helen King, Roy Porter, G. S. Rousseau, and Elaine Showalter. *Hysteria Beyond Freud.* Berkeley: University of California Press, 1993.

Gorham, Deborah. *The Victorian Girl and the Feminine Ideal*, London and Canberra: Croom Helm, c.1982.

Gosse, Sir Edmund William. *Robert Browning, Personalia.* Boston and New York: Houghton, Mifflin, 1890.

Gregory, Dr. John. *A Father's Legacy to His Daughters.* London, 1774; rpt. in A Garland Series. New York: Garland, 1974.

Greville, Charles C. F. *The Greville Memoirs: A Journal of the Reigns of King George IV. King William IV and Queen Victoria.* Ed. Henry Reeve. New ed. 8 vols. London: Longmans, Green, 1888. Vol. IV.

Griffin, W. Hall and Harry Christopher Minchin. *The Life of Robert Browning*. New York: Macmillan, 1912.

Gronow, Rees Howell. *Reminiscences and Recollections of Captain Gronow: Being Anecdotes of the Camp Court Clubs & Society 1810-1860*. Abr. ed. New York: Viking Press, 1964.

Haight, Gordon S., ed. *The George Eliot Letters*. 9 vols. New Haven: Yale University Press, 1954-55.

Hall, S. C. [Samuel Carter]. *Retrospect of a Long Life*. 2 vols. London: Richard Bentley & Son, 1883.

Hardy, Hon. Alfred E. Gathorne, ed. *Gathorne Hardy, First Earl of Cranbrook. A Memoir, with Extracts from His Diary and Correspondence*. 2 vols. London: Longmans, Green, 1910.

Hare, Augustus J. C. *The Story of My Life*. New York: Dodd, Mead; London: George Allen, 1901.

Hatton, Joseph. *Journalistic London, Being a Series of Sketches of Famous Pens and Papers of the Day*. London: Sampson Low, Marston, Searle, & Rivington, 1882.

Hawthorne, Nathaniel. *The English Notebooks*. Ed. E. Randall Stewart. Oxford University Press, 1941; rpt. New York: Russell and Russell, 1962.

Helps, Sir Arthur. *Realmah By the Author of "Friends in Council."* New ed. London: Macmillan, 1869.

Highfill, Philip, Jr., Kalman A. Burnim, and Edward A. Langhans. *Biographical Dictionary of Actors, Actresses, Musicians, Dancers, Managers, and Other Stage Personnel in London, 1660-1880*. 16 vols. Carbondale: University of Southern Illinois Press, 1973-93.

Hillebrand, Harold N. *Edmund Kean*. New York: Columbia University Press, 1933.

Hobson, Harold, Phillip Knightley, and Leonard Russell. *The Pearl of Days: An Intimate Memoir of The Sunday Times 1822-1972*. London: Hamish Hamilton, 1972.

Hollingshead, John. *My Lifetime*. 2 vols. London: Sampson Low, Marston, 1895.

Howarth, T. E. B. *Citizen-King: The Life of Louis-Philippe King of the French*. London: Eyre and Spottiswoode, c.1961.

Howe, Julia Ward. *Reminiscences 1819-1899*. Boston: Houghton, Mifflin, 1899.

Howe, Susanne. *Geraldine Jewsbury: Her Life and Errors*. London: George Allen and Unwin, 1935.

Hudson, Derek. *Munby: Man of Two Worlds: The Life and Diaries of Arthur J. Munby 1828-1910*. London: John Murray, [1972].

Hunter, Robert E. *Shakespeare and Stratford-upon-Avon, a "Chronicle of the Time": Comprising the Salient Facts and Traditions … together with a Full Record of the Tercentenary Celebration*. London: Whittaker, 1864.

[Jenkin, Henrietta Camilla (Jackson)]. *Once and Again. A Novel. By the Author of "Cousin Stella" … etc. etc.* 3 vols. London: Smith, Elder, 1865.

Jewsbury, Maria Jane. *Maria Jane Jewsbury: Occasional Papers, Selected with a Memoir by Eric Gillett*. London: Oxford University Press: Humphrey Milford, 1932.

Jewsbury, Geraldine Endsor. *Selections from the Letters of Geraldine Endsor Jewsbury to Jane Welsh Carlyle*. Ed. Mrs. Alexander Ireland [Annie Elizabeth Nicholson Ireland]. London: Longmans Green, 1892.

Jones, Sara Pugh. *A Hurried History of Llangollen*. Llangollen Blue Guide Sheets. Bala: A. J. Chapple Bala Press, 1961.

Kemble, Frances Anne. *Records of a Girlhood*, 2nd ed. New York: Henry Holt, 1879.

--- *Records of Later Life*. New York: Henry Holt, 1882.

Kendal, Madge [Margaret Grimston, née Robertson]. *Dame Madge Kendal. By Herself.* London: John Murray, 1933.

Knowles, James Sheridan. *Love*. 3rd ed. London: E. Moxon, 1839. (Bound in rose watered silk with gold design on the cover and gilt-edged pages. Inscription on the flyleaf: "To my most dear Helen from her affectionate and true Friend – E. B. Decr 7th – 1839." Shakespeare Centre Library.)

Koss, Stephen. *The Rise and Fall of the Political Press in Britain*. Vol. 1: *The Nineteenth Century*. London: Hamish Hamilton, 1981.

Laver, James. *Taste and Fashion*. New York: Dodd, Mead, 1938.

Lawrence, W. J. *The Life of Gustavus Vaughan Brooke, Tragedian*. Belfast: W. & G. Baird, 1892.

Lawson, Robb. *The Story of the Scots Stage*. Paisley: Alexander Gardner, 1917.

Leach, Joseph. *Bright Particular Star: The Life and Times of Charlotte Cushman*. New Haven: Yale University Press, 1970.

Leathers, Victor. *British Entertainers in France*. Toronto: University of Toronto Press, c.1959.

Lehmann, Rudolf. *An Artist's Reminiscences*. London: Smith, Elder, 1894.

Lerry, George G. *Henry Robertson, Pioneer of Railways into Wales*. Oswestry: Woodalls, 1949.

Lewes, George Henry. *On Actors and the Art of Acting*. Leipzig: Tauchnitz, 1875.

Le Livre du Centenaire du Journal des débats 1789-1889. Paris: E. Plon, Nourrit, 1889.

Lochhead, Marion. *The Victorian Household*. London: John Murray, 1964.

[Lockhart, John Gibson]. *Peter's Letters to His Kinsfolk*. 2nd ed. 3 vols. Edinburgh: Blackwood, 1819.

Lowther, James William, Viscount Ullswater. *A Speaker's Commentaries*. 2 vols. London: Edward Arnold, 1925.

MacDermot, E. T. *History of the Great Western Railway*. 2 vols. London: Great Western Railway Co., 1927.

Mackaye, Percy. *Epoch: The Life of Steele Mackaye, Genius of the Theatre, in Relation to His Times and Contemporaries. A Memoir by His Son Percy Mackaye*. New York: Bon and Liveright, c.1927.

Macready, William Charles. *Macready's Reminiscences and Selections from His Diaries*. Ed. Sir Frederick Pollock, 2 vols. London: Macmillan, 1875.

--- *Diaries of William Charles Macready 1833-1851*. Ed. William Toynbee. 2 vols. London: Chapman and Hall, 1912.

Mander, Raymond and Joe Mitchenson. *The Theatres of London*. London: Rupert Hart-Davis, 1963.

Marchand, Leslie A. *The Athenaeum: A Mirror of Victorian Culture*. Chapel Hill: University of North Carolina Press, 1941.

Marston, John Westland. *Our Recent Actors: Some Recollections Critical, and, in Many Cases, Personal, of Late Distinguished Performers of Both Sexes. With Some Incidental Notices of Living Actors*. London: Sampson Low, Marston, Searle & Rivington, 1890.

--- *The Patrician's Daughter: A Tragedy in Five Acts (As Represented at the Theatre Royal, Drury Lane)*, 2nd ed. London: C. Mitchell, 1842.

Martin, Helena Faucit, Lady. *On Some of Shakespeare's Female Characters*. New and enl. [4th] ed. Edinburgh: Blackwood, 1891.

Martin, Theodore, Sir. *Helena Faucit (Lady Martin)*. Edinburgh: Blackwood, 1900.

--- *Essays on the Drama*. [1st ser.] London: Printed for private circulation, 1874.

--- *Queen Victoria as I Knew Her*. 3rd imp. Edinburgh: Blackwood, 1908.

--- *Memoir of William Edmonstoun Aytoun*. Edinburgh: Blackwood, 1867.

Masson, Rosalie Orme. *Pollok and Aytoun*. Famous Scots Series. Edinburgh, and London: Oliphant Anderson & Ferrier, 1898.

Mathews, Mrs. [Anne Jackson]. *Memoirs of Charles Mathews, Comedian*. 4 vols. London: Richard Bentley, 1838.

McGregor, O. B. *Divorce in England: A Centenary Study*. London: Heinemann, 1957.

Merivale, Herman and Frank T. Marzials. *Life of W. M. Thackeray*. Great Writers Series. London, New York, and Melbourne: W. Scott, 1891.

Micale, Mark S. *Approaching Hysteria: Disease and Its Interpretations:* Princeton: Princeton University Press, 1995.

Mitchell, Charles. *The Newspaper Press Directory: Containing Full Particulars Relative to Each Journal Published in the United Kingdom and British Isles*, 3rd ed., rev. London: Benn Bros., 1851.

Moody, Richard. *Edwin Forrest: First Star of the American Stage*. New York: Knopf, 1960.

[Morgan, Sydney Owenson, Lady]. *Lady Morgan's Memoirs*. [Ed. W. Hepworth Dixon]. 2 vols. London: William E. Allen, 1862.

Morison, Stanley. *The English Newspaper: Some Account of the Physical Development of Journals Printed in London between 1822 and the Present Day*. Cambridge: Cambridge University Press, 1932.

Morley, Henry. *The Journal of a London Playgoer: From 1851 to 1866*. London: George Routledge & Sons, 1891.

Morley, Malcolm. *Margate and Its Theatres*. London: Museum Press, 1966.

Mursell, Arthur. *Memories of My Life*, London: Hodder and Stoughton, 1913.

The Museums Area of South Kensington and Westminster. Ed. F. H. W. Sheppare. London: Athlone Press, University of London; pub. for the Greater London Council, 1975. Vol. 38 of *Survey of London*. 1900-. 44 vols. to date.

Odell, Mary Theresa. *Mr. Trotter of Worthing: The Theatre Royal, 1807-1855*. Aylesbury: Aldridge Bros., 1944.

Oliphant, Mrs. [Margaret O. Wilson]. *Autobiography and Letters of Mrs. M. O. W. Oliphant*. Ed. Mrs. Harry Coghill. Edinburgh: Blackwood, 1899.

Oswald, Harold. *The Theatres Royal in Newcastle upon Tyne: Desultory Notes Relating to the Drama and Its Homes in That Place*. Newcastle-upon-Tyne: Northumberland Press, 1936.

Partridge, Eric. *The French Romantics' Knowledge of English Literature (1820-1848)*. Paris: E. Champion, 1924.

Peddie, Alexander. *Recollections of Dr. John Brown Author of "Rab and His Friends," etc, With a Selection from His Correspondence*. London: Percival, 1893.

Pettit-Dutaillis, Ch. *The Feudal Monarchy in France and England from the Tenth to the Thirteenth Century*. London: Routledge and Kean Paul, 2nd imp. 1949.

Pigot & Co.'s National London and Provincial Commercial Directory. London, 1827.

Pollock, Juliet Creed, Lady. *Macready as I Knew Him*. London: Remington, 1884.

Ponsonby, Arthur. *Henry Ponsonby: Queen Victoria's Private Secretary*. New York: Macmillan, 1943.

Porter, Henry C. *History of the Theatres of Brighton, from 1774 to 1885*. Brighton: King & Thorne, 1886.

Rees, James. *The Life of Edwin Forrest with Reminiscences and Personal Recollections*. Philadelphia: c.1874.

Reynolds, Frederick. *The Life and Times of Frederick Reynolds. Written by Himself.* 2 vols. London: Henry Colburn, 1846.

Ritchie, Anne Thackeray. *Letters of Anne Thackeray Ritchie. With Forty-two Additional Letters from Her Father William Makepeace Thackeray*. Ed. Hester Ritchie. London: John Murray, 1924.

--- Ritchie, Anne Thackeray. *Records of Tennyson, Ruskin, and Browning*. London: Macmillan, 1892. [Dedicated to Sir Theodore and Lady Martin]

Rosenberg, Marvin. *The Masks of Macbeth*. Berkeley: University of California Press, 1978.

Rowell, George. *Queen Victoria Goes to the Theatre*. London: Paul Elek, 1978.

St. Helier, Lady [Susan Mary Elizabeth (Stewart-Mackenzie) Jeune]. *Memories of Fifty Years*. London: Edward Arnold, 1909.

Sala, George Augustus. *The Life and Adventures of George Augustus Sala written by Himself.* 3rd ed. 2 vols. London: Cassell, 1895

--- *Twice Round the Clock; or the Hours of the Day and Night in London*. London: Houlston and Wright, [1859].

Saxon, A. H. *The Life and Art of Andrew Ducrow and the Romantic Age of the English Circus*. Archon Books. Hamden, Conn.: Shoe String Press, 1978.

Scott, William Bell. *Autobiographical Notes of the Life of William Bell Scott H.R.S.A., LL.D., and Notices of His Artistic and Poetic Circle of Friends 1830 to 1882*. Ed. W. Minto. 2 vols. London: James R. Osgood, McIlvane, 1892.

Sellar, E. M. [Eleanor May]. *Recollections and Impressions.* Edinburgh and London: Blackwood, 1907.

Shakespeare, William. *The Riverside Shakespeare,* Ed. G. Blakemore Evans et al. 2nd ed. Boston: Houghton Mifflin, 1997.

Shakespeare Birthday Book. (Red cloth with gold lettering on gilt-edged pages; illustrated with reproductions of paintings. Inscribed on the flyleaf: "To Mrs. Theodore Martin from Victoria R & I/ Windsor Castle/ Jan. 3. 1877." Signed at their birthdates by various members of the royal family. Shakespeare Centre Library.)

Shattuck, Charles H., ed. *Bulwer and Macready: A Chronicle of Early Victorian Theatre.* Urbana: University of Illinois Press, 1958.

--- *Mr. Macready Produces AS YOU LIKE IT.* Urbana: Beta Phi Mu, 1962.

--- *Shakespeare on the American Stage: From the Hallams to Edwin Booth.* Washington: Folger Shakespeare Library, c.1976.

--- *The Shakespeare Promptbooks: A Descriptive Catalogue.* Urbana: University of Illinois Press, 1965.

--- *William Charles Macready's "King John."* Urbana: University of Illinois Press, 1962.

Showalter, Elaine. *The Female Malady: Women, Madness, and English Culture, 1830-1980.* New York: Pantheon Books, 1985.

Sillard, Robert M. *Barry Sullivan and His Contemporaries.* 2 vols. London: T. Fisher Unwin, 1901.

Simms, William Gilmore. *The Letters of William Gilmore Simms.* Ed. Mary C. Simms Oliphant, Alfred Taylor Odell and T. C. Duncan Eaves. 6 vols. Columbia: University of South Carolina Press, 1952-56, 1982.

Simon, Brian. *Studies in the History of Education 1780-1870.* London: Lawrence and Wishart, 1960.

Smith, F. Hopkinson. *In Thackeray's London: Pictures and Text.* London: Smith, Elder, 1913.

Soubies, Albert. *Le Théâtre italien de 1801 à 1913.* Paris: Libraire Fischbacher, 1913.

Southern, Richard. *Changeable Scenery: Its Origin and Development in the British Theatre.* London: Faber and Faber, 1952.

Sprague, Arthur Colby and Bertram Shuttleworth, eds. *The London Theatres in the Eighteen-Thirties* [selections from Charles Rice's "Dramatic Register"]. London: Society for Theatre Research, 1950.

Stebbins, Emma. *Charlotte Cushman: Her Letters and Memories of Her Life. Edited by Her Friends, Emma Stebbins*. Boston: Houghton, Osgood, 1878.

Stirling, Edward. *Old Drury Lane: Fifty Years' Recollections of Author, Actor, and Manager*. 2 vols. London: Chatto & Windus, 1881.

Stoddart, James H. *Recollections of a Player*. New York: Century, 1902.

Stoker, Bram. *Personal Recollections of Henry Irving*. 2 vols. New York: Macmillan, 1906.

Stokes, Sir William. *William Stokes His Life and Work (1804-1878)*. Masters of Medicine. London: T. Fisher Unwin, 1898.

Strickland, Walter G. *A Dictionary of Irish Artists*. 2 vols. Dublin, 1913, rpt. New York: Hacker Art Books, c.1968.

Talfourd, Thomas Noon. *The Athenian Captive. A Tragedy in Five Acts*. London: Edward Moxon, 1836.

Terry, Ellen. *The Story of My Life: Recollections and Reflections*. London: Hutchinson, 1908.

Thomas, William Beach. *The Story of the* Spectator, *1828-1928*. London: Methuen, 1928.

[*The Times* Staff Members]. *The History of The Times*. 2 vols. New York: Macmillan, 1955.

Towse, John Ranken. *Sixty Years of the Theatre: An Old Critic's Memories*. New York: Funk and Wagnalls, 1916.

Trewin, J. C. *Mr. Macready: A Nineteenth-Century Tragedian and His Theatre*. London: George G. Harrap, 1955.

Trewin, Wendy. *The Royal General Theatrical Fund: A History 1838-1988*. London: Society for Theatre Research, 1989.

Trollope, Anthony. *The Small House at Allington*. 1864. New York: Dutton, 1963.

Vandenhoff, George. *Leaves from an Actor's Note-Book*. New York: D. Appleton, 1860.

Veith, Ilza. *Hysteria: The History of a Disease*. Chicago: University of Chicago Press, 1965.

Vizetelly, Henry. *Glances Back through Seventy Years: Autobiographical and Other Reminiscences*. 2 vols. London: Kegan Paul, Trench, Trubner, 1893.

Walker, Archibald Stodart, ed. *The Letters of John Stuart Blackie to His Wife*. Edinburgh: Blackwood, 1909.

Wallack, Lester. *Memories of Fifty Years*, New York: Charles Scribners's sons, 1889.

White, Terence De Vere. *The Parents of Oscar Wilde: Sir William and Lady Wilde*. London. Hodder and Stoughton, 1967.

Williamson, Jane. *Charles Kemble, Man of the Theatre*. Lincoln; University of Nebraska Press, c. 1964.

Wilson, Mrs. C. Baron. *Our Actresses: or, Glances at Stage Favourites. Past and Present*. London: Smith, Elder, 1844.

Wilson, T. G. *Victorian Doctor. Being the Life of Sir William Wilde*. New York: L. B. Fischer, 1946.

[Winston, James]. *The Theatric Tourist: Being a Genuine Collection of Correct Views, with Brief and Authentic Historical Accounts of All the Principal Provincial Theatres in the United Kingdom … By a Theatric Amateur*. London; T. Woodfall, 1805.

Wood, Christopher. *Dictionary of Victorian Painters*. Antique Collectors Club. Woodbridge, Suffolk: Baron, c.1871.

Wright, G. N. *An Historical Guide to the City of Dublin*. 2nd ed. London: Baldwin, Cradock, & Joy, 1825.

Wyndham, Henry Saxe. *The Annals of Covent Garden Theatre*. 2 vols. London: Chatto and Windus, 1906.

Wyndham, Horace. *Speranza: A Biography of Lady Wilde*. New York: Philosophical Library, 1951.

Youngson, A. J. *The Making of Classical Edinburgh*. Edinburgh: University of Edinburgh Press, [1967].

2. Articles and Chapters in Books

Abraham, L. A. and S. C. Hawtry. “Bill, Private” and “Parliamentary Agent.” *A Parliamentary Dictionary*. London: Butterworth, 1956.

“Adams, John Couch (1819-1892).” *Dictionary of National Biography*. 1901-1911.

“Ainger, Alfred (1837-1904).” *Dictionary of National Biography*. 1901-1911.

“Alison, Sir Archibald (1792-1867).” *Dictionary of National Biography*. 1885.

“The Antient Drama – Antigone.” *Glasgow Theatrical Review* 10 Mar. 1847: 122.

Archer, William. “Ophelia and Portia: A Fable for Critics.” *The Theatre* ns 6 (1 July 1885): 17-27.

Armstrong, Joseph, ed. "Helena Faucit Martin's Unpublished Letters to Robert Browning" and "From Sir Theodore Martin." *Baylor Browning Interests*. 2nd series, XXXIV, 4 (July 1931): 9-21, 21-24.

"Armstrong of Cragside." *The Complete Peerage of England Scotland Ireland Great Britain and the United Kingdom Extant Extinct or Dormant by G[eorge] E[dward] C[okayne]*. New ed., rev. and enl. Ed. the Hon. Vicary Gibbs. 13 vols. London: St. Catherine Press, 1910-59. Vol. I: 218-19.

Barker, Kathleen. "Charles Dillon: a Provincial Tragedian." *Shakespeare and the Victorian Stage*. Ed. Richard Foulkes. Cambridge: Cambridge University Press, 1986. 283-94.

--- "The Decline and Rise of the Brighton Theatre 1840-1860." *Nineteenth Century Theatre Research* VIII (Spring 1980): 29-51.

Barrett, Daniel. "'Shakespeare Spelt Ruin and Byron Bankruptcy': Shakespeare at Chatterton's Drury Lane, 1864-1878." *Theatre Survey* XXIX (Nov. 1988): 155-73.

Bulwer-Lytton, Robert, First Earl Lytton. "Miss Anderson"s Juliet." *Shakespeariana*. 10 vols. 1883-93; New York: AMS, 1965. II: 1-22.

Carlisle, Carol J. "Constance: A Theatrical Trinity." *King John: New Perspectives*. Ed. Deborah Curren-Aquino. Newark: University of Delaware Press, London and Toronto: Associated University Presses, c.1989. 149-54.

--- "The Faucit Saville Brothers; or, Theatre and Family." *Scenes from Provincial Stages: Essays in Honour of Kathleen Barker*. Ed. Richard Foulkes. London: Society for Theatre Research, 1994. 114-26.

--- "Helen Faucit's Acting Style." *Theatre Survey* XVII (1976): 38-56.

--- "Helen Faucit's Lady Macbeth." *Shakespeare Studies* XVI (1983): 205-33.

--- "Helen Faucit's Rosalind." *Shakespeare Studies*. XII (1979); 65-94.

--- "Lofty Tragedy for Mundane Audiences: John Westland Marston's *The Patrician's Daughter and Strathmore*." *When They Weren't Doing Shakespeare: Essays on Nineteenth-Century British and American Theatre*. Ed. Judith L. Fisher and Stephen Watt. Athens: University of Georgia Press, 1989. 152-62.

--- "Macready's Production of *Cymbeline*." *Shakespeare on the Victorian Stage*. Ed. Richard Foulkes. Cambridge: Cambridge University Press, 1986. 138-52.

--- "The Other Miss Faucit." *Nineteenth Century Theatre Research* VIII (1978): 71-88.

--- "Passion Framed by Art: Helen Faucit's Juliet." *Theatre Survey* XXV (1984): 177-92.

--- "Two Notes on Helen Faucit." *Theatre Notebook* XXX (1976): 99-102.

"Church Rates." *A Dictionary of English Church History*. Ed. S. L. Ollard, Gordon Crosse, and Maurice F. Bond. 3rd ed., rev. London: A. R. Mowbray, 1948. 118-19.

"Darbyshire, Alfred (1839-1908)." *Dictionary of National Biography*. 1901-1911.

Davis, Tracy. "The Actress in Victorian Pornography." *Theatre Journal* XLI (October 1989); 294-315.

De Quincey, Thomas. "The Antigone of Sophocles, as Represented on the Edinburgh Stage in December 1845." *Tait's Edinburgh Magazine* n.s. XIII (Feb. 1846): 111-16; (Mar. 1846): 157-62

Dimock, George E., Jr. Introduction. *Iphigenia at Aulis*. By Euripides. Trans. W. S. Merwin and George E. Dimock, Jr. The Greek Tragedy in New Translations. Ed. William Arrowsmith. New York: Oxford University Press, 1978. 3-21

Dowden, Edward. Rev. of *On Some of Shakespeare's Female Characters*, by Helena Faucit, Lady Martin. *Academy* 27 June 1885: 447-48.

Downer, Alan S. "Mr. Congreve Comes to Judgement." *Humanities Association Bulletin* XXVII, No. 2 (Autumn 1966): 5-12.

Fletcher, George. "Shakespeare's Female Characters and Their Present Representatives on the Stage." *Athenaeum* 4 Feb. 1843: 110-11.

--- "Female Characters in 'King John.' Present Acting of the Lady Constance …" *Athenaeum* 18 Feb. 1843: 161-63.

--- "Characters in 'As You Like It.' " *Athenaeum* 13 July 1844: 647-49; 20 July: 670-73; 27 July: 695-97.

Fox-Davies, Arthur Charles. "Martin, Sir Theodore." *Armorial Families: A Directory of Some Gentlemen of Coat-Armour, showing Which Arms in use at the Moment Are Borne by Legal Authority*. 3rd ed. Edinburgh: T.C. & E. C. Jack, 1899

"Froude, James Anthony (1818-1894)." *Dictionary of National Biography*. 1901.

Gunnis, Rupert. "Durant, Susan" and "Foley, John Henry, R.A." *Dictionary of British Sculptors 1660-1851*. Cambridge, Mass.: Harvard University Press, 1954.

"Hall, Anna Maria (1800-1881)." *Dictionary of National Biography*. 1890.

"Hall, Samuel Carter (1800-1889)." *Dictionary of National Biography*. 1890.

"Hamley, Sir Edward Bruce (1824-1893)." *Dictionary of National Biography*. 1901.

Hankey, Julie. "Helen Faucit and Shakespeare: Womanly Theater." *Cross-Cultural Performance Differences in Women's Re-Visions of Shakespeare*. Ed. Marianne Novy. Urbana: University of Illinois Press, 1993. 50-69.

Hazlitt, William. "Characters of Shakespeare's Plays." *Complete Works of William Hazlitt.* Centenary Edition. Ed. P. P. Howe after A. R. Waller and Arnold Glover. 21 vols. London: J. M. Dent, 1930-34. IV: 165-360.

"Helen Faucit." *The Theatre* 1 Dec. 1851 and I Jan. 1852.

"Helps, Sir Arthur (1813-1875)." *Dictionary of National Biography.* 1891.

Holmes, Martin. "A Regency Cleopatra." *Theatre Notebook* XVIII (1954): 46-47.

"In The Pit of a Theatre." Extract from an unnamed book or journal, 282-87, pasted in a volume of reviews of Lady Martin's *On Some of Shakespeare's Female Characters.* MS. 16442. National Library of Scotland.

Irwin, David and Francina Irwin. "History-Painting: Sir William Allan." *Scottish Painters: At Home and Abroad 1700-1900.* London: Faber and Faber, 1975. 204-15.

Japp, Alex. "Lady Martin's Female Characters of Shakespeare." *Gentleman's Magazine* 250 (May 1886): 451-62.

Juden, B, and J. Richer. "Le Théâtre anglais à Paris. Saison de 1844-1845." *La Revue des lettres modernes.* Nos. 74-75 (1962/63): 3-35, 63-66, 67-71.

"Kingsley, Charles (1819-1875)." *Dictionary of National Biography.* 1892-93.

Lewes, George Henry. "Article IV." *Westminster Review* XXXVII (Jan.-Apr. 18412): 321-47.

--- "Poetry and the Drama." *Westminster Review* XXXIX, Pt. 2 (Feb.-May 1843): 603-4.

"Marcet, Mrs. Jane (1769-1858)." *Dictionary of National Biography.* 1893.

Martin, Helena Faucit. Extracts from *On Some of Shakespeare's Female Characters.* In *A New Variorum Edition of Shakespeare.* Ed. Horace Howard Furness. Philadelphia: Lippincott. Vols. on *The Merchant of Venice* (c.1888) 441-42; *The Winter's Tale* (1898) 366-67; *Much Ado about Nothing* (c.1899; 3rd ed., 1904) 386-87. Vol. on *Macbeth*, rev. ed. (3rd ed.). Ed. Horace Howard Furness, Jr. (1903) 485-86.

"Martin, Sir Theodore." *Dictionary of National Biography* (1816-1909). 1912-21.

[Martin, Theodore]. " 'As You Like It' à l'Americaine." *Blackwood's Edinburgh Magazine* (Sept. 1890): 421-430.

[---]. "Bouquet of Ballads. By Bon Gaultier." *Dublin University Magazine* (May 1849): 608-11.

[---]. "The Drama in Connection with the Fine Arts," *Dublin University Magazine.* (July 1846): 97-106.

--- trans. "King René's Daughter. A Lyrical Drama. From the Danish of Henrik Hertz. By Bon Gaultier." *Dublin University Magazine.* (June 1848): 671-96.

--- "Plays, Players, and Critics." *Fraser's Magazine* LXVIII (Dec. 1863): 767-76.

[---]. "Theatrical Reform: The 'Merchant of Venice' at the Lyceum." *Blackwood's Edinburgh Magazine* (Dec. 1879): 641-656.

[Martin, Theodore and William Aytoun]. "Bon Gaultier and His Friends." *Tait's Edinburgh Magazine* n.s. XII (Feb. 1844): 119-31.

"Memoir of Mr. E. F. Saville." *Theatrical Times* 29 Aug. 1846: cover and 90.

"Memoir of Mr. William Farren." *Oxberry's Dramatic Biography and Histrionic Anecdotes.* 5 vols. London, 1825. III3: 37-47.

"Memoir of Mrs. Faucit." *Oxberry's Dramatic Biography and Histrionic Anecdotes.* 5 vols. London, 1825. III: 17-35.

"Merivale, Herman Charles (1839-1906)." *Dictionary of National Biography.* 1901-1911.

"Miss Helen Faucit." *Glasgow Theatrical Review.* 24 Feb. 1847: 106-7.

"Miss Helen Faucit in *Richelieu.*" *Theatrical Journal* 16 Jan. 1841: 17; 19; 23 Jan. 1841: 25-66.

"Mr. Edward [sic] Faucit Saville." *Theatrical Journal* 11 Mar. 1843: 79.

"Mr. and Mrs. Theodore Martin at Braich-y-Gwynt." No. 120 of the series "Celebrities at Home." *The World* 4 Dec. 1878; 4-5

"Mrs. Faucit." In "The Dramatic Gallery" V: 31-34, a section of an unidentified periodical in the Library of the Performing Arts, New York Public Library, Lincoln Center.

"Mrs Faucit." *Authentic Memoirs of the Green-Room.* London, 1814:1848.

"Mrs. Faucit." *La Belle Assemblée* Aug. 1817: [51].

Murray, Christopher. "Macready, Helen Faucit, and Acting Style." "*Theatre Notebook* XXIII (1968): 21-25.

Nerval, Gerard de. "Les Acteurs Anglais." *L'Artiste* 22 Dec. 1844.

--- "Les Acteurs Anglais (1845)," *La Revue Théatrale*, No. 29 (1 er Trimestre 1955): 5-8 (Republished from *La France Musicale*, 19 Jan. 1845.)

Ormond, Richard and Leonée. "Helen Faucit as Antigone." *Country Life.* 7 Dec. 1967: 1507-8.

"Our Actors: And Their Originally Intended Trades, Crafts and Callings. By Asmodeus. Pry" [4th and 5th parts of a multi-part article]. *Metropolitan Magazine* XVIII (Jan. 1837): 85-91, and (Feb. 1837): 138.

Rev. of *On Some of Shakespeare's Female Characters*, by Helena Faucit, Lady Martin. *The Times* (London) 26 Nov. 1885: 16.

Rev. of *On Some of Shakespeare's Female Characters*, by Helena Faucit, Lady Martin. *Athenaeum* 12 Sept. 1885: 345.

Rev. of *On Some of Shakespeare's Female Characters*, by Helena Faucit, Lady Martin. *Pall Mall Gazette* 13 June 1885: 5.

Rinear, David. "From the Artificial towards the Real: The Acting of William Farren." *Theatre Notebook* XXXI (1977): 21-28.

Rosenfeld, Sybil. *A Short History of Scene Design in Great Britain*. Drama and Theatre Studies. Totowa: Rowman and Littlefield, 1973.

--- "Muster Richardson – 'The Great Showman,' " *Western Popular Theatre*. Ed. David Mayer and Kenneth Richards. London: Methuen, 1977. 105-21.

Rowell, George. "Another View of Macready." *Theatre Notebook* XLVIII, No. 2 (1994): 63-76.

Salter, Denis. "A Picturesque Interpretation of History: William Charles Macready's *Richelieu*, 1839-1850." Fisher and Watt 39-63.

Seef, Adele. "Charles Kean's *King Lear* and the Pageant of History." *Shakespeare, Man of the Theatre*, Ed. Kenneth Muir, Jay L. Halio, and D. J. Palmer. Newark: University of Delaware Press, 1983. 231-42.

Shattuck. Charles H. "Macready's *Comus*: A Prompt-Book Study." *Milton Studies in Honor of Harris Francis Fletcher*. Ed. G. Blakemore Evans et al. Urbana: University of Illinois Press, 1961. 731-48.

Sorrell, Mark. "Edmund Kean and Richardson's Theatre." *Theatre Notebook* L (1996): 29-38.

Sprague, Arthur Colby. "Shakespeare and Melodrama." *Essays and Studies*. n.s. XVIII (1965): 1-12.

"Stokes, Margaret McNair (1832-1900)." *Dictionary of National Biography*. 1901-1911.

[Stokes, Margaret, with contribution from Georgianne Colmache, and edited by Theodore Martin]. "Helen Faucit." *Blackwood's Edinburgh Magazine*. CXXXVIII (Dec. 1885): 741-60.

"Stokes, Whitley (1830-1909)." *Dictionary of National Biography*. 1912-21.

T.A.C. "Helen Faucit. Recollections of a Great Actress. By an Old Theatrical Hand." *News and Post* 24 May 1889.

Thompson, Fred C. "A Crisis in Early Victorian Drama: John Westland Marston and the Syncretics." *Victorian Studies* IX (1966): 375-98.

Turner, Henry. "Recollections of Ryder." *The Theatre* 1 May 1885: 224.

Waller, E. W. Rev. of *On Some of Shakespeare's Female Characters*, by Helena Faucit, Lady Martin, *The Theatre* ns VI (1 July 1885): 28-34.

"William Farren." *Theatrical Journal* 28 Dec. 1870: 410-11.

Williams, M. J. "The Egyptian Campaign of 1882." *Victorian Military Campaigns*. Ed. Brian Bond. New York and Washington: Frederick A. Praeger, 1967. 243-78.

[Wilson, John – "Christopher North"]. "Dies Borealis, Christopher under Canvas." *Blackwood's Edinburgh Magazine* (Nov. 1849): 620-54.

"Wingfield, Lewis Strange." *Dictionary of National Biography*. 1900.

Ziegler, Georgianna. "The Actress as Shakespearean Critic: Three Nineteenth-Century Portias." *Theatre Survey* XXX (1989): 93-109.

3. Newspapers and Theatrical Journals

(Theatrical News and Reviews)

Note: Various periodicals that provided useful information about Helen Faucit's provincial engagements are not included here. Only those named in the text and notes are listed. The starred periodicals are particularly significant because of long-term coverage and/or unusually interesting reviews.

Aberdeen: *Aberdeen Herald.*

Belfast: *Belfast Daily Mercury; Belfast Commercial Chronicle.*

Brighton: *Brighton Herald, Sussex Monthly Advertiser* ("Lewes" column}.

Bristol: *Bristol Mirror; Bristol Times and Bath Advocate; Western Daily Press; Bristol Mercury.*

Buxton: *Buxton Herald.*

Carlisle: *Carlisle Journal; Carlisle Patriot; Carlisle News.*

Cork: *Constitutional; Cork Evening Herald; Cork Examiner*; Southern Reporter.*

Derby: *Derby and Chesterfield Reporter; Derby Mercury.*

Dublin: *Dublin Evening Post; Evening Freeman*; Evening Packet*; Nation*.*

Dundee: *Dundee Courier.*

Edinburgh: *Caledonian Mercury*; Edinburgh Courant; Edinburgh Observer*;Scotsman*; Weekly Review and Dramatic Critic.*

Glasgow: *Glasgow Argus; Glasgow Citizen; Glasgow Constitutional; Glasgow Courier*; Glasgow Dramatic Review*; Glasgow Herald*; Glasgow Theatrical Review*; North British Daily Mail*; Scotch Reformer's Gazette*.*

Greenock: *Greenock Advertiser.*

Limerick: *Limerick Chronicle.*

Liverpool: *Liverpool Albion*; Liverpool Chronicle; Liverpool Daily Post*.*

London: *Age; Actors by Daylight; Argus; Art Journal; Athenaeum*; Atlas; Bell's Weekly Message; Bell's Life in London; Britannia; British Stage and Literary Cabinet; British Statesman; Conservative Journal; Court Journal; Daily News*; Daily Telegraph*; English Chronicle; Era; Evening Star, Examiner*; Graphic; Idler; Illustrated London News*; John Bull; Literary Gazette*; London Review; Metropolitan Magazine; Metropolitan Conservative Journal; Morning Advertiser; Morning Chronicle*; Morning Herald*; Morning Post;* New Monthly Magazine; Observer*; Pall Mall Gazette*; Planet; Satirist; Scourge; Spectator*; Sun; Sunday Times*; Tallis's Dramatic Magazine; Theatrical Chronicle; Theatrical Inquisitor; Theatrical Journal*; Theatrical Observer; Theatrical Times; The Times*; Weekly Chronicle; World.*

Manchester: *Manchester Advertiser and Chronicle; Manchester Courier*; Manchester Guardian*; Manchester Examiner* (1846-48); *Manchester Examiner and Times* (called *Manchester Daily Examiner and Times* during one period, 1855-74)*; *Manchester Express.*

New York: *New York Herald; Spirit of the Times.*

Newcastle: *Newcastle Advertiser*; Newcastle Chronicle; Newcastle Courier.*

Paris: *Le Constitutionnel* (review signed "R." [Rolle]); *Journal des débats* (reviews signed "J. L." – probably John Lemoinne)*; *Le Messager des chambres* (review by Edouard Thierry)*; *La Presse* (reviews by Théophile Gautier)*; *Le National; L'Artiste and La France musicale* (see entries for Nerval under "Articles," above); see also *La France théâtrale* and *Courrier des spectacles* as quoted by Leathers, *British Entertainers in France*, and *Le Siècle* and *La Quotienne* as quoted by Juden and Richer.

Perth: *Constitutional and Perthshire Agricultural and General Advertiser.*

Richmond: *Hiscoke and Sons Richmond Notes, A Monthly Record of local Information for Richmond and Its Neighbourhood* Apr. 1865; 41. Letter, "Miss Helen Faucit," signed "A Friend to Dramatic Reminiscences."

Sheffield: *Sheffield and Rotherham Independent.*

Stratford-upon-Avon: *Stratford-upon-Avon Herald.*

Unidentified: Clipping in the Saville Scrapbooks, f.2 (verso), Nottingham Public Library; clipping pasted on the back of a Covent Garden playbill for 2 June 1816, Theatre Museum, London.

4. Obituaries, Funerals, Monuments

"Death of an Old Inhabitant." *Thames Valley Times* 10 April. 1889.

"Death of Helen Faucit." Unidentified newspaper clipping, 1 Nov. 1898, in the Extra-Illustrated *Actors and Actresses.* Harvard Theatre Collection.

"Funeral of Helen Faucit." Unidentified clipping in the Extra-illustrated *Actors and Actresses.* Harvard Theatre Collection.

"Funeral of Lady Martin." *Times* 5 Nov. 1898.

"The Late Lady Martin." *Times* 7 Nov.1898.

"The Late Miss Saville." *Nottingham Journal* 19 Sept. 1851.

"Memorial to Helen Faucit." *Illustrated London News* 21 Oct. 1899.

Obituary of John Faucit Saville, Sr. Unidentified clipping in the Library of the Performing Arts, New York Public Library, Lincoln Centre.

Obituary of John Harris *Irish Times* 16 Mar. 1874.

"Our Little Chatter Box." *Theatrical Journal* 13 Aug. 1851: 265 (death of John Faucit Saville's youngest daughter).

"Sudden Death of a Veteran Actor." *Sunday Times* 6 Nov. 1853.

Unidentified clipping (no newspaper name or date) telling of Harriet Faucit Bland's grave in Mt. Auburn Cemetery (Boston, Mass.), Harvard Theatre Collection.

5. Clipping Files and Scrapbooks

Birmingham Central Reference Library, Shakespeare Library: Files of newspaper reviews of provincial performances.

Manchester Central Public Libraries, Arts Library: Scrapbooks containing playbills and newspaper reviews for Manchester theatres. (Note: These were a valuable resource for me, but they have since been lost or removed from the library.)

Nottingham Public Library: Saville Scrapbooks, 2 vols.

Shakespeare Centre Library, Stratford-upon-Avon: Marie Corelli-Theodore Martin controversy, newspaper clippings.

Shakespeare Centre Library, Stratford-upon-Avon: "Theatre Records," Vol. 1.

6. Playbills

Birmingham,Local Studies Library and Shakespeare Library, both in the Central Public Libraries: Birmingham playbills; also, in Shakespeare Library, volumes of playbills for Shakespearean performances in various towns, each volume devoted to a single play.

British Library: Playbills 182 (Bath); 196 (Birmingham); 202 (Brighton); 206 (Birmingham and Bristol); 274 (Bury and Buxton); 275 (Chesterfield); 276 (Cork); 210 and 214 (Dublin); 220 (Glasgow); 242 and 243 (Liverpool); 259 (Manchester); 262 (Newcastle-on-Tyne); 263 (Plymouth); 296 (Norwich); 297 (Nottingham); 298 (Penzance); 299 (Richmond, Surrey); 318 and 319 Edinburgh); 327 (York); 396 (Sheffield).

Edinburgh Library, Central Public Library, Edinburgh (Edinburgh playbills).

Folger Shakespeare Library: Cork and Margate playbills.

Glasgow University library: Glasgow playbills inserted in BG39-a12, a volume of Glasgow Ephemera in the Smith Collection.

Harvard Theatre Collection: Playbills for Belfast, Brighton, Cork, Derby, Dublin, Edinburgh, Glasgow, the Haymarket (London), and Sheffield.

Liverpool, Local History Library in the Central Public Libraries (Liverpool playbills).

Manchester, Arts Library and Local History Library in the Central Public Libraries: Manchester playbills.

Margate, Public Library: Margate playbills.

Mitchell Library, Glasgow: Glasgow playbills.

Morab Library, Penzance: Penzance playbill.

National Library of Ireland: Dublin playbills, MS Dublin Jurymen 1852 NL (microfilm).

National Library of Scotland: Edinburgh playbills, Vol. R283.c.23-25

Norwich, Local History. Central Public Library: Norwich playbills.

Richmond, Surrey, Public Library: Richmond playbills.

Theatre Museum, London: Covent Garden, Drury Lane, Haymarket, Lyceum.

York, Central Public Library: York playbills, Vol. Y/792/YOR.

Personal Collection of the Author: Covent Garden (London), Glasgow, Lyceum (London). Manchester. Newcastle-on-Tyne.

7. Public Records

Boston, Massachusetts: Health Department – Registry Division, City of Boston (Deaths).

Brighton: Sussex Public Record Office, Lewes: Brighthelmston Parish Registers.

Falmouth: International Genealogical Index, Church of Jesus Christ of Latter-Day Saints, Columbia, S.C. – from Falmouth Parish Register.

Greenwich: (1) Local History Library – Rate Books. (2) St. Alphege Church, Parish Registers.

London: (1) Church of St. Mary Abbot, Kensington – Parish Registers. (2) City of Westminster Public Library – Parish Register, Church of St. Martin-in-the-Fields. (3) Office of Population Censuses and Surveys, St. Catherine's House – Marriage and Death Certificates. (4) Public Record Office – 1851 Census. (5) London County Hall Record Office – Bishop's Transcript, Parish of St. George, Southwark; Consistorial and Episcopal Court of London, Assignation Book 1820.

Norwich: Norwich and Norfolk Public Record Office – All Saints Church, Parish Registers.

8. Promptbooks

Anderson, James R. Promptbook of Sheridan Knowles's *Woman's Wit*, Harvard Theatre Collection.

Faucit, Helen. Promptbook of *As You Like It*. By William Shakespeare. PROMPT *AYL* 40. Folger Shakespeare Library. (Shattuck, *As You Like It* #15). Based on John Philip Kemble's acting edition.

--- Promptbook of *Cymbeline*. By William Shakespeare. PROMPT *Cymb* 2. Folger Shakespeare Library. (Shattuck *Cymbeline* #14). Based on Charles Knight's Cabinet Edition, 1843.

--- MS part of Iphigenia, bound with five other parts. Shakespeare Centre Library, 82.99 (Acc. 4004), under the title "Miss Helen Faucit. Stage Parts."

--- Promptbook of *King René's Daughter*. Library of the Garrick Club, London. Based on *King René's Daughter. A Danish Lyrical Drama by Henrik Hertz*. Trans. Theodore Martin. 2nd ed. Edinburgh and London, 1864.

--- Promptbook of *The Lady of Lyons*. By Edward Lytton Bulwer, Based on an edition of 1849. MS part of Pauline, bound in same volume, at the end of the printed text. Shakespeare Centre Library, 82.5 collns. (Acc. 4002).

--- Promptbook of *Macbeth*. By William Shakespeare . Shakespeare Centre Library. S.R./P.72.19 (Acc.4010). (Shattuck, *Macbeth* #28). Based on an edition of 1814 as "Revised at the Theatre Royal, Drury Lane." Fanny Kemble's rehearsal copy, given to Helen Faucit by Charles Kemble. Contains Helen Faucit's markings.

--- First Promptbook of *Romeo and Juliet*. By William Shakespeare. PROMPT *Rom* 8. Folger Shakespeare library. (Shattuck, *Romeo and Juliet* #14). Based on a Cumberland acting edition using Garrick's version.

--- Second Promptbook of *Romeo and Juliet*. By William Shakespeare . PROMPT *Rom* 9. Folger Shakespeare Library. (Shattuck, *Romeo and Juliet* #21). Based on Knight's Cabinet Edition, 1843.

Macready, William Charles. Promptbook of *Cymbeline*. By William Shakespeare. Transcribed by George Ellis. PROMPT *Cymb* 17. Folger Shakespeare Library. (Shattuck *Cymbeline* #10). Based on an edition of George Steevens.

Moore, John. Promptbook of *As You Like It*. By William Shakespeare. PROMPT *AYLI* 23. Folger Shakespeare Library. (Shattuck, *As You Like It* #37).

9. Manuscript Sources

Note: Individual manuscripts are identified in the chapter notes. Asterisks indicate collections with the greatest number of relevant manuscripts.

Armstrong Browning Library, Baylor University, Waco, Texas.

Beineke Library, Yale University: Osborn Collection.

Brighton Public Library.

British Library: Ashley Collection.

*Folger Shakespeare Library.

Furness Library, Charles Patterson Van Pelt Library, University of Pennsylvania.

Greenwich Local History Library.

Harry Ransome Humanities Research Centre, University of Texas, Austin.

*Harvard Theatre Collection, Houghton Library.

Huntington Library.

National Library of Ireland.

**National Library of Scotland.

National Library of Wales.

Personal Collection of the Author.

Raymond Mander and Joe Mitchenson Theatre Collection.

Royal Archives, Windsor Castle.

Shakespeare Centre Library: Royal Shakespeare Company collections

Theatre Museum, Victoria and Albert Museum, London.

10. Letters to the Author

Aird, Mrs. Cathrine. 3 Sept. 1971.

Dawson, Barbara. 22 Apr. 1983. ts.

Ellmann, Richard 19 Apr. 1989. ts.

Gedge, Mrs. Catherine J. 7 July 1967 and 12 July 1967. mss.

Greenhill, R. A. 6 Dec. 1978. ts.

Hoskins, Mrs. Leila 12 Aug. 1967 and 29 Aug. 1967. mss

Howard, Diana. 19 Dec. 1973. ts.

Hubbard, Edward. 4 Sept., 26 Sept., and 29 Nov. 1978. ts., with a conjectural plan of Bryntysilio's interior as it was in the Martins' day.

Hudson, Derek. 21 Nov. 1973. ms.

Irwin, Eric. 1 Jan. 1983. ts.

Jones, Gwyneth. 3 Aug. [1967]. ms.

McCullough, Thomas, M.D. 16 Feb. 1990. ts.

Olsen, Gerald, M.D. 26 Jan. 1990. ts.

Stephenson, Mrs M. H., 10 July 1967. ms.

White, Terence De Vere. 21 Nov. 1973. ms.

11. Interviews with the author

Gedge, Mrs. Catherine J. 15 July 1967.

Jones, Gwyneth. Aug. 1981.

Jones, Mrs. R. H. 10 Aug. 1969.

Omand, Mrs. James., Autumn, 1971.

Index